With love to
Matt from
Mother and Dad

Xmas, 1970

D0210964

BY DUMAS MALONE

.~.~.~.~.~.~.

JEFFERSON AND HIS TIME
(of which the following volumes have been published)

JEFFERSON THE VIRGINIAN

JEFFERSON AND THE RIGHTS OF MAN

JEFFERSON AND THE ORDEAL OF LIBERTY

JEFFERSON THE PRESIDENT
FIRST TERM, 1801–1805

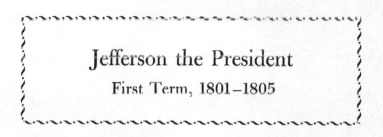

Jefferson the President

First Term, 1801–1805

THE THIRD PRESIDENT LATE IN HIS FIRST TERM
Portrait of Jefferson painted in January, 1805, by Rembrandt Peale

JEFFERSON AND HIS TIME

VOLUME FOUR

Jefferson
the President

First Term, 1801–1805

BY DUMAS MALONE

With Illustrations

Boston
LITTLE, BROWN AND COMPANY

1970

LIBRARY OF CONGRESS CATALOG CARD NO. 48–5972

FIRST EDITION

Published simultaneously in Canada
by Little, Brown & Company (Canada) Limited

PRINTED IN THE UNITED STATES OF AMERICA

This work as a whole is for
ELISABETH

This volume on the presidency is for
GIFFORD and PAMELA

Contents

Introduction   xxiii

Chronology   xxv

THE REPUBLICAN TACK

I	A Troubled Transition	3
II	Profession and Promise: The First Inaugural	17
III	From Capitol Hill to the President's House	29
IV	The Captain and His Mates	50

DEMOCRATIZING THE GOVERNMENT

V	The Dreadful Burden of Appointments	69
VI	Congress and the Man of the People: Peace and Economy	90
VII	The Jeffersonians and the Judiciary, 1801–1802	110
VIII	Politics and the Marbury Case, 1802–1803	136

THE MEASURE OF A MAN

IX	"A Small but Cherished Society"	159
X	The Presiding Scientist	177
XI	The Religion of a Reasonable Man	190
XII	Torrent of Slander	206
XIII	Freedom and Licentiousness, 1802–1805	224

FREEDOM'S EMPIRE

XIV	Impending Crisis in the West	239
XV	The Mississippi Question, 1802–1803	262
XVI	The Louisiana Treaty	284
XVII	The Constitution and the Expanding Union	311
XVIII	The Precarious Periphery, 1803–1805	333
XIX	The Government and the New Citizens	348

DEMOCRACY AND PARTY POLITICS

XX   Without Benefit of Protocol: The Merry Affair   367
XXI   Partisans and Irreconcilables, 1803–1804   393
XXII Tragic Interlude   408
XXIII An "Interview" and an Election, 1804   425
XXIV John Randolph and the Yazoo Question   440
XXV   Judges on Trial   458

APPENDICES

I   The Charge of a "Deal" in 1801   487
II   The Miscegenation Legend   494
III Notes on the Merry Affair   499

     Acknowledgments   501
     List of Symbols and Short Titles   505
     Select Critical Bibliography   509
     Index   525

Illustrations

Thomas Jefferson by Peale   *Frontispiece*

The President's House   39

Plan of the Principal Story of the President's House in 1803   45

The Secretary of State Madison   53

The Secretary of the Treasury Gallatin   55

Vice President Aaron Burr   125

Chief Justice John Marshall   146

Monticello from the West and South   169

Charles Willson Peale   183

Dr. Benjamin Rush   187

Map of the West and Southwest, 1803   242

Marqués de Casa Yrujo   267

Robert R. Livingston   290

James Monroe   300

Map of the Spanish Floridas   305

Benjamin Henry Latrobe   369

Senator William Plumer of New Hampshire   372

Jefferson's Polygraph   420

Jefferson in Profile   438

Congressman John Randolph   445

Justice Samuel Chase   475

Introduction

THIS volume, the fourth in the comprehensive biographical study of Thomas Jefferson on which I have been long engaged, covers his first term as President, and, like its predecessors, is a unit in itself. It has been virtually complete for several years but was withheld because of my desire to finish my study of the entire presidency before putting any part of it into print. At this writing my work on the second term is so well advanced that I now feel warranted in releasing this account of the first administration. I have learned from painful experience the unwisdom of precise predictions about my progress in exploring the life of this extraordinarily versatile and seemingly inexhaustible man, but I feel relatively safe in promising that, barring accidents, the lapse of time between this volume and its sequel will not be great.

On turning the leaves of the calendar backward I am dismayed by the discovery that I have been unable to proceed through Jefferson's presidency as an investigator and writer any faster than he himself did as a living man. I have met with a number of unforeseen interruptions, but my main difficulties have arisen from the very nature of the task. His presidency was much the most complicated part of Jefferson's career and the materials bearing on it are considerably more extensive than in any other equivalent period of his long life. During his presidential years, as in no others, his story merges with the history of the country. He has to be related to far more events and persons than when he was a lesser official or when, retired at Monticello, he was above the battle. He repaired to that cherished sanctuary regularly while First Citizen, but not even there could he be a private man. He received communications about public affairs by every post, and only when riding on horseback about his farms, or tinkering with some gadget, or enjoying the companionship of his beloved family, could he be oblivious of what was going on in the country and the world.

Anyone who essays to write the biography of a President must familiarize himself as best he can with major events and developments in the country as a whole, and, if dealing with an age when international relations were of prime importance to the Republic, he should try to see things in their world setting. He can hardly know too much about times and circumstances and, as I am well aware, he is likely to know too little to orientate his subject properly. On the other hand, he can easily make the mistake of saying so much about the larger scene that the reader will lose sight of the supposedly central figure. If the biography of a public man may be likened to a concerto there can be too much of the orchestra.

The present book does not purport to be a history of the United States during Jefferson's first term as President, but it can hardly help being in large part the history of an administration. There are chapters in which the President himself may seem offstage, as in the last two, when John Randolph is making most of the noise, and in those dealing with diplomatic episodes whose outcome was chiefly determined by the actions of others. Events that importantly affected the administration cannot be ignored, even though Jefferson himself had little or nothing to do with them. Insofar as possible I have sought to view these from the President's House in Washington or the mansion at Monticello, going to particular pains to ascertain just when and what he learned about them. In reaching decisions he did not have the benefit of hindsight, nor did he have access to valuable sources of information, especially diplomatic sources, that are available to modern scholars. It is important to know not only what he actually did, but what options he rejected, what he did not do. Often we cannot be absolutely sure, but we need not accept partisan assertions and exaggerations, either pro or con; we have to rely on the available record.

My first concern has been to determine and to report accurately what happened and how it happened. The task of separating demonstrable truth from the myths, legends, and downright misrepresentations that gather around an eminent public man and highly controversial figure is difficult and exacting, but no one who would tell a true and honest story can escape it. In the course of this narrative I frequently point out what I regard as mistakes and misjudgments by Jefferson's contemporaries, but my general policy has been to let the facts, as I have ascertained them, speak for themselves. At times I refer specifically to what I believe to be errors on the part of modern writers, but I have made no special attempt to measure this account against the works of others. While I am much indebted to certain monographs and have greatly benefited from the labors of other scholars, this is a fresh study, based on original sources, and it must stand on its own feet.

The biographer or historian, besides trying to answer the questions "what" and "how," should do everything he can to find out *why* things happened, and his effort to arrive at the fullest possible understanding should not subject him to the charge of trying to explain things away. I hope this work constitutes a contribution to knowledge, but knowledge can avail little if it does not contribute to understanding. The difficulty of reading the minds of men, great in any case, is magnified in that of the many-sided Jefferson, who wrote incessantly but rarely revealed his innermost thoughts and feelings. It is not at all surprising that his aims and motives have been variously interpreted. There is something in him for almost everybody, and, through the years, the tendency has been for observers to see in him what they wanted to see. This has been especially true of persons whose interest in him has been primarily political.

Without claiming to have arrived at the whole truth about him as a public man, I shall venture some reflections on the relations between his political ideas, as previously expressed, and his conduct of the presidency in the period covered by this book. It should be remembered that, despite the range of his personal interests, he had been primarily a man of affairs since he attained maturity, and that he never cast his thought in systematic form. He was no theorist, remote from life, but he was a characteristically thoughtful as well as a highly articulate man who sought to guide his steps by truth as he perceived it and by principles which, as he believed, had been adduced by reason.

During the first decade of his public life Americans were inquiring into the "principles of politics" to an unexampled degree, and he was in the mainstream of revolutionary ideology at the beginning of the Republic. A score of years later, writing to a discouraged supporter, he said that the "spirit of 1776" was not dead but merely slumbering.[1] He identified this with republicanism. He could never forget that John Adams, who was now President, had shared with him the pangs and hopes that attended the nation's birth, but it seemed to him that this old comrade had become unmindful of the "spirit of 1776." Judging from his own words after he assumed the first office, he believed that the "revolution of 1800" marked the revival of that spirit and a return to first principles. It should not be supposed, however, that his political ideas had remained unchanged through a quarter of a century.

[1] TJ to Thomas Lomax, Mar. 12, 1799 (Ford, VII, 373).

He never ceased to look back with nostalgia on the early years of the American Revolution, but this is not to say that he was unaffected by the events and developments that occasioned the Federal Convention and the framing of the Constitution of 1787. He reacted against the anarchic libertarianism and the trend toward "democratic despotism" that marked the period, though he was less disillusioned with his countrymen than were his friends Washington and Madison. Out of the country during the most critical years, he was less disturbed than they by the domestic turmoil and more fearful of autocracy such as he had observed at first hand in Europe.[2] He certainly viewed the aftermath of the American Revolution with no such distaste and dismay as Alexander Hamilton, with whom Madison parted company in Washington's first administration and whom Jefferson then regarded as a would-be monarchist. The term may have been too strong, but Hamilton had slight sympathy with republicanism as Jefferson understood it at the dawn of American independence, and more recently his fears of popular rule had been quickened by the sanguinary events in France. Jefferson himself was disillusioned with the French Revolution before he became President, but he feared that the reaction against it and toward autocratic government in Europe would engulf the western world, including his own land. High Federalism was politically reactionary; and, at a time when counter-revolution was gaining momentum elsewhere, the election of Jefferson signified that it was checked in the United States. He himself undoubtedly regarded his victory as a vindication of the American Revolution, but to what extent did he purpose to restore republicanism in its earlier American form?

He was not above voicing clichés for political purposes, but, beyond any doubt, he was convinced that the Federalists, in the time of the Sedition Act, had attacked individual liberties which he had expected the American Revolution to establish. Unquestionably he intended, by the conduct of his administration, to reaffirm the "truths" he had proclaimed so eloquently in the Declaration of Independence and his Bill for Establishing Religious Freedom in Virginia. He regarded these as self-evident and immutable.

As for the doctrine of the sovereignty of the people, in the American context this was so fundamental that virtually everybody paid it lip-service. Some did little more than that, however, and there was much difference of opinion with respect to the immediate implications of the doctrine. Jefferson's distrust of rulers and of oligarchies of birth and

[2] See *Jefferson and the Rights of Man*, ch. IX. I am much indebted to Gordon S. Wood's stimulating study of American political thinking in these years, *The Creation of the American Republic, 1776–1787* (1969); see especially chs. II, X.

wealth, and his reliance on the common sense of the people generally, were notable throughout his career, but he was well aware of the practical limitations of direct democracy ("participatory democracy" in our idiom). This had been carried to grave extremes in the decade following the adoption of the Declaration of Independence, and it was pressed by followers of his during his presidency. He fully recognized that, except in a small locality, a viable government must be based on a system of representation, and that certain affairs of state, especially foreign affairs, cannot be effectively conducted in public view or be safely subjected day by day to popular control, necessary though ultimate public approval of foreign policy is in a self-governing country. While he was an egalitarian with respect to rights and opportunity, he might also have been called an elitist, for he believed in an aristocracy of talent and virtue. As President he was as concerned for efficiency in the offices of government as the Federalists had been and considerably more than many members of his own party. He was never an undiscriminating democrat, but clearly he was more democratic than the Federalists in that he sought to set the government on a broader base and was more concerned than they that it be administered in the interest of the people generally rather than in that of special groups. As President he never ceased to think of himself as the representative of the whole people. Recognized on the strength of his famous writings as a herald of freedom, this aristocrat on grounds of birth and tastes well deserved the appellation "Man of the People" which was accorded him by his followers.

Whether or not he should be described as a revolutionary at any time after the winning of American independence depends, of course, on one's definition, but his moderation as President has inevitably caused historians to wonder if, in speaking of the "revolution of 1800," he was not merely engaging in partisan exaggeration. This brings us back to the "spirit of 1776." Nothing was more characteristic of the Patriots at the birth of the Republic than the conviction that the American people were unique in their character, their opportunity, and their mission, and that their experiment in self-government was destined to set an example for the world. To that faith and that vision Jefferson purposed that the country should return. The revolution, or the restoration, he sought to bring about was largely, perhaps chiefly, in the realm of the spirit. The results of his efforts to revive in others the faith of 1776 that he himself had never lost cannot be measured with precision, but if one can judge from the letters and resolutions that flooded his desk, he was notable among Presidents for his success in inspiriting individual human beings.

Besides the "truths" he regarded as axiomatic and the doctrine of the sovereignty of the people, which may perhaps be designated as a corollary, there were other doctrines he accepted and principles he believed in without attributing to them the same qualities of timelessness and immutability. Some of the most important and also the most enduring of these related to the American constitutional system under which he operated as President. Jefferson adhered to the doctrine of the separation of powers and believed in a balanced government. His unhappy experiences as war governor of Virginia did not permit him to share the extreme distrust of the executive and emphasis on the legislative branch of government that had been manifest in the years following the Declaration of Independence; and, before the adoption of the Constitution of 1787, he was on record as being as opposed to legislative omnipotence as to any other. A few years before his election as President, however, when describing the differences between the two parties, he said that the Federalists favored the executive, while the Republicans, believing that branch already too strong, inclined to the legislature.[3]

He himself thought that the Federalists tended to exalt the executive unduly and he reacted strongly against presidential pomp and ceremony. His own unceremoniousness, while not out of character, went so far that he may be charged with putting on something of an act. It seems safe to say, however, that as chief executive he was disposed neither to aggrandize his own authority nor to encroach on the prerogatives of Congress. He was consistently respectful of that body, which he called the Great Council of the nation and recognized as the branch of the government closest to the people. Nonetheless, he exercised influence on legislation which has been rarely matched in presidential history and which probably went considerably beyond his own original expectations. The circumstances under which he did this, and the means he employed, are described in detail in various chapters of this book. His procedure exemplified his practicality and ability to adjust himself to the facts of political life. Perceiving at an early stage that, if desired legislation was to be enacted, he could not stand aloof and content himself with mere recommendations, he acted chiefly through the congressional leaders of his own party, whom he treated with due respect and relied on for counsel. Clearly recognizing the sensitivity of the legislators, he sought to keep his own leadership out of sight. Accordingly, he was described by enemies at the time, and has been by critics since then, as devious, secretive, and hypocritical. More complimentary adjectives may be applied — tactful, discreet, and mod-

[3] TJ to John Wise, Feb. 12, 1798 (*A.H.R.*, III, 488–489).

est, for example — and it seems clear that, in that climate of opinion and those circumstances, he followed the course most likely to be both fruitful and acceptable. He himself may have had some qualms, but the results demonstrated his political sagacity.[4]

Though his relations with the legislative branch, or to be more precise with the majority in Congress, were notably harmonious until almost the end of his first administration and were not marked by open conflict even then, the situation was very different with respect to the third branch of the federal government. He was at odds with the judiciary throughout his first term; and the duel, as it has been called, between the President and the Chief Justice was resumed in his second. The battle between Jefferson and his supporters on the one hand and John Marshall and the champions of the judges on the other was waged intermittently and indecisively. I hope my detailed account of its successive phases will serve to illuminate it, but I should run a grave risk of over-simplifying highly complicated matters if I should attempt to summarize it here.[5] Though marked by doctrinal differences, in my judgment this conflict was basically political and should therefore be viewed in its full setting of events and circumstances.

At this time and afterwards Jefferson privately set forth his views of the proper relationship between the independent but coordinate branches of the government. Considered in the light of his times, these have much to commend them on grounds of reasonableness and realism. It seems sufficient to say here that in nothing that he had said previously and in nothing he said as President did he manifest hostility to the judiciary as such or the desire to make it subservient to either or both of the other branches. He thought it should be genuinely representative of the people, however, and responsible to them. How to make it so without denying judicial tenure and destroying judicial independence was a problem which baffled him, as it has others until our own day. One possible course, which office-hungry supporters of his clamored for, was to replace Federalists by Republicans. What his government did, however, was merely to repeal the act whereby the Federalists in their last days of power created and filled a number of new judgeships. At his behest his first Congress restored the *status quo ante bellum*. He initiated impeachment proceedings against an insane judge who could be removed in no other way, and, less directly, against a justice of the Supreme Court who had flagrantly abused his high office. With the trial of Samuel Chase, however, he had virtually nothing to do. It is

[4] I discuss this matter more fully in my paper "Presidential Leadership and National Unity" (*Jour. Sou. Hist.*, Feb., 1969).
[5] See chs. VII, VIII, XXV, below.

often difficult to distinguish between the policies he himself favored and those the congressional majority actually pursued, but his role in this conflict was much exaggerated and misinterpreted by his political enemies. Attributing to him purposes he never avowed and giving him no credit for the moderating influence he exercised on his own followers, they sought to conceal their own partisanship beneath the mantle of constitutional righteousness.

It was fortunate for Jefferson and his party that their repeal of the Federalist Judiciary Act was upheld by the Supreme Court, for they had previously accused their rivals of taking liberties with the Constitution and were themselves identified with the doctrine of strict construction. Hamilton had said that this doctrine would put the government in a strait jacket, and certain historians have made much of the embarrassment it caused Jefferson in connection with the Louisiana Purchase. He has been twitted for not seeking an amendment to the Constitution when he believed that one was needed. To anyone who follows the course of events leading to the acquisition of the province of Louisiana it should become clear, I think, that Jefferson's decision not to raise the constitutional question was unavoidable.[6] It might be said that in this case constitutional purism yielded to the national interest and that realism triumphed over consistency. It seems to me, however, that the significance of the episode has been overemphasized. Jefferson's scruples, which were voiced only in private, did him credit. The crucial question was whether the government had the right to incorporate such a vast area and thus ultimately change the character of the Union. Jefferson believed that this fateful step should not be taken without the consent of the existing states, but he became less concerned when he saw so many signs of overwhelming public approval. The episode did not show that he had abandoned the doctrine of strict construction, but it did show that he was no rigid doctrinaire.

Others may arrive at a different judgment, but, on viewing this administration as a whole, I find no more inconsistency between Jefferson's public conduct and his previously expressed convictions and beliefs than might have been expected of a sensible man who, after having played the part of critic when in opposition, was faced with the responsibility of governing the country. If, under the pressure to which he was subjected, he had lived up to his own ideals at all points he would have been more than human, and unquestionably there were times when he manifested the proneness to self-deception that is common

[6] See ch. XVII.

to mortals. One is more impressed with his pragmatism in this period than in those that preceded it, but I perceive no indication that he abandoned his high aspirations for his countrymen. At a time when he had many other things to think about besides the "inherent and inalienable rights of man," he countenanced a few actions that could be interpreted as attacks on the freedom of the press.[7] But these were most exceptional and not remotely comparable to the repressive actions of the previous administration. Meanwhile, he himself was subjected to scurrilous attacks which went far beyond any that either of his predecessors had endured and which, in fact, would be difficult to match in the whole of American history. In the face of bitter clerical hostility he strongly and consistently upheld the "illimitable freedom of the human mind." The air his countrymen breathed during this administration was freer than it had been in that of John Adams. One cannot speak with full assurance in such a matter, but it would appear that he presided over the most tolerant government on earth and the most democratic society. There was nothing comparable in the chief nations of Europe at any rate.

When Jefferson took office nobody had any reason to anticipate the most memorable achievement of his presidency, the acquisition of the province of Louisiana. This was clearly in line, however, with the policy he had advocated when secretary of state. There could be no possible doubt of his determination to maintain the free navigation of the Mississippi River on which the economic life of the trans-Appalachian states and territories was so dependent. If denied it, he doubted if they would be content to remain in the Union. The events and circumstances bearing on this diplomatic triumph, which added so much to the popularity of an already popular administration, are amply described in this volume. Here I am merely pointing out that it was the crown and culmination of a policy which was fixed with respect to ends though flexible with respect to means. Jefferson was determined that his country should get New Orleans at some time in one way or another, and by a combination of shrewd diplomacy and good luck he got it, along with much more territory than he was seeking at the moment and a number of fresh problems.

The dismal failure of his efforts to acquire West Florida was not revealed until his second term. In this volume I deal with the beginnings of the ill-fated negotiations and I hope I have cast some light on these. In the end Jefferson was shown to have done some bad guessing about the

7 See ch. XIII.

attitudes of foreign courts, but in launching this diplomatic venture he was pursuing the same policy as in the negotiations for New Orleans and showed the same clear recognition of the western and the national interest. This Virginia landholder was no localist, no sectionalist. He was willing to go to great lengths to procure this coastal region and the river outlets it contained, but he did not accept the advice of his major foreign representatives that he seize it by force. Even if he had believed himself warranted in taking such action, as he may have, it would have run counter to another, and at the time a more important, policy — the maintenance of the peace which he regarded as essential not only to the growth of his young country but also to the success of the American experiment in self-government. The success or failure of the peaceful diplomacy he relied on depended largely on the course of events in Europe over which he had no control and of which he could not be quickly informed. In these circumstances he pursued in foreign affairs a course which may seem tortuous, but he did not lose sight of his long-range goals while giving some of them priority over others.

On the domestic side his most immediate problem, as the first chapter in this book seeks to show, was to effect a peaceful transfer of authority and to unite a politically divided country. The latter aim he never lost sight of and, in the continuing effort to attain it, he followed more moderate policies than many of his own partisans desired. At the same time, he sought to maintain unity within his own party, and in terms of loyalty to himself was highly successful in doing so. In this period he reached the highest point of his career as a party leader, and, if we may judge by the election returns in 1804, he gained the support of an overwhelming majority of his countrymen, including the moderate Federalists.

Jefferson's presidency must be viewed in its own setting of time and circumstance, not in ours. The sort of government he conducted would be as unsuited to the requirements of today as the horse-drawn vehicle he rode in. The proper question is whether it was well adapted to the country's needs in the first quadrennium of the nineteenth century. Opinions may be expected to differ, but mine is that it clearly was. That it was a limited government is certainly not surprising. At that stage hardly anybody outside of Hamilton's little coterie saw any reason why the federal government should do much except in foreign affairs. What the country needed and what the people wanted were not neces-sarily the same, but the immense popularity of Jefferson's policy of *laissez faire* strongly suggests that most people wanted the government to let them alone. Putting his faith in individuals, he sought to increase their freedom and lighten their burdens. Hamilton, the supreme early American advocate of a positive government, charged him with catering to the populace in order to gain popularity. He might have said more about the responsibilities of citizenship, which he had so clearly recognized throughout his own career, and about the dangers of excessive individualism; but he recognized far better than Hamilton the genius of the American people.

His popularity was probably owing primarily to his policies, but he himself symbolized freedom and democracy. His personal contacts with the citizenry were necessarily very limited, but in those he had he showed clearly his respect for the dignity of personality. There is a good deal about him as a person in this volume, especially in the section entitled "The Measure of a Man." He did not cease to be a devoted father while President, and this period was saddened by the early death of the younger of his two daughters. As never before he was now recognized as the chief American patron of science and learning, whose interest extended to everything that bore on human knowledge or well-being and whose universality of spirit transcended all boundaries. Paradoxically, he manifested ardent national patriotism in this same period and achieved his greatest success as a party leader. He has been viewed by some as a man of paradox whose contradictions cannot be resolved. I would not seek to rob him of his fascination by reducing him to a dull level of uniformity, but few things about him have impressed me more than his extraordinary ability to hold diverse and even contradictory things in equilibrium. He showed more composure when in the highest office than he had in opposition, and conducted a balanced government as a well-balanced man.

Elsewhere I am making particular acknowledgment of aid rendered me and kindnesses shown me in connection with this book.

DUMAS MALONE

Alderman Library
University of Virginia
May, 1969

Chronology

1801

Jan. 27   Senate consents to nomination of John Marshall as chief justice.

Feb. 3   Convention with France is consented to by Senate with conditions.

13   Judiciary Act of 1801 becomes effective.

17   TJ is elected President by the House of Representatives on the 36th ballot.

18   He informs Gallatin he will eventually nominate him as secretary of the treasury.

24   He offers R. R. Livingston appointment as minister to France.

March 2   Adams nominates judges and justices of the peace for the District of Columbia.

4   TJ is inaugurated as President.

8   First meeting of executive officers is held.

14   Gallatin sends TJ rough sketches relative to finance.

18   TJ offers passage to Thomas Paine (news reaches America from France in July).

19   He moves from Conrad's to the President's House.

April 1   He leaves Washington for Monticello, arriving April 4. Meriwether Lewis arrives in Washington soon after his departure.

26   He leaves Monticello for Washington, arriving April 29.

May 1   The Madisons arrive in Washington, staying with TJ about three weeks.

14   Gallatin begins service as secretary of the treasury (on recess appointment).

By this date TJ apprehends cession of Louisiana to France by Spain.

Pasha of Tripoli declares war on U.S.

20   American naval squadron is dispatched to Mediterranean.

29   By this date Callender visits Washington.

June 18   Merchants of New Haven remonstrate against appointment of Samuel Bishop.

July 4   Celebration is held at President's House.

12   TJ replies to merchants of New Haven.

30   He leaves Washington for Monticello, arriving August 2.

31   Bonaparte ratifies convention with the U.S., with a proviso.

August   During the month, TJ has his family inoculated against smallpox with vaccine from Dr. Benjamin Waterhouse.

22 Virginia Jefferson Randolph is born at Monticello.
Sept. 20 Francis Eppes, TJ's grandson, is born at Monticello.
27 TJ leaves Monticello for Washington, arriving September 30.
Oct. 1 Preliminaries of peace are signed by France and Great Britain (known in N.Y. Nov. 20).
15 R. R. Livingston sails for Europe from N.Y.
Nov. 6 TJ addresses Circular to Heads of Department.
28 Gideon Granger becomes postmaster general.
Dec. 7 First session of the 7th Congress begins.
8 TJ sends his first annual message to Congress.
19 Senate resolves that convention with France is duly ratified.
20 TJ tells Dr. Rush he has discovered a "flaw" in his health.
21 Petition of William Marbury and others for writ of mandamus is presented to Supreme Court.
24 Peale's mastodon is exhibited to members of American Philosophical Society.

1802

Jan. 1 Mammoth cheese is presented to Jefferson.
In his reply to an Address by Baptists, he gives his position regarding the separation of church and state.
8 Debate on repeal of the Judiciary Act of 1801 begins in the Senate.
Convention with Great Britain is signed by Rufus King.
During the month, charges against Burr of intrigue with the Federalists are circulated.
March 8 Judiciary Act of 1801 is repealed.
16 U.S. Military Academy is established by act of Congress.
29 Convention with Great Britain is communicated to the Senate.
April 6 Internal taxes are repealed.
18 TJ writes R. R. Livingston about the crisis created by the cession of Louisiana.
24 He suggests that Caesar A. Rodney of Delaware run for Congress.
26 Agreement with Georgia for Cession of Western Land Claims is presented to Congress.
29 New Judiciary Act is passed.
30 A convention to form a constitution for the new state of Ohio is authorized by Congress.
May 3 First session of the 7th Congress ends.
5 TJ leaves Washington for Monticello, arriving May 8.
27 He leaves Monticello for Washington, arriving May 30.
July Callender's attacks on TJ begin.
21 TJ leaves Washington for Monticello, arriving July 25.
Aug. 5 Rufus King resigns as minister to Great Britain.
23 By this date TJ has learned of declaration of war by Morocco.
September The Thorntons visit Monticello.
Oct. 1 TJ leaves Monticello for Washington, arriving October 3.

	18	Deposit in New Orleans is closed.
	30	Thomas Paine arrives in Baltimore.
Nov.	*15*	Paine's first letter "To the Citizens of the U.S." is published in *National Intelligencer*.
	21	TJ's daughters arrive in Washington for a visit which lasts until early January.
	23	TJ becomes aware about this time of closing of deposit in New Orleans.
	29	A convention forms a constitution for the new state of Ohio.
Dec.	*6*	Second session of the 7th Congress begins.
	15	TJ sends his second annual message to Congress.

1803

Jan.	*5*	TJ's daughters leave for Virginia.
	11	He nominates Monroe for an extraordinary mission to France.
	18	He sends to Congress a confidential message on a projected expedition to the Pacific.
	31	Senate debates the petition of William Marbury and others.
Feb.	*1–3*	TJ writes Du Pont de Nemours and Livingston about Monroe's mission.
	3	He transmits to House of Representatives complaints against Judge John Pickering.
	19	The new state of Ohio is admitted to the Union.
		TJ suggests a prosecution to Governor McKean.
	24	Decision in the case of Marbury *vs.* Madison is announced.
	25	Ross Resolutions are defeated in Senate.
	28	TJ writes Dr. Rush about his health.
Mar.	*2*	Decision is made in case of Stuart *vs.* Laird.
		House of Representatives resolves that Judge John Pickering be impeached.
	3	Second session of the 7th Congress ends.
	6	TJ offers B. H. Latrobe the surveyorship of public buildings.
	7	He leaves Washington for Monticello, arriving March 11.
	9	Monroe sails for France.
	28	TJ discusses the "schism" in Pennsylvania with Gallatin.
	31	He leaves Monticello for Washington, arriving April 3.
Apr.	*21*	He sends Rush a syllabus dealing with the doctrines of Jesus.
	30	Treaty for the cession of Louisiana to the U.S. is signed in Paris.
		During the month Thomas Mann Randolph and John W. Eppes are elected to Congress.
May	*1*	By this date TJ regards the resumption of the European war as inevitable.
	13	He writes Nicholson about the conduct of Justice Chase.
	17	The right of deposit is formally restored.
	18	Rufus King leaves London.
June	*1*	TJ sends Levi Lincoln an article for publication.
		He answers Gabriel Jones.
	20	He gives instructions to Meriwether Lewis.

July 4 News of Louisiana Purchase is published in *National Intelligencer*.

14 TJ receives documents of Louisiana Purchase.

19 He leaves Washington for Monticello, arriving July 22.

He discusses the constitutionality of the Louisiana Purchase in private.

Sept. 22 He leaves Monticello for Washington, arriving September 25.

Oct. 3 Polygraph is advertised for sale by C. W. Peale; TJ begins to use one several months later.

17 First session of the 8th Congress begins

TJ sends Congress his third annual message.

He submits treaty with France to the Senate.

21 The Louisiana treaty is proclaimed.

During the month Thomas Mann Randolph and John W. Eppes, new members of Congress, arrive and stay at the President's House.

31 Louisiana Enabling Act is approved.

Nov. 24 TJ sends John Breckinridge the outline of a constitution for Louisiana.

Dec. 2 He has Anthony Merry and his wife for dinner.

12 Resolution requesting the President to transmit copies of the 12th Amendment to the states is passed by Congress.

20 The U.S. takes formal possession of Louisiana.

1804

Jan. 6 Impeachment articles against Judge John Pickering are in the Senate.

10 Debate on Louisiana Government Bill begins in Senate.

16 Formal acquisition of Louisiana is reported in the *National Intelligencer*.

17 TJ says he will stand for re-election.

26 Burr calls on him.

Feb. 18 Louisiana Government Bill is passed by Senate.

25 Republican congressional caucus nominates TJ and George Clinton.

28 TJ writes Latrobe concerning difficulties with Dr. Thornton about completing House chamber.

Mar. 12 After impeachment trial, Senate finds Judge Pickering guilty.

House of Representatives votes to impeach Justice Chase.

26 Act for the Organization of Orleans Territory and Louisiana District is approved.

TJ offers private secretaryship to William A. Burwell, succeeding Lewis Harvie.

27 First session of 8th Congress ends.

Apr. 1 TJ leaves Washington for Monticello, arriving April 4.

By this time he is aware of separatist movement in New England.

17 Maria Jefferson Eppes dies at Monticello.

25 Burr is defeated in gubernatorial election in New York.

May	*11*	TJ leaves Monticello for Washington, arriving May 13.
	26	He writes General Armstrong about his appointment to succeed Livingston in France.
June	*2*	He receives a letter of condolence from Abigail Adams.
	4	C. W. Peale and Baron Humboldt dine with TJ.
July	*11*	Burr-Hamilton duel takes place.
	23	TJ leaves Washington for Monticello, arriving July 26.
Sept.	*25*	12th Amendment is declared ratified.
	27	TJ leaves Monticello for Washington, arriving September 30.
Nov.	*5*	Second session of 8th Congress begins.
	8	TJ sends his fourth annual message to Congress.
		During the latter part of the month he sits to Saint-Mémin for a portrait.
		In the course of the month, electors are chosen in the states.
Dec.	*4*	House adopts articles of impeachment of Justice Chase.
	8	James Monroe leaves Paris for Madrid.

1805

Jan.	*6*	TJ tells John Taylor he expects to retire at the end of his second term.
	18	William A. Burwell asks temporary relief as TJ's secretary; Isaac Coles serves in his place.
	25	Pennsylvania Senate acquits three judges of state supreme court.
	29	Debate on Yazoo compromise begins in House (lasts through February 2).
	31	"Libels" on TJ are debated in Massachusetts House of Representatives.
Feb.	*4*	Trial proper of Justice Samuel Chase begins.
Mar.	*1*	Justice Chase is acquitted by the Senate.
	2	Vice President Burr bids farewell to Senate.
		Act further providing for government of Orleans Territory is approved.

The Republican Tack

[1]

A Troubled Transition

SHORTLY before noon on the first Wednesday in March, 1801, a tall and plainly dressed gentleman repaired to the north or Senate wing of the United States Capitol in the new federal city of Washington. Thomas Jefferson, who was nearing fifty-eight, had walked — perhaps he may be said to have strolled — from his nearby lodgings at Conrad and McMunn's to the only part of the projected Capitol that was yet erected; and there, in the chamber where he had recently presided over the Senate as Vice President, he was inaugurated as the third President of the Republic. The Republic itself was nearly twenty-five years old, and for a dozen years it had been conducted under the Constitution which was framed in Philadelphia during the troubled period that followed the winning of American independence. That instrument was destined to endure, this straggling settlement beside the Potomac was fated to grow into a majestic city, and a succession of chief magistrates were to be inducted here as quadrennium followed quadrennium. It was his distinction to be the first of the line in this place, in this first year of a new century.

At ten o'clock that day the company of Washington artillery and the company of Alexandria riflemen paraded in front of Conrad and Mc-Munn's, just off Capitol Hill; and there was a discharge of artillery when he entered the north wing, accompanied by the heads of department, the marshal of the District, and his officers. The President-elect was attended by friends on his walk from his lodgings, but there was no cavalcade on Pennsylvania Avenue.[1] When he arose to speak he faced hundreds of persons in a crowded room, but certain notables were conspicuously absent. Both his predecessor and the bitterly hostile Speaker of the House, Theodore Sedgwick of Massachusetts, had left town by daybreak. John Adams, in fact, vacated the President's House

[1] Most of these details are from the *National Intelligencer*, Mar. 6, 1801. Other accounts are referred to in the next chapter.

at four o'clock. Jefferson's old friend and recent rival was not as lacking in good will as his abrupt and ungracious actions implied: later letters and comments showed that. But to a man of his vanity, still desolate because of the untimely death of a son, the scene in the Senate chamber would have been virtually intolerable, and no doubt his successor was glad he was spared it. The presence of John Marshall, the new Chief Justice who administered the oath to his distant kinsman, was ironical, though mutual distrust had not yet turned into implacable mutual hostility; and, in the light of recent circumstances, very probably Jefferson would have preferred another Vice President to Aaron Burr. But, while averse to ceremony and indifferent to protocol, he was as a rule scrupulously mindful of civilities. And at this time, minimizing both political and personal animosities, he deliberately and wisely sought to be conciliatory and reassuring.

It is easier to see why he did so if we consider not merely his temperament but also the events of the preceding weeks and the spirit which still prevailed among those who had most bitterly opposed him. He had maintained extraordinary serenity in the midst of bedlam, but he was well aware of what one of his contemporaries described as "the uncommonly extravagant ravings" of the times.[2] In the young Republic, thus far, the nineteenth century had been notable for unreconciled political animosities. On this inauguration day any citizen in Boston could have read in the leading Federalist newspaper the following epitaph within a black border:

YESTERDAY EXPIRED
Deeply regretted by MILLIONS of grateful Americans,
And by *all* GOOD MEN,
The FEDERAL ADMINISTRATION
of the
GOVERNMENT of the *United States:*
Animated by
A WASHINGTON, an ADAMS: — a HAMILTON, KNOX,
PICKERING, WOLCOTT, M'HENRY, MARSHALL,
STODDERT AND DEXTER
Aet. 12 years.[3]

Several weeks earlier this same party organ, after listing Massachusetts Federal and Antifederal names in contrasting columns, had con-

---

[2] Expression of Christopher Gadsden, in a letter of Mar. 11, 1801, to John Adams (Adams, *Works*, IX, 579).
[3] Boston *Columbian Centinel*, Mar. 4, 1801.

cluded that the former were clearly superior in "talents, virtues, probity, property, and public services." [4] The generalization may have been nearer the truth in New England than in other regions, but wherever such arrogance was rife the accession of the opposing party to power was viewed with consternation. What the alarmists feared, they said, was "the general ascendancy of the worthless, the dishonest, the rapacious, the vile, the merciless and the ungodly." [5] Since the success of the Republican standard bearers was attributed to the support of such men as these, the defeat of the Federalists was held to mean far more than a change of men: the triumphant party represented a "brutal menace" to public order and the just administration of the Constitution.

Extravagance of language was specially pronounced in the partisan press, but these sentiments can be matched in the private letters of party leaders. Even John Adams, who had broken with the extremists, went so far as to say: "A group of foreign liars, encouraged by a few ambitious native gentlemen, have discomfited the education, the talents, the virtues and the property of the country." [6] He believed, however, that the Federalists were as unpatriotic as the "antis" and blamed his party for deplorable lack of common sense. He himself cannot be fairly charged with lack of patriotism, and his robust skepticism commands respect in any age, but he shared the distrust of popular sovereignty which lay at the root of his party's failure in an allegedly self-governing society. The central political fact of the first weeks of the new century was that the Federalists would not accept the outcome of the election. Thus it came about that for two months after their unmistakable defeat the political future of the country was shrouded in uncertainty.

The occasion of this obstructionism was the accidental tie between the two Republican candidates, owing to a grave flaw in the original electoral system. [7] To Jefferson, the major personal victim of the mishap, the sins of his foes were painfully apparent. It was not merely that, in the years 1798–1800, the dominant group had sought to destroy political opposition, designating this as subversive. It was not merely that he himself had been attacked with a virulence which surpassed that of

[4] Jan. 14, 1801.
[5] Communication, "To the Public," reprinted in *Columbian Centinel*, Jan. 21, 1801, from *Gazette of the U.S.*, Jan. 10, 1801.
[6] Adams to Benjamin Stoddert, Mar. 31, 1801 (*Works*, IX, 582).
[7] Under this each elector voted for two men without indicating which was his choice for President and which for Vice President. For the events see *Jefferson and the Ordeal of Liberty*, pp. 491–505.

the Republican journalists against John Adams. (In fact, this was rarely to be matched in the entire history of American presidential campaigns.) After the popular preference for the party of opposition had been clearly shown in the election, the group in power had sought to defeat the obvious will of that party by electing Burr instead of the universally acknowledged Republican leader. Even worse than that, Jefferson himself had no doubt that, if they had been able to do so, some of the Federalists in Congress would have prevented the election of either, hoping to slip one of their own crowd in. At any rate, the country did not know until two weeks before the expiration of Adams's term which of two men would succeed him or whether, in fact, there would be a legally elected President to inaugurate. There was grave uncertainty and at least a threat of chaos. There was even talk of civil war.

Soon after he became aware of the unanticipated tie with Burr, Jefferson remarked that his fate lay in the hands of his enemies.[8] This was not strictly true, for he had strong and determined friends in Congress, but we may ask what would have happened if these enemies had prevented his election there. No answer to such a question can rise above the level of speculation, and our concern is with what actually occurred rather than with what might have been. Nevertheless, in view of the charges of disunionism which were hurled back and forth at the time, the plans of the responsible Republican leaders and their frame of mind are worth inquiring into. Were they prepared to use force if need be and thus risk the disruption of the Union? Did they contemplate any other form of resistance? How far was Jefferson personally involved in Republican plans and maneuvers?

We have sufficient testimony from key men and crucial areas to venture some tentative answers to these questions. The place where the decisive conflict occurred was the chamber of the House of Representatives. There, according to the Constitution, a choice must be made. In that body Albert Gallatin was unquestionably the Republican leader, and he appears as the key figure on that side in this crisis. He drew a full plan of procedure, with a view to various contingencies. This was communicated to Jefferson and his friend Wilson Cary Nicholas, senator from Virginia, and, according to its author, it was fully approved by Jefferson and by the party.[9] According to the Federalists, the cen-

---

[8] TJ to Monroe, Dec. 20, 1800 (LC, 18511).

[9] This important document, presumably drafted before Feb. 9, 1801, is in Gallatin's *Writings* (1960), I, 18–23. He himself commented on it and on the struggle in a letter of May 8, 1848, to Henry A. Muhlenberg (Henry Adams, *Life of Albert Gallatin* [1943], pp. 248–251).

ters of "disaffection" outside Washington were in Jefferson's own Virginia, where his devoted friend James Monroe was governor, and Pennsylvania, which had a resolute Republican executive in Thomas McKean. It was from these two states that excited Federalist editors said troops would march. Important letters from the two governors, showing their attitude in the crisis, have been preserved. Also, we have some private comments from Jefferson himself in letters and memoranda.[10]

One conclusion which emerges from these and other contemporary records is that the most responsible Republican leaders did not contemplate resistance in the event the House of Representatives should elect Burr instead of Jefferson, much as they would have deplored that outcome. Governor McKean stated explicitly that his state would have acquiesced; and the Republicans properly insisted from the first that the House must perform its constitutional function and choose between the two men who had received an electoral majority. In view of the complexion of the House, where the Republicans controlled more state delegations than the Federalists though the latter had a numerical majority, Gallatin himself did not doubt that they could prevent Burr's election if they stood firm; and, in any case, neither they nor Jefferson saw any choice but to follow the procedure prescribed in the Constitution.[11] Their chief fear was that the Federalists would circumvent this somehow; and they won the first round in the fight when the House, on February 9, 1801, adopted the rule not to adjourn until after it had made an election.[12] Obstructive tactics might have prevented a decision by this body before March 3, but on the face of the record the House was now formally committed to constitutional procedure.

A second inescapable conclusion from what the Republican leaders said at the time is that the designation, by congressional act, of anybody *except* Jefferson or Burr as President would have been viewed as usurpation and resisted. Gallatin, for one, regarded as impracticable and improbable any attempt to make a President by law; he doubted that the necessary bill could be passed or that Adams would sign it. Governor Monroe, indignant though he was at rumors of Federalist purposes, thought it unwise for the legislature of Virginia to take any step founded on the expectation of usurpation, but he stood ready to reconvene that body without delay and went to the utmost pains to keep himself informed of developments. Since he found no need to act we

[10] Most of the more important sources are cited hereafter. See also TJ to John Breckinridge, Dec. 18, 1800 (Ford, VII, 469); Monroe to TJ, Jan. 6, 18, 27, 1801 (S.M.H., III, 253–257).

[11] The vote in the House on this question was by states.

[12] The rules adopted on that day are in *Annals*, 6 Cong., pp. 1009–1011.

have no way of knowing precisely what the non-submission of Virginia would have amounted to, but it might well have been accompanied by the display, even by the use, of force.

Speaking of his own plan years later, Gallatin said: "No appeal whatever to physical force was contemplated, nor did it contain a single particle of revolutionary spirit." [13] The statement seems accurate enough as applied to the purposes of the man who actually directed the successful fight in the House. The only contingency he really feared was that this body would adjourn without reaching a decision, thus bringing on an interregnum; and in that case he was disposed to await the meeting of the next Congress, which would be safely Republican, rather than that the Republicans should themselves assume the executive power. He feared that this might result in the withdrawal of New England from the Union. In the remote contingency of "usurpation" on the part of the Federalist majority in the present Congress, he favored peaceful refusal to submit to unconstitutional authority. Yet he afterwards recognized that, if necessary, this "usurpation" would have been put down by force.

As might have been expected, Jefferson kept aloof from this controversy insofar as he could, but he afterwards said that he conversed with John Adams about the state of affairs when he chanced to meet the President walking on Pennsylvania Avenue. At the moment he was disturbed by reports that "a very dangerous experiment was then in contemplation, to defeat the Presidential election by an act of Congress," devolving the government in any interregnum on a president of the Senate, who would be elected by that Federalist body. This alleged plan was the more dangerous because it contemplated provision for a contingency in advance of the voting and thus would have encouraged the Federalists to prevent a constitutional election.[14] He asserted to Adams that "such a measure would probably produce resistance by force and incalculable consequences," which the President could prevent by negativing it. He got no satisfaction out of Adams, whom he reported as having suggested the simplest and quickest way out — that is, that he insure his election by giving assurances that he would honor the public debt, maintain the navy, and not displace the federal officers.

Jefferson spoke more categorically in a few letters to intimate political friends. After the House had been balloting for four days and while the issue was still uncertain, he wrote Governor Monroe:

[13] Gallatin to H. A. Muhlenberg, May 8, 1848 (Henry Adams, *Life*, p. 248).

[14] TJ reported the conversation with Adams in a memo. of Apr. 15, 1806 (Ford, I, 313), and in a letter to Benjamin Rush, Jan. 16, 1811 (Ford, IX, 297–298). It probably took place before the House adopted its rules of procedure on Feb. 9, 1801.

If they could have been permitted to pass a law putting the government into the hands of an officer, they would certainly have prevented an election. But we thought it best to declare openly and firmly, one & all, that the day such an act passed, the middle States would arm, & that no such usurpation, even for a single day, should be submitted to. This first shook them; and they were completely alarmed at the resource for which we declared, to wit, a convention to re-organize the government, & to amend it. The very word convention gives them the horrors, as in the present democratical spirit of America, they fear they should lose some of the favorite morsels of the constitution.[15]

When reporting his election to Madison soon thereafter, he said that the Federalists were confronted not only with the impossibility of electing Burr, but also with "the certainty that a legislative usurpation would be resisted by arms, and a recourse to a convention to reorganize and amend the government." [16] A few weeks later, after his inauguration and at a time of calm, he wrote differently to his learned friend Joseph Priestley. "There was no idea of force, nor of any occasion for it," he then said.[17] A more correct statement, nearer the full truth, would have been that there was no idea of force among the responsible leaders, *except in the case of attempted usurpation by the Federalists*, and that the occasion for employing it did not arise. At the moment Jefferson, who was congratulating the country on the peaceful settlement of this dispute, presented a half-truth to a lover of peace. Also, he described the probable course of events in the case of the non-election of a President, when the federal government would have been like a clock that had run down.

> A convention, invited by the Republican members of Congress, with the virtual President & Vice President, would have been on the ground in 8 weeks, would have repaired the Constitution where it was defective, & wound it up again.

This surmise was not in accord with Gallatin's later recollection. Many years after the crisis the leader of the congressional Republicans said that there was no intention or even suggestion that a convention be called to reorganize the government and amend the Constitution; only when Jefferson's correspondence was published and when Gallatin read Jefferson's letters to Monroe and Madison did he learn that "such a measure floated in the mind." He said that Jefferson might have wished

15 TJ to Monroe, Feb. 15, 1801 (Ford, VII, 491).
16 TJ to Madison, Feb. 18, 1801 (L. & B., X, 202).
17 TJ to Priestley, Mar. 21, 1801 (Ford, VIII, 22).

for something of the sort or believed that the threat of it would frighten the Federalists, but asserted that under no circumstances would this have been done by the Republicans, whose real strength lay in their devotion to the Constitution.[18] In his plan of 1801, however, Gallatin did refer to the possibility of a Republican meeting in case a new election should be required or usurpation be attempted — a meeting "to form an uniform plan of acting." [19] This contemporary document had greater validity than his letter of old age. Jefferson may have been thinking of this suggestion and have read into it more than Gallatin intended.

That he himself would have summarily seized the position to which he was morally entitled is virtually unthinkable in view of his temperament and philosophy. Judge Hugh Henry Brackenridge of western Pennsylvania, who thought the Federalists quite capable of usurpation, had suggested bold measures. Writing Jefferson in January, he said:

> Were I in the place of President designate, in my present mind I would not hesitate one moment, to announce myself on the fourth day of March next President, and to convene the legitimate authorities instantly to ratify that annunciation.

His thought was that in the meantime the consent of "the rival candidate if he might be so called" could have been obtained in writing; and that in such a case everything depended on "the decision and rapidity of the movement." [20] It is hard to think of Jefferson's playing a part in such a *coup d'état*, and impossible to think of him as initiating it. The role of an American Bonaparte did not suit him. His letter to Priestley may perhaps be viewed as a rationalization after the event, as a description of a possible solution of a desperate situation to which he could have acceded. He could have accepted the first office if backed by the sort of convention that had framed the Constitution, and this convention could have repaired the inadequate provisions for the election of a President. Thus, after he was secure in office, his mind turned to the "peaceable and legitimate resource" which was always in reach, "superseding all appeal to force," and he found comfort in the thought of it.

The actualities of the case in the strategic state of Pennsylvania were better described in a letter written him that day by its governor.[21] Thomas McKean, while saying that his state would have acquiesced in

---

[18] Gallatin to H. A. Muhlenberg, May 8, 1848 (*Life*, pp. 248–249).
[19] Gallatin, *Writings*, I, 20.
[20] Brackenridge to TJ, Jan. 19, 1801 (LC, 18645–18649a); received Jan. 30.
[21] McKean to TJ, Mar. 21, 1801 (LC, 19021).

the election of Burr, asserted that it would *not* have submitted to the appointment of any person who had not received a majority of the electoral vote. In fact, he had framed a proclamation, enjoining the obedience of all officers to Jefferson as President and Burr as Vice President, in case they should agree, as was expected. A resolution, approving the proclamation and pledging support to it, had been drawn for adoption by the state House of Representatives, which his party controlled, along with an instrument to be signed by the Republican senators, in case they were in a minority. The militia would have been warned to be ready, arms for 20,000 having been secured along with brass fieldpieces. An order would have been given for the arrest and trial of any member of Congress or other person found in Pennsylvania who should have been concerned with the "treason" of appointing somebody other than Jefferson or Burr as President. All this, however, the Governor had committed to the flames on his receipt of the pleasing intelligence of Jefferson's election. Had the event been different, he said, the consequences might have been deplorable indeed.

While the Governor and legislature of Pennsylvania were standing by and Monroe was on the alert in Virginia, the issue was decided in the federal House of Representatives in Washington according to constitutional procedure, just as Albert Gallatin had confidently expected. In later years he was disposed to minimize Jefferson's personal part in these events, and that gentleman himself said that it was his duty to be passive and silent. Congressional supporters of his cause chatted with him at Conrad's during all the weeks he was there, but they waged their final fight behind closed doors, ably directed by Gallatin. The loyalty that Jefferson commanded among them stood the crucial test, for their lines held firm, and he did not need to rally them. We may ask, however, if he did anything whatever to win over the reluctant Federalists.

Shortly before his election he wrote Monroe that many attempts had been made to obtain terms and promises from him. "I have declared to them unequivocally," he said, "that I would not receive the government on capitulation, that I would not go into it with my hands tied." [22] Yet he was afterwards charged with having made a "deal" with the Federalist representatives who permitted his election by withholding their votes against him, especially James A. Bayard of Delaware, who actually held the decision in his hands. Since this charge did not become a matter of formal record until his second term and was not widely publicized until after his death, the precise circumstances under which

[22] TJ to Monroe, Feb. 15, 1801 (Ford, VII, 491).

it was made and denied need not be described here.[23] However, the episode on which it was based has some bearing on the vexatious problem of appointments which the new President faced, and on his broad policy of reassurance after a period of intolerant partisan warfare and a crisis which threatened to disrupt the country.

According to Jefferson's own record, President John Adams and Senator Gouverneur Morris told him that all he had to do to gain the election over Burr was to give assurance on the points which most disturbed the Federalists — the public debt, the navy, and the retention of Federalist officeholders. If such reassurance should be regarded as a promise or a deal, the suggestion that he make one came from these high officials. His own reply, he afterwards said, was that the world must judge of his future course by his conduct in the past.[24] He undoubtedly believed that a public statement would have been improper and unwise, and he claimed that it was unnecessary. It should be remembered, however, that in this campaign there was no official party platform, that he had made no public speeches, and that, ever since his retirement from the secretaryship of state at the end of 1793, his views on current questions had been set forth almost entirely in private letters and conversations. It was by no means as clear to his opponents as it was to his intimate friends then, and as it is to students now, just how he himself stood on public issues. Therefore, it was not unnatural for Federalists — especially moderates who were disposed to prefer him to Burr — to seek assurance of some sort. And, by the same token, it was not improper for friends and supporters who were familiar with his views to be as reassuring as they honestly could, while avoiding specific commitments.

On one of the points at issue in the minds of the Federalists, anybody who was acquainted with Jefferson's past record could have spoken with entire confidence. He had never wavered from the position that the national debt was a sacred obligation. There was no reason to expect him to repudiate Hamilton's fiscal policy as established by law, whether or not he liked it. What he had recently objected to was his former colleague's *conduct* of the Treasury and Hamilton's indifference, as he saw it, to the actual payment of the debt. His attitude toward the navy was more ambiguous. He himself regarded that attitude as realistic and flexible, but if his enemies had had access to all the things he had said they could not have satisfied John Adams and Secretary Benjamin Stoddert on this point. But it was not the main point. The crucial question was that of Jefferson's attitude toward the Feder-

[23] For fuller details, see Appendix I.
[24] Memo. of Apr. 15, 1806 (Ford, I, 313).

alists then in public office. With reference to these, James A. Bayard admitted that he himself tried to make a "deal." [25]

Speaking for himself and the Federalist representatives from Maryland and Vermont with whom he was acting, the sole representative from Delaware said: "In determining to recede from the opposition to Mr. Jefferson, it occurred to us that probably, instead of being obliged to surrender at discretion, we might obtain terms of capitulation." [26] His employment of the language of war suggests the deep animosities of the time but was in fact unfortunate: this was a question of bowing to the obvious will of the American electorate, not of surrendering to a victorious military chieftain. First approaching Representative John Nicholas of Virginia, a close friend of Jefferson's, Bayard set forth his terms. He raised the same questions as Adams and Gouverneur Morris — that is, about the public debt, the navy, and present officeholders. But he spelled out the last and crucial one more fully, claiming that subordinate public officers should not be removed "on the ground of their political character, nor without complaint against their conduct."

Though Nicholas said that he considered these points reasonable and in accordance with the views and intentions of Jefferson, Bayard was not content with reassurance in such general terms. He wanted an "engagement" and asked Nicholas to seek one from Jefferson. When the Representative from Virginia declined to do this, Bayard turned to General Samuel Smith, a Republican congressman from the divided state of Maryland who had already shown a proclivity for maneuvering behind the scenes and who, at this stage, enjoyed the confidence of Jefferson.[27] To Smith, Bayard was specific: he mentioned by name the collectors of the ports of Philadelphia and Wilmington, George Latimer and Allen McLane, of whose security he was particularly solicitous. Five years later Bayard said that Smith, after consulting Jefferson, brought back the desired assurances, whereupon he and the other gentlemen named by him withheld their votes from Burr, enabling Jefferson to be elected. Writing his friend McLane on the day of the election, Bayard reported that he had direct information that Jefferson would not engage in a general proscription of Federalist officeholders. "I have taken good care of you," he said, "and think if prudent, you are safe." [28] Thus, from his own account of the episode, it could be argued

[25] In his deposition of Apr. 3, 1806. (M. L. Davis, *Memoirs of Burr*, II, 129–133). See Appendix I, below.

[26] *Ibid.*, II, 130.

[27] For Smith's earlier activities in connection with the presidential tie, see *Jefferson and the Ordeal of Liberty*, pp. 497–498.

[28] Bayard to McLane, Feb. 17, 1801 (*A.H.A. Report for 1913*, II [1915], 128–129).

that Bayard's personal decision in this fateful presidential contest hinged on his friend's security in a minor office. In view of the high character that was given him by both friends and foes, one would prefer to believe that his major motive in 1801 was the preservation of constitutional government and the Union, as he also stated at the time.[29]

The assumption that Jefferson would not make an indiscriminate sweep of Federalist officeholders, such as Bayard had now come to fear from Burr, could have been honestly made, without special consultation, by Samuel Smith or Congressman John Nicholas or any other Republican leader who knew him well. Five years later Smith recalled, however, that he did consult Jefferson after Bayard had asked him to, and that he raised the three points at issue. Jefferson himself said, after the same passage of time, that he did not remember this particular conversation, among the many he had in which such matters were discussed, but that it may have occurred. Presumably it did take place, and Smith's further statement, many years later, that Jefferson was unaware of his purposes was disingenuous, for no doubt the most distinguished boarder at Conrad's expected his views to be passed on. Obviously it would have been unwise, however, for Smith to have mentioned Bayard's name; and such a conversation as occurred must have been informal and casual. The Marylander was no recognized emissary, and in reporting back to Bayard he spoke with only such authority as he himself had assumed. In giving his own opinion of Jefferson's intentions, he probably made these more palatable than he had a right to, overreaching himself in his zeal. He said later that he mentioned the name of McLane, about whom somebody else had already spoken to Jefferson, and that the latter stated that the reports he had received of McLane led to the supposition that this officer was meritorious. Jefferson may have said that at the moment, without committing himself to act otherwise than on the merits of the case when he looked into it further. Actually, McLane underwent an official inquiry but was not removed.[30] Altogether, the charge of a "deal," based on fallible human memory, turns out to be a gross distortion; and if there was discredit in this episode it appears to belong far more to Bayard and Smith than to Jefferson.

If he gave any special assurances, either Bayard did not inform the Federalist caucus of them or the information he gave had very slight effect. Though a little handful of Federalist congressmen abstained on

[29] See, especially, his letter to Samuel Bayard, Feb. 22, 1801 (*ibid.*, 131–132). It should be noted, however, that TJ himself was and continued to be highly suspicious of Bayard.

[30] For further details about the statements of Smith and TJ after the event, and about what happened in the confused case of McLane, see Appendix I.

the final ballot, they did not vote for Jefferson; and all the others remained adamant, supporting Burr to the very last. Far from yielding with grace and proper sportsmanship, they did not yield at all. Jefferson's first conclusion from this was that they had issued a new declaration of war on him and meant to maintain an unbroken phalanx. At the moment he was referring to the House of Representatives. His departure from the presiding officer's chair in the Senate, the day after the publication of his *Manual of Parliamentary Practice*, was marked by an exchange of compliments, but on the senatorial side these were affected in some degree by continuing bitterness.[31] The reply to his graceful farewell address which was presented by Gouverneur Morris for an all-Federalist committee, though laudatory only with respect to the recent Vice President's conduct as a presiding officer, was likewise marked by felicity. It expressed confidence that his official conduct as President would be directed to the honor and interests of the country — "a confidence derived from past events." An amendment was moved, however, to strike out the words we have quoted and nine senators voted for it, to nineteen against.[32]

Whether or not Jefferson was aware of this futile final gesture of disapproval in the Senate, he believed that his unyielding foes in Congress had alienated the large body of moderates within their own party. Looking backward, we can see that these representatives needlessly prolonged partisan animosity and exposed their country to unnecessary danger, compounding the offense by continued intransigence. At the same time they made the conciliatory policy of the new President all the more appealing by contrast. That policy was owing to no deal he had made with his foes, but it was congenial with his own temperament and admirably adapted to the country's immediate needs.

He had no doubt that his election met with popular approval. If the Republican papers may be believed, the news of it was received in the various parts of the country not merely with relief but with joy. Bells were rung and cannon fired in Baltimore, Philadelphia, New York, and even in Boston. Since inauguration day was now so near, major celebrations were generally delayed till then, but one gentleman of the Federalist persuasion in Philadelphia asserted that there had been too much

---

[31] On inauguration day, Mar. 4, 1801, the *National Intelligencer* reported the publication of the *Manual* on Feb. 27. A long review of it appeared in this paper on his birthday, Apr. 13.

[32] Mar. 2, 1801 (*Annals*, 6 Cong., pp. 755–756); see also *Jefferson and the Ordeal of Liberty*, pp. 457–458. The nine die-hard Federalists were Chipman and Paine of Vt., Hindman and Howard of Md., Livermore of N.H., Read of S.C., Ross of Pa., Tracy of Conn., and Wells of Del. Morris and the other two committeemen, Dayton of N.J. and J. Mason of Mass., were among the 19.

bell-ringing already. To the celebrants he addressed this bit of irate doggerel:

> Oh ye rascally Ringers and Jacobin foes,
> Ye disturbers of all who delight in repose,
> How I wish, for the quiet and peace of the Land,
> That ye had round your *necks* what ye hold in your *hands*.[33]

The night before the inauguration, a citizen of a neighboring town, whom the now-jubilant *Aurora* identified with the irreconcilable "aristocrats," acted on another idea. He removed the clapper from a churchbell, so that the triumphant "democrats" would not have the pleasure of hearing it next day.[34] This minor episode may perhaps be dismissed as a mere political prank, though the humorlessness and self-righteousness of implacable Federalism argue against such designation. A protesting witness saw a lesson in it: he remarked that the man who removed the clapper was defeating his own ends, for now the bell would be heard all over the continent, instead of merely in that single town. A similar observation may be made on the conspicuously obstructive tactics of the Federalists in Congress and their uncharitable extremism elsewhere. They provoked a reaction of which the new President, who sought a consensus and tried to guide his conduct by the light of reason, hastened to avail himself.

[33] *Gazette of the U.S.*, Feb. 20, 1801.
[34] *Aurora*, Mar. 10, 1801, speaking of Burlington, N.J.

[II]

Profession and Promise: The First Inaugural

SINCE the House of Representatives did not elect him until February 17, Jefferson had only a little more than two weeks in which to prepare his inaugural address. This was somewhat less time than he had to write the Declaration of Independence. He drafted both documents without any secretarial assistance, consulting no book or paper in the earlier instance and having no need to do so now. As the author of the immortal Declaration, he was out of sight at the climactic moment; that paper issued from the Continental Congress as a manifesto, not as a personal pronouncement. He spoke for the Patriot party then, as he now did for the Republican, but more particularly he now spoke for himself, with his own voice. It was not a loud voice; only a portion of the persons assembled in the crowded Senate chamber could hear it. But, since he gave an advance copy of his address to the publisher of the *National Intelligencer* and Samuel Harrison Smith had it set in type beforehand, the new President's auditors could quickly become readers if they wanted to.

The speech made great noise out of doors, according to contemporary report, and it echoed through subsequent generations. No precise estimate of its immediate impact is possible, but this was undoubtedly considerable, and the first presidential inaugural in Washington proved to be one of the most memorable in the long series. Its enduring appeal may be attributed to its verbal felicity and to the fact that much of it has been deemed timeless, but first emphasis must be laid on the timeliness of this utterance. Whatever may be thought of its bearing on the twentieth century, the address was admirably adapted to the particular circumstances of March 4, 1801.

One of the auditors in the Senate chamber, Margaret Bayard Smith, clearly perceived the significance of the occasion. Writing her sister-in-law, she said: "The changes of administration, which in every government and in every age have most generally been epochs of confusion, villainy and bloodshed, in this our happy country take place without any species of distraction, or disorder. This day, has one of the most amiable and worthy men taken that seat to which he was called by the voice of his country." [1] Since there had been grave doubt until the last two weeks that the transition would be peaceful and orderly, and the people's choice confirmed, the most obvious meaning of this event was that constitutional processes had been maintained and popular sovereignty vindicated. The good lady, who was a cousin of the Federalist Congressman from Delaware as well as the wife of the local Republican publisher, did not refer to previous uncertainty or cast reproach on anybody. Neither did the new President, but he seized upon this occasion to define succinctly the proper relations between the majority and minority in a self-governing society. His words bore directly on recent events and the existing situation, but they also set a pattern for future conduct. That is, they were both timely *and* timeless.

Putting the most polite and magnanimous interpretation on the fierce conflict in which his countrymen had recently been engaged, he characterized this as a contest of *opinion*. He recognized that its violence might have surprised strangers not accustomed to American freedom of expression, thus anticipating the comments of innumerable later visitors on American presidential campaigns. But, he added, the issue now being decided by the voice of the country under the rules of the Constitution, all would "*of course*, arrange themselves under the will of the law, and unite in common efforts for the common good." [2] By assuming this to be a matter of course he helped to make it so, then and thereafter. The acquiescence of the minority and of defeated candidates was not merely a manifestation of good political manners — or, as one would say in the twentieth century, of good sportsmanship. He correctly saw it as a necessary maxim of self-governing society, "a vital principle of republics," the only alternative to which was an appeal to force, "the vital principle and immediate parent of despotism."

Assuming the acquiescence of the bulk of the minority as he did, Jefferson was not disposed to chide or lecture his defeated foes, though some of them appeared obdurate. The main purpose of this man who so

---

[1] Margaret Bayard Smith to Susan B. Smith, Mar. 4, 1801, in *First Forty Years of Washington Society* (1906), p. 25.

[2] Italics inserted. In quoting from TJ's first inaugural, I have used the draft in his papers (LC, 18836–18837). This is full of abbreviations but does not appear to be a first draft, as Ford says the one printed by him is (VIII, 1–6). With the abbreviations spelled out and capitals placed at the beginning of sentences, this differs in only a few minor respects from the text in the *National Intelligencer*, and in the journals of the legislative and executive proceedings of the U.S. Senate. More editorial changes were made in the text in *A.S.P.F.R.*, I, 56–57; and in J. D. Richardson, *Messages and Papers of the Presidents*, I (1907), 321–324.

disliked contention was to assure them, and in seeking to do this he proclaimed a "sacred" principle:

> that though the will of the majority is in all cases to prevail, *that will, to be rightful, must be reasonable;* that the minority possess their equal rights, which equal laws must protect, and to violate would be oppression.[3]

Few passages in this memorable address better deserve to be remembered. Though he did not speak of the "tyranny of the majority," as Tocqueville was to do in classic phrase, he showed that he was fully aware of its possibility and of the necessity to guard against it. One of the things he had striven for, and which his election had served to vindicate (if not yet, perhaps, to establish fully), was the right of political opposition; but, judging from a later portion of his address in which he virtually repeated the guarantees of the constitutional Bill of Rights, he was now thinking more of individuals than of a minority party.

He did not speak here of divisions that were based on the rivalry of organizations or on a continuing struggle between the "ins" and "outs." He believed that parties represented, or should represent, differences of opinion; and in his effort to restore the social harmony which he so greatly prized he now tended to minimize even these. Recent experience warranted his assertion that political intolerance could be as despotic and wicked as the religious intolerance which, as he optimistically averred, had been banished from these shores. But, wisely refraining from uttering a public rebuke to anyone, he attributed the loss of harmony and affection chiefly to the struggle in Europe and concern for national security. In one of his most moving passages he said:

> During the throes and convulsions of the ancient world, during the agonizing spasms of infuriated man, seeking through blood and slaughter his long lost liberty, it was not wonderful that the agitation of the billows should reach even this distant and peaceful shore; that this should be more felt and feared by some and less by others, and should divide opinions as to measures of safety.

One may doubt if the aspirations and excesses of the French Revolution and its aftermath, and the mixed American reaction to these, could be better summed up than they are in this single poetical sentence. Allowance must be made for rhetoric, but beyond question the political bitterness of the last decade of the eighteenth century in the young American Republic was enormously accentuated by the exigencies of the international situation. Then it was that domestic partisans were

[3] Italics inserted.

termed "Anglomen" and "Jacobins." Fortunately for the new President, there was now little excuse to harp on external danger and the time was ripe to remind Americans of their essential unity. This he did by making a distinction between principles and opinions and then resorting to a seeming paradox:

> But every difference of opinion is not a difference of principle. We have called by different names brethren of the same principle. We are all republicans: we are all federalists.

In viewing the last sentence of this famous passage, one should observe that Jefferson did not capitalize the key words and thus turn them into unquestionable party names, as later editors of this address took the liberty of doing. Allowance may be made for his characteristic dislike for capitals, and also for his failure to use terms with the precision of an academic philosopher, but his thought can be best understood if the words are left just as he wrote them. From other things he said about this time, it is evident that he regarded the hard core of the Federalists as unyielding and irreconcilable. He could only have meant that nearly all Americans favored a republic rather than a monarchy and accepted the federal system of government, as contrasted with consolidation on the one hand and full state sovereignty on the other. In this sense, he had used almost the same language several years earlier.[4] This was another way of saying that nearly everybody approved of the Declaration of Independence and the American Revolution, which in his opinion had been clearly vindicated in the election, and the Constitution, which the House of Representatives had so recently maintained. Also, this was another way of saying that they were all loyal Americans, whose patriotism should not be impugned and who should not be at one another's throats. They were not enemies, as might have been supposed by a foreigner viewing the recent election and reading the rival newspapers, but brethren. Presumably he was thinking of those whom he elsewhere designated as "monocrats" when he referred to such as might wish to "dissolve the Union or change its republican form." Not even they need be disturbed, however, since "error of opinion may be tolerated where reason is left free to combat it."

While pronouncing what he regarded as abiding truth he was brushing off the diehards; but they did not need to apply these words to themselves unless they accepted the designation of monocrats, which they could not have been expected to do. Actually, Jefferson's minimiz-

---

[4] To John Wise, Feb. 12, 1798, saying: "both parties claim to be federalists and republicans, and I believe with truth as to the great mass of them: these appellations therefore designate neither exclusively . . ." (See *Jefferson and the Ordeal of Liberty,* pp. 364–365).

ing of differences, along with his conciliatory tone, was agreeable at the moment to the Federalists of all shades — more so than to many members of his own party, as George Cabot and others soon said. What his recent opponents most feared was political proscription, and these words pointed away from that.

The new President touched on a basic difference between himself and the High Federalists when he spoke of the fear of some that a republican government, and more particularly this government, was not strong enough. It was in this connection, in one of the most memorable of his many memorable phrases, that he referred to it as "the world's best hope," anticipating Lincoln's "the last best hope of earth." He himself believed this government the strongest on earth, because of the personal concern of its citizens for it; and he was convinced that it would grow in strength as self-government was extended. Otherwise, he showed no disposition to make the government any stronger, but he spoke of its being "in the full tide of successful experiment," and from this one might have supposed that he did not intend to weaken it.

This hope was implicit in the public approbation Hamilton gave the speech a few weeks later. Seizing upon the reference to "successful experiment," and also on what Jefferson had said about the honest payment of the national debt and the sacred preservation of the public faith, he interpreted the address "as virtually a candid retraction of past misapprehensions, and a pledge to the community, that the new President will not lend himself to dangerous innovations, but in essential points will tread in the steps of his predecessors." [5] This was an overstatement, made with a political purpose of its own, but Hamilton correctly surmised that, in practice, his inveterate foe would recognize the desirability of continuity in public policy and of the obligation to honor past commitments. He rightly sensed Jefferson's desire that the transition from the previous administration be orderly and gradual, as well as peaceful.

Hamilton was not being wholly complimentary when he privately predicted, early in the year, that Jefferson would follow a temporizing rather than a violent policy; he did not say, as he could have said truthfully, that his ancient foe was experienced in government and realistic when confronted with actual problems.[6] But neither before the inauguration nor after it did he view Jefferson as a reckless revolutionary. The

[5] In Address to the Electors of the State of New York, 1801 (Lodge, VII, 194–195). He was opposing the candidacy of George Clinton for governor and comparing the latter unfavorably to TJ on grounds of moderation.

[6] To J. A. Bayard, Jan. 16, 1801 (Lodge, VIII, 581–582). At the time he was urging the Federalists to support TJ rather than Burr; see *Jefferson and the Ordeal of Liberty*, pp. 500–501.

same can be said of John Marshall, though he had had less opportunity to observe his distant kinsman's practicality and made no allowance for it. On the morning of inauguration day, the Chief Justice wrote: "The democrats are divided into speculative theorists and absolute terrorists. With the latter I am *not* disposed to class Mr. Jefferson." [7] Adding a postscript in the afternoon, Marshall aptly characterized the inaugural address: "It is in general well judged and conciliatory. It is in direct terms giving the lie to the violent party declamation which has elected him, but it is strongly characteristic of the general cast of his political theory." The Chief Justice did not care for that "general cast" and Hamilton must have liked it even less, for he was the most conspicuous champion of political positivism in his day while Jefferson sounded here like an apostle of negation.

After recounting his country's many blessings, the new President asked what else was necessary for the happiness and prosperity of its people. His own answer, which was destined to be quoted out of its context of time and circumstance through generations of growth and change, was as follows:

> a wise and frugal government, which shall restrain men from injuring one another, shall leave them otherwise free to regulate their own pursuits of industry and improvement, and shall not take from the mouth of labor the bread it has earned. This is the sum of good government, and this is necessary to close the circle of our felicities.

Judging from this passage alone, he would reduce the functions of the federal government virtually to those of a disinterested policeman and unexacting landlord. The system he would set up, as one might suppose from this, was the absence of a system.

At a later time he said that his first inaugural address, from the nature of the case, was "all profession and promise." [8] The professions were of undaunted confidence in the future of his fortunately situated country, and in the loyalty of its citizens and their ability to direct their own affairs. This was a testament of faith in freedom and self-government, wholly in accord with the Declaration of Independence and presenting a refreshing contrast to the doubts of the High Federalists. It assumed loyalty to the Constitution, which had recently been less conspicuous

---

[7] To C. C. Pinckney, Mar. 4, 1801. The correct text of this letter is in *A.H.R.*, April, 1948, pp. 518–520. Quoting it in his *Life of John Marshall*, III (1919), 11, A. J. Beveridge, who may have had a defective copy, omitted the word "not," which I have italicized.

[8] To John Tyler, Mar. 29, 1805 (L. & B., XI, 69).

among them than among the Republicans. Though he said little here about the construction of that document, he gave some clues in listing "essential principles" which amounted to promises. One of these was:

> the support of the state governments in all their rights, as the most competent administrations for our domestic concerns and the surest bulwarks against anti-republican tendencies.

This suggested a shift of emphasis in the direction of state rights, without specifying just what these were. It was followed by another principle or promise:

> the preservation of the general government in its whole constitutional vigor, as the sheet anchor of our peace at home and safety abroad.

Elsewhere he spoke somewhat more specifically of the distribution of functions within the federal structure. Replying a few weeks later to an address from the General Assembly of Rhode Island, he said:

> To the united nation belong our external & mutual relations: to each state severally the care of our persons, our property, our reputation, & religious freedom. This wise distribution, if carefully preserved, will prove, I trust from example, that while smaller governments are better adapted to the ordinary objects of society, larger confederations more effectually secure independence and the preservation of republican government.[9]

To Hamilton and Marshall, words like these may have seemed the reflection of a pale nationality, but at that time, when communication was so difficult and slow, this view of federalism was far from unrealistic. And the fact that he advocated a limited national government did not necessarily mean that this would be feeble within those limits, or that he himself would be inflexible.

Some of his other "promises" need not be regarded as negative. The rendering of "equal and exact justice to all men" would require diligence no less than fairness; and, even as a policeman, the federal government could extend its power far. The "encouragement of agriculture, and of commerce as its handmaid" might necessitate positive action, despite the present presumption that it would not. The assurance that entangling foreign alliances would be avoided was a negative statement, but the man who made it had already shown positiveness and initiative in the conduct of foreign affairs. Other promises of his can be stated affirmatively, but mostly he talked of rights which must not be disregarded, laying major emphasis on what his government should *not*

[9] May 26, 1801 (LC, 19340).

do. The "sum of good government" as given here was intended to be small.

In his thinking about the proper relations between the majority and minority, he had emerged from the mood of a leader of the opposition and become the responsible leader of a united people. The revelation of this in his address was probably the most important fact about it in the eyes of his contemporaries, and for this reason it was all but universally acclaimed. In his views of governmental functions, however, he had advanced little beyond the mood of opposition — partly, perhaps, because he had had so little time. He was saying essentially what he had said in letters in the last few years.[10] With a felicity which no one else could match, he was setting forth the tenets of his party, which he believed to be also those of the vast preponderance of Americans. He was listing the maxims of republicanism. Fully approving of them, his friend Dr. Benjamin Rush wrote him: "You have concentrated whole chapters into a few aphorisms in defense of the principles and *form* of our government." Margaret Bayard Smith expressed the sentiments of others as well as herself when she said that the address contained "principles the most correct, sentiments the most liberal, and wishes the most benevolent, conveyed in the most appropriate and elegant language and in a manner mild as it was firm." [11] The expressions which seemed most "visionary" to his former foes were those that reflected faith in the sovereign people, and their earliest criticisms of his conduct of the government chiefly related to removals from and appointments to office. The negativeness of his political philosophy was more remarked upon at a later time than it was then.

One of the most pungent early comments on it came from a friend of Hamilton's, as might have been expected. Robert Troup, while admitting that he did not apprehend the serious mischiefs from Jefferson's administration that had been predicted, gave the opinion that it would be "the little contemptible thing that grows of a trimming system and a studied adherence to popular notions." [12] To the High Federalists the designation of the new President as the "Man of the People" carried a connotation of reproach. But the author of the Declaration of Independence took it as a matter of course that in this sort of political society the chief magistrate should "lead things into the channel of harmony between the governors and governed"; and few of his successors

---

[10] See especially TJ to E. Gerry, Jan. 26, 1799 (Ford, VII, 327); *Jefferson and the Ordeal of Liberty*, pp. 408–409.

[11] Rush to TJ, Mar. 12, 1801 (Butterfield, II, 831; M. B. Smith, *First Forty Years*, pp. 25–26).

[12] R. Troup to R. King, May 27, 1801 (King, III, 461).

have doubted that the President must.[13] It was by rendering it truly representative and responsive that he hoped to strengthen the government. Troup added that in Hamilton's judgment Jefferson and his friends could not really conduct the political vessel in "the tempestuous sea of liberty." Perhaps more people would have expressed similar doubts if the affairs of the country had been in as critical a state as they were in 1793 or 1797. But, since the foreign storm had largely subsided and the new President himself was pouring oil on the home waters, it may be doubted if there were many outside of Hamilton's circle who saw any pressing need for the government to do much.

If the former Secretary of the Treasury was not the American originator of the idea of powerfully positive national government, he was unquestionably its most conspicuous early exponent, but he was now in an eclipse from which in fact he never emerged. If it may be claimed that he defeated himself by his own excesses, it may also be said that he could now be ignored *because of* his past successes in establishing the public credit and strengthening the government. An arm like his was not now needed, or at least did not seem to be. The major problems of the Adams administration had lain in the field of foreign relations, with which the domestic turmoil of the time was directly related. But Adams no more conceived of the federal government as a positive instrument in domestic affairs than Jefferson now did, and actually his mind was less flexible. He thought of it primarily as a guardian of public order, and he was likewise concerned to splinter power in order to render it less dangerous. Even if one grant that Hamilton, in seeking a greater degree of consolidation, was doing so in the national interest as he perceived it, one cannot deny that the immediate benefits of his policies accrued to a relatively small group; they did not appear to be in the popular interest. The idea of central power wielded positively in behalf of the people as a whole had dawned on none of these men; and, after allowing for the true Hamiltonians, one may doubt if any considerable number of people now desired much more of the federal government in the domestic field than the maintenance of order, the rendering of impartial justice, and the faithful administration of other affairs expressly assigned to it.

The issue was not between *laissez faire* and the welfare state, for in pre-industrial America nobody envisioned the latter. The extreme against which Jefferson had recoiled was despotism such as he had observed in pre-revolutionary Europe, and which his countrymen had revolted against in a much milder form in their own Revolution. When

[13] TJ to Monroe, July 10, 1796 (Ford, VII, 89).

he was in France, viewing a higher degree of tyranny than anything he had seen previously, he said that European society was divided into wolves and sheep, that officials of all sorts tended to become wolves, that governments tended to devour the governed, while the rich preyed upon the poor.[14] In viewing the economic and social contrasts in the Old World, he expressed the opinion that people living under no government but that of public opinion, like the Indians, were happier than those living under existing European governments. An astute modern commentator suggests that what Jefferson himself aimed at was "a government too weak to aid the wolves, and yet strong enough to protect the sheep." [15] It may be doubted, however, if he ever regarded this figure of speech as applicable to his own fortunate country, whose inhabitants had been schooled for so long a time in self-government, and surely he did not think so now, when his faith in them had been sustained and strengthened. Shortly after his inauguration he wrote: "It is rare that the public sentiment decides immorally or unwisely, and the individual who differs from it ought to distrust and examine well his own opinion." [16] He had deep respect for public opinion, never doubting that government must rest on the consent of the governed. He had not lost, and never did lose, his distrust of governors. His hopes lay in a society of relatively unrestricted individuals. His desire was that all artificial restrictions be removed and men left to master their environment and attain their natural potentialities. Thus, on the American scene at least, his negativeness on the side of government was matched by positiveness on the side of persons. Herein lies a clue to a seeming paradox. For all his gentleness, this advocate of minimal government was not weak or pale as a person; he was vibrant and multi-dimensional, attesting throughout his long, incessantly active, and unceasingly useful life what a man can do under freedom. In his own personality he rounded out an otherwise one-sided philosophy.

During the last decade of his life, in a private letter, he spoke of the "revolution of 1800," saying that, although effected by the suffrage of the people and not by the sword, it was "as real a revolution in the principles of our government as that of 1776 was in its form." [17] The question of the accuracy of this expression can be resolved, in part at

---

[14] TJ to Edward Carrington, Jan. 16, 1787 (Ford, IV, 360). For a stimulating discussion of this, see D. J. Boorstin, *The Lost World of Thomas Jefferson* (1948), pp. 177–178.

[15] Boorstin, p. 190.

[16] TJ to William Findley, Mar. 24, 1801 (Ford, VIII, 27).

[17] TJ to Spencer Roane, Sept. 6, 1819 (Ford, X, 140). Early in his administration he spoke privately of the "two revolutions," but this is his most familiar quotation on the subject.

least, into one of semantics. The term "revolution" assumed in the twentieth century new dimensions of economic and social upheaval which he could not have been expected to anticipate. To him the word had a predominantly political connotation, and if Americans were basically agreed on the principles of the government, as he said in his inaugural address, he might just as well have used the word "restoration." The most accurate statement of the matter, it seems, is that in 1801 he was seeking to return to the principles of the American Revolution, especially by recognizing the sovereignty of the people more fully, and that, in the United States, on the political front at least, he checked what he regarded as a counter-revolution. At the moment he sounded like no revolutionary; indeed, he hardly sounded like a reformer. On the last day of March, reflecting on the difficulty of effecting social change, he recognized the wisdom of Solon's remark, "that no more good must be attempted than the nation can bear." The chief thing was "to reform the waste of public money, and thus drive away the vultures who prey upon it, and improve some little on old routines." To this statement he added another rather tentative one: "Some new fences for securing constitutional rights may, with the aid of a good legislature, perhaps be attainable." [18] The major change that he anticipated was in the spirit of the government. He was promising very little and appears to have been content, now that the danger of tyranny was removed, to let nature take its course.

Yet there can be no possible doubt of his belief, at this dawn of a century, that he and his country were in the morning of a new era. Nowhere did he express this better than in a letter to Dr. Joseph Priestley, the clergyman-scientist whom he recognized as a kindred spirit.

As the storm is now subsiding, and the horizon becoming serene, it is pleasant to consider the phenomenon with attention. We can no longer say there is nothing new under the sun. For this whole chapter in the history of man is new. The great experiment of our Republic is new. Its sparse habitation is new. The mighty wave of public opinion which has rolled over it is new. But the most pleasing novelty is its so quickly subsidizing over such an extent of surface to its true level again. The order & good sense displayed in this recovery from delusion, and in the momentous crisis which lately arose, really bespeak a strength of character in our nation which augurs well for the duration of our Republic; & I am much better satisfied now of its stability than I was before it was tried.[19]

[18] TJ to Dr. Walter Jones, Mar. 31, 1801 (L. & B., X, 255–256).
[19] TJ to Joseph Priestley, Mar. 21, 1801 (Ford, VIII, 22).

In the ringing words of his inaugural address, this "rising nation, spread over a wide and fruitful land," was "advancing rapidly to destinies beyond the reach of mortal eye." To his mind the attainment of these "transcendent objects" lay far less with political governors than with the people, who were intent on possessing and developing this land. His chief domestic task, as he now saw it, was to maintain freedom and approximate equality of opportunity. If, in theory, he carried the minimization of government too far even for that time, and also created confusion by speaking of current policies as though they were abiding principles, one who believed that the earth belongs always to the living generation could adjust himself to changed circumstances and newly perceived realities. His actual conduct of the presidency conclusively proved that. If he was prone to be too sanguine, his hope, in essence, was the historic American dream. The predominantly agricultural setting in which he placed it was destined to change far beyond his expectations, and problems were to arise that he could not imagine. But in that century, except perhaps in the years of civil war, relatively few of his countrymen doubted the ultimate fulfillment of this dream of unparalleled individual achievement and human happiness in the invigorating air of freedom. And until this day he remains its historic embodiment.

If, however, he had been a mere dreamer the great new experiment of the Republic, which as he believed had been interrupted and was now resumed, might have failed or faltered. Nothing of the sort was being attempted elsewhere: the French Revolution had issued in one-man rule, and the counter-revolutionary spirit generally prevailed elsewhere in the Old World. His first task was to make the federal government more nearly a government of the people, and at the same time to make it work. His manners were conciliatory and his preferred methods those of gradualism and patience, but within a year he had manifested a degree of presidential leadership which he himself probably did not anticipate and actually tried to keep out of sight. Thus it came about that the herald of freedom wrote a notable chapter in the history of the American presidency, and, on the national scene, established his historic claim to the title of father of American political democracy. This he did by force of the public opinion he always cherished and now cultivated with conspicuous success.

[III]

From Capitol Hill to the President's House

FOR two weeks after his inauguration Jefferson remained at the boarding-house near the Capitol; not until March 19 did he remove to the big box of a President's House a mile away. He still ate at the common table — where the food was indifferent if Gallatin was any judge. The story that he took the lowest and coldest seat at this table, even on inauguration day, was reported too many years later to be recognized as authentic, but no doubt he continued to be personally unpretentious.[1] Some of the congressmen and senators left before he did, but during these days Conrad and McMunn's continued to be a seat of consultation, and the chief magistrate of the United States attended to the business of his high office in the parlor adjoining his bedroom. He had already invited Captain Meriwether Lewis to be his private secretary, but did not learn of his acceptance until he himself moved to the President's House. At first, therefore, he even lacked a messenger. With the ready consent of John Marshall, acting secretary of state, the chief clerk of the State Department bore the first presidential message to the Senate, which was meeting briefly in special session.[2] This was an unpretentious start, but by common consent it was auspicious.

He could read in the papers of impressive celebrations in his honor elsewhere — notably the one on inauguration day in Philadelphia. In size and splendor the procession there was said to have exceeded anything ever seen in that city, except for the one in celebration of the Constitution.[3] A notable feature of this was the elegant schooner *Thomas Jefferson* on a carriage drawn by sixteen horses, one for each state, with a youth dressed in white on each. William Duane's paper,

[1] In reminiscences of Margaret Bayard Smith (*First Forty Years*, p. 12), said to have been written in 1837.

[2] TJ to Marshall, and Marshall to TJ, Mar. 2, 1801 (LC, 18821, 18825). Their exchange was wholly friendly.

[3] *Aurora*, Mar. 6, 1801. Victory celebrations in Virginia are described by N. E. Cunningham in *Virginia Cavalcade*, VIII (summer, 1958), 4–9.

the *Aurora*, noted that Federalists had no part in this procession, but the rival *Gazette of the United States*, after expressing the hope that the new President, unlike the King of France, would never have to expiate with his blood "a misplaced confidence in unruly and insatiable demagogues," commended the decorum and moderation of the day's proceedings. Perhaps repenting of its own magnanimity, this paper soon observed, however, that while the toasts at one of the democratic dinners were such as might be drunk by patriotic Americans, at other feasts the sentiments expressed were truly "Jacobinical," while their music was "Ça ira, The Rights of Man, Marseilles hymn, &c." [4] Neither side would yet surrender its clichés and old slogans.

More to the point, in fact, were certain new songs and music. What was called "Jefferson's March" was played that day, though one is uncertain just what was referred to.[5] There is some confusion, also, about "Jefferson and Liberty." Designated as "A Patriotic Song, for the Glorious Fourth of March, 1801," this appeared in the *Aurora* several weeks before the identity of the new President was sure, but by inauguration day no good Republican could doubt its appropriateness. From fourteen stanzas we quote two, along with the chorus:

> O'er vast Columbia's varied clime;
> Her cities, forests, shores and dales,
> In shining majesty sublime,
> Immortal Liberty prevails.

> *Rejoice! Columbia's sons, rejoice!*
> *To tyrants never bend the knee,*
> *But join with heart, and soul, and voice,*
> *For* JEFFERSON *and* LIBERTY.

> From Georgia up to Lake Champlain,
> From seas to Mississippi's shore,
> Ye sons of freedom loud proclaim,
> THE REIGN OF TERROR IS NO MORE.

> *Rejoice! Columbia's sons,* &c.[6]

---

[4] *Gazette of the U.S.*, Mar. 5, 9, 1801.

[5] The *Aurora* said it was composed for the occasion, but a march by this name, composed by J. Womrath, was performed in Norfolk "with universal applause" on Feb. 20, while "The People's March" by John I. Hawkins was printed in March in Philadelphia. (Notations of Carleton Sprague Smith and Helen D. Bullock on program of Founder's Day Concert, University of Virginia, 1943.)

[6] *Aurora*, Jan. 24, 1801, printed 14 stanzas and gave the tune as "Willy was a Wanton Wag." The program of the bicentennial concert at the University of Virginia in 1943 contained six stanzas and gave the tune as the traditional Irish air "The Gobby-O." An undated clipping in TJ's political scrapbook (UVA) contains 14 stanzas.

There were other songs, like one beginning "I sing great Jefferson's fair praise," which the Federalist press ironically characterized as an "inimitable ode" without fear of contradiction.[7] But the modern observer, accustomed to the display of presidential trivia by avid journalists and commentators, is most struck by the relative shortage of references to this President as a person, and by the proneness of people at that time to endow abstractions with the attributes of personality. Everywhere Jefferson shared honors with Liberty. In an elaborate pageant in his own state she was depicted as a beautiful virgin, assailed by a king, a bishop, a soldier, an orator (who denounced her as a Jacobin), and various evil statesmen. At the moment of gravest danger, a trumpet sounded and a courier proclaimed that Jefferson was President, whereupon her enemies fled, she resumed her customary intrepidity and, after various symbolic acts like trampling the crown, was surrounded by sixteen beautiful and adoring women — one for each state, of course. By this time Liberty appears to have become a guardian angel; she pointed at "Union" in gold capitals, but all these actions were designed to show that this could not be maintained without her.[8] That was truly an important observation, but there was danger in this apotheosis of abstractions; it was to dog a leader who shared the thought habits of his age but tended and in fact had to be a relativist in practice. The rule of Liberty could never be absolute and any pragmatic limitation of it was likely to offend her votaries. Liberty and union were inseparable, as Daniel Webster was also to say, but they were not always as congenial bedfellows as during this brief presidential honeymoon.

Celebrations in Boston and neighboring towns were on a smaller scale, and, according to the struggling Republican newspaper in the New England metropolis, they were orderly and respectable.[9] The more strongly intrenched Federalist organ, which had gone into mourning on inauguration day, remarked that the fertile valley of the Connecticut River produced "abundant harvests of Federalism and unwavering attachment to right principles," while Jacobinism and yellow fever were endemic in seaports. This paper, however, described Jefferson's speech as neat and conciliatory, and took the line that actually he had announced Federalist principles, to the disappointment of his own followers.[10] No objection was voiced to his "creed," and it

[7] *Gazette of the U.S.*, Mar. 11, 1801.

[8] Described in *National Intelligencer*, Mar. 6, 1801. My brief account gives an inadequate impression of this complicated and, to our minds, extremely artificial performance.

[9] Boston *Independent Chronicle*, Mar. 5, 1801.

[10] *Columbian Centinel*, comment of Mar. 14, 18, 1801. A contributor, LEONIDAS,

was averred that time would attest or disprove his sincerity. This probably meant that future judgment depended on what he did about appointments, seagoing commerce, and the navy. Jefferson's own early judgment, which in fact remained essentially unchanged, was that "appearances of reunion" were very flattering everywhere below New England.[11]

We cannot be sure how many of the newspaper reports and comments he saw but may suppose he read the letters that came to him from all quarters. One of the most encouraging was from Dr. Benjamin Rush, who said that his speech had opened a new era. Never before had this man of science and learning in Philadelphia known the public mind to be more agreeably affected by a publication. "Old friends who had been separated by party names and a *supposed* difference of *principle* in politics for many years shook hands with each other immediately after reading it, and discovered, for the first time, that they differed in *opinion* only, about the best means of promoting the interests of their common country." He could fill a page, he said, with the names of persons, formerly called Federalists, who had praised the speech and he mentioned several. As for himself, he summed things up by saying: "I consider it as a solemn and affecting address to your fellow citizens, to the nations of Europe, to all the inhabitants of the globe, and to posterity to the latest generation, upon the great subject of political order and happiness." [12]

Jefferson got these cheering comments the day before he moved into his new quarters. Several weeks passed before he got from his predecessor at Quincy the brief expression of good will which closed their correspondence for upwards of a decade. The occasion for this was a formal note from Jefferson, written in the third person a few days after the inauguration. In this he said he was enclosing a letter which had come into his hands but was obviously a private one, intended for Adams. Actually, the letter and the papers within it related to the funeral of the ex-President's son Charles, to whose recent tragic death the melancholy father now referred, expressing the hope that Jefferson would never experience such an affliction. Then Adams said: "This part of the Union is in a state of perfect tranquility and I see nothing to obscure your prospect of a quiet and prosperous administration, which

on Mar. 18, describing the speech as "a model of eloquence" and praising his "creed," said that he seemed "determined to kick down the *ladder* by which he ascended."

[11] TJ to TMR, Mar. 12, 1801 (LC, 18923).

[12] Rush to TJ, Mar. 12, 1801 (Butterfield, II, 831), received Mar. 18. In the account of the inaugural I have already drawn on this exceedingly quotable letter.

I heartily wish you." [13] We can regret that Adams had not sent his good wishes sooner, and also that Jefferson did not now send a brief private note of sympathy. To read the mind of either in their silence is impossible, but we may surmise that each of them was embarrassed and fearful lest anything he might say would be misinterpreted. It was to be a long time before they came to understand each other, though happily they did so before they died.

Before his first term was over, Jefferson said that only one act of Adams's had given him personal displeasure: he considered his predecessor's last appointments to office as personally unkind. "They were from among my most ardent political enemies, from whom no faithful cooperation could ever be expected," he said, "and laid me under the embarrassment of acting thro' men whose views were to defeat mine; or to encounter the odium of putting others in their places. It seemed but common justice to leave a successor free to act by instruments of his own choice." [14] Adams's conduct at the end of his administration unquestionably left much for friendship to forgive; and, after due allowance for the pressures of partisan politics, it must be recognized that he unnecessarily complicated the most vexing and pressing of his successor's domestic problems, that of appointments to office. Other comments on the retiring President were much more severe. "You can have no idea of the meanness, indecency, almost insanity, of his conduct, specially of late," wrote Gallatin to his own wife the day after the inauguration.[15]

A degree of personal pique entered into the judgment of the man who was to achieve lasting fame as secretary of the treasury but was at this time more obnoxious to the "Federal phalanx" in the Senate than any of Jefferson's other prospective lieutenants. Gallatin viewed the action of Adams in calling the Senate to meet in special session on March 4 as improper, since time was too short for certain newly elected Republican senators from the West to get there. Accordingly, the overwhelming Federalist majority might be expected to thwart Jefferson's nominations.[16] In fact, Adams was following the precedent Washington had set four years earlier, but he himself had submitted no nominations to the special session of the Senate his predecessor had

[13] TJ to Adams, Mar. 8, 1801; Adams to TJ, Mar. 24, 1801 (*A.-J. Letters*, I, 264), received Apr. 9.

[14] TJ to Abigail Adams, June 13, 1804 (*A.-J. Letters*, I, 270).

[15] Mar. 5, 1801 (Henry Adams, *Life of Albert Gallatin*, p. 265).

[16] Gallatin to his wife, Feb. 19, 1801 (*ibid.*, p. 263). See also TJ to Madison, Feb. 18, 1801 (Ford, VII, 495).

called, since he retained the whole of the existing official family. Strictly speaking, his action in 1801 was not improper, but under these circumstances it was embarrassing.

On the short list of nominations that the new President submitted to the Senate the day after the inauguration, the name of Albert Gallatin did not appear; after the members of the "Federal phalanx" had gone home, and he was ready to assume the duties of office, he received a recess appointment. In any case this list would have been short, for Jefferson could do nothing specific about organizing an administration until assured that he would head it. That is, he had had only two weeks. He already had an understanding with his most intimate friend, James Madison, with regard to the secretaryship of state. For secretary of war he nominated Henry Dearborn, and for attorney general Levi Lincoln, both from Massachusetts. In December he had prematurely offered the post of secretary of the navy to Robert R. Livingston of New York. The Chancellor wisely declined that offer, but he afterwards agreed to accept appointment as minister to France.[17] Jefferson nominated no secretary of the navy now, since he had not been able to find one. His entire list consisted of Madison, Dearborn, Lincoln, and Livingston. After promptly consenting to these nominations the Senate adjourned, leaving to the President the task of organizing the executive branch of the government from these modest beginnings.

He could not quickly assemble his small official family. Madison, besides being unwell, was kept at home by the death of his father and did not get to Washington till May. Since Levi Lincoln, who had served in the recent Congress, was in town, Jefferson asked him to perform the duties of secretary of state in the interim; he was not overburdened as attorney general. John Marshall had continued to serve as secretary of state until March 5. Jefferson's request that he do so is a sufficient answer to the story that at midnight on March 3, Lincoln, on his order, took forcible possession of the office and stopped Marshall from signing the commissions of recent Adams appointees.[18] Dearborn assumed his duties promptly, while Gallatin lingered long enough to attend a couple of meetings with him, Lincoln, and the President, and to give the latter some rough sketches relative to finances. He then went home to Pennsylvania to collect his family, returning about the middle of May. Not until then did he actually receive his appointment, but everybody antic-

[17] TJ wrote Dearborn Feb. 18, 1801 (Ford, VII, 495–496); Livingston, Feb. 24 (Ford, VII, 499).
[18] TJ to Marshall, Mar. 4, 1801 (LC, 18835). Beveridge (*Marshall*, II, 561–562) also denies this story.

ipated it and the Federalists sharply criticized it in newspapers and private letters.

The most important conference that the new President had in his parlor at Conrad and McMunn's with Gallatin, Dearborn, and Lincoln bore on the most immediate of his problems, that of removals from and appointments to public office; and the judgment of his advisers undoubtedly entered into the decisions that were then made, as it did in others made thereafter.[19] Also, this little group shared or approved the early decision to relieve those persons who were still suffering under the Sedition Act or threatened by it. Only three such persons were mentioned at the time and clemency appears to have been extended to no others in this category. One man was still in prison. David Brown, who had been charged with responsibility for the erection of a liberty pole at Dedham, Massachusetts, and with seditious libel against the Adams administration, had received from Justice Samuel Chase the most severe sentence imposed under the Sedition Act, and that despite his plea of guilty. Even after he completed his term of eighteen months, in December, 1800, he remained in jail because of his inability to pay his fine of $480. Adams rejected two petitions from him for pardon; but without waiting for a petition Jefferson pardoned him, on March 12, 1801, remitting his fine. The crucial feature in the pardon of James Thomson Callender four days later was also the remission of a fine ($200), for that notorious pamphleteer had just completed his nine months' sentence and made the payment. His delay in gaining a refund of this caused Jefferson much embarrassment in the next few months and kindled the resentment which led to Callender's later attacks on his benefactor. The only other name mentioned at the meeting at Conrad's was that of William Duane, whose case was still pending. Jefferson stopped the proceedings against him later in the year.[20]

While Adams did nothing to facilitate the transition from one administration to another, two members of his staff were generously cooperative. Samuel Dexter, after a conversation with Jefferson, agreed to postpone his retirement from the Treasury Department; he remained at

[19] TJ's memo. of meeting of Mar. 8, 1801 (Ford, I, 291–293). This continuing problem is dealt with in ch. V, below.

[20] Pardons of Brown and Callender, Mar. 12, 16, 1801 (National Archives, Book of Pardons and Remissions, No. I (1793–1812), ##37, 38; TJ to Edward Livingston, Nov. 1, 1801, regarding Duane (Ford, VIII, 57–58n.). The cases of Brown and Callender are admirably described by J. M. Smith in *Freedom's Fetters* (1956), pp. 257–270, 334–358. Further reference to Callender is made in ch. XII, below. TJ had decided to remit Callender's fine before consulting his advisers, as his letter of Mar. 4, 1801, to George Jefferson shows (MHS).

its head until about a week before Gallatin's return.[21] And Benjamin Stoddert, who lived in Georgetown, stayed on as secretary of the navy while Jefferson was unsuccessfully offering this unpromising post to General Samuel Smith (who at length assumed it temporarily), John Langdon of New Hampshire, and William Jones of Philadelphia. Stoddert did not attend the dinner in Alexandria ten days after the inauguration, which was the major local celebration, but both he and Dexter were invited. The President, Vice President, Secretary of War, Attorney General, and General James Wilkinson attended. "The utmost liberality of sentiment prevailed," according to one report. "The toasts were axioms from the President's inaugural speech." [22] The Postmaster General, Joseph Habersham, who was not of secretarial rank, remained in office until fall. But for the problem of finding a head for the Navy Department, the President himself would have gone home sooner to attend to his personal affairs. He did go on April 1 and can be readily forgiven for remaining at Monticello for nearly the whole of the loveliest of months there. He could not do much organizing or working out of procedure until May, a couple of months after his inauguration. The ship of state, which he proposed to put on its republican tack, got under way very slowly — if, indeed, she may be said to have left the harbor. This was largely by force of circumstances, but time was not of the essence when there were hardly any pressing problems.

One relatively important item of unfinished business was connected with the sailing of a ship. A month before the inauguration the Senate had consented to the Convention of 1800 with France, provided that one article be expunged and another inserted. Thus modified, the treaty was ratified by Adams fifteen days later. Meanwhile, he nominated James A. Bayard minister to France. After the House broke the tie between Jefferson and Burr, Bayard wisely declined this appointment, believing that his acceptance might arouse suspicions of his motives in ceasing to oppose Jefferson's election and that, in all probability, the new President would promptly recall him anyway.[23] Jefferson sent the

[21] Gallatin said Dexter acted "with great civility" (letter to Mrs. Gallatin, Mar. 5, 1801; Life, p. 265). TJ wrote him Feb. 20, and Stoddert, Feb. 21 (Ford, VII, 498–499).

[22] Dinner of Mar. 14; report of Mar. 16 from Alexandria in Boston Columbian Centinel, Mar. 28, 1801.

[23] Borden, Bayard, pp. 97–98. On the whole question of the treaty and its ratification, see Hunter Miller, Treaties and Other International Acts of the U.S.A., II (1931), esp. 482–487. Adams, saying that he had made the nomination in order to hasten the exchange of ratifications, informed the Senate on Mar. 2 that he would leave this entire business to his successor (Journal of Executive Procs. of the Senate, I, 388).

documents to France by Congressman John Dawson of Virginia; and William Vans Murray, minister at The Hague, conducted the negotiations in Paris. In accepting the appointment as minister to France, Livingston attached the proviso that he should not leave for two months; and Jefferson informed him that he would not be expected to go until after the return of Dawson with the ratification by France which would probably take four.[24] There was considerable delay in the full restoration of diplomatic relations, for which Adams had striven so hard; and, by his nomination of Bayard, he added to the impression that he was trying to embarrass his successor. No historic example of bipartisanship in international matters was afforded here, but the Franco-American question, which had so long been vexatious and divisive, disappeared over the horizon with Dawson's boat and stayed out of sight till fall.[25] Meanwhile, it was generally assumed in Federalist circles that Rufus King would remain in Great Britain as minister, and this impression was soon confirmed.

ii

When Jefferson removed from Conrad's to the "great castle" that Abigail Adams found so uncomfortable, this was not yet known as the White House; indeed, a boarding establishment near the Capitol had given itself that name.[26] The President's House, as it was called throughout his occupancy of it, was built of freestone or sandstone, as the North Wing of the Capitol was. It had been painted or whitewashed, but the whiteness of the building was more remarked upon after the War of 1812, when its blackened stone was freshly painted. It had the same external walls as the present main structure, along with the four engaged Ionic columns on the north front, but lacked the north and south porticos which so greatly relieve the severity of the original building. Though these were not added until the 1820's, Jefferson deserves much of the credit for them, since in most respects they followed drawings made by Benjamin H. Latrobe which he approved during his second term.

He bore no direct responsibility for the original design. In the com-

---

[24] Livingston to TJ, Mar. 12, 1801 (LC, 18931); TJ to Livingston, Mar. 24, 1801 (Ford, VIII, 29–30).

[25] TJ received the French notification, with a proviso on their part, in November, 1801. He asked the advice and consent of the Senate on Dec. 11, got it on Dec. 19, and proclaimed the Convention on Dec. 21.

[26] Advertisement in *National Intelligencer*, Jan. 14, 1801. Abigail Adams described the President's House vividly in letters to her daughter and sister, Nov. 21, 1800 (*Letters* [1848], pp. 382–383; *New Letters* [1947], pp. 256–260).

petition for the President's House that he instituted when secretary of state, he himself had submitted a plan, modeled on Palladio's Villa Rotonda and calling for a dome and porticos. Though the prize-winning design, by James Hoban, appears to have been approved by President Washington and the commissioners without Jefferson's having seen it, it was one that he might have been expected to like, or at least not to dislike. Apparently based on a plate in James Gibbs's *Book of Architecture* and bearing considerable similarity to Leinster House, Dublin, it was essentially Palladian in character. A British visitor in Jefferson's first term, describing the house as plain, said that the epitaph of Vanbrugh might be applied to its builder:

> Lie heavy on him Earth; for he
> Has laid a heavy hand on thee.[27]

Jefferson was responsible for the addition of low arcaded wings in his second term, but the President's House did not change externally during the first years he was in it. Abigail Adams, despite her sufferings from the discomfort and inconvenience of the huge mansion, admired the wild but romantic view over the Potomac to distant Alexandria; and she sensed the great possibilities of both the house and grounds while lamenting that the place was so unfinished. Her old friend Mr. Jefferson was more accustomed to unfinished houses: he still had one at Monticello, even though he had ceased to live among flying brickbats and had finally got his whole roof on. This widower had a keen eye for domestic detail and a passion for improvements, but as a builder he liked the start and carrying on of things better than their completion. In a real sense, therefore, this incomplete but promising house suited him, just as this raw new capital city did — as, indeed, this ever-growing, ever-changing American society did.

During his first months in office, the presidential grounds were cleaned up somewhat. A post and rail fence was then erected, and midway in his first term, after he had availed himself of the talents of Latrobe, the leaky roof was wholly replaced. The great stone house was described in a newspaper as "big enough for two emperors, one pope and the grand lama in the bargain."[28] Irreverent Federalist writers

[27] John Davis, *Travels of Four Years and a Half in the U.S.A.* (1803), pp. 171–172. Hoban's elevation of the north front, TJ's, Leinster House, and a design from Gibbs can be conveniently seen in *The White House: An Historic Guide* (Washington, 1962). For expert comments see Fiske Kimball, *Jefferson, Architect* (1916), pp. 53–54, 176–179; see also *Jefferson and the Rights of Man*, pp. 384–385.

[28] W. B. Bryan, *History of the National Capital*, I (1914), 406, quoting Alexandria *Advertiser*, May 25, 1801, from Washington *Federalist;* jocular references in *Columbian Centinel*, May 23, 1801, and elsewhere.

The President's House

Engraving on the title page of Charles Janson's *Stranger in America* (1807)

asked if this was to be the home of the Secretary of State and the Secretary of the Treasury as well as the President. The Madisons stayed there for several weeks in May, but Jefferson's only regular companion in this emptiness was his private secretary. He said they felt like two mice in a church after the Madisons left. A sympathetic observer commented that the President's salary was not adequate to his house, the one being very circumscribed while the latter was of vast dimensions.[29] The salary was actually $25,000, which was a princely sum in those days, but the house had twenty-three rooms, and, according to Abigail Adams, it needed thirty servants.

Jefferson's most pressing immediate problem was that of manning it. During the period of less than two weeks that he camped there before going home to Monticello, he appears to have had at least a steward, a housekeeper, and three servants. They took care of Meriwether Lewis very well, when he arrived just after Jefferson left. In the fall he had another steward, Étienne Le Maire, who stayed with him to the end, and the domestic staff went beyond a dozen before the year was out. Jefferson carefully listed in his account book the members of this staff with their wages. The cook, who often appears in his records as M. Julien, was French as his steward was. Both of them were brought from Philadelphia.[30] His records leave many domestic questions unanswered, but they exemplify his extraordinary attention to detail. They also show that, despite his sincere effort to administer the affairs of the government economically, he conducted those of the First Citizen on an impressive scale of personal generosity.

At the end of his first year as President, he summed up his expenses — continuing to use "D" and not the dollar sign, as we do for convenience here.[31] During this first year he expended in Washington more than $6500 for provisions and groceries, nearly $2700 for servants (some of whom were liveried), and more than that for wines. The latter, to which this connoisseur gave personal attention, are the subject of numerous entries. Among the most interesting of his early expenses were those for a carriage and horses. It was not the fault of his predecessor that he incurred these, as the following episode will show.

[29] Davis, p. 177.

[30] Most of the details here are from the Account Book. The succession of Le Maire was arranged by his predecessor, Joseph Rapin, in August. Among the servants was an occasional slave from Monticello who appears to have received nothing beyond pocket money. Whether or not any of the others were slaves does not appear on the face of the record, but they all received wages.

[31] The summary, Mar. 4, 1801–Mar. 4, 1802, is printed from the Account Book in Randall, III, 21–22, the dollar mark being inserted. TJ was not even using this mark in 1826, when the record ends. A similar summary for 1802–1803 is in the Account Book.

Shortly after Jefferson's election over Burr, John Adams informed him that there were already in the stables seven horses and two carriages which were the property of the United States and available for his use.[32] No doubt this was intended as a considerate act and a gesture of good will. But unhappily, soon thereafter, members of the legislative branch found out that Adams had purchased these vehicles and animals out of an appropriation for furnishings. Republican representatives criticized him sharply for his interpretation of the law, and Congress, in one of its final actions, ordered that these horses and carriages be sold and the proceeds added to the furniture account of the new President. The British representative in Washington believed that Adams's mortification over this was one of the reasons for his leaving town before the inauguration, as it may have been. The episode may also have been embarrassing to his successor, wholly apart from monetary considerations.[33]

Early in the year Jefferson had bought a new riding horse; and, while at home in April, he received four carriage horses which he had commissioned his son-in-law, John W. Eppes, to buy for him in Petersburg.[34] These were dear, as he admitted, but he regarded one of them as the finest gelding in America and said that less perfect animals would not have answered his purpose at all. No more would the Adams horses have suited him, probably, since most of them were advanced in years. Meanwhile, a chariot was being made for him near Philadelphia. After he got this in the fall he described it as neat without any tawdriness. With four horses, plated harness, and two postilions, it must have been impressive, but it appears to have been unused until he was visited by his daughters.[35]

Opinions differed with respect to the adequacy of the furnishings in the President's House at the end of the Adams regime. The economy-minded Republicans tended to be optimistic on this subject and were chiefly responsible for the failure of Congress to make a fresh appropriation for the benefit of the new President. A number of purchases had been made in 1800, however, and approximately $12,000 was available

[32] Adams to TJ, Feb. 20, 1801 (*A.-J. Letters*, I, 263).

[33] Thornton to Grenville, Mar. 4, 1801 (FO, 5:32). For the discussion in which Adams was criticized, see *Annals*, 6 Cong., pp. 1068–1071; for the act including a provision for the sale of all property other than furniture in the presidential establishment, see p. 1572.

[34] For letters of April and June, 1801, about these horses and Account Book entry of Apr. 20, see *Farm Book*, pp. 101–102. The total cost was $1600.

[35] Dr. Enoch Edwards attended to this commission for him, writing him Apr. 17, May 18, Aug. 31, 1801 (LC, 19193, 19290–19291, 19336–19338). TJ expressed his satisfaction Oct. 11, 1801 (LC, 20131). The cost of some $1200 included the harness and two postilion saddles.

from the appropriation of that year and other sources.[36] Jefferson was inquiring into the precise state of this fund by May, hoping that, after the purchase of indispensable articles, enough would be left to buy part of a service of plate which Gouverneur Morris was offering. Actually, Morris sold this service to Robert R. Livingston, before that minister sailed for France. Jefferson said he was glad, since the fund was largely exhausted by the purchase of necessities, and the only articles of plate they really needed were a half dozen casseroles, which he would have to import.[37] Apparently he did that sooner or later, for six silver casseroles were listed in the inventory he drew on leaving office.

By that time the President's House appears to have been well furnished, and there can be no doubt that Jefferson himself contributed directly to the elegance of its appointments. During his first months in office the place may still have given an impression of bareness, but at least by May, when he got back from Monticello and had largely assembled his official family, he made it a center of hospitality. The Madisons were with him when Margaret Bayard Smith, after dining with him, said that he had company every day, though his table was rarely laid for more than twelve. Soon thereafter he wrote his son-in-law: "We find this a very agreeable country residence. Good society, and enough of it, and free from the noise, the heat, the stench, and the bustle of a close built town." [38] Congress was not then in session, problems of protocol had not yet arisen among the diplomats, and it seemed that he could be a country gentleman such as he was at home. But, as the first citizen and a perennial host, he had assumed heavier financial burdens than he realized.

He had supposed that, with his handsome salary, his situation would be sufficiently improved for him to help his two sons-in-law substantially. But, as he wrote young Randolph in the autumn after his inauguration, the extraordinary expenses of his "outfit" made it impossible for

[36] An inventory of furniture, dated Feb. 27, 1801, is in *Historic Preservation* (quarterly of the National Trust), XV (1963), 90–93, at the end of a brief article by Margaret Brown Klapthor. This may be compared with TJ's at the end of his administration, in *Antiques*, June, 1929, pp. 485–486, appended to an article by Marie Kimball. From a statement in TJ's papers (MHS) in the writing of Thomas Claxton, Oct. 6, 1801, it appears that about $6760 of the appropriation of $15,000 in 1800 was spent in the Adams administration. With the balance from this and from the appropriation of 1797, the proceeds of the sale of the horses and carriages, etc., about $12,000 was available to TJ at the start. By Oct. 6, 1801, the expenditures from this amounted almost exactly to those under Adams in the previous year.

[37] TJ to Morris, May 8, 1801 (Ford, VIII, 48–50), Nov. 1, 1801 (LC, 20221). Morris's letters to TJ, such as May 20, 1801 (LC, 19320) were friendly and rather jocular.

[38] Margaret Bayard Smith to Maria Bayard, May 28, 1801 (*First Forty Years*, p. 29); TJ to TMR, June 4, 1801 (LC, 19390).

him to do what he had planned. Accordingly, he then proposed to give each of them something he still had a good deal of — that is, land. He would lay off for them two parcels of from 600 to 1000 acres at Poplar Forest.[39] While he no longer expected to have anything left over from his salary, he thought it sufficient for his own maintenance; and he believed that the returns from his lands would enable him to pay off the burdensome inherited debt he was still bearing. Such was not to prove the case.

To get ahead of the story, he found at the end of his first year as President that his outgo exceeded his income. However, his expenses included building at Monticello, payments on debt, and non-recurring expenditures for his outfit. During the following year, 1802–1803, he attained a virtual balance.[40] That is, his salary then maintained him, though it was no more than adequate for his vast house at any time and in the end proved insufficient.

Not until his second winter as President was Jefferson visited in Washington by his daughters and he frequently bemoaned his lack of family life. His private secretary lived in the household, just as William Short did in Paris. Meriwether Lewis, a native of Albemarle County, was well known to Jefferson, and personal considerations undoubtedly entered into his appointment. In offering it, however, the President said that he especially valued this young officer's knowledge of the army and the West, where he had been serving. After a couple of years the brave and enterprising captain was entrusted with a highly congenial western mission; and in the meantime he was an aide and courier rather than a clerk or an amanuensis. Jefferson wrote his own letters, which were very numerous, making copies on a press.[41] It seems that the present East Room, which had been designed by Hoban as a public audience chamber but in which Abigail Adams had hung out her clothes when its walls were still unplastered, was divided into two rooms for the secretary.[42] The partition was unsubstantial, no doubt, and this end of the house was still in an unfinished state a couple of years later, when the ceiling had given way. Meriwether Lewis was inured to hardship

[39] TJ to TMR, Oct. 8, 1801 (LC, 20116); also, Nov. 16, 1801 (LC, 20289).

[40] Account Book, Mar. 4, 1803. Apparently he did not draw up similar summaries for later years.

[41] TJ to Lewis, Feb. 23, Mar. 31, 1801 (LC, 18766, 19106); Lewis to TJ, Mar. 10, Apr. 5, 1801 (LC, 18909, 19134); TJ to W. A. Burwell, Mar. 26, 1804, defining secretary's duties (Bixby, pp. 105–106). TJ paid his secretary out of his own pocket, the annual salary being $500 at first, $600 later.

[42] William Cranch, nephew of Abigail Adams, reported the division and disposition of the big room to Samuel Shaw, May 15, 1801 (Mass. Hist. Soc. Miscell. MSS, Vol. XVIII). Judging from the order of rooms in the inventory of furniture of 1809, the secretary had two on the first floor.

and imperturbable in danger, but these quarters may have contributed to the depressed spirits which Jefferson observed at times in that intrepid soldier. The President had better working and living quarters.[43] His library or cabinet was at the southwest corner on the principal floor; he had there a desk and an abundance of tables, large and small, as well as a letter press of the latest model. This was an excellent place for writing and for meeting with his official family. Next to it was what Latrobe called the President's antechamber and he himself called his sitting room.[44] Beyond it was the oval drawing room, now the Blue Room, through whose windows the memorial to him can now be seen in the distance. At the end of his presidency and probably earlier, it contained the full-length portrait of George Washington by Stuart, the only thing known to have been in the house during his occupancy that is there at this writing.

During Adams's brief residence, visitors usually entered through this beautiful oval room, which was thus turned into a vestibule, but Jefferson quickly shut off that approach. This was the room on which at first he spent most for furnishings. His visitors made a more dignified entrance on the north front, but until almost the end of his presidency they had to ascend wooden steps and cross a wooden platform before coming into the great hall. The common dining room was on the south front, corresponding to the Green Room of the twentieth century. Though smaller than the public dining room on the northwest corner, it eventually contained an extra large mahogany table in six pieces and a complement of fifteen chairs. The notable thing about Jefferson's dinner parties was not their size but their number. The flat silver was kept in this room, and he may be presumed to have done his entertaining here.

The main stairway, between the public dining room and the library, was not put in until after the middle of his first term, but there was another, on the left as one entered the great hall. Since Jefferson minimized stairways, he was probably quite content with this, though access to his own quarters was not as easy as at Monticello, where they were on the main floor. Here, in the opinion of his daughters, they were too remote. He had a bedroom and dressing room on the south-

[43] See the "Plan of the Principal Story in 1803," drawn by Latrobe, with designations of rooms and comments. Some of these can be read only with the aid of a magnifying glass. In *Restoration of the White House* (57 Cong., 2 sess., Senate Doc. No. 197 [Washington, 1903]) there is a plan of the upper floor in 1903. TJ's inventory of 1809 matches the rooms closely except in the east end of the house, where the chief changes were made.

[44] This corresponds to the present Red Room. His library corresponds to the southern half of the present state dining room, as built in 1903.

PLAN OF THE PRINCIPAL STORY OF THE PRESIDENT'S HOUSE IN 1803
Original drawing by Benjamin H. Latrobe

west, above his library, and besides these there was a chamber which he seems to have used as a sitting room. The oval room upstairs was the ladies' drawing room. Abigail Adams liked it, as apparently everybody did. There was plenty of space for Martha and Maria when they paid their long-awaited visit, but some of the rooms on this floor remained unfinished during Jefferson's first two years in office — that is, until after he made Latrobe surveyor of public buildings.

By 1801 the President's House was flanked by two brick departmental buildings — the Treasury at the corner of Fifteenth and Pennsylvania Avenue on the east, and the home for State, War, and Navy on the west. The latter could not be fully occupied for some time, but relatively adequate provision had been made for the executive branch of the government. Jefferson's own quarters, though not wholly comfortable, were more than commodious, and it was the part of wisdom for him to make the best of them while initiating a policy of public economy. The available funds were insufficient to construct the South Wing of the Capitol, though its foundations were laid. This situation imposed a serious problem, for the membership of the House of Representatives would be increased after the reapportionment based on the census of 1800, and the temporary quarters of that body in the Senate Wing had already proved much too cramped for comfort. During the recent session, the members of Congress had been exceedingly dissatisfied with their accommodations in the federal city, private as well as public, and it was said there were still "prodigious clamors" against the place. It was also reported that the new President was doing all he could "to induce a continuance of the government at Washington," and that presumably he would succeed.[45] At this stage, however, despite his "noble spirit of building" and his vision of a monumental city, he had to reconcile himself to makeshifts.

To the commissioners of public buildings and grounds he indicated the priorities in the summer of 1801, referring to the two "most important objects for ensuring the destinies of the city" which could be undertaken. All others he deemed subordinate.[46] One of these major immediate objects was the building of a temporary chamber for the House of Representatives, an operation already in progress. Alternative plans had been drawn by James Hoban and submitted to Jefferson. He approved the one to raise to the height of one story the elliptical wall in the foundations of the South Wing, the external walls being left to the future. His idea was that what was thus built could be incorporated with

[45] R. Troup to R. King, May 27, 1801 (King, III, 461).
[46] TJ to Commissioners, Aug. 29, 1801 (Padover, pp. 226–227).

relatively little cost in what should be built later. The chief and perhaps the only merit of this plan was its immediate feasibility. The "Oven" was ready for the representatives in the autumn, when fortunately the hot season was past. This low brick building was without beauty, and there was no long-range economy in erecting it in this wise; a couple of years later, Latrobe was compelled to tear it down. By that time the President, having established his reputation for economy, had been granted a respectable building appropriation by Congress, and things were beginning to be done as they should have been from the first.

The other item of top priority at the beginning of the administration was the making of a good gravel road from the new Rock Creek bridge (at M Street) along Pennsylvania and New Jersey avenues to the Eastern Branch. These were the only avenues that existed anywhere except on paper. The District of Columbia included Georgetown, which Abigail Adams regarded as a dirty little hole; and south of the river it took in the larger town of Alexandria, which she only saw in the distance from the President's House.[47] Communication between these relatively old river towns was by road and the Georgetown ferry, or by boat all the way. Viewed from the water the wooded shores were beautiful. What was euphemistically called Washington City, but was really a mere segment of the countryside, extended from Rock Creek to the Eastern Branch of the Potomac (or the Anacostia River), where the Navy Yard was. In 1800 it contained 3210 people out of a total of somewhat more than 14,000 in the entire District and 8000 on the Maryland side.[48] Not for years would this thinly settled area be a city in anything but name, and its means of transportation and communication long remained deplorable.

The "good gravel road," which seemed to Jefferson so imperative, would join the President's House and the buildings grouped around it to Georgetown on the west, and to Capitol Hill on the east, crossing the Tiber or Goose Creek on a recently built stone bridge at Second Street. Then, proceeding onward by New Jersey Avenue, it would lead from the Capitol to the virtually inaccessible Navy Yard and Marine Barracks. Little was done on the last leg of this projected road for some time; and what was done on Pennsylvania Avenue between the President's House and the Capitol was so inadequate that this stretch required Jefferson's personal attention in 1803, when more money was

[47] The retrocession to Virginia of the part of the original District south of the river did not occur until 1846.
[48] For a table, giving the figures from successive censuses, see Constance M. Green, *Washington, Village and Capital, 1800–1878* (1962), p. 21. North of the river, besides Georgetown and Washington proper, there was a division called Washington County.

available; not until after that did it become a real road, bordered with rows of Lombardy poplars. In the meantime, they worked on a foot-way from Rock Creek to the Capitol, using chips of stone from the buildings on the hill to mitigate the dust and mud. In roads as in major public buildings the new era was really a couple of years getting started. Meanwhile, the President could get around much more easily on horseback than in the new chariot which he seems to have been saving for a visit from his daughters.

Jefferson's relationship with the national capital was unique. Next only after George Washington among public men, he was the creator of the federal city. Since his predecessor sojourned there only a few months, he was the first President really to live there; and, because of the smallness of the population if for no other reason, his relations with the residents were unusually intimate. He was in close touch with local officials, the most important of whom were appointed by him under existing law, and his deep interest in local affairs could not have failed to become a matter of common knowledge.

As President he had been able to do relatively little for the place when, for the first time during his stay there, the most important date in the American calendar came round, but his celebration of the Fourth of July was in character. About noon a hundred citizens of Washington and Georgetown, along with a group of Cherokee chiefs, paid their respects to him in the big stone house, incidentally disposing of vast quantities of the refreshments he generously provided in his usual dining room. Though the marines and their band were there, the spirit of the occasion would have been more martial if General Washington had been present. The first President might possibly have "mingled promiscuously with the citizens" as the third did, but the third unbent more easily than the first and lacked the brusqueness of the second.[49]

Most of the persons who went to the President's House that day, and most of those at a festive dinner at his old boarding-house afterwards, were Republicans no doubt; but in community matters in this society there was little ground for political partisanship — especially when Congress was not in session. When Jefferson left this rural capital for good, some eight years later, a spokesman for the citizens said that his "mild and endearing virtues" had made all of them his friends.[50] Over-statement was to be expected at the moment of parting, but, next to Albemarle County, the federal district was his home country, and, as in

[49] This occasion was described by Margaret Bayard Smith in a letter to Mary Ann Smith, July 5, 1801 (*First Forty Years*, pp. 30–31).
[50] Washington Citizens to TJ, Mar. 4, 1809 (Padover, p. 459).

Albemarle, he was not without honor there. On his first Independence Day as First Citizen he was only in the beginning of his unique relationship with his local fellows, but they were already coming to know him as a generous neighbor and a characteristically kindly man.

$\begin{bmatrix} \text{IV} \end{bmatrix}$

The Captain and His Mates

JEFFERSON was by no means the only person of his time who had recourse to nautical metaphors when speaking of the national government, but it was somewhat ironical that he should have done this to the degree he did. A lover of the land and perfectly at home on horseback, he was very likely to be sick at sea and dreaded ocean voyages. Whether justly or not, seafaring New Englanders accused him of indifference to commerce and passed grim jokes about his navy. But reference to the ship of state was so natural as to be virtually inevitable, and in that age of sail he did not have to explain what he meant by putting the vessel on its "republican tack." That is the best-remembered nautical expression of this man of the hills who had assumed the helm. "The storm through which we have passed has been tremendous indeed," he wrote one of his associates of 1776. "The tough sides of our Argosie have been thoroughly tried. Her strength has stood the waves into which she was steered, with a view to sink her. We shall put her on her republican tack, and she will not show by the beauty of her motion the skill of her builders." [1] This was at the beginning of his administration. At the end of it he talked plaintively of having gained the harbor, sounding as though he wished he had never set sail.[2] At that time, acutely conscious of the discomforts and perils of the voyage he had made, he was in no position to realize that it was to prove one of the most memorable in the annals of his country. We shall not attempt to assess it here, but we may ask what sort of captain he essayed to be, and what sort of men he had with him as mates. Metaphors aside, how did he administer affairs of state? At the moment we arbitrarily limit this inquiry to the executive branch of the government, with special reference to his early years in the first office.

Now fifty-eight years old, the new President had been for a genera-

[1] TJ to John Dickinson, Mar. 6, 1801 (Ford, VIII, 7).
[2] TJ to Du Pont de Nemours, Mar. 2, 1809 (*J.D. Correspondence*, p. 122).

tion almost continuously in public life. He had gained his first, and to his own mind his brightest, laurels as a legislator and a draftsman. The Declaration of Independence and the bills he drew within the next few years in the legislature of his own state were in themselves sufficient to ensure him lasting fame; and, through the generations, his countrymen have honored him most, perhaps, because of the noble beauty of his words. But it was frequently alleged, in his own day and thereafter, that he was considerably less impressive as an executive than as a spokesman. It was often claimed by his political foes that he was no helmsman for bad weather. Until this time the charge was largely based on his ill-fated governorship of Virginia during the Revolution. That he was notably conscientious in the performance of his administrative duties at that time, his papers unmistakably reveal; and it is clear that as the chief executive of his own newly constituted state he had little actual power. No one so weakly armed with authority could have been expected to cope with the situation in which the British invasion of Virginia placed him, and we may doubt if he could have done so by asserting the power of a dictator.[3] In other words, his governorship afforded no fair test of his executive capacity, and least of all a test of his competence in normal times. That traumatic experience left an ineffaceable mark on his memory, and unquestionably he learned one thing from it: the necessity of a higher degree of executive power vis-à-vis the legislature than he had had. This particular lesson he did not need to apply immediately as President, for Congress was not in session. His first actions were within the executive branch and the matter of first concern was its organization and direction.

In this he had the advantage of his own experience as secretary of state in Washington's administration and his observations of the Adams government. He followed the procedure of the first President in many ways, while avoiding that of the second. The most obvious weakness of Adams's position as an executive was that, until nearly the end, he was surrounded by department heads not of his own choosing and far from loyal to him. From first to last, Jefferson's lieutenants or mates were loyal. No presidential Cabinet was ever more harmonious. This was partly because of the temperaments of the ministers themselves, and the habit of cooperation they had gained as members of the opposition. Even more, probably, it was due to the President, who made a special point of harmony and to whom they were all personally devoted. In his ability to command the loyalty of his subordinates without needing to ask it, Jefferson was an executive beyond compare.

[3] See *Jefferson the Virginian*, chs. XXII–XXV.

Not until a couple of months after his inauguration was he able to assemble his chief assistants. In the month of May he held a couple of meetings at which five of his officers attended: the Secretaries of State, the Treasury, and War, with the acting Secretary of the Navy and the Attorney General. Madison, who was now fifty-one, had driven up from Orange County, Virginia. His long-time friend the President had advised him particularly about the difficulties of the journey. Regarding Bull Run hill as the worst he had ever seen on a public road, Jefferson had arranged for a couple of men to be there with horses to help the Madisons get up it.[4] In the middle of May the childless couple were still guests at the President's House, but toward the end of the month they set up housekeeping, presumably in one of the Six Buildings at what is now Washington Circle (Pennsylvania Avenue and Twenty-second Street), where the State Department was temporarily quartered. Not until autumn did they move to the house in the 1300 block of F Street, next door to Dr. William Thornton's, which Dolley Madison was to make a noted center of hospitality.

Madison, seven years younger than Jefferson, was the oldest of the advisers. He was not in good health, but fortunately there were few problems in his department at first. He was not really settled for some months, but he was always at home in Jefferson's presence. A physically unimpressive man and a modest one, he evoked respect rather than enthusiasm. He had been relatively little in the public eye since his retirement from Congress in 1797, though he had been extremely active behind the scenes in connection with the legislative protests against the Alien and Sedition Acts in his own state and had been in close touch with his tall neighbor in Albemarle County. While in rustication he had rendered important service to his party as a strategist and draftsman, but his role as party leader had necessarily declined in relative importance as that of Jefferson had grown. He gave no sign whatsoever of personal jealousy, however, and this wise and experienced statesman, whose grasp of constitutional matters was surer than that of the President, could have been expected to be invaluable as a balance wheel. The two men had no secrets from each other, and, throughout their long and extraordinarily harmonious association, Madison was a man whom Jefferson could not do without. The extent of his influence cannot be measured accurately, since their conversations were rarely recorded, but in general it may be said that in both foreign affairs and domestic politics the voice of the Secretary of State was that of prudence and moderation. The most severe criticism of him came, not from Federalists, but from Republicans.

[4] TJ to Madison, Apr. 30, 1801 (MP, 22:55).

JAMES MADISON.

Albert Gallatin faced a more difficult problem than Madison in getting his family moved from western Pennsylvania to Washington. He had two small children and his wife was expecting a third. They lived successively for a brief time in two houses in the general vicinity of the President's, but in order to endure the summer they afterwards took one near Capitol Hill, on the Bladensburg Road. This physical fact was to prove important, for the place became a haunt for congressmen. Gallatin did more than any other member of the administration except the President himself to bridge the gap between the executive and legislative branches.

Jefferson had anticipated that the appointment of Gallatin would arouse more opposition than any other of the major ones, and gave him a recess appointment for just that reason.[5] Some went so far as to call him a "venal Swiss," but the most common taunt against this native of Geneva was that he could not speak the English language intelligibly, and that he was French in spirit as well as accent. Judging from the portrait of him by Gilbert Stuart, made in this period, he had a distinct French look, with his prominent nose and the black hair on each side of his conspicuous bald spot.[5a] This look was not now as great a disadvantage as it had been while he was marshaling the harassed Republicans in the House of Representatives during the half-war with France, but his features lent themselves to caricature. The assertion by the friendly *National Intelligencer* that he was no more a foreigner than Hamilton was met with disdain by the Federalist press. His connection with the opponents of the excise tax in Pennsylvania, prior to the Whiskey Rebellion, was also held against him; and he was described as one who had always opposed the policy of the national government. At this early stage, before his conservative approach to fiscal questions was fully manifest and his extraordinary diligence had become widely known, this even-tempered man was the best available target in the administration.

The blindness of the Federalist leaders to the true character of the new Secretary of the Treasury is revealed by the words of one of Hamilton's intimates. Writing Rufus King, Robert Troup said that all the "virtuous and enlightened" Federalists regarded Gallatin's appointment

[5] May 14, 1801. In March, before leaving Washington to bring back his family, Gallatin attended informal meetings with TJ, Dearborn, and Lincoln. Also, he sent TJ rough sketches relative to finances which anticipated the policy of the administration (Mar. 14, 1801; Gallatin, *Writings*, I, 24–26).

[5a] See the engraving shown here. Henry Adams (*Life of Gallatin*, p. 301) reads more into this portrait than I am disposed to do, despite my admiration for the man.

THE SECRETARY OF THE TREASURY ALBERT GALLATIN
Engraving from the portrait by Gilbert Stuart, 1803, reproduced from the
frontispiece of Henry Adams's *Life of Albert Gallatin* (1879)

as "a violent outrage on the virtue and respectability" of the country.[6] Actually, the despised Genevan could have been properly described as an aristocrat by right of birth; and his wife, Hannah Nicholson, formerly of New York, was a lady by any proper definition. Her social gifts, which may have been wasted in western Pennsylvania, were to prove a valuable asset to him in Washington. Gallatin himself was a man of the highest respectability. Forty years old at the time of his appointment, he was the youngest of this group and was to prove the most industrious. His were the tasks requiring the most assiduous attention. He told his son that during his first two years, while he was familiarizing himself with his office and its details, his labors required every hour of the day and many of the night.[7]

Early in the autumn of this first year a hostile paper paid him a left-handed compliment by saying that, whereas he had been formerly accused of doing his utmost to "*stop the wheels of government*," he now appeared to be the only one of the new rulers who was keeping them going, since he alone was in Washington.[8] It was true of him as it had been of Hamilton that he had to be at the seat of government more than any of his colleagues, and in single-minded devotion to business he represented an improvement on his over-ambitious and over-political predecessor. Far from attempting to build up a political machine, Gallatin, who had much the largest department to administer, conducted it with notable non-partisanship. It is significant that there was no speedy replacement of the most important Treasury officials whom he inherited from the previous administration. Samuel Meredith, the treasurer of the United States, remained in office until he resigned in October, 1801. John Steele, the comptroller, stayed a year longer; his resignation, because of illness in his family, occasioned general regret.[9]

[6] Troup to King, May 22, 1801 (King, III, 454). Henry Adams says that Gallatin was "perhaps of the whole administration the one who suffered least from Federal attacks" (*Life*, p. 277). Such was certainly not the case during the early months of the administration.

[7] Albert to James Gallatin, Feb. 19, 1825 (*ibid.*, p. 607). He then said that it was out of the question to accept again the office he held for twelve years.

[8] Boston *Columbian Centinel*, Oct. 3, 1801. Samples of early attacks on Gallatin can be seen in *Gazette of the U.S.*, Mar. 24, 1801; *Columbian Centinel*, Apr. 18, 1801; and elsewhere. A strong defense appeared in Boston *Independent Chronicle*, May 11, 1801. A good modern evaluation is in Alexander Balinky, *Albert Gallatin: Fiscal Theories and Policies* (1958), ch. 1.

[9] The case of Steele, a moderate Federalist from North Carolina and close friend of Congressman Nathaniel Macon, is of particular interest. He left the government on the best of terms. In *Papers of John Steele*, ed. by H. M. Wagstaff, I (1924), there is much friendly correspondence with TJ and Gallatin. His resignation of Sept. 30, 1802, was finally accepted Dec. 10 (*ibid.*, I, 316, 337-338). He was succeeded by Gabriel Duval of Maryland, while Thomas Tudor Tucker succeeded Meredith.

A more objective observer than the Federalist journalists and leaders sized Gallatin up much more accurately at the outset. Writing his home office, Edward Thornton, the British chargé, said that Gallatin and Madison were the ministers most likely to enjoy Jefferson's full confidence and influence his actions. Others made the same prediction and nobody was surprised when it was fulfilled. But the young Britisher also thought there might be a contest between the two for the President's favor, and in that case he gave the odds to Gallatin, because of the latter's talents for business, his intense application and superior art, and most of all "the greater force and decision" of his character[10] In fact, no rivalry worthy of the name developed between them — partly because neither of them was overly ambitious for himself — partly because Jefferson surpassed them both in art and commanded from both unswerving devotion. During the early months, however, when Madison was unwell, when relatively little was stirring on the foreign front, and when the main concern was that of domestic administration, Gallatin appears upon the face of the record to have been the more important of the two. Jefferson was capable of being his own secretary of state but not of being his own secretary of the treasury. In matters of general policy he conferred freely with both of them, treating them both as peers. The term "triumvirate" which has been so often applied to them is fitting, but the implication that Jefferson was not wholly the head of his official family is incorrect. No one can read the notes and letters that passed between its members and its head without perceiving the deference that he evoked from all.

The British chargé correctly predicted that the other ministers would have little influence outside their own departments, but all or nearly all of them performed some degree of political service. Gallatin made a favorable early report on the two New Englanders in this group. Writing privately he said:

General Dearborn is a man of strong sense, great practical information on all the subjects connected with his Department, and what is called a man of business. He is not, I believe, a scholar, but I think he will make the best Secretary of War we [have] as yet had. Mr. Lincoln is a good lawyer, a fine scholar, a man of great discretion and sound judgment, and of the mildest and most amiable manners. He has never, I should think from his manners, been out of his own State or mixed much with the world except on business. Both are men of 1776, sound and decided Republicans; both are men of the strictest integrity; and both, but Mr. L. prin-

[10] Thornton to Hawkesbury, June 2, 1801 (FO 5:32).

cipally, have a great weight of character to the Eastward with both parties.[11]

The political reasons for these two appointments were obvious, and Jefferson's correspondence leaves no doubt of his strong desire to build up his party in the region of his bitterest enemies. He knew Levi Lincoln of Worcester, Massachusetts, thought highly of his abilities, and recognized him as one of the most reputable Republicans in his state. The practice of having the Attorney General attend meetings of the Executive Council was established in Washington's administration, but that officer headed no department and was not required to live in the capital. He was expected to have other clients than the government, and had his office wherever he chanced to be. Besides the legal counsel he gave Jefferson on occasion, Lincoln provided him with detailed information about politics and public opinion in New England, along with his own political advice. Similar service was performed by Gideon Granger of Connecticut, who became postmaster general in the autumn, weighting the executive branch further on the side of New England. He had an organization to administer but was not recognized as a member of the Executive Council.[12]

Political considerations also entered into the appointment of Dearborn, who came from the part of Massachusetts known as the district of Maine. Much to the point, however, was his excellent military reputation in the Revolution and his opposition to expensive military and naval establishments during his brief and inconspicuous service in Congress.[13] Madison had known him there and may have suggested him to Jefferson, who appears not to have met him before his appointment. There was good reason to believe that he would be a satisfactory administrator of the modest army which existed and which the Republicans were not disposed to augment. He could hardly have failed to be an improvement on James McHenry in the previous administration. By and large, he played his minor role acceptably, and he was an agreeable addition to the official circle. Most of his children were married, and he did not get personally established in the City of Washington until the autumn of this first year, when he brought his family to a rented house on Capitol Hill. Judging from the report of the publisher of the *National Intelligencer*, he was a friendly host and provided abundant champagne from a well-stocked cellar. Jefferson himself said after an

[11] Gallatin to Maria Nicholson, Mar. 12, 1801 (*Life*, p. 276).

[12] Granger became postmaster general on Nov. 28, 1801. On his appointment, see ch. V, below.

[13] I have benefited from reading the dissertation of R. A. Erney, "The Public Life of Henry Dearborn" (Columbia University, 1957).

acquaintance of four years: "General Dearborn and his lady . . . are plain and excellent people, he very much of a farmer . . . You will find them both to be without ceremony, he a man of business and well informed in various branches of it." [14] Dearborn, like all the others, was much concerned about matters of health in the climate of Washington, but he appears to have endured more of its summer heat than any of them except Gallatin.

The new President had been in office more than four months before he acquired a secretary of the navy. He said privately with grim humor that he would probably have to advertise for one. His difficulties must have amused the Federalists, especially in maritime New England, but eagerness to head a declining department was hardly to be expected. After the settlement with France, reduction of the navy was likely in any case; and no one who was familar with the past record of the Swiss Secretary of the Treasury could doubt where the axe of economy would chiefly fall. While Jefferson was waiting for replies to his various offers, the unwanted post was filled temporarily by General Samuel Smith of Maryland; and in the middle of July it was accepted by his brother Robert, a lawyer who had a large admiralty practice in Baltimore.[15] Jefferson made this appointment in desperation; and, after consultation with his advisers, especially Gallatin, he had already laid down the lines of naval policy. Under these circumstances, no doubt the appointee seemed as good a man as he was likely to find. To some extent, however, political considerations probably entered into his effort to attach Samuel Smith to his official family and, failing that, to get Robert. The General was a man of very considerable influence in Maryland and in congressional circles; as a member of the House he had been an important figure behind the scenes in connection with the presidential election. The naval office, which so long went begging, could hardly have been regarded as a rich reward, but Jefferson would have been politically realistic in wanting to keep Samuel Smith on his side. The General was translated to the Senate after a couple of years, and long before this administration was over he was the leader of a recognized faction. How well his brother, a less forceful man, administered his department is until this day a matter of dispute. Gallatin thought him less efficient than Dearborn, and considerably less co-operative in economy. Some conflict between the head of the Treasury and the head of the department most affected by the demands of economy and strict

[14] S. H. Smith to M. B. Smith, Apr. 26, 1803 (*First Forty Years*, pp. 35–36); TJ to John Strode, Aug. 26, 1805, quoted by Erncy, p. 42, from LC.
[15] Robert Smith to TJ, July 13, 1801 (Bixby, pp. 87–88, replying to a letter of July 9 from TJ). The post had been offered previously to R. R. Livingston, John Langdon of New Hampshire, Samuel Smith, and William Jones of Philadelphia.

accounting might have been anticipated. Time was to show that this was the greatest threat to the harmony which Jefferson cherished for his official family. But to a much greater degree than either his immediate predecessor or his immediate successor he maintained it.[16]

One reason for this was that his official family was composed of "mild and amiable men," as a political foe admitted.[17] But this ministerial amiability might have counted for little had not the President himself laid such stress on harmony and set an example for the rest. Harmony was for Jefferson a principle of administration which extended far beyond the circle of his most intimate advisers.[18] He sought it in the relations between the executive and legislative branches, between the federal government and the states, between the governors and the governed. This emphasis was in full accord with his own relations with his daughters, sons-in-law, and numerous other kinspeople. Without a high degree of social harmony, life seemed to him hardly worth living; and in the American context government not based on the approval of the governed would have been a travesty. He was to find that, at best, national unity was incomplete, but unity at the center proved to be attainable.

Here we find him, in theory and practice, in both agreement and disagreement with Hamilton, who laid great emphasis on unity but in his imperious way sought to impose it from above, relying far more on formal organization. Jefferson, though an amazingly orderly man who was characteristically careful about procedure, relied little on mechanism as such and feared the growth of bureaucracy. That was a reason for favoring rotation in office. While a highly efficient person himself and an admirer of efficiency in others, he sought to simplify operations and avoid confusion. Speaking of public administration in the last decade of his life, he minimized its problems. "There are no mysteries in it," he said. "Difficulties indeed sometimes arise; but common sense and honest intentions will generally steer through them." [19] He may have consciously or unconsciously blinded himself to complications he disliked, but he never ceased to put his faith in persons. Having taken care that, unlike John Adams, he should be surrounded by advisers in

[16] Reference may be made here to a letter from Gallatin to TJ, May 30, 1805 (Gallatin, *Writings*, I, 234).

[17] Henry Lee to R. King, June 18, 1801 (King, III, 475). This comment antedated the appointment of Robert Smith.

[18] See the admirable discussion in L. K. Caldwell, *The Administrative Theories of Hamilton & Jefferson* (1944), ch. IX. I am disposed to press the point even further than this discerning author does. He discusses Hamilton's theories in ch. III.

[19] TJ to Dr. J. B. Stuart, May 10, 1817 (L. & B., XV, 112).

basic agreement with himself, he trusted them, deliberately overlooking minor faults as he did in members of his own family. In weak hands such forbearance might have been dangerously imposed upon; but he was a strong man, commanding respect for his character and achievements, an amiable man who was most loved by those who best knew him. It was no embarrassment to him to yield upon occasion to the judgment of Madison or Gallatin, both of whom he deeply respected; and it was in his nature to be respectful of the opinions of them all; but there was no doubt that the head of the table was wherever he happened to be sitting. If his grasp weakened toward the end of his administration, under circumstances which were enough to shatter anyone's morale, that consideration need not concern us yet. In these early years he was the indubitable master of his official household, albeit a kindly one. This degree of mastery could not have been expected to extend to the whole of the officialdom of the time, or to the entire country; but rarely if ever in the history of the presidency has there been equally skillful and successful administration that was based to the same extent on personality.

As Jefferson well remembered from Washington's administration, the first meetings of the department heads and the Attorney General were held in order to discuss dangers which concerned them all. These dangers arose from the Indians in the West and the warring nations of Europe. The executive council, as it was then called, met in the first instance to consider questions of national security. No serious question of this sort was pending when Jefferson himself became President, and during his early months in office he availed himself of the collective wisdom of his assistants with respect to the most pressing of his domestic problems — that of appointments to and removals from public office.[20] To some extent he continued to do this in later months, and he never specifically limited Council meetings to matters of national security; but they soon assumed much the same pattern as in Washington's time, and, because of relative calm on both the western and the Atlantic front, they soon became infrequent.[21] Gallatin favored a general conference once a week, but Jefferson regarded this as unduly wasteful of time, and he appears not to have averaged one a month in any year of his presidency.

The practice he really preferred, or so he afterwards said, was the

[20] This matter is discussed in the next chapter.
[21] For the year 1801, see TJ's memoranda in the Anas (Ford, I, 291–296). The number of meetings sharply declined in 1802 and did not greatly increase until 1806, though some of those in intervening years dealt with important questions.

one that Washington followed at the outset: taking the opinions of his assistants individually in conversation or writing and then reaching his own decision without necessarily revealing what they had said. This was precisely what the first President did with the opinions of Edmund. Randolph, Jefferson, and Hamilton respecting the constitutionality of the first Bank of the United States.[22] Jefferson was disappointed with the result in that instance but liked the method. He believed in a single, not a plural, executive and spoke slightingly of the French Directory as a form of government. Also, he greatly disliked open contention and looked back with no pleasure on the time when he and Hamilton were "daily pitted in the Cabinet like two cocks." Contrasting that situation with the one in his own Cabinet, he said: "the harmony was so cordial among us all, that we never failed, by a contribution of mutual views on the subject, to form an opinion acceptable to the whole." He claimed that there was no instance to the contrary in any matter of importance during his entire presidency.[23] The surviving record shows that there were instances of dissent, but as a rule he and his counselors were so successful in arriving at a consensus that there was no need to take a formal vote. Had there been a sharp division, Jefferson would probably have reverted to Washington's first practice and sought opinions privately. He did that anyhow in an informal way, in effect employing both methods. His most influential advisers, Madison and Gallatin, did not have to wait for infrequent Council meetings to see him.

He followed Washington most closely in the conduct of the ordinary or day-to-day business of the government, showing a diligence comparable to that of the first President and surpassing that of Adams, whom he regarded as an indifferent administrator. The basic idea was that the President should keep his finger on the business of all the departments, and on the affairs of the entire Union, by seeing all the significant correspondence every day and passing judgment on it as he liked. He formalized the procedure in the autumn of 1801, when he addressed a circular to the department heads, describing in some detail the Washingtonian method he wished to follow.[24] Previously, the department heads had submitted correspondence to him in no inconsiderable quantity, but not in the same proportion. His action was intended as no rebuke or indication of doubt as to the wisdom and rectitude with which the public business had been conducted. With pardonable exaggeration he said: "If I had the universe to choose from, I could not

[22] See *Jefferson and the Rights of Man*, ch. XX.
[23] TJ to Dr. Walter Jones, Mar. 5, 1810 (Ford, IX, 273–274). By that time the term "Cabinet" had come into use.
[24] Nov. 6, 1801 (Ford, VIII, 99–101).

change one of my associates to my better satisfaction." But he wished to be informed every day about what was going on and to serve as a unifying factor. Like Washington but unlike Adams, he intended to be the hub of the executive wheel.

Gallatin, who had more business to attend to than anybody else, protested that his correspondence was generally insipid and filled with petty details, sending at the same time a bundle of it which was not wanted, as Jefferson promptly made clear. The President reassured his exceedingly diligent Secretary of the Treasury that experience would soon show the department heads the sort of letters he really ought to see.[25] He did not wish to be swamped with routine business, but it is hard for anyone going through his papers in this period to escape the impression that he often must have been. Even though he and his department heads were in what was little more than a village and the major offices were close together, a continuous stream of notes and memoranda passed between them. Often in the third person, these now seem quaint but they suggest that, in the top echelon, the public business was conducted with politeness and grace. "Th: Jefferson" or "Th: J," after presenting his compliments to one of his secretaries, made a request or suggestion. The Secretary of State or Secretary of the Navy extended his complimentary greetings before passing on a bit of information. Gallatin, who had so many notes to write, avoided wasteful preliminaries, but nobody appears ever to have been informal, and everybody ended his communications with a polite flourish. The words "affection" and "affectionate" were often conjoined with "respect" and "attachment," but the use of first names would have been unthinkable. Besides a certain quaintness, there is some humor in these interminable departmental communications. It appears to have been quite unconscious in a note from a lesser official of the Navy Department who had the honor of enclosing to the President a letter "containing the pleasing intelligence that the beef and pork ordered for the *Chesapeake* about the safety of which some apprehensions were entertained had safely arrived." [26]

Daily communication between the departments and the President was rendered impossible in the previous administration, Jefferson said, because of Adams's "long and habitual absences" in Massachusetts. Toward the end of the first summer of his own presidency, an unfriendly newspaper said that it would be difficult to say just where the

[25] Gallatin to TJ, Nov. 9, 1801 (Gallatin, *Writings*, I, 58); TJ to Gallatin, Nov. 10, 1801 (LC, 20260).
[26] Mar. 6, 1802 (LC, 20885).

government then was. The President was at Monticello, the Secretary of State somewhere in Virginia, and others at various places away from Washington, though admittedly the Secretary of the Treasury was there.[27] Writing Gallatin from his own house a few weeks later, Jefferson took note of such complaints; and, after congratulating Gallatin on the improved health of his family and the recent addition to it, explained his own policy and practice with respect to absence from the seat of government.

> I consider it as a trying experiment for a person from the mountains to pass the two bilious months on the tide-water. I have not done it these forty years, and nothing should induce me to do it. As it is not possible but that the Administration must take some portion of time for their own affairs, I think it best they should select that season for absence. General Washington set the example of those two months; Mr. Adams extended them to eight months. I should not suppose our bringing it back to two months a ground for grumbling, but, grumble who will, I will never pass those two months on tide-water.[28]

His unvarying practice, then, was to spend the months of August and September on his mountain; and, far from berating his major officers for being away from the seat of government in these unhealthy months, he chided them for being there. The person he admonished most was Gallatin, who, a year later, remained through August in what Jefferson regarded as a dangerous situation. On his arrival in New York in early September, Gallatin admitted the bad effects of his stay in Washington, lamenting that the situation of the place should be "an impediment to that constant superintendence which is so essentially necessary in the Treasury Department." [29]

Complaints about the absence of high officials were answered in the friendly Washington paper, the *National Intelligencer*. There it was pointed out that both of Jefferson's predecessors, and especially Adams, went considerably farther from the capital. He was only a hundred miles away, and had so arranged things that information could reach him in two days and an answer be back within a week.[30] For those times, this communication was generally fast enough; and actually the Secretaries of War and the Navy, as well as Gallatin, remained in the unhealthful city when there seemed to be real need. When he himself

[27] Boston *Columbian Centinel*, Aug. 12, 1801.

[28] TJ to Gallatin, Sept. 18, 1801 (Ford, VIII, 95).

[29] Gallatin to TJ, Sept. 9, 1802; see also TJ to Gallatin, Aug. 23, 1802 (Gallatin, *Writings*, I, 94, 96).

[30] *National Intelligencer*, Sept. 25, 1801.

was at home the presence of Madison in the neighboring county of Orange was a real convenience, for communication between them was relatively quick and easy.

At Monticello he breathed more salubrious air than in low-lying Washington, and, at the end of his first presidential summer, he was glad to be at home for paternal and grandpaternal reasons. Both of his daughters were there, and each presented him with a new grandchild during this visit.[31] On human grounds these few weeks on the mountaintop were also notable for the fact that, during them, the President of the United States inoculated against smallpox his family, among whom he included slaves, with virus he had received from Dr. Benjamin Waterhouse of Boston. Not only did he safeguard his own household by supporting this noble medical pioneer; he caused vaccine inoculation to "commence its career" in Virginia (and shortly in the District of Columbia) "under more favorable circumstances than in any other state." [32]

He contributed to public as well as private health by repairing to Monticello, but he hardly enjoyed a real vacation. He claimed, indeed, that he was more pressed than when at the seat of government, since he often had to write a letter instead of settling a matter with a few words. Nor did he enjoy the privacy he had counted on; he was so besieged by guests and callers that he told his daughter Martha in the first year of his presidency that he must henceforth make his visits home by stealth.[33]

From his own record of correspondence it appears that he received more letters during his first presidential vacation than he normally did in the same length of time in Washington, and that he answered a larger proportion of them. There can be no possible doubt that he was enormously occupied with the public business. His private secretary was not with him and would have been of no help with correspondence, for Jefferson wrote his own letters, making press copies for the record. In Washington his secretary served him chiefly as an aide de camp, a messenger, and a helper with guests. In the President's House he could do more by word of mouth, but if his own statement is to be believed he

31 Virginia Jefferson Randolph and Francis Eppes. For family details, see pp. 160–161, below.

32 Benjamin Waterhouse to TJ, Oct. 1, 1801 (LC, 20093–20094). TJ reported to Dr. Shore of D.C. on Sept. 12, 1801, that with perfect success he had inoculated about 50 members of his "family," while his two sons-in-law had respectively inoculated 60 and 70 of theirs. This letter and others on the subject were printed by Dr. R. H. Halsey in *How the President, Thomas Jefferson, and Dr. Benjamin Waterhouse established vaccination as a public health procedure* (Privately printed, New York, 1936).

33 TJ to Martha, Oct. 19, 1801 (*Family Letters*, p. 209).

rarely laid down his pen. Writing his son-in-law in the autumn about his business, he said: "It is now got to a steady and uniform course. It keeps me from 10 to 12 and 13 hours a day at my writing table, giving me an interval of 4 hours for riding, dining and a little unbending." [34]

Before Congress met he had to draft important official papers, such as his annual message to that body, but he must have arisen often from his writing table to receive callers, since he was always accessible to them. His personal contacts were of the first importance, and the record of these is in the nature of the case incomplete, but his extraordinary industry is sufficiently revealed by his surviving papers. These leave no possible doubt of his exceptional diligence in the performance of the public business, both in its larger aspects and in its daily processes. Rarely if ever has the first office in the Republic been occupied by a more capable administrator.[35]

By contemporary standards, his chief associates in the executive branch were competent, Gallatin and Madison being highly so. The question of administration, however, cannot be separated from that of appointments to lesser office. The life of this captain would have been much simpler and his days much less laborious if he had not had to give so much of his attention to the crew.

[34] TJ to TMR, Nov. 16, 1801 (LC, 20289).
[35] L. D. White, in *The Jeffersonians* (1951), ch. 1, recognizes TJ's important contributions to administration in the larger sense; but the statement that he was not interested in "the normal process of day-to-day administration" should not be interpreted as meaning that he played only a minor part in this.

Democratizing the Government

[V]

The Dreadful Burden of Appointments

THE problem of appointments to public office was not the gravest that Jefferson faced during his presidency, but it was the most burdensome and vexatious, especially in the first year or two. His papers do not reveal the whole burden he bore, for they report few of his conversations, but they show unmistakably that the load was very heavy. His situation was less difficult than that of Lincoln, whose accession sixty years later also marked a change of parties. In a time of dire national peril the strange tall man from Illinois was beset by a "mob of candidates" and, according to report, was handling the whole patronage, great and small.[1] He was appointing a consul at Hamburg, an agent to the Choctaws and Chickasaws, and a marshal for Kansas while the Southern Confederacy was forming. Fortunately, Jefferson operated in no such atmosphere of crisis. One reason for the great emphasis on appointments in letters and newspapers during his first months in office was that there was little else to talk about. Both his political enemies and friends were watching him as he set about organizing his government, and in filling its offices he met his first test after the inauguration.

The federal establishment in his time was small in comparison with that of Lincoln, and a pygmy by contrast with the giant of the twentieth century, but the roll of civil, military, and naval officers communicated by him to Congress early in 1802 fills nearly sixty pages in a folio volume. The growth under Federalist rule is suggested by a comparison between this roll and one prepared by Hamilton a decade earlier which fills only eleven pages.[2] Jefferson and Gallatin were unable to go back to that, though they had considerable success at first in shortening the list they inherited. Many of the officers on it got most or all of their remuneration from fees. Notable among these were the collectors at

---

[1] J. G. Randall, *Lincoln the President*, I (1945), 311.
[2] The roll as communicated on Feb. 17, 1802, is in *A.S.P., Class X, Misc.*, I (1834), 260–319. For the list for the year ending Oct. 1, 1792, see pp. 57–67.

the chief ports, who were the best paid public employees after the President himself. A few of them got almost as much as the Secretary of the Treasury and the Chief Justice together.[3] Though it may be said of Jefferson as it was of Lincoln that he concerned himself with offices both large and small, his relation with the minor posts was generally nominal. More to the point are lists of presidential appointments that he himself drew up. The fullest of these, covering his entire administration, occupies more than a dozen closely written pages.[4] Of even more immediate interest is the statement he made, after he had been head of the government more than two years, that 316 officers in the United States were subject to appointment and removal by him.[5] One reason why he drew up lists with such care was that he was blamed on the one hand for making too many new appointments and on the other for making too few. The crux of the matter was the removal of Federalist incumbents. As he lamented, he was cast in the unwelcome role of public executioner; and while his own supporters were shouting "Off with their heads," his political opponents were describing his victims as holy martyrs. This kindly man, who claimed that in private life he had had hardly any enemies, was in a most uncongenial situation.

In attempting to understand removals from office in the first decade of the nineteenth century, the modern reader must bear in mind that this was long before there was assured tenure under civil service regulations. The germs of a permanent bureaucracy might have been seen in the Hamiltonian system of administration, with its emphasis on stability. The Federalists were seeking to perpetuate this system, but Jefferson, who thought of public service more as a duty than a career, was basically unsympathetic with what we now call bureaucracy. As a country gentleman from Virginia he might have been expected to be. Himself a notably efficient man, he had slight tolerance for vested incompetence; and, at a time when relatively few public offices were highly technical, he regarded change as salutary except in minor clerical or menial posts. But, since he was basically a gradualist as well as a

---

[3] There were reductions during TJ's administration, but on his accession the collectors at Philadelphia, Petersburg, and Charleston got from c. $8250 to $8500, while at this time the Secretary of the Treasury got $5000 and the Chief Justice $4000. The postmasters at New York and Philadelphia got over $4500. Representatives and senators were paid $6 per diem when in attendance. One day's pay was allowed for each 20 miles to and fro.

[4] LC, 33095–33101.

[5] TJ to William Duane, July 24, 1803 (Ford, VIII, 258), a letter which was not sent. He did not include the judiciary and military, nor the internal revenue offices now abolished, nor the postmasters, who were named by the Postmaster General. In May, 1803, he drew up a list of appointments, arranged in classes (LC, 20545–20546).

kindly person, no one who knew him well would have expected him to be ruthless, and he had strongly implied in his inaugural address that he would not be. Of his extensive power to make removals, however, there was no legal doubt. He himself distinguished between the judiciary and military, who were removable only by established process, and officers who had been appointed to serve at the pleasure of the President. Among the latter at the time were not only the collectors at the ports, who held the most lucrative posts, but also the federal attorneys and marshals.[6] With respect to such of these officers as Jefferson removed, there was no question of the legality of his action but merely of its wisdom.

He had abundant advice about policy from his own political supporters. Judge Hugh Henry Brackenridge of Pittsburgh discussed the alleged proscription of political opponents in his state by Governor Thomas McKean, a Republican whose judgment Jefferson admired and with whom his relations were cordial. According to Brackenridge, the results of McKean's policy were salutary and he would never have been re-elected if he had not pursued it. This observer thought it a discriminating policy, however, and Jefferson rightly regarded Brackenridge as an advocate of moderation.[7] Much the same opinion of the success of McKean's policy was held by the astute John Beckley, who sent Jefferson a long letter of advice from Philadelphia. The recommendation he regarded as most important was that changes be made of men in office, "so as *gradually*, but certainly and effectively, to place the executive administration in the hands of decided republicans, distinguished for talents and integrity." Though this practical politician favored gradualism, he candidly stated his opinion that a policy based on conciliation or compromise would tend to confirm the charges of Jefferson's foes that he lacked political firmness.[8]

The fears of his intimate friend James Monroe were similar. To the mind of the Governor of Virginia there could be no graver political error than to arouse suspicion of accommodation with the defeated party; and he urged Jefferson to follow his excellent judgment rather than the "benevolent suggestions" of his heart.[9] Monroe said this before reading the inaugural address. The new President quickly assured Monroe and others that his hopes of conciliation did not extend to the

---

[6] As the commissions from this period on file in the National Archives show, some of these officers were appointed for a term of years, unless the President should be pleased to revoke their commissions sooner. Federal judges were appointed to serve during good behavior.

[7] Brackenridge to TJ, Feb. 17, 1801 (LC, 18652), received Mar. 6.

[8] Beckley to TJ, Feb. 27, 1801 (LC, 18801–18802), received Mar. 3.

[9] Monroe to TJ, Mar. 3, 1801 (S.M.H., III, 261–264), received Mar. 7.

Federalist leaders, whom he recognized as implacable; he was trying to reconcile the large body of moderates. Nonetheless, there is unmistakable evidence that his address not only aroused false hopes in Federalist circles but also fears in the minds of Republicans, even in his own state.

Monroe was specially disturbed by the thought that Jefferson would make a gesture to the Federalists by appointing one of them to high office. To Monroe the principles of the Republicans and their foes differed as light from darkness. Within a few weeks he made the suggestion, on his own behalf and that of other Republican leaders in his state, that Rufus King be recalled from London, though he quickly withdrew this and wished he had not made it.[10] Jefferson showed no disposition to consider such an action, but he let it be known that under existing circumstances he would appoint only Republicans to vacancies as they occurred.[11] This resolution was not improper, since the Federalists had monopolized the offices of the government. From the beginning Jefferson realized the desirability of attaining an approximate equilibrium, but he was not disposed to force matters. Therefore, he was not gratified by the statement of Congressman William Branch Giles that a pretty general "purgation" was expected by the friends of the new order.[12]

During his first month as President, Jefferson reported to Dr. Benjamin Rush that he had to withstand a torrent of pressure from his friends.[13] Characteristically respectful of their counsel, he went to pains to explain his position about removals to almost every supporter of his who wrote him. His mind told him that general approbation was not to be expected. Stating this to one of his sons-in-law, he added: "Still I shall hope indulgence when it shall be seen that removals are on fixed rules, applied to every case without passion or partiality. The rule may be disapproved, but the application shall be beyond reproach." These first rules, by which he was hoping to abide faithfully, he set down in almost identical terms in letter after letter.[14]

Failure to observe the rule that no good man should be disturbed for mere difference of opinion, he said, was exactly what Republicans had complained of in the former administration. He told Monroe that removals must be as few as possible, that they must be made gradually,

[10] Monroe to TJ, Apr. 29, May 4, 1801 (S.M.H., III, 279–280).

[11] TJ to Monroe, Mar. 7, 1801 (Ford, VIII, 10).

[12] Giles to TJ, Mar. 16, 1801 (LC, 18967–18969). Giles was one of those who were dubious about the retention of Rufus King, but he was specially grieved about the Federalist judiciary.

[13] TJ to Rush, Mar. 24, 1801 (Ford, VIII, 32).

[14] Perhaps they are best stated in this letter of Mar. 27, 1801, to J. W. Eppes (Edgehill-Randolph Papers, UVA) and in one to Giles, Mar. 23, 1801 (Ford, VIII, 25–26).

and he "bottomed on some malversation or inherent disqualification."
Thus he started with two categories.

1. He saw "inherent disqualification" in the appointments made by
Adams after the latter's defeat was known (December 12, 1800), since
these should not have been made in the first place. Such of them as
were made subject to presidential pleasure he would treat as nullities.
He claimed that even Adams's friends agreed to the rightfulness of this,
and few will now deny that there was impropriety in the rush of
Adams's final appointments. But Jefferson enlarged the period of impropriety to almost three months, and a rigid adherence to the principle
that a President should make no appointments whatever from the time
that he learns of the election returns might have embarrassed the adminis
tration, as it actually did in his own last months in office. Government
had to go on. Furthermore, his designation of this entire group of appointments as "midnight appointments" was an obvious exaggeration
for effect. Finally, the most important of them were judicial; and the
judges, who were appointed for good behavior, were beyond his reach.
This category provided him with only limited opportunities.[15]

One batch of minor appointments to which the term "midnight"
could be aptly applied and which entered into later controversy need
only be mentioned here. On March 2, by authority of an act of February 27, Adams nominated forty-two persons as justices of the peace for
the District of Columbia, and the Senate confirmed them on the last
day of the session. Treating these appointments as nullities because of
the non-delivery of the commissions, and availing himself of the discretion vested in the President by the law, Jefferson, on his second day in
office, gave recess appointments of his own to thirty persons. These
included twenty-five who had been nominated by Adams, but did not
include William Marbury. He was to figure in a *cause célèbre* when
Jefferson's first term was half over, but during the recess of Congress in
1801 his name does not appear to have been noised about. At that time
the major criticisms of the new President arose from other actions.[16]

2. Malversation or, in less pretentious language, official misconduct
seemed to him a sufficient ground for removal, as well it might to any
fair-minded person, though there could be disagreement as to what

---

[15] His own list (LC, 20545-20546) shows that the largest number of removals
that he put in this category for the years 1801–1803 consisted of federal attorneys
or marshals (11), whose removal he also justified on other grounds. Next in number
were foreign commercial agents and consuls (9), who were of minor consequence.

[16] The circumstances of the case of Marbury *vs.* Madison are described in ch.
VIII, below. For Section 11 of the act of Feb. 27, 1801, see *Annals*, 6 Cong., p.
1554. See also *Journal of Executive Procs. of the Senate,* Mar. 2–3, 1801, and Jan.
6, 1802, pp. 388–390, 404.

misconduct actually consisted of. Most of the persons removed on this ground were customs officials or others within the domain of the vigilant Secretary of the Treasury, the most common charge being delinquency in accounts. The brother of Elbridge Gerry was one of these, to Jefferson's grave embarrassment. A couple of marshals, alleged to have packed juries, were included here, among them David M. Randolph of Virginia, but these officers most often fell in another category, not clearly distinguished at the outset but always in Jefferson's mind. Since the courts were "so decidedly" Federalist and the judges were irremovable, he held that attorneys and marshals should be replaced by Republicans in order to protect the Republican citizenry — that is, the main body of the people. Even when allowance is made for partisan exaggeration, this position does not seem unreasonable.[17]

Republican fears that Jefferson might pursue his conciliatory policy too far soon diminished in Virginia, and the pressure on him to remove Federalists from office was far less in the southern and western states than in those to the north and east, where partisan strife was fiercer. One of his friends and county neighbors not only opposed the proscription of all Federalists but believed that party lines might be obliterated. Senator Wilson Cary Nicholas, writing him early in the summer of 1801, voiced the ardent hope that at the next election the President would be hailed as "the chief magistrate of the American people, and not the head of a party." [18] But the present chief magistrate, unlike his predecessors, was the recognized head of a party, and actually it was as President that he came into full maturity as a party leader.

This advocate of freedom recognized that, within the framework of basic principles that were agreed to, there would always be differences of opinion; but, as he showed in his inaugural address, he also recognized that in a republican government there must be peaceful acquiescence in the will of the majority. What he hoped for in his sanguine moments was the acquiescence, at least, of the extreme Federalists and the support of the moderates. About the former, however, he was never free from doubt, and his immediate effort was to isolate them and render them powerless. That is, he wanted to destroy them politically. When he said that conciliation had failed, as he did a number of times within a year or two, he probably meant that the "ultras" were more numerous and less acquiescent than he had expected.

[17] In the brief section "Attornies & marshals removed for high federalism, & republicans appointed as a protection to republican suitors in courts entirely federal & going all lengths in party spirit" TJ included, as attorneys: David Fay, Vt., replacing Charles Marsh, and Edward Livingston, replacing Richard Harrison in N.Y. (LC, 20546).

[18] Nicholas to TJ, June 24, 1801 (LC, 21388).

In partisan politics he was pragmatic rather than doctrinaire. He played by note when he could, but was not averse to playing by ear, and his extraordinary success as party leader while President could never have been achieved had he been less skillful in adjusting himself to changing circumstances. His original policy with respect to removals from office was that, besides being very gradual, these should be made for assignable reasons. Some of the reasons he listed in the first place as sufficient had a political coloration, but he wanted to avoid the charge that political conflict really boiled down to a struggle for office. Furthermore, he had high standards of administration. His original policy was never abandoned, but it was modified and somewhat quickened in the light of developing circumstances. There were two main reasons: the hungry demands of his own followers whose continued support he deemed essential, and the irreconcilability of his chief enemies, whom he sought to weaken. Republican hunger was probably at the peak in New York and Pennsylvania, where his most important early removals and appointments were made, but Federalist intransigence was greatest in Connecticut. His action there in the summer of 1801 was so bitterly protested that he seized upon this occasion to make a public statement of policy. Of all the things he said on the subject of appointments to public office it is this that is most often quoted.

The removal of Elizur Goodrich from the relatively remunerative post of collector of the port of New Haven required no departure from the "principles" that Jefferson had already set forth in private letters. The appointment of Goodrich, made by Adams about two weeks before he left office, was one of those that Jefferson attached the word "midnight" to and described as nullities. This official, who was commissioned to serve during the pleasure of the President, was unquestionably removable. But the "principles" of the new President with respect to removals had not yet been made public. Furthermore, Goodrich, a learned lawyer and recent congressman, had impressive local connections in the state where Federalism was strongest. To deprive him of the best political plum in Connecticut when he was believed to merit and had hardly begun to enjoy it was to court fierce resentment and vigorous protest.

The name of this particular officer appeared on Jefferson's memorandum of his first Council meeting. At that time Levi Lincoln of Massachusetts was asked to consult Pierpont Edwards, a Republican leader in New Haven who happened also to be the son of Jonathan Edwards. Jefferson himself conferred about Goodrich in correspondence with Edwards and with Gideon Granger, his most trusted informant about politics in Connecticut. He stated his "principles" to these men, asked their advice, and based his action on what they told him.[19] These advisers and the other Republican leaders consulted by them agreed that the "cause" required the removal of Goodrich. Their judgment was based on the rancor and intolerance of the dominant Federalists in the state, which in their opinion exceeded anything of the sort elsewhere, and on the weakness of the Republicans. Even if their account of the local ruling group was exaggerated, though seemingly it was not, it was one to which Jefferson himself gave ready credence since the government of Connecticut represented to him the most conspicuous American example of the union of church and state. He had not forgotten that the "established clergy," as Edwards designated them, had inveighed against him in the presidential campaign; and he had no difficulty in accepting Granger's statement that incredible torrents of abuse were still pouring from the pulpits. This had been notably the case in connection with a recent state election; and at a late meeting of the legislature the Federals had shown a determination to exclude all Republicans from state and local office.[20] "They talk here as though all power was still in their hands," wrote the son of Jonathan Edwards to the President whom they had not accepted. "If you administer the government, say they, according to former administration, they will support you, but if you displace officers they will turn you out at the next election." [21] Against the "phalanx" of civil officials and clergymen the Republicans thought themselves at a greater disadvantage than their brethren anywhere else in the Union. The Federals were saying that Jefferson had appointed none of his own party in Connecticut because none was fit for appointment. The "federal orthodoxy" were assumed to have a monopoly of intelligence and virtue, along with most of the property, while the Republicans were "disorganizers."

The leaders of the despised minority in the state were convinced that to leave intolerant Federalists in offices from which they could be legitimately removed would be to strengthen the party of irreconcilables — that a temporizing policy, however desirable it might be elsewhere, would be ruinous in Connecticut.[22] They did not single out Elizur Goodrich for special blame but designated all the Federalists in high office as "bitter persecutors." As his successor they recommended Sam-

[19] TJ to Edwards and to Granger (not yet postmaster general), Mar. 29, 1801 (Ford, VIII, 43–46, and note); Granger to TJ, Apr. 15, 1801, and Edwards to TJ, May 12, 1801 (*A.H.R.*, III, 272–277), received May 16.

[20] Specific actions were cited by Ephraim Kerby in a letter to Burr, May 24, 1801. This must have been sent to TJ, since it found its way into his papers (LC, 19334–19335).

[21] *A.H.R.*, III, 275.

[22] This view was supported by numerous later letters, including one of June 11, 1801, signed by more than twenty (LC, 19395–19398).

uel Bishop, mayor of New Haven, judge of the county court, and a deacon in one of the "established" churches. "In him will be embraced respectability, integrity, religion, steady habits, and firm republicanism." [23] So said the Republican spokesman. In the opinions of the dominant Federalists such a combination was rare among supporters of the President in New Haven, seat of that citadel of political and religious orthodoxy, Yale College.

On the letter containing this recommendation Jefferson wrote, "Goodrich to be removed." A week later, the collector was removed and Samuel Bishop appointed to replace him.[24] Though the motives of this presidential action may be accurately described as political, it is easily understandable in view of the total circumstances. In certain respects it was faulty as a test case. Jefferson made no allegations of official misconduct against Goodrich during the latter's brief tenure, and according to his lights needed to make none, provided that he himself maintained the standards of the service. But the ousted collector had one considerable advantage over his successor, besides the support of the shippers he served: he was forty years old, while Samuel Bishop was approaching seventy-eight. Thus local critics of the President could say that in effect the appointment was given to Samuel's son Abraham, who would have to do the work. They were said to hate Abraham beyond all men, because of his political activity. They had not forgotten that, a week after Jefferson's inauguration, he had delivered an oration at nearby Wallingford before the Republicans at their "General Thanksgiving." [25]

The expected protest from New Haven merchants against the removal and appointment was not slow in coming.[26] The signers, who were certified as the owners of more than seven-eighths of the navigation of the port, not only testified that Goodrich had been an unexceptionable official; they also claimed that Bishop lacked the necessary qualifications. While giving Jefferson the dubious credit of ignorance of this, they left the appointee himself in no doubt as to their attitude. A committee of them waited on the old man and one of them read their remonstrance to him before sending it to Washington. He himself would have had great difficulty in reading it if what they said was true: namely, that his eyesight had failed to the point that he could hardly write his name. This particular allegation appears to have been an exaggeration: within a year he sent Jefferson an unusually legible letter,

[23] *A.H.R.*, III, 276.
[24] May 23, 1801. TJ got Edwards's letter of May 12 on May 16.
[25] Mar. 11, 1801, published as a pamphlet, New Haven, 1801; P. Edwards to TJ, June 10, 1801 (LC, 19422–19423).
[26] June 18, 1801 (LC, 19484–19486).

saying that he retained his handwriting sufficiently to express his gratitude.[27] At that time, however, he had only just recovered from a long
spell of sickness, and he may have been noticeably infirm at the time of
his appointment. The original suspicions of the protesting merchants
were substantiated when his son was appointed his successor, after his
death in 1803.

In his reply to the merchants in 1801, Jefferson defended the elder
Bishop adroitly, reminding the remonstrators that the legislature of
Connecticut had manifested its sense of his competence very recently
by bestowing local offices on him, and also remarking that, at a much
more advanced age, Benjamin Franklin had ornamented human nature.[28] This paper was most notable, however, as a public statement of
the removal policy at which the first President who was also the recognized head of a party had arrived. Believing that his pleas for tolerance
and harmony had been misconstrued into assurances that no officer
would be disturbed, he seized this opportunity to deny the policy of
perpetuating the monopoly of a "particular sect." Though he avoided
the names of the parties, he now officially recognized their existence.
The Federalists, who had so long claimed that they constituted the government, probably winced at his designation of them as a sect; and
some of them may have been annoyed by his reference to them as a
minority in the nation. He asserted that the national majority (Republican) as well as the minority had its rights, including a proportionate
share in public office. He would have denied the later charge that he
introduced the spoils system, since considerations of political alignment
had unmistakably entered into John Adams's appointments, even
though these had not been made with noteworthy political skill. "If a
due proportion of office is a matter of right," he now asked, "how are
vacancies to be obtained? Those by death are few; by resignation none.
[Commonly quoted as: "Few die; none resign."] Can any other mode
than that of removal be proposed? This is a painful office; but it is made
my duty, and I meet it as such." In the strict sense, he did not regard
the replacement of Goodrich as a removal, since the latter had a "midnight" appointment, but he now added another category to his earlier
list — namely, removals to correct the political imbalance in officialdom. The blame for this imbalance he placed squarely on the previous
Federalist proscription of Republicans. He would gladly have left to
time and accident the raising of the latter to their just share, he said, but
their "total exclusion" called for "prompter correction." When he had
corrected the situation, he would "return with joy to that state of

[27] Samuel Bishop to TJ, Mar. 27, 1802 (LC, 20967).
[28] TJ to Elias Shipman and others, July 12, 1801 (Ford, VIII, 67-70).

things, when the only questions concerning a candidate shall be, is he honest? Is he capable? Is he faithful to the Constitution?"

Judging from what Jefferson's correspondents told him, his action with respect to the collectorship in New Haven heartened his supporters, there and elsewhere in New England. He himself believed that he had given mortal offence to the "monarchical Federalists," but he reflected that they were already mortally offended. He believed that Connecticut was a very special case, as did his major advisers on New England politics, Levi Lincoln and Gideon Granger, both of whom generally favored a policy of gradualism. Faced with extreme intolerance there on the state level, Jefferson was disposed, for a time at least, to meet it in kind on the national level.[29] The dominant group in Connecticut aroused his latent anticlericalism as well as his partisanship. He promptly removed a few other officers there but moved slowly after that.

His most important appointment from this area at this stage was that of Gideon Granger as postmaster general in the autumn of 1801, following the rather reluctant resignation of Joseph Habersham of Georgia. The President well described to this intensely loyal supporter his purposes in the matter of appointments. After expressing his appreciation of the domestic obstacles which caused Granger to demur, he said:

> But nobody knows better [than Granger], because no one has encountered more steadfastly, the formidable phalanx apposed to the republican features of our constitution. To bear up against this, the talents & virtues of our country must be formed into phalanx also. My wish is to collect in a mass round the administration all the abilities, & the respectability to which the offices here can give employ. To give none of them to secondary characters. Good principles, wisely & honestly administered cannot fail to attach our fellow citizens to the order of things we espouse. Under this view of the circumstances in which we are placed, we cannot dispense here with your aid.[30]

Since the Postmaster General appointed the postmasters, Jefferson was making this trusted New Englander a major distributor of patronage. At the same time he was giving him an important role as watchman, for the abuse of authority in post offices was notorious. Jefferson was always fearful lest his own letters be opened for partisan purposes. This appointment illustrates the great confidence he showed in individual New Englanders and the valuable political service he received from

29 TJ to Lincoln, July 11, 1801 (Ford, VIII, 66–67).
30 TJ to Granger, Oct. 31, 1801 (LC, 20210). The date of the actual appointment was Nov. 28.

them. Both in the executive and legislative branches he gave note-worthy encouragement to men in that region whom he regarded as promising. But he withdrew Granger from the Connecticut scene and one may doubt if there was a state in the Union where his own party made slower progress. On the other hand, it should be noted that his partisans there did not waver in their loyalty to him, even when he be-came the object of outrageous personal attacks on religious and moral grounds during his second year in office.[31]

The general effect of Jefferson's answer to the remonstrance from New Haven was to arouse Republican hopes of further removals. No one was more aware of this than the Secretary of the Treasury, whose department offered the largest number of potential appointments, in-cluding the remunerative collectorships of the ports. The President gave color to these hopes by removing the collector of New York, admittedly for political reasons, and appointing in his place Aaron Burr's lieutenant, David Gelston.[32] Gallatin believed that anything less than what had been done thus far would have been unjust to the Re-publicans, but he hoped that little more would be done, preferring to displease political friends rather than give the Federalists a talking point. The department head who faced the greatest administrative task, and who believed that the government could best command public sup-port by demonstrating its effectiveness, was specially fearful of "the arts of those men whose political existence depends on party" — pro-fessional partisans, he might have called them. Among these he included William Duane of the *Aurora*, to whom he sought to show "the impro-priety of numerous removals." He was particularly concerned about Pennsylvania, the state of his recent residence, where he believed Re-publicanism to be so firmly established in the minds and hearts of the people that the displeasure of particular individuals involved little danger. He regarded New York as a more doubtful case, but, until the meeting of Congress, wanted to go slowly on removals, especially in Pennsylvania. Alexander J. Dallas, who had been recently appointed federal attorney for that state and was emerging as the leader of the more conservative faction there, agreed with this judgment.[33] No high officer of the government was to suffer so much as Gallatin from the professional partisans in his own party, but not the least of his services to his revered chief was to offset the pressure of the "sweeping Repub-licans" on him.

[31] Republicans of Connecticut to the President, Oct. 27, 1802 (LC, 21890–21892).
[32] July 9, 1801, which was before his Reply. TJ himself classified this action among those designed to correct the political imbalance. (LC, 20546).
[33] Gallatin to TJ, Aug. 10, 17, 1801 (*Writings*, I, 32–33, 38–40). Also, Sept. 14, 1801 (I, 49–53).

The latter expression was that of Jefferson himself, who admitted that his answer had given this group greater expectations than he thought its terms justified.[34] But, especially in these early months, he was more disposed than Gallatin to bear with extremists in his own party, believing that it would be unwise to risk the loss of tried friends for new converts. Besides being chief of state he was the head of a party and he saw no choice but to reconcile his two functions. Neither of his predecessors had recognized such a dual task, and few of his successors performed it so successfully. In more ways than one he sought to maintain a balance.

The response to the New Haven merchants had other repercussions in high administrative circles. A couple of weeks after it was made, Gallatin sent Jefferson a draft of a circular he proposed to send to the collectors. To these men, who had the appointment of various minor officers subject to his approval, he wanted to say that the door of office should be no longer shut against anyone because of his political opinions, as it had been in the Federalist era, but that only integrity and capacity should be considered. After consultation with Madison, however, Jefferson requested the Secretary of the Treasury to hold up this circular until such time as an equilibrium should be established. The collectors were *not* to be advised that they might appoint Federalists, and the assumption was that, for the present, they were to appoint only Republicans.[35]

Gallatin also intended to say to the collectors that no appointee should be permitted to exercise his influence to affect other men's freedom of opinion and suffrage. With this part of the circular Jefferson was in full agreement, and no doubt he, like Gallatin, meant the injunction to apply to members of both parties. But its more immediate implication was that electioneering activity by Federalist officeholders was sufficient ground for their removal. Jefferson had taken this position from the beginning. During his second year, while saying that he still preferred to depend on the slow operations of death, resignation, and delinquency to restore the balance, he made this further statement to Levi Lincoln: "Every officer of the government may vote at elections according to his conscience; but we should betray the cause committed to our care, were we to permit the influence of official patronage to be used to overthrow that cause." [36] Thus he made room on his list for additional officers who were properly removable on political grounds. But a definition of electioneering was hard to agree on, and he

[34] TJ to Gallatin, Aug. 14, 1801 (*ibid.*, I, 37).
[35] Gallatin to TJ, July 25, 1801; TJ to Gallatin, July 26, 1801 (*ibid.*, I, 28–29).
[36] TJ to Lincoln, Oct. 25, 1802 (Ford, VIII, 176).

had trouble with ardent Republicans who were less concerned than he that removals should be defensible at the court of public opinion.

The prolonged struggle over Allen McLane, collector of the port of Wilmington, Delaware, was a case in point. In connection with this, Jefferson remarked that, compared with questions of removal and appointment, all his other difficulties were as nothing.[37] Demands for the removal of McLane, an intolerant and obstreperous Federalist who held the most lucrative appointive office in the state, were made by Delaware Republicans very early in the administration. An inquiry into his official conduct was instituted, but to the great disappointment of his local foes, who had regarded his ouster as certain, he was cleared of the charges. The pressure for his removal continued, taking the form of petitions in the spring of 1802 and occasioning vast correspondence on the part of Jefferson. The burden of the complaint was that the Collector, and the Federalists of the state generally, continued to be bitterly hostile to Republicanism.

From the local point of view, Jefferson's retention of McLane appears to have been politically unwise. The survival of the offensive Collector may perhaps be attributed to presidential procrastination, after the original inquiry, until removal became even more difficult because of his modification of his policy. It may be attributed to the opposition of Gallatin to political reprisals in his department. It may be cited as an example of Jefferson's overall policy of requiring defensible reasons for removals. At all events, he made only a few of them on grounds of electioneering alone and was generally more moderate than his own partisans.

Reactions to the removal policy, as announced in Jefferson's first summer as President, closely followed party lines. Federalist leaders and newspapers, especially in the North and East, assailed it as a direct contradiction of the inaugural address. Few were as discerning as John Quincy Adams, who believed that, prior to the meeting of Congress, there was nothing else for which they could blame the administration.[38] Congressman Theodore Sedgwick, the former Speaker of the House who had absented himself from the inauguration, asserted that nothing could be more mischievous than this policy, which rendered the emoluments of office "a mass of electioneering corruption." While seeing no justice whatever in it, he reluctantly expressed the opinion that Jeffer-

---

[37] TJ to John Dickinson, June 21, 1801 (LC, 19504). For a fuller account of the McLane case, with numerous references, see Appendix I, below.

[38] J. Q. Adams to Rufus King, Oct. 13, 1801 (King, III, 525).

son had lost no influence by avowing it.[39] During the first session of the Seventh Congress (December 7, 1801, to May 3, 1802) the Federalists had much more than the removal policy to talk about, and Jefferson himself stated privately that it was modified at the end of that session. Up to that time, according to his own count, there were sixteen removals "on political principles alone, in very urgent cases." He afterwards said that he determined at that time to make no more removals except for "delinquency, or active and bitter opposition to the order of things which the public will had established." Ten were removed on the latter ground in the next year, but he did not include these among the officials displaced "to make room for some participation for the Republicans," of whom he claimed there were only sixteen altogether.[40] Other calculations of his differ somewhat from this one in detail, and he was not wholly consistent in his designation of "political" dismissals.[41] The lines between his various designations and categories were inevitably blurred, and he did not gain Federalist approval of his assumption that Adams's "midnight" appointment were nullities and did not count, agreeable as this was to Republicans.[42]

After the first session of his first Congress the *New York Evening Post*, established by Hamilton and a notably well-edited paper, asserted that the only important office in that city not yet conferred on some democrat was one that no "anti-federalist" of sufficient ability could be found to fill. This comment reflected the continued arrogance of the former ruling group.[43] The best of the Federalist papers, discerning no principle whatever in Jefferson's policy, attributed it wholly to partisan revenge. In the summer of 1802, the *Evening Post* had this to say:

> The truth is, it has become ridiculous in Mr. Jefferson and his supporters to pretend that, in their present system of hunting the Federalists like wild beasts, they are governed by any principle or principles which will bear avowal or can be for a moment sup-

[39] Sedgwick to King, Dec. 14, 1801 (King, IV, 35).

[40] TJ to J. H. Nicholson, May 13, 1803 (L. & B., X, 388–389), replying to a letter of May 10 in which this important congressman expressed approval of the policy pursued (LC, 22696).

[41] About this time, presumably, he drew up A Correct View of Certain Appointments arranged in classes (LC, 20545–20546).

[42] Typical of Republican approval was the discussion "Removals from Office" in *Aurora*, May 27, 1802.

[43] Quoted from *New York Evening Post* in *Aurora*, June 29, 1802, with a spirited reply. The position in New York was that of naval officer, then held by Richard Rogers, whom TJ afterwards described as a Revolutionary Tory. The appointment of Samuel Osgood, postmaster general under Washington, to the office on May 10, 1803, occasioned further unpleasant comment from the *Evening Post* (referred to by TJ in Ford, VIII, 234n).

ported under any pretence whatever. A deadly revenge, an inexorable rancour, a vindictive malice against all and every one who has dared to differ in sentiment from them, however good, however virtuous, however meritorious he may be, marks and controuls the measures of those now in power; . . . to be a federalist is a sure mark for destruction, if destruction be within their power to command.[44]

Allowance may be made for the fact that the purge in New York City was especially sweeping, and for the further fact that Jefferson regarded Hamilton, patron saint of this paper, as a monocrat and was implacable to him. But at just this time the President was resisting the pressure to remove Allen McLane from the collectorship of Wilmington, Delaware, and was trying to retain John Steele, a moderate Federalist from North Carolina, as comptroller of the Treasury. It would have been surprising, therefore, if he had not viewed the failure of Federalist spokesmen to concede any discrimination or sense of justice to him as a rebuff of his efforts at conciliation. A Republican orator interpreted motives more realistically. Elder John Leland, a notable Baptist Republican of New England, said this at Cheshire, Massachusetts:

Had he [Jefferson] retained all the officers which he found in office, he would have disappointed that majority which promoted him, and likewise committed himself to the opposition party, to reproach him for being too cowardly to change men or measures, or stick to his friends. The truth is, the federal *ins* made their calculations to be eternal *ins*, and those three letters, o, u, t, have been made a handle to raise a mighty fog.[45]

The redoubtable Elder mixed his metaphors but indubitably approached the truth. This issue was primarily one between the "ins" and the "outs," and the extreme Federalists, who were disposed to condemn whatever the administration did, played into the hands of the "sweeping Republicans." Jefferson and Gallatin were caught in the crossfire.[46] But the middle way the administration followed was the wise way. This lay between a policy of no removals whatever on political grounds, which would have dismayed loyal supporters while safeguarding disloyal obstructionists, and a policy of thoroughgoing proscrip-

[44] July 8, 1802.

[45] July 5, 1802 *Writings of the Late Elder John Leland* [1845], p. 265). We shall meet him again in connection with the mammoth cheese (see pp. 106–108, below).

[46] They were subjected in the summer of 1803 to a concerted attack by a Republican faction in Pennsylvania led by Duane and Michael Leib, but that episode belongs in the later story of party politics.

tion, which would probably have injured the civil service and would almost certainly have alienated the moderates whom Jefferson was trying to win over. In unexampled circumstances and under unremitting pressure from both the right and left he pursued a reasoned course with essential though not invariable consistency, manifesting far more moderation, patience, and forbearance than his critics.[47]

If the success of his policy may be measured by the attainment of the desired balance between parties in the entire federal establishment, as reflected in total figures, that success was gained slowly. Not even in the middle of his first term did the Republicans have what he regarded as a due proportion of offices. Indeed, the citizens of that political complexion had so increased in number because of the popularity of the administration that they amounted, in his estimation, to two-thirds or even three-fourths of the whole. Yet they still had fewer than half of the offices.[48] For that reason he continued to appoint only Republicans to vacancies, but he had the situation sufficiently in hand by that time to leave the creation of vacancies to the course of nature. The judiciary represented a special case, but in both the executive and legislative branches the peaceful transition to his regime had been effected.

Toward the end of his presidency, addressing a friendly state governor, Jefferson reflected that solicitations for office were the most painful incidents to which an executive magistrate was exposed, and that the "gift of office" was his most dreadful burden. "A person who wishes to make it an engine of self-elevation, may do wonders with it," he said; "but to one who wishes to use it conscientiously for the public good, without regard to the ties of blood and friendship, it creates enmities without numbers, many open, but more secret, and saps the happiness and peace of his life." [49] The problem of removals, acute during only his first year in office, or at the most his first two years, was inseparable from the problem of appointments, which was perennial. That he gave extraordinary care to the latter can be doubted by no one who has gone through his papers and read only a fraction of his correspondence bearing on this subject. How many of the applications and recommendations that are still extant were personally examined by him it is

---

[47] A discerning contemporary appraisal of his removal policy is in "A Vindication of the Measures of the Present Administration" by Algernon Sidney (*National Intelligencer*, Apr. 15, 18, 1803). For an authoritative modern judgment see L. D. White, *The Jeffersonians* (1951), pp. 347–354.

[48] He made this point in a communication which, contrary to his custom, he wrote for anonymous publication in a newspaper; TJ to Levi Lincoln, June 1, 1803 (Ford, VIII, 233–234), with text of communication (Ford, VIII, 234–239n).

[49] TJ to Gov. James Sullivan of Mass., Mar. 3, 1808 (L. & B., XII, 3).

impossible to determine, but his notations show that he handled a very great many.[50]

From the voluminous records the inescapable impression emerges that he wielded the appointive power with notable conscientiousness. This is certainly not to say that he made no unfortunate appointments, and was therefore unique among Presidents; nor is it to deny that he tended to identify the public good with the success of his own party, as Lincoln and others did. It is to say that, in his particular political circumstances, he strove to maintain the high standards that he had observed from within the Washington administration, and that he himself had exemplified as a public servant. Since he wondered if he did not make more enemies than friends by the exercise of appointive power, he can hardly be believed to have employed it as an engine of self-elevation. The consolidation of his own position of leadership was owing to his appeal to the citizenry generally and to his skillful management of Congress far more than to his appointments.

He unquestionably disregarded ties of blood, sedulously avoiding the nepotism which had marred the record of John Adams. At the very beginning he made clear his unwillingness to appoint even distant relatives to office.[51] Did he disregard ties of personal friendship? In certain of his removals for misconduct he undoubtedly did, but the appointment of John Page remains to be considered. From college days Page had been to him a friend very like a brother. This gentleman and scholar, with his enormous house (Rosewell), which young Jefferson had so often visited, and with his huge family, was in grave need of a steady income; and this former congressman was fully worthy of public office on grounds of character. The problem, in Jefferson's phrase, was to place his friend's talents in an office to which they were analogous. Toward the end of his first year as President he offered Page, for lack of anything more suitable, the post of collector at Petersburg, Virginia. Though the emoluments of this had been reduced, it was a desirable post; it was also a very responsible one because of the large sums passing through the collector's hands. Obviously doubting whether Page's talents were "analogous" to this position, he frankly said that the

[50] *Letters of Application and Recommendation during the Administration of Thomas Jefferson, 1801–1809* (1936), a pamphlet issued by the National Archives, lists the persons applying or recommended. The letters have been reproduced as microcopy No. 418. There is no file of replies because of the policy of not answering applications. An enormous number of letters about appointments from and to TJ are preserved in his own papers.

[51] George Jefferson to TJ, Mar. 4, 1801 (MHS), reluctantly forwarding a letter of application from his brother; TJ to George Jefferson, Mar. 27, 1801 (Ford, VIII, 38).

proneness of his old friend to be over-trustful of others constituted a danger which would have to be guarded against. Page himself hesitated, then accepted, and finally resigned because of the condition of his health. Thus Jefferson was spared an unsuitable appointment; and, fortunately, the Virginia General Assembly came to the rescue in the autumn of 1802 by electing this lovable man governor of the commonwealth, regardless of his precarious health and trustful nature. After reading Page's modest and grateful letters and those of his distressed wife, one can better understand and even condone Jefferson's amiable weakness in this episode. But, to get well ahead of the story, in his second term he provided Page a sinecure, which he described as such, at a time when the ex-Governor's health was worse and he was clearly unequal to any exacting task. From this single case it might be supposed that the humane President, toward the end of his own service, relaxed his official vigilance or became careless in the exercise of accustomed power, but it would not be safe to argue from this one appointment among hundreds that he put the benefit of friends above the public interest.[52]

Very early in the administration a Federalist leader was reported to have predicted that Jefferson would not nominate for office any man who would be admitted into decent company in New England.[53] In the region of his most implacable foes he was compelled to draw on the politically disinherited to a greater extent than in most other places, but one of the characteristic features of his policy was his emphasis on respectability and good local standing in his appointees. In Congress during his first term the weight of ability lay with the Federalist minority. How successful he was in his effort to create in the executive branch the phalanx of talent and virtue of which he spoke to Gideon Granger and others is a matter of opinion, but he increased the likelihood of this by broadening the base of his appointments. Wisely minimizing the claims of birth and wealth as such, he recognized ability wherever he found it. Yet the official personnel in his administration actually differed little in character and status from that in the Federalist era. As has been well said, the country was still governed by gentlemen,

[52] Most of TJ's letters bearing on this case, beginning with that of Feb. 20, 1802, are given in Ford, VIII, 132–137. The unsympathetic editor remarks that this story "furnishes perhaps the most curious instance of the use of public office for private benefit." If his superlative is warranted, which may be gravely doubted, it is only with respect to the episode of TJ's second term, into the background of which we do not enter here. Letters of Page to TJ about the earlier appointment are Mar. 27, 1802 (LC, 20968); Apr. 19 (LC, 21081); June 1 (LC, 21286); Aug. 9 (LC, 21583). Mrs. Page wrote TJ, Aug. 23, 1802 (LC, 21658).

[53] Reported in *Aurora*, Mar. 17, 1801.

though the Jeffersonian concept was broader than the Federalist.[54] And if, despite the flood of office-seekers, he had difficulty in finding competent appointees in particular localities and in inducing the most suitable men to serve for modest salaries at the seat of government, Washington and Adams had faced the same problem.

He gave preference to supporters of the two "revolutions" of 1776 and 1800, having no patience with men who could be designated as Tories and tending to equate these with "monarchists." To appoint a monarchist to office in the United States, he said, would have been like appointing an atheist to the priesthood.[55] That he gave recognition to past political service is undeniable, but his personal political debts were few; and the catalogue of his appointments of men who helped elect him, as presented by James A. Bayard in the first session of his first Congress, was short and unimpressive.[56] Perhaps the clearest case of this sort was the appointment of Charles Pinckney of South Carolina to be minister at the court of Madrid; Republican leaders in Jefferson's own state were dubious of this at the time and it proved to be unfortunate.

Aaron Burr had influence on appointments at the very first but soon lost it. John Swartwout, who was named marshal for the New York district, was Burr's man; so was David Gelston, the new collector of the port. The latter was referred to as Burr's devoted tool by a Federalist leader who conjectured that the Vice President was laying a trap for Jefferson.[57] Doubts about the actions of Burr in connection with the presidential tie and about the loyalty of his supporters to Jefferson were sown in the latter's mind very early, and he soon took counsel with Governor George Clinton about appointments in New York.[58] That a factional struggle was impending in New York soon became apparent. Jefferson made it a practice to keep out of this sort of thing insofar as possible; in general he sought to reconcile factions. But nowhere was the appointive authority a more potent weapon than in struggles within the party, and it was not used in Burr's behalf after the midsummer of 1801.

Because of Gallatin's familiarity with New York politics through his father-in-law, James Nicholson, and other connections, Jefferson placed special reliance on his judgment with respect to appointments in

---

[54] L. D. White, considering the period 1801–1829 as a whole, sums up these matters well in *The Jeffersonians*, especially pp. 354–357, 548–550.

[55] Ford, VIII, 238n.

[56] *Annals*, 7 Cong., 1 sess., pp. 640–641.

[57] R. Troup to R. King, Aug. 8, 1801 (King, III, 495–496).

[58] Samuel Osgood to Madison, Apr. 24, 1801, cited by Cunningham, *Jeffersonian Republicans in Power*, p. 39; TJ to Clinton, May 17, 1801 (Ford, VIII, 52–54). It should be noted, however, that Gelston was appointed after that, on July 9.

that state as well as in Pennsylvania. Gallatin himself hated to enter into local feuds, and, longer than most of the high officers, he remained friendly to Burr. The latter appealed to Gallatin in the interest of his loyal supporter Matthew L. Davis, whom he had recommended as naval officer in New York and against whom he claimed there were "secret machinations." Davis was not appointed at this or any other time, though he made a special trip to Monticello in September, 1801. Jefferson put him off then and brushed Burr off a little later, explaining his failure to answer the latter's letters about appointments by stating his rule that the only answers to such letters must be found in what was done or not done about them. This was in fact a signal that Burr would not be consulted thereafter, though his full insulation was not generally perceived until after Congress had been several weeks in session.[59] Jefferson's attitude to him at this time need be attributed to no vindictiveness; it was warranted on grounds of prudence.

Factional quarrels complicated his problem of appointments more than Federalist criticism did. As time went on, the worst of these developed in Pennsylvania; and, while trying to keep out of that and generally managing to do so, he supported the moderates against the professional partisans when the test came. He never ceased to seek and receive advice about appointments from local leaders in all parts of the country, but, from the time that his first Congress assembled, he came to rely most on the judgment of representatives and senators. The doctrine of senatorial courtesy was not yet established, and he exercised his influence so skillfully that hardly any of his nominations were rejected.[60] At the very start he established efficacious relations with Congress such as had been attained by neither of his predecessors and were to be matched by few of his successors.

[59] TJ to Burr, Nov. 18, 1801 (Ford, VIII, 102-103). Among numerous letters bearing on the Davis episode, the following may be cited: Burr to Gallatin, June 28, Sept. 8, 1801 (Adams, *Life*, pp. 283-284); Gallatin to TJ, Sept. 12, 14, 1801; and TJ to Gallatin, Sept. 18, 1801 (Gallatin, *Writings*, I, 47-55). Richard Rogers was retained as naval officer until May 10, 1803, when Samuel Osgood was appointed.

[60] Alexander B. Lacy, in his unpublished dissertation on "Jefferson and Congress," ch. III, says there were only four in TJ's first term. Three of these were military; the fourth, that of William Walton as commercial agent to Santo Domingo, was apparently rejected because of objections of Senator Samuel Smith. Lacy thinks this the only possible case of "senatorial courtesy" in TJ's administration (citing J. Q. Adams, *Memoirs*, I, 340).

$\lceil$ VI $\rceil$

Congress and the Man of the People:
Peace and Economy

EVEN when he was secretary of state Jefferson viewed with dread
the sessions of Congress, which added so greatly to the burdens of
the chief executive and department heads. Since he did not call a special
session after his inauguration as President, he had a respite of nine
months during which he could set his executive house in order and get
ready for the troublesome legislators — an advantage that had not been
accorded his predecessor. By the end of the first week in December
enough senators and representatives had straggled into the raw settlement on the Potomac to constitute a quorum in both chambers.[1] Most
of them lived rather uncomfortably as transients in lodgings or board-
ing-houses near the Capitol. There the senators now had the North
Wing to themselves; the representatives took over the "Oven," which
had been built on the foundations of the projected South Wing. In the
House, where the Republicans had a majority approaching two-thirds,
the veteran Nathaniel Macon of North Carolina, who was on the best
of terms with the President, was promptly elected Speaker, and John
Beckley was returned to the post of clerk from which the Federalists of
a previous Congress had ejected him. Though this action was a recognition of genuine competence, it may also be attributed to gratitude to
an unusually effective party worker. Some of the Republican senators
from remote states were so slow in arriving that the party majority in
the North Wing was uncomfortably small, but it was sufficient to procure the election of Abraham Baldwin of Georgia, a staunch supporter
of the administration, as president *pro tempore*. Vice President Burr
did not come for several weeks and his attitude was dubious after he

---

[1] The first session of the 7th Congress began Dec. 7, 1801, and ended May 3,
1802.

got there.[2] It was to the closely divided Senate that the President must submit his long list of recess appointments. He withheld this for a month until his margin of support had become greater. His appointments then went through without real difficulty, though not without further delay.[3]

Considering the difficulties of transportation, it was a long mile between Capitol Hill and the President's House, around which the chief departmental offices were clustered. There could be no doubt that the legislative and executive branches were separate. During the days that the Federalists controlled the latter, the Republicans tended to magnify the former in their doctrine. Some of the opponents of the new administration direfully predicted that it would seek to restore the principles of the Confederation, one of which was congressional dominance of the federal structure. During his years in opposition Jefferson was identified with criticism of the executive, but his own experiences as the governor of his commonwealth during the American Revolution, and what he learned of troubles in other states, had indelibly impressed on him the dangers of executive impotence and legislative omnipotence. Like virtually all thoughtful Americans, he accepted without question the theory of separation of powers and a balanced government, but he gave some sign at the beginning and more as he went along that he was pragmatic with respect to the actual operations of that government. He wrote his friend Du Pont de Nemours: "What is practicable must often control what is pure theory: and the habits of the governed determine in a great degree what is practicable." [4]

If he was speaking primarily of a legislative program, he was also describing, perhaps unwittingly, his approach to the problem of procedure. His method with respect to Congress developed in the light of circumstances and varied with them. The first practical necessity he perceived was that there be harmony and co-operation rather than conflict between these two branches of the government. The events of the congressional session were to show that this was to be brought about primarily by his own personal influence and the party loyalty he engendered and husbanded, but he always tried to keep within the bounds of

[2] Writing on Jan. 1, 1802, to JWE (Edgehill-Randolph Papers, UVA), and to TMR (LC, 20590), TJ said that the relative strength of the parties in the House was 66 to 37, though the Republican margin would be increased by the arrival of an absentee and the filling of a vacancy; in the Senate it would be 18 to 14 if all were there.

[3] Submitted Jan. 6, 1802, and as best I can make out from the confusing record of the proceedings, largely approved Jan. 26 (Senate *Executive Journal*, I, 400–405).

[4] TJ to Du Pont, Jan. 18, 1802 (Ford, VIII, 127*n*.).

official propriety and it may appear that in his first message to Congress he emphasized these unduly. Out of consideration for that body and its independence of judgment, he said, he did not deliver this message in person. He sent it by his secretary, Captain Meriwether Lewis. This action was regarded by some as an "insidious reflection" on the conduct of his predecessors, but in his opinion it made good sense.

He was breaking the precedent which George Washington had set and starting a tradition which lasted more than a century. One reason which has been alleged for his procedure is that he did not like to make speeches and in fact could hardly be heard. No doubt he realized that his pen was more potent than his tongue, but there is merit in his claim that this method was more considerate of Congress.[5] Physical circumstances in the new capital differed from those in the old. If the condition of Pennsylvania Avenue discouraged him from using his chariot and four or he was undisposed to employ that stylish conveyance, as good a rider as he could have readily traversed the long mile on horseback. But, according to the custom which began as a mark of respect to the first President, senators and representatives returned the visit, bearing their replies with them. In Philadelphia a large number of carriages had been assembled to take the legislators a couple of blocks to the residence of John Adams — a circumstance which many regarded as ridiculous. The present problem was of another sort. How could so many carriages be found for the journey of a mile over the creek and through the swamp to the President's House?

Other difficulties had arisen after partisan conflict grew. Presidents referred to controversial questions in their addresses, and replies suggested a degree of approval which was not felt by all members. Objections were chiefly raised by Republicans, many of whom scoffed at the whole business as an aping of English procedure. Some objectors pointed out that Congress was outdoing Parliament, for that body did not wait upon the King *en masse;* it customarily ordered that the reply to the Throne be delivered by a committee. There were sufficient practical reasons for the abandonment of a practice which was not yet firmly entrenched. Jefferson's successors, previous to Woodrow Wilson, did not return to it, and even when that eloquent President did, Congress wisely refrained from replying to him.

While Jefferson believed that his procedure would be acceptable to Congress as a whole, he was well aware that it would be specially pleas-

[5] The best account is that of Charles Warren, "How the President's Speech to Congress Was Instituted and Abandoned," in *Odd Byways of American History* (1942), ch. VIII.

ing to his own supporters. Soon after the inauguration he had assured Nathaniel Macon that he would abandon the presidential address, along with levees and other ceremonial foolishness.[6] His own objections to the trappings of royalty and aristocracy as improper in a republic had been voiced at least as early as his stay in France, where he had abundant opportunity to observe them, along with the imbecilities of kings and nobles. At that time he was hoping to continue in the diplomatic service, where he could serve his fellow citizens silently and remain invisible.[7] His fears of monarchy in his own country, as voiced then and thereafter, now appear exaggerated, but his dislike of monarchical forms, and indeed of all sorts of pageantry and ceremonialism, was no politician's affectation. While he highly approved of noble public buildings as civic temples, he strongly objected to any glorification of rulers. To him public officials in a self-governing society were public servants and should appear as such. This was sound republican doctrine, predestined to acceptance in a country like the United States; and to him at that time the danger that the public itself might tyrannize over its servants probably seemed remote.

Certain of his critics, less averse to the distinctions of rank and class in the Old World and less aware of their essential incompatibility with the mobile society of the New, saw in him the chief promoter of the "wild doctrines of equality" of the French Revolution. One of these was the British chargé, Edward Thornton, who was rather friendly to Jefferson, but whose comments were influenced by High Federalist opinion. He described the new President as being "careful in every particular of his personal conduct to inculcate upon the people his attachment to a republican simplicity of manners and his unwillingness to admit the smallest distinction, that may separate him from the mass of his fellow citizens."[8] The ranking British representative also reported with dismay that Jefferson, setting apart no special day for receiving visits, admitted any person at any time, "with a most perfect disregard to ceremony both in his dress and manners." Thornton saw no leveling spirit in the expensive style of living in the President's House, though he reported that there was less form and ostentation than in the time of General Washington.

The contrast between the Jeffersonian concept of an unceremonious chief executive who was always accessible, and the Federalist ideal of a

[6] TJ to Macon, May 14, 1801 (L. & B., X, 261).
[7] TJ to Francis Hopkinson, Mar. 13, 1789 (Boyd, XIV, 651); see *Jefferson and the Rights of Man*, p. 212.
[8] Thornton to Hawkesbury, Dec. 9, 1801 (FO, 5:32).

remote dignitary shielded by protocol, is borne out by Hamilton's original advice to Washington about the access of officials to him.[9] The
ablest of the High Federalists was generally more concerned with the
reality of power than with forms, but he believed that only department
heads, foreign ministers, and senators wanting to consult the President
on public business should have ready access to him; Hamilton would
have denied it to congressmen. This was an impossible ideal, as that of
complete accessibility also was, but the policies were purposeful in both
cases. One was designed to enhance the dignity of the presidential
office, the other to emphasize its representative character, and each was
needed in its own time.

Hospitality was an essential element in the Jeffersonian technique.
The fact that he hated to dine alone and had no family at hand partially
explains his practice of having company for dinner every day, but it
was no accident that this so often consisted of senators and congressmen. One of the latter, Dr. Samuel Lathrop Mitchill, a representative
from New York who chanced also to be a man of science and learning,
thus described him about a month after he sent his first message to
Congress:

> I have had several opportunities of seeing and conversing with
> him since my arrival in Washington. He is tall in stature and rather
> spare in flesh. His dress and manners are very plain; he is grave, or
> rather sedate, but without any tincture of pomp, ostentation, or
> pride, and occasionally can smile, and both hear and relate humor-
> ous stories as well as any other man of social feelings. . . . He is
> more deeply versed in human nature and human learning than al-
> most the whole tribe of his opponents and revilers.[10]

By this time it had probably become second nature to him to be
unceremonious and unostentatious, but he could not have been unaware that he had long since become a symbol and that his political
strength had very considerably derived from it. That he carefully
guarded his image as the unassuming man of the people can no more be
doubted than that George Washington guarded his dignity. The third
President needed it to offset the counter-image of an ambitious schemer
and reckless visionary which for a decade his enemies had sought to
imprint on the public mind. Also, it served to reduce suspicions of his
intellectuality among the unlearned. Insofar as the egalitarianism of this
cultivated gentleman was self-conscious, it may be regarded as his particular variety of showmanship and protective coloration.

The basic question is not whether he guarded or projected his demo-

[9] Hamilton to Washington, May 5, 1789 (Lodge, VII, 45-46).
[10] Dr. S. L. Mitchill to his wife, Jan. 10, 1802 (*Harper's Mag.*, LVIII, 743-744).

cratic image too zealously in matters which now seem trivial; it is whether he conscientiously used this major political asset in the larger public interest. What he said in his first message to Congress was far more significant than the way he transmitted the document. The public demand for it implies that it was immediately recognized as important. The *National Intelligencer*, having run out of printed copies on the day of its delivery, issued several successive editions in the next three days, saying that the demand gained strength from a more general perusal of the message. To this editor it offered bright evidence that its author deserved the noble title of Man of the People.[11] Also, it showed him as the bearer of good tidings of peace and the lightening of human burdens.

In the first words the President addressed to what he tactfully called the "great council" of the nation he announced the restoration of peace in the world. Toward the end of November he had learned that, on October 1, preliminary articles had been signed in behalf of Great Britain and France; and soon thereafter he said that the only real danger to the success of his domestic policies was now removed. To a Republican governor he wrote: "We can now proceed without risk in demolishing useless structures of expense, lightening the burthens of our constituents, and fortifying the principles of free government." [12] He fully recognized that governmental controls and exactions necessarily increase, and human liberties inevitably shrink, in a state of war; they tend to do so even under the threat of external danger. For just that reason he persistently sought peace and tried to keep out of the broils of Europe. For that reason, also, he could have congratulated himself that his administration began in 1801, instead of 1797, when the launching of such an experiment in democratic and economical government as his would hardly have been possible.

Grave difficulties in foreign relations were to arise before the next congressional session, but at the outset he was much luckier in his times than John Adams was at any point in the latter's administration, and he benefited directly and greatly from negotiations his predecessor had started. In midsummer Bonaparte ratified the convention which the American emissary, Congressman John Dawson, bore to France as amended by the Senate before Adams left office. The First Consul attached a proviso which meant in effect that, as his country renounced

[11] *National Intelligencer*, Dec. 14, 1801. The message of Dec. 8, 1801, with the comments and suggestions of Gallatin, can be conveniently seen in Ford, VIII, 109–125.
[12] TJ to Gov. Joseph Bloomfield of N.J., Dec. 5, 1801 (LC, 20360).

the old treaties with the United States, the latter renounced its claims for spoliations. Because of the irregularity in the form of ratification, Jefferson was impelled to ask a second advice and consent from the Senate. One Federalist member of that body, Gouverneur Morris, thought this a foolish and demeaning action, but it forestalled criticism on the ground that he had accepted a weakened convention because of his French sympathies. As a gesture of deference it was politically wise and in the event quite harmless. The Senate readily consented since practically everybody was glad to settle with Bonaparte on even terms and get out of the French imbroglio once and for all.[13] They did not know as yet that fresh dangers were to rise from the First Consul's colonial policy in this interim of European peace. Meanwhile, the arrival of Livingston in France marked the resumption of normal diplomatic relations. He did not sail until autumn but a French chargé, L. A. Pichon, had arrived in March and talked with Jefferson at length thereafter. He found the President friendly and communicative, with pacific intentions toward all the world, and reported to his own government that nothing beyond passive neutrality was to be expected of him.[14] He also reported that relations between the United States and Great Britain were improving.

The British had no representative of ministerial rank in the United States at this time. After Robert Liston left, they had a chargé in the person of Edward Thornton. He conversed with Jefferson before Madison arrived and on occasion afterwards, finding the President more communicative than the Secretary of State. At the earliest of these meetings Jefferson asked the young Britisher to assure his government that they could expect as sincere friendship from the new administration as from the old. Thornton reported to his own superior in England that Jefferson dismissed the representations of him as anti-British as mere newspaper talk for electioneering purposes. "For *republican* France he might have felt some interest," said Thornton, paraphrasing the President, "but that was long over, and there was assuredly nothing in the present Government of that country which would naturally incline him to show the smallest undue partiality to it at the expense of Great Britain or indeed of any other country." [15] Jefferson's reference

---

[13] TJ submitted the ratification to the Senate on Dec. 11, three days after he sent his message to Congress as a whole, and the Senate consented Dec. 19 (*A.S.P.F.R.*, II, 345; Hunter Miller, *Treaties and Other International Acts*, II, 483–484; G. Morris, *Diary and Letters*, II, 416, entry of Dec. 19, 1801).

[14] Pichon to Minister of Foreign Affairs, May 14, July 22, 1801 (AECPEU, 53:-115–118, 177–184).

[15] Thornton to Grenville, Mar. 7, 1801, describing conversations in late February and on Mar. 5 (FO, 5:32).

to his attitude toward France can be readily supported by comments from Federalists. Writing from Boston to Rufus King in London a year after this, one of them said: "The sect and even the philosopher openly inveigh against Bonaparte. . . . One source of apprehension is therefore removed, and at present there is not much reason to fear that we shall be thrown into the arms of France, should the present European armistice end." [16] After so long a time, it seemed, *that* ghost was laid.

Rufus King had been wisely left in London by Jefferson and instructed to conclude the negotiation of a convention dealing with private American debts to British creditors, as assumed by the United States in Jay's Treaty. John Adams and his secretary of state, John Marshall, deserve the credit for starting this negotiation, as King does for successfully pursuing it. The convention was not signed until Jefferson had been ten months in office and was not submitted to the Senate until nearly the end of the congressional session, but it was anticipated before he transmitted his first message. One of its articles provided that the United States should pay a lump sum of £600,000 as compensation for the debts, thus settling a vexing question which was of particular concern to Virginians. One of them, Senator Wilson Cary Nicholas, expressed his pleasure that an accommodation with the traditional enemy was likely. "I do not believe that any event would produce more mischievous consequences to the U.S. than a rupture with G.B.," he said. Since Jay's Treaty many things had changed. [17]

As for the other country with which American relations were important, the Chevalier Casa de Yrujo, envoy of Spain and son-in-law of that good Republican, Governor Thomas McKean of Pennsylvania, was on such friendly terms with the President that, soon after the inauguration, he was helping him find a cook. [18]

Jefferson perceived only one exception to the state of general peace: the weakest of the Barbary states of North Africa, Tripoli, had declared war on the distant American Republic, and trouble was likely with some of the others. In order to inform Congress fully of developments in the Mediterranean theater he communicated a mass of letters and other documents which are much more colorful than any brief summary of them can be. [19] Treaties had been made with these petty

[16] Joseph Hale to King, Apr. 13, 1802 (King, IV, 107).
[17] Memo. of Council meeting, June 13, 1801, at which it was unanimously agreed that King should conclude his negotiations on the subject of Art. VI of Jay's Treaty (Ford, I, 296); Convention of Jan. 8, 1802, in Miller, *Treaties*, II, 488–490, submitted to Senate Mar. 29, consented to Apr. 26. Nicholas commented in a letter to TJ, Oct. 30, 1801 (LC, 21914).
[18] Yrujo to TJ, Mar. 13, 1801, from Philadelphia (Bixby, pp. 79–80). Also, see ch. XIV, below.
[19] *A.S.P.F.R.*, II, 347–361.

piratical powers in the past, all of them calling for what amounted to tribute. The United States was acting like the other nations with commerce to protect, but Jefferson had opposed this sort of policy from the time he was in France, believing that the only effective language to employ against these brigands of the sea was that of force.[20] He never believed in buying peace with them, and actually he was the first President to use force against them. John Adams was not undisposed to do so, but the Father of the United States Navy stayed his hand because of the troubles with France.

The current trouble with the Bey of Tripoli arose from his dissatisfaction with his treaty and tribute; he resented the fact that the Dey of Algiers enjoyed a much better arrangement. He declared war by having the pole carrying the American flag cut down. Before learning of this, Jefferson, in answer to earlier threats, had ordered to the Mediterranean a squadron of four vessels under Commodore Richard Dale, whom he instructed to protect American commerce while showing full respect for friendly powers.[21] The main results of this mission were the blockading of Tripoli and the victory of the schooner *Enterprise* over a Tripolitan polacca without loss of life. The latter vessel, completely dismantled, was then permitted to return to port.

In reporting the first naval exploit of his administration, Jefferson remarked that, under the Constitution, actions beyond the line of defense were unauthorized without the sanction of Congress. In the first of the series of newspaper articles in which Hamilton, writing in the *New York Evening Post* as LUCIUS CRASSUS, critically examined the President's message, this advocate of governmental power and executive authority protested against any denial of the right to capture and detain vessel and crew.[22] His constitutional argument was that when a foreign nation declared war or openly made it on the United States, a declaration by Congress, if not nugatory, was at least unnecessary. If President Franklin D. Roosevelt had believed that, he would not have needed to go to Congress after Pearl Harbor. Hamilton was not merely engaged in constitutional hairsplitting, however: he wanted to demonstrate that the President, in his deference to Congress and his defensive tactics in the Mediterranean, had shown himself to be pusillanimous. The Colossus of Federalism asked, "What will the world think of the fold which has such a shepherd?"

Since the Tripolitan War dragged on for four years, in the course of which the United States became briefly embroiled with Morocco, the

[20] See *Jefferson and the Rights of Man*, pp. 27–32.
[21] Secretary of State to Wm. Eaton, May 20, 1801 (*A.S.P.F.R.*, II, 347–348).
[22] Dec. 17, 1801 (J.C.H., VII, 745–747).

charge could be readily made during Jefferson's first term that he was pursuing an inconclusive and indecisive policy with respect to the Barbary powers. But, since his government applied more force against these pestiferous states than any other power did, gaining relatively favorable terms in the end, there are insufficient grounds here for characterizing the President as a timid and foolish shepherd.[23]

He had initiated a limited action, but its limitations were not owing to theoretical pacifism, nor chiefly to constitutional scruples, but to severely practical considerations. In dealing with these states the question was whether the game was worth the candle—whether it was cheaper to buy peace with them than to compel it. Convinced that the payment of blackmail, besides being humiliating, was the more expensive in the long run, Jefferson definitely preferred forceful action. This, however, might prove embarrassingly costly in the short run. The limitations were imposed by the actualities of naval power and available financial resources and by presumable public sentiment. He was carefully regarding all of these at the moment. He figured that the maintenance of the American frigates in the Mediterranean would be little more expensive than in American waters. Also, he believed that this mission would serve a purpose in the training of officers and men, as it did. The nearest approach to a rift in the official family was occasioned by this enterprise. The Secretary of the Navy wanted to press it, while Gallatin feared that it would strain the financial resources of the government.[24] The task of the President was to keep it from getting out of hand, for he had made economy and the discharge of the public debt basic in his domestic policy and with these had coupled tax reduction.

ii

The severest critics of Jefferson's financial policy asserted that, like his social practice, it was primarily designed to gain popularity. "*Good patriots must at all events please the people,*" wrote Hamilton sarcastically.[25] In the lexicon of the High Federalists that was what demagoguery meant; to them there was ignobility as well as peril in any conscious attempt to give the people what they wanted, though they themselves made no objection to the granting of governmental favors to special groups. The man whom they characterized as a demagogue never believed that the voice of the people was the voice of God, but

[23] Ray W. Irwin, *Diplomatic Relations of the U.S. with the Barbary Powers* (1931) is an excellent account; see ch. VIII for the years 1801–1802 and ch. XIII for a summing up.
[24] The difference of opinion was clear by the late summer of 1802, if not earlier.
[25] In the first article of his "Examination," Dec. 17, 1801 (J.C.H., VII, 745).

he was notable in his time, and has been ever since, for his confidence in the common-sense judgment of the people generally. Shortly after his inauguration he said to a former congressman: "It is rare that the public sentiment decides immorally or unwisely, and the individual who differs from it ought to distrust and examine his own opinion." [26] To his mind the adoption of agreeable rather than disagreeable measures, when possible, was the duty of public officials. This was not a matter of seeking popularity for its own sake, though he could hardly have been blamed for liking it after all the abuse he had been subjected to. Governors and government had to be supported, and reliance must be placed on public approbation if it was not placed on force, which he detested, and habits of obedience, which were not deeply engrained in his country.[27] He did not trust the people implicitly, but as between the wishes of the many and those of the few this member of the gentry saw no choice but to recognize the former, if he could do so safely. To say that he wanted his government to be popular is another way of saying that he wanted it to be supported.

No one can question the political sagacity which led him to emphasize at the earliest opportunity measures of assured popularity. Before the first annual message was delivered, John Taylor of Caroline prophesied: "A rigid economy will enable the administration to repeal some of the most obnoxious tax laws, and this will acquire a confidence which will enable them to do either right or wrong." [28] Jefferson recommended the immediate repeal of *all* the internal taxes, though the more cautious Gallatin thought such action premature. The British chargé, after observing that economy and relief from taxes were the great instrument whereby Jefferson's partisans secured the election, said "it must be owned that he has availed himself with great art of this powerful engine, and has afforded a complete triumph to his party." [29] Few could doubt that a foundation for popular administration had been quickly and skillfully laid.

His decision to advocate the prompt repeal of the internal taxes, when Gallatin was counseling delay, had a political coloration, but in this matter there was no real difference between the two men except with respect to timing. Gallatin believed that unless taxes were reduced by this administration they never would be, and he recognized practical advantages in getting rid of all the internal taxes at one time, since the

26 TJ to William Findley, Mar. 24, 1801 (Ford, VIII, 27).

27 Rightly or wrongly, the British chargé regarded the South and West as less "friendly to subordination" than New England (Thornton to Hawkesbury, Oct. 1, 1801; FO, 5:32).

28 Taylor to W. C. Nicholas, Sept. 5, 1801 (*Papers, MHS*, p. 102).

29 Thornton to Hawkesbury, Dec. 8, 1801 (FO, 5:32; Duplicate No. 56).

collection of a part of them would be disproportionately expensive. The policy as a whole was that of both men, and it reflected the convictions of both. It may be divided into four closely related parts: strict governmental economy, tax reduction, definite provision for the retirement of the national debt, and specific rather than general appropriations. Reference to the last was made in the message on Gallatin's suggestion, and in his own report to Congress he spelled out his plan to retire the debt. But Jefferson heartily approved of both of these, and the entire program was in full accord with his current philosophy and past utterances.

Since he was an excessively generous man who maintained expensive establishments at the President's House and Monticello, he may seem out of character as an advocate of any sort of economy. He liked handsome surroundings, served the best of food and drink, and in the realm of furnishings and books was a compulsive buyer. But he hated waste, and his personal regimen was marked by moderation, even by austerity. He kept detailed records of his receipts and expenditures, never being careless in financial matters though often over-optimistic; and his inability to get out of the debt he inherited can be largely attributed to factors beyond his control.[30] Private and public finance are two different matters, but his advocacy of public economy can be attributed in part to his personal experience and observation. The plantation society in which he grew up was still bearing the burdens of past prodigality and excessive recourse to credit, and he himself was caught in the toils of debt from which he could not escape. He did not want the country as a whole to repeat this experience. In speaking of the extravagance of his predecessors he indulged in partisan exaggeration. Writing one of his sons in law a few months after the inauguration, he said: "We are hunting out and abolishing multitudes of useless offices, striking off jobs, etc., etc. Never were such scenes of favoritism, dissipation of treasure, and disregard of legal appropriations seen." [31] He had undoubtedly observed far greater extravagance and favoritism in France, and the example he was most anxious to avoid was provided by European governments, but he was suspicious of high officials anywhere and insisted on their strict accountability for the use they made of the people's money.

Coupled as this doctrine was with the recommendation of specific rather than general appropriations and insistence on rigid observance of the letter of the law by all officials from the President down, it may be regarded as a parallel to that of strict construction of the Constitu-

[30] See *Jefferson the Virginian*, pp. 441–445.
[31] TJ to TMR, June 18, 1801 (LC, 19483).

tion. After a period of Federalist rule which had been strongly tinctured by Hamiltonian arrogance and highhandedness, Jefferson's reminder that the control of public expenditure really lay with the branch of the government which was supposedly closest to the people was salutary, as was his insistence that executive officers regard themselves as stewards rather than rulers. In his effort to democratize the government he was reiterating first principles. But his financial doctrine, if rigidly adhered to, involved dangers similar to those perceived by Hamilton in strict construction of the Constitution; in theory at least he appeared to be putting the high executive officials, including himself, in strait jackets by sharply limiting their discretion. But if he sounded to Hamilton like a visionary theorist, he was to act like a pragmatist at certain crucial points in his administration, strongly supported by the ultimate power — public opinion. In purchasing Louisiana he wisely veered from his customary financial procedure, though he did not abandon his financial objective.

The program of governmental economy, reduction of taxes, and systematic curtailment of the national debt was not based merely on the expectation that peace could be maintained; it was inseparable from his concept of a limited federal government. In his message he said that this government was "charged with the external and mutual relations only of these states," the principal core of the great human concerns of person, property, and reputation being left to the states themselves.[32] Acting in cases subject to his discretion, he had begun to cut the roll of federal officials; he wielded his shears in the spirit of a gardener, pruning shrubs of their excess foliage. He had reduced the foreign missions to three — in Great Britain, France, and Spain; and he had discontinued the inspectors of internal revenue, whom Gallatin regarded as more an obstruction than a help. With the repeal of the internal taxes the collectors of these would also be discontinued, but Gallatin, who sought efficiency along with economy, thought it undesirable to make much further reduction in the civil service. The best hope for savings that he saw was in the armed services, and in the prospect of continuing peace the administration speeded the process of demobilization.

Sending Jefferson rough sketches relative to finances shortly after the inauguration, Gallatin said they could save hundreds of thousands in the Departments of War and the Navy, while they could only save thousands in the others.[33] One reason why the President gave first attention to naval reduction was that, by an act passed at the end of the Adams administration, he was given discretion to sell all naval vessels

[32] Ford, VIII, 120.
[33] Gallatin to TJ, Mar. 14, 1801 (Gallatin, *Writings*, I, 25).

except thirteen frigates and to take all except six of the latter out of active service.[34] Almost immediately Jefferson began to avail himself of this discretion, which he afterwards described euphemistically as a direction. In June he wrote his son-in-law that, while the law required him to keep six frigates armed, he believed that three would be quite enough.[35] He had recently dispatched precisely that number, along with a sloop of war, to the Mediterranean. He had long favored the use of naval power against the Barbary pirates, but at this time he apparently saw no other service that American frigates could be expected to render. Regarding any competition with the major sea powers as hopeless, he saw no point in building expensive vessels which would shortly become obsolete. He was concerned only with defense and believed that if difficulties with those powers should arise, these would have to be met by other means than force.[36] This philosophy did not commend itself to naval enthusiasts in his age or thereafter, but his position was reasoned and he himself regarded it as realistic.

Since naval reduction did not seem dangerous during his first year in office his first reports of it were undoubtedly gratifying to members of his own party and probably to most other people. In his message to Congress he stated that five frigates had been laid up and that two others would be as soon as repaired. The roll of officers in all departments, which he communicated several weeks later, contained an impressive list of offices abolished since the passing of the Naval Act of 1801, nineteen captains among them.[37] There were still fifteen captains when the Council met in October, 1801. Voting on them one by one, the President and his Secretaries then reduced the list to nine. Expenditures for the navy never reached as small a figure as Gallatin originally recommended, but very substantial savings are reflected in the statistics. Expenditures were least in the year 1802, when they fell to $915,000, which was less than half what they were in 1801. Their rise after that may be attributed to the actions against the Barbary States, for which Gallatin showed more reluctance than Jefferson, but they always remained low by Federalist standards.

[34] Act of Mar. 3, 1801 (*Annals*, 6 Cong., pp. 1557–1559).

[35] TJ to TMR, June 18, 1801 (LC, 19483); also, May 14, 1801 (*Papers, MHS*, pp. 95–96).

[36] A good statement of his matured thought about naval power is in his letter of May 27, 1813, to John Adams; see also one of Nov. 1, 1822 (*A.-J. Letters*, II, 324, 584). Adams thought him more friendly to the navy than Hamilton, whom he regarded as an army man.

[37] Communicated Feb. 17, 1802 (*A.S.P., Class X, Misc.*, I, 319); see TJ's memo. of Oct. 22, 1801 (Ford, I, 296). The condensed tables of receipts and expenditures, 1801–1811, in D. R. Dewey, *Financial History of the U.S.* (1912), pp. 123–124, can be conveniently consulted.

The economy-minded President was able to do little about the army at first, but, as he told Congress, he regarded the present military forces as larger than they need be. "For defence against invasion, their number is as nothing," he said; "nor is it conceived needful or safe that a standing army should be kept up in time of peace for that purpose." [38] He asked Congress to perfect the laws relating to the militia, which he regarded as the country's first and readiest reliance, and it may be said by way of anticipation that within a couple of years the expenses of the regular establishment had been cut in half.

At the beginning of his critique of the presidential message Hamilton said that it conformed to "the bewitching tenets of that illuminated doctrine, which promises men, ere long, an emancipation from the burdens and restraints of government; giving a foretaste of that pure felicity which apostles of this doctrine have predicted." [39] One of these burdens was taxation. Hamilton, who had seized upon the Whiskey Rebellion as an opportunity to demonstrate the might of the federal government in support of its authority to tax, had no sympathy with what he regarded as the coddling of the people. The view of Jefferson, by contrast, was that unnecessary taxation of those for whose benefit the government had been established was absurd, and that in an emergency, such as war, the public would rise to the occasion and accept the burdens that would then be necessary. Though taxes in America had never been high by European standards, he and Gallatin did not forget that in the Federalist era there had been two revolts against them, the Whiskey Rebellion in Washington's second term and the Fries Rebellion in the Adams administration. Objection in both cases was to internal taxes, which, unlike imposts, were clearly visible. Believing that government must be based on consent rather than the suppression of dissent, the administration chose to dispense with the most unpopular taxes. What Hamilton interpreted as a sign of weakness may be regarded in a self-governing society as a matter of common sense.

The specific plan to reduce the national debt and provide for its ultimate extinction was that of Gallatin, who believed that he was appointed for the primary purpose of performing this task. [40] When he assumed office the debt amounted to $83,000,000 and he believed that it could be paid off in sixteen years by annual appropriations of $7,300,000.

[38] Ford, VIII, 121.
[39] Dec. 17, 1801 (J.C.H., VII, 744).
[40] His plans are well summarized by Raymond Walters in *Gallatin*, pp. 145–146 (citing *A.S.P. Finance*, I, 701–717). They are described in detail and more critically by Alexander Balinky in *Albert Gallatin: Fiscal Theories and Policies* (1958), chs. 3–5.

Jefferson's enthusiastic support of this central endeavor was thoroughly consistent with his own past. It reflected not only his personal experience in the debt-ridden society of his own state but also his observations of European governments. While he was contemplating the public debt of France he penned one of the most characteristic of all his sayings: "The earth belongs always to the living generation." [41] One of the meanings he perceived in this is that every generation should be free from the incubus of inherited debt, and should not transmit its own burdens to posterity. While in France he became so deeply concerned over his country's debt in Europe that he drafted specific proposals for its amortization; and he made detailed calculations of the sort a number of times thereafter.[42]

In the light of his actual record the absurdity of the charge, so long current in Federalist circles, that he was a repudiationist is obvious, though he unquestionably believed that Hamilton increased the public debt unnecessarily. Furthermore, he was convinced that Hamilton was not really interested in paying it off. If we can imagine these two men as translated into the era in which corporate and public debt underlies the economic structure of every capitalistic society, we have abundant reason to suppose that Jefferson, a countryman with old-fashioned financial ideas, would be ill at ease. The analogy that he drew was not between public and corporate debt but between the debts of a nation and those of an individual. Hamilton would be much more at home in twentieth-century finance, and he was more modern than his historic rival in thinking of public debt as an investment in the future of the country. To Jefferson it was an incubus to be removed as soon as possible.

Toward the end of his service his mind turned with that of Gallatin to the possibility of using part of the revenue for roads and other constructive improvements, but his aversion to public debt persisted through his administration. A few months after his retirement he wrote Gallatin:

> I consider the fortunes of our republic as depending, in an eminent degree, on the extinguishment of the public debt before we engage in any war: because, that done, we shall have revenue enough to improve our country in peace and defend it in war, without recurring either to new taxes or loans. But if the debt should once more be swelled to a formidable size, its entire discharge will be

[41] TJ to Madison, Sept. 6, 1789 (Boyd, XV, 396). For an ample account of the circumstances of this famous letter, see *ibid.*, XV, 384-391.

[42] *Ibid.*, XIV, 190-209. No fewer than eight calculations of his are scattered through his papers under various dates, beginning in 1788 and extending into his presidency.

despaired of, and we shall be committed to the English career of debt, corruption and rottenness, closing with revolution. The discharge of the debt, therefore, is vital to the destinies of our government, and it hangs on Mr. Madison and yourself alone. We shall never see another President and Secretary of the Treasury making all other objects subordinate to this.[43]

The eight years of Jefferson's administration covered half the time that Gallatin originally regarded as necessary to extinguish the debt. During that period it was actually reduced by almost a third, despite extraordinary expenses that were not allowed for in the beginning.[44] It is now clear that this high degree of success could not have been achieved but for the large increase in revenue from import duties that accompanied the growth of American commerce in this period. The President and Secretary of the Treasury gave too much credit to their economies, some of which now seem petty. Beyond any doubt, however, the administration was in earnest. Although the pay-as-you-go policy, with a reduction in the armed forces, did not commend itself to the bold and positive mind of Hamilton, most people could be expected to approve of rigorous financial management on the part of their government regardless of their own practices.

Though Jefferson gave major emphasis to his financial program in his first recommendations to his first Congress, the resulting bills were not the first to be passed by that body. Indeed, the most controversial measure of the session, the repeal of the Judiciary Act of 1801, was passed a month before the law repealing the internal taxes.[45] But, once proposed, the latter was sure of passage. The financial policy of the administration was a major reason for the waxing popularity of the President.

If this popularity was commensurate with certain tokens he received from admirers, it was already enormous before the legislators really got down to business. On his first New Year's Day as President he was presented with the "mammoth cheese," which was more than four feet in diameter, fifteen inches thick, and weighed 1235 pounds. Sometimes called the "Cheshire cheese" from the town of its origin in Massachu-

[43] TJ to Gallatin, Oct. 11, 1809 (Ford, IX, 264). At the moment he was deeply concerned lest Gallatin leave Madison's Cabinet.

[44] Chiefly the Barbary Wars and the Louisiana Purchase. For a table showing the reduction from $83,000,000 in 1801 to $57,000,000 in 1809, and comments on this, see Dewey, pp. 125–126. Describing the performance of the Treasury, 1801–1808, Balinky (ch. 6) goes further in attributing its success to the fortunate increase in revenue from imposts.

[45] Approved Mar. 8, 1802. The act repealing the internal taxes was approved Apr. 6, and the one providing for the redemption of the debt Apr. 29.

setts, where Elder John Leland had proclaimed him to a Baptist constituency as the Man of the People, this attracted some ridicule along with much good-humored curiosity. Less excitement was created by the "mammoth veal," received a little earlier from the butchers of Philadelphia. Not only did they describe themselves as the most loyal of Republicans; they addressed the President as patriotic Americans who particularly admired him for overcoming European prejudice that the animals of the New World were inferior and degenerate. To support his arguments, as advanced in the *Notes on Virginia* and elsewhere against Buffon and other foreign scientists, they sent him the hind quarter of the largest calf of her age (115 days) ever seen in their part of the country. He confessed that, despite the care and hopes of the senders, it arrived in too advanced a state for table use but claimed that it retained its full beauty of appearance. Also, he assured his patriotic admirers that the repetition of "such successful examples of enlarging the animal volume" would do far more than any words of his to correct erroneous European opinion. Whether or not this lover of Nature's marvels chuckled when he penned these spacious phrases we have no way of knowing.[46]

The great cheese was made in the summer of 1801 by members of Leland's congregation, reputedly from the milk of 900 cows at one milking, not one of them a Federalist. Because of its size it required a cider press, and the term "mammoth," which was being popularized about this time by Charles Willson Peale, another sturdy Republican, in connection with a specimen he was mounting in his Philadelphia museum, was quickly applied to it. In the fall Leland and a companion took it by sleigh or wagon to the Hudson, then by sloop to New York and Baltimore, whence it went to Washington by wagon. At the various stopping places it was viewed by big crowds; and Elder John Leland, now called the "mammoth priest," preached to large and curious congregations both going and coming. He delivered it to the President's House on New Year's morning, along with an address. In this the cheese was described as a "pepper-corn" of the esteem of the signers for the chief magistrate, as a "sacrifice to republicanism," as a mite in the scale of democracy. In his reply Jefferson, besides reiterating his devotion to republican principles, including the prohibition of religious tests, referred to the cheese as an extraordinary proof of skill in the domestic arts and expressed special gratitude for this mark of esteem from free-

[46] Messrs. Fry and Coleman to TJ, Oct. 17, 1801; TJ to them, Oct. 21 (LC, 20151, 20164). John Beckley, who spoke of them as Fry and Chapman, delivered TJ's reply, afterwards writing him that, since they were Germans and did not understand English, it had to be translated by one of their brethren. The letter to TJ was in English and must have been written for them.

born farmers. Writing his son-in-law, he further described the offering as "an ebullition of the passion of republicanism in a state where it has been under heavy persecution." He did not accept it as a gift from these impecunious farmers, however, for he gave Leland $200 a few days later. This may have taken the form of a contribution to Leland's church, and it figured out as a considerably higher rate per pound than was ordinarily paid for cheese.[47] A Federalist congressman from Massachusetts viewed with disgust this "parade of Democratic etiquette," and referred to Leland, who preached before members of the two houses and the President soon thereafter, as "a poor, illiterate, clownish creature." [48] But Manasseh Cutler and many others viewed the mammoth cheese on that New Year's Day and the next one, by which time some sixty pounds had been removed from the middle because of symptoms of decay. What finally happened to it is uncertain: some said that the last of it was served at a presidential reception in 1805, others that it was dumped into the Potomac. At all events, the episode was not soon forgotten, and in the twentieth century it may be described as a highly effective publicity stunt. The address and the reply appeared in Republican papers under the heading: "THE GREATEST CHEESE IN AMERICA, FOR THE GREATEST MAN IN AMERICA." According to this view the country had a mammoth President.[49]

Jefferson scrupulously declined valuable gifts and said that he was averse to receiving addresses, but one that came from another group of New England Baptists offered him a welcome opportunity. His answer to the Danbury Baptist Association of Connecticut, bearing the same date as the reply to his cheese-making admirers in Massachusetts, was to be quoted long thereafter. In it he declared that by means of the prohibitions in the first amendment to the Constitution, a "wall of separation" had been built between church and state. He was seeking to encourage the dissenting minority in Connecticut and to rebuke the politico-religious rulers of that commonwealth. The controversy which raged during his administration between him and his clerical foes in that part of the country is dealt with more specifically hereafter.[50] At this point

[47] Account Book, Jan. 4, 1802; TJ to TMR, Jan. 1, 1802 (LC, 20590). The best account is L. H. Butterfield, "Elder John Leland, Jeffersonian Itinerant," in *Procs. Am. Antiq. Soc.*, Vol. 62, Part 2, esp. pp. 219–227, giving both addresses, quotations, and ample references. The address and TJ's reply both appeared in *National Intelligencer*, Jan. 20, 1802. Leland referred to his journey in his *Writings* (1845), p. 32. Among the communications ridiculing the cheese episode, one in *N.Y. Evening Post*, Mar. 5, 1802, offers a good example of Federalist sarcasm.

[48] Manasseh Cutler to Dr. Joseph Torrey, Jan. 4, 1802, in Cutler's *Life, Journals and Correspondence* (1888), II, 66–67.

[49] *National Intelligencer*, Jan. 20, 1802, from *Baltimore American*.

[50] See ch. XI, below.

we are primarily concerned with the popularity which was so vital a factor in his presidential leadership. He gained this over Congress very quickly, though never over the rulers of Connecticut. The Danbury Baptists, who said that such privileges as they enjoyed in that state were "as favors granted, and not as inalienable rights," honored him as an apostle of religious liberty. Much of their address sounded like his bill for establishing religious freedom in Virginia, and they hoped that the sentiments of their "beloved President" would prevail so that "hierarchy and tyranny" would vanish from the earth.

After drafting a reply, Jefferson submitted it to his chief consultants on New England, Gideon Granger and Levi Lincoln. The former believed that it expressed truths that were actually held by the great majority of the people of the region and by almost half the people of Connecticut. Though it might occasion "a temporary spasm among the Established Religionists," the Postmaster General wanted nothing in it changed. The Attorney General thought differently. In his draft Jefferson said that, since Congress was inhibited by the Constitution from acts respecting religion, and the executive was authorized only to execute their acts, he had refrained from prescribing "even occasional performances of devotion" — that is, as he told Lincoln, from proclaiming fastings and thanksgivings as his predecessors had done. On Lincoln's advice that this might give uneasiness even to Republicans in the eastern states, where they had long been accustomed to proclamations of thanksgiving by their governors, he wisely left it out.[51] In his opinion, Southerners would not have objected to his explanation, presumably because of their indifference to Thanksgiving and indisposition to fasting.

His rigid secularism was more of a disadvantage to him in the East than elsewhere, but he had the support of the "dissenters" there, as he had that of repressed groups everywhere. Others besides the Danbury Baptists, seeing in his past services "a glow of philanthropy and good will shining forth in a course of more than thirty years," believed that God had raised him up to fill the chair of state. His enemies might castigate him as an unbeliever, but the devotion of his followers had a religious fervor.

[51] The address of the Danbury Baptist Asso., dated Oct. 7, 1801, is in LC, 20111. The draft of TJ's reply as submitted to Granger and Lincoln, and a press copy of it as sent, are in LC, 20593–20594; the latter is printed, under the date Jan. 1, 1802, in L. & B., XVI, 281–282. The important letters are: Granger to TJ, Dec. 31, 1801 (LC, 20521); TJ to Lincoln, Jan. 1, 1802 (Ford, VIII, 129); Lincoln to TJ, Jan. 1, 1802 (LC, 20600).

[VII]

The Jeffersonians and the Judiciary

1801–1802

JEFFERSON'S success in his dealings with Congress was bottomed on his nationwide appeal as a symbol of freedom and democracy, and on the general popularity of his policies. Federalists might be reluctant to concede the former, but the more discerning of them quickly perceived the latter.[1] He could not have done what he did without the support of public opinion, and it is highly significant in the history of the presidency that he so fully recognized the necessity of this. The adoption of some of his proposals, such as tax reduction, might have been expected without any effort on his part beyond that of making them. But during most of his administration Congress not only accepted practically all of his recommendations; it passed virtually no bills of any significance without his recommendation or tacit approval. That legislative record was not to be matched in American history until the presidency of Woodrow Wilson.[2] It cannot be explained on grounds of popularity and timeliness alone; it required presidential leadership.

By exercising this to the degree that he did in his relations with Congress, Jefferson laid himself open to the charge of disregarding the doctrine of separation of powers and the independence of the legislature which he and his party had previously emphasized. Since full consistency in the face of changed circumstances is not desirable in a statesman and not to be expected of a wise one, we are warranted in regard-

---

[1] See, for example, J. Q. Adams to R. King, Jan. 18, 1802 (King, IV, 59–60).
[2] E. S. Corwin, *The President: Office and Powers* (1948), p. 21, quotes N. J. Small, *Some Presidential Interpretations of the Presidency* (1932), p. 172, to the effect that, considering the differences in the times, the legislative leadership of TJ and Wilson approached equality. With respect to that of TJ, I am much indebted to the unpublished dissertation of my former student A. B. Lacy, "Jefferson and Congress, 1801–1809" (UVA, 1963).

ing the charge of inconsistency as relatively unimportant. The fact is, however, that few of Jefferson's words and actions before becoming President bore directly on this question. He had said a great deal about the dangers of monarchy but surprisingly little about the relations between the executive and legislative branches, except in connection with the actions of Hamilton when he himself was secretary of state.[3]

At that time he charged his colleague with trying to establish the influence of the Treasury Department.[4] By the same token, Hamilton was trying to weaken the influence of Jefferson's department, but the latter's objection had broader grounds. While he was in the Washington administration, except perhaps during his last months, it had no such unified policy as his own administration had from the beginning. Hamilton assumed the right to speak for it and to influence Congress in the field of foreign as well as fiscal affairs. Jefferson regarded himself as limited to his own field, and as free to approach Congress only in the name of the President or with the latter's consent when specifically asked to do so.[5] No such presumptuousness as he had seen in Hamilton marked the conduct of his own ministers. Because of the terms of the law creating the Treasury Department, Gallatin had more direct dealings with Congress than any of the others, and he sometimes sharply disagreed with Jefferson in conference, but he never ceased to be a spokesman of the President and of this notably unified administration. Thus executive participation in legislative matters became unmistakably presidential. Also, it would be nearer the truth to say that Jefferson embodied himself with Congress, as John Marshall had predicted, than that he sought to establish executive supremacy. While he markedly exercised executive influence over Congress, there were often times when, after he had pointed the way, his own partisans went considerably farther than he wanted them to go, and he deferred to them. What he sought and gained was not subservience but a high degree of cooperation.

In performing his constitutional duty to make recommendations to the legislature, Jefferson outlined a purposeful program at the very beginning. But, as he said later, if he had limited himself to formal recom-

[3] In the fight over Jay's Treaty he supported the position of the congressional Republicans with respect to the rights of the House of Representatives vis-à-vis the President and Senate, but the partisan position he took at that time has little bearing on the present discussion. See *Jefferson and the Ordeal of Liberty*, ch. XVI.

[4] See TJ to Washington, Sept. 9, 1792 (Ford, VI, 101–104).

[5] As in various reports. TJ's connection with the Giles Resolutions in the last year of his secretaryship may be regarded as an exception, but, if so, his very secretiveness reflected his compunctions. See *Jefferson and the Ordeal of Liberty*, ch. II.

mendation, his government would have been a "government of chance and not of design." [6] Believing in his proposals, he was not willing to abandon them to chance from the moment of their birth. In seeking to exert his own influence in their behalf without encroaching on the prerogatives of Congress, he quickly perceived and never lost sight of the need to keep open the line of communication with the legislative body. To be more precise, it was with the majority since they were ready to listen to him. He had more to tell them than he felt like saying in a public message. Though his popular appeal as a symbol was the original basis of his political strength and he was characteristically considerate of the lowly, he had directly exercised his political influence on leaders throughout his career. It is not surprising, therefore, that he fell into the way of communicating with his party in Congress through members "in the confidence and views of the administration." The extent to which these men consulted him cannot be measured because of the lack of records of conversations, if for no other reason, but he undoubtedly treated them with deference and valued their counsel, sometimes yielding to it rather against his own judgment. In view of his temperament and conscious effort to avoid all appearance of dictation, one would suppose that he left tactics to the field commanders as a rule. Events were to prove, however, that no one could be floor leader without being in sympathy with him and that, almost invariably, the members of his party in Congress loyally carried out his wishes as these became known. When the test came they were Jeffersonians.

Thus, without employing force or corruption, he bridged, or at least narrowed, the gap between the executive and legislative branches. This he was able to do because, unlike both of the Presidents before him and most of those after him, he was the undisputed head of his party. Members of the opposition gained no comfort from these developments and, as might have been expected, raised cries of one-man rule. But his partisans honored his wishes for good reasons: his popularity was an invaluable asset to them and he towered above them in talents as well as prestige. Such dissension as appeared within his party during his first years in office was chiefly at the local level rather than in Congress, where there was remarkable Republican unity and loyalty to the Chief.

This became apparent in the first major legislative battle — over the repeal of the Judiciary Act of 1801. That fight demonstrated the effectiveness of the congressional majority when working in conjunction with the President, and the victory foreshadowed many others.

[6] To Barnabas Bidwell, July 5, 1806 (LC, 27995–27996). This letter contains one of the best statements of his matured ideas about executive-legislative relationships.

But the issue which was then raised was destined to abide. The judicial branch of the government was the least susceptible to democratization, and one result of the struggle was to solidify opposition which Jefferson had once hoped to dissolve by conciliation. Furthermore, this action fell short of the desires of certain members of his own party.

The judiciary act which aroused such ire among the Republicans became effective on February 13, 1801, less than three weeks before the expiration of the last Congress the Federalists ever controlled, and most of the officers authorized by it were commissioned less than two weeks before the administration of Adams ended. On his very last day in office the retiring President transmitted the names of three circuit court judges to succeed persons who had declined appointment, along with those of three judges for the District of Columbia; among the latter was William Cranch, his wife's nephew.[7] His signing of commissions on the eve of Jefferson's inauguration gave rise to the expression "midnight judges." No other action of Adams was so hard for his successor to forgive as his exercise of the appointing power to the bitter end, and the late conduct of the Federalists in Congress showed unmistakably that they saw no need to guide themselves in any way by the popular verdict. Because of the shamelessness of this court-packing, the genuine merits of the measure the Federalist die-hards had enacted were not unnaturally obscured in the minds of the President and party they were so eager to thwart.

Actually, the law corrected genuine defects in the organization of the federal judicial system which many responsible leaders had recognized for years. A major improvement was the relief it afforded the Supreme Court justices from circuit court duty, which was onerous in those days of difficult travel.[8] Another objection to the previous system was that justices might sit in the same case in circuit court and on appeal. To correct these ills, sixteen new circuit court judges were provided for, some changes were made in the districts, and, on the supposition that the work of the Supreme Court would be lightened, its membership was to be reduced from six to five with the next vacancy. In political terms this meant that the next President would be debarred from naming a successor to the first justice who died or retired. Jefferson had missed by only a few weeks the chance to select a chief justice. The High Federalists were not as satisfied with John Marshall as John Adams was, but Jefferson, who does not appear to have underestimated

[7] List with dates in *National Intelligencer*, Apr. 17, 1801.
[8] There had been no provision for it in the outlying regions of Kentucky, Tennessee, and Maine.

him at any time, could expect the antagonism of this distant relative throughout his own administration even if he did not anticipate that Marshall would serve for a generation. Meanwhile, the third President on his accession was faced with the fact that there was no Republican in the entire federal judiciary, which had been heavily reinforced at the eleventh hour by members of the defeated party.

The likelihood that this measure would increase the effectiveness of the national judiciary was no solace to the Republicans, since most of them held that branch of the government in detestation. The act was designed to enlarge the jurisdiction of the federal courts and make them more accessible; but in the South and West there was fear that the extension of their authority would be inimical to certain local interests. One reason commonly alleged by Federalists for the hostility of Virginians to their regime was the desire of planters to escape from their debts to British creditors, the expectation being that federal courts would insist on a strict compliance with treaty obligations. Since this particular problem was approaching settlement by the time the new Congress assembled, it had ceased to be pertinent. A more immediate question in the South and West was that of land titles, which were in great confusion and constant litigation. Leading Virginians and Kentuckians preferred to leave them with state rather than federal courts — within local rather than "foreign" jurisdiction. By contrast, persons with a stake in the great land companies, from the Holland Company in New York and Pennsylvania to the Yazoo Company in Georgia, had feared state actions against their speculative interests and sought to have the unresolved questions of land titles settled by federal courts.[9] These interested persons included some of the most important Federalist leaders, while those contesting their claims, for public or private reasons, and emphasizing state courts, were as a rule Republicans.

There were abundant additional reasons for the hostility of Republicans to the federal judiciary, which they rightly regarded as an arm of the Federalist party. They viewed the judges who tried the sedition cases as agents of tyranny and were infuriated by the arrogant and domineering spirit that had been displayed on the bench. Some Federalists believed that the unpopularity of the judiciary was a sure sign that it was meritoriously performing its major function, checking the excesses of the populace; but advocates of public order should not have expected conspicuous contempt for public opinion to remain unrebuked in a self-governing society.

There were signs that the judges had undergone no change of heart

[9] This point is emphasized in the admirable article of Kathryn Turner, "Federalist Policy and the Judiciary Act of 1801" (*W. & M.*, Jan., 1965, esp. pp. 23-30).

since Jefferson became President. At the first session of the new circuit court of the District of Columbia the nephew of Abigail Adams, Judge William Cranch, and Judge James M. Marshall, brother of John, sought the prosecution of the publisher of the *National Intelligencer* because of a communication in that paper which severely criticized the federal judiciary. Since the Sedition Act had expired, they wanted libel proceedings to be instituted under the common law. They were blocked by the Republican judge on the court, recently named by Jefferson, and by the grand jury, but their actions appeared to be in full accord with earlier efforts of the judiciary to muzzle the Republican press.[10]

Summing things up, a distinguished twentieth-century writer said: "Thus, unhappily, democracy marched arm in arm with State Rights, while Nationalism found itself the intimate companion of a narrow, bigoted, and retrograde conservatism." [11] If we regard both state rights and nationalism — both political democracy and judicial independence — as absolutes, we cannot escape the judgment that the country faced an unresolvable contradiction, that it must be impaled on one horn or the other of a dilemma. If certain contemporary comments on the two sides are to be taken at face value, a choice had to be made between anarchy and tyranny, between private property rights and confiscation. In the inexact science of government one should beware of absolutes, and when viewing political history we must allow for the exaggerations of partisanship, but there is no denying that this situation was serious. Statesmanship had failed in permitting it to become so. Republicans were not all of the same hue, and there was no justification in reason for their complete exclusion from the judiciary in the past because of the excesses of some of them. The implacable Federalists in a dying Congress, with a vain President at the end of his power, had compounded the difficulties; and the Man of the People came into a heritage of intransigent judges.

Political enemies of Jefferson in his own lifetime and numerous later writers contended that he planned a "campaign" against the judiciary from the very start, but that, as a cautious politician, he put this into effect only step by step lest he jeopardize the popularity of his party.[12] It seems more likely that he took one step without being sure of or nec-

[10] Warren, I, 194–198, citing *National Intelligencer,* June 12, Nov. 18, 1801, and other papers. The one Republican member of this court was appointed by TJ when an Adams nominee declined appointment.

[11] A. J. Beveridge, *Marshall,* III, 48. This author, whose sympathies are with the federal judiciary, gives an impressive statement of the causes of the public fear and hatred of it. Present-day writers, like Mrs. Turner, lay additional stress on economic considerations.

[12] Beveridge, III, 19.

essarily committed to the next one. At any rate, we should stick to the available record and remain aware of attendant circumstances.[13] Ten days after his inauguration, referring to his irreconcilable foes, whom he did not then regard as numerous, Jefferson said: "The principal of them have retreated into the judiciary as a stronghold, the tenure of which makes it difficult to dislodge them." A few weeks later, speaking of one of the last-minute appointments of Adams which he so deeply resented, he said: "The judge of course stands till the law is repealed, which we trust will be at the next Congress." [14] When he addressed Congress in the fall, he did not specifically recommend this course. Late in his message he said: "The judiciary system of the United States, and especially that portion of it recently erected, will of course present itself to the contemplation of Congress." [15] At the same time he laid before that body a statement of the business of the national judiciary, with the obvious intent of proving that no enlargement of it was necessary. He needed to do no more, for in the meantime other leaders in his party had been much more violent and verbose with respect to the judiciary in general.

Among these was Congressman William Branch Giles of Virginia, who believed he was describing the predominant sentiment of Republicans in his state when he said: "It is constantly asserted that the revolution is incomplete, so long as that strong fortress is in possession of the enemy." To this pugnacious partisan it seemed a singular circumstance that public sentiment should have forced itself into the executive and legislative branches, and that the judiciary "should not only not acknowledge its influence, but should pride itself in resisting its will under the misapplied idea of 'Independence!.' " After making this diagnosis he prescribed a drastic remedy: "an absolute repeal of the whole judiciary system, terminating the present officers and creating an entirely new system, defining the common law doctrine, and restraining to the proper constitutional extent the jurisdiction of the courts." [16] Jefferson never advocated that degree of demolition.

What he may have said in private we have little way of knowing, but (apart from filling a vacancy in the District of Columbia) the only thing he did before the meeting of Congress to remedy what he undoubtedly regarded as judicial ills, and the only thing he could do officially, was to replace a number of Federalist attorneys and marshals who

[13] One of the best accounts of the repeal of the judiciary act is in Warren, ch. IV.
[14] To Joel Barlow, Mar. 14, 1801 (L. & B., X, 223); to Archibald Stuart, Apr. 8, 1801 (Ford, VIII, 46).
[15] Ford, VIII, 123.
[16] Giles to TJ, June 1, 1801 (LC, 19373-19374).

held their posts at the pleasure of the President. Included among these were a good many persons whom he designated as "midnight" appointees, and for the removal of whom he saw no need to assign other reasons. On one of his own lists, however, he had a category designated as: "attornies and marshals removed for high federalism, and republicans appointed as a protection to republican suitors in courts entirely federal and going all lengths in party spirit." [17] Since many such officials impaneled juries consisting wholly of persons of their own political persuasion and often made a mockery of jury trials, this action of his may be interpreted as a move toward impartial justice, as well as one of counterpartisanship.[18]

ii

A resolution calling for the repeal of the act of the previous Congress respecting the judiciary was introduced in the Senate on January 6, 1802, by John Breckinridge of Kentucky. This was seconded by Stevens Thomson Mason of Virginia, the recognized majority leader in the Senate at this time and a man who was in the President's full confidence. So was Breckinridge, who had been Jefferson's intermediary in the matter of the Kentucky Resolutions in 1798.[19] He was a new member of the Senate, however, and may have taken the initiative because of strong pressure for repeal from his own constituents. Jefferson himself had laid first emphasis on economy and tax reduction, and it might have seemed better politics to let the most popular and least controversial part of his program be enacted first. The Senate could not initiate financial legislation, however, and pressure for immediate action on the question of the judiciary may have been brought to bear on Jefferson by Breckinridge and by impatient critics of the judges in Virginia. If he was disposed to resist this on grounds of expediency, a particular action of the Supreme Court a couple of weeks after the delivery of the presidential message may have convinced him that the issue must be faced without delay.

In its December term in 1801, meeting in the small room in the North Wing of the Capitol known as the Senate Clerk's Office, John Marshall and his five associates took the first step toward the famous decision of Marbury vs. Madison (1803). The Court granted a preliminary motion to show cause why a writ of mandamus should not be

---

[17] LC, 20546; see above, p. 74 and note 17.
[18] Beveridge fully recognizes the sins of the marshals and attorneys (see III, 42–43).
[19] See *Jefferson and the Ordeal of Liberty*, pp. 401–402, 405.

issued to the Secretary of State, requiring him to deliver commissions as justices of the peace in the District of Columbia to William Marbury and three others who had not received them though their appointments had been duly confirmed.[20] Both Breckinridge and Mason regarded this action as an attack by the judiciary on the President through the Secretary of State, and it was thus referred to in the subsequent debate in both the Senate and the House. It was also interpreted by Republicans as an attempt to delay the repeal of the judiciary act, which many Federalists expected, and as such it was regarded as a threat against Congress.[21] In this light the movement for repeal may be viewed as a defensive offense, or as a counterattack. It merely sought to restore the *status quo ante bellum* and the President seems to have revealed to nobody whether or not he would afterwards seek more.

Important Virginians besides Giles hoped the offensive would proceed further, and Jefferson had to allow for the constitutional doctrines now being advanced in his own state. It does not necessarily follow, however, that he subscribed to them at all points or that, as the responsible head of the government, he believed they could be put into operation. His immediate task was to democratize the government and to make it effective within the limits he had set. This he was endeavoring to do by changing its spirit rather than its framework. Sympathetic as he was with the desire of his old friend Judge Edmund Pendleton, head of the Virginia Court of Appeals, "to erect new barriers against folly, fraud and ambition," he could not have been expected to push all the constitutional amendments proposed by that highly respected jurist, and he need not be supposed to have wholly approved of them. Pendleton's article, "The Danger Not Over" was destined to enter into the Virginian canon of sacred political writings, along with Madison's *Report* of 1800, which purified the doctrines of the Kentucky and Virginia Resolutions.[22] Judge Pendleton did not suggest that in a working government there must be close cooperation between the executive and legislative branches under presidential leadership. His emphasis was on the separation of functions and in his redistribution of these he would have diminished those of the executive and increased those of the legislature. Following the analogy of the Virginia state government, he would have committed to Congress the appointment of federal judges, and he would have made them removable on joint address of House and Senate. In the present connection, Pendleton's influential article is chiefly

[20] Warren, I, 200–206; Beveridge, III, 110–111; see above, p. 73.

[21] Warren accepts this interpretation, but cites only a single newspaper reference.

[22] Pendleton's article appeared in Richmond *Examiner*, Oct. 20, 1801; see D. J. Mays, *Pendleton*, II, 332–336. On Madison's *Report*, see *Jefferson and the Ordeal of Liberty*, pp. 422–423.

significant because of its implied criticism of the existing federal judiciary and its emphasis on legislative control. The faith of this jurist lay chiefly in the popularly elected lower House rather than in the Senate, whose future power he feared and predicted. He was clearly on the side of popular rule, though he and other leading Virginians, while supporters of state courts against federal, were not distrustful of all courts, like certain Republicans in Pennsylvania.

More specific reference to the immediate situation was made by John Taylor of Caroline, Pendleton's foster son, who was consulted by Senator Wilson Cary Nicholas, a close associate of Jefferson's, and by John Breckinridge. Besides advocating the repeal of the judiciary law and providing useful arguments regarding the constitutionality of the proposed action, he expressed strong hopes of "constitutional reform" under Jefferson.[23] Noting the depression of the "monarchists" after the message to Congress, he wrote Breckinridge: "They deprecate political happiness — we hope for the president's aid to place it on a rock before he dies." He feared, however, that going farther into the judiciary system beyond the repeal of the offensive law was not feasible at the time. "All my hopes upon this question rest, I confess, with Mr. Jefferson," he said, "and yet I know not how far he leans to the revision." We may doubt if anybody knew, or if the President had determined his future course. Later events and the actions of his enemies as well as his friends were to help him make up his mind.

Apart from the question of timing, there was no doubt whatsoever in his mind about the desirability of repealing the judiciary law, since he believed that the expiring Federalist Congress had no real right to pass it. Morally he regarded it as a nullity, just as he did all of Adams's "midnight" appointments. Less than two weeks after his message to the new Republican Congress he described it as a "parasitical plant engrafted at the last session on the judiciary body," and by that time at least he expected it to be lopped off.[24] He himself did not need to brandish an axe in public, but the repealing bill was as truly his as any that he specifically recommended. Furthermore, in this connection the congressional Republicans hewed to the line of procedure he had marked in his *Manual of Parliamentary Practice*, setting a legislative pattern which became characteristic of his administration. A notable feature of this was the emphasis on the committee of the whole. That is, questions

[23] Notably in a letter of Sept. 5, 1801, to Nicholas which found its way into TJ's files (*Papers, MHS*, pp. 100–103), and in one of Dec. 22, 1801, to Breckinridge (printed by Beveridge, III, 609–610, from Breckinridge Papers, LC). Very likely the letter was shown to TJ.

[24] To Benj. Rush, Dec. 20, 1801 (Ford, VIII, 128). This was the day before the motion in the mandamus case, though that was probably anticipated.

were presented in the form of resolutions which were debated by the whole House; not until after the adoption of these were committees named to work out details and draft bills.[25]

In his *Manual*, Jefferson had pointed out that rules of procedure had special value in affording protection to the minority, but this particular rule enabled the majority to determine what bills should be introduced. The Federalist minority protested against it in the present instance, as they often did thereafter. But the procedure did not prevent full discussion. No one was more anxious than Jefferson that Congress be a truly deliberative body and he honored it as such, though he must have squirmed at some of the things the Federalists said in the heat of debate and have regretted some of the utterances of his own partisans. The Jeffersonian emphasis on open discussion is illustrated further by the action of both houses of Congress early in the session in providing a place on the floor for stenographers and note-takers, an action which Gouverneur Morris described as "the beginning of mischief." [26] Samuel Harrison Smith reported the judiciary debate. Because of his political leanings this was regarded by some as an advantage to the Republicans, but the reports in the *National Intelligencer* were generally esteemed and they were undoubtedly an improvement on those of earlier congressional sessions.

When John Breckinridge opened the debate in the Senate, he set out to demonstrate that the judiciary act was unnecessary and improper, and that Congress had the constitutional right to repeal it.[27] For theoretical arguments the Senator from Kentucky relied chiefly on John Taylor of Caroline, sometimes using almost the words of that rural philosopher. From things that Breckinridge said later in this debate, one may suppose that he had had some constitutional discussion with the President. We may assume, also, that Jefferson had no doubt whatever of the constitutional right to repeal the act and that his supporters all knew it. But ostensibly their specific dependence on him was on the practical side. They drew heavily on the document he had submitted with his message containing statistics about cases instituted in the federal courts since their organization and those then pending. Federalist speakers soon pointed out omissions in what appears to have been a hasty tabulation. Senator Uriah Tracy of Connecticut claimed there

[25] See Section XII of the *Manual* and *Jefferson and the Ordeal of Liberty*, p. 457. Procedure was more uniform in the Senate than in the House, where questions were sometimes referred to committees in advance of general discussion. This matter is ably discussed by A. B. Lacy in his dissertation "Jefferson and Congress."
[26] Morris, *Diary and Letters*, II, 416–417. The Senate acted Jan. 5 and the House Jan. 7 (*Annals*, 7 Cong., 1 Sess., pp. 22, 406–408).
[27] Jan. 8, 1801 (*Annals*, 7 Cong., 1 sess., p. 25).

was a total error of five hundred to six hundred cases.[28] Eventually the President sent a revised tabulation, based on later reports, admitting an underestimate of eighty two cases instituted and ninety pending.[29] The episode may have been somewhat embarrassing to Jefferson, who was characteristically careful in public matters, and the Federalists had ground for charging that Republicans underestimated the services of the national judiciary and exaggerated the costs of the additional judges. On the other hand, it appears that litigation in the federal courts had begun to decline even before Jefferson became President, and there was reason to suppose that it would decline further with the expiration of the Sedition Act and the cessation of debt cases in Virginia.[30] Economy in the courts of justice might seem unwise and even petty, but it was in full accord with the policy which was being followed in the executive departments.

For almost two months the repealing bill was the chief concern of Congress — first in the Senate, where it was passed on February 3, 1802, by a vote of 16 to 15, and then in the House, where the Senate bill was passed without amendment a month later by a large majority.[31] The Apportionment Act, which the census of 1800 necessitated, had been passed in the meantime, but no other important measure was adopted until after the judiciary question was disposed of, and no other led to such debates.[32] Obviously, it was much the most controversial question of the session and the one on which party lines were most sharply drawn. In fact, it was the only one of which the opposition could make an issue with any hopefulness. The magnification of it, therefore, was to the political interest of the Federalists. Jefferson and the Republican congressional leaders, who were so confident that public opinion was on their side, probably did not expect this measure to meet with such strong and bitter opposition. Senator Gouverneur Morris, who was not the most reliable of reporters but was unquestionably in the thick of

[28] *Annals*, 7 Cong., 1 sess., p. 55. For samples of critical comments in the House, see pp. 571, 743–745.

[29] Feb. 26, 1802. For this and the original estimate see *A.S.P. Misc.*, I, 319–323. Since the reports came to the President through Madison, perhaps his department should be blamed in part at least for the errors. Madison said the aggregate was not materially altered, and that the actual variance was between 1½ and 2 per cent.

[30] W. S. Carpenter, *Judicial Tenure in the U.S.* (1918), pp. 54–55. Reference to probable further decline was made in many speeches.

[31] *Annals*, 7 Cong., 1 sess., pp. 183, 982.

[32] The main debates took place in the Senate, Jan. 8–19, and in the House, Feb. 15–Mar. 1. The bill to repeal the internal taxes was introduced in the House on Mar. 8 and passed by a larger margin (61 to 24) on Mar. 22 after little debate. There was more debate and a smaller margin in the Senate, where it passed Mar. 31 by a vote of 15 to 11.

this fight, said afterwards that they had counted on an easy victory. Before Congress met, Fisher Ames, anticipating the repeal and the ouster of the new circuit judges, predicted that this action would be received with patience by all Federalists and with approbation by some.[33] That is, it would be considered as but another phase of the removal policy, which he regarded as unprincipled but not worth making much fuss about. The Republican leaders may have been surprised by the cohesion of the opposition. At all events, this became an out-and-out party fight which was marked by mutual recrimination. No one observing these clamorous contestants would have said that they were all federalists and all republicans.

The President, though increasingly aware of his responsibilities as the leader of his party, had not openly abandoned the policy of conciliation; and he would have been unlike himself if he had not personally regretted the extreme political rancor this fight engendered. Gouverneur Morris was among the members of both parties who had late tea at the President's on the evening of the day the debate in the Senate opened and he delivered a perfervid speech against repeal. He described Jefferson as "very civil, but with evident marks of constraint." Before the final vote in the Senate he had dinner with the President. Of his host he then said: "His constrained manner of reception shows his enmity, and his assiduous attentions demonstrate his fear." [34] These comments by a hostile and rather patronizing guest need not be taken at face value. The President, who had not ceased to be a gentleman, was continuing to perform his social function assiduously and was maintaining to foe and friend alike the forms of politeness. Morris was neither the first nor the last to make the mistake of seeing in his good manners a sign of hypocrisy and timidity. Except for the corrected document he transmitted toward the end of this fight, ostensibly he was out of it from the time it started in the North Wing of the Capitol, and he would have been out of character if he had told his spirited followers what to say or had sought to direct their movements in detail. But it may be safely assumed that the Republican congressional leaders — Mason and Breckinridge in the Senate and William Branch Giles in the House — kept in close touch with him.

Though the legislative history of the repealing bill belongs to the story of Jefferson's lieutenants rather than to his, some reference should be made to events in the Senate, where the fate of the measure

[33] Morris to R. R. Livingston, Aug. 21, 1802 (*Diary and Letters,* II, 426); Ames to R. King, Oct. 27, 1801 (King, IV, 5).
[34] Jan. 8, 26, 1802 (*Diary and Letters,* II, 417–418).

was decided. The Republican majority in that body was so slim that any defection was perilous. Actually, they had one defection and were endangered at critical moments by absences.[35] The bill passed its second reading by the vote of Vice President Burr, who began to preside in the middle of January. On the third reading, however, Burr broke another tie in favor of the Federalists, with the result that the bill was referred to a committee, a majority of whose members were unfriendly. A few days later, taking advantage of the arrival of an absentee, the Republicans carried a motion to discharge the committee, bringing the bill back on the open floor, and on the next day it passed its third and final reading by the margin of one vote.[36] Though this sharp bit of tactics obviated obstruction and delay, such was the cohesion of the actual though slight Republican majority that they might have carried the bill in any case. But there can be no doubt of the significance of the episode in the political career of Aaron Burr.

Since the early weeks of his presidency Jefferson had been aware of reports that Burr was seeking to build up a personal following, loyal to himself only, and by the late summer of 1801 he was turning a deaf ear to the Vice President's suggestions about appointments. Before the arrival of Burr in Washington, Jefferson knew of allegations that he had engaged in pre-election moves in his own interest. The President had been particularly informed by James Cheetham, a New York journalist who had broken with Burr and associated himself with the Clintonian faction. By the end of December, Cheetham had written Jefferson that Burr was planning a coalition with the Federalists. In his reply the President, while admitting that he liked to be informed, was noncommittal with respect to Burr and clearly indicated that he did not want to engage in this sort of correspondence.[37]

Had the Republican leaders in the Senate known all that Burr was doing they might have been more careful. Whatever his motives were, he called on Gouverneur Morris promptly and informed him that he was disposed to go along with the Federalists with respect to the repeal measure, though he could not directly break with his party.[38] The result of his ambiguous performance in breaking tie votes was that he

[35] Senator John E. Colhoun of S.C. voted with the Federalists.

[36] Jan. 26–Mar. 3, 1802 (*Annals*, 7 Cong., 1 sess., pp. 147–150, 154–160, 183).

[37] Cheetham was the author of the bitter pamphlet, *A View of the Political Conduct of Aaron Burr* (New York, 1802). On Dec. 10, 1801, he submitted to TJ what he designated as Some Account of the Plans and Views of Aggrandisement of a Faction in the City of New York (LC, 20396–20401). On Dec. 29, he wrote TJ that John Wood's history of the administration of Adams would probably be suppressed by Burr (for $1100) in order to avoid offense to the Federalists (LC, 20511–20512). TJ discreetly replied Jan. 17, 1802 (Ford, VIII, 129–130).

[38] Jan. 15, 1802 (Morris, *Diary and Letters*, II, 417).

offended one side without satisfying the other. A few weeks after these events a prominent Federalist congressman reported that Burr was "completely an insulated man at Washington; wholly without personal influence." While Hamilton was disquieted by the "cabal" between Burr and some of the Federalists, he gained, during the next few months, a certain satisfaction from the Republican "schism." [39] So far as Republican congressional opinion went, this was very one-sided; Burr was thoroughly discredited, and Jefferson more firmly established than ever as the idol of the party.

The beginnings of another "schism," which had already appeared in the struggle over appointments in Pennsylvania, are suggested by another episode in the final days of the Senate fight. Senator James Ross from that state, a Federalist, presented a memorial from the Philadelphia bar approving the newly created system as exceedingly convenient in that district, and protesting against a return to the old one. Somewhat to the embarrassment of the Republican senators, the name of Alexander James Dallas, whom Jefferson had appointed attorney for the East Pennsylvania district, appeared on this, along with those of other Republican lawyers. On the strength of this memorial, Ross moved the exception of that particular circuit from the repeal.[40] By squelching this motion the Republican majority, led by Southerners and Westerners, manifested indifference to any inconvenience they might cause in eastern professional circles.[41] But the objection of Senator Ross to what he described as "a measure more pernicious in its nature, and more fatal in its consequences than any ever proposed in this House" was owing to no mere consideration of the convenience of bar and bench. This sort of exaggerated language must be attributed to the intemperance of partisanship unless there was in fact a mortal threat to impartial justice and the Constitution, as does not appear to have been the case.

The Republicans in both houses based their constitutional arguments on the indisputable power of Congress to establish inferior federal courts and the corresponding right to abolish them, which they regarded as an inescapable consequence. One senator asked: "Are we to

---

[39] T. Sedgwick to R. King, Feb. 20, 1802, and R. Troup to R. King, Apr. 9, 1802 (King, IV, 74, 103–104); Hamilton to King, June 3, 1802 (Lodge, VIII, 601–602).
[40] *Annals*, 7 Cong., 1 sess., pp. 152–153, 160–161.
[41] Dallas had already taken a relatively conservative stand on this issue on professional grounds (to W. C. Nicholas, Jan. 4, 1802, in TJ's *Papers, MHS*, pp. 106–109). Before TJ's first term was up Dallas was to find himself in conflict with a faction in his own state opposed not merely to the existing federal judiciary but to state judges also.

Vice President Aaron Burr
Portrait by John Vanderlyn

be eternally bound by the follies of a law which ought never to have been passed?" [42] The Federalist debaters fell back on the constitutional provision that judges should serve during good behavior and that their compensation should not be diminished while they remained in office. Gouverneur Morris presented this argument in its baldest form: "A contract . . . is made between the Government and the Judiciary; the President appoints; the Legislature fixes his salary; he accepts the office; the contract is complete. He is then under the protection of the Constitution, which neither the President nor Congress can infringe. The contract is a solemn one. Can you violate it? If you can you may throw the Constitution into the flames — it is gone — it is dead." [43]

In more appealing form the argument was that security of tenure was essential to the independence of the judiciary. A congressman voiced the faith which has been cherished by generations of Americans when he said: "If it is within the power of human contrivance to select a spot where the streams of justice will flow pure and uncontaminated, it is in a tribunal of independent judges." [44] It could hardly have been denied, however, that in the recent past these streams had been polluted by politics; and Stevens Thomson Mason and others asserted that not even the courts could claim independence of the nation — that even they must depend in some degree on public opinion. If the fear on the one hand was of an omnipotent legislature, on the other it was of an irresponsible and untouchable judiciary. Said Senator Jackson of Georgia: "I am more afraid of an army of judges, under the patronage of the President, than of an army of soldiers. The former can do us more harm." [45]

The argument that Congress could establish judgeships but not abolish them occasioned the Republican counter-argument that any administration before leaving office could create a host of them and that this policy could be continued *ad infinitum*. In his final speech in the House, John Randolph asked: "Will not the history of all Governments warrant the assertion, that the creation of new and unnecessary offices, as a provision for political partisans, is an evil more to be dreaded than the abolition of useless ones? . . . And does not the doctrine of our opponents prove that, at every change of administration, the number of your judges will probably be doubled?" [46]

In reply to similar comments on the illimitable power of Congress to

[42] Robert Wright of Maryland (*Annals*, 7 Cong., 1 sess., p, 36).
[43] Jan. 8, 1802 (*ibid.*, p. 41).
[44] Joseph Hemphill of Pa. (*ibid.*, p. 543).
[45] Jan. 12, 1802 (*ibid.*, p. 47).
[46] Feb. 20, 1802 (*ibid.*, p. 659).

create offices, James A. Bayard, chief spokesman for the minority in the House, had said that the Constitution was "predicated on a certain degree of integrity in man"—that it had entrusted to government "powers liable to enormous abuse, if all political honesty be discarded." [47] But as Randolph rejoined, the Federalists claimed for themselves the integrity they denied their opponents, charging the latter with designs of usurpation they themselves disowned. It appeared that their recent defeat had by no means cured them of self-righteousness. Hamilton had not escaped from his, but few if any of the congressional leaders of his party presented the issue as clearly as he. From the beginning he perceived that the right to abolish courts would have to be conceded, and the practical suggestion he offered in behalf of the judges boiled down to their compensation during the rest of their lives.[48] But even if this had been acceptable to the Federalists, which may be doubted, it was not to the economy-minded Republicans and probably would not have been supported by public opinion. It has been said that "Congress has in every subsequent alteration of the federal judiciary respected the tenure of the judges of the courts abolished." [49] The arguments advanced by the Federalists in 1802 may have influenced later law makers, but in after years such a policy was facilitated by the increasing needs of a growing country, permitting the transfer of displaced judges to other courts, and also by the decline of political partisanship in the judiciary. If the situation in Jefferson's first year as President was not positively unique it was most unusual, and the Republicans had no practicable alternative between outright repeal and no repeal, which of course was what the Federalists really wanted.

In the debate in the Senate, where the outcome was actually determined, the Republican spokesmen were generally more temperate than their opponents. Little was added to the argument by the much more lengthy debate in the House. While the Republicans had a commanding majority there and were well organized under the leadership of William Branch Giles, they did not curtail the discussion, as the space devoted to it in the official record clearly shows. No estimate of the relative intemperance of the two sides can be readily made, but there was less occasion for verbal violence on the part of the Republicans, who had the votes, than on that of their opponents. Giles himself, who had a reputation for immoderation, overstated the case in presenting

[47] Feb. 20, 1802 (*ibid.*, p. 637).
[48] Best stated in his article of Mar. 19, 1802, in his "Examination" (J.C.H., VII, 821). See also that of Jan., 1802 (J.C.H., VIII, 771).
[49] W. S. Carpenter, *Judicial Tenure in the U.S.* (1918), p. 78.

the issue as one between despotism and democracy; and in his attack on the historic record of the Federalists he made extreme charges and unwarranted allegations. The seven-hour speech of James A. Bayard, before crowded galleries, was hailed by Federalists of high rank as the greatest of the debate. It deserved these encomiums as a spirited defence of his party, but it was a most immoderate speech in many passages and full of denunciation. Jefferson himself perceived in it a threat of forcible resistance. "They expect to frighten us," he wrote his son-in-law, "but are met with perfect sangfroid." [50]

Of the judges he was defending Bayard said in his peroration: "The present measure humbles them in the dust, it prostrates them at the feet of faction, it renders them the tools of every dominant party." In the trenchant reply which John Randolph made in Giles's absence, the most brilliant of the Republicans sagely remarked that the whole of Bayard's argument was "founded on the supposition of a total want of principle in the Legislature and Executive"— a lack which he by no means perceived in the previous Federalist Congress and President. The Congressman from Delaware blamed everything on Jefferson. "The Legislature will be the instrument of his ambition, and he will have courts as the instruments of his vengeance. He uses the Legislature to remove the judges, that he may appoint creatures of his own." No such interpretation could be properly placed on the terms of the repeal act, which the House was supposedly discussing: it called for removals only, not fresh appointments. In Bayard's opinion, the effect of this diabolical legislation would be to concentrate all the powers of government in one man. His misunderstanding or misstatement of the Republican philosophy could hardly have been more complete.

To this alarmed Federalist it seemed that his country stood on the brink of the revolutionary torrent which had deluged France with blood. He concluded his address by saying: "The meditated blow is mortal, and from the moment it is struck, we may bid a final adieu to the Constitution." Another defender of the sacred document, a man who had enjoyed the kindness of Jefferson in France in other days, John Rutledge, Jr., of South Carolina, was equally hysterical. Though the "friends of the Constitution" might be overcome by numbers, he hoped that when the "ministerial phalanx" burst into the temple they

[50] TJ to TMR, Feb. 21, 1802 (*Papers, MHS*, pp. 111–112). Giles's speech of Feb. 18, and that of Bayard Feb. 19–20, are in *Annals*, 7 Cong., 1 sess., pp. 579–602, 603–650. These are well described in *Federalism of James A. Bayard*, pp. 109–124, by Morton Borden, who is notably fair to both of them. For an analysis of the former he cites G. M. Betty in *John P. Branch Hist. Papers*, III (June, 1911), 173–198. John Randolph replied to Bayard on Feb. 20 (*Annals*, 7 Cong., 1 sess., pp. 650 ff.) — quite effectively, in my opinion.

would be "in the portico, the vestibule, and around the altars" defending it to the death against all change.[51]

Before these wild words were spoken, a Federalist paper had described the "precipitate repeal" of the judiciary act as "a wanton, if not a perfidious abuse of power," saying that "almost the only barrier against licentiousness and party tyranny" was being broken down. Such comments, endlessly repeated, occasioned a correspondent, friendly to the administration, to say after the end of Congress that never in a comparable period had such "an overwhelming torrent of falsehood" deluged the country. "Federalism, having nothing to do, has become a Hercules of words; and the legislator, to whom was confined the performance of public duties, is transformed into a mere public crier." [52] The Federalist Hercules or town crier devoted himself chiefly to the judiciary question. Extreme items can easily be culled from contemporary Republican papers, but in this matter the chief ones, Duane's *Aurora* and the *National Intelligencer*, whose publisher was reporting the speeches, were relatively restrained. Just after the Senate passed the repeal bill the latter said:

> It pre-eminently marks the triumph of republican principles. . . .
> Economy in the public expenditure, distrust of extravagant executive patronage, a dread of whatever tends to the unnecessary aggrandisement of the powers of the general government, constitute a few of the features of the repealing act; and they are features which, it is not hesitated to say, will recommend it to national approbation. Indeed, so conclusive and irresistible have been the arguments used in its support, that among the dispassionate part of the community, among those who have not taken their ground with a resolution not to abandon it on any conviction, in short among the nation, it is confidently believed that not one man in a thousand will condemn the repealing act.[53]

The Republican editor ended this optimistic statement with an expression of respect for those voting with the minority. The chief Federalist spokesmen against the measures in Congress showed no such tolerance of the majority. James A. Bayard even doubted their solidarity. Writing his father-in-law, who was displaced as judge by this act, he said: "Notwithstanding the Party adhered together, they were much shaken. They openly cursed the measure, and if it had been possible for

[51] *Annals*, 7 Cong., 1 sess., p. 762. On the association of young Rutledge with TJ in France, see *Jefferson and the Rights of Man*, pp. 115–117, 149.
[52] SIDNEY in *National Intelligencer*, Apr. 28, 1802. The previous Federalist comment was from New-England *Palladium*, quoted in *National Intelligencer*, Feb. 12.
[53] *National Intelligencer*, Feb. 5, 1802.

them to recede, they would have joyfully relinquished the project. But they had gone too far, and were obliged to go through." [54] However, he named only one Republican who had joined his side in opposing it, Congressman William Eustis of Massachusetts. Republicans were not of one mind at this or any other time about desirable procedure against a partisan judiciary which claimed immunity, and no doubt their cohesion in support of this bill may be attributed to their clear recognition that it was a party measure. But the Federalists opposed it to a man for precisely the same reason.

The repealing act appears to have heightened hostility to the President on the part of those he himself already regarded as irreconcilable and to have solidified the congressional opposition while mobilizing the majority. But, despite the furor in the press, Federalist leaders complained that the public had not been sufficiently aroused against its dangers. The Republican interpretation of the measure as one of correction was reflected in the headline in the *Aurora*, "MIDNIGHT LAW REPEALED," and this probably gained wide public acceptance. The displaced circuit court judges might have been regarded, even by Republicans, as innocent sufferers for the sins of others, but as "midnight" appointees they made no such appeal to human sympathy as the victims of the Sedition Act. Jefferson gave his own opinion of this legislative action when he said: "We have restored our judiciary to what it was while justice and not federalism was its object." [55] He was referring to partisan Federalism, for he was a staunch supporter of constitutional federalism as he understood it and no foe to the judiciary as such. In the heat of controversy, however, he was often charged with being one; and in the babel of politics constitutional and partisan terms became so confused that they were often indistinguishable.

iii

The conflict over the repealing act can be readily interpreted as political, as an episode in the continuing struggle between rival parties for power and preferment. Thus viewed under existing circumstances, it appears as a relatively moderate action whose immediate practical effect was slight. It created no new offices and failed to meet the desires of the more clamorous Republicans. But, while its constitutional implications were exaggerated, it impinged on unsettled constitutional questions and is historically connected with the controversy over the power

---

[54] Bayard to Richard Bassett, Mar. 3, 8, 1802, quotation from latter (Bayard, *Papers*, p. 150).
[55] *Aurora*, Mar. 8, 1802; TJ to Volney, Apr. 20, 1802 (LC, 21086–21088).

of the judiciary vis-à-vis one or both of the other branches of the government which has continued in one form or another until our own day. During the debates much was said on both sides about the seat of authority in the determination of questions of constitutionality. That issue came to a head in the case of Marbury vs. Madison, and it can be best discussed when we consider that in the next chapter. Passing reference must be made to it, however, in connection with the measure by which the Republican majority, after repealing the Federalist Act of 1801, amended the judicial system of 1789 they had restored.[56]

Though this "new system" was described by Congressman Bayard as a "miserable patchwork," John Marshall said a score of years later that it was a "great improvement of the pre-existing system." [57] Apparently the Chief Justice was referring to the provisions respecting the circuit courts, roundly condemned by Federalists at the time, which constituted a major feature of the act. Instead of three circuits there were now to be six, within each of which a justice of the Supreme Court was to reside; he was to serve with the various resident district judges on the circuit court twice a year. The framers of the act probably expected circuit riding to be less arduous under this arrangement; and by the residence provision they may have hoped to localize the justices somewhat and cause them to become familiar with at least one geographical segment of public opinion. At any rate, one result of the resumption of circuit riding under these conditions was to reduce the remoteness of the highest court.[58] There was also to be a reduction in traveling to and from the seat of the federal government, for the amendatory law provided for one term of the Supreme Court each year instead of two. This provision, however, was the most controversial of the bill, for it meant that there could be no session until another year. Under the law of 1801 the justices would have sat in June, 1802, and according to that of 1789 they would have sat in August, but now they could not do so till February, 1803. Thus there was to be a gap of fourteen months between sessions.

The argument of the supporters of the bill that only one term was needed in view of the small number of pending cases, and that, under existing conditions of travel, a single session of four weeks rather than

[56] An Act to Amend the Judicial System of the U.S., approved Apr. 29, 1802 (Annals, 7 Cong., 1 sess., pp. 1332–1342). It was passed by the Senate on Apr. 8, by a vote of 16 to 10; and by the House on Apr. 23, by a vote of 46 to 30, the major debate being in that chamber.

[57] Warren, I, 209, note 2, citing U.S. vs. Duvall (1821), 6 Wheaton, 542, 547. Warren does not correctly distinguish between the act of repeal and the amendatory act, attributing the change in the circuits to the former rather than the latter.

[58] See D. G. Morgan, Justice William Johnson (1954), p. 52.

two sessions of two weeks would be to the convenience of all concerned, had more merit than Federalist critics conceded, but the obsti-
nacy of the majority with respect to the session of June, 1802, seemed
inexplicable on practical grounds. Since the repealing act of 1801 was
not to become effective until July 1, a June session of the Supreme
Court had been expected by judges, lawyers, and litigants, and it was
wholly natural that somebody should ask why the majority went out of
their way to prevent it. Bayard asked if the Republicans were afraid the
Supreme Court would declare the repealing law void; and, when the
bill was finally voted on, he specifically charged that the prevention of
the meeting of the Supreme Court was its real purpose. Joseph H.
Nicholson, for the Republicans, denied this, but his recorded rejoinder
is unconvincing and it is no wonder that the charge stuck.[59] Nicholson
claimed that he wanted harmony to prevail between all the branches of
the government, but by flaunting legislative power the congressional
majority appeared to be deliberately affronting the highest officials of
one of them. They were risking a psychological reaction in favor of the
judiciary.

The unwisdom of their action from a partisan point of view was
recognized by Governor James Monroe of Virginia, from whom
Jefferson received a letter on the very day he signed the amendatory
bill.[60] "If the repeal was right," said this friend and party leader, "we
should not shrink from the discussion in any course which the Constitution authorises, or take any step which argues a distrust of what is
done or apprehension of the consequences." He added, as a further
objection, that an enforced postponement of the meeting of the Court
might be "considered as an unconstitutional oppression of the judiciary
by the legislature, adopted to carry a preceding measure which was also
unconstitutional." He was uncertain whether a collision with the Court
could be avoided in any case but believed that such a measure invited
one. He did not fear the outcome of a collision if it should occur, he
said, but preferred that the onus be on the Court and the Federalists,
rather than on the legislature and the Republicans.[61]

Jefferson, whose mild temper had occasioned doubts in the minds of

[59] *Annals,* 7 Cong., 1 sess., p. 1235. For an example of Federalist threats, see the
prediction of Supreme Court action by Samuel W. Dana of Conn. (*ibid.,* pp.
919–920).

[60] Monroe to TJ, Apr. 25, 1802 (S.M.H., III, 341–344), received Apr. 29. TJ did
not refer to this question in writing Monroe May 9 (N.Y. Pub. Library).

[61] There is ambiguity in this letter. Monroe may seem to be arguing against a
"collision" in the first part and for one in the last part, but he certainly did not
want one to occur under unfavorable political circumstances.

many ardent Republicans and who was identified by the Governor of Virginia with mild policies, signed the bill containing the provision which his friend regarded as provocative.[62] In itself that fact has slight significance, for he never employed the weapon of veto while President and would hardly have done so now even if he had objected to some feature of the measure. We can safely assume that he regarded a single annual session of the Supreme Court as sufficient and had no doubt whatever of the authority of Congress to prescribe one, but there appears to be no record of anything he said about the matter of postponement. He could not have been unaware of this particular provision, however; it was in the bill which originated in the Senate and emanated from a committee including two senators who were close to him.[63] Whether or not they consulted with him on this point is unknown, but the presumption is that he consented to the provision at the outset by silence if not by positive affirmation. There appears to have been no significant Federalist protest against it in the Senate; it became controversial toward the end of the debate in the House. By that time the Republican leaders were committed, and intervention by the President would have looked like letting them down.

Whatever his personal preference may have been in this particular matter, his general attitude toward the judiciary can be described with confidence. Unquestionably he wanted to keep it within what he regarded as proper bounds, and the doctrine of absolute judicial supremacy was to him another name for tyranny; but he was seeking a viable government, marked by the harmonious cooperation of the three coordinate branches. In controversial matters his vision might be obscured by partisanship, as that of most others was, but it is harder to believe that he would knowingly invite a collision with the Supreme Court than that he would seek to avoid one. If he favored the postponement of its session, therefore, he probably did so for the latter reason, believing that time was working in his party's favor.

In any case, this legislative action was highhanded, and it appears to have been superfluous. Later events suggest that, contrary to the threats of certain Federalists in Congress and the fears of Republicans, there was no real likelihood that the Supreme Court would overrule the repeal of the Federalist judiciary act and directly challenge congressional authority. John Marshall promptly let it be known privately that

[62] On the doubts, see Duane to Abraham Bishop, Aug. 28, 1802 (*Procs. Mass. Hist. Soc.*, 2 ser., XX, 274-276). Duane himself did not share them.
[63] W. C. Nicholas and John Breckinridge, who replaced an absentee on Apr. 2, 1802. The chairman was Joseph Anderson of Tenn. (*Annals*, 7 Cong., 1 sess., p. 251).

he favored peaceful acceptance of the situation by the displaced circuit judges.[64] The two Federalist leaders in the fight against repeal, Senator Gouverneur Morris and Congressman Bayard, whose father-in-law was one of the judges, agreed at the time that this was the proper course. The major question was whether the Supreme Court justices would respect the repeal by resuming the circuit court duties of which they had been temporarily relieved and which they had hoped to escape. On consulting his associates in the summer, Marshall found that no one of them except Samuel Chase was disposed to raise the constitutional question; and before Congress met again they had resumed their old duties, as he had wanted them to do.[65] Furthermore, at the next session which Congress permitted the Court, in the case of Stuart *vs.* Laird it affirmed the constitutionality of the repealing act.[66]

This decision has been cited as an illustration of the fortunate truth that in the American Republic "party taint seldom contaminates judicial functions." [67] One would be equally warranted in saying that a contrary decision would have afforded a conspicuous example of political partisanship. Six days before this, the Chief Justice, in the case of Marbury *vs.* Madison, had made an assertion of judicial authority which was to prove memorable but which was regarded as gratuitous by the President and his supporters at the time. The postponement of the session of the Supreme Court by legislative act may have been a factor in provoking Marshall's action, but that cannot be fairly described as non-partisan.

The emphasis we have laid on the most controversial question of the first session of the Seventh Congress may have given a distorted impression of that session and have obscured its notable accomplishments. On the day that Jefferson approved the act amending the judicial system he also signed the one providing for the redemption of the whole public debt; and the Republican majority, in their effort to correct the errors of the past, not only repealed the Federalist judiciary act but also

[64] As Hamilton reported to C. C. Pinckney, Apr. 25 (quoted by Warren, I, 224, note 1); and as Bayard wrote Judge Richard Bassett on Apr. 24 (Borden, p. 125). The fact that a memorial of protest from Bassett and other displaced circuit judges was presented to the Senate, Jan. 27, 1803, need not discredit the testimony regarding Marshall's attitude in the spring of 1802. (On the memorial, which was rejected Feb. 3, 1803, see *Annals*, 7 Cong., 2 sess., pp. 30–31, 51–78.)

[65] Warren, I, 269–271, citing correspondence of which Beveridge was unaware. The latter gives the erroneous impression that the Chief Justice remained aloof (Beveridge, III, 130–131).

[66] 1 Cranch, 309; Warren, I, 271–272; Beveridge, III, 130. Marshall did not participate because he had sat on the case in a lower court.

[67] Warren, I, 272, quoting William Rawle.

passed a liberal naturalization law. Reference to other important acts will be made hereafter, when matters that they deal with are considered.[68] Suffice it to say here that this record of legislative accomplishment was not to be matched in any other session during Jefferson's administration, and rarely in later American history in time of peace.

After the adjournment of Congress the *National Intelligencer* said: "The measures of this session may be pronounced to be in magnitude only secondary to the establishment of the Constitution, which, indeed, in some respects they rival, as the legitimate spirit of that instrument is perhaps alone to be found in the principles on which they rest." [69] This may be designated as a partisan exaggeration, and these measures may be regarded as predominantly corrective rather than constructive; by many, indeed, they were thought to be actually destructive. But, considered as a whole, they constituted a notable legislative success, under skillful presidential leadership, in the effort to democratize the government and make it more truly representative of the people it was designed to serve.

[68] Such as the acts dealing with the military establishment and trade with the Indians and the Ohio enabling act. The acts of the session can be seen in *Annals*, 7 Cong., 1 sess., pp. 1300–1379.
[69] *National Intelligencer*, May 5, 1802.

[VIII]

Politics and the Marbury Case

1802–1803

THE debate over the judiciary was addressed more to passion than to understanding. So at least the ranking British representative in the United States reported to his home government, saying that he had never witnessed anything like it. He was half inclined to believe that if the President had foreseen this he would not have called the subject to the attention of Congress.[1] One congressman reassured his wife that the violence of the speeches on Capitol Hill was not to be taken too seriously, since the men who delivered them often laughed about them afterwards.[2] Jefferson's loathing for controversy exceeded his ability to laugh things off; he was not conspicuously a man of humor, and, both literally and figuratively, his skin was thin. Without minimizing the denunciatory rhetoric of the congressional minority, he described these men as "the bitterest crop of the remains of Federalism rendered desperate and furious by despair." [3]

Whatever explanation may be given, the most passionate utterances in the first session of his first Congress centered on an issue which, though exaggerated, was real — the only issue that the Federalists could genuinely hope to exploit. During the interim between the first and second sessions of this Congress, no public event of material importance happened on the domestic scene; John Quincy Adams described the period as one of extraordinary tranquility. Furthermore, when Congress met, the President, who had been so signally successful the previous year, had hardly anything to propose to it. This was as he

[1] Thornton to Hawkesbury, Mar. 1, 3, 1802 (FO 5:35).
[2] Dr. S. L. Mitchill to his wife, Feb. 10, 1802 (*Harper's Mag.*, LVIII, 744). He also said that the printed and spoken versions were often different, since the authors edited them.
[3] TJ to Joel Barlow, May 3, 1802 (Ford, VIII, 149). He was referring to the Senate but undoubtedly felt the same way about the House.

wanted it. "A noiseless course, not meddling with the affairs of others, unattractive of notice, is a mark that society is going on in happiness," he said.[4]

These months were not happy ones for him as a human being: during them, in the absence of promising public issues, certain of his enemies made unparalleled attacks on his religion and private morals. Since these continued long thereafter and require more extended treatment than can be given here without interrupting the narrative, they are treated by themselves hereafter.[5] We also defer consideration of foreign questions, such as that of Louisiana, which came to a climax during this session. Our concern here is with domestic political developments, including the revival of the politically promising judiciary question through the actions of Chief Justice Marshall.

Federalist despondency during and immediately following the congressional session of 1801–1802 is nowhere better revealed than in the private comments of Alexander Hamilton. The gloom of the Colossus of the party was deepened by his consciousness that he had not regained his influence in it. Shortly after the passage of the repealing bill by the Senate, he lamented his "odd destiny":

> Perhaps no man in the United States has sacrificed or done more for the present Constitution than myself; and contrary to all my anticipations of its fate . . . I am still laboring to prop the frail and worthless fabric. Yet I have the murmurs of its friends no less than the curses of its foes for my reward. . . . Every day proves to me more and more, that this American world was not made for me. . . . The time may erelong arrive when the minds of men will be prepared to make an effort to *recover* the Constitution, but the many cannot now be brought to make a stand for its preservation. We must wait a while.[6]

References to their own undying devotion to the Constitution, and to violations of it by their foes, abounded in the writings of the Federalists in this administration, just as they did in the writings of the Republicans in the previous one. But, since such expressions were part of the common parlance of politicians, as they have continued to be, the sensible procedure is to seek to reduce the grounds of political disagreement to more meaningful terms. Hamilton himself did that, better than

[4] J. Q. Adams to R. King, Oct. 8, 1802 (King, IV, 176); TJ to Thos. Cooper, Nov. 29, 1802 (Ford, VIII, 178).

[5] See chs. XI–XII, below.

[6] Hamilton to Gouverneur Morris, Feb. 27, 1802 (Lodge, VIII, 591–592).

most of his fellow partisans, after the session was over, when he still regarded the prospects of the country as extremely dim.

> The mass is far from sound. At head-quarters a most visionary theory presides. . . . No army, no navy, no *active* commerce; national defence, not by arms, but by embargoes, prohibitions of trade, etc.; as little government as possible within; — these are the pernicious dreams which, as far and as fast as possible, will be attempted to be realized.[7]

This political positivist and champion of national power was saying that Jefferson was dangerously weakening the Republic, under the spell of the visionary theory and pernicious dream that its strength lay primarily in the character of the people which a mild and limited government would help to foster. Even if these two men had been operating within another constitutional framework, Hamilton would have focused on the powers of the government and the governors, while his historic rival would have emphasized the rights and trustworthiness of the governed. The practical question was the same as the one raised by Lincoln in his Gettysburg address under more dangerous circumstances: whether a nation conceived in liberty and dedicated to the equal rights of men could in fact endure. In the existing state of world peace, Jefferson was confident that it could endure, and, in his effort to make it what it was supposed to be, he had availed himself of the force of the legislative majority, backed as he believed by majority opinion. As a champion of governmental power, Hamilton bewailed the theoretical limitations Jefferson had set, but the immediate grievance of the Federalists was that within these his administration had manifested such efficacy.

The ambivalence of Federalist criticism was especially evident in the private comments of Gouverneur Morris, who had launched many shafts of flaming oratory in the senatorial debate, and who, perhaps, should not be taken very seriously. On the one hand he asserted that the administration was too weak to prosper; on the other that the Republicans sought to exalt the executive and had laid the foundations of a "consolidated government." The Republicans did not know how to govern, he said, and could not possibly last; but at the same time he recognized that there was "a considerable mass of genius and courage, with much industrious cunning," in those working to overturn the Constitution. Unless this was met by a "phalanx" of talents and property, he believed that large estates would be cast into the melting pot.[8]

---

[7] Hamilton to Rufus King, June 3, 1802 (Lodge, VIII, 601–602).
[8] Morris to R. R. Livingston, Mar. 20, Aug. 21, 1802 (*Diary and Letters*, II,

That Morris's rhetoric surpassed his judgment is shown by his statement that Jefferson had already outlived his popularity and was de-
scending to a condition which no decent word could designate. Thus
he implied at least that he accepted the charges of gross personal immorality which James Thomson Callender had launched against his former
benefactor, and that Morris himself was oblivious of the weakness in
the position of the Federalists which caused them to take these up so
gleefully.

John Quincy Adams did not make that mistake. Recognizing that
these charges originated in "personal resentment and revenge," he connected them with the internal feuds among the Republicans. On these
the Federalists based great hopes without recognizing that Republican
disunity naturally increased with the decline of their fear of the Federalists, which had previously done so much to bind them together. Writing after the summer was over and the political trends more percep-
tible, John Adams's son stated that, apart from these feuds, the strength
of the administration was steadily increasing, and that Republican leaders themselves were needlessly fearful of the precariousness of the democratic popularity on which the success of their party rested.

> The power of the Administration rests upon a support of a much
> stronger majority of the people throughout the Union than the
> former administrations ever possessed since the first establishment
> of the Constitution. Whatever the merits or the demerits of the
> former administrations may have been, there never was a system
> of measures more completely and irrevocably abandoned and re-
> jected by the popular voice. It never can and never will be re-
> vived. The experiment, such as it was, has failed, and to attempt
> its restoration would be as absurd, as to undertake the resurrection
> of a carcass seven years in its grave. The alarm of the pilots at the
> helm is therefore without cause. What they take for breakers are
> mere clouds of unsubstantial vapour. The only risque to which
> they are exposed is the shallowness of their waters.[9]

The chief helmsman admitted no alarm. Jefferson said that Federalism could not revive under that discredited name. Among his bitterest
opponents, however, the results of the spring elections in the East gave
some ground for the resurgence of hope. The *New York Evening Post*
reported the returns under the headings "The Sun of Federalism Once
More" and "The Sun of Federalism Emerging." [10] The President him-

---

422–424, 426–429). The last comment and some of the others may have taken form
because of Morris's desire to sow seeds of doubt in Livingston's mind and separate
him from the Republicans.
   [9] J. Q. Adams to King. Oct. 8, 1802 (King, IV, 176–177, quotation from 177).
   [10] *N.Y. Evening Post*, Apr. 12, May 5, 1802.

self recognized that the tide of Republicanism had suffered a small check in Massachusetts, but was pleased with the showing elsewhere in New England. He even believed that his party had gained ground in Connecticut, the state generally regarded as an impregnable bastion of the old order.[11] While the behavior of Connecticut's sons, in and out of Congress, was regarded by High Federalists as noble, and Massachusetts was believed to be "slowly assuming her ancient consequence and imposing posture," the die-hards found no ground for encouragement in the reports from the South and West and little in what they heard from the middle states. Thus one of them sagely remarked: "I believe the safest rule is to look to the eastward." [12]

In terms of political geography the question arises: where did the East end and the South and West begin? In the eyes of the British chargé the Delaware River marked the "moral and political division" of the country between the New England group and the Virginia group.[13] Though Jefferson's slant was different, he described the situation in much the same way. Late in the summer of 1802, in the interim between congressional sessions, he wrote to one of his supporters in Massachusetts:

> Our information from every quarter is that republican principles spread more and more. Indeed the body of the people may be considered as consolidated into one mass from the Delaware southwardly and westwardly. New Jersey is divided, and in New York a schism may render inefficacious what the great majority would be equal to. *In your corner alone priestcraft and lawcraft are still able to throw dust into the eyes of the people.* But, as the Indian says, they are clearing the dust out of their eyes there also.[14]

The young Britisher who so greatly admired the character of the New Englanders was less sanguine: he doubted if they could be expected to be content with a government, dominated by Virginia, which denied them their "just ascendancy."

Whatever the long-range prospects might be, the results of the fall elections were highly encouraging to the administration. Before he had the full returns, Jefferson said that the Federalists could command a popular majority in only three of the sixteen states. Besides conceding Connecticut, Massachusetts, and New Hampshire, however, he admitted that New Jersey and Delaware were rather doubtful.[15] A couple

[11] TJ to Joel Barlow, May 3, 1802 (Ford, VIII, 149).
[12] J. McHenry to R. King (King, IV, 111).
[13] Thornton to Hawkesbury, Oct. 1, 1801 (FO 5:32).
[14] TJ to Elbridge Gerry, Aug. 28, 1802 (Ford, VIII, 170). Italics added.
[15] TJ to R. R. Livingston, Oct. 10, 1802 (Ford, VIII, 174). Probably he had seen

of weeks later, on the basis of further returns, he declared that the Republicans had gained ground everywhere except in a single district in Delaware.[16] Some of the elections to the Eighth Congress, including those in Virginia, were not to be held until spring, and the Congress he was to face during the winter of 1802–1803 was the Seventh, in its second session. But, while the congressional alignment was not yet changed, his political position was already strengthened.

The greatest political danger lay in the divisions within his party and the possible coalescence of dissidents with the Federalists. Up to this point the bitterest intraparty conflict was between the Clintonians and Burrites in New York, which had been largely resolved in favor of the former and stronger faction. The charges which were being circulated bore directly on Burr's loyalty to the head of the party, for he was accused of maneuvering for the presidency from 1800 to the present and of conniving with the enemy.[17] This feud gratified many zealous Federalists, but the Hamiltonians would have no commerce with Burr and believed the charges against him fully warranted.[18] The general impression was that in his own party he was a "gone man," but some Federalists outside New York were looking on him with hope.

The movement against Burr was not initiated by Jefferson, and during the summer of 1802 he counseled forbearance. While recognizing the likelihood of divisions within his own party as it became preponderant, he was disposed to ignore them as long as possible and tried to stand above them. Because of his exercise of the appointing power he could not avoid entering into them to some degree; to all practical purposes he sided against Burr when he ceased heeding the Vice President's recommendations for office.[19] But his remarkable success as a party leader, commanding the support of all factions, can be explained in part by what he did *not* do. Through his many correspondents he was informed of developments everywhere, and he always kept his finger on the public pulse, but rarely did he intervene in local matters, and with relatively few exceptions he recognized the party leaders who were locally approved.

---

the calculations in the *National Intelligencer*, Oct. 6, based on returns to that date, to the effect that if a presidential election were to take place then, the Republicans would have a majority of almost three to one.

[16] TJ to Levi Lincoln, Oct. 25, 1802 (Ford, VIII, 175).

[17] Most notably in James Cheetham's pamphlet *A View of the Political Conduct of Aaron Burr* (1802). Cheetham published additional pamphlets in 1803, was answered by William P. Van Ness as ARISTIDES, and replied to him in 1804. TJ had all of these (Sowerby, III, 387–388).

[18] R. Troup to R. King, May 6, June 6, Aug. 24, 1802 (King, IV, 120–121, 135–136, 160–161).

[19] See above, p. 88.

In this congressional election year he made one conspicuous departure from his characteristic hands-off policy and this became a matter of public knowledge. He urged Caesar A. Rodney to run for Congress against James A. Bayard in the troublesome little state of Delaware. This action could be readily interpreted as one of personal revenge against the Federalist leader of the House of Representatives for what he had done and said in the judiciary fight and it was of doubtful political wisdom for that reason. But, at a time when the weight of talent was still on the Federalist side in Congress, Jefferson sought by one stroke to get rid of Bayard and to add an able representative to the Republican forces. He had a high opinion of Rodney and was prepared to groom him for congressional leadership. As things turned out, Rodney defeated his personal friend and political rival Bayard by fifteen votes. The Federalists lamented that Delaware was disgraced by such trampling on talents and merit, while Republicans rejoiced at a signal victory. But the net result of Jefferson's intervention was disappointingly slight: Rodney served only one term in Congress and Bayard afterwards failed to return to the House only because he was chosen by the legislature to serve in the Senate.[20]

A milder example of Jefferson's intervention was provided by the case of Senator Stevens Thomson Mason of his own state. Mason, whose health was bad, suggested that he resign and that James Monroe, whose term as governor of Virginia was nearing its end, should succeed him. This would have been natural enough, since he was originally appointed to fill out Monroe's term. At Mason's insistence Jefferson, when at home in the late summer, discussed the matter with his neighbor Monroe and found that the latter had decided to resume law practice. Jefferson finally persuaded Mason to finish his term and serve again if re-elected, as Monroe was sure he would be. Unfortunately, he died soon after the close of the second session of the Seventh Congress. Jefferson's actions in this episode stemmed naturally from his friendship with both men as well as his concern to keep effective leaders in Congress. Even so, he wisely tried to keep out of sight and to avoid any appearance of dictation.[21] This continued to be his policy, also, in his relations with the legislature itself. Charges of despotism and dictatorship were bandied about in Federalist circles, but rarely if ever at this stage by Republicans. The real ground for the protests of the

[20] TJ to Rodney, Apr. 24, 1802 (Ford, VIII, 147–148), Rodney to TJ, Apr. 30, 1802 (LC, 21163–21164); Oct. 6, 1802 (LC, 21800); Oct. 15, 1802 (LC, 21823); TJ to Rodney, Nov. 28, 1802 (LC, 22006); Dec. 31, 1802 (Ford, VIII, 187–188). The episode is well described in Borden, *Bayard*, ch. X.

[21] TJ to Mason, Sept. 3, 1802 (LC, 21712); TJ to Monroe, Dec. 11, 1802 (LC, 22053); Monroe to TJ, Dec. 17, 1802 (LC, 22078).

opposition was the effectiveness of Republican leadership and party discipline. During the congressional session of 1802–1803 this was notably maintained.

Jefferson preferred a noiseless course and, judging from his own words, he expected little action in the second session of a Congress which had made such an outstanding record in its first. If circumstances would permit, he was quite willing to coast along. Actually, the legislative accomplishments of this session in the domestic field were relatively slight, and because of changes in the status of Louisiana foreign affairs took the center of the stage.[22] In terms of presidential leadership, the emphasis shifted from legislation to diplomacy, but legislative cooperation was essential. That it was given is an exceedingly important fact of history. Because of illness, William Branch Giles could not resume his post as majority leader in the House, but John Randolph, who succeeded him, was signally effective despite his youth, his ghostly appearance, and his personal eccentricities. Thus the party which had received a fresh mandate from the country and was undoubtedly supported by the vast majority of the American people was in full control of the legislative branch. Within the executive branch the Council was united and harmonious, and by means of presidential removals and appointments loyal Republicans were gradually replacing die-hard Federalists in the civil service.

The major obstacle to the attainment of a unified and viable government, reflective of the popular will, was still the judicial branch, which remained overwhelmingly Federalist and could be expected to be unresponsive if not obstructive. Whether or not the judges were "rendered desperate and furious by despair," as Jefferson had said the congressional leaders of the opposition were, they constituted the irremovable "remains of Federalism." His own partisans had prevented the Supreme Court from meeting in June, 1802, but the Justices did gather in February, 1803. Late in the month the Chief Justice, whom Jefferson afterwards described as crafty, made a pronouncement in which even John Marshall's ardent admirers have perceived much guile. This was his decision in the case of Marbury *vs.* Madison, which was destined to be a landmark in constitutional history but was most noteworthy as an episode in party history at the time. It was a Federalist counterattack, directed primarily at the executive.

Viewing this now, in its actual circumstances, one cannot escape the impression that the questions at immediate issue were trivial. The complaints against the executive branch of the government with which the

22 See below, ch. XV.

proceedings began closely followed the Federalist line of objecting to the removal of any member of that party from public office. But the alleged action of Jefferson which was objected to fell within his first days as President, when he was striving to be conciliatory and was moving very cautiously against Federalist officeholders. It will be recalled that William Marbury was one of the justices of the peace for the District of Columbia whom Adams nominated on his next to the last day in office and who never got his commission.[23] Jefferson was greatly vexed by the "midnight" appointments of his predecessor, but these particular appointments were minor and his response in this instance was mild. The bill authorizing them left with the President the determination of their number; Adams had determined on forty-two for the counties of Washington and Alexandria, while Jefferson, intent on economy, held that thirty would suffice. In this, later events demonstrated the soundness of his judgment. He promptly gave recess appointments to thirty, including twenty-five of Adams's original appointees and five selected by himself. If this was a punitive and partisan action it was moderate, and it appears to have attracted little attention at the time, but the Federalists asserted months later that he had no right to take any action whatsoever.

Since the commissions of the Adams appointees disappeared, nobody now knows just how they read. According to the law, these officers were to be appointed for five years, and the Federalists contended that they were as irremovable as judges. Presumably nothing was said in the commissions about either "good behavior" or the "pleasure of the President." [24] The administrative principle or theory on which Jefferson proceeded, as he said afterwards, was that delivery was essential to give validity to a commission, as to a deed or bond, and that until delivery it was in the power as well as the possession of the executive who was entitled to withhold it at his discretion.[25] But for the distortions of partisan politics this supposition would probably have been generally accepted at the time as natural and reasonable. That the commissions of the original Adams appointees as justices of the peace in the District of Columbia were not delivered was owing in the first place to John Marshall himself, who continued to act as secretary of state on March 4, Jefferson's first day in office, at the latter's request. Marshall's failure to send them out may be attributed to his "customary negligence of details," though he seems to have held consistently that the signing and

[23] See above, p. 73.
[24] The commissions of TJ's own appointees as sent out contained neither expression and mentioned no term of years.
[25] TJ to George Hay, June 2, 1807 (Ford, IX, 53–54n).

sealing completed the transaction, delivery being a mere formality.[26] Years later Jefferson said that, finding the commissions lying on a table in the State Department, he forbade their delivery.[27] This was his response to what he regarded as an impropriety on Adams's part in appointing these minor officials at the last minute. He could not have issued such an order to James Madison, as has been often stated in works of law and history, for Madison did not assume office until some weeks thereafter. He may have done so to Levi Lincoln, who served *ad interim*, but it seems likely that he gave instructions to one of the clerks. This action on his own part could not be proved at the time, however. He reported to the Senate in the following winter that he had reduced the number of justices of the peace, and that body confirmed a list of thirty, as later modified after several declinations.[28]

A motion in behalf of William Marbury and three others, looking toward a writ of mandamus to compel Secretary of State Madison to deliver their commissions, was made by Charles Lee, late attorney general, at the December session of the Supreme Court in 1801. It was then regarded by the Republicans as an attack on the executive and interpreted as an attempt to delay the repeal of the judiciary act of the last congressional session.[29] No one can be sure that the edge of Republican resentment against the Federalist judiciary would have been blunted if the Court had dismissed this minor case for lack of jurisdiction at the outset, as it did eventually, but its agreement to hear the argument was *not* a conciliatory gesture. The Court assigned a day in the next term for a hearing, but since that term was abolished by Congress, the case could not come up until February, 1803. By that time the business of the District of Columbia was sufficiently cared for by thirty justices of the peace and the term for which Marbury was originally appointed was almost half over. On practical grounds this case, dealing with a petty office, could have had little meaning to anybody. Jefferson correctly described it as a moot case and we may still wonder why it was kept alive.

The most important reason in Marshall's mind, according to his best-known biographer, was that the "fundamental question as to what

---

[26] Beveridge, III, 124–125, quoting extract from a letter of Mar. 18, 1801, from John to James M. Marshall. This is the position the Chief Justice took in his decision.

[27] TJ to Justice William Johnson, June 12, 1823 (L. & B., XV, 447). I know of no record that he said this sooner.

[28] Nominations submitted Jan. 6, Apr. 5, 1802; approved Apr. 27 (*Journal of Executive Procs. of the Senate*, I, 404, 417–418, 423). Blanket commissions for the two counties, dated Apr. 27, 1802, and each containing fifteen names, are in the National Archives.

[29] See above, pp. 117–118.

CHIEF JUSTICE JOHN MARSHALL
Portrait by J. W. Jarvis

power could definitely pass upon the validity of legislation must be answered without delay." [30] This interpretation reflects later views of the historic significance of the case rather than the contemporary opinion of it. One may doubt if, when he granted a preliminary motion and set a date for a hearing, the Chief Justice had it in mind to invalidate an act of Congress and thus demonstrate the authority of his court. His fears of the exercise of legislative power doubtless increased in the months that followed; he must have become very anxious to put himself on record or he would not have gone so far out of his way to do so. His admiring biographer credits him with "perfectly calculated audacity," but the prevailing contemporary impression was that he was gunning for the executive rather than the legislature. It has been said that he seized an occasion to announce "rules of procedure which the Executive branch of the Government must observe." That was just what Jefferson and the Republicans believed him unwarranted in doing.[31]

The centrality of this issue was made clear in a debate in the Senate shortly before the case was tried.[32] Embarrassed because of their inability to offer legal proof that they had been appointed in the first place, Marbury and two others petitioned the Senate for an attested copy of the proceedings insofar as these related to their nomination and confirmation. By a close vote, on which only Federalists supported the petition, it was denied.[33] The debate itself followed strict party lines. The Republicans charged that the purpose of the petition was to pry into executive secrets and enable the Supreme Court, assuming "unheard of and unbounded power," to exercise authority over the President. On the other side, Gouverneur Morris asserted that the President's supporters were arguing for "the most momentous system of tyranny ever to be brought before a national assembly." Obviously the Federalists were doing all they could to aid, and the Republicans to obstruct, the judiciary in its conflict with the executive. Partisanship on both sides was virtually complete, and one would find difficulty in determining which set of fears was the more unreasonable.

Between the debate on Marbury's petition and the beginnings of the hearings on the case before the Supreme Court, Jefferson submitted to

---

[30] Beveridge, III, 109.

[31] *Ibid.*, III, 132; see also 110. Charles Warren in his admirable account of this episode in *Supreme Court in U.S. History*, I, ch. V, clearly recognizes that this, rather than the question of judicial review of legislation, was the major issue in the minds of the people at the time. Beveridge does not, and, in my opinion, frequently makes the mistake of "reading back" and getting things out of chronology.

[32] Jan. 31, 1803 (*Annals*, 7 Cong., 2 sess., pp. 34–50); well discussed by Warren and by A. B. Lacy in his dissertation "Jefferson and Congress," ch. VI.

[33] The vote was 13 to 15, and would have been a tie if Theodore Foster of R.I. had not voted with the Republicans.

the House of Representatives complaints he had received against District Judge John Pickering of New Hampshire.[34] This message led to the vote of the House at the very end of the session to impeach a man whose improper conduct was actually attributable to insanity, and to his conviction about a year later. Federalists were afterwards to designate this action as the opening gun in a general campaign of impeachment, and champions of Marshall were later to claim that the Chief Justice was in peril. Unquestionably there was talk among Republicans of impeaching judges, but much of it was loose and there is no way of proving that he was in actual danger.[35]

Meanwhile, a direct attack of indubitable peril on presidential authority was launched in the Senate by James Ross of Pennsylvania, an irreconcilable Federalist who could be counted on to present an extreme partisan position with ability. This attack arose from the most burning question of the moment — that of the free navigation of the Mississippi and the right of deposit at New Orleans. These "rights" were imperiled by the actions of the Spanish Intendant and by the retrocession of Louisiana to France. Jefferson was sending James Monroe to France and seeking to settle this vital question by diplomacy — as in the course of time he did to the vast benefit of the country. But Senator Ross introduced resolutions authorizing immediate military action and thus infringing on the prerogatives of the President in the conduct of foreign affairs and as commander in chief.[36] Not until the day after the Marbury decision were these dangerous resolutions defeated. They were supported by Federalists and opposed by Republicans on strict party grounds.

It is uncertain whether the Chief Justice was or was not in danger, but by consenting to consider the case of Marbury he unquestionably confronted himself with a dilemma. If he were to issue a mandamus he would have no way to enforce it, and it would be ignored by the executive branch. On the other hand, a rejection of Marbury's petition would have been regarded as a vindication of the executive to whom Marshall was implacably hostile. The Chief Justice must have regretted at times that he ever picked up this hot potato. The means he adopted to escape his predicament, to do a maximum of damage to the President and at the same time enhance the authority of his Court vis-à-vis both the legislature and executive were indeed amazing. He could not have accomplished this *tour de force* had he not taken up the several questions in the precise order that he did. At a number of points he closely

---

[34] Message dated Feb. 3, 1803; received Feb. 4 (*Annals*, 7 Cong., 2 sess., p. 459).
[35] Warren, I, 226–230, sums up the talk.
[36] Resolutions introduced Feb. 16, 1803 (*Annals*, 7 Cong., 2 sess., pp. 95–96).

followed the argument of Charles Lee, the former Attorney General of the United States who represented Marbury.[37] But the question that Lee sought to answer first was the one Marshall put off to the last — that of the authority of the Supreme Court to issue a writ of mandamus. Starting the other way round, Marshall asked three questions in the following order: Did the applicant have a right to the commission? If he had the right and this had been violated, did the laws afford him a remedy? If they did, was the remedy a mandamus issuing from that court?[38] Had he answered the crucial question of jurisdiction negatively in the first place, as he did finally, he would not have needed to raise the others. As Jefferson said later, the judges disclaimed all cognizance of the case, but stated what their opinion would have been if they had had cognizance of it. A contemporary critic said of the three questions: "The last decision was that the Court had no jurisdiction to decide the other two, which they nevertheless decided." [39] Nathaniel Macon said the Court reminded him of a member of Congress who always spoke on one side and voted on the other. Marshall denied Marbury's petition after having elaborately argued for its rightfulness, thus managing both to have his cake and eat it.

From the point of view of the administration the most vexatious thing in the opinion was the assertion that the withholding of Marbury's commission was an act "not warranted by law, but violative of a vested legal right." [40] Charles Lee had great difficulty in establishing the fact that this commission had ever existed, if indeed he did prove it. Madison, against whom the action was directed, could not be held responsible for what happened before he assumed office, and in fairness Marshall might have said so. Legal proof that Jefferson had withheld the commission was lacking, but the Chief Justice's dictum was interpreted as a rebuke of the chief executive as a lawbreaker and could hardly have been otherwise intended. He held that the President's authority and discretion with respect to a particular appointment ended when he signed a commission and transmitted it to the Secretary of State for the affixing of the seal.[41] In performing this act that officer, in

[37] Attorney General Levi Lincoln was summoned as a witness, but on the side of the government the case was not contested.

[38] Report of proceedings, with opinion, in 1 Cranch, 136–179, opinion beginning p. 152.

[39] Argument of LITTLETON, quoted by Warren, I, 250; see also 254; TJ's comment in letter to George Hay, June 2, 1807 (Ford, IX, 53n).

[40] 1 Cranch, 162.

[41] For authoritative comment on the power of the President in the matter of commissions, see E. S. Corwin, ed., *Constitution of the U.S.A.: Analysis and Interpretation* (1953), p. 454. Here, after a summary of Marshall's doctrine, it is noted with apparent approval that the Attorney General, more than sixty years

Marshall's opinion, was not the political or confidential agent of the executive but an officer of the law, amenable to the law like anybody else.

While concluding that the direction of a mandamus to the Secretary of State was entirely proper, Marshall was aware of what had been said by supporters of the administration in the Senate and went to some pains to answer the charge that he was attempting to meddle with .the prerogatives of the executive. He said: "The province of the court is, solely, to decide on the rights of individuals, not to inquire how the executive, or executive officers, perform duties in which they have a discretion. Questions in their nature political, or which are, by the constitution and laws, submitted to the executive, can never be made in this court." But, in his opinion, a head of department, when directed by law to perform an act affecting the rights of individuals, was liable like everybody else. This performance was not under the particular direction of the President and could not be forbidden by him. The present case was of that sort — a plain case for a mandamus "either to deliver the commission, or a copy of it from the record." [42]

Those who heard these words must have expected that a mandamus would follow and the executive be thus directly challenged by the judiciary. That it did not follow and that an interdepartmental crisis did not ensue was owing to the further declaration of Marshall that the grant of authority to his court to issue such an order was itself an unconstitutional legislative action. The *necessity* of this declaration has been denied or questioned by highly competent constitutional authorities, and we may wonder if it was not owing to the exigencies of the practical situation — that is, to the undesirability of forcing the issue with the executive — rather than to the requirements of logic. [43] Admirers

---

later, held that the President has the right to withhold a commission after signing it. In the case of Marbury, to be sure, TJ withheld a commission that had been signed by his predecessor; but one may doubt if many members of Congress in 1801 questioned this right or recognized the transmission to the Secretary of State as the point of no return.

[42] See especially 1 Cranch, 168. A distinction between the executive and ministerial functions of members of the executive branch of the government was clearly drawn a generation later, when the Supreme Court upheld the issuance of mandamus as ordered by the Circuit Court of the Dist. of Columbia. This was in the case of Kendall *vs.* U.S. (1838), following the refusal of the Postmaster General to pay certain claims authorized by Congress. While the power of the Supreme Court to review, through appellate proceedings, administrative actions of a "ministerial" nature was thus affirmed, this power does not appear to have been exercised again until 1880. Quite clearly it amounted to little, in practice, until relatively recent times. (See F. P. Lee, "The Origins of Judicial Control of Federal Executive Action," in *Georgetown Law Journal*, March, 1948, pp. 287–295.)

[43] See Warren, I, 242; Corwin, *op. cit.*, p. 560.

of Marshall, however, have held and later writers have generally not denied that such a declaration was desirable in view of current attacks on judicial authority. Whatever may have been thought about this specific exercise of judicial review, the statement of the necessity for it under the American system with which Marshall closed his historic opinion has been widely hailed as a classic. What is more to the point here is that there appears to have been relatively little objection to it at the time.[44] The contemporary objection was almost wholly to Marshall's condemnation of the conduct of the executive, which was regarded as officious, gratuitous, and distinctly partisan in spirit and purpose. In temper, he lacked the self-righteousness which had made High Federalism so intolerable, but the Chief Justice's rebuke carried the implication, if indeed it was not based on the assumption, that Jefferson could not be trusted to be law abiding.

Besides the fact that public attention was now centered on the Louisiana question, a major reason for the relative disregard of the declaration that a portion of an act of Congress was unconstitutional, which was to be considered in later years the most important thing in Marshall's opinion, was the practical consideration that he actually decided against Marbury when the Republicans had probably expected a decision for the latter. Furthermore, while lecturing the executive for what he regarded as remissness, he admitted that his Court could do nothing about it. It would have been difficult indeed to question the general principle the Chief Justice pronounced at the very end of his opinion: "that a law repugnant to the constitution is void, and that courts, as well as other departments, are bound by that instrument." On this foundation he was to build a superstructure of vast judicial power, but the rival powers he was to humble were not those of Congress but of the states. Never again was he to exercise the right which he here proclaimed to declare an act of Congress unconstitutional. This was not known in the year 1803, to be sure, but his statement of the general principle, and his reference to oaths of office — which were imposed on legislators and President as well as judges — seemed to leave place for the exercise of constitutional judgment to other branches of the government.[45] According to this view, Marshall was not asserting judicial monopoly.

Jefferson's fears of judicial power varied with circumstances. When he first contemplated the Constitution of the United States he had little

[44] Warren, after an extensive examination of contemporary newspapers, takes this position (I, 245).

[45] See E. S. Corwin, *Court over Constitution* (1950), pp. 66–68, 76.

fear of that power; indeed, he thought of it as a safeguard against the greater present danger of legislative or executive tyranny, especially legislative. In his opinion, the judiciary could be a particular guardian of the rights of individuals.[46] Suspicious of Marshall's motives in the Marbury case though he undoubtedly was, he could only have approved of the Chief Justice's assertion that the sole province of the court was to decide on such individual rights. He did not now or ever thereafter deny that the judiciary had to square its decisions with the Constitution: he agreed with Marshall that all three branches of the government must do that. The Chief Justice had asserted that the court could *not* enter into political matters. The crucial question remained as to what was political and what was reviewable. Jefferson could hardly have agreed that the judiciary had the sole right to answer this question, and he left no possible doubt of his opposition to the claim that it had the *exclusive* right to rule on questions of constitutionality.

He was now proceeding on a theory of constitutional interpretation which allowed for the participation of all three of the co-ordinate branches. This has been designated by scholars as the "tripartite" theory and his version of it has been further designated as "political," in distinction from the "juristic" version of Marshall. The latter theory may have pointed toward "judicial monopoly," which Jefferson would no more have consented to than to monarchy, but during his lifetime the Supreme Court had not arrived at that doctrine.[47] While ever desirous of enhancing the prestige of the judiciary and asserting its authority, in order to establish the rule of law and check the excesses he associated with democracy, Marshall had overruled the national legislature in only a trivial matter, and throughout his career he showed healthy respect for its constitutional judgment. In later years his sharpest conflict was with state courts and state legislatures, and, within the federal government, he was more at odds with the executive than with Congress.[48]

[46] Writing Madison, Mar. 15, 1789, he said that an important argument for a declaration of rights was that it put a "legal check" into the hands of the judiciary (Boyd, XIV, 659); see also *Jefferson and the Rights of Man*, p. 163. The question whether his position on judicial review changed by the time of his presidency is argued *pro* and *con* by Wallace Mendelson and Samuel Krislov in *Jour. of Pub. Law*, X (1961), 113–124; *Univ. of Chicago Law Rev.*, XXIX (1962), 327–337; and elsewhere. It seems to me that there was undoubtedly a change in emphasis.

[47] Both in the matter of terminology and that of interpretation I am deeply indebted to Prof. Donald G. Morgan of Mount Holyoke College, part of whose study *Congress and the Constitution* (1966) I was privileged to read in advance of its publication and from whose personal counsel I have profited. He holds that the theoretical differences between TJ and Marshall have been exaggerated.

[48] The examples of TJ and Andrew Jackson come readily to mind.

Prior to the adoption of the Constitution, Jefferson had good reason to be aware of the dangers of legislative dominance such as he himself had experienced as an impotent war governor. Though, as Hamilton correctly observed, he was no advocate of executive weakness, he showed little or no fear of legislative omnipotence after the establishment of a better balanced federal system under the Constitution. His trust in the legislature was naturally more manifest after his party had gained control of it and it was working harmoniously with him; but his confidence in it was inseparable from his faith in representative government, his belief that Congress reflected popular opinion to a greater degree than either other branch, and his view of it as a genuinely deliberative body. Accordingly, he was convinced that the federal legislature had a vital part to play in constitutional interpretation. He emphasized this considerably more at a later time than now — because he saw much greater need to do so, if for no other reason. At the moment Congress could speak for itself; some of its Republican members, in fact, said too much. Quite naturally, at the outset of his administration he was concerned to uphold the constitutional rights of the executive as he perceived them. It was in connection with his own responsibilities respecting the Sedition Act that he made his first known declaration of the tripartite theory. This was in a passage in his first annual message to Congress that he struck out.

The Sedition Act, which expired with the Adams administration after the failure of Federalist efforts in the Sixth Congress to renew it, had not been brought before the Supreme Court, but the Justices and federal judges who tried the cases under it had viewed it as constitutional. John Marshall had objected to it, but only on the ground of its unwisdom. In pardoning those who were still suffering under it when he assumed office, Jefferson acted within indisputable presidential authority.[49] But he did not justify this action afterwards as an exercise of executive clemency. The explanation he gave was that, believing the law to be in "palpable and unqualified contradiction to the Constitution," he was duty bound to disregard it. In the passage he had intended to transmit to Congress he presented his constitutional theory. According to his own marginal note, he left out the passage because it might be "chicaned" and furnish the opposition something "to make a handle of." The message, he concluded, should be clear of everything which the public might be made to misunderstand.[50]

[49] Art. II, Sec. 2 of the Constitution. He pardoned David Brown on Mar. 12, 1801, and James Thomson Callender on Mar. 16. See above, p. 35.

[50] The beautifully clear copy he retained, showing the omission, is in LC, 20381–20385. The omitted paragraph was printed by Beveridge, III, Appendix A,

In deleting this passage he showed good political judgment, for it would unquestionably have been interpreted by the opposition as an avowal of arbitrary presidential authority — as a claim to the right to nullify any law, signed by a previous President, of which he did not personally approve. The sincerity of Jefferson's avowal of zealous devotion to the Constitution would have been denied by his political enemies, and his assertion that under his solemn oath of office he was obligated to declare unconstitutional an act which had already expired might have seemed gratuitous even to his friends. If he had presented his theory in this form it would have been widely hailed, not as an attempt to maintain a balanced and viable government, but as an invitation to chaos.

In terms of theory, the most significant portion of this long-hidden document is as follows:

> Our country has thought proper to distribute the powers of its government among three equal & independent authorities, constituting each a check on one or both of the others, in all attempts to impair its constitution. To make each an effectual check, it must have a right in cases which arise within the line of its proper functions, where, equally with the others, it acts in the last resort & without appeal, to decide on the validity of an act according to its own judgment, & uncontrouled by the opinion of any other department. We have accordingly, in more than one instance, seen the opinions of different departments in opposition to each other, & no ill ensue. The constitution, moreover, as a further security for itself, against violation even by a concurrence of all the departments, has provided for its own reintegration by a change in the persons exercising the functions of those departments.[51]

Recognizing that infractions of the Constitution might be committed from inadvertence, or panic, or momentary passion, he believed that these should be corrected in good faith as soon as discovered.

To what extent he communicated his theory of constitutional interpretation to his own partisans it seems impossible to determine, but in a speech in the Senate his intimate friend John Breckinridge echoed this.[52] Breckinridge's idea of the subject was "that the Constitution intended a

---

TJ's marginal note and Beveridge's comment being on pp. 51–53. Part of the passage appeared, apparently for the first time in print, in C. A. Beard, *Economic Origins of Jeffersonian Democracy* (1915), pp. 454–455.

[51] Except for the substitution of "its" for "it's" and the insertion of an occasional comma, this passage is given just as TJ wrote it.

[52] Feb. 3, 1802 (*Annals*, 7 Cong., 1 sess., pp. 178–180). Breckinridge did not refer to the Sedition Act and directed his fire chiefly against the alleged right of the judiciary to annul acts of Congress.

separation of the powers vested in the three great departments, giving to each exclusive authority on the subjects committed to it." This was a year before the decision in the Marbury case and Marshall may be assumed to have been aware of the argument, whether or not he attributed it to Jefferson.

About a year and a half after that decision, Jefferson reaffirmed the tripartite theory in the course of an unhappy exchange of letters with Abigail Adams, and again this was with reference to Callender's pardon and the Sedition Act. Then he said vehemently: "I considered and now consider that law to be a nullity as absolute and as palpable as if Congress had ordered us to fall down and worship a golden image; and that it was as much my duty to arrest its execution in every stage, as it would have been to have rescued from the fiery furnace those who should have been cast into it for refusing to worship their image." Here he spoke of the executive as a check on the legislative authority. Arguing further with this unconvinced lady a little later, he defined the respective powers of the judiciary and the executive somewhat more precisely than hitherto:

> The judges, believing the law constitutional, had a right to pass
> a sentence of fine and imprisonment, because that power was
> placed in their hands by the constitution. But the Executive, be-
> lieving the law to be unconstitutional, was bound to remit the
> execution of it; because that power has been confided to him by
> the constitution. That instrument meant that its co-ordinate
> branches should be checks on each other. But the opinion which
> gives to the judges the right to decide what laws are constitutional,
> and what not, not only for themselves in their own sphere of ac-
> tion, but for the legislature and executive also in their spheres,
> would make the judiciary a despotic branch.[53]

Circumstances never provided Jefferson with an occasion to present a full-bodied exposition of his tripartite doctrine, and he does not appear to have referred to it often in private letters. Quite clearly, he never abandoned it, and with the passing years he refined and clarified it to some degree. Perhaps the best statement of it in its developed form was made in a letter he wrote six years after his retirement.[54] He then repeated that there was no word in the Constitution which gave the judiciary, more than the executive or legislative branches, the right to decide on the constitutionality of a law. "Questions of property, of character and of crime being ascribed to the judges, through a definite

[53] TJ to Abigail Adams, July 22, Sept. 11, 1804, *A.-J. Letters*, I, 275, 279.
[54] TJ to W. H. Torrance, June 11, 1815 (L. & B., XIV, 303–306). See also TJ to George Hay, June 2, 1807 (Ford, IX, 53–54*n.*).

course of legal proceeding, laws involving such questions belong, of course, to them; and as they decide on them ultimately and without appeal, they of course decide for *themselves*." So, in turn, the executive must decide with respect to laws prescribing executive action, and Congress those governing legislative proceedings. "And, in general, that branch which is to act ultimately, and without appeal, on any law, is the rightful expositor of the validity of the law, uncontrolled by the opinions of the other co-ordinate authorities. It may be said that contradictory decisions may arise in such case, and produce inconvenience. This is possible, and is a necessary failing in all human proceedings. Yet the prudence of the public functionaries, and authority of public opinion, will generally produce accommodation."

This view of the matter he still believed to be sound and this procedure practicable. He now said, however, that if there *had* to be an "exclusive expounder of the sense of the Constitution," the legislature had the best claim, because alone of the three it had the right to impeach and punish members of the other branches, and also because it was most subject to the control of the people. Between these two views he saw no meritorious alternative. The idea of the exclusive authority of an irresponsible judiciary was never one that he could tolerate.

To jurists of our day the Jeffersonian theory of constitutional interpretation may seem vague and remote. In his own day, however, and for some decades thereafter it approximated the actualities of the governmental situation. The Republican Congress continued its conflict with the judiciary for a time by means of the impeachment process, and the duel between Chief Justice and President was resumed in the Burr trial.[55] But to all practical purposes the legislature and the executive continued to determine for themselves whether or not they were acting within the bounds of the Constitution. Marshall's words of warning in the Marbury case may have caused them to be more careful, but the constitutional significance of these words really lay in the distant future. In Jefferson's administration, even in his generation, they amounted to a political gesture, and little more.

[55] In his second term.

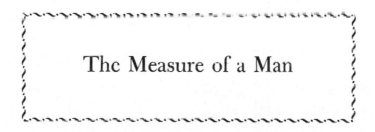

The Measure of a Man

[IX]

"A Small but Cherished Society"

SOON after he assumed the presidency, Jefferson remarked that it was an unenviable post because it afforded little exercise for "social affections." [1] Later in his first year he wrote his younger daughter: "I have here company enough, part of which is very friendly, part well enough disposed, part secretly hostile, and a constant succession of strangers. But this only serves to get rid of life, not to enjoy it. It is in the love of one's family only that heartfelt happiness is known. I feel it when we are all together and alone beyond what can be imagined." A few months after that he said, "I count from one meeting to another as we do between port and port at sea." [2] Comments of the sort from his pen can be endlessly multiplied, and he supported his words with deeds. This unfailingly generous *paterfamilias* seized upon every opportunity to gather his children and grandchildren round him, gladly going to inordinate trouble to that end. In his native region devotion to one's family was traditional, but he manifested it in superlative, almost in excessive, degree.

What with his own homecomings and the annual visits to Washington that he originally expected from his two daughters, he had hoped that they could all be together four or five months in the year. Despite the pressure of public business he carried out his projected schedule better than his daughters could. Washington was much nearer their homes than Philadelphia, where he had served as Vice President and secretary of state, but a journey of three or four days by carriage over rough or muddy roads was exceedingly difficult for young children and positively dangerous for expectant mothers.

[1] TJ to Catherine Church, Mar. 27, 1801 (*Papers, MHS*, p. 94), replying to a letter of congratulation. This friend of Maria Jefferson's was the daughter of his old friend from Paris days, Angelica Church, sister-in-law of Alexander Hamilton.

[2] TJ to Maria, Oct. 26, 1801; July 1, 1802 (E. M. Betts and J. A. Bear, Jr., eds., *The Family Letters of Thomas Jefferson*, 1966, pp. 210, 231; referred to as *Family Letters*).

By the end of his only long visit home in his first year — in the sickly season of August and September, when he always sought the hills — his daughter Martha Randolph, not yet thirty, had five children ranging downward from the age of ten. Maria Eppes, who was twenty-three, had one. All had gathered at Monticello for his visit; and there, under the roof that had finally been put on his still unfinished mansion, his two latest grandchildren were born.[3] Martha and her brood had moved over from Edgehill, some five miles away, and no doubt Thomas Mann Randolph rode back and forth day by day. John Wayles Eppes had brought Maria, by way of the family seat at Eppington on the Appomattox River, from Bermuda Hundred below the James, where he had a place his father had settled on him. Presumably he followed the instructions of his father-in-law that they proceed at the pace of a snail.

The accouchements fitted neatly into the calendar, falling within the span of Jefferson's scheduled visit, but in the case of young Francis Eppes the margin of safety was slight. He appeared only a week before his paternal grandfather set out for Washington and was one of the most delicate infants his Aunt Martha ever saw. On the other hand, her own youngest, her daughter Virginia, proved to be the largest and healthiest baby she had ever had. Once her father jokingly referred to the bearing of children as woman's "trade." For all his solicitude he, like virtually everybody in that age, expected women to pursue it continuously; and, in view of the colossal wastefulness of Nature, no doubt he regarded it as necessary that they should. Since so many infants died a great many must be born. His daughter Martha was exceptionally good at the trade, giving birth to a dozen all told and losing only one. Time was to show even more clearly than it had shown already that the case was quite otherwise with Maria.

During the few precious weeks in his first presidential year when he had his entire family beneath the paternal roof, he himself conducted, by means of correspondence, almost as much public business as he did in Washington, and both he and his daughters resented the flood of visitors. It seemed that they never could see him alone, Maria said. For four weeks after he left, the sisters remained at Monticello with their progeny, seeing much of each other. Martha then returned to Edgehill, and, a little later, Maria and her husband went back to Bermuda Hundred by way of Eppington. At this time and for several years afterwards they talked of building a house at Pantops, across the Rivanna from Monticello on the land Jefferson gave them when they were married. He eagerly offered to have their hilltop leveled, but nothing had come of this plan as yet. For a time both Maria and her father hoped

[3] Virginia Jefferson Randolph was born Aug. 22, 1801; Francis Eppes, Sept. 20.

that she could be back in the spring, when he expected to make a brief visit home after Congress rose, but the state of her health and the delicacy of her little son made the journey impossible. By force of geography and physical necessity, therefore, she was more remote from her father than Martha was, but in the winter season, even between Washington and Albemarle County, an exchange of letters required a week.

Jefferson himself frequently complained that he was far too busy to write as much or as often as he liked. Martha said that, because of incessant domestic duties, she generally had to dash off her letters in a hurry; and Maria found writing difficult even when she was well, as she rarely was at this stage of her life. Nonetheless, the total body of these intimate letters is considerable and they permit us to glimpse the human problems that this extraordinarily devoted family faced from day to day.[4] Nobody then spoke of the country's First Family, and this one was not in the public eye. Actually, there were two families, though the First Citizen made it his particular business to keep them as one. At times his sons-in-law must have regarded him as too possessive, but he disarmed them by his never-failing solicitude and his wholehearted acceptance of them. Their only real complaint was that he tried to do too much for them. His correspondence with them was more extensive in this period than that with his daughters. According to the custom of the times he addressed them as "Dear Sir" in letters, and referred to them as Mr. Randolph and Mr. Eppes, as indeed their young wives did, but they could not doubt that he regarded them as sons. Maria consistently addressed him as "My dear Papa," as Martha generally did, though she sometimes said "My dearest Father." Her children called him "Grand Papa."

In writing to his sons-in-law the President often spoke of public affairs, sometimes making highly significant comments, but in his letters to his daughters he largely confined himself to matters personal and domestic. No modern reader can fail to be impressed with the reiterated avowals of affection and devotion, both on his side and theirs. This degree of sentimentality, which now seems excessive, may perhaps be regarded as a sort of antidote to the formality of that age. Jefferson, who was in so many respects restrained, obviously hungered after such avowals and liked to make them. That they were not empty words the actions of all of them clearly showed.

The main topics of correspondence at this stage, besides personal

4 The correspondence between TJ and his daughters and grandchildren is in *Family Letters*. When I do not cite individual letters, or do not give the location of those I do cite, my reliance on this collection, which was generously made available to me in advance of publication, may be assumed.

plans, were health and the children. Jefferson never wearied of chatter about the youngsters. "I long to be in the midst of the children," he once wrote Martha, "and have more pleasure in their little follies than in the wisdom of the wise." [5] He was an adoring grandfather, unfailingly solicitous and notably assiduous in his attentions. From the moment his grandchildren began to read he kept them supplied with books, and he took enough time from matters of state to correspond with them after they began to write. Anne Cary and Thomas Jefferson Randolph now shared regularly in these exchanges, and Ellen Wayles Randolph was beginning to. He encouraged all of them in their pursuit of learning, seeking at the same time to impress upon them the importance of good dispositions.[6] From the point of view of modern youth his tone was excessively didactic and moralistic, but it was in the convention of that age and apparently these young children did not mind it from one who was in most respects indulgent. Unless the family tradition is wholly wrong, they quite adored their grandfather at this time and ever afterward.

The recurring references to illness in this family correspondence remind us that in those days health was an exceedingly precarious commodity. While saying that the state of his own health was so consistently firm that they need be in no uncertainty about it, Jefferson was always urging on his daughters and their husbands and even on his grandchildren that, if there was time for nothing else, somebody must write him at least once a week the three words "All is well." In the lack of gynecologists and pediatricians such as civilized society knows today, rarely could it then be said of young matrons and their offspring that all was well. Several weeks after his return to Washington in the autumn of his first presidential year, he received the disturbing news that all of the children had whooping cough. He especially dreaded that disease, for good reason: it had cost him his youngest daughter two years after he lost his wife.[7] He learned that Maria's little Francis, though coughing himself black in the face, gave promise of survival. The baby was still in a precarious state, however, when they took him to Southside Virginia. In desperation Maria "borrowed" one of the Monticello house servants to go along as nurse, expressing more contrition afterwards than her father thought warranted. Critta would have had nothing to do at Monticello, he said, though actually he received word that, when she was gone, there was no one to sweep up after the

[5] Jan. 26, 1801 (*Papers, MHS,* p. 85).
[6] As, for example, in a letter of Mar. 2, 1802, to the three of them (*Family Letters,* p. 218).
[7] Lucy Elizabeth, whom he left with the Eppes family when he went to France, died in 1784, along with one of her little cousins.

plasterers who were still at work there. The whooping cough created even more anxiety in the Randolph household, where there were five children to suffer from it. Ellen and Cornelia became delirious, their mother said, and their father fell into such an agonized state that she had to act in the double capacity of nurse to her children and comforter to her husband.[8] Nevertheless, this extraordinarily robust young matron quickly recovered from her fatigue and reported that she had not been in such good health in years. Maria, on the other hand, apparently suffering again from an abscessed breast, was unable to use her hands for six weeks. That was a sufficient explanation of her delay in writing to her father.

Jefferson's frustrations in his persistent attempts to get his daughters to visit him in Washington can be correctly attributed to unfavorable physical circumstances, but he also encountered a degree of reluctance on their part that had other causes. They had spent many months in Paris, and by any standard that could be properly applied in their own land they were gentlewomen, but for years now they had lived remotely in the country. No doubt they exaggerated the glamor and polish of the raw capital city, which in reality was little more than a segment of the countryside, but these thoroughly domesticated young matrons were undisposed to venture from home into the larger world. This was especially the case with Maria, the less robust and more diffident of the two. Early in 1802 she wrote her father: "It would make me most happy to go to Washington to see you but I have been so little accustomed to be in so much company as I should be in there to receive the civilities and attentions which as your daughter I should meet with and return, that it is sensible to remain where I am." [9] These sentiments greatly perturbed Jefferson, and in trying to argue her out of her reluctance he revealed something of the social philosophy at which he himself had arrived.

I think I discover in you a willingness to withdraw from society more than is prudent. I am convinced our own happiness requires that we should continue to mix with the world, and to keep pace with it as it goes; and that every person who retires from free communication with it is severely punished afterwards by the state of mind into which he gets, and which can only be prevented by feeding our sociable principles. I can speak from experience on this subject. From 1793 to 1797 I remained closely at home, saw none but those who came there, and at length became

[8] Martha to TJ, Nov. 18, 1801 (*Family Letters*, pp. 212–213).
[9] Maria to TJ, Jan. 24, 1802, from Eppington (*ibid.*, p. 217).

very sensible of the ill effect it had on my own mind, and of its direct and irresistible tendency to render me unfit for society and uneasy when necessarily engaged in it. I felt enough of the effect of withdrawing from the world then to see that it led to an anti-social and misanthropic state of mind, which severely punishes him who gives in to it; and it will be a lesson I never shall forget as to myself. I am certain you would be pleased with the state of society here, and that after the first moments you would feel happy in having made the experiment. . . .[10]

At the time he was definitely counting on receiving Martha in the spring and hoped the two daughters would make their first visit to the President's House together. His specific plan was to take Martha and her children back to Washington with him at the end of his own spring visit to Monticello and to keep them there until he went home for his long stay in August. This well-laid scheme, which he worked out in characteristic detail only to have it fail, was connected with certain plans of Thomas Mann Randolph that he played a part in and are of interest in themselves.

His son-in-law had conceived the idea of acquiring lands in the Mississippi Territory to put into the profitable culture of cotton. Jefferson talked him out of that, pointing out that this was remote and dangerous country and suggesting that he consider Georgia instead. The removal of Martha and the children to another home was not being considered; her father would have taken violent exception if it had been. He wrote his son-in-law: "You may visit your possessions in Georgia spring and fall with greater ease and much less danger to your health than you could the Mississippi territory once in half a dozen years. In fact I should be delighted to own a cotton estate in Georgia, and go and pass every winter under the orange trees of that country." [11] Beyond knowing that the weather was warmer than in Virginia, he does not seem to have been very well informed about "that country," but he quickly made inquiries in Washington of representatives from Georgia. He arranged for a couple of them to stop in Albemarle for a conference with Thomas Mann Randolph on their way home after the congressional session; he even drew up an itinerary for a prospecting trip. His zeal may have been quickened by his anticipation of a highly pleasing situation: he could take care of his daughter and her children in Washington while her husband and their father was away.

[10] TJ to Maria, Mar. 3, 1802 (*ibid.*, p. 219).
[11] TJ to TMR, Mar. 12, 1802 (LC, 20904). Among other letters bearing on this scheme are TJ to TMR, Mar. 20, 28, 1802 (LC, 20938, 20971); TJ to Maria, Mar. 29, 1802 (*Family Letters*, pp. 220–221).

Wanting Maria and Francis at the same time and disregarding her reluctance, he sent her careful instructions about the best route from her part of the state. But a fresh obstacle to the movement of that branch of the family now appeared: no horses for the journey could be spared from plantation operations at this season. Jefferson countered this objection by saying that he would send for Maria, but the only promise he could get was from John Wayles Eppes that they would be at Monticello late in the summer. This son-in-law saw no reason, however, why the work of leveling a housesite at Pantops should not be undertaken. He had to come to Albemarle periodically to look after that property and apparently was not averse to living on it eventually, since his place at Bermuda Hundred was remote and uncomfortable. Jefferson had proposed that he occupy Monticello, but Eppes would not consider an immediate move to Albemarle, for he had consented that his name be brought forward as a representative from his district.[12]

It turned out that the other son-in-law postponed his prospecting trip to Georgia. He appears to have been agreeable to his family's visiting Washington anyway, and the President made modified but detailed plans for their journey. These came to naught, however, because the children were threatened with measles.[13] Thomas Mann Randolph's Georgia scheme entered into much correspondence in the fall and did not receive the *coup de grâce* until another year, when he also decided to stand for Congress. Our immediate concern, however, is with the summer of 1802, when Jefferson suffered these domestic frustrations and the lonely President's House was still unvisited by his descendants. He managed to get them all together at Monticello on the occasion of his second long visit home, but not until after much correspondence about the measles.

Jefferson reported to Maria that the disease was going through the family at Edgehill and might be expected to take a month before finishing its course. Therefore, he advised her to avoid that place and go straight to Monticello, whence any and everybody suffering from measles would be removed. Though he was determined to take every safeguard, his instructions would have actually affected very few: the plantation slaves were a mile and a half away, and on the mountain, besides a few nailboys, there were only the children of a couple of domestic servants. He specifically designated the places where these were to go if necessary.[14] Soon it appeared that Martha's children had

[12] JWE to TJ, June 25, 1802 (UVA).

[13] TJ to Martha, Apr. 24, June 3, 1802 (*Family Letters*, pp. 224–225, with instructions for the road on verso; *ibid.*, pp. 226–228, from MHS).

[14] TJ to Maria and Martha, July 1, 2, 1802 (*ibid.*, pp. 230–231, 232).

escaped the measles — a circumstance she regretted, since they were ready for the disease and she wanted them to get it behind them. Relaying the news to Maria, Jefferson assured her that she could now proceed with confidence. "I am satisfied Francis will have more to hope from the change of air, than to fear from the measles," he wrote. Getting out of Tidewater in the bilious season and into the hills always seemed to him a matter of supreme importance. On precisely what day Maria put her fears behind her the records do not show, but she got to Monticello while her father was on his longest visit of the year, and *paterfamilias* again had the pleasure of gathering his entire flock around him.[15] He also served as host to other relatives and friends.

They never lacked for company in summer, he said. From the neighboring county of Orange the Madisons brought over Dr. William Thornton with his wife and mother-in-law, who were visiting them. Dr. Thornton, designer of the Capitol, was a neighbor of the Secretary of State in Washington. His wife in her diary left a rather gloomy account of Monticello, partly because of the circumstances of her arrival. Reaching the foot of the little mountain after dark, all except the oldest lady left their vehicles and ascended three-quarters of a mile through the woods on foot while the lightning flashed; they got to the house shortly before the breaking of a thunderstorm. Though Mrs. Thornton had expected an unfinished house she was shocked by this one. Going through a large unfinished room, lighted by a dull lantern and with loose planks on the floor, they entered a large room, with a small bow room separated from it by an arch. (This was the dining room with the tea room opening from it.) The company were seated at tea — part of them in the unlighted larger room — and she thought the appearance "irregular and unpleasant." No modern visitor to the famous house is likely to think of it as a place of gloom and darkness, but those who have ascended beyond the first floor will appreciate a further comment of this guest. "When we went to bed," she said, "we had to mount a little ladder of a staircase about two feet wide and very steep, into rooms with the beds fixed up in recesses in the walls — the windows square and small turning on pivots. Everything has a whimsical and droll appearance."[16]

Mrs. Thornton could have surmised that she and her husband did not draw the best guest room, but when she counted up the family and visitors she might have wondered how beds could have been found for

15 TJ to Maria, July 16, 1802; Maria to TJ, July 17, 1802 (*ibid.*, pp. 234, 235).
16 Entry for Saturday, Sept. 18, 1802, in Mrs. William Thornton's Diary, Vol. 1 (LC). Entries of great interest continued through Wednesday, Sept. 22.

everybody. If they all came down to breakfast at eight on Sunday, after having been awakened by a bell at seven, there were nearly a score of adults around the board. Besides the President, his two daughters and their husbands, his brother (Randolph Jefferson), his son-in-law's sister (Virginia Randolph), his former secretary (William Short) lately from France, and the Madison-Thornton party of six (including Dolley's sister), there were at least four others. Additional guests appeared for dinner at five. Mrs. Thornton also became aware of the children. She said that Mrs. Randolph, "a very accomplished, sensible woman," had five fine ones whom she went to great pains to instruct. In the opinion of this observer, as of others, Mrs. Randolph was not handsome, while Mrs. Eppes was "very beautiful but much more reserved." The doctor came to see her little son, who was "very sick."

Upon examining the plan, Mrs. Thornton concluded that the house would be handsome and convenient when completed, though she doubted if it ever would be. A great deal had been done to improve the grounds, but much more was needed. The setting was beautiful, but this was "a place you would rather look at now and then than live at." Another visitor by the name of Thornton, the British chargé, who began a three days' stay before this lady left, was also appalled by the incompleteness. Edward Thornton said the place was in "a state of commencement and of decay," adding that only in Virginia did people strive to bring these two extremes together "by inhabiting an unfinished house till it is falling around their ears."[17] Jefferson's frequent changes and interminable building operations at Monticello attained sufficient notoriety to inspire Federalist writers who may be presumed never to have seen the place. One versifier thus described the builder:

> Still restless, still chopping and changing about;
> Still enlarging, rebuilding, and making a rout,
> Fickle Mammoth, however outré it appear,
> Pulls down, and builds up again, ten times a year.
> With this altering rage, poor dissatisfied elf,
> What a pity it is he don't alter himself.[18]

This writer gave him no credit for taking the long view. Mrs. Thornton was kinder when she said of her host: "He is a very long time maturing his projects." For example, he was much concerned with a phaeton that he had constructed after *eight* years of preparation. She thought that the President of the United States ought to occupy his

[17] Edward Thornton to Sir Robert Liston, Oct. 4, 1802 (photostat UVA; original in National Library of Scotland, Edinburgh).
[18] *Port Folio*, Mar. 26, 1803.

mind with more important things. No doubt there were other guests besides herself, however, who were impressed with the extensive library, one of the best on the continent. Here he displayed some of his fine prints when he had let in his guests.

As Mrs. Thornton observed, the master's bedroom was separated from the library only by an alcove and he always kept his door locked. That was the only way he could be assured of freedom to devote himself to matters she herself would have recognized as important. He had letters to write about inescapable public business even when he had guests. His wing of the house had to be regarded as a sanctuary, and so apparently it always was. Presumably it was finished by this time so far as carpentry was concerned. Before he got home he had written James Dinsmore about the framing over his bed, the original intention of which was to enable him to have another room above his chamber if ever he wanted one.[19] Whether or not the walls in the connecting rooms at his end of the house were yet lined with books is uncertain, but during the year he had paid for bookshelves.

One can speak with somewhat greater confidence about the state of his overall plan for the mansion house and its dependencies. Apparently the rooms off the southeast arcade were done, though it may be that some of them were still being plastered. The foundations of the nail-house on Mulberry Row and of the southwest "offices" had been laid. The southwest pavilion was certainly not built, and actually these "offices" were chiefly coachhouses. For the icehouse at the end of the arcade next the main house he had sent very special instructions.[20] Mrs. Thornton might have regarded this as a misuse of presidential time. On this or a later visit she made a watercolor drawing of the west front, showing the plinths on the dome. If these had not yet been placed she may have known they would be; other details suggest that she may have been drawing from the plan as well as the finished structure. She showed a sunnier and more pleasant place than the one she described in her diary.[21]

Earlier that year, writing an old Paris friend from the big and still unfinished house he was tenanting in Washington, Jefferson had said:

[19] TJ to James Dinsmore, June 22, 1802, in Monticello construction file.

[20] Part of these can be conveniently seen in *Garden Book*, p. 278 and Plate XVIII. On Dec. 10, 1802, he asked Dinsmore to install a tube and bucket, to draw up the water collected at the bottom, describing this in detail (Monticello construction file). On Nov. 22, 1802, he wrote J. W. Eppes (MHS) that he had paid for the completion of the southeast "offices."

[21] Shown in this volume and in J. A. Bear, Jr., *Old Pictures of Monticello* (1957), p. 9. When she was there again in 1806, Mrs. Thornton found the house and grounds "amazingly improved."

MONTICELLO FROM THE WEST AND SOUTH

Watercolor by Mrs. William Thornton, circa 1805

"My strongest predilections are for study, rural occupations and retirement within a small but cherished society." He then uttered one of his characteristic lamentations that, because of the times in which his life was cast, he had been thrown into "the bitter and deadly feuds of party." [22] In pursuance of his ideal of retired and elevated life he was slowly proceeding with his architectural plans on his own place. As a generous *paterfamilias* and host he briefly enjoyed the society he most cherished. And when, perforce, he returned to the scene of party feuds he expected soon to have his daughters with him. At last they were really coming to the President's House, but they were so slow about it that he had to continue to draw on his extraordinary store of patience. He got back on October 4, 1802, and they finally arrived on November 21, to remain with him about seven weeks.

Long before they set out he had provided an itinerary, with full details about roads that were often hard to follow and taverns that were generally indifferent.[23] For the journey of some 120 miles they must allow four days, though they would actually travel only about three and a half. They would encounter the worst hills on the last day, and he planned to send fresh horses to an intermediate point. Expecting his elder son-in-law to conduct them, Jefferson sent him, by way of Martha, a hundred dollars to cover expenses. His purse was always open to the members of his family. It turned out that Randolph was called to Richmond and Eppes set out with them. He was on horseback, while the women and children were in a carriage. At the end of the second day Captain Meriwether Lewis met them with fresh horses and another carriage; this was at Strode's Tavern, one of the good ones. Martha had said that she would bring none of the five children except Jefferson — that is, Thomas Jefferson Randolph, whom to avoid confusion we shall refer to as "Jeff" even though his grandfather appears never to have done so. She finally included Ellen, who was now six. Virginia, aged fifteen months, was left behind with a nurse, as was the slightly younger Francis Eppes, though this must have been a wrench to Maria. She wondered if, at this late season, they should not wait till spring, but Martha, while describing this as only a flying visit, said they must make it to show that they were really in earnest about Washington. That they seized on this opportunity was fortunate, for father and daughters were never again to be together in that place.[24]

[22] TJ to Madame de Corny, Apr. 23, 1802 (Gilbert Chinard, *Trois Amitiés Françaises de Jefferson* (1927), p. 206.
[23] On verso of letter of June 3, 1802, to Martha (*Family Letters*, pp. 227–228).
[24] Correspondence of Oct. 7–Nov. 9, 1802. TJ sent $100 on Oct. 18, as his Account Book shows.

The doings of the President's family were not news in those days, and personal records tend to become sparse in periods when there was no need for letters. Therefore, we have little beyond fragments of information about this long-awaited visit. Such contemporary comments on the daughters as have come to light bear out the impressions about their personalities that Mrs. Thornton had gained at Monticello. The most familiar of these comments, and still the most precious, were from Margaret Bayard Smith, wife of the publisher of the *National Intelligencer*, who dined with them at their father's table, called on them a couple of times in the morning, and was called on several times by them. On the day after Christmas this friendly observer wrote:

> Mrs. Eppes is beautiful, simplicity and timidity personified when in company, but when alone with you of communicative and winning manners. Mrs. R. is rather homely, a delicate likeness of her father, but still more interesting than Mrs. E. She is really one of the most lovely women I have ever met with, her countenance beaming with intelligence, benevolence and sensibility, and her conversation fulfils all her countenance promises. Her manners, so frank and affectionate, that you know her at once, and feel perfectly at your ease with her.[25]

Throughout her long and useful life, friends and observers of Martha Randolph were saying the same sort of things about her friendliness and intelligence and her attractiveness despite the lack of what commonly goes by the name of beauty. Her resemblance to her father grew closer with the passing years, and her unusual accomplishments were often remarked upon. Among the fewer surviving comments on Maria Eppes there are references to her intelligence and accomplishments, also, but she herself did not esteem her attainments highly. On the contrary, there is abundant evidence that she had what a later generation would call an inferiority complex with reference not merely to her prodigious father but also to her robust and outgoing sister. That is one explanation of the reserved and retiring disposition that her contemporaries observed. But they also remarked upon her rare beauty. Years later, one who had known her sister better but had had the pleasure of looking at her remembered her face as divine. "Her complexion was exquisite," he said; "her features all good, and so arranged as to produce an expression such as I never beheld in any other countenance: sweetness, intelligence, tenderness, beauty were exquisitely blended in her countenance. Her eye, fine blue, had an expression that cannot I think

[25] To Susan B. Smith, Dec. 26, 1802 (*First Forty Years of Washington Society*, p. 34).

be described." [26] It may be supposed that she looked like her mother. She might have regarded that as sufficient compensation for her relative unlikeness, in mind as in body, to the father who towered over her, but seemingly she did not.

Margaret Bayard Smith was much taken with little Ellen Randolph, who talked with her at the President's House and spent a day with her afterwards by special invitation. Mrs. Smith described the six-year-old as "without exception one of the finest and most intelligent children I have ever met with." Because of her marked friendliness toward the entire family, perhaps we should discount all of this lady's superlatives, but special interest attaches to her comment that Ellen was "singularly and extravagantly fond of poetry." The poetry that the child's grandfather preferred was mostly in Greek and Latin, but he supplied her and her elder sister with a great deal of English verse in the course of time.

If the recollections of the other visiting grandchild are to be believed, Jeff Randolph was the most adventurous of the family. Years afterward, speaking of his stay in Washington when he was ten, he described an unauthorized trip with the coachman to the Navy Yard, where he was received with salutes and other honors and served a collation. He reported that his mother reprimanded him, that his grandfather thought the trip a good joke, and that he himself "skulked out of the way" to avoid possible unpleasantness. Apparently he went to the Navy Yard behind a pair of the President's fine horses, rather than in the chariot with four. For the first time, however, this elegant vehicle, which had been received more than a year earlier, now came into some use. To his great disappointment, the coachman, Joseph Dougherty, had been given no opportunity to show himself on his box before the young ladies came.[27] Normally the President himself went everywhere on horseback, without attendants, to the disapproval of certain diplomats. He would never have acquired the chariot if he had not been thinking of his daughters.

Maria afterwards said that the total cost of this visit to her father must have been immense; and, while blaming herself for her abuse of his indulgence, she asked him to excuse it in part on the ground of her inexperience. He replied that in fact she and her sister did not indulge themselves as much as he wished, and that nothing prevented his supplying their "backwardness" but his total ignorance of articles that

[26] Peachy R. Gilmer, quoted in R. B. Davis, *Francis Walker Gilmer* (1939), p. 373.
[27] TJ, in a letter to Martha, June 18, 1802 (*Family Letters*, pp. 228–229) spoke of the coachman's chagrin that she was not then coming for a visit. The visit to the Navy Yard is described in the Memoirs of T. J. Randolph, 2nd ms., p. 3 (UVA).

might suit them. Coming from remote country life as they did, they undoubtedly needed numerous articles of dress and toilet; and, while Washington was no teeming mart, it was more of an emporium than anything they had access to in Bermuda Hundred or Albemarle County. Therefore, they probably purchased or ordered a good many things. Their father made at least one concession to fashion in their behalf: through Mrs. Madison he procured for them two wigs at a cost of $38.[28] The dinners that he gave habitually were no more ceremonious than those at Monticello. At this board, therefore, his daughters probably felt quite at home. He took them regularly on Sundays to religious services in the Hall of Representatives. At a later time these gatherings partook of the character of social assemblies, where the beauty and fashion of the federal city were displayed. There could not have been much display as yet, and this President was not supposed to like it, but he would not have been human if he had not enjoyed showing off his daughters.[29] No special festivities marked the Christmas season. Jefferson was largely oblivious of that, though his gifts to charity appear to have become greater and more numerous as it approached. The only festival day besides the Fourth of July that he recognized officially was New Year's, when he held a levee. The presence of his daughters at this celebration was noted; and they themselves must have been impressed by the officers of state and foreign representatives and accompanying ladies who came to pay their father, the President, the compliments of the season.[30] The guests gathered in the "octagon hall," now the Blue Room, where wine, punch, and cake were served. The mammoth cheese might still be seen in the present East Room, though in somewhat shrunken form.

This was on Saturday, and the President's daughters started homeward on the following Wednesday. Besides giving them a hundred dollars for expenses, he sent along a slave named John, normally assigned to the dining room, who afterwards brought back the carriage and horses. Jefferson himself crossed the Potomac on the Georgetown ferry with them and accompanied them a little way into Virginia on horseback.[31] What he saw of the road was so bad that he anticipated for them a dreadful journey and wished they had waited for a better time.

[28] Account Book, Nov. 20, 1802, and references in previous letters; Maria to TJ, Jan. 11, 1803; TJ to Maria, Jan. 18, 1803 (*Family Letters*, pp. 240, 241).
[29] Margaret Bayard Smith describes them as social assemblies in *First Forty Years*, pp. 13-14. Specific reference to the attendance of the President and his family was made by Manasseh Cutler (*Life, Journals and Correspondence*, II, 113, 116).
[30] Good account in the diary of Cutler.
[31] Account Book, Jan. 4, 5, 1803.

He did not learn of their safe arrival until ten days later. Meanwhile, having heard the rumor that they had to stop two or three days on the road in a miserable hovel, he had suffered greatly in imagination. As Maria informed him, it was a distressing journey, but her most depressing remembrance was of his parting with them and turning back. Her most painful thought was of the "unsafe and solitary manner" in which he slept upstairs. The top floor of the President's House had indeed become a lonely place, as he confessed.

After seven weeks, Martha's youngest did not recognize her until she put on an old dress that the child remembered. Also, it turned out that little Francis Eppes had at length been exposed to measles, which he actually had some weeks later. But there could be no possible doubt that the visit had been successful. Its success lay, not so much in supplying the "backwardness" of young matrons whose lives had been too long remote and in giving them a glimpse of their father's other world, but in cementing further their ties with him as a human being. For all his unceremoniousness, they could hardly have failed to gain some thrill from seeing him in his role and at his seat as President, but what Maria talked about was the pleasure of being with him as a person. Apparently they spent many hours with him apart from company — in the evening, when he never went out. His callers came, and he did his entertaining, in the daytime. Nobody said so, but the association with his daughters may be presumed to have been more intimate because neither husband was around. This was not a situation that could be expected to continue, and certainly not in the case of Maria, who was in so many ways an Eppes rather than a Jefferson. But as she reflected on the generosity and devotion that had been lavished on her, filial sentiment engulfed her. "Adieu dearest and most beloved of fathers," she wrote. "I feel my inability to express how much I love and revere you. But you are the first and dearest to my heart." [32]

John Wayles Eppes would have been surprised to hear this, but that level-headed young husband probably would have been undisturbed. He himself had strong filial affection for his father-in-law, whom he had known all his life and with whom he had lived as a boy. Furthermore, Jefferson had long been and never ceased to be very fond of him. In due course he reported the arrival of his wife and baby son at Eppington. Maria, enjoying a blessed interval between pregnancies, was in good health; but on the road the little boy, from cold or colic or some other cause, apparently became lifeless in the carriage. Martha's husband, who was conducting them on this journey, took the child in his

[32] Jan. 11, 1803 (*Family Letters*, p. 240).

arms to a nearby house, where a warm bath gradually restored him.[33] Despite the perils of the road, Eppes expected to bring Maria to Monticello in March, when her father would make a brief visit at the end of Congress, and to leave her there while he himself made the circuit of the county courts in his district before the congressional elections. This plan was carried out, and things were going well with her when her father's first term passed its halfway mark.

Martha's husband was more temperamental and more self-conscious than Maria's; and, because of the facts of geography, Randolph was more aware from day to day of what his father-in-law was doing for his branch of the family. Also, because of propinquity, it was more difficult for him to emerge as a personality from the shadow of this giant. Like Maria, he suffered from an inferiority complex, and shortly before the daughters made their trip to Washington he indicated as much in a letter, simultaneously depreciating himself and avowing his filial affection.[34] Since Jefferson relished avowals of devotion, he may be said to have invited them, but a major secret of his success in dealing with Randolph and Eppes was that he treated them as peers, or at least as full-grown sons. So, after stating that he looked upon Randolph as part of himself, and also that no alliance on earth could have been more pleasing to him than the one into which his elder daughter had entered, he asserted that there was and ever must be mutual regard and respect between himself and his son-in-law. The only thing that had ever pained him was that his old debts prevented his being of as much service as he would have liked. "In matters of interest I know no difference between yours and mine," he said. "I hope therefore that you will feel a conviction that I hold the virtues of your heart and the powers of your understanding in a far more exalted view than you place them in; and that this conviction will place your mind in the same security and ease in which mine has always been."

At this time and for weeks thereafter he was assiduously engaged in procuring for this self-doubting young planter information bearing on the latter's projected acquisition of cotton lands in Georgia. A new difficulty had appeared: according to the existing laws of South Carolina, no Negro slave could be carried through that state. After receiving various letters on the subject from South Carolina, he concluded that, while no obstacle might actually be imposed and special dispensation might be granted, the best hope was that the legislature would change the law. Whatever the reason may have been, that is what the

[33] JWE to TJ, Feb. 10, 1803 (Edgehill-Randolph Papers, UVA).
[34] Letter of Oct. 29, 1802, which has not been discovered, but the character of which can be readily surmised from TJ's reply of Nov. 2 (LC, 21926).

legislature did, and, after going to a vast amount of trouble, he reported the fact to his son-in-law.[35] There had been much ado about nothing, as he found out in the spring. Randolph wrote that he expected to be disappointed in his Georgia scheme and was unsure that he would make a trip there. He was now inclined to dispose of such of the slaves that he had thought of settling there as were of bad character, and to keep the others for improvements on his present lands.[36]

His decision may have been reached on economic grounds, but in the meantime he, too, had got into a race for Congress. Unlike that of Eppes it involved Jefferson in political embarrassment, for it looked to the displacement of one of the President's old supporters. Jefferson received the blame for it, but he showed lack of political acumen if he recommended it. To have discouraged it, on the other hand, might have been to strike a blow at the self-esteem of his doubt-ridden son-in-law. The chances are that he had nothing to do with it one way or the other, fully recognizing the right of self-determination in the small but cherished society of which he was the undisputed head.

[35] Jan. 17, 1803 (LC, 22219).
[36] TMR to TJ, Apr. 29, 1803 (Edgehill-Randolph Papers, UVA).

[X]

The Presiding Scientist

IF Jefferson's own words may be taken at face value, what he enjoyed most, with the single exception of intimate family relationships, was the pursuit of knowledge. Again and again he lamented that public affairs had deflected him from the path of study and inquiry for which Nature really intended him. His political talents, which ostensibly he minimized, were never so effectively employed as during his early years as President, but, by the same token, his tasks as the head of state and of his party left him little time to contribute personally to the advancement of knowledge on which, more than on anything else save freedom, he based his hopes for the progress and increased happiness of mankind. From the beginning of his presidency, however, he occupied a pre-eminent position in his country as a patron of science and learning, such a position as was held by only Benjamin Franklin before him, and by no American public man after him. His political enemies might and did mock his learning — Timothy Pickering dubbed him the "moonshine philosopher of Monticello" — but he was held in highest honor in the hall of the American Philosophical Society, though the facts of geography now precluded his physical presence there.

His election, in 1797, to the presidency of a body which, in his opinion, comprehended whatever distinction in science and philosophy the Republic had, was described by him as the "most flattering incident" of his life. At the time he was about to become Vice President of the United States. The removal of the capital from Philadelphia to Washington in 1800, while facilitating his visits home and association with his own family, deprived him of the pleasure of presiding over the sessions of the Society and mingling happily with its resident members. Therefore, he offered to resign its chief office. He was re-elected, nonetheless, and continued to be thereafter until he had been six years retired at Monticello. His standing is suggested by the words addressed to him by a leading member of the Society about that time: "To you, Sir, the first thoughts of a friend to American Science and Literature are naturally turned." [1] Repeated honor was not paid him by this society for political reasons, though he had many staunch political supporters as well as close personal friends among its members. One of the most zealous of these was the artist Charles Willson Peale, who lived with his family in Philosophical Hall and long housed his museum of natural history there. To him Jefferson was "not only the champion but almost the incarnation of Reason and Wisdom." [2] Others may not have gone quite that far, but many members unquestionably shared that feeling.

Early in 1802 one of them, Du Pont de Nemours, addressed a letter as follows:

> To His Excellency Thomas Jefferson
>   President of the American Philosophical Society,
>   Member of the Institut National de France
>   President of the United States

Apparently this letter gave the bearer of the first and third of these titles his earliest information of the second. [3] When Du Pont, as a member of the Institute, was asked to suggest names for consideration as foreign associates, he replied: "You will find few men in Europe, even for the other branches of learning, and none in the world for our *class* of morals and politics, who can be compared to President Jefferson." The Institute acted before hearing from him, and assigned the newly elected member to Du Pont's class, though they would have been warranted in putting him in either of the others: sciences, or literature and beaux-arts.

In the certificate of his election, which arrived a good many months later, he was described as "President of the Congress of the United States." The inexactitude may have reflected French ignorance of the form of the American government, but his election was probably not owing to his official position. The only person ahead of him on the list as announced was Joseph Banks, president of the Royal Society; and the likelihood is that, insofar as the choice of Jefferson was not based on his own intellectual achievements, it was due to his presidency of

---

[1] TJ's relations with the American Philosophical Society in this period are described by Gilbert Chinard in its *Proceedings*, Vol. 87 (1944), pp. 267–271. The letter quoted was from P. S. Du Ponceau, Nov. 14, 1815.

[2] C. C. Sellers, *Charles Willson Peale*, I (1939), 19.

[3] Du Pont to TJ, Feb. 20, 1802 (in my edn. of the *Correspondence* of the two men [1930], pp. 41–43). TJ was elected, on Dec. 26, 1801, a foreign associate of the Institute in the class of moral and political sciences (Comte de Franqueville, *Le Premier Siècle de l'Institut de France*, II [1896], 55). When this class was abolished in 1803 he passed to that of history and literature; and in 1816, after another change in organization, he passed to l'Académie des Inscriptions et Belles-Lettres.

the American Philosophical Society. That society did not reciprocate by putting the name of Napoleon Bonaparte on its rolls, though actually he was a member of the Institute and had participated in its deliberations. Nor did the Institute grant its honors to Madison, Monroe, or John Quincy Adams, who followed Jefferson in the office of chief magistrate. Indeed, during his lifetime, it elected no other person who was American by both birth and residence. A signal honor was conferred on him as the most noted American intellectual of his generation, and he probably cherished it as he did no public office.[4]

Official notification was slow in reaching the *associé étranger*, but he received it "with that sensibility which such an expression of respect from a body of the first order of science, is calculated to inspire." In the spirit of modesty that characterized all his relations with the learned, he said: "Without pretensions or qualifications which might do justice to the appointment, I accept it as an evidence of the brotherly spirit of Science, which unites into one family all its votaries of whatever grade, and however widely dispersed through the different quarters of the globe." [5] These words were written at a time when he was much perturbed by the aggressive imperialism of the French, and considerably after the course of their revolution had disillusioned him about a brotherhood of free peoples. He found consolation and hope, however, in the international brotherhood of science, and of this he himself was ever a loyal member. Besides writing letters to foreign men of learning as time and opportunity were afforded, he sent to the Institute, while still President, a collection of fossil bones that was afterwards described as magnificent. The French were aware of his services to vaccination, and in the course of his presidency one of their agricultural societies gave him a medal for his "perfectioning" of the plow. They recognized him as a man of learning who strove incessantly to be useful.[6]

During his first term as President of the United States he said that he had to make it a rule not to indulge in correspondence on "philosophi-

---

[4] Priestley was elected to the Institute in 1802. Two men of American birth, then living abroad, were also honored: Count Rumford in 1802, and Benjamin West in 1803. The next American to be chosen was Edward Livingston in 1833.

[5] TJ's letter of Nov. 14, 1802, addressed to the president and secretaries, is printed in Gilbert Chinard's *Jefferson et les Idéologues* (1925), p. 21. An almost identical letter, dated Nov. 3, is in LC, 21931. His certificate (MHS) may have reached him before he got an official letter.

[6] On the plow, see *Jefferson and the Ordeal of Liberty*, pp. 216–217. Some of the services I have referred to, and many others, were mentioned in eulogies of him in France after his death. Long before then he had become a member of numerous other foreign societies.

cal subjects" despite his fondness for them.[7] His correspondence itself raises a strong doubt that he was able to carry out his self-denying resolution. To him "science" meant all knowledge, and the term "philosophy" as he used it included what we call natural science — a subject that appealed to him much more than metaphysics. People knew that he was interested in all varieties of learning, in every form of inquiry into Nature and its laws, in every invention or device that might contribute to human comfort and well-being. He could not keep people from writing him about these things even if he really wanted to prevent them. He had no disposition to rebuff foreign savants or members of the American Philosophical Society, and, while brushing off or ignoring eccentrics, he was nearly always a patient and appreciative listener who probably replied to more letters than he needed to.

Many believed, as one man said, that "the mild and philanthropic Jefferson" might be addressed "with the freedom and familiarity of a *fellow citizen and friend.*"[8] At the beginning of the administration, Charles Willson Peale, an actual friend and a very assiduous one, expressing the hope that the President could still find leisure to give some attention to "the minutiae of public good," addressed him on kitchen fireplaces, a subject that had occupied most of his own spare time that winter.[9] The presidential attention was called to many minutiae: a corn sheller in Newburyport, the account of which caused him to draw up a statement of the labor it would save; "animated oats" from Pennsylvania, which performed curiously when dropped briefly into water: a "butter refrigeratory," which he was invited to go twenty miles to see. One good lady made a more surprising suggestion about refrigeration: since frost put an end to yellow fever, would not a similar purpose be served if a person suffering from this disease were put into a frosty place?

His miscellaneous correspondence, however, was more than a melange of curious and relatively inconsequential items. He himself was seeking "a refracting telescope, suited both for terrestrial and celestial objects," and presumably it was at his request that Andrew Ellicott sent him a highly mathematical account of his own method for calculating the rising and setting of heavenly bodies.[10] Among his own

[7] This particular expression is from a letter of Oct. 22, 1803, to Caleb Brickham (LC, 23433), replying to one on the fascinating subject of the tides, but he said much the same thing earlier.

[8] Samuel Elliott to TJ, November, 1802, received Dec. 19 (LC, 22018). This person was commending his brother for an appointment, while sending some sort of pamphlet of his own.

[9] Peale to TJ, Mar. 8, 1801 (LC, 18896–18898).

[10] Ellicott to TJ, May 11, 1802 (LC, 21376); on the telescope, see *Papers, MHS,*

letters about books was one in which, while subscribing for half a dozen copies of a proposed work on language, he gave his own ideas about ways of learning them. In another, when ordering a book in French, he said that he never read translations.[11] Through Joel Barlow he got a letter of Robert Fulton's describing experiments in submarine navigation; and one of his Connecticut supporters, introducing Eli Whitney to him, spoke of the latter's manufacture of arms and invention for cleaning cotton.[12] Jefferson had previously corresponded with Eli Whitney and already knew about the cotton gin, which interested him particularly because of its bearing on agriculture. Toward industrial development he had appeared more indifferent, but he was deeply concerned about locomotion and not unaware of the future possibilities of steam in this connection. Special interest attaches, therefore, to his reply to one who had presented the fascinating idea of using it to move carriages.

> That the introduction of so powerful an agent as steam will make a great change in the situation of man I have no doubt. To extend its application nothing is wanting as you observe, but to simplify the machinery and make that & the fire apparatus more portable. No law of nature forbids us to hope this, and the ingenuity of man leaves us to despair of nothing within the laws of nature. Some effective steps towards this simplification have been lately taken, but nothing which approaches to your object of moving carriages by that agent. That you may succeed in it, I sincerely wish. I should suppose no place in the US so likely as Philadelphia to furnish artists equal to the execution of the requisite machinery, & persons willing to embark in the enterprise itself, for a just share in its profits. . . .[13]

Though he was to live nearly a quarter of a century longer, he was never to witness the success of such a project; not only was he generations away from automobiles; never did he even see a train. But, believing as he did that "the ingenuity of man leaves us to despair of nothing within the laws of nature," this holder of his country's highest political office was a prophet of the science and invention that were to revolutionize man's situation in the modern world.

---

p. 99. TJ consulted this surveyor and mathematician for the benefit of Meriwether Lewis before the latter set out on his expedition.

[11] TJ to N. G. Dufief, Nov. 15, 1802, and order of Nov. 17 (LC, 21967–21968).

[12] To TJ from Barlow in Paris, Oct. 26, 1801 (LC, 20184); Pierpont Edwards to TJ, Oct. 27, 1801 (LC, 20190).

[13] TJ to James Sylvester McLean, Oct. 25, 1802 (LC, 21867), replying to a recent letter.

The interest of this universal scientist and scholar in the future possibilities of steam, while unquestionably genuine, was less characteristic of him than his enthusiasm for the mastodon that Peale procured and mounted in Philosophical Hall, thereby causing the word "mammoth" to come into more common use. A pioneer paleontologist in his own right, Jefferson was the real instigator of this particular activity of the indefatigable Peale, who was artist, collector, and exhibitor all in one. Early in Jefferson's presidency of the American Philosophical Society, while he was Vice President of the United States, a committee was set up at his instigation to inquire into the antiquities and present state of their own country. Of this committee he and Peale were members, and if he did not draft the circular they distributed through the country, a document of great importance in the history of American science, it bears the unmistakable imprint of his ideas and aspirations. One of the expressed objects of the committee was to acquire skeletons of the mammoth and other ancient animals. Another, bearing out the claim that this circular was a charter of American ethnology, was to inquire into the customs and language of the Indians. By means of the Indian relics he caused to be collected, the vocabularies he acquired, and the instructions he gave Meriwether Lewis for the latter's famous expedition, Jefferson was to make genuine contributions, direct and indirect, in this field of inquiry. At the outset of his administration he manifested his interest in paleontology, as well as his characteristically American enthusiasm for bigness, in the support he gave to Peale.

At every stage that dauntless collector reported to the most distinguished American friend of science his efforts and adventures in his successful quest for prehistoric bones. Returning to his museum with findings from New York State, he hoped that the "grandeur" of this skeleton, when set up, would excite Jefferson's curiosity and produce a visit; and, while setting it up in Philosophical Hall, he made regular reports of progress.[14] The President was not among the members of the Philosophical Society to whom the mastodon was exhibited on Christmas Eve, 1801, before the public was admitted at a price, but unquestionably he was there in spirit. Only a few days later he was presented with the mammoth cheese, and in this period other stupendous things were reported avidly in the papers while sober Federalists made sport of them. Whether or not the President saw any advantage in connecting the word "mammoth" with his party and administration, he was

[14] Peale to TJ, June 29, Oct. 11, 1801 (LC, 19556, 20132–20134) and at other times. The story of Peale's "mammoth doings" is told by Sellers, II ch. 5. Chinard prints and discusses the historic circular in the Society's *Proceedings*, Vol. 87, pp. 269–271. For TJ's previous contributions to paleontology and interest in Indians, see *Jefferson and the Ordeal of Liberty*, ch. XXII.

CHARLES WILLSON PEALE
Self-Portrait, circa 1804

glad to attach it to things American and to have these made known abroad. He had not forgotten his argument with Buffon and other foreigners regarding the size of animals in the New World. Peale had another skeleton, which he sent his sons Rembrandt and Rubens to display abroad. Highly approving the venture, Jefferson advised him how to exhibit it.[15]

The President himself was responsible for an addition to Peale's bone collection in Philadelphia, and the mammoth continued to figure in their correspondence. After completing the gigantic task of mounting the skeleton, however, the exhibitor could turn his attention to the other interests of his museum. He kept on writing Jefferson about his hopes and purposes, knowing that he would always find a friendly ear. The director was counting on his museum to provide him support such as he could not gain from portrait painting, but he brought to his task philosophy as well as art. Justifying his idea of presenting natural subjects to the public in the closest approximation of a natural environment, he averred to his learned and eminent friend that "a knowledge of the wonderful and various beauties of Nature" was "more powerful to humanize the mind, promote harmony, and aid virtue, than any other school yet imagined." [16] No one would have been quicker than Jefferson to agree that, for his own good, man should go to school to Nature.

In his opinion the medical profession of the day had hardly begun to do that. His old-time friend and fellow member of the Philosophical Society, Dr. Benjamin Rush of Philadelphia, was well aware of his lack of faith in the "principles" of the profession.[17] Modern historians of medicine will readily agree that his skepticism was warranted and his empiricism wise. In all his correspondence with his daughters about the physical ills of their children, he showed a disposition to rely on remedies that had been tested by experience and on the healing powers of nature. The toll of death in his own family was not calculated to increase his faith in doctors, and in spirit he was more scientific, in the modern sense, than most of them. This is not to say that he made no use of them: he paid many medical bills for the members of his household, including servants, both in Washington and at Monticello. Also, he had great friends in the medical fraternity, Dr. George Gilmer of Albemarle County in earlier days and Dr. Rush at this time being conspicu-

---

15 TJ to Peale, May 5, 1802 (Ford, VIII, 151–152).

16 Peale to TJ, Jan. 12, 1802 (LC, 20660).

17 Rush to TJ, May 5, 1803 (Butterfield, II, 863). As Rush's editor says, a monograph on the subject of TJ and medical science is needed.

ous examples. What is more, he gave unstinted support to such innovations in practice as gained the sanction of his mind.

His personal services in connection with Jennerian vaccination
against smallpox offer proof of that; and Dr. Benjamin Waterhouse of
Massachusetts, who had to overcome so much fear and prejudice as a
pioneer in this field, was deeply grateful to this eminent patron. In his
first presidential year Jefferson had caused his family and "people" in
Virginia to be inoculated with virus he got from Waterhouse, and his
sons-in-law had followed his example. He exchanged letters frequently
with doctors on this subject, and in his third year, on another visit
home, he used vaccine matter he brought from Washington to inocu-
late a large deputation of persons from a neighborhood thirty miles
away, where smallpox had appeared. Reporting this episode to the man
who was surest to be interested in it, he said that thus he was able to
"communicate the blessing" for which they were indebted to Dr. Waterhouse.[18] From his description it appears that he vaccinated these persons with his own hand. Nothing was more characteristic of him than
his concern to free mankind from the scourge of communicable disease; and, just as he hoped that farmers could make their own plows
after his model, he wanted vaccination to be brought to the level of
common capacities, so that it could be practiced by the mass of the
people in their own homes without expense. It was supremely important, therefore, that uncontaminated virus matter should be made available to them.[19]

Though Jefferson's intimate correspondence abounds in references
to the physical ills of others, it is not burdened with comments on his
own health, which he consistently reported to his family as firm. He
wrote Dr. Rush, some nine months after he assumed the burdens of the
highest office, that his health had always been so uniformly good as to
arouse his grave fears that he might live too long. He now reported to
this intimate friend, but to no other mortal, that he had discovered a
flaw that dispelled those fears without immediately threatening his
effectiveness. "It will probably give me as many years as I wish," he
said, "and without pain or debility." He did not say just what it was,
and the busy doctor, perhaps concluding that time was not of the essence, waited nearly three months before asking him. Jefferson's reply
was even more unhurried: he waited another year. Rush then pre-

18 Waterhouse to TJ, Mar. 1, 1803; TJ to Waterhouse, Mar. 21, 1803 (LC, 22435,
22512). For the inoculation of 1801, see p. 65, above; for TJ's own inoculation
as a young man by the more dangerous method known as "variolation," see
Jefferson the Virginian, pp. 99–100.
19 TJ to Dr. John Redman Cox of Philadelphia, Apr. 30, 1802 (LC, 21159).

scribed for an ailment that had ceased to distress him, but that did occasion his death, after a much longer span of years than he anticipated or may have thought desirable.[20]

Dr. Rush said that if his own reading and experience should prove insufficient, he would lay the history of Jefferson's case before the most intelligent members of the profession in Philadelphia, without mentioning his friend's name. Until he himself reached the grave he would treat this entire subject as utterly confidential. The main reason that Jefferson was so long in describing his ailment was that he saw no real need for counsel. For the first time in his life he had suffered from diarrhea, after dining moderately on fish, and he conducted experiments in diet and regimen thereafter on his own account. The net result of these was to confirm his original judgment about fish, apparently without causing him to rule out any other specific article of food, and to remind him of the importance of moderation in eating. He perceived a remedial effect in his daily ride of an hour or two, and said that his "complaint" was now in a state of innocence. He regarded his case as chronic, however, and doubted if medicine could help it at his age, if it could at any period of life. While laying at Rush's feet ideas that he described as "unlettered," he obviously saw no present need for a physician. Comments from his friend would be helpful, however, if his complaint should become really troublesome. He made it perfectly clear that he wanted facts, not theories.

Rush's suggestions about diet and regimen, which seem generally sensible even now, accorded with the moderation with respect to food and drink that Jefferson was already practicing. Avoiding ardent spirits altogether, he drank only light wines, and he did not use tobacco, even though he raised it at Poplar Forest.[21] The doctor approved of riding on horseback under normal conditions, but he thought exercise should be gentle and laid great emphasis on rest. "Carefully avoid fatigue of body and mind from all its causes," he urged. "Late hours and midnight studies and business should likewise be avoided. It will be unsafe for you to sit up later than 10 o'clock." [22] The imperfect illumination of an age of candles and sperm-oil lamps would have discouraged most people from midnight studies, but Jefferson may have needed to be

[20] TJ to Rush, Dec. 20, 1801 (Ford, VIII, 128); Rush to TJ, Mar. 12, 1802 (Butterfield, II, 847); TJ to Rush, Feb. 28, 1803 (Ford, VIII, 220–221); Rush to TJ, Mar. 12, May 5, 1803 (Butterfield, II, 856–859, 863–864).

[21] A couple of boxes of fine cigars were sent him with the suggestion that Mr. Burr and Mr. Gallatin would enjoy them if he did not. It is more likely that the latter gentleman was given the opportunity than the former (Thos. Newton to TJ, Feb. 12, 1802 [LC, 20802]).

[22] Butterfield, II, 857, in Rush's letter of Mar. 12, 1803.

DR. BENJAMIN RUSH
Portrait by Charles Willson Peale

warned against them. There was no reason to urge him to get up early, since he arose with or before the sun throughout life. Apparently he did not heed one injunction. Rush recommended that at his age he discontinue in winter his habitual practice of bathing his feet in cold water the first thing in the morning, but he seems to have been still doing this more than a decade later, when he attributed to it his remarkable exemption from colds.[23]

Denying that medicines were futile in Jefferson's case, the doctor prescribed some for his use if his ailment should become serious. Despite skepticism, his friend carefully preserved this letter for possible future use, but we may doubt if he soon had recourse to the laudanum that was recommended, or to a syrup made from "powder of oak galls," cinnamon, brandy, and sugar. It is unlikely that he applied "blisters" to his feet and ankles, or that he availed himself of a remedy Rush himself described as radical — mercury to be used internally in combination with opium or externally as an ointment. He may have doubted if there was as much sympathy between the skin and the bowels as Rush averred. If he was really worried about the likelihood of excessive longevity, he gained little support from this generally reassuring friend, who claimed on the basis of observation that intestinal ills rarely shortened life if the stomach was unimpaired, as Jefferson said his was. The sanguine doctor was not dismayed by chronic cases. Among those he reported to a patient who insisted on facts was that of a highly respected Philadelphian who, at the age of sixty-six, was cured of long-continued diarrhea "by the use of the cold bath." For all his preference for natural remedies over drugs, this must have strained Jefferson's credulity.

The President's physical flaw would have occasioned unseemly merriment among his political enemies, no doubt, if they had known and talked about it. Apparently they did not, but at times somebody spread wholly unwarranted stories about his state of health. Once when he was at Monticello, late in the summer before Dr. Rush prescribed for him so lengthily, the rumor ran through Washington that he was so ill as to require the constant attention of half a dozen doctors.[24] Even if the details of his private correspondence with his amiable medical friend in Philadelphia had been made known, there would have been no ground for public concern over his physical condition, and as time went on this became even better. In the summer of 1804, a few months before his re-

[23] TJ to James Maury, June 16, 1815 (L. & B., XIV, 319). He made very interesting comments on his regimen and health to Dr. Vine Utley, Mar. 21, 1819 (Ford, X, 125).
[24] Henry Dearborn to TJ, Aug. 15, 1802 (LC, 21611).

election to the presidency in his sixty-second year, he reported to a friend in Europe: "My health, which at one time threatened an unfavorable turn, is now firm." [25] Before his final retirement from public office he began to complain that the burdens were beyond his strength, but this was certainly not the case during his first term. His incessantly active mind was housed in a sound and exceptionally durable body. His life was temperate, orderly, and exceedingly industrious. He was not without critics, however, who raised questions about the state of his immortal soul.

[25] TJ to Philip Mazzei, July 18, 1804 (L. & B., XI, 40).

[XI]

The Religion of a Reasonable Man

DURING the campaign of 1800, Jefferson's political foes had frequently denounced him in press and pulpit as an atheist. These
"name callers," like others in other times, did not bother to define their
terms with precision, and they arrogantly assumed that God was on
their side in a conflict into which many mundane considerations entered. However, there always were clergymen — generally outside
New England or among less favored sects there — who supported
Jefferson. Before his inauguration one of these, regarding the reports of
his hostility to the Christian religion as a Federalist artifice and finding
no ground for them in his writings, suggested that he make a public
avowal of his belief.[1] He was no more disposed to do that than to publicize intimate details about his health or family: to him any man's relations with God were a strictly private matter. In his inaugural address,
however, when recounting his country's many blessings, he referred to
its religion, clearly implying that he shared in this:

> . . . enlightened by a benign religion, professed, indeed, and prac-
> ticed in various forms, yet all of them inculcating honesty, truth,
> temperance, gratitude, and the love of man; acknowledging and
> adoring an overruling Providence, which by all its dispensations
> proves that it delights in the happiness of man here and his greater
> happiness hereafter . . .

A friendly Boston paper soon commented that the leading Federalist
journal in the city left this "affecting passage" out.[2] His beleaguered
New England supporters still had to defend him against the charge of
atheism; and, before his presidency was over, he was to be designated in
that region as Anti-Christ. The bitterness of the dominant Congrega-

[1] William Arthur to TJ, Jan. 8, 1801 (MHS); on denunciations during the
campaign, see *Jefferson and the Ordeal of Liberty*, pp. 480–483.
[2] Boston *Independent Chronicle*, Mar. 16, 1801, commenting on the much more
powerful *Columbian Centinel*.

tional clergy toward him can be considerably attributed to his insistence on the complete separation of church and state, just as the support of the "dissenting" Baptists can be. In a real sense, if not a technical one, the Congregational clergy, magistrates, and more prosperous citizens of New England constituted an Establishment. Members and defenders of this found ready reason to oppose him, while those who were contending against it tended to become his supporters. In that region he was for the "Outs" against the "Ins," and the latter could not forgive him.

Nowhere else was there just this form of vested religious interest, but there was much in the Jeffersonian philosophy that might have been expected to disquiet authoritarians, absolutists, and dogmatists of any sort. The rigidly orthodox adherents of any sect could have found disturbing language in the preamble of his famous Bill for Establishing Religious Freedom and in sections of his *Notes on Virginia*. In the latter he had said: "The legitimate powers of government extend to such acts only as are injurious to others. But it does me no injury for my neighbor to say there are twenty gods or no god. It neither picks my pocket nor breaks my leg." [3] He himself was no atheist, no polytheist, but such tolerance of all beliefs, and of no belief, is not in the spirit of the devotee who has planted his feet on what he regards as the true and only way to salvation, whether this be Congregational, Baptist, Catholic, or any other. In fact he offered, as in word he promised, complete freedom to all, showing no disrespect for any. During his first year as President, he recommended to the commissioners of the District of Columbia that they grant the application for the purchase from them of a site for a Roman Catholic church, recognizing that the establishment of this would be highly advantageous. He wrote Bishop Carroll that he would be happy on this and every other occasion to show his respect and concern for the "religious society" over which that prelate presided. The Bishop may have winced at the language, but he would have been at fault if he had not recognized the respect and concern as genuine.[4]

In the matter of religious organizations and opinions, Jefferson's philosophy was pluralistic: he regarded a multiplicity of sects as desirable, seeing safety against tyranny in numbers. Since he attacked no sect on religious grounds, no one could rightly charge him with being personally antireligious. He had long been a generous contributor to churches, and he made a special point of attending divine services while President. It was fortunate that he did not encounter much ceremony,

[3] *Notes on the State of Virginia,* Peden edn. (1955), p. 159.
[4] TJ to Bishop Carroll, Sept. 3, 1801 (LC, 19966).

since he did not care for that; he abhorred mystery and anything he regarded as obfuscation. The God he worshiped was the God of Nature. Viewing the Great Creator with an awe and reverence beyond that of most moderns, he sought with rare diligence to discover and obey His laws. To him there was no field or area that the mind might not and should not freely examine, and he himself would accept only what had gained the sanction of his critical and enlightened intelligence. Entirely apart from politics, it is no wonder that some devout men, without comparable faith in human intelligence and with more devotion to inherited tradition, should have been disquieted by him. His failure to issue Thanksgiving proclamations was an act of omission rather than commission. Before his first Thanksgiving Day came round, however, he raised a storm of criticism by offering Thomas Paine passage to America on a ship-of-war. At a time when his enemies had hardly anything of a public nature to talk about, they seized on this as an overt act. If on his part it was a calculated rather than an impulsive act, it cannot be regarded as shrewd politics since it gave a handle to his critics and gained him no votes.

The President did not invite the return of the highly controversial pamphleteer nor did he need to. Paine invited himself back to America, describing it as the country of his heart and the place of his political and literary birth. Here this hitherto unsuccessful and inconspicuous Englishman had written *Common Sense* and the *Crisis*, making thereby a contribution to the cause of American independence of which Jefferson, who embodied the spirit of 1776, was ever mindful. Paine's *Rights of Man*, which, as he boastfully said, had the greatest run of any work yet published in English, fell within the French Revolutionary phase of his tempestuous literary career. This work caused him to be outlawed in his native land and aroused grave fears in America — notably in John Adams, who regarded its author as the greatest mischief maker of the age. It seems, however, to have been generally approved in the United States when it first appeared here, as it undoubtedly was by Jefferson and the Republicans.[5] The vicissitudes of Paine in France, where he broke with the Terrorists and was imprisoned almost a year in the Luxembourg, should have gained him some favor among Americans who had feared him as a revolutionary, but the circumstances of his release at the instance of James Monroe, the American Minister in France at the time, served to identify him anew with the Republicans against the Federalists. In his *Letter to George Washington* he bitterly assailed

[5] For the controversy over the work when the first part of it was published in America, see *Jefferson and the Rights of Man*, ch. XXI.

one who, as he believed, had wholly failed him in his time of greatest need but who certainly did not deserve to be described as "a hypocrite in public life," and as either "an apostate or an impostor." [6] Appearing in the *Aurora* about a month after Washington's Farewell Address, this diatribe against a man whose heroic stature the clouds of political controversy might obscure but could not conceal did the Republican cause a disservice. It by no means represented Jefferson's judgment of Washington even at that moment of extreme partisan conflict, but the silence with which he greeted it was interpreted by his enemies as approval of it. Whatever reservations he may have had about Paine — and he must have had many on the score of manners, if on no other — he did not now or ever repudiate him. In customary personal procedure and conduct he was very unlike Paine, but as a party leader he tended to be uncritical of those who were on his side, and with respect to public issues he seems never to have doubted that he and this ill-mannered pamphleteer were in basic agreement. Believing that they were seeking the same ends, and also, no doubt, that Paine was much less extreme than he sounded, Jefferson tolerated in him a degree of impatience and egotism that he himself rarely if ever showed.

It was as the author of *The Age of Reason*, more even than as the writer of a violent letter against Washington, that Paine became suspect in America, for his supposed religious views were unpalatable to many who approved of his politics. In this work, partly written while he was still in prison and continued while he was enjoying the hospitality of Monroe in Paris, he coupled his declaration of belief in one God and immortality with a declaration of disbelief in the creeds of all the churches he knew of. Not unnaturally he was viewed as an enemy of all varieties of organized religion. "My own mind is my own church," he said, and in the course of the work he applied that mind mercilessly to the sacred Scriptures. Many of the same things have been said by scholars at one time or another in more solemn language, and this author avowed his reverence for the God of Nature in some deeply moving passages. Certain of his references, however, such as those to the Virgin Mary, approached or attained obscenity. Jefferson worshiped the same sort of God, laid the same sort of emphasis on conduct and humanity, and applied similar critical tests to the Bible. However, he did not ridicule the religious beliefs of others, and in procedure he was a patient pragmatist, not an impatient iconoclast. That would not have been enough to commend him to the rigidly orthodox in any age, and we

[6] M. D. Conway, *Writings of Thomas Paine*, III (1895), 213–252; dated July 30, 1796, published in *Aurora*, Oct. 17, 1796. See *Jefferson and the Ordeal of Liberty*, p. 307.

may be sure that relatively few of his contemporary countrymen concerned themselves with such fine distinctions. Also we may be reasonably sure, on the basis of human experience, that only a relatively small
proportion of those who condemned Paine's work had actually read it.
It was well known by name, however, by the time that his prospective
return to America was reported, and this may perhaps be described as
the first *cause célèbre* of Jefferson's administration.

No doubt the author of *The Age of Reason* would have come back
from France some months sooner than he did but for his justifiable fear
that the English would take him off any French vessel on which he
might take passage. These circumstances shed light on the request he
made of Jefferson in the autumn of 1800, when the outcome of the
election was still uncertain. "If any American frigate should come to
France, and the direction of it fall to you," he said, "I will be glad you
would give me the opportunity of returning." [7] Not long after the
inauguration Jefferson offered him the opportunity on the *Maryland*,
which was taking Congressman John Dawson to Le Havre with the ratification of the French treaty. Considering the dangers to which Paine
was exposed and his past services to the American Republic, the offer
of transportation in a public vessel was not as gratuitous as it might
otherwise appear, but Jefferson, in this private letter, went a good deal
further than was necessary in praise of its recipient:

> I am in hopes you will find us returned generally to sentiments
> worthy of former times. In these it will be your glory to have
> steadily laboured and with as much effect as any man living. That
> you may long live to continue your useful labours and to reap the
> reward in the thankfulness of nations is my sincere prayer. Accept
> assurance of my high esteem and affectionate attachment. [8]

Paine did not accept this offer. For a variety of reasons he did not
return to America until the autumn of 1802, by which time the cessation of the war permitted him to come on a private vessel. Nor did he,
like Philip Mazzei, give out the letter at the time he got it. [9] He waited
more than a year after his return to do that. However, a report of it,
which could have come from him only, reached America in the
summer of 1801. According to this, he received from Jefferson a "very
affectionate letter," inviting him to return to America, and offering him

---

[7] Oct. 1, 1800, at the end of a long letter, Paine to TJ (Conway, *Writings*, III,
378). He explained the circumstances more fully on Dec. 2, 1802, in the fourth of
his letters *To the Citizens of the United States* (*ibid.*, III, 402–403).

[8] TJ to Paine, Mar. 18, 1801 (Ford, VIII, 19).

[9] For the famous episode of TJ's letter to Mazzei five years earlier, see *Jefferson
and the Ordeal of Liberty*, pp. 267–268, 302–307, 366–367.

a "national vessel" for passage.[10] This report did not include Jefferson's complimentary remarks, but it gave the erroneous impression that he took the initiative, when actually Paine did.

The hungry Federalist papers hastened to make the most of what they had, hurling epithets against the distant pamphleteer with furious abandon and striking at the man whom they charged with standing behind him. Paine was referred to as an "obscene old sinner," as the "living opprobrium of humanity," as an "infamous scavenger." One writer even suggested that Jefferson as an agriculturist wanted to use him as manure.[11] He was associated with the "foreign convicts and renegadoes" whom the Republicans, according to this view, had long encouraged to insult the nation. The major counts in his indictment were his alleged vilification of Washington, which was indeed a fact though capable of partial explanation, and his character and conduct as an "infidel" — a term that was meaningless in his eyes. The real target, of course, was Jefferson.

Thus spoke the strongest journalistic champion of "the wise, the rich, and the good" in Boston, whose rule the President and his followers had challenged:

> But the importation of THOMAS PAINE . . . is most of all to be deprecated in a moral view — not on account of any ascendancy which *so notorious a drunkard*, and *so impious a buffoon* can be supposed to gain over the minds, or manners of *true Americans*; but because he comes under the sanction, and with the *co-operation* of the *highest officer* in the Union. . . . It would be unavailing to say, that a congeniality of political sentiments (which doubtless exists) is the *only* inducement which actuates Mr. JEFFERSON in this affair, and that he may still be that *good christian*, which his friends have represented him. . . . Will *charity itself* be able to erase from the public mind, the conviction of Mr. JEFFERSON's hostility to revealed religion, while he cherishes and patronizes its most rancorous, though by no means its most *decent, refined, or elegant foe?* And will any human exertions suffice to stop the progress of blasphemy, and profligacy, when thus "*respectfully*" countenanced and encouraged? [12]

[10] An item, reportedly from a Paris paper, appeared in *National Intelligencer*, July 15, 1801. Paine published the full letter in his seventh *Letter to the American People*, Apr. 21, 1803, saying that Federalist critics had not previously known its precise contents (Conway, III, 427–428). Writers on the subject have generally assumed that these were known from the beginning.

[11] Communication in *Gazette of the U.S.*, Sept. 7, 1801.

[12] Boston *Columbian Centinel*, Aug. 22, 1801. For this and numerous other quotations from newspapers I am indebted to my former student Dr. Jerry W. Knudson. He treats this topic in his dissertation "The Jefferson Years: Response by the

In this campaign of invective at a time when journalistic manners were abysmally low, the Federalist papers had much the better of it — partly because Republican publishers like Samuel Harrison Smith and William Duane had genuine reservations about the religious views of Paine. His defenders did not fail to remind the public of his signal services during the American Revolution and of his hostility to every form of tyranny everywhere, but their main effort was to dissociate Jefferson from him in the matter of religion and to claim that far too much was being made of the episode — as was unquestionably the case.[13] Sense of proportion is a rare accompaniment of partisanship in any era and the controversialists of that one were far from reasonable.

Paine landed at Baltimore on October 30, 1802. His own statement that every newspaper from New Hampshire to Georgia was filled with abuse or applause was one of his egotistical exaggerations, but references to him began to multiply several weeks before his arrival and reached their peak that winter.[14] During the days he remained in Baltimore, the case of mechanical models, wheels, etc., this ingenious man had brought with him was unloaded. Accounts of his reception varied with the reporters. His red nose served to authenticate Federalist allusions to his frequent sipping of brandy. The truth of the allegation that he was shunned by respectable people is much more difficult to prove but may have been substantially correct. Whatever difficulties he may have met in the matter of lodging, he found a place at Lovett's Hotel in Washington, and remained a couple of months in the capital. His contribution to the gaiety of the Federalists, whose editors had so little of a public nature to cavil about at the moment, is suggested by a song entitled "Thomas Paine and the King." We quote from a couple of its twenty-three stanzas:

Tom Paine is come from far . . .
His coming bodes disastrous times,
His nose is a blazing star! . . .

Press, 1801–1809" (UVA, 1962), ch. VI, and in an article, "The Rage around Tom Paine" (N.-Y. Hist. Soc. Quart., Jan., 1969, pp. 34–61).

13 The National Intelligencer and the Aurora took this line from the beginning. The Boston Independent Chronicle defended TJ's religion, as on Aug. 24, 1801.

14 Paine to T. C. Rickman, Mar. 8, 1803 (P. S. Foner, ed., Complete Writings of Thomas Paine [1945], II, 1439). Gazette of the U.S. had a series of articles in the fall of 1802 which were duly copied in N.Y. Evening Post, best of the Federalist papers. The strongest defense of Paine appears to have been made by Duane in the Aurora; he continued to emphasize politics rather than religion. Relatively little was said by Smith in National Intelligencer.

The ship came into port,
King Thomas he sent his coach and six,
To bring Tom Paine to court.[15]

King Thomas's coach was being used by his daughters at the time, and their presence in the President's House along with two of his grandchildren no doubt provided a sufficient argument against Paine's sleeping there on his first arrival, if that question came up. Prior to the opening of Congress in early December he undoubtedly dined there, but apparently he did not do so afterwards. He dined at Gallatin's, where Dr. Samuel Latham Mitchill, a representative from New York, heard him recite some of his verses, like an old schoolboy speaking his piece, and found this rugged-faced and red-nosed veteran with lively black eyes very entertaining. Senator William Plumer of New Hampshire, making his first visit to the President, had a more shocking experience. Besides giving a description of Jefferson's sartorial informality that was destined to be much quoted, he reported that Paine entered the room while he was there, "seated himself by the side of the President, and conversed and behaved towards him with the familiarity of an intimate and equal!" The startled Senator, whose Federalism was not yet tempered by admiration for this President, asked: "Can Virtue receive sufficient protection from an administration which admits such men as Paine to terms of intimacy with its chief." [16] Paine might have assumed a manner of intimacy whether his host liked it or not, but there is no reason to doubt that Jefferson, believing that the visitor's past services to the cause of human freedom entitled him to genuine respect, showed it to him.

Other Federalists reported that Jefferson found Paine embarrassing. Congressman Manasseh Cutler believed that the President sensibly felt "the severe, though just, remarks" that had been made on his "inviting" Paine to the country.[17] He could not have failed to be sensitive to these remarks, both as a man and a politician, but it does not follow that he admitted their justness; and disloyalty to political supporters and those whom he regarded as friends of freedom was wholly uncharacteristic of him. When he erred, it was on the other side. There were signs, however, that Paine himself thought that he had received insufficient

[15] N.Y. Evening Post, Jan. 10, 1803. "To the tune of Malbrouk, vulgarly called Moll Brookes."

[16] Plumer to Judge Smith, Dec. 9, 1802 (quoted in Wm. Plumer, Jr., Life of William Plumer [1857], p. 242). Dr. Mitchill commented on Paine in a letter to his wife, Dec. 11, 1802 (Harper's Mag., LVIII, 745–746).

[17] Manasseh Cutler to Dr. Joseph Torrey, Jan. 3, 1803 (Cutler, II, 118–119).

presidential attention. On the eve of his departure for Philadelphia and New York after Congress had been about five weeks in session, he rather abruptly asked Jefferson to send his models back, expressing regret that he had been unable to talk about them and other matters. "But," he said, "you have not only shown no disposition towards it, but have, in some measure, by a sort of shyness, as if you stood in fear of federal observation, precluded it. I am not the only one who makes observations of this kind." [18] Such observations might have been expected, for critics of the President were in the enviable position of being able to blame him for doing too much or for doing too little.

"You have certainly misconceived what you deem shyness," wrote Jefferson. "Of that I have not had a thought towards you, but on the contrary have openly maintained in conversation the duty of showing our respect to you and of defying federal calumny in this as in other cases, by doing what is right. As to fearing it, if I ever could have been weak enough for that, they have taken care to cure me of it thoroughly." He reminded Paine of the pressure of public business, which in fact was unrelenting during the congressional session; he did not mention, as he might have, the visit of his daughters and grandchildren and his devotion of his few spare hours to them. He said to the inventive Paine, as to others, that he had been obliged to forego mechanical and mathematical matters. However, he thought well of the models, especially one for planing, saying that he would like a couple of them if ever they should be made and sold.[19] He may have been merely going through the motions with Paine, impelled by a sense of duty, but he appears to have done as much as could have been expected of a busy chief magistrate. It appears, also, that neither at this time nor thereafter did he utter a word of complaint against one who was doing him far more political harm than good.

There was some disposition among Republican leaders to welcome the support of Paine's trenchant pen. Thus Caesar A. Rodney, while expressing disapproval of his religious views, wrote the party chieftain: "His style is calculated for the plain understanding of every good citizen. He will be a masterly hand at detecting and exposing federal misrepresentations." [20] William Duane of the *Aurora*, who also disliked his religious ideas, said repeatedly that no Federalist writer could stand up to him. However, his major contribution to political literature during

[18] Paine to TJ, Jan. 12, 1803 (Foner, II, 1439). On Christmas Day, 1802, Paine had given some gratuitous but sensible advice on the question of Louisiana (*ibid.*, II, 1431–1432). The wording of his later letter suggests, however, that he was not referring to that.
[19] TJ to Paine, Jan. 13, 1803 (Ford, VIII, 189).
[20] Rodney to TJ, Nov. 4, 1802 (LC, 22968).

the first months after his arrival, a series of letters *To the Citizens of the United States, and Particularly to the Leaders of the Federalist Faction*, bore far more on his own past achievements and controversies than on the present situation.[21] The report had been going around that he meant to add another part to the *Age of Reason*. After his third letter appeared, William Duane, fearful lest he take up the subject of religion, tried to dissuade him. Duane wrote Jefferson: "I have fairly told him that he will be deserted by the only party that respects or does not hate him, that all his political writings will be rendered useless, and even his fame destroyed." [22] Duane's remonstrances may have been more successful than he thought at the time, but Paine published in the *National Intelligencer*, whose editor apparently thought it necessary to accept his offerings whether or not he himself approved of them, a letter from Samuel Adams, urging him not to try to "unchristianize" the mass of the American people, along with his own reply.[23] As a statement of his own position and of the circumstances under which he wrote the offensive work, which he believed Samuel Adams had not read, this is reasonable and informative, but most of the Republican leaders would have liked it better if he had not gone into the matter at all.

Jefferson himself appears to have maintained entire silence on the subject. Of all issues, that of religious freedom was the one on which he was least likely to be coerced. Unquestionably, however, he was going to great pains to attend divine services in the House of Congress. One Federalist observer, while regarding this as no kind of evidence of the President's own religion, believed that it went far to prove that "the idea of bearing down and overturning" the religious institutions of the country, which in his opinion had been "a favorite object," had been given up.[24] Jefferson did not need to give up that object since he had never had it.

Not until after his return to his old home in Bordentown, New Jersey, did Paine give to the world the text of the letter Jefferson had written him two years earlier, the reports of which had occasioned such an outcry. It appeared in a lesser paper and may have attracted little attention during the excitement over the Louisiana question.[25] It occasioned a further private statement of Jefferson's, however, more

---

[21] The first seven of these, dated Nov. 15, 1802–Apr. 21, 1803, are in Conway, III, 381–429; Foner, II, 908–948. An eighth was dated June 5, 1805 (Foner, II, 949–957). The first five, written in Washington, appeared in *National Intelligencer*.

[22] Duane to TJ, Nov. 27, 1802 (*Procs. Mass. Hist. Soc.*, 2 ser., XX, 279).

[23] *National Intelligencer*, Feb. 2, 1803 (Conway, IV, 200–208).

[24] Manasseh Cutler, Jan. 3, 1803 (Cutler, II, 119).

[25] In Paine's seventh letter *To the Citizens*, dated Apr. 21, 1803, and said to have appeared in Trenton *True American* (Conway, III, 427–428).

than two years later. Early in his second term he assured Paine that he himself had nothing whatever to do with an alleged "half denial" of it in the *National Intelligencer*. "With respect to the letter," he said, "I never hesitated to avow and to justify it in conversation. In no other way do I trouble myself to contradict anything which is said." [26]

Only a few months after that, John Adams, whom Paine had gone out of his way to castigate, said privately that he was willing to call the age anything but the Age of Reason. He doubted if any man had so influenced it as Tom Paine, and believed that there could be no more severe satire on an age than to say this. "For such a mongrel between Pigg and Puppy, begotten by a wild Boar on a Bitch Wolf, never before in any Age of the World was suffered by the Poltroonery of mankind, to run through such a Career of Mischief. Call it then the Age of Paine." [27]

In American intellectual history this was definitely *not* the Age of Paine. The reaction against the "infidelity" associated with the French Revolution was far from checked, and rationalism was actually less acceptable in the country than it had been when Adams signed the Declaration of Independence. But his detestation for Paine was based on no prime concern for the Establishment in New England or for traditional theology, since he was fiercely independent of both. Judging from his later correspondence with Jefferson he himself was a freethinker in the literal meaning of the term.

At that later time Jefferson himself said: "I not only write nothing on religion, but rarely permit myself to speak on it, and never but in a reasonable society." [28] He had had ready access to "reasonable society" in far off student days, when he dined at the Palace in Williamsburg with Governor Francis Fauquier, William Small, and George Wythe; and in old age he could give his pen free rein in religious dialogue with John Adams. During his presidency, when he could not turn to that alienated friend and deemed it a political necessity to be careful, he found "reasonable" company in Dr. Benjamin Rush, to whom he had proclaimed in immortal phrase his eternal hostility to every form of tyranny over the human mind. He also found it in Dr. Joseph Priestley, the renowned chemist and Unitarian clergyman who had been the target of William Cobbett and other Federalist writers but now rejoiced in freedom from all fear of persecution. In theology neither fully agreed

[26] TJ to Paine, June 5, 1805 (Ford, VIII, 361).
[27] Adams to Benjamin Waterhouse, Oct. 29, 1805 (*Statesman and Friend* [1927], p. 31).
[28] TJ to Charles Clay, Jan. 29, 1815 (L. & B., XIV, 233).

with Jefferson, but for the former he prepared what was perhaps the fullest statement of his religious position he ever made, and he received the immediate stimulus for this action from the latter.

Priestley, who had recently dedicated to Jefferson the final volumes of his *General History of the Christian Church*,[29] sent him in the spring of 1803 a pamphlet entitled *Socrates and Jesus Compared*. Receiving this when on his spring visit home, after the adjournment of Congress, he reflected on it on the road back. Soon after his return he suggested that Priestley enlarge his treatment, so as to compare the moral doctrines of the chief philosophers of Greece and Rome, and the doctrines of the Jews, with those of Jesus. He himself had thought of doing this, in fulfillment of a promise to Dr. Rush five years earlier to give him, some day, a statement of his views on the Christian system. In fact, he had formulated an outline in his mind — perhaps while he was joggling over those rough Virginia roads — and he now presented it to a scholar whom he believed to be far better qualified to perform the task than he. He never did find time to elaborate this outline; but when Priestley demurred on grounds of age and ill health he drew it up in somewhat fuller form and called it a syllabus. In a couple of beautifully penned pages he estimated the merit of the doctrines of Jesus, as compared with those of others. It is no mere skeleton, but an epitome and a most unusual testament.[30]

From his early manhood he had been familiar with the classical philosophers, and he was succored by them after he espoused natural law and rejected supernaturalism.[31] He decried any belittlement of teachers who had done so much for him, but had come to view them far more critically than he did as a young man. "Their precepts related chiefly to ourselves," he now said, "and the government of those passions which, unrestrained, would disturb our tranquility of mind." While recognizing their greatness as advocates of self-mastery who pointed the way to inner peace, he thought them "short and defective" in developing man's duties to others. The patriotism they inculcated was too restrictive; their justice and benevolence did not embrace all mankind.[32]

Just when this lifelong classicist began to turn himself into a biblical scholar is difficult to determine, but by now he was thoroughly familiar

---

[29] Dedication dated July, 1802; last four volumes published 1802–1803.

[30] Pertinent passages from related letters are in Sowerby, II, 172–174, along with a reproduction of the manuscript. The printed text is in Ford, VIII, 223–228, with letters. TJ wrote Priestley, Apr. 9, 1803, and Rush, Apr. 21, sending the syllabus on Apr. 23. He sent it to Priestley on Apr. 24.

[31] See *Jefferson the Virginian*, pp. 106–107, with references to *Literary Bible*, and Adrienne Koch, *Philosophy of Thomas Jefferson*, ch. 2.

[32] He was concerned with only their *moral* principles; and he mentioned particularly Pythagoras, Socrates, Epicurus, Cicero, Epictetus, Seneca, and Antoninus.

with the Gospels, which he could readily read in Greek. From his young manhood he was very fond of the psalms in English translation, but wide as his learning was it did not extend to Hebrew. And, while thoroughly modern in his desire to subject the Scriptures to tests of the same sort as those applied to any history or literature, he could not have been expected to disentangle the diverse elements in the Old Testament. Whatever the reason may have been, he was far more critical of the doctrines of the Jews than of those of the classical philosophers. He called their system "deism," defining this as belief in only one God — that is, monotheism.[33] Their ideas of God, however, this critic regarded as "degrading." He did not like the idea of a jealous and wrathful deity. Also, he disliked the idea of a "peculiar people": he rejected the ethics of the Jews chiefly on the ground that they were antisocial with respect to other peoples. He believed, therefore, that they stood in grave need of reformation when Jesus came. He did not realize the extent to which one whom he regarded as the greatest of teachers drew on the precepts of his own people.

Jefferson did not refer to the Messiah, the Savior, or the Christ, but he had unbounded admiration for Jesus, whom he now introduced in moving language:

> In this state of things among the Jews, Jesus appeared. His parentage was obscure; his condition poor; his education null; his natural endowments great; his life correct and innocent: he was meek, benevolent, patient, firm, disinterested, & of the sublimest eloquence.[34]

His unvarnished and uninhibited account of the disadvantages under which the doctrines of Jesus appeared reflects the difficulties he himself had encountered in his effort to discover them in their pure form. That life and those doctrines, he said, had been committed to writing by unlettered men, who drew on memory long afterwards. "According to the ordinary fate of those who attempt to enlighten and reform, he fell an early victim to the jealousy and combination of the altar and the throne," and thus did not have time to develop and present a complete moral system. The doctrines Jesus actually pronounced came down only in fragments, "mutilated, misstated, and often unintelligible." Worst of all, his simple doctrines were corrupted through the years by followers who engrafted on them "the mysticisms of a Greek sophist [Plato], frittering them into subtleties, and obscuring them with jargon."

[33] Irrespective of definition, he appears to have been relatively unfamiliar with Jewish religion.

[34] Ford, VIII, 227.

Jefferson's view of the corruptions of Christianity, which he described elsewhere as "invested by priestcraft and established by kingcraft, constituting a conspiracy of church and state against the civil and religious liberties of mankind," was reinforced by a book of Joseph Priestley on this subject.[35] That writer and others contributed to his appreciation of the doctrines of Jesus, but his admiration may be largely attributed to his own thorough and unaided study of the Gospels themselves. After commenting on the "corruptions" he detested, he said:

> Notwithstanding these disadvantages, a system of morals is presented to us, which, if filled up in the true style and spirit of the rich fragments he left us, would be the most perfect and sublime that has ever been taught by man.

Jefferson admired the doctrines of Jesus because he believed that these gave juster notions of the attributes and government of God than had been held previously, and he approved of this teacher's emphasis on the future life as a supplementary motive to moral conduct. Even more important, however, was the inculcation of "universal philanthropy, not only to kindred and friends, to neighbors and countrymen, but to all mankind." Herein Jefferson saw the "peculiar superiority" of the system of Jesus. Not only so. "He pushed his scrutinies into the heart of man; erected his tribunal in the region of his thoughts, and purified the waters at the fountain head." Brushing aside the trappings of ceremony and the obscuring mantle of theology, the President of the United States had arrived at the heart of the matter.

Concerning himself with ethics alone, he had deliberately avoided the question of divinity in the syllabus itself. Sending it to Dr. Rush, he said that his views, "the result of a life of inquiry and reflection," were very different from the anti-Christian system imputed to him. "To the corruptions of Christianity I am indeed opposed," he declared; "but not to the genuine precepts of Jesus himself. I am a Christian, in the only sense he wished any one to be; sincerely attached to his doctrines, in preference to all others; ascribing to him every *human* excellence; and believing he never claimed any other." Dr. Rush was pleased to learn that his friend was "by no means so heterodox" as his enemies had supposed, but agreed to disagree with him as to the "character and mission of the Author of our Religion." [36] Jefferson had described Jesus

---

[35] *An History of the Corruptions of Christianity, in two volumes.* TJ owned the 2nd edn. of 1793, and presumably became acquainted with the work after that date. (See Sowerby, II, 120, with extracts from pertinent letters.) He appears to have gained little beyond stimulus from Priestley's *Socrates and Jesus Compared.*

[36] Rush to TJ, May 5, 1803 (Butterfield, II, 864). TJ wrote him Apr. 23.

to Priestley as "the most innocent, the most benevolent, the most eloquent and sublime character that has ever been exhibited to man"; but
the old minister was surprised at Jefferson's opinion that Jesus never
laid claim to a divine mission, and wrote him at length on the subject in
order to provide him with further food for thought.[37] Whether Priestley now regarded Jefferson as almost a Christian or altogether one is
uncertain, but he did not question the latter's perfect right to his own
opinions. Dr. Rush, on the basis of his own observations of the slight
influence of religious opinions on morals, and of the evil practices of
many orthodox people, fully agreed that the only real test, and the
only one God would apply at the judgment seat, was that of conduct.
Along with Jefferson, whom he liked, and with Paine whom he disliked, he could have quoted Alexander Pope's familiar lines:

> For modes of faith let graceless zealots fight;
> His can't be wrong whose life is in the right:
> In faith and hope the world will disagree,
> But all mankind's concern is charity.

The author of the syllabus sent copies of it to his two daughters,
with whom normally he did not discuss religious matters, although he
had delivered countless moral exhortations to them while they were
growing up. Also, he wanted to send copies to three or four particular
friends. Knowing what uses his political and clerical foes would make
of the syllabus if they got hold of it, he prudently asked that it be
returned to him after it was read. One of these friends, Levi Lincoln,
asked the privilege of making a copy and was granted this on the
understanding that he would not put Jefferson's name on it.[38] The syllabus did not get out, to be trampled underfoot, but fortunately it has
been preserved into a time when anybody who regards it as a gem need
have no fear in saying so.

Before the end of his first term Jefferson began a compilation which,
when completed in his old age, he entitled *The Life and Morals of Jesus
of Nazareth*. This consisted of extracts from the Gospels that he re-

[37] Priestley to TJ, May 7, 1803 (LC, 22679). For an admirable brief account of
Priestley's theology and writings on the subject of religion, see Caroline Robbins,
"Honest Heretic: Joseph Priestley in America" (*Procs. Am. Philos. Soc.*, Vol.
106 [1962], esp. pp. 68–72. Following TJ's suggestion, Priestley finally wrote *The
Doctrines of Heathen Philosophy, compared with those of Revelation* (1804).
While commending this, Jefferson afterwards agreed with John Adams that
Priestley "did not do justice to the undertaking," adding that "he felt himself
pressed by the hand of death." (Sowerby, II, 121–123, giving extracts from letters.)

[38] Accompanying note, TJ to Lincoln, Apr. 26, 1803 (Ford, VIII, 225–226). I
have not yet determined whether or not TJ actually sent out other copies, and,
if so, to whom. After the deaths of Priestley and Rush, TJ was much concerned
to get hold of their copies.

garded as genuine and was ultimately done in Greek, Latin, and French as well as English. In its first form it had another title and it was originally designed for the benefit of the Indians. He claimed that he spent only two or three nights on it in this period. He must have spent more than that, but it is a notable fact that this chief of state devoted even that time to such a task. Since it was finished so much later it need not concern us here. We may note, however, the judgment of a scholarly Unitarian clergyman in the middle of the twentieth century that Jefferson's "knowledge of and admiration for the teachings of Jesus have never been equaled by any other president." [39]

Apparently he had not yet called himself a Unitarian, as he did occasionally in extreme old age, while always avoiding identification with any particular denomination. John Adams, whose theology was much the same, said afterwards that Jefferson had as much religion as Priestley. Whether or not he could be properly described as religious while President depends largely on one's definition. This apostle of spiritual freedom regarded himself as a Christian, and unquestionably he was one in his ethical standards. As he well knew, a full revelation of his reasoned opinions about religion and morality would have merely served to provide his political and ecclesiastical foes with ammunition for further attacks. To him himself and to those who really knew him, the tactics of his enemies could not have failed to seem cruelly unfair. A parody on a familiar song in a hostile publication is a case in point:

> All bigot chains our chief unites,
> For Devil nor for God to care:
> Or if variety we prize,
> Has *twenty Gods* or more to spare.
> Rejoice, ye Infidels, rejoice,
> From law and conscience quite set free,
> And curse the Priests with Lincoln's voice,
> For J——N and Liberty.[40]

[39] Henry Wilder Foote, in his edn. of *The Life and Morals of Jesus of Nazareth* (1951), p. 13. The work was first published by order of Congress in 1904.

[40] *Port Folio*, Feb. 19, 1803. The references are to the passage in the *Notes on Virginia* quoted on p. 191, above; and to Levi Lincoln, the Attorney General, who was from New England. The reason for the reference to the latter is obscure.

[XII]

Torrent of Slander

THOUGH Thomas Paine was unquestionably a political liability to Jefferson at this stage of his career, and his own alleged "infidelity" served to accentuate hostility to him in certain quarters, especially in New England, his unquestionable anticlericalism won him support, notably among the Baptists in that region and elsewhere. There were those who believed that his philosophy of complete religious freedom and consistent practice of *laissez faire* were actually conducive to the spread of religion in the country. Such was the opinion of a general assembly of the Presbyterian church that met in Philadelphia after he had been two years in office. It was then said that during his administration a "preached gospel" had prospered greatly.[1] Under these circumstances the attacks on him on religious grounds may have done his reputation little harm except among those who were already opposed to him, and may even have done him some good.

The attacks on his personal character had no compensatory advantage whatsoever, but the historical significance of these can be easily exaggerated. They were largely if not wholly irrelevant, since they related not to public but to private conduct and to episodes, real or imagined, most of which fell in the distant past. In comparison with the enormous effect on the President's popularity of the public measures of his first term, these charges appear to have had only slight political consequence. To lay on them the same degree of emphasis that his enemies did at the time would be to distort this story. It is nonetheless true that he suffered open personal attacks which in severity and obscenity have rarely if ever been matched in presidential history in the United States, that he writhed under them even though he said hardly anything about

---

[1] David Jackson to TJ, Aug. 6, 1803 (LC, 23112), sending him extracts from the proceedings, and giving interesting comments on the political alignment of the various religious groups. The Rev. William Bentley commented, Jan. 24, 1802, on the attachment of the Baptists to the administration, attributing the remarkable growth of that sect to this (*Diary*, II, 1907, p. 409).

them, and that some of them were destined to re-echo through the generations. With only one significant exception, these virulent attacks were without substantial foundation; and, except for some reiteration of charges that had been made in the campaigns of 1796 and 1800, they emanated from a single poisoned spring. The grossest of them were given to the world by James Thomson Callender, whom he had unwisely befriended.

Jefferson's relations with this impecunious and disreputable journalist offer the most extreme example of the gullibility of a personally generous man who was insufficiently critical of those who were, or seemed to be, in basic agreement with his political position.[2] There is no reason to believe that he ever told Callender what to say, but for a time at least he had welcomed the support of this unsparing critic of the Federalists and had tolerated excesses that he himself would not have engaged in. His financial contributions to this needy man amounted to very little until Callender became an object of persecution. If he wanted to dissociate himself from the fugitive by that time, he could not do so either in consistency or charity; and in his effort to have as little to do with him personally as possible — that is, to answer as few of his letters as possible — Jefferson did not challenge Callender's intimation that the gifts to him were for party services rendered. Thus by force of circumstances, as well as by too-ready generosity and excess of party loyalty, Jefferson unwittingly subjected himself to the danger of blackmail. Callender was fully aware of that if his benefactor was not, and, like any blackguard dealing with a reputable gentleman, he had the advantage of unscrupulousness.

Republican support of Callender when on trial for sedition was occasioned by considerations of party loyalty and by resentment of the bullying tactics of Justice Chase. Jefferson encouraged such support, but James Monroe had far more hand in it. His turn came when as President he pardoned Callender. In view of his expressed opinion that the Sedition Act was unconstitutional his action was consistent, entirely apart from what he may have thought of this particular victim. Actually, he pardoned a more appealing object of sympathy first: David Brown, who had been more than eighteen months in jail in Massachusetts.[3] Since both men had completed their prison terms, the practical significance of the two pardons consisted solely in the remission of the fines. Callender had actually paid his fine of $200 by that time, but

[2] For his relations with Callender prior to his presidency, see *Jefferson and the Ordeal of Liberty*, pp. 332–333, 466–467, 469–472. I have also summed them up in *Thomas Jefferson as Political Leader* (1963), pp. 56–60.
[3] See p. 35, above.

Jefferson sent word to him that it would be remitted as promptly as possible.[4] There were unforeseen delays, unfortunately, and Callender himself, shortly before his death, said that his "chastisement" of the President was in return for these. As he put it, Jefferson refused to pay the fine.[5] That was not the whole story by any means nor did he give a fair account of any part of it.

The impatient writer did not get his money back until three months after he was pardoned.[6] The main reason he had to wait so long was that the Federalist United States marshal to whom he originally paid the fine imposed obstacles to its repayment. That marshal was David Meade Randolph, who was married to Thomas Mann Randolph's elder sister Mary. Despite the embarrassingly close relationship, Jefferson removed him within three weeks of his own accession, on the ground that he had packed juries and withheld money from the government. In reporting this action to his own son-in-law, Jefferson laid stress on jury packing.[7] It is not unlikely that he was thinking of the marshal's conduct in Callender's trial, where the jurymen were all Federalists, though David Randolph afterwards denied charges of partisanship and collusion with Justice Samuel Chase in procuring the panel.[8]

Whatever the degree of his partisanship may have been, the marshal who had personally apprehended Callender in the first place was now expected to restore the fine; and, before his own removal from office, he intimated that he would raise no objection. But Callender — either because of illness or fear or perversity — did not immediately come for the money; and, after learning of his own removal, the marshal began to voice doubts about Callender's legal right to get the fine back. Did he not pay it *before* he was pardoned? After some time Levi Lincoln, the attorney general and acting secretary of state, ruled that the fine could and should be restored since it had not been turned into the Treasury by the former marshal — who actually owed the government a considerable additional sum on his own account. Thereupon, David Randolph, by no means averse to embarrassing the administration, proceeded to report the fine as a credit item in rendering his account, though he did not yet send the money or discharge his further debt to

[4] TJ to George Jefferson, Mar. 4, 1801 (MHS).

[5] Richmond *Recorder*, May 28, 1803.

[6] June 20, 1801. He was pardoned Mar. 16.

[7] TJ to TMR, Mar. 12 (*Papers, MHS*, p. 93). The decision to remove D. M. Randolph was made by Mar. 8, 1801, when TJ noted it in his memo. of his meeting with Gallatin, Dearborn, and Lincoln (Ford, I, 292). This was more than a week before Callender's pardon. The formal removal was on Mar. 24.

[8] He defended himself vigorously in *Gazette of the U.S.*, Jan. 29, 1802, and on Feb. 16, 1805, in the Chase trial. (*Trial of Samuel Chase . . . Taken in Short-hand by Samuel H. Smith and Thomas Lloyd*, I [1805], 248–254.)

the government. After Gallatin assumed office and took the same position as Lincoln, the former marshal was explicitly instructed to pay Callender. This he finally did, getting a receipt, but for a time it looked as though the liberated journalist could not get his money without instituting a lawsuit.[9]

Just when and to what extent Callender was informed of the complicated circumstances is uncertain, but it may be doubted if any explanation would have been acceptable to one who had begun to complain of his shabby treatment by the party while he was still in prison and who was ever prone to exaggerate his own deserts. He probably did not exaggerate his financial distress, but he appears to have disregarded and denied certain friendly offers. It was said after his death that provision would have been made by loyal Republicans for the payment of his board, after his emergence from jail, and that he would have thus been able to continue his political writing — presumably having access to the columns of the Richmond *Examiner*, whose publisher, Meriwether Jones, had previously befriended him.[10] He admitted an offer for help from James Monroe, but his eye was obviously on the post office in Richmond and the burden of his complaint was that he was unappreciated. He wrote the President at least once after the inauguration, but, saying that he "might as well have addressed a letter to Lot's wife," he then turned to Madison, for whom he now professed particular attachment.[11] By this time, as he reported to the Secretary of State, he had written the following words of explanation to Thomas Leiper, to whom he owed money for taking care of his motherless boys in Philadelphia: "Mr. Jefferson has not returned one shilling of my fine. I now begin to know what Ingratitude is." Charging the President with breach of promise, he asserted that he himself was no man "to be oppressed or plundered with impunity." He said he was being sacrificed

[9] On request, Gallatin, departing from his "habit of opposing nothing but silence to party calumnies," described the entire course of events in a letter to Samuel Harrison Smith, Aug. 20, 1802, sending copies of supporting documents. (Gallatin Papers, N.Y. Hist. Soc.) Again departing from his custom, he drafted an article which was published anonymously in *National Intelligencer*, Oct. 20, 1802. Madison described the major complications to Monroe, June 1, 1801 (Hunt, VI, 421–422), making no reference to a letter from Callender, May 7, saying that Randolph had offered to repay the money if he would come for it. This Callender declined to do because of fears for his personal safety and his resentment at the tone of Randolph's communication. This and other letters of Callender, referred to here only by date, may be seen in W. C. Ford, "Thomas Jefferson and James Thomson Callender," in *New Eng. Hist. and Geneal. Register*, Vol. 51 (1897). Cunningham treats this episode briefly but well in *Jeffersonian Republicans in Power*, pp. 250, 252, 263.

[10] Editorial in *Examiner*, July 27, 1803.

[11] Callender to Madison, Apr. 27, 1801, after TJ had failed to respond to a letter of Apr. 12.

to political decorum, and, while claiming to recognize Jefferson's exemplary probity and to admire the man and his policies exceedingly, he now admitted that, because of the "ostentatious coolness and indifference" that had been manifested toward himself in the past, he did not love or trust him. This was the first time he had given even a hint of this, he said, but he also gave more than a hint that what he really wanted was public office.

Jefferson had no intention of giving him that; but, greatly embarrassed by the delay in the refunding of the fine, the President unwisely acted in a way that would have laid him open to the charge of yielding to blackmail if it had become known. Agreeing too quickly with the suggestion of Monroe that, in order to remove from Callender all cause for complaint, they had better refund his fine by private contributions, he sent the Governor an order for $50. Before any use could be made of this, Callender himself arrived in Washington. "He did not call on me," wrote the President to the Governor; "but understanding he was in distress I sent Captain Lewis to him with 50 D. to inform him we were making some inquiries as to his fine which would take a little time, and lest he should suffer in the meantime I had sent him, &c." If Jefferson had expected his action to be gratefully accepted he was greatly disappointed. The report on Callender continued: "His language to Captain Lewis was very high-toned. He intimated that he was in possession of things which he could and would make use of in a certain case: that he received the 50 D. not as a charity but a due, in fact as hush money; that I knew what he expected, viz. a certain office, and more to this effect. Such a misconstruction of my charities puts an end to them forever." [12] He asked that Monroe make no use of the order sent him. Actually, the Governor had already returned it, with an expression of regret that Meriwether Lewis had paid Callender anything, after hearing him express his views.[13] Now terming Callender a wretch and serpent, Monroe hoped that, through Meriwether Jones, they could get back from him even the most unimportant letters. Jefferson had never written him many letters, but apparently nobody persuaded Callender to part with any of them.

In Washington the burden of dealing with his claims fell on Madison, who found him implacable toward Jefferson and impossible to reason with. The Secretary of State concluded that he was under the tyranny of love, besides other passions, and had persuaded himself that his suit would be successful if he could gain the dignity and emoluments of the post office in Richmond. Madison disabused him of all illusions with

[12] TJ to Monroe, May 29, 1801 (Ford, VIII, 61).
[13] Monroe to TJ, June 1, 1801 (S.M.H., III, 289).

respect to that appointment and hoped that his plain dealing might have done Callender some good.[14] Actually, the obstreperous fellow did not trouble the administration for a good many months after the repayment of his fine, but before the beginning of Jefferson's second year in office he had found a new journalistic medium. In the summer of 1801, Henry Pace began to print the Richmond *Recorder*, and in February, 1802, Callender became his partner. According to the *Examiner*, whose publisher had formerly shown him generous and patient hospitality, he vented his misanthropy not only by his acts of political apostasy, but also by his efforts to destroy that paper. He carried on a running fight against it all summer.

At least by March, Callender was training his guns on the administration, with particular reference to the Postmaster General into whose service he had not been permitted to enter. Before long he got around to William Branch Giles, the Republican legislative leader, and to Albert Gallatin. Accusing the Secretary of Treasury of "barefaced and matchless contradictions," he wondered how the President could let such a man come into his presence.[15] Taking up the cudgels for Aaron Burr, he engaged in heated altercation with James Cheetham, who had accused the Vice President of machinations against Jefferson. Samuel Harrison Smith of the *National Intelligencer*, whom Callender derisively called "Miss Smith," followed the wise policy of ignoring him or brushing him off, thus denying him the controversy he sought and thrived on; but William Duane of the *Aurora* pitched into the fray, indulging at times in personal attacks on Callender in which, it seemed, he tried to match him in virulence.[16]

Jefferson's chief personal embarrassment at first arose from his previous connection with Callender and his gifts to him. These were fully exploited by Federalist papers, including the best of them, Hamilton's organ, the *New York Evening Post*. By the end of the summer Callender was attacking the President directly — saying among other things that it would have been advantageous to his reputation if his head had been cut off five minutes before he began his inaugural speech.[17] The vengeful campaign of the embittered journalist reached its crescendo in the autumn of 1802. His fury was diminished or dissipated in the spring of 1803, but it ended only with his death in July, in the James River in three feet of water — an event that was largely ignored outside the local press. The death was officially designated as accidental, proceeding

[14] Madison to Monroe, June 1, 1801 (Hunt, VI, 420–422).
[15] *Recorder*, May 26, 1802; also Aug. 11, 18.
[16] For example, *Aurora*, Sept., 15, 1802.
[17] *Recorder*, Sept. 15, 1802.

from intoxication, but the *Examiner* regarded it as suicidal, claiming
that this unfortunate man had descended to the lowest depths of misery
after having been fleeced by his partner.[18] Such was the pitiable end of
one of the most notorious scandalmongers and character assassins in
American history. The evil that he did was not buried with him: some
of it has lasted through the generations.

During the last four months of 1802, besides publishing his correspondence with Jefferson and continuing to snipe at the policies of the
administration, Callender vented his wrath in sensational charges
against the character and private conduct of his erstwhile benefactor.
Specifically, he gave to the world the Sally story, the Walker story, and
the Gabriel Jones story. According to the first, Jefferson had a slave
mistress; according to the second, he had sought to seduce a friend's
wife; according to the third, he had tried to pay a debt to a friend in
depreciated currency. The two last referred to events prior to or during the American Revolution, a quarter of a century before this date.
The Gabriel Jones episode presents no real problem since the debt was
unquestionably discharged and we have treated the Walker affair in
considerable detail in an earlier volume.[19]

The story of Sally, sometimes known as Dusky Sally, should therefore concern us first, as it did Callender. There was a contemporaneous
element in this as he proclaimed it, for he alleged that the man *"whom
it delighteth the people to honor"* was still keeping a concubine. It may
be noted that Jefferson was nearing sixty at this time and that his journalistic critic had never visited Monticello.

Without mentioning any source of information, Callender asserted
that what he was stating was well known. According to his first version
of the story, Sally went to France with Jefferson and his two daughters. The journalist subsequently corrected his dates somewhat, while
saying that the liaison began in France. He claimed that she had a son
named Tom, ten or twelve years old, who strikingly resembled the
President, and that the "wench" had borne Jefferson several other children. References to these varied but the highest alleged number appears
to have been five. At one time Callender described these youngsters as
mahogany-featured; at another he spoke of "yellow Tom" and said that
the Republicans might be called the "mulatto party." The vulgar terms
that he and others applied to the alleged mistress will not bear repeat-

[18] Editorial of July 27, 1803. He died July 17.
[19] *Jefferson the Virginian*, pp. 153–155, and Appendix III. The allegations in the
Jones episode are well disposed of in Boyd, II, 260–261, under the date Apr. 29,
1779. Callender publicized the Sally story in Richmond *Recorder*, Sept. 1, 15, 22,
29, 1802, and later that fall.

ing; one of the kindest was to the "African Venus" who was said to officiate as a housekeeper at Monticello.

Factual accuracy was of no concern to Callender, but if he had gone to the little mountain he would have found there a household slave named Sally Hemings, who by all accounts was nearly white and very good-looking. She had accompanied Polly Jefferson to France, being then aged fourteen, and she was now twenty-nine. There was no yellow Tom, but she had lost a daughter and had two living children: a son, Beverley, now in his fifth year, and a daughter, Harriet, who was less than two. Callender imagined the others, categorically asserting that the President of the United States was the father of them all. No one can deprive the disgruntled editor of the dubious honor of launching this lush story, but an English writer afterwards surpassed him in luxuriance of imagination. A few years after Jefferson's death, Mrs. Trollope wrote that he was said "to have been the father of children by almost all his numerous gang of female slaves," and to have taken particular pleasure in being waited upon by them at table.[20]

Whatever Callender might have thought of this later elaboration, he claimed in December, 1802, to be greatly pleased with the results of his disclosures. While Mrs. Randolph and Mrs. Eppes were visiting their father in the President's House, he said:

> The strokes of the *Recorder* have been sufficiently felt: not from an uncommon share of abilities in the subscriber [Callender], for he pretends to none. But because he was resolved to disclose a few entertaining facts. By the indulgence, or partiality of other editors, they have made the "grand tour" of the continent. If this paper could acquire ten times its present circulation, it would not make so much impression upon the public mind, as has been made by the innumerable extracts in other newspapers. These are accompanied and illustrated by copious commentaries, the collected labors of a thousand intellects. Thus, the people get information; and, until the people are well informed, there cannot be a correct and firm government.[21]

Beyond question, Callender's charges were widely disseminated by the Federalist press of the day; and, whether or not they engaged "a thousand intellects," they occasioned a number of poetic effusions. One of the best known of these, which Callender himself reprinted from the

[20] Frances Trollope, *Domestic Manners of the Americans* (1949), p. 72; see also p. 317. For an account of Sally's children, see the present work, Appendix II, n. 1.

[21] *Recorder*, Dec. 8, 1802. He was referring to his publicizing of both the Sally and the Walker stories.

Boston Gazette, was a song, sung to the tune of "Yankee Doodle" and purported to have been written by the Sage of Monticello himself. The first verse and chorus of this ran as follows:

> Of all the damsels on the green,
> On mountain, or in valley,
> A lass so luscious ne'er was seen,
> As the Monticellian Sally.

> Yankey doodle, who's the noodle?
> What wife were half so handy?
> To breed a flock of slaves for stock,
> A blackamoor's the dandy.[22]

Some of the other verses were even more salacious, and one of them, following Callender's lead, referred vulgarly to a passage in the *Notes on Virginia* in which Jefferson had spoken of the physical characteristics of the Negroes.

The obscenity and vulgarity of these extracts, from Callender and others, serve to illustrate the low taste of the journalism of the era, but in our own time the pertinent question is whether there was any validity whatever in the tale he told. A trifold answer can be given to this. (1) The charges are suspect in the first place because they issued from the vengeful pen of an unscrupulous man and were promulgated in a spirit of bitter partisanship. (2) They cannot be proved and certain of the alleged facts were obviously erroneous. (3) They are distinctly out of character, being virtually unthinkable in a man of Jefferson's moral standards and habitual conduct. To say this is not to claim that he was a plaster saint and incapable of moral lapses. But his major weaknesses were not of this sort; and while he might have occasionally fallen from grace, as so many men have done so often, it is virtually inconceivable that this fastidious gentleman whose devotion to his dead wife's memory and to the happiness of his daughters and grandchildren bordered on the excessive could have carried on through a period of years a vulgar liaison which his own family could not have failed to detect. It would be as absurd as to charge this consistently temperate man with being, through a long period, a secret drunkard.

He himself said, after his retirement, that he never wished slanders of him by political enemies to be answered by anything but the tenor of his life. "I should have fancied myself half guilty," he said, "had I condescended to put pen to paper in refutation of their falsehoods, or

---

[22] *Recorder,* Nov. 17, 1802. Douglass Adair attributes this to Joseph Dennie, editor of the *Port Folio.* On Dec. 1, 1802, "A Philosophic Love Song," and on Apr. 27, 1803, "Black and White," were reprinted from *Boston Gazette.*

drawn to them respect by any notice from myself." [23] This was nearly always his policy with respect to attacks on his public conduct, and it appears to have been almost invariable in matters that he regarded as strictly private.[24] He ignored attacks on his religion and morals, relying on the good sense of the public and believing that his assailants would defeat their ends by their own excesses. There seems to be no record of his ever having referred specifically, even in private, to the story connecting him with his slave Sally Hemings. In the autumn of 1802, when his optimism about the political prospects of his party was to be fully confirmed by the elections, he attributed the increased bitterness of the Federalists to their desperation. At the same time he believed that every decent man among them was revolted by Callender's filth. Some of his political advisers feared that many respectable people, though affecting displeasure at "calumny," secretly countenanced it. Such was almost certainly the case, but Jefferson had no intention of taking any notice of his most unscrupulous calumniator.[25]

Neither had the editor of the *National Intelligencer*, the paper often described as the organ of the administration. Declining to publish a communication respecting the character and conduct of Callender, Samuel Harrison Smith said:

> The Editor has determined not to disgrace the columns of a Paper that entertains a respect for decency and truth, by republishing the infamous calumnies and vulgarities of a man who has forfeited every pretension to character, or refutations of falsehoods which may recoil on those who propagate them, but cannot impair the well earned esteem in which the first talents and virtues of the nation are held. Without incurring any responsibility for the future, the Editor has prescribed to himself for the present the duty of suffering these base aspersions to perish unnoticed in their own infamy.[26]

About a month later this editor modified his policy sufficiently to copy a communication from the Richmond *Examiner*. This constituted the most effective sort of counterattack on Callender, since it revealed

---

[23] TJ to Dr. George Logan, June 20, 1816 (Ford, X, 27).

[24] Three exceptions may be noted: an article dealing with appointments that he asked Levi Lincoln to insert in a Massachusetts paper (June 1, 1803; Ford, VIII, 233–234); "Answer to Gabriel Jones" (June, 1803; Ford, VIII, 235–240); reply in *Aurora*, Feb. 13, 1804, to paper on etiquette in *Washington Federalist*, Feb. 1, 1804 (see pp. 387, 499–500, below).

[25] TJ to R. R. Livingston, Oct. 10, 1802, and to Gallatin, Oct. 13, 1802 (Ford, VIII, 173–176); Levi Lincoln to TJ, Oct. 16, 1802 (LC, 21842). On the elections see pp. 140–141, above.

[26] Sept. 29, 1802, declining a communication signed LUCULLUS.

the generosity of Jefferson to another needy man who did *not* requite him by ingratitude. Without referring specifically to Callender's charges and thus advertising them further, the writer described him as a second Judas, whose treason might be applauded by the Federalists but whom they must abhor as a traitor. The writer was specific about the gifts of Jefferson to him, fifty dollars at one time and thirty at another, and he spoke of "that good man, the President, whom I have known for thirty years, whose character as a man of benevolence, talents and virtue dignify the human heart." [27]

Whether or not "public resentment was aroused against the calumniator," as William Duane of the *Aurora* informed Jefferson, the tenor of the latter's life was the best answer to him then, as it is now.[28] Callender said he would gladly go to court to prove the truthfulness of his charges, but that would have been to give them more publicity and to have smeared Jefferson further, regardless of the result. The President of the United States could have submitted to no such indignity. The fact that this story was not expressly and publicly denied proves nothing whatsoever. Without referring to it explicitly, Jefferson did deny it in private a few years later, when it was included in a list of charges against his morals that was hotly debated in Massachusetts. When he said that only one of these was based on truth, he was not speaking of this one.[29] That statement did not become public knowledge during his lifetime, however, nor in his century; and in the generation after his death the "miscegenation legend" was elaborated beyond Callender's version, taking on new dimensions of improbability. These later developments, and the reasons for them, belong to the history of the Jefferson image in the minds of his countrymen, and do not bear on the phase of his life we are now considering. We refer to them elsewhere in the present volume, but at this point in our narrative we leave the story of his slave Sally wrapped in the mantle of silence he himself placed upon it, believing that it deserved nothing more.[30]

A few weeks after opening the most scurrilous phase of his attack on his former benefactor, Callender announced in bold type: "Mrs. Walker in our next." When he actually got around to this topic, he paid his

[27] Robert Lawson, writing from Richmond, Oct. 16; reprinted from *Examiner* by *National Intelligencer*, Oct. 27, 1802.

[28] Duane, writing Oct. 18, 1802, wanted more information before repelling Callender's "monstrous calumnies," and hoped to get it on a projected visit to TJ (*Procs. Mass. Hist. Soc.*, 2 ser., II, 278). Apparently he did not do so.

[29] See p. 222, below.

[30] On the later developments, see Appendix II, below.

compliments to John Walker and his wife, while pillorying a "certain great personage," but there was real danger that his exposé would reflect on them as well.[31] The sensation-loving journalist, by publicizing a personal episode of a previous generation that had no bearing on public questions, was reopening a wound that time had partially if not wholly healed. He did this, he said, because the public have a right to be acquainted with the real character of officeholders. Also, no enemy could object to being attacked with his own weapons: a few years earlier the democrats had made a great noise over a personage of the other party (Hamilton), who had had illicit commerce with another man's wife, and what was sauce for the goose was sauce for the gander.[32] Since he himself was chiefly responsible for that noise, it may be said that Callender was now atoning for one ill deed by performing another. But the two cases did not represent a close parallel because a public issue was involved in the earlier one, if for no other reason. Nor could anybody at that time know as surely as we can that Jefferson, even in private, characteristically refrained from critical comments on the private morals of his political enemies. In such matters his standards were conventional and strict, but it was John Adams, not he, who waxed violent regarding the carnal sins alleged against Hamilton.

The nearest thing to such a sin that can be pinned on him occurred in connection with Mrs. Walker. As best we can construct a story of which no contemporary record has been found, Jefferson, at the age of twenty-five, made advances to the wife of an absent friend and neighbor that he himself described long afterwards as improper.[33] Without describing the circumstances in any way, he said that when young and single he "offered love to a handsome lady." That he did so more than once while still single is possible, but Walker's later private statement that, despite repeated rebuffs, he pursued the lady over more than a decade is virtually incredible. One of Jefferson's secretaries reported him as saying while President that his action was wholly unpremeditated and resulted from an accidental visit.[34] According to Walker's own account, his wife did not tell him of Jefferson's advances until after that neighbor had gone to France — which was a number of years

[31] The most important references to this affair in the *Recorder* in the fall of 1802 were on Oct. 13, 27 and Nov. 17.

[32] For this episode see *Jefferson and the Ordeal of Liberty*, pp. 326–331.

[33] In *Jefferson the Virginian*, I described the affair briefly, pp. 153–155, and at considerable length in Appendix III. Since then I have learned something more about developments in TJ's presidency, when Callender broke the story, but I remain uncertain about just what happened in the first place.

[34] W. A. Burwell in his Private Memoir in LC. I did not have this memoir when writing the account in *Jefferson the Virginian*.

after the event or events by any reckoning. The ensuing correspondence is not now known to exist, but it contained an admission on Jefferson's part that was described by Callender and others as a confession of baseness. Though the journalist threatened to publish the correspondence, the likelihood is that he had merely heard about it from Federalist friends of Walker.[35]

To what extent the affair was known and talked about prior to Jefferson's presidency is difficult if not impossible to ascertain. He himself is reported by his secretary to have said that it had long been known, and that Hamilton had threatened him with the exposure of it about the time of the Reynolds affair. His friends and supporters claimed, however, that there was no gossip among his neighbors about happenings *after* his marriage. It seems likely that local talk, such as there was, died down until he was involved in the fierce partisan conflicts of the last four or five years of the century, when the earlier story could easily have been exaggerated. He is reported to have believed that Mrs. Walker herself gave countenance to the *exposé* in his presidency.[36] If so, her personal enmity and political partisanship beclouded her judgment, for this sort of publicity could hardly have failed to bring her great embarrassment. Callender, contemplating the effects of his disclosures toward the end of the season in which he made them, said that if Jefferson's next election depended on the ladies of Virginia, he would hardly get a half dozen votes in the state.[37] Regardless of the political uses and effects of this story, its public resurrection caused John Walker to seek satisfaction from Jefferson beyond what he had received already. No doubt he was egged on by others, and John Page must have been thinking of these, as well as of Callender, when he wrote Jefferson in the spring of 1803: "Perdition seize the wretches who would open the scars of wounded friendship, to gratify private resentment and party spirit." [38]

By this time Madison had written confidentially to Monroe, who was already privy to it, that the affair had been happily cleared up.[39] Whether or not the two men met in person, or Walker was represented by an intermediary, Jefferson appears to have made some sort of written statement that was not to be published. Soon, however, he heard a

[35] Reference here is to correspondence *before* Callender publicized this matter, not to later exchanges.

[36] Report of W. A. Burwell.

[37] *Recorder,* Dec. 15, 1802.

[38] Page to TJ, Apr. 25, 1803. Slightly modernized from the exact quotation in *Jefferson the Virginian,* p. 451.

[39] Madison to Monroe, Apr. 20, 1803 (Hunt, VII, 48n.). Monroe had gone to France.

Republican report that the correspondence between him and Walker was being shown to Federalists with little discrimination.[40] Walker himself said that because of the failure to devise some way to inform the world that satisfaction had been given (as in private it had been), the only way he could protect his good name was to show the correspondence to friends.[41] There is clear evidence, also, that these papers were in demand among Federalists of high standing. Perhaps at the request of Francis Kinloch, a member of a prominent South Carolina family, Walker sent that gentleman a letter giving a brief account of the discussion with Jefferson early in 1803, along with a copy of a letter from Jefferson, containing the latter's admission. Neither document gave details about the original event or events that caused the trouble. Going abroad, Kinloch left these letters with his distinguished fellow South Carolinian and Federalist, Thomas Pinckney. Senator Uriah Tracy of Connecticut learned of them from David Meade Randolph who, after his dismissal as United States marshal, had sought as a bitter enemy of the administration to delay the remittance of Callender's fine. Senator Tracy, who gained the erroneous impression that all the papers bearing on what he called "the famous affair of our virtuous great man and Mrs. Walker" were in Pinckney's hands and subject to the latter's discretion, expressed a strong desire that they be sent to him. He preferred to receive them without restriction, but would be glad to do so under almost any restriction rather than not see them. In reply, besides describing what they actually were, Pinckney said they were not to be published. However, he agreed that if Walker did not object, the letters might be sent to Tracy, as presumably they were.[42] While Pinckney, a gentleman of the old school, was shocked by Jefferson's admission, he considered the trust that had been reposed on himself a "security from calumny" to the reputation of the injured person, not as a "political engine." But for Callender's vindictiveness, however, and Federalist eagerness to get something on Jefferson, the reputation of the person who was admittedly the injured party would not have been endangered. And this fragment of a story out of another generation was unquestionably used as a "political engine." This was shown early the next year in Massachusetts, where, after Jefferson's overwhelming re-election as President, the scandalous charges against him were debated in the House of Representatives, and both he and his old friend

[40] Unsigned letter received by TJ on May 20, 1803 (LC, 22772).
[41] Walker to Gen. Henry Lee, Mar. 28, 1805 (LC, 25833, originally from Lee Papers).
[42] Tracy to Pinckney, Mar. 6, 1804; Pinckney to Tracy, Apr. 3, 1804, and to Walker on the same date (all in Pinckney Papers, LC). No reply from Walker has been discovered.

Walker were discomfited anew. This episode occurred at a later date than we have reached in our political narrative, but it can be fittingly considered here.

Viewed in its setting of time and place, the attack on the conduct and character of the President that was made in the *New-England Palladium* of Boston on January 18, 1805, was clearly an act of political desperation.[43] In an unsigned article for which the publishers Messrs. Young and Minns, also printers to the State of Massachusetts, accepted responsibility, there were lunges at public acts and policies, because of or in spite of which the Republicans had swept the country. The article was an expression of utter irreconcilability. But, primarily, it was a sweeping attack on the private morals and personal character of Jefferson. It repeated the charges of cowardice during his governorship of Virginia made by a couple of his political enemies in the election campaign of 1796, fifteen years after the event, and never substantiated from contemporary records.[44] It renewed charges of irreligion such as had been made in connection with the return of Thomas Paine. It charged Jefferson with hiring Callender to invent scandalous lies and circulate violent falsehoods concerning Washington and every other good man in the country, referring to the deceased journalist as a "base calumniator." Nevertheless, without blanching, the author or authors accepted at face value all of Callender's scandalous calumnies of Jefferson. For palpable unfairness and undiscriminating castigation this tirade could hardly be matched in the writings of that wretch himself.

Not unnaturally it was regarded as outrageous by Republican members of the Massachusetts House of Representatives, who had greatly increased in number but still constituted a minority in that body. Instead of leaving the article to defeat itself by its own excess, one of these delegates moved that the House express disapproval of it. He consented to withdraw this motion when a fellow Republican offered a resolution that the printers of this "indecent and libelous publication" be no further employed by the General Court. This unwise resolution led to debates that impinged at times on public questions but in the course of which the indecent allegations were further exposed to view. Taking the position that an inquiry should be made to determine

[43] In an article entitled "The Monarchy of Federalism," which was ostensibly an attempt to ridicule charges of monarchy against the Federalists by attributing to the "Democrats" worse conduct than they reprobated. Its emphasis is better suggested by the title given it in the *N.Y. Evening Post*, Feb. 12, 1805: "Mr. Jefferson's Character." In that paper, on Feb. 27, appeared the first of a series entitled "Commonwealth of Massachusetts vs. Thomas Jefferson."
[44] See *Jefferson and the Ordeal of Liberty*, pp. 279–283.

whether or not the statements were actually misstatements, the Federalist majority caused the resolution to be referred to a committee. The printers defended themselves before this committee in writing, thus elaborating their allegations. The report of the committee showed that there was no need for any of this procedure. It properly held that the House had no right to censure or punish individuals except in the case of the breach of its own privileges, and that the rescinding of the contract with the printers was inexpedient since they had been guilty of no such breach. That is, Jefferson's moral guilt or innocence had nothing to do with the matter one way or the other. Nonetheless, his friends in the legislature insisted on seeking to vindicate his character, with the result that it was subjected to further debate in the course of which the lengthy written defense of the printers was read to the House. Not only so, it was shortly published, along with the debate.[45] The committee report was adopted, as it should have been, but the margin was slight: 91 to 85. The vote was not really on Jefferson's character, but no doubt his supporters thought it was, while his enemies were by no means averse to blackening him.

In the debate John W. Hulbert of Sheffield, the leader on the Federalist side, assumed a tone of condescension when referring to the accusation that Jefferson had taken a "sable damsel" to his bosom: he knew not whether the charge was true or false but had no disposition to scrutinize it. "If it be true," he said, "it is to be presumed that Mr. Jefferson considers it excusable." The legislator had been told that the custom of the country where Mr. Jefferson resided "warranted the practice, and, de gustibus non est disputandum." [46]

As to the Walker story, Messrs. Young and Minns said they had this on the testimony of reputable gentlemen, and that nothing in Jefferson's character provided presumptive evidence against it. Indeed, they argued that other things he had done and the religious unbelief he had expressed showed that he might be expected to make such an attempt. "He might think, with Hume and other infidels, that even adultery, when known, was a small crime; when unknown, none at all." [47] The chief spokesman for the Federalists did not need to argue from the tenor of Jefferson's moral life, thus adjudged to be evil. Hulbert showed such a knowledge of events, as revealed in confidence to Francis Kinloch and others by John Walker, as to cause the latter gentleman

[45] Alexander Young, *The Defence of Young and Minns, Printers to the State, before the Committee of the House of Representatives.* With appendix, containing the debate, etc. (Boston, 1805). The debate on the resolution was on Jan. 31, 1805; that on the report on Feb. 14.

[46] *Ibid.*, p. 55.

[47] *Ibid.*, p. 14.

to express wonderment at his sources of information. The legislator even mentioned the name of General Henry (Light Horse Harry) Lee as the bearer of a letter demanding satisfaction.[48]

At some time in the course of this reopened controversy Walker sent Lee, his wife's nephew and his trusted agent in it, a detailed account of the original events as reported by his wife years after they purportedly occurred. For reasons that are more fully given elsewhere, the story in this form may be regarded as grossly exaggerated and unbelievable.[49] It was considerably worse than the one told by Hulbert in the Massachusetts House of Representatives and may be assumed not to have circulated in Federalist circles at this time.[50] There is no reason to suppose that Jefferson ever saw it or that he ever attested to its accuracy by any private admission to Walker. The only statement of his about the affair that can now be quoted in so many words was made after the Massachusetts debate. That debate was promptly reported to him by an indignant supporter who urged him to take suitable measures to bring Hulbert to "condign punishment." [51] He did not follow that advice but, some weeks later, he took occasion to enlarge the very small circle of friends who shared his intimate confidence with respect to the charges against his moral character, particularly the Walker affair. Madison, Monroe (before going abroad), and the President's secretary were already in his confidence; and before revealing himself to lesser members of the Cabinet he must have done so to Gallatin, and also to Dearborn. In the summer of 1805, he wrote a letter to Robert Smith, secretary of the navy, which has been fortunately preserved. In this he said:

> The inclosed copy of a letter to Mr. [Levi] Lincoln will so fully explain it's own object, that I need say nothing in that way. I communicate it to particular friends because I wish to stand with them on the ground of truth, neither better nor worse than that makes me. You will perceive that I plead guilty to one of their charges, that when young and single I offered love to a handsome lady. I acknowledge its incorrectness. It is the only one founded on truth among all their allegations against me. . . .[52]

---

[48] Walker to Lee, Mar. 28, 1805 (LC, 25833, formerly in Lee Papers). He had received from a friend a copy of the debate.

[49] See *Jefferson the Virginian*, pp. 449–450, where it is given in full from an undated copy in Lee's handwriting. Originally in the Lee Papers, it is now filed with the Jefferson Papers in LC through no choice of his.

[50] Perhaps Walker drafted this account after the Massachusetts debate in a mood of exacerbation. I previously thought it likely that he sent it to Lee with his letter of Mar. 28, 1805, but am now less disposed to that opinion.

[51] Isaac Story of Marblehead to TJ, Feb. 8, 1805, sending the *Columbian Centinel* of Feb. 6, reporting debate of Jan. 31 (Bixby, pp. 110–111).

[52] TJ to Smith, July 1, 1805 (Bixby, pp. 114–115). Originally he had planned to

This private statement contains all that we really know about Jefferson's original part in this widely publicized affair. It does not quite end the private story, for there were further negotiations looking to the satisfaction of John Walker, though information about these is fragmentary. Early in the following year, John Randolph heard and sarcastically reported the rumor that the President and Walker had met at Madison's, through his mediation and that of Lee, but if this was true the report that peace was fully restored was premature.[53] A few weeks later and again in September, while visiting at nearby Belvoir, Lee conferred with Jefferson at Monticello. Apparently Walker wanted something further in writing, and a paper of some sort may have been drafted soon after the latter meeting. This seems unlikely, however, and nothing was to be published at any rate, though Jefferson was quite willing to exculpate the lady in private.[54] Silence seems to have fallen on the episode during the last years of his presidency, but social relations between him and the Walkers appear never to have been restored. Both of them died in 1809 and toward the very end Jefferson sent to Belvoir a little present of fruit, which was graciously received. The disappearance and presumable destruction of the papers relating to this private affair strongly suggest that there was a desire on both sides to relegate it to oblivion.[55]

---

send also papers relating to the charges against him as governor of Va., but these were to be otherwise taken care of. His reference was to a defense of his conduct in a series of articles in the Richmond *Enquirer*, beginning Aug. 23, 1805. It should be noted that the letter to Smith did not appear in print until 1916. The fuller letter to Lincoln has not been discovered. Presumably it was returned to TJ with accompanying papers. We have, therefore, little more than a covering letter.

[53] Randolph to J. H. Nicholson, Feb. 24, 1806 (Nicholson Papers, LC, 3:1354a). Henry Lee, Jr., in a letter of Aug. 24, 1833, to Richard T. Brown, which was intended for the perusal of President John Tyler, said this meeting did occur at the insistence of his father (Tyler Papers, LC, ser. 1, vol. 1, folio 6322). The purpose of the letter was to demonstrate that the younger Lee, known to have been guilty of an act of gross immorality, was no more blamable than Jefferson, whom he claimed Tyler idolized.

[54] Later negotiations are referred to in Lee's letter of Sept. 8, 1806, to TJ (now in LC, 28252–28253), and in Stephen Sayre's to TJ, Nov. 15, 1806 (LC, 28454–28457). The great question was how to let this exculpation become known without making it public, and we do not know what the precise answer was.

[55] The few intimate documents we have cited were preserved by Henry Lee, whose personal relations with TJ were generally unfriendly.

[XIII]

Freedom and Licentiousness

1802–1805

CONSIDERING the extent and severity of the attacks on Jefferson's morals during his presidency, his apparent ability to brush them off is remarkable. No doubt his progressive disillusionment with the press during his administration was, in part at least, a reflection of his resentment of the outrageous charges against him as a person, but his philosophy impelled him to distinguish sharply between private and public matters, as he did so notably in the field of religion. The scurrilous newspapers of the day made no such distinction; everything was grist for their mill. That the line should sometimes have become blurred in his own mind is not surprising; he had not reached such a height of sainthood or philosophical detachment that it made no difference to him whose ox was gored. But greater than the temptation to interpret unreasonable attacks on his public conduct as personal was that to regard them as unfair attempts to defeat the will of the sovereign people, which he had increasing reason to believe his government represented. In opposing the Sedition Act, however, he and his followers had urged the necessity of public discussion and emphasized the danger of restrictions of the press. If the country had emerged from a reign of terror, into what sort of regimen had it come? The question of President Jefferson's attitude toward the press deserves asking, though we are concerned here with his first term only.

Shortly before reaching the halfway point in that term, he strongly expressed himself on this subject in a private letter to a man of learning in Europe. After saying that the citizens of the country generally were enjoying "a very great degree of liberty and security in the most temperate manner," he added these words of warning against what might be seen in print: "Our newspapers, for the most part, present only the caricatures of disaffected minds. Indeed, the abuses of the freedom of the press here have been carried to a length never before known or borne by any civilized nation." [1] In this statement he made no distinction between the papers opposing and those supporting him, but, being human, no doubt he had the former particularly in mind. Political enemies of his attributed his election to the effectiveness of the Republican press when his party was in opposition. Fisher Ames had written: "The newspapers are an overmatch for any government. They will first overawe and then usurp it. This has been done, and the jacobins owe their triumph to the unceasing use of this engine." [2] Though the Republicans had considerably fewer papers than their rivals during the Adams administration, they may have had as many or more that were strongly partisan. Jefferson's administration was marked by the creation, either by establishment or transformation, of Federalist "electioneering papers," the virulence of which increased as time went on.[3] Meanwhile, the Republican papers increased in number, partly because they now had the advantage of the official printing, and as supporters of the administration they naturally tended to be more restrained than they had been in opposition. By and large, however, they were not well edited and their standards of taste were low.

The one most closely associated with the administration, the *National Intelligencer*, was moderate in tone and tried to avoid controversy. William Duane of the *Aurora* (Philadelphia) was a vigorous champion of the measures of the government, but he spent much of his energy on local vendettas and in Pennsylvania was a rather divisive factor. Jefferson regarded him as over-zealous but treated him with great respect and retained his confidence.[4] The Republican chieftain had tolerated excess in his loyal supporters when seeking to oust the Federalists, but such personal influence as he exercised on the party press as President, directly or indirectly, was on the side of moderation. This was particularly true with respect to partisanship in the matter of appointments. In 1804, after the demise of the *Examiner* in Richmond, Thomas Ritchie established the *Enquirer* in that Federalist stronghold in Jefferson's own state. This came to be an immensely influential regional paper, noted for high ethical standards, but it played relatively little part in the controversies of his first term. In dealing with national

[1] TJ to M. Pictet, Feb. 5, 1803 (L. & B., X, 356–357).
[2] Ames to John Rutledge, Jr., Oct. 16, 1800, quoted in D. H. Fischer, *Revolution of American Conservatism: The Federalist Party in the Era of Jeffersonian Democracy*, (1965), p. 135. The discussion of the Federalist press in this work, ch. VII and Appendix III, is informative and illuminating.
[3] The apt expression "electioneering paper" is used by Fischer, who gives on p. 424 the tests applied. See also his tables in Appendix III.
[4] TJ to Madison, Aug. 29, 1803 (MP, 26:27).

affairs, the *Enquirer* was much more like the *National Intelligencer* than the *Aurora*, and there is significance in the fact that Duane, the aggressively partisan publisher of the latter, and moderate Thomas Ritchie disliked each other.[5]

Whether the newspapers of the country as a whole were more scurrilous than they had been during Adams's presidency, and whether the opposition journals were less scrupulous than the Republican, are arguable questions, but undoubtedly the Jeffersonian experiment in self-government was conducted in a dark era in American journalism, an era in which the papers evinced a degree of irresponsibility and licentiousness hardly conceivable to those who have not actually read them.[6] As newsgatherers they made distinct advances in this period, but all too often the editorial comment, which was now coming to be a recognized feature of a newspaper, was bitter and unreasonable. The same can be said of many of the contributions. Under these circumstances many things were said by papers of the opposition that would have rankled in the breast of any chief executive. Jefferson, who was confident of popular support and determined to retain it, did not brush off these taunts, gibes, and misrepresentations as readily as he did unwarranted and irrelevant strictures on his private morals, but he was rarely disposed to do anything about them.

He had been in office only slightly more than a year when he informed his attorney general of his position with respect to the highly offensive journalists. It was that of a practical man, facing an actual situation. More than two decades earlier, in his noble Bill for Establishing Religious Freedom, he had asserted that "the opinions of men are not the object of civil government, nor under its jurisdiction." Contemporaries of his in the legislature of his state, unwilling to go that far, had deleted this, but he himself could have been fittingly described from that point onward as an absolutist with respect to the freedom of religious opinion. For that cause he suffered much. But, as the responsible head of the government, he voiced no approval of the doctrine, recently advanced by a Republican writer, that freedom of the press, like chastity, is either absolute or non-existent; and, in comparison with other formulators of libertarian philosophy in his own party, he appears to have been in important respects a relativist rather than an absolutist at this stage.[7] Thus, while dismissing the idea of governmental

[5] C. H. Ambler, *Thomas Ritchie, A Study in Virginia Politics* (1913), pp. 19–20.
[6] See F. L. Mott, *American Journalism* (1941), pp. 167–208.
[7] The statement about the absolute freedom of the press was that of George Hay in *Essay on the Freedom of the Press* (1799, reprinted 1803), as cited by L. W. Levy in *Jefferson and Civil Liberties* (1963), p. 53. Levy takes the position, rightly in my opinion, that TJ contributed little to the "new libertarianism," ad-

action against abuses of the press, he spoke of the impracticability and inexpediency of this, rather than its impropriety. He summed up his current thinking in these words:

> While a full range is proper for actions by individuals, either private or public, for slanders affecting them, I would wish much to see the experiment tried of getting along without public prosecutions for *libels*. I believe we can do it. Patience and well doing, instead of punishment, if it can be found sufficiently efficacious, would be a happy change in the instruments of government.[8]

Thus he candidly stated that his own policy was experimental; and, while hoping that prosecutions by government itself could be avoided at all levels, he held that the power to prosecute and punish gross abuses of the freedom of the press existed somewhere. In constitutional discussions before this time he had made clear his belief that this regulatory authority lay with the several states. All of them, he said, had made provisions for punishing slander, and those persons who had time and inclination could resort to these laws for the "vindication of their characters." He approved these laws, by and large, but held that they went too far where they did not permit the truth of allegations to be presented as a defense.[9] The few prosecutions of Federalist journalists, allegedly licentious, that occurred in his first term were instituted in behalf of states, the cases being tried in state courts. In this period there appear to have been only two of these worthy of note, as compared with some fourteen indictments under the federal Sedition Act and three at common law in the last two years of the Adams administration.[10]

Also, it may be noted that in states where Federalists controlled the courts, they were by no means averse to legal proceedings against Republican journalists in "vindication of their characters." A case in Massachusetts in the spring of 1803 is of special interest. The printer of the Salem *Register*, William Carlton, convicted at the court in Ipswich

---

vanced in theory by Tunis Wortman and other Republicans about the turn of the century. To this one can agree, however, without accepting this critic's value judgments.

[8] TJ to Levi Lincoln, Mar. 24, 1802 (Ford, VIII, 139). Though apparently referring to attacks on the government and its officials, he did not use the expression "seditious libel," and may have deliberately avoided it.

[9] TJ to Abigail Adams, Sept. 11, 1804 (*A.-J. Letters*, I, 279). See also his statement in the Kentucky Resolutions (*Jefferson and the Ordeal of Liberty*, p. 403).

[10] Possibly there were other cases that have not come to my attention, but these can hardly have changed the *relative* situation. Speaking of Jefferson's entire presidency, a liberty-loving historian has said that, when put to the test, "he rated far above his predecessor but somewhat under A Plus." (Irving Brant, *The Bill of Rights: Its Origins and Meaning* [1965], p. 312.)

in April of libel on Timothy Pickering, was imprisoned for sixty days, fined $100, and required on release to give security for good behavior to the amount of some $800. According to that rare Jeffersonian among New England clergymen the Reverend William Bentley, who loathed Pickering and his "enraged faction," such were the consequences of "touching the contentious Ex-Secretary." [11] In his diary, Bentley also wrote that, even if the charge against the Republican printer should be deemed just, "yet when we consider the great provocations which have been given from the licentiousness with which the President and all his friends have been treated, we can but be astonished at the effrontery of such proceedings." [12]

Of the two notable prosecutions of Federalist editors by Republicans, those of Joseph Dennie in Pennsylvania and Harry Croswell in New York, the former should concern us more, since Jefferson appears to have been connected with it. The first move toward it was not made by him, however, but by the state authorities.[13] Dennie was the editor of the *Port Folio*, a weekly devoted to literature and politics, in which all things Jeffersonian were castigated. In the middle of January, 1803, the following bit of editorial comment appeared in this Philadelphia publication:

> We have seen, in the speech of one state executive officer, to the legislature, a pointed allusion to what he is pleased to call "the abuse of the noblest invention of man, the best preservation of civil liberty, a *free press*," and to which he ascribes all the discord and discontent prevalent in the country. As a corrective of these abuses, the same speech suggests the expediency of "the discipline of the laws." [14]

About three weeks later, Governor Thomas McKean wrote President Jefferson a long letter, describing in detail the political situation in Pennsylvania.[15] This was highly gratifying to the Republicans, he said:

[11] Pickering, whom Adams had dismissed from his Cabinet, had recently returned from Pennsylvania to his native state. He suffered unexpected defeat as a candidate for the national House of Representatives in the autumn of 1802, but recouped his political fortunes sufficiently to be elected by the legislature to the U.S. Senate in the following year.

[12] Apr. 25, 1803, the day Carlton was sentenced; see also entries for Apr. 21 and June 25 (William Bentley, *Diary* [1802–1810], III, 20, 28–29).

[13] The account of TJ's connection, actual or supposed, with these cases by L. W. Levy in *Legacy of Suppression* (1960), pp. 300–301, and *Jefferson and Civil Liberties*, pp. 58–59, in my opinion is based on inadequate knowledge of the circumstances and is unfair to TJ.

[14] *Port Folio*, Jan. 15, 1803.

[15] McKean to TJ, Feb. 7, 1803 (LC, 22325–22326), received Feb. 11; apparently not seen by Levy.

in the last general election the sense of the people had been "unequivocally declared in favor of our democratic representative government and the present administration." But, while pleased with the conduct of the people, he was far from pleased with that of the press and asked Jefferson's advice and consent before doing something about it:

> The infamous & seditious libels, published almost daily in our newspapers, are become intolerable. If they cannot be altogether prevented, yet they may be greatly checked by a few prosecutions: I have had it for some time in contemplation to make the experiment but as the President, Congress, and several of the principal officers of the U.S. have been frequently implicated, I have declined it until I should obtain your advice & consent. This vice is become a national one, and calls aloud for redress.

The recipient of this letter was generally less disposed to advise local leaders in whom he had confidence than to consent to whatever tactics they thought desirable in their own localities. Rarely if ever did he exercise a veto on their measures. The situation in Pennsylvania was specially delicate because of the feuds in the party there. Into these Jefferson was careful not to enter, but his sympathies and those of Gallatin lay with the moderates, with whom at this time he identified McKean. The Governor was also a fellow signer of the Declaration of Independence, always a consideration of weight with the author of that document. Jefferson may have been forewarned about the rigorous attitude of McKean, a former judge, toward critics, but he himself had recently, in private, condemned the newspapers in even more sweeping terms. At the same time, however, he had described the policy that he had thought best to follow thus far: namely, to rely wholly on the good judgment of the public to distinguish between the abuse and wholesome use of the press.[16] His assent to the Governor's suggestion a couple of weeks later signalized no change in federal procedure, but it revealed a lessening in his faith, as the fresh arguments now advanced by him showed his increased fears.

> The federalists having failed in destroying the freedom of the press by their gag-law, seem to have attacked it in an opposite form, that is by pushing its licentiousness & its lying to such a degree of prostitution as to deprive it of all credit. And the fact is that so abandoned are the tory presses in this particular that even the least informed of the people have learnt that nothing in a newspaper is to be believed. This is a dangerous state of things, and the press

16 TJ to M. Pictet, Feb. 5, 1803 (L. & B., X, 357).

ought to be restored to its credibility if possible. The restraints provided by the laws of the states are sufficient for this if applied. And I have therefore long thought that a few prosecutions of the most prominent offenders would have a wholesome effect in restoring the integrity of the presses. Not a general prosecution, for that would look like persecution: but a selected one. . . .[17]

This, then, was to be a limited experiment, conducted under the laws, not of the United States, but of Pennsylvania. He hoped that similar action would be taken in some other states, believing that the results would be salutary. During the period we are considering, apparently he did nothing directly to encourage such action anywhere else, but while writing McKean he made a specific suggestion with reference to Pennsylvania. He enclosed a paper which seemed to him "to offer as good an instance in every respect to make an example of" as could be imagined. However, he left the Governor to judge.

Since we do not have the paper that he sent McKean, we cannot surely know what or whom he had in mind. The editor actually indicted, five months later, was Joseph Dennie of the *Port Folio*, a publication better described as a magazine than a newspaper. What is more, the specific libel with which he was charged did not appear until two months after the President wrote the Governor.[18] Whoever may have been responsible for selecting Dennie, he was undeniably a likely subject: no one in that period satirized Jefferson more unmercifully or with comparable wit and literary skill.[19] Among passages the President could have read in the *Port Folio* by this time were a number that were much more personal than the one selected by the Pennsylvania authorities. From this treasurehouse of Federalist satire could have been drawn such a gem as this:

> The *circle* of our President's *felicities* is greatly enlarged by the indulgence of Sally, the sable, and the auspicious arrival of Tom Paine, the pious.[20]

As a classicist, the President himself might have been impressed by an ode in imitation of Horace, which was addressed to him a week later, and as a naturalist by one paragraph in particular:

[17] TJ to Gov. Thomas McKean, Feb. 19, 1803 (Ford, VIII, 218–219).

[18] Respublica *vs.* Dennie (4 *Yeates'* [Pa.] *Reports* [1805], 266–268). An indictment for libel, based on a passage in the *Port Folio*, Apr. 23, 1803, was found in the July sessions, 1803, in the Mayor's Court. The case was removed to the Pa. supreme court in its December term. A decision of "Not Guilty" was rendered in Philadelphia in November, 1805.

[19] See H. M. Ellis, *Joseph Dennie and His Circle* (1915), ch. X.

[20] *Port Folio*, Jan. 15, 1803.

> Resume thy shells and butterflies,
> Thy beetle's heads, and lizard's thighs,
>   The state no more controul:
> Thy tricks, with *sooty Sal,* give o'er;
> Indulge thy body, Tom, no more;
>   But try to save thy *soul.*[21]

The passage cited in the libel action, however, did not refer to the President. It was a tirade against democracy by a literary man who did not bother to define his terms but was incensed by any and all attempts to broaden the base of government and popularize its operations. After asserting that the futility of democracy had been demonstrated wherever this form of government had been tried, he continued:

> It is on its trial here, and the issue will be civil war, desolation and anarchy. No wise man but discerns its imperfections, no good man but shudders at its miseries, no honest man but proclaims its fraud, and no brave man but draws his sword against its force. The institution of a scheme of polity so radically contemptible and vicious, is a memorable example of what the villainy of some men can devise, the folly of others receive, and both establish, in despite of reason, reflection, and sensation.

The term democracy had by no means gained the general acceptance it was to attain in later years in America, and in fact was very rarely employed by Jefferson, who never forgot that in the morning of the Republic it had been commonly equated with mobocracy. But to him and his followers this violently reactionary language could not have failed to seem deserving of stern rebuke. The propriety of the attempt to prove it libelous in a court of law is, however, quite another question, and even on practical grounds the action was unwise. According to the provision of the Pennsylvania constitution under which Dennie was tried, the jury could decide on libel by the fact as well as the law, and the defendant could introduce evidence in attestation of the truthfulness of his alleged libel. This, in Jefferson's view, was his right. But neither the truthfulness nor the untruthfulness of what was in reality a violent expression of opinion could be satisfactorily demonstrated. Many times postponed, the case was not tried until Jefferson had entered upon his second term, and the defendant was then acquitted. The editor regarded himself as triumphant thus far in his warfare with the "fiend" Democracy, but in the meantime his violence had considerably abated. The same could not be said of McKean's zeal against "libeling";

[21] *Ibid.,* Jan. 22, 1803.

this was more extreme in later years than when the President first sanctioned it.[22]

There is no known comment of Jefferson's on the more famous case of Harry Croswell, who was actually tried sooner than Joseph Dennie and, unlike the latter, was convicted. Another difference was that the alleged libel of Croswell, editor of a sheet called *The Wasp* in Hudson, New York — a paper which "became a symbol of unrestrained scurrility" — was not an attack on the principles of the existing federal government but on the President himself.[23] On September 9, 1802, this paper said:

> Jefferson paid Callender for calling Washington a traitor, a robber, and a perjurer; for calling Adams a hoary-headed incendiary; and for most grossly slandering the private characters of men whom he well knew were virtuous. These charges, not a democratic editor has yet dared, or ever will dare, to meet in an open and manly discussion.[24]

Governor George Clinton of New York did not enjoy Jefferson's intimacy, but he was a powerful ally. Republican officials initiated and conducted this case in a spirit of thoroughgoing partisanship. We can only speculate about Jefferson's attitude toward it.[25] Since he stated specifically to McKean that more than one prosecution of licentious journalists was desirable, he might have been expected to approve of this one; and disapproval of it, after it got started, would not have been in line with his general policy of non-interference in state matters. George Clinton was not the sort of man he would normally have told what *not* to do in his own commonwealth.

There is, however, no ground for assuming the President's approval of the illiberality that marked the procedure in this case. New York law did not require that truth be recognized as a defense; and at the trial in the circuit court in July, 1803, the Republican presiding judge ruled that it could not be, saying that the only question before the jury was whether the defendant had actually published the libelous passage. It was not for them to decide that it was or was not libelous. Though

---

[22] For Dennie, see Ellis, p. 184. For McKean, especially in 1806–1807, see S. W. Higginbotham, *The Keystone in the Democratic Arch* (1952), pp. 123–125.

[23] The characterization of *The Wasp* is that of Fischer, p. 141.

[24] Quoted in People *vs.* Croswell (3 *Johnson's* [N.Y.] *Cases*, 336, 339 [1904]).

[25] Levy in *Legacy of Suppression*, p. 299, says it would not be surprising if a letter from TJ to Clinton, recommending this sort of action, should be discovered. This is a presumptuous statement, though of course there is the *possibility* of such a discovery.

Jefferson did not specifically mention this case when writing Abigail Adams a few months later, and could not have been expected to welcome the exposure of the Callender episode in open court since it had been exposed too much already, he explicitly said that when a state denied a defendant the opportunity to prove his charges it went too far.[26] This particular case derives much of its historic significance from the fact that Alexander Hamilton, as counsel for Croswell, appealed to the supreme court of the state for a new trial on this ground, and said some notable things about freedom of the press in his argument.[27] He lost his appeal, but in 1805 the law of the state was liberalized and in the August term of that year Croswell was granted a new trial.[28] In the meantime, however, *The Wasp* had gone out of existence and ceased to sting the President. This immediate victory of New York Republicanism appears to have been the only tangible success of the limited experiment in selected prosecutions in state courts.

In the light of what actually happened in Jefferson's first term, we must ask if he was warranted in saying what he did about the press and its freedom in three eloquent paragraphs of his second inaugural.[29] With due allowance for rhetoric, he was clearly justified in asserting that the "artillery of the press" had been directed against his administration, "charged with whatsoever its licentiousness could devise or dare." As one who was fully aware of the importance of the press to science as well as to freedom and who had conspicuously encouraged it, he deeply and properly regretted its indubitable abuses. His own partisans shared the blame for the excesses, to be sure, but he probably thought that he had been more assailed than his predecessor, with less reason. His assertion that the abuses might have been corrected by the "wholesome punishments" provided by state laws against falsehood and defamation has been disapproved of, in our own day, by libertarians more absolutist than he, but it was consistent with what he had said elsewhere, in public and private. The following statement is more questionable: "but public duties more urgent press on the time of public

---

[26] TJ to Abigail Adams, Sept. 11, 1804 (*A.-J. Letters*, I, 279).

[27] Feb. 13, 1804. Extracts from his argument are conveniently assembled in R. B. Morris, *Alexander Hamilton and the Founding of the Nation* (1957), pp. 480–485. It can be seen in full form in Julius Goebel, Jr., ed., *Law Practice of Alexander Hamilton*, I (1964), 775–848.

[28] In *Legacy of Suppression*, p. 299, Levy points out that Judge Brockholst Livingston, who was against the appeal and held "reactionary views" regarding freedom of the press, was afterwards appointed to the U.S. Supreme Court by TJ. It does not follow, however, that TJ approved of Livingston's position in this particular matter and appointed him for that reason.

[29] Mar. 4, 1805 (Ford, VIII, 346–347).

servants, and the offenders have therefore been left to find their punishment in the public indignation." Had he conveniently overlooked
occurrences in New York and his own private letter to the Governor
of Pennsylvania?

Probably he was not speaking of public servants in states; he would
not have thought it proper to speak for them, and his reference to the
enforcement of state laws against "false and defamatory publications"
was unmistakable. It was "a service to public morals and public tranquillity," he said, to reform these abuses by these "salutary coercions." If
he incorrectly implied that, in furtherance of such purpose, Republican
state officials had taken no time whatever, he would have been warranted
in saying that they had taken relatively little. And if he had been disposed
to dwell on the danger of employing legal means for purposes of political persecution, he could have found examples in Federalist conduct in
New England. Most likely, his intended reference was to himself and
the federal government, no direct action of which against an offending
newspaperman in this period has been alleged. He might have truthfully added that he had gone to great pains to maintain a hands-off
policy with respect to the affairs of the several states, and that he spent
far more effort in discouraging excessive zeal among his own partisans
than in exciting them.

If, however, he had been called upon to answer allegations that he
had failed to live up to his own ideals and public representations, his
best response would not have been an attempt to explain away particular episodes. Just as the most convincing answer to the charges against
his morals is provided by the tenor of his private life, his attitude toward the press and its freedom is best and most fully revealed in the
general tenor of his policy and conduct as he bore the enormous responsibilities of his high office, seeking to make democratic government
a success as well as a reality and to control his party while leading it.
Lapses and unwise actions need not be palliated, but the wisdom and
success of the major experiment should not be obscured by these. The
main question, as he correctly said, was "whether freedom of discussion, unaided by power, is not sufficient for the propagation and protection of truth — whether a government, conducting itself in the true
spirit of its constitution, with zeal and purity, and doing no act which it
would be unwilling the whole world would witness, can be written
down by falsehood and defamation." His government did not attain
that degree of purity and candor; he made more concessions to political
expediency than he would admit, and he veered at times from a constitutional path that was too narrow for large movement; but on balance
he conducted in his first term a highly successful experiment. The suc-

cess of this, as he perceived much more clearly than did his two presidential predecessors and as a number of Federalist leaders during his presidency grudgingly admitted, was contingent on popular support. With some important exceptions, chiefly in New England, he gained that support in notable measure, and the fortunate course of international developments permitted him to minimize the importance of force in the conduct of government. The extraordinary support the people gave him may be attributed chiefly to the public recognition of the democratic spirit and the actual achievements of his government.

If the counsel he gave Governor McKean marked the lowest point of his faith and the highest of his fears in his first term, a letter he wrote in the summer of 1804 to an ardent admirer in Virginia showed that his characteristic mood of confidence had returned. In this he said: "The firmness with which the people have withstood the late abuses of the press, the discernment they have manifested between truth and falsehood, show that they may safely be trusted to hear everything true and false, and to form a correct judgment between them." [30] While admitting that he might err in his measures, he asserted that nothing would deflect him from the "*intention* to fortify the public liberty by every possible means." In this light, such countenancing of public prosecutions for libel as he may have been guilty of, in this period, may be viewed as a momentary aberration on the part of a devotee of freedom who recognized, nonetheless, that politics is the art of the possible.

[30] TJ to Judge John Tyler, June 28, 1804 (L. & B., XI, 33; replying to a letter of June 10 [LC, 24425-24426]). Italics added.

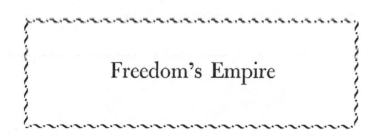

Freedom's Empire

[XIV]

Impending Crisis in the West

A S Jefferson had anticipated, the peace that descended on war-weary Europe and the Atlantic world in the autumn of his first year as President provided a climate favorable to the sort of domestic regime he purposed to establish.[1] Accordingly, in 1801–1802 he pursued with increasing confidence policies designed to minimize government while democratizing it, and to lighten the burdens and enlarge the freedom of the citizenry. In the domestic field his administration was an immediate beneficiary of the peace. It was ironical, therefore, that the gravest diplomatic problems of his first term should have arisen during the brief lull in the European war — problems which occasioned belligerent talk at home and threatened the Union. The most critical period roughly coincided with the second session of his first Congress in the winter of 1802–1803, and the major problem was not resolved by the acquisition of Louisiana until after the war had been resumed.

At the outset this was not a territorial but a commercial question, centering on provisions of the treaty of San Lorenzo of 1795 with Spain, the possessor of Louisiana and the Floridas. That settlement, which was highly favorable to the United States, was negotiated on the American side by Thomas Pinckney after Jefferson's retirement from the secretaryship of state, but in a real sense he was its architect, since it followed the lines he had laid down.[2] By the second year of his presidency the men of the western waters had taken extensive advantage of the free navigation of the Mississippi in all its length and breadth, which was recognized as an American right, and also of the permission to deposit their goods in New Orleans, pending their exportation, without the payment of custom duties. Perhaps a dozen American flatboats floated down the river to New Orleans in 1792, while upwards of 500

---

[1] See above, p. 95.
[2] See *Jefferson and the Rights of Man*, pp. 406–411.

river craft did so ten years later.[3] There were other reasons for the rapid growth and increased prosperity of the trans-Appalachian region, but the treaty of San Lorenzo was a very important one; and, fortunately for the Union, this growing commerce was redounding to the economic advantage of Easterners as well, especially merchants and shippers in Middle Atlantic cities.

The basic cause of the crisis of 1802–1803 was the retrocession of the province of Louisiana by Spain, whose hard-pressed officials had granted Americans privileges beyond what the treaty actually called for, to France, the most rapacious and aggressive of the Powers. There was a secret agreement in 1800, to be carried into effect later, news of which gradually leaked out. The precipitating cause of American excitement was the closure of the deposit at New Orleans by the Spanish Intendant in the autumn of 1802. This surprising action, which was regarded by high Spanish officials in the New World no less than by Americans as a violation of the treaty of San Lorenzo, precipitated a domestic political crisis in the United States. By weathering this and keeping the channels of diplomacy open until the controversy was settled more advantageously than even he had hoped, Jefferson gained an overwhelming political victory while assuring the welfare of the Mississippi Valley and the physical greatness of his country. There was a considerable element of luck in his diplomatic triumph, but his success was greatly facilitated by the powerful backing he had from the region most involved — the West.

A score of years earlier he had expressed a "peculiar confidence in the men from the western side of the mountains." [4] The events of his administration were to show that these men, and especially their political leaders, had a "peculiar confidence" in him as one who, fully understanding their problems, was doing all he could to help them while leaving them the freedom to help themselves. His record as an advocate of western development and self-government was clear and consistent. He had favored the formation of the state of Kentucky from Virginia's counties below the Ohio, and had played a stellar role in the cession by his own commonwealth of its claims to the imperial domain afterwards incorporated in the Northwest Territory. Then, as a member of the Continental Congress, he laid down the lines on which the expansion of

[3] A. P. Whitaker, in his admirable study *The Mississippi Question, 1795–1803* (1934), pp. 150–154, gives these figures and other valuable statistics. He points out, on p. 52, that the first exercise of the right of free navigation of the Mississippi by an American vessel was in December, 1796, and that the formal establishment of the deposit in New Orleans was in April, 1798.

[4] TJ to J. P. G. Muhlenberg, Jan. 31, 1781 (*Boyd*, IV, 487).

the Union from the original thirteen states actually occurred. The basic principle, which came to be commonly accepted but which he recognized from the very first and explicitly stated, was that new states were to be created out of the national domain by successive steps, being admitted to the Union, when sufficiently populous, as peers of the older commonwealths.

No one more than he deserves to be described as the architect of orderly expansion, and at every stage he upheld the interests of the actual settlers, seeking to facilitate their acquisition of land and to prevent the exploitation of the vast interior by privileged land companies. He sought to bind the West to the East by extending to it the full benefits of political union and the right of self-government. If he had erred it was through excess of faith in the region, not fear of its development. The same could not be said of the most conspicuous Federalist leaders, and Westerners naturally preferred him to them. In the presidential election of 1796 he got no votes north and east of the Delaware River and expected none, but there was no doubt then or in 1800 of his support by the men beyond the mountains. This support might be accounted for on the ground of his policies and democratic emphasis alone, by contrast with those of the Federalists, but it is an important historical fact that the first settlers and their first political leaders naturally gave allegiance to Virginia because of their origins. Furthermore, although Jefferson himself never went beyond the Shenandoah Valley, he maintained close personal and political ties with these leaders at all times.

Before he became President, only two states had been formed in the trans-Appalachian country, Kentucky and Tennessee. Until after the treaty of Greenville with the Indians in 1795, following the victory of "Mad" Anthony Wayne at Fallen Timbers, settlement north of the Ohio River was slow, but it proceeded rapidly during the latter half of the last decade in the century, and the state of Ohio was admitted to the Union in the middle of Jefferson's first term. From the outset all three of these new commonwealths were strongly Republican. With the political leaders of Kentucky, which was an outpost of Virginia and had acted in close accord with the mother state in the controversies of the Adams administration, Jefferson's connection was intimate. John Breckinridge, who had come to the bluegrass country from Albemarle County and was the spokesman of his former neighbor in the Kentucky Resolutions of 1798, enjoyed Jefferson's full confidence in the struggles in Congress after Breckinridge succeeded the Federalist Humphrey Marshall in the Senate. With the other senator, John Brown, Jefferson had been on the friendliest of terms since they were fellow lodgers and

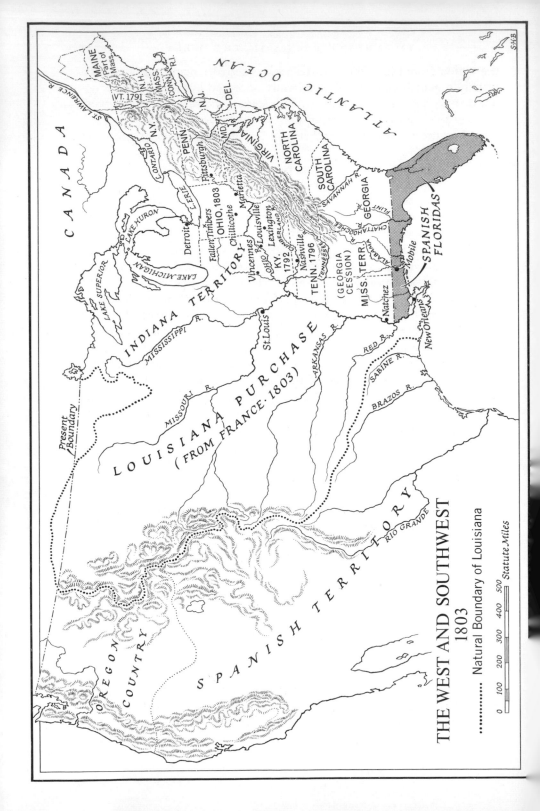

THE WEST AND SOUTHWEST
1803
········· Natural Boundary of Louisiana

0 100 200 300 400 500
Statute Miles

CANADA

ATLANTIC OCEAN

MAINE
Part of
Mass.

VT. 1791   N.H.   MASS.   CONN.   R.I.

N.Y.   N.J.   DEL.

PENN.   MD.

VIRGINIA

NORTH CAROLINA

SOUTH CAROLINA

GEORGIA

SPANISH FLORIDAS

ST. LAWRENCE R.

LAKE ONTARIO   L. ERIE

LAKE HURON   LAKE MICHIGAN

LAKE SUPERIOR

Detroit

Fallen Timbers

OHIO, 1803   Marietta

Chillicothe

Pittsburgh

Vincennes   Louisville   Lexington

OHIO R.   KY. 1792   CUMBERLAND R.

Nashville

TENN. 1796   (TENNESSEE)

(GEORGIA CESSION)

MISS. TERR.

Natchez   Mobile

New Orleans

CHATTAHOOCHEE   FLINT   ALABAMA R.   SAVANNAH R.

INDIANA TERRITORY

MISSISSIPPI R.   MISSOURI R.   St. Louis

LOUISIANA PURCHASE
(FROM FRANCE · 1803)

ARKANSAS R.

RED R.

SABINE R.

BRAZOS R.

RIO GRANDE

Present Boundary

OREGON COUNTRY

SPANISH TERRITORY

SHB

messmates in Philadelphia during his vice presidency, and he was a friend and correspondent of many other Kentuckians. His personal relations with leading citizens of the less developed state of Tennessee were not so close, but Senator William Cocke and Tennessee's only congressman, William C. C. Claiborne, were both native Virginians, and the latter became the President's protegé when appointed in 1801 as governor of the territory of Mississippi.

In Ohio, which attained the status of a separate territory in 1798 and had a legislature of its own, there were settlers from New England and the Middle Atlantic States as well as the upper South, but political leadership centered on the southern tier of counties along the river which were predominantly Virginian. The name "Chillicothe Junto" was given the group of leaders who carried to success the movement for statehood. The most prominent of these were Edward Tiffin, speaker of the legislature, and his brother-in-law, Thomas Worthington, a member of that body, both of whom had come to Ohio from Virginia. When the latter visited Washington in the winter of 1801–1802 in the interest of statehood he became acquainted with Jefferson, who gave him a friendly welcome. The enabling act, passed by the Republican Congress, was approved by the Republican President on April 30, 1802 — as it deserved to be on the merits of the case, though it was of obvious partisan advantage. The necessary constitutional convention was scheduled for the fall, and it duly met at Chillicothe.

Concurrent with the movement for statehood was one for the removal of Arthur St. Clair, who had been Governor of the Northwest Territory from its beginning and who bitterly opposed statehood at this time — partly, it may be supposed, because of his Federalist politics, and partly because he objected to the shrinkage of his own authority. Certain actions of his, in disregard of the territorial legislature, showed that he clung to powers which were no longer his by law. Besides this he was accused of acceptance of improper fees and other illegal acts. Early in 1802, Jefferson received from Worthington a list of charges against General St. Clair. After the passing of the enabling act, these received his careful attention and that of all the members of his Council. The consensus was that enough of the charges were proved to warrant the Governor's removal but that the wisdom of this was questionable in view of his long public service and the fact that his authority in Ohio was nearing an end anyway. He seemed deserving of an expression of disapprobation, however, and this he got in the letter the Secretary of State wrote him on June 23, 1802, in the President's behalf. The Republicans in Ohio were disappointed but they had no doubt they would control the constitutional convention in the fall.

When that body met, St. Clair's implacable hostility to statehood expressed itself in conduct too outrageous to be overlooked. In an address to the convention he said, among other things, that the enabling act was a nullity. Gallatin, who had previously opposed his removal, now regarded it as imperative. In the letter of dismissal in which Madison spoke for Jefferson, reference was made to St. Clair's "intemperance and indecorum of language" toward Congress, to his disorganizing spirit, and to his gross violation of the rules of conduct enjoined by his public station.[5]

As a responsible administrator, Jefferson could have taken no other action, but the net result of these events was to his distinct political advantage. St. Clair would have lost all authority in Ohio in any case, but he was now powerless in the rest of the old Northwest Territory. As Worthington had predicted to Jefferson, the Republicans had an overwhelming majority in the convention, over which Tiffin presided. He became the first governor of the new commonwealth while Worthington, elected by an overwhelmingly Republican legislature, became one of the first United States senators. He did not begin to serve until the fall of 1803, but in the meantime there was no doubt that the President had the loyal support of Ohio.

From the point of view of Jefferson, the course of events in Ohio led to a well-rounded achievement. While aiding the movement for increased self-government on the local level he and his party bettered their position both locally and nationally, and he strengthened his ties with the most influential local Republican leaders. Somewhat earlier, results not dissimilar to these were attained under more confused circumstances in the territory of Mississippi. As established by act of Congress in 1798, the year when the Spanish actually withdrew below the thirty-first parallel, it consisted of what was known as the Natchez Strip, extending from the Mississippi River to the Chattahoochee and lying between the Spanish border and a line parallel to this, beginning at the mouth of the Yazoo River. Adams's appointee as governor of this strategic territory was Winthrop Sargent, a New England Federalist who had been secretary of the Northwest Territory. When he went to

[5] Besides the articles on Tiffin, Worthington, and St. Clair in *D.A.B.*, see R. C. Downes, "The Statehood Contest in Ohio," *Miss. Valley Hist. Rev.*, Sept., 1931, pp. 155–171, and "Thomas Jefferson and the Removal of Governor St. Clair in 1802," *Ohio Arch. and Hist. Pubs.*, XXXVI (1927), 62–77. The main documents about the St. Clair episode are in C. E. Carter, ed., *Territorial Papers of the U.S.*, III, 211–214, 224, 231, 259–260 (referred to as Carter). TJ's consultation with the heads of department in the spring is shown by his letter of Apr. 29, 1802, to all of them (LC, 21155), and by their replies, of which those of Gallatin, Apr. 30 (LC, 21167–21169), and Madison, June 19 (LC, 21359–21360), are most important. These are partially printed in the article by Downes.

Natchez the Mississippi Territory was in the first stage of government as prescribed by the Northwest Ordinance, which provided the model for the congressional action — that is, the territory was governed by appointed officials (a governor and three judges) who had authority to adopt such laws of the original states as seemed necessary and suitable. Following sharp criticism of the authorities and pressure from dissatisfied inhabitants, in 1800 Congress advanced the territory to the second stage of government by granting the citizenry the right to elect a legislature of their own — and this despite uncertainty whether there was the requisite number of inhabitants (5000).[6] This action was objected to, however, by a large number of persons whom Governor Sargent described as "the most respectable inhabitants" and with whom he agreed.[7] Thus when the Governor's three-year term neared its end in the spring of 1801, shortly after Jefferson's accession to the presidency, the territory was split in two factions. Andrew Ellicott, the American commissioner charged with drawing the boundary line between Mississippi and Spanish Florida, agreed that the faction opposing Sargent consisted of the less reputable members of the community and believed that the inhabitants in general were insufficiently mature for the second stage of territorial government, as indeed they may have been.[8]

But Jefferson could not have been expected to reappoint a Federalist who was identified with a local faction that wanted Congress to reverse itself. In place of Sargent he appointed William C. C. Claiborne, who had been representative from the frontier state of Tennessee in the last three Congresses. The President's opinion of the local situation can be best judged from what he wrote Claiborne privately.[9] He recognized that the faction favoring the first grade was "richer and better informed," but believed that the other consisted of the "body of the people."[10] To Claiborne he said: "Our love of freedom and the value we set on self-government disposes us to prefer the principles of the second grade." Since the territory had actually been granted that grade by a Federalist Congress, a man of his democratic proclivities could hardly have countenanced what he regarded as a backward step, even

[6] The act of Apr. 7, 1798, and the supplemental act of May 10, 1800, are in Carter, V, 18–22, 95–98. Among other documents in this collection is a petition of a committee of inhabitants, dated Oct. 2, 1799, asking for advancement to the second stage (pp. 78-82); it was signed by Cato West and fourteen others.

[7] Sargent to President of U.S. Senate, Dec. 20, 1800, sending petition of Dec. 20, 1800, with many signatures (Carter, V, 109–117).

[8] Ellicott to Madison, May 27 and Dec. 29, 1801 (Carter, V, 126-127, 131–134).

[9] TJ to Claiborne, July 31, 1801 (Ford, VIII, 71–72).

[10] It was in unquestionable control of the territorial legislature. On Dec. 21, 1801, that body expressed approval of TJ's declination to reappoint Sargent. See his letter of Mar. 2, 1802, in Carter, V, 141.

though the forward step may have been taken too hastily. As an executive he really had no choice but to support the existing law, but he urged the Governor to try to bring around the dissident group and reconcile the warring factions. Since the richer group feared an increase in taxes in the second stage of territorial government, the President emphasized the desirability of keeping expenses low. His counsel was wise from both the national and the partisan point of view, and he continued to believe that he had made a wise choice of a territorial governor. There was no doubt of Claiborne's loyal support of the President, but unfortunately he did not assume his duties for six months and factionalism by no means disappeared after his arrival. At the time of the Burr conspiracy in Jefferson's second term the richer group tended to support that adventurer rather than the administration.[11]

When the Mississippi Territory was created, the State of Georgia had not formally relinquished its claim to the lands included in it and to the rest of the area of the present states of Alabama and Mississippi. The Georgians had already given strong evidence, however, of their desire to cede these lands to the United States under certain conditions, and they soon put themselves unequivocally on record.[12] The territorial act of 1798 called for the setting up of a federal commission to negotiate with representatives of the state with respect to boundaries and land claims. Adams named such a commission, but nothing came of it in his administration. Jefferson's appointees — the Secretaries of State and the Treasury and the Attorney General — met with a solidly Republican commission from Georgia, and the agreement of April 24, 1802, resulted.[13] By this Georgia formally ceded to the United States the entire region between its present western boundary and the Mississippi, receiving in compensation $1,250,000 along with the promise that, as soon as possible, the federal government would extinguish the Indian titles within the borders of the state as then drawn. The agreement provided that the federal government might set aside five million acres to settle land claims in the region ceded. Most of those that were presented afterwards arose from the sales to land companies by the state under the notorious Yazoo Act of 1795, which had been repealed by a later legislature in response to public indignation. The proposed settlement

[11] Claiborne was appointed May 25, 1801, and arrived in the territory Nov. 23.

[12] By action of a state constitutional convention in May, 1798, following a resolution of the Georgia House of Representatives of Jan. 29, 1798. See T. P. Abernethy, *The South in the New Nation* (1961), p. 153 and references.

[13] Text of articles, with extensive notes, in Carter, V, 142–146. Adams had appointed the corresponding officers from his government. The Georgia commissioners were Senators Abraham Baldwin and James Jackson and Congressman (later Governor) John Milledge.

of the Yazoo claims aroused in Congress one of the bitterest controversies of Jefferson's presidency, and this question was not disposed of finally until after he had left office. But this particular storm was several years in gathering, and the agreement seemed satisfactory to both the state and federal government when it was reached in 1802. Then it offered the promise that order would be brought out of vast confusion.[14] After this agreement the northern boundary of the frontier Territory of Mississippi was moved to the Tennessee line.

In a real sense Georgia was still a frontier state. This was chiefly owing to two facts: on the south it bordered on Spanish Florida, and a very large portion of its area was still occupied by Indians. In the latter respect it was now much worse off than Ohio. The slowness of the federal government in extinguishing Indian titles within the borders of the state was a major grievance of the impatient Georgians in later decades. In the first year of Jefferson's administration his Indian policy, as carried out by the Secretary of War, was essentially a continuation, or a moderate extension, of the policy he inherited. Of the actions occasioned by developments and new dangers in Louisiana we shall speak hereafter. It may be noted at this point that the four cessions negotiated in the years of 1801–1802 were in the Territory of Mississippi and the State of Georgia. Three of them, including one in southern Georgia, were on the Spanish border, and the fourth marked a gain for the land-hungry Georgians in the more fertile interior of their state.[15] No frontier region could be expected to be wholly satisfied with the speed and effectiveness of governmental actions with respect to the Indians, but what this administration had done thus far had given a strong impression of concern for the well-being of the ordinary settler; and all along the arc from Ohio to Georgia the democratic President had gained the loyal support of the chief political leaders. On the political frontier his fortifications were well manned.

According to his enemies in his own day, however, and to certain historical critics in after years, he was culpably indifferent to the military and naval defenses of his country in the face of fresh dangers. Within three months of his accession, after informing his son-in-law

14 The claims settlement recommended by the presidential commission was attacked by John Randolph in the House in 1804, and even more bitterly a year later. (See ch. XXIV, below.) Congress did not act decisively in this matter until 1814, following Marshall's decision of 1810 in Fletcher vs. Peck.

15 A list of cessions, 1801–1809, with a map, based on C. C. Royce, "Indian Land Cessions in the United States," in Eighteenth Annual Report of the Bureau of American Ethnology, Part 2, is in R. A. Erney's dissertation "The Public Life of Henry Dearborn" (1957), pp. 86–87.

that the government was selling off surplus frigates and greatly reducing expenses, he stated that he feared the cession of Louisiana by Spain to France, saying it would be "an inauspicious circumstance to us." [16] Not until the following winter did he receive from Rufus King in London indubitable confirmation of the fateful treaties between these two countries, but during the summer of 1801 that minister had left him in no doubt about the probabilities of the cession.[17] Lacking confirmation of it, Jefferson could not properly have mentioned it in his first annual message to Congress, but by then he was aware that a momentous change of neighbors was likely to take place on the North American continent.

In this message he said that the regular army was larger than necessary, but that the laws relating to the militia — which he had described in his inaugural address as the country's "best reliance in peace and for the first moments in war" — should be improved. The army was considerably below its authorized strength when he took office. At this session, Congress reduced it further, taking no action with respect to the militia.[18] The British representative in the United States, writing his home office, said that it was "perfect infatuation" in the administration to choose this moment to leave the frontier almost defenseless by the reduction of the military establishment.[19] The administration would have denied the allegation, since most of the regulars were in western posts, but beyond any doubt the President, during his first year in office, acted as though he expected no early breach of the peace, pursuing his program of economy and democratization to the utmost while the sun was shining.

There were good political reasons for his early emphasis on domestic matters; and, in view of the uncertainties with respect to France and Spain, it is hard to see what other foreign policy would have been better than one of watchful waiting. In the long run his reliance had to be

[16] TJ to TMR, May 14, 1801 (*Papers, MHS*, p. 95).
[17] The secret treaty of San Ildefonso was signed Oct. 1, 1800. The treaty of Aranjuez, Mar. 21, 1801, referring to Louisiana as already ceded, promised the Grand Duchy of Tuscany to the Spanish Prince of Parma in return. It was a copy of the later treaty, enclosed by Rufus King in a letter of Nov. 20, 1801, to Madison (*A.S.P.F.R.*, II, 511–512) which gave the administration the first confirmation of the cession. The French government had not officially admitted it, however, and TJ did not have this confirmation when he sent his first annual address to Congress. In King's letter of Mar. 29, 1801, to Madison (*A.S.P.F.R.*, II, 509), he spoke of the probability of the cession, as he did in other dispatches during the summer.
[18] Act of Mar. 16, 1802 (*Annals*, 7 Cong., 1 session, pp. 1306–1312). At the outset of the administration, the army's strength in officers and men was about 1000 below the 5438 authorized by law. By this act the authorized strength was reduced to 3312. Returns for 1802–1809 are in *A.S.P. Mil. Aff.*, I, 159 ff.
[19] Thornton to Hawkesbury, Jan. 26, 1802 (FO, 5:35).

on diplomacy, and he undoubtedly thought himself realistic in not em-
barking on a hopeless naval race with the great Powers. His countrymen
would have been intolerant of such naval expenditures as had seemed
necessary during the half-war with France, and the large majority of
them shared his opinion about the army. If he had run any risk thus far
it was a calculated one and in his opinion small. The reports of the
American military establishment which the representatives of foreign
governments sent home could not have been expected to overawe European chancelleries or strengthen the hands of American negotiators;
but arguments of great persuasiveness could be drawn from the facts of
geography and long-range American potentialities.[20]

i i

At the outset, Jefferson had few diplomats to rely on. Quite properly, he did not want to send a minister to France until the convention
with that country had been ratified.[21] For that reason and also because
Robert R. Livingston was not ready to go, that gentleman's sailing was
delayed until the autumn of 1801, and he did not reach Paris until December. Fortunately, Rufus King was still in England, where he was
skillfully effecting a settlement of outstanding issues in Anglo-
American relations. The earliest reliable information about the prospects with respect to Louisiana came from him. He fully realized the
dangers in the situation. In his first dispatch bearing on it he reported
the opinion of influential persons in France that there was a natural line
of separation between the American people on the two sides of the
mountains. He believed that the cession was intended to weaken the
Union. Afterwards he reported that the British feared the extension of
French power up the Mississippi and through the lakes to Canada. In
one of his conversations with Lord Hawkesbury, he quoted the saying
of Montesquieu that the existence of the Turks and Spanish was fortunate, since they of all nations were "the most proper to possess a great
empire with insignificance." [22] The same could not have been said of
France.

Spanish consent to the diminution of their empire was more of a
mystery to American statesmen of the time than it is to modern scholars, who have access to more documents. Louisiana was more than an
expensive luxury to Spain; because of her inability to defend it, and its

---

[20] Pichon, the French representative, gave detailed military information in his
dispatch of July 8, 1802 (AECPEU, 54:416–426).

[21] See above, p. 37.

[22] King to Madison, June 1, 1801 (*A.S.P.F.R.*, II, 509–510).

progressive penetration by Americans, it was a dangerous liability.[23] Jefferson himself had long been confident that, if Nature were left to take its course, the mouth of the river would inevitably become the possession of his own country. He did not need to be told that the Spanish were better neighbors than the French would be, but he regarded it as wise to issue reminders that the administration thought so. Madison wrote Charles Pinckney, who had reached his post in Madrid, and the President himself sent a special private word to Claiborne, who was designated as governor of the territory nearest New Orleans and the mouth of the Mississippi.[24] The American preference for the Spanish as neighbors was emphasized in both of these early communications, and the maintenance of friendly relations with them was urged. "Everything irritating to be avoided, everything friendly to be done for them," Jefferson said. So long as there was hope that they would remain where they were he wanted to risk no disturbance. What to do in case France should come into possession of Louisiana he did not say, except that "profound reconsideration" of American conduct would then be necessary.

More explicit directions were given Livingston before he sailed for France, where the real issue lay.[25] Like Pinckney, he was instructed to do everything possible to find out what had actually happened. Assuming success in this quest, he was then to follow one or the other of two courses. (1) If the project was not yet carried through, he was to try to dissuade the French from it by presenting the American position — that is, that the transfer was not in the interest of the United States and would imperil relations with France. (2) If the cession had irrevocably taken place, he was to avoid irritating the French and inquire into the possibility of the cession to the United States of the Floridas, especially West Florida. Livingston could read French well enough, but he could not speak it adequately; and, because of deafness, he could not hear it. These were disadvantages, but he was regarded as a Francophile and was a man of unquestionable personal distinction. He was probably as competent a diplomatist as Jefferson could have sent to France and he pursued his objectives with great diligence.[26] His major difficulties did not arise from his own limitations. He soon became convinced that the business between France and Spain had been concluded, but Talley-

23 Whitaker, *Mississippi Question*, p. 182.
24 Madison to Pinckney, June 9, 1801 (*A.S.P.F.R.*, II, 510); TJ to Claiborne, July 13, 1801 (Ford, VIII, 71).
25 Madison to Livingston, Sept. 28, 1801 (*A.S.P.F.R.*, II, 510–511).
26 On his appointment, see George Dangerfield, *Chancellor Robert R. Livingston of New York* (1960), pp. 304–305. This author describes his career in France in Part V of that excellent biography.

rand, who was definitely anti-American and enjoyed snubbing Livingston, continued to insist that nothing had been settled. Effective negotiation was virtually impossible under these baffling circumstances.

Early in 1802, however, the administration in Washington became
considerably more active behind the scenes. Jefferson could no longer
harbor any doubt that the cession of Louisiana to France had been
agreed to. By March, indeed, the treaty of which he had received
copies from King and Livingston got into the papers, to the considerable embarrassment of certain Republican editors — especially William
Duane of the *Aurora*, who had decried the alarms sounded in the *New
York Evening Post* and other Federalist organs a few weeks earlier.[27]
Meanwhile, an expedition under Bonaparte's brother-in-law, General
Leclerc, had arrived in St. Domingo with the actual but unavowed purpose of overthrowing General Toussaint Louverture, the extraordinary
Negro who had made himself ruler of the island and whom Bonaparte
himself had designated as captain general when, because of involvement
in Europe, the First Consul could not act against him.[28] Jefferson had
been assured by Rufus King that no part of this expedition was designated for Louisiana — as we now know it could not have been at the
time, since no order for the transfer of that province to France had yet
been issued. Present-day scholars, with access to once-secret documents, also know that this move represented a commitment of Bonaparte to the revival of the French colonial empire in America, after the
turmoil of revolution; and, in the light of later events, they can now see
that the fate of Louisiana hinged on it. Jefferson could hardly have
been aware of this as yet; and even if he had recognized that the interests of his own country would have been served by the failure of the
Leclerc expedition, he was in no position to oppose it. In fact, he had
previously expressed approval of the purpose of the French to restore
their rule by overthrowing the "Bonaparte of the Antilles."

He did this in the summer of 1801, while the European war was still
going on and he was waiting for the French ratification of the convention of 1800, by which their half-war with the United States was
ended. Under these circumstances he could hardly have failed to recog-

[27] The treaty of Mar. 21, 1801 (Aranjuez), was published in the *Aurora*, Mar. 29,
1802, along with an editorial which reflected the previous confusion of the public
mind on this subject. On Mar. 26, the *Aurora* had asserted that no definite knowledge of the cession was possessed in America at that time; and on Mar. 30, Duane
assured the "anti-republicans" that he had not been in the particular confidence of
the administration. Federalist papers had been prophesying the cession for three
weeks, he said. The *National Intelligencer* appears to have virtually ignored the
subject.

[28] The expedition sailed from Brest Nov. 22, 1801, arriving about Feb. 1 in St.
Domingo, as Americans designated united Sainte Domingue and Santo Domingo.

nize St. Domingo as a French colony and, understandably, he did not want to risk offending the capricious First Consul. But in his conversations with the French chargé, showing less restraint than Madison, he appears to have gone further than was wise or necessary. According to Pichon, he said that, in case of peace between France and Great Britain, "nothing would be easier than to furnish your army and fleet with everything, and to reduce Toussaint to starvation." [29] He was reported as saying that neither the United States nor Great Britain wanted St. Domingo to become another Algiers — that is, a piratical state — and Bonaparte afterwards availed himself of this expression in discussions with the British. Jefferson also recognized that Toussaint and his country of emancipated blacks could be regarded as a menace to the institutions of American states wherein slavery was legalized, but he minimized that danger.

His own state had very recently put down the slave insurrection which bears the name of Gabriel, and it suppressed sporadic revolts in the years immediately thereafter. Jefferson had counseled Governor James Monroe not to go beyond absolute necessity in the matter of executions, and early in his presidency he was asked by this friend to help him find a place to which convicted insurrectionists might be sent. In his first response to the Governor's request he said that Nature seemed to have formed the islands of the West Indies "to become the receptacle of the blacks transplanted into this hemisphere." [30] That is, he harbored the thought that all the slaves in the United States might eventually be sent there. It seemed to him at the moment that the most promising asylum was St. Domingo, where the blacks were established in a *de facto* government. The prospect did not frighten him. He said:

> The possibility that these exiles might stimulate & conduct vindictive or predatory descents on our coasts, & facilitate concert with their brethren remaining here, looks to a state of things between that island & us not probable on a contemplation of our relative strength, and of the disproportion daily growing; and it is overweighed by the humanity of the measures proposed, & the advantages of disembarrassing ourselves of such dangerous characters. Africa would offer a last & undoubted resort, if all others more desirable should fail us. . . .

[29] Statement as reported by Pichon to Talleyrand, July 22, 1801 (AECPEU, 53:178). This episode is described in considerable detail by C. L. Lokke in "Jefferson and the Leclerc Expedition" (*A.H.R.*, XXXIII, [Jan. 1928], 322–328), and more briefly by Brant in *Madison*, IV, 62–65.

[30] TJ to Monroe, Nov. 24, 1801 (Ford, VIII, 105), replying to Monroe's letter of June 15, 1801 (*S.M.H.*, III, 292–295). On the Gabriel revolt of 1800, see *Jefferson and the Ordeal of Liberty*, p. 480, and references there cited.

In the opinion of the Virginia legislators, however, an asylum in Africa or South America was preferable in the case of those who had been convicted. Turning to Africa, therefore, in the second year of his presidency Jefferson inquired of Rufus King in London about possibilities in Sierra Leone. The results of this action were wholly negative.[31]

In his reference to St. Domingo as a possible receptacle of exiled American slaves, Jefferson implied a degree of complacency with respect to the rule of Toussaint which did not accord with Pichon's report of an earlier conversation. At that moment, when French action was not imminent, he seems to have indulged in overstatement in his effort to be conciliatory. Bonaparte, in turn, accepted Pichon's report at even more than its face value: in Leclerc's instructions the claim was made that the President had promised to take all necessary measures to reduce Toussaint to starvation and aid the French army immediately on its arrival.[32] Jefferson would almost certainly have denied doing more than hint at the possibility of concert with the French, and it is most unlikely that his attitude was a determining factor in the mind of the First Consul anyway, but Bonaparte was warranted in assuming that the expedition to St. Domingo would arouse no American objection. Since formal American protest would have been improper as long as the island was recognized as a part of France, Jefferson had not appreciably weakened his hand by his diplomatic indiscretion. Indeed, one can perceive method in his excess: having convinced Pichon of his excellent dispositions toward the French, he was in position to speak candidly about the effect the taking of Louisiana would have on the relations between the two countries. By the beginning of 1802 he was telling the chargé that the result would be, at the first European war, a rupture between the United States and France and an alliance between the former and Great Britain. Also, he was saying that the French could remain in Louisiana only so long as the Americans would permit.

He undoubtedly expected this strong language to be reported to the French Minister of Foreign Affairs, as it was.[33] Soon thereafter the British representative in America wrote home that he had met scarcely a person of either party who would not prefer almost anybody to the French as neighbors, and that the likely effect of a vigorous colonial

[31] Other references to this interesting episode include: Monroe to TJ, Dec. 8, 1801; Feb. 13, May 17, June 11, 1802 (S.M.H., III, 318–319, 336–337, 348–349, 351); TJ to Monroe, June 2, 1802 (Ford, VIII, 152–154); TJ to King, July 13, 1802 (Ford, VIII, 161–164); replies of Christopher Gore, Oct. 10, 1802, and King, Dec. 20, 1802 (King, IV, 173–174, 197–198).

[32] Quoted from Leclerc's instructions by Lokke, in A.H.R., XXXIII, 327.

[33] Pichon to Talleyrand, Jan. 2, 1802 (AECPEU, 54:17).

policy on their part would be to drive the United States into a closer connection with Great Britain.[34] He was reading the mind of the administration correctly. A few weeks later, following a conversation in which the President himself introduced the subject of Louisiana, he reported Jefferson as saying that the occupation of the province by France would give an entirely new character to all American relations with her, and that the only sure way of avoiding trouble was for her to cede the island of New Orleans.[35] The President was sowing seeds in the minds of these foreign representatives which he hoped would bear future fruit. In neither case, however, was the soil fully prepared as yet, for at this stage Pichon was doubtful of the political success of the administration, while Thornton believed that its domestic policies would weaken the country, thus making the friendship of the United States less important to the British, and its enmity less formidable.[36] Furthermore, Jefferson had not gained the personal regard of these two men to the extent that he did later.

His freedom in talking with them about a question which Madison avoided need not be attributed to disregard of propriety and certainly not to any basic difference of opinion between him and his Secretary of State. The two men were notably harmonious in spirit and worked out all important policies between them. But, besides differing in temperament and style, they were playing roles which were distinctive though supplementary. To foreign representatives in the United States and to American representatives abroad the official position was generally presented by Madison with traditional diplomatic caution and restraint. Jefferson, off the record, spoke more freely, more experimentally, and at times more violently. This he did, not only to Pichon and Thornton, but also to Livingston in France.

The letter he wrote that minister toward the end of his first congressional session, during which he had launched with such success his domestic program of economy and democratization, is the fullest and most colorful presentation of his position with respect to the Mississippi question prior to the Louisiana Purchase; and it shows, better than any other document, how far he was willing to go in this matter if necessary. It has been quoted at length by historians for just these reasons. But it was a private letter which he did not communicate to Congress at a later time as part of the official correspondence bearing on the

34 Thornton to Hawkesbury, Jan. 26, 1802 (FO, 5:35).

35 Thornton to Hawkesbury, Mar. 6, 1802 (FO, 5:35). He found TJ much less difficult of access on this subject than Madison, who avoided discussing it.

36 Pichon to Talleyrand, Feb. 23, 1802 (AECPEU, 54:161–165); Thornton to Hawkesbury, Feb. 1, 1802 (FO, 5:35).

Louisiana Purchase.[37] He was wise in withholding it, for by that time he no longer needed to threaten the French with an Anglo-American alliance, and the revelation of the fact that he had done so might have added to diplomatic complexities and domestic political difficulties. His strongest verbal effort to prevent the carrying out of the agreement between France and Spain was made off the record.

He was providing background material for Livingston and also for Du Pont de Nemours, who bore the letter on a visit to his native France and was permitted to read it. To use a friend as a courier was a common practice in an age when all correspondence was subject to grave dangers, but special interest attaches to Jefferson's procedure in this case. Du Pont was to seal the letter after perusing it, and was cautioned to deliver it to Livingston with his own hands. If anything should happen to him, his wife was to follow the same instructions. In a closely guarded private letter the President could use threatening language without issuing an official ultimatum or formal instructions.[38]

The specific threat, which did not appear in Madison's official letter to Livingston, also carried by Du Pont, was of an American alliance with Great Britain and eventual war with France.[39] In his explicit reference to war, Jefferson went a little further than in his talk with Pichon, though that talk pointed in the same direction. The major significance of this letter in history arises chiefly from the fact that, better perhaps than any other single source, it reveals his contemplation of a diplomatic revolution. It provides a striking illustration of his flexibility with respect to diplomatic means in pursuit of ends which were constant. The fixed goal in this case, the *sine qua non*, was the free navigation of the Mississippi. By possessing herself of New Orleans, France, with whom hitherto there had been so few points of basic conflict that she had seemed a natural friend, would turn herself into a natural enemy. By "placing herself in that door," he said, France would assume to the United States "the attitude of defiance." Abiding friendship between

[37] TJ to R. R. Livingston, Apr. 18, 1802 (Ford, VIII, 143–147). The Louisiana documents were communicated to Congress in October, 1803 (*A.S.P.F.R.*, II, 506–583). They then became a matter of record and were accessible to the legislators to whom they were communicated, even though they were not published until later. The Livingston letter appeared in the first edition of TJ's writings, the *Memoir*, edited by T. J. Randolph (1829), III, 491–494. A lengthy extract from it was printed in *State Papers and Correspondence bearing upon the Purchase of Louisiana* (1903), without indication that it was not communicated to Congress.

[38] He described the procedure in a letter to Du Pont, Apr. 25, 1802 (*J.-D. Correspondence*, pp. 46–49). Another reason for his great care was that he enclosed a cipher for Livingston's use. He sent letters to other friends in France by Du Pont.

[39] Madison to Livingston, May 1, 1802 (*A.S.P.F.R.*, II, 516).

the two countries would thus become impossible, as the French themselves would be blind not to see. On the American side, new arrangements and a new alignment would inevitably follow.

> The day that France takes possession of New Orleans fixes the
> sentence which is to restrain her forever within her low water
> mark. It seals the union of two nations who in conjunction can
> maintain exclusive possession of the ocean. From that moment we
> must marry ourselves to the British fleet and nation.

Coming from one who had so often and so bitterly condemned British policy, and had labored so long and hard to free his countrymen
from British commercial thralldom, this was startling language. Equally
surprising were his references to the navy, which he was sharply reducing. "We must turn all our attentions to a maritime force, for which
our resources place us on very high grounds," he said. And the first
cannon fired in Europe was to be the signal for the forcible exclusion of
France from the New World. That she could be ejected from New
Orleans he had no doubt whatever; and, assuming an Anglo-American
alliance and naval superiority, his confidence was warranted, for the
military potentialities of his own country could be realized upon when
necessary. Therefore, the French could count on retaining Louisiana
only during the interval of peace, whether this should prove long or
short.

He did not want the French to be on the continent of North America
at all, but his immediate concern was for the island of New Orleans and
the Floridas, which he assumed to be at the disposal of France. If she
were to cede these to the United States, while retaining the lands west
of the Mississippi, there would be no immediate need for a British alliance; but, as he told Du Pont, he regarded this as a mere palliative. By
now his fears had revived that the troops on St. Domingo would proceed to Louisiana after completing their task on the island, but in his
opinion this would require a considerable time. Every American eye
was fixed on "this affair of Louisiana," he said. Not since the War of
the Revolution had anything "produced more uneasy sensations
through the body of the nation." But there was no strong domestic
pressure on him as yet to do something tangible, and he himself believed there was still time for negotiation. He also believed that, because of the physical situation and potentialities of the United States,
his diplomatic hand was strong.

Hoping that Du Pont, a former French official, could do something
to impress on the present government the "inevitable consequences of

their taking possession of Louisiana," the President wanted him to be fully informed on this subject; and, to make sure that he did not miss the point, Jefferson summed up his own argument in a covering letter to this friend.[40] Du Pont got the point, beyond question, but he took it more as a challenge to his French patriotism than Jefferson had anticipated. Viewing the threat of war very seriously, Du Pont, while fully agreeing that the free navigation of the Mississippi must be maintained, distrusted the British and minimized the danger to the United States and Mexico, a country which he himself did not doubt that the Americans really wanted to conquer. In his opinion, also, freedom of commerce could be assured by France just as well as it had been by Spain. If, however, the Americans wanted land rather than a guarantee of rights, they should renounce all desire with regard to the west side of the river. That is, they should seek New Orleans and the Floridas, offering the French enough to tempt them before they took possession.[41]

Claiming that he had been misunderstood, Jefferson sent Du Pont an explanatory letter in which he said that his observations were not to be considered as menaces.[42] "It is as if I foresaw a storm tomorrow and advised my friend not to embark on the ocean today," he said. "My foreseeing it does not make me the cause of it, nor can my admonition be a threat, the storm not being produced by my will. It is in truth our friendship for France which renders us so uneasy at seeing her take a position which must bring us into collision." He also denied any present thought of conquest and any desire to extend American territory beyond the Mississippi; he wanted that river to be the western boundary throughout its course. That is, he wanted New Orleans and the Floridas, though he did not think the country able to pay more for them than the sum due the United States on spoliation claims under the recent convention. He was fully aware of the danger of allying the country with Great Britain. "It would only be better than to have no friend," he said. Finally, he asked Du Pont to show Livingston this letter.

Writing a few lines to that minister on the same day, he said that in his earlier letter he had gone further into the province of the Secretary of State than he had intended, thus reminding Livingston that he was speaking off the record.[43] He certainly had no designs on Mexico and

[40] TJ to Du Pont, Apr. 25, 1802 (*J.-D. Correspondence*, pp. 46–49).
[41] Du Pont to TJ, Apr. 30, 1802 (*ibid.*, pp. 52–61).
[42] TJ to Du Pont, May 5, 1802 (courtesy of Jefferson Papers, Princeton).
[43] TJ to Livingston, May 5, 1802 (LC, 21197).

was not panting for war. The official line was laid down by Madison, speaking in more general terms. The Secretary of State did not minimize the seriousness of the situation. He said that if the French should take possession of the mouth of the Mississippi, the "worst events" were to be anticipated.[44] But Livingston's specific instructions were in line with those he had received in the first place: he was to try to dissuade the French from carrying out their project; he was to inquire into the extent of the cession and try to find the price at which New Orleans and the Floridas could be acquired. No offer was authorized, however, and in the matter of argument and inquiry Livingston, in effect, was left to his own devices while his home government awaited developments.

During the summer the Minister drafted an elaborate memoir, designed to show that the possession of Louisiana would not be advantageous to France.[45] In certain places this essay clearly reflected Jefferson's private letter to him. While Livingston did not refer specifically to a British alliance — which, if we may judge from his past, would have been most unwelcome to him personally — he did so indirectly, as he did to the possibility of open American hostility to France. And in language less colorful than that of Jefferson but reminiscent of it, he spoke of the paramount importance of New Orleans, which France would be wise to cede to the United States.[46] In the summer of 1802 he thought that the Floridas were not included in the cession, though he afterwards changed his mind about that. Talleyrand promised to read Livingston's memoir, but during the summer there seemed no way to get through to Bonaparte. On September 1, the frustrated Minister wrote the Secretary of State: "There never was a Government in which less could be done by negotiation than here. There is no people, no Legislature, no counsellors. One man is everything. He seldom asks advice, and never hears it unasked. . . . Though the sense of every reflecting man about him is against this wild expedition, no one dares to tell him so." [47]

Livingston's reference was to a prospective expedition to Louisiana, which he had reported to his government several months earlier. Originally he had been unduly alarmed about the immediacy of this and had

[44] Madison to Livingston, May 1, 1802 (*A.S.P.F.R.*, II, 516).

[45] Aug. 10, 1802 (*A.S.P.F.R.*, II, 520–524); discussed by Dangerfield, *Livingston*, pp. 331–336. Livingston said that, after having this translated, he struck off twenty copies and distributed these where he thought they would do good.

[46] Especially, *A.S.P.F.R.*, II, 523. TJ wrote Madison, Sept. 13, 1802, that Livingston asked too little, specifically, of France (Ford, VIII, 171–172).

[47] Livingston to Madison, Sept. 1, 1802 (*A.S.P.F.R.*, II, 525).

exaggerated its size, but he was now minimizing the danger.[48] Except for the uneasiness it was exciting in America he would not be disturbed, he said, for he was sure that in the end France would relinquish Louisiana and cede New Orleans to the United States.[49] Later events, including the renewal of the European war which he was predicting, demonstrated the astuteness of his judgment. Within a few months Bonaparte himself was to conclude, as Livingston had done, that St. Domingo required more than the French could furnish. This was not his opinion in the summer and autumn of 1802, however. By June word had reached Paris of the complete success of Leclerc on the island. Toussaint, unwisely trusting French professions, had delivered himself up to Bonaparte's brother-in-law, who subsequently sent the black chieftain to France to die in a dungeon. The projected expedition to Louisiana under General Victor was hampered by physical difficulties, and it could not be dispatched until the Spanish had ordered the delivery of the province to France anyway. Actually, this order was not issued until October 15, 1802, though the French were assured in the summer that it would be. At that time, therefore, it was a fair assumption that the French *would* take over Louisiana.

Reports which got into the American press in these months strengthened this impression. In June, 1802, certain reflections on the Louisiana question in the *Gazette de France* were published in America, where they were generally regarded as representative of the views of the French government.[50] In this publication the United States was charged with assistance to the rebels in St. Domingo and with the desire to extend its yoke over the West Indies. Also, because of the alleged necessity of establishing a barrier to American ambitions, and a counterpoise to American domination, the reattachment of Louisiana to France was described as very wise and important.

Reporting this to his own government, Pichon said that the opposition papers sometimes treated this question satirically — felicitating the Republicans on the prospect of having good friends as neighbors and being able to take at the source doctrines they greatly admired. More often they blamed the administration for lack of foresight, for feeble-

---

[48] He wrote the Secretary of State about it Apr. 24, 1802 (*A.S.P.F.R.*, II, 515–516). The story of this projected expedition, which actually did not come off, is well told on the basis of French sources by E. W. Lyon in *Louisiana in French Diplomacy, 1759–1804* (1934), ch. VI.

[49] Livingston to Madison, Sept. 1, 1802 (*A.S.P.F.R.*, II, 525).

[50] N.Y. *Spectator*, June 9, 1802, from *Gazette de France* of the last of April; extensively commented on by Pichon in his dispatch to Talleyrand, July 7, 1802 (AECPEU, 54:410 ff.).

ness, for imprudence in reducing military and naval strength at a time when the Union was menaced by the proximity of a turbulent people, directed by a government of boundless ambition. He reported also that the newspapers on the side of the administration were equally uncomplimentary about the French. Meanwhile, the British representative, though not claiming that Jefferson's party was cured of its bitterness to his own country, felt warranted in saying that Republican predilection for France scarcely existed, even in name.[51]

Observing that the Louisiana question was "peculiarly interesting" to the President, Thornton reported that Jefferson talked with him about it many times with perhaps too little caution. In fact the President was talking to the young Britisher in much the same language he had used to Livingston, and was adding some unqualified comments on Bonaparte, whom he cordially detested.[52] He was more cautious in his conversations with Pichon, and, while convinced of the unfriendliness of the French government, he warned Livingston to maintain a friendly though independent tone in all his communications. He wanted his country to remain disengaged as long as possible, taking sides against one or the other of the chief rival nations only when circumstances should make it absolutely necessary.[53] Du Pont had asserted that the French would respect American rights as well as the Spanish had done, and the British Foreign Secretary had told Rufus King that they would have no "colorable pretext" for excluding American citizens from the navigation of the Mississippi. On acquiring Louisiana, France would be subject to all engagements appertaining to it at the time of its cession.[54] This opinion was duly reported to Madison, but not until November did Livingston receive any assurance of the sort from France. Talleyrand finally told him that the provisions of the treaty between Spain and the United States would be observed, but the American Minister was obviously dubious.[55]

Long before his report reached the United States, the Mississippi question became critical — though, ironically, this was no fault of the French. In mid-October the Spanish Intendant in New Orleans closed the deposit in that port, and news of his startling action reached Washington by the last week in November. Jefferson got it shortly after his two daughters arrived for their long-anticipated visit, and a couple of weeks before the beginning of the congressional session. The forebod-

[51] Thornton to Hawkesbury, July 3, 1802 (FO, 5:35, No. 29).
[52] Thornton reported more of these Aug. 4, 1802 (FO, 5:35, No. 35).
[53] TJ to Livingston, Oct. 10, 1802 (Ford, VIII, 173).
[54] Hawkesbury to King, May 7, 1802 (*A.S.P.F.R.*, II, 517).
[55] Livingston to Madison, Nov. 11, 1802 (*A.S.P.F.R.*, II, 526–527).

ings of Westerners about their commerce down the great river had assumed tangible reality, and the tendency among Americans everywhere was to blame this situation on the French. Also, clamor inevitably arose that something should be done about it.

[XV]

The Mississippi Question

1802–1803

WHEN the President transmitted his second annual message to Congress ten days before Christmas in 1802, the speck he had observed on the western horizon in the previous spring had not yet turned into the tornado that he feared.[1] The French had not taken physical possession of the province of Louisiana and forced an agonizing reappraisal of the diplomatic posture of the United States. He had been informed, however, that they were assembling an expedition, in defiance of wind and wave; and he now knew that the Spanish Intendant in New Orleans had provoked a local storm by closing the deposit there. His awareness of these dangers could hardly have been suspected from the words he addressed to Congress; not without warrant did Alexander Hamilton describe his message as a lullaby. His first reference was to pleasing circumstances which showed the goodness of God, and his major emphasis was on the unquestionable success of his program of economy and freedom. He referred, it is true, to the retrocession of Louisiana to France, recognizing that if carried into effect it would change the aspect of foreign relations, but he did not admit the early likelihood of this and made no mention whatever of recent developments in New Orleans. The country was "still blessed with peace and friendship abroad," he said, and quite obviously the image he wanted to impress on the public mind was that of an administration intent on preserving these.

To be sure, he stated that the country was still engaged in warfare with Tripoli and that other piratical Barbary powers threatened to join the fray. Morocco had done so briefly in the summer, and the sending

[1] TJ to Du Pont, Apr. 25, 1802 (*J.-D. Correspondence*, p. 48). For the message, see Ford, VIII, 181–187.

of an additional frigate to the Mediterranean had occasioned much excited correspondence between Jefferson and his department heads during his latest visit home. Gallatin, who was a persistent advocate of economy and generally suspicious of the navy, wrote him from Washington by every post, obviously regretting the absence of the President and Secretary of State during days of stress that chanced to fall in the hottest and most unhealthful months. This particular conflict of opinion, in which the Secretary of the Treasury opposed the dispatching of the vessel and the Secretary of the Navy favored it, was resolved in favor of the latter. Meanwhile, apprehensions about Morocco had receded; and, while the blockade of Tripoli was not entirely effective and there had been American losses, the President had no doubt that in the end American pressure would prevail. In fact, the administration was diligent in this matter, and its patience was ultimately rewarded, but at the moment the dangers were being minimized and the difficulties kept out of sight.[2]

While recognizing that troubles with the Barbary powers might require the augmentation of the navy and some increase in expenses, he made his most interesting proposal with respect to naval vessels that were *not* in use. At this time he proposed to add to the Navy Yard in Washington a dock in which vessels could be "laid up dry and under cover from the sun." Since he figured that the cost of this would be little more than that of one vessel and it would save many ships from decay, he regarded the measure as one of economy. In connection with this project he had brought Benjamin Henry Latrobe to Washington, and that architect and engineer produced a plan so pleasing to him that he afterwards made Latrobe surveyor of public buildings. Some doubts were expressed by congressmen when they discussed the project of a drydock — Federalist Roger Griswold regarded it as a "visionary scheme" such as might be expected from the philosophy of the administration — and nothing came of it. The British chargé, who reported the proposal without apparent disapproval, seemed to think Jefferson sincere in his desire to preserve a decent navy. But the President did not now suggest the creation of a maritime force which could

[2] Following the declaration of war by Morocco, of which TJ knew by late August, 1802, the frigate *John Adams* was ordered to the Mediterranean. On the receipt of news that, in effect, the Emperor had declared a state of peace, TJ ordered the sailing of the frigate held up. Smith protested and, after consulting Madison, TJ ordered that she sail. Numerous letters bearing on this minor but interesting episode, chiefly in September, 1802, are in LC, Vol. 126; and the printed correspondence of Gallatin with TJ in August is full of references to Barbary affairs.

join with the British in driving the French from the seas and confining them behind their high-water mark.[3] And, while repeating his suggestion of the year before that Congress review the institution of the militia, he was proposing no change in the military establishment. He gave no sign that he anticipated any need for his country to assume a belligerent posture while the European powers were at peace.

The immediate danger lay in the situation at New Orleans, which he ignored in his official message to Congress. Two days after he sent this, however, the House of Representatives by unanimous vote adopted a resolution calling upon him for such papers as the government had relating to the removal of the deposit.[4] It seemed that the vigilant congressmen would not let him pursue the noiseless course he preferred. The French representative in Washington, who was still having difficulty in figuring the President out but had become convinced of his prudence, feared that he now faced a dilemma. However timid Mr. Jefferson might be, said Pichon, and whatever value he might set on his pacific policy, he would be impelled toward vigorous action in order not to lose the support of his own partisans.[5] Such might have been the case eventually, but the Frenchman misinterpreted the political situation at the moment. The resolution was introduced by John Randolph, the majority leader, and this was no unfriendly action. It beat the Federalists to the draw and gave Jefferson the chance, while supplementing his message in the light of the latest information, to speak words of reassurance. Furthermore, the limitation of the inquiry to developments in New Orleans was in accord with the effort of the administration to keep these entirely separate from the question of the cession of Louisiana to France.

When communicating to the House the papers requested by it, Jefferson asserted that the government had lost no time in taking every step required by the situation. Also, he reported the opinion of the administration that Morales, the Intendant at New Orleans, had acted on his own authority. He underlined this some days later by sending a copy of a letter from the Governor General of Louisiana to the Governor of the Mississippi Territory, denying responsibility for the Intendant's action and saying that this was not authorized by the govern-

[3] The episode of the drydock is dealt with by Talbot Hamlin, in *Benjamin Henry Latrobe* (1955), pp. 230, 257–258, and he shows Latrobe's preliminary design in Plate 21. TJ wrote Latrobe, Nov. 2, 1802, and Latrobe sent drawings and an estimate of cost ($167,968), Dec. 4 (LC, 21927–21928, 22026–22033). For discussion in the House of Representatives, Jan. 19, 20, 1803, see *Annals*, 7 Cong. 2 sess., pp. 401–411. Thornton reported TJ's proposals to Hawkesbury, Dec. 28, 1802 (FO, 5:35).
[4] Dec. 17, 1802 (*Annals*, 7 Cong., 2 sess., pp. 280–281).
[5] Pichon to Talleyrand, Dec. 23, 1802 (AECPEU, 55:125–127).

ment of Spain.[6] The same position was taken by the Spanish representative in the United States, the Marqués de Casa Yrujo, with whom
Madison had communicated promptly and who had promised his immediate interposition. The assumption on which the administration was
proceeding — that Morales had acted independently — was supported
by the best information available, and it warranted the hope that the
protest Madison quickly dispatched to Pinckney in Madrid would be
heeded by the Spanish government.[7] Even if Jefferson and his secretary of state had actually been less confident than they claimed to be,
they were wise in leaving a way of escape that the Spanish might take
without losing face.

The question of responsibility for what happened in New Orleans
has occasioned speculation among historians until this day. It now appears that Morales acted on instructions from home which he was enjoined to conceal from everybody, including Spanish officials of higher
rank than he, and that the French were neither responsible for what he
did nor informed of it by the Spanish court. Thus the blame which was
generally cast on them by the American public was actually unjustified,
and the administration was right in trying to keep this question distinct
from that of the cession of Louisiana. The motives of the Spanish government still remain rather mysterious, but a major reason for this ill-
timed order now appears to have been the abuse of the right of deposit
by Americans as a means of smuggling, and if diplomatic considerations
were involved they appear to have been connected with the anti-
French sentiments of Spanish officialdom of the moment.[8] Publicly, the
Intendant took the position that privileges granted neutrals in time of
war need not be continued in time of peace. By his proclamation he
closed the port of New Orleans to foreign commerce, thus striking a
blow at American shippers in Atlantic coastal cities who had been doing a lucrative business with New Orleans. The legal right of the Spanish to exclude these ships was unquestionable, however. The closure of
the deposit was another matter. Morales sought to justify this by de-

---

[6] TJ's communications to the House of Representatives were dated Dec. 22, 30,
1802 (*A.S.P.F.R.*, II, 469–471). On his suggestion, the letter from the Governor
General was not published, but it is identified and described in Madison's letter of
Jan. 10, 1803, to Pinckney (*ibid.*, II, 528). Claiborne wrote a letter of protest to
Governor Manuel de Salvado on Oct. 29, the same day that he transmitted to the
Secretary of State the proclamation of Morales, the Intendant, which he had re-
ceived from the Vice Consul in New Orleans.

[7] Madison to Pinckney, Nov. 27, 1802 (*ibid.*, II, 527).

[8] This matter is discussed by A. P. Whitaker in *The Mississippi Question*, ch.
XI, and by E. W. Lyon in *Louisiana in French Diplomacy*, ch. VIII, and "The
Closing of the Port of New Orleans" (*A.H.R.*, XXXVII, 280–286). The former
scholar is more doubtful than the latter that the problem of motive and responsibility has been finally solved.

scribing the deposit as a privilege granted by treaty for a term of three years, which had now expired. He disregarded the provision of the treaty that if the deposit were not continued at New Orleans it should be at an "equivalent establishment" elsewhere on the banks of the Mississippi.[9] Contrary to the opinion of many at the time, and of some later historians, the proclamation of the Intendant did not deny to Americans the free navigation of the Mississippi. Flatboats coming down the river could load their cargoes on vessels lying in the harbor, and there were other ways of meeting the new situation.[10] But fresh difficulties had been imposed on the exercise of American treaty rights, and Westerners could not have been expected to make fine legal distinctions. To them, as Madison correctly said, the Mississippi was everything — "the Hudson, the Delaware, the Potomac, and all the navigable rivers of the Atlantic States, formed into one stream."

This graphic statement was in the letter of protest the Secretary of State sent to the American Minister to Spain.[11] When Jefferson reported that the administration had done all the situation called for, he was referring chiefly to actions on the diplomatic front; and, while fully aware of the seriousness of the difficulty, he was convinced that this battle must be waged with diplomatic weapons. The protests of Governor Claiborne and Madison were prompt, vigorous, and proper. Even more important, as later events were to prove, were the representations of Yrujo. The Spanish representative was deeply obligated to Jefferson, who at the beginning of the administration had urged that he be retained in the post from which Timothy Pickering as secretary of state had sought his dismissal.[12] Also, the fact that he was married to the daughter of Governor Thomas McKean of Pennsylvania disposed him favorably to the Republican party, and he was on the best of personal terms with the President at this time. The Spanish Minister, who promptly agreed that the proclamation of the Intendant was in violation of the treaty with the United States, had already promised his immediate interposition in New Orleans. Though his representations were to prove ineffective there, they were ultimately to be influential in Spain, and the administration showed notable astuteness and skill in eliciting his full support. But no public statement about his co-operation

---

[9] Article XXII of the treaty.

[10] Senator John Brown wrote TJ from Frankfort, Ky., Nov. 26, 1802 (received Dec. 9) that relatively little western produce was then at New Orleans or on the way there, but that large quantities would be ready for exportation at the rise of the rivers in the spring (LC, 22002).

[11] Madison to Pinckney, Nov. 27, 1802 (*A.S.P.F.R.*, II, 527).

[12] TJ to Don Joseph Yznardi, Mar. 26, 1801 (Ford, VIII, 33–34). On this matter, see Whitaker, *Mississippi Question*, pp. 205–206, 313 (note 10).

THE SPANISH MINISTER: MARQUÉS DE CASA YRUJO
Portrait by Gilbert Stuart

could properly be made as yet, and diplomatic processes were painfully slow in an age when two months were generally required to get an official communication from Europe. Fortunately, the President could take into his confidence the leaders of his party in Congress, with whom he had established such cordial relations. And the record shows that the Republicans, including representatives from the West, were disposed to give him the time he needed. Also, they were willing to go along with him in his effort to maintain as much privacy as possible in delicate diplomatic matters. The opposition, which centered in the East, sought to gain political capital out of all these difficulties, but the Republican majority in the House of Representatives blocked the Federalists effectively and gave the President a vote of confidence.

On January 7, 1803, after a debate behind closed doors, resolutions on the New Orleans question were adopted by a vote of two to one. While affirming an "unalterable determination" to maintain American boundaries and rights of navigation on the Mississippi as established by treaties, the House expressed willingness to ascribe the recent action in New Orleans to the "unauthorized misconduct of certain individuals" rather than to ill faith on the part of the Spanish government. That is, the interpretation of this action by the administration was accepted for the time at least. What was more, the Representatives, "relying, with perfect confidence, on the vigilance and wisdom of the Executive," expressed willingness to await the issue of such measures as that branch of the government was pursuing. A Federalist amendment which would have stricken out this expression of confidence was beaten down.[13]

The Federalists had tried to secure the passage of a resolution of their own. Introduced by Roger Griswold of Connecticut early in the new year, this called upon the President for documents relating to the cession of Louisiana, together with a report on the circumstances, unless he should deem it improper to submit these at this time. If the Federalists did not know how incomplete the information in the possession of the government actually was they may have suspected it, and they could easily have guessed that Jefferson was not ready to show his hand. Clearly, they wanted to face him with the blame of a refusal to comply with their request and to publicize their concern over the problems of the West. John Randolph sought to set the record straight by showing who the "unshaken friends" of the navigation of the Missis-

[13] *Annals*, 7 Cong., 2 sess., pp. 339–342. The amendment was defeated, 30 to 53. Other clauses were approved by the Federalists, even though as a group they voted against the resolution as a whole. The resolution carried, 50 to 25. It is attached to the documents submitted by TJ in *A.S.P.F.R.*, II, 471.

sippi and western interests really were. The chief ammunition he employed was a speech by James Monroe in the debate in the Virginia ratifying convention of 1788, which he read to the House despite its wearisome length.[14] Monroe had castigated John Jay and the eastern states supporting him in his famous negotiations with Gardoqui, when he was secretary for foreign affairs under the Confederation, alleging that he would have bartered away western interests for eastern commercial advantage.

The net result of this sparring and maneuvering in the House of Representatives was that consideration of Griswold's resolution was postponed until the Randolph resolution could be passed and that, finally, the Federalist motion was defeated. This was on the very day when Jefferson cut the ground from under the opposition and gratified the Westerners by sending to the Senate the nomination of Monroe as minister extraordinary, to negotiate with the French and, if need be, with the Spanish.[15] The synchronization of these legislative and executive actions was perfect, and the appointment of the recent Governor of Virginia to this mission was a skillful stroke.

Though the administration had the House of Representatives under firm control, Jefferson was well aware of the extreme agitation of the public mind and of the necessity of doing something to quiet it. The legislature of Kentucky had adopted a memorial to the President and Congress respecting the closing of the deposit, and Madison said that representations were expected from every quarter of the West. Jefferson himself spoke privately of the "fever" of the western mind, of the "ferment" of the whole country which threatened its peace, and of the necessity of adopting "measures of urgency." The ones he had been pursuing were invisible, or largely so, and thus insufficient to quiet the minds of the Westerners. The appointment of Monroe was calculated to reassure them, and Randolph's extended reference to his past efforts in behalf of the free navigation of the Mississippi, while certainly not accidental, may in fact have been unnecessary. In Jefferson's opinion, he had the "unlimited confidence" of the western people, as he had that of Jefferson himself.

Monroe, who had just ended his term as governor of Virginia, was actually on the point of setting out for the West when he got word of his appointment.[16] Before resuming the practice of law he was going to look after his interests in Kentucky, where he had large landholdings.

[14] Jan. 6, 1803 (*Annals*, 7 Cong., 2 sess., pp. 330–335). Griswold's resolution was introduced Jan. 4 (*Ibid.*, pp. 312–313).

[15] Jan. 11, 1803 (*Ibid.*, p. 368).

[16] Monroe to TJ, Jan. 7, 1803 (S.M.H., IV, 1); TJ wrote him Jan. 10 (Ford, VIII, 188).

His chief adviser with respect to these lands was Senator John Breckinridge of that state, formerly of Albemarle County, Virginia.[17] Jefferson was at pains to point out to the prospective envoy that the financial arrangements for his services abroad were not so good as those the Federalists had made for their extraordinary missions. Time was to show that the President, while seeking to avoid all appearance of granting special favors to a friend, was requiring of him a great personal sacrifice.[18] Monroe himself was painfully aware of the danger that his diplomatic venture might prove a failure, but this inveterate public man was glad to be brought back into the current of national and international affairs in behalf of a cause to which he had long been committed. Since the Federalist senators voted on strict party lines against his confirmation, quite obviously they chose to treat his appointment as political.[19] Jefferson himself claimed that it had silenced the Federalists. Within a few weeks he was to discover that such was by no means the case, and even now they were saying that he had "taken special care that a stone which the builders rejected should become the first of the corner." [20] The Federalists had not forgotten that Washington had recalled Monroe from France, and, according to their party line, he returned home in disgrace. But his appointment was pleasing to Republicans generally, and particularly to the men of the western waters. It was a tangible action which, for a time at least, was reassuring.

An accompanying legislative action was only partially visible to the general public. Congress implemented the mission by appropriating $2,000,000 "to defray any expenses which may be incurred in relation to the intercourse between the United States and foreign nations." Thus the resolution read, but the full purpose of the appropriation was made clear only in secret session. This was to enable the executive to begin negotiations with the French and Spanish governments for the purchase of the island of New Orleans and the provinces of East and West Florida.[21]

[17] Whitaker, p. 313, note 19, cites Monroe to Breckinridge, Mar. 4, 1803, from Breckinridge Papers, saying that he had one tract of 20,000 acres and that he instructed his attorney to follow Breckinridge's advice in connection with these lands during his own absence in Europe.

[18] TJ to Monroe, Jan. 13, 1803 (Ford, VIII, 190–192). In his unpublished biography of Monroe, Harry Ammon points out that he never fully escaped from the burden of debt he assumed as a result of this costly mission.

[19] The nomination was sent to the Senate on Jan. 11, 1803, and confirmed by a vote of 15 to 12 (*Journal of Executive Procs. of the Senate*, I, 431–432, 436).

[20] Gouverneur Morris to James Parrish, Jan. 14, 1803 (*Diary and Letters*, II, 431).

[21] Jan. 12, 1803. Report of Committee of House of Representatives recommending the adoption of the resolutions (*Annals*, 7 Cong., 2 sess., pp. 370–374). The burden of the argument was that possession of these territories was necessary for

The desire of the administration to acquire New Orleans and the Floridas, now revealed to Congress, had already been made known to Livingston. While Jefferson refused to blame the French government for the action of the Spanish Intendant in the coveted city, there could be no doubt that New Orleans was included in the cession to France. The latest word from Livingston was that the provinces of East and West Florida were not included, though they were greatly desired by Bonaparte. Thus the negotiations that Congress had agreed to support were shrouded in uncertainties. To Senator Gouverneur Morris the faith of Jefferson was not as a grain of mustard seed but as a full-sized pumpkin. Probably it was never as great in fact as the President himself averred, but it had been augmented by a letter he got on the last day of the year from Du Pont de Nemours, who took a more favorable view of the situation than Livingston.[22]

Assuming, as he really had no right to do, that the French would possess themselves of the Floridas as well as New Orleans, and believing that there would be no obstacle to negotiations with the United States after they had done so, Du Pont set forth certain proposals that he would make if his advice were sought. The settlement he described was one that he regarded as mutually desirable and that actually coincided with the immediate desire of the administration — namely, the cession to the United States of all the territory east of the Mississippi. In return for this Du Pont proposed that the French be granted the same freedom as Americans to conduct business in the ceded region without paying duties, and that all the territory west of the Mississippi be absolutely reserved for France. Finally, he suggested $6,000,000 as the selling price for the eastern region. Outstanding American spoliation claims against France plus the appropriation by Congress approximated that sum, and Jefferson probably had these facts in mind when he requested $2,000,000 of that body.

He may have been considerably less sanguine than Du Pont. Correctly assuming, however, that things were still in a state of flux, he believed that even a faint hope of successful negotiation should be pursued, that he must continue to play for time, that he must follow a policy of patience. Events were to vindicate his judgment. At this very

<hr>

the safety of the country and that acquisition of them by purchase was preferable to acquisition by war. It was recognized that more money might be required.

[22] Du Pont to TJ, Oct. 4, 1802, received Dec. 31 (*J.-D. Correspondence*, pp. 68–71). Presumably Madison referred to this in his letters of Jan. 18, 1803, to Livingston and Pinckney (*A.S.P.F.R.*, II, 529). TJ's reply of Feb. 1, 1803 (Ford, VIII, 203–208), was carried by Monroe and left open for Livingston's perusal. He and Monroe agreed, however, that it would be best not to deliver it for the present. (Livingston to TJ, Apr. 14, 1803 [LC, 22586].)

juncture, the death of General Leclerc in St. Domingo and the virtual annihilation of his army by disease were being mourned in Paris; and the French expedition designed for Louisiana was icebound in a Dutch port. Unfortunately, Monroe's mission to France was also delayed. Not until two months after his nomination did he set sail, and in the meantime there were further signs of impatience at home, especially among the Federalists in Congress.[23] Shortly after Gouverneur Morris voted against the confirmation of Monroe, that senator summed up his judgment of the President's policies: "He believes in payment of debts by diminution of revenue, in defence of territory by reduction of armies, and in vindication of rights by appointment of ambassadors.[24]

Jefferson himself afterwards claimed that at least from the spring of 1802, when he first had authentic information of the cession of Louisiana to France, the administration had clearly recognized the possibility of war and prepared for that eventuality. The grumblers would be mortified, he believed, if they could see the files of the government. "They would see," he wrote, "that tho' we could not say when war would arise, yet we said with energy what would take place when it should arise." [25] His reference was to a general war such as actually broke out, not to a localized conflict in which his own country might become engaged with Spain or France, and he appears to have been thinking primarily in long-range terms. An examination of the records of the War Department does in fact reveal that he did considerably more for national defense, outside the field of diplomacy, than many later historians gave him credit for, and more than was known to the American public at the time.[26]

Whether the military preparations on the frontier were adequate or inadequate is an unanswerable question, since they were not tested, but against partisan criticism it could have been safely asserted that Dearborn was a much more effective secretary of war than his Federalist predecessor, James McHenry. During the winter of 1802–1803 he undoubtedly gave his major attention to frontier defense. It may be that

[23] Monroe sailed from New York on Mar. 9, 1803.

[24] Morris to James Parish, Jan. 14, 1803 (*Diary and Letters,* II, 431). See also Manasseh Cutler to Dr. James Torrey, Jan. 15, 1803 (Cutler's *Life,* II, 122).

[25] TJ to Horatio Gates, July 11, 1803 (Ford, VIII, 250).

[26] Mary P. Adams, in "Jefferson's Reaction to the Treaty of San Ildefonso" (*Jour. Sou. Hist.,* XXI [May, 1955], 173–188), challenging the statements of Henry Adams and other historians who do not credit TJ with military preparations, gives a spirited account of his actions. She refers particularly to military preparations on the Mississippi and the northern boundary, to land policy, Indian policy, and the Lewis and Clark Expedition.

the things he did were long overdue, but he did as much as could reasonably have been expected, considering the means at his disposal.[27] It is
a question whether or not more means should have been provided, but
the President did not want to alarm the country and, given the
total circumstances, he thought the provisions sufficient. The crucial
area was the Mississippi Territory. Early in January, Governor Claiborne wrote from Natchez: "We have in this part of the Territory,
about two thousand Militia, pretty well organized, and with a portion
of this force (say six hundred men) my opinion is, that New Orleans
might be taken possession of provided there should be only Spanish
troops to defend the place." About the same time Dearborn took steps
to strengthen Fort Adams, on the river just above the Spanish border,
and he afterwards reinforced it further.[28]

More interest attaches to policies and actions with respect to the Indians, with which Jefferson was more directly concerned and which
had more long-range significance. Because of their nature, these could
not be publicly proclaimed; they were described in communications to
the Secretary of War and other officials and a confidential message to
Congress. They suggest that the President had divested his mind of the
sentimentality he had previously manifested toward the American abo-
rigines. He was now under no necessity to defend them against the
aspersions of French naturalists, but he was well aware of the danger of
their falling under French influence with the reversion of Louisiana to
its former owners.[29] His present concern was to protect his own borders by removing the Indians from them as soon as possible and replacing the redmen with white settlers; but, rationalizing his position in his
own mind no doubt, he claimed that he was seeking to lead them into
the paths of peace and the blessings of agricultural society. Perhaps no
President ever addressed visiting delegations of Indians in more gracious fraternal language. Speaking to one group early in 1802, he said,
characteristically: "We shall, with great pleasure, see your people become disposed to cultivate the earth, to raise herds of the useful animals, and to spin and weave, for their food and clothing."[30] An
important result of their adoption of a life of agriculture and herding,

[27] This is the judgment of Erney in his dissertation on Dearborn, p. 108.

[28] Claiborne to the Secretary of State, Jan. 3, 1803 (*Official Letter Books of
W. C. C. Claiborne* [1917], I, 253). For other actions of Dearborn in the spring,
see Mary P. Adams, pp. 176–179.

[29] For his previous defense of the Indians, see *Jefferson the Virginian*, pp. 385–
387; *Jefferson and the Rights of Man*, pp. 101–102; *Jefferson and the Ordeal of
Liberty*, pp. 346, 355.

[30] Jan. 7, 1802 (L. & B., XVI, 390). For other addresses of 1802 and early 1803,
see pp. 391–400.

rather than hunting, would be that they would require less land, and the circumstances of the time sharply accentuated his desire to speed the process.

Before revealing his purposes in confidence to Congress early in 1803, he wrote Dearborn a long letter in which he described them without restraint. By procuring Indian lands along the Mississippi and its tributaries, he hoped to establish on the western boundary a "strong front," so that the great river would serve as a barrier like the Atlantic on the East.

> Our proceedings with the Indians should tend systematically to that object [he said], leaving the extinguishment of title in the interior country to fall in as occasion may arise. The Indians being once closed in between strong settled countries on the Mississippi & Atlantic, will, for want of game, be forced to agriculture, will find that small portions of land well improved, will be worth more to them than extensive forests unemployed, and will be continually parting with portions of them, for money to buy stock, utensils & necessities for their farms & families.[31]

Also, he was thinking of more than the interests of the Indians when he referred to the system of trading posts or "factories" that Dearborn had already extended. These were to provide at slightly more than cost such necessities and comforts as the Indians might wish — except for spirituous liquors, which he wisely excluded. By means of these "factories" the administration sought to counteract not only the influence of foreign traders but also that of irresponsible American traders, and by contrast with the practices of others the conduct of the government was relatively benevolent, as Jefferson always claimed it was. But, with a degree of candor which was possible only in private communications, he suggested that the Indians be encouraged to run into debt and thus be rendered amenable to the cession of land in order to rid themselves of it.

Thus expressed, his policy sounds cold-blooded; and quite clearly, in this time of crisis, he was making a virtue of what he regarded as necessity. His private communications as well as his public utterances abound in expressions of good will, however. To Governor William Henry Harrison of Indiana Territory he wrote:

> Our system is to live in perpetual peace with the Indians, to cultivate an affectionate attachment from them, by everything just & liberal which we can do for them within the bounds of reason, and

---

[31] TJ to Dearborn, Dec. 29, 1802 (LC, 22110–22112). This letter served as one of Dearborn's guides in Indian policy thenceforth.

by giving them effectual protection against wrongs from our own people.[32]

Despite all he had said in the past about the noble savages, he assumed that the "bounds of reason" were to be determined, not by them, but by paternalistic authority. He undoubtedly thought of himself as a promoter of social evolution, however, and as a humane man. To Harrison he also wrote:

> In this way our settlements will gradually circumscribe & approach the Indians, & they will in time either incorporate with us as citizens of the U.S. or remove beyond the Mississippi. The former is certainly the termination of their history most happy for themselves, but, in the whole course of this, it is essential to cultivate their love. As to their fear, we presume that our strength & their weakness is now so visible that they must see we have only to shut our hand to crush them, & that all our liberalities to them proceed from motives of pure humanity only.

Specifically, he sought cessions of land in the Northwest, and by the treaty with the Kaskaskia tribe, whose weakness he pointed out, the United States gained title, later in this year, to a tremendous area from the Illinois River to the Ohio, amounting to about a third of the present state of Illinois. He began to create a "broad front" there at any rate. No special effort was made at this time to get lands on the Mississippi from the Yazoo to the Illinois, because that country belonged to the Chickasaws, a notably friendly tribe that was specially averse to the alienation of its lands. A trading post was set up at Chickasaw Bluff, however, as were others at strategic points elsewhere. In terms of frontier defense and the promotion of settlement the Indian policy of the administration was realistic, and it could hardly fail to be popular among the settlers as it became known. Its results were not immediate, however, and it was fully revealed only in private. Jefferson described it, in somewhat more restrained language, in a confidential message to Congress which had a further and even more secret purpose. He was seeking support for a western expedition in which commercial, scientific, and military objectives would be conjoined.[33]

He presented a request for an appropriation of $2500 for an exploring expedition as though it were a direct outgrowth of the Indian policy he was now describing in confidence to the Great Council of the

---

[32] TJ to Gov. W. H. Harrison, Feb. 27, 1803 (LC, 22410–22413; also L. & B., X, 368–373).
[33] Jan. 18, 1803 (*Annals*, 7 Cong., 2 sess., pp. 24–26; Ford, VIII, 192–202, with letters about the Lewis and Clark Expedition).

nation. One result of extending the trading houses would be to drive Americans as well as foreigners from the Indian trade east of the Mississippi. Compensatory opportunity should be sought for the former in the trans-Mississippi region, and it would be to American advantage to supplant or anticipate foreigners in the fur trade there. He was thinking of the British, operating from Canada, and his reference to the exploration, not merely of the course of the Missouri, but also of the "whole line even to the Western Ocean," showed that he was well aware of Oregon. Thus presented, his proposal appears to have been motivated primarily by commercial considerations such as should have commended him to men of business enterprise.

In public, the commercial purposes of the expedition were to be masked by its avowed scientific objects. That the latter were important to Jefferson himself could be questioned by no one who knew him well; and he may have presented the matter to Congress as he did because he doubted the constitutional authority of that body to make an appropriation for a "literary expedition." This is what he told the Spanish envoy beforehand, at any rate.[34] Presenting the project to Congress in what he regarded as its most appealing form, he gained speedy approval of it. The bearing of the expedition on frontier defense was not immediate, but information about the Indians might prove very valuable; and if Louisiana had not been acquired before Meriwether Lewis and William Clark set out, these two army officers would have made what amounted to a military reconnaissance. Since their famous expedition did not get started until another year and was not finished in his first term, it need not concern us further here. Viewed in retrospect it affords a notable example of his continental vision, and by proposing it to Congress he may be presumed to have strengthened his already strong hold on the Westerners in that body. But only indirectly could he reach the general public by this action; and he did not thus satisfy scorners of long-range measures who clamored for immediate results. Nor was it to be expected, at a time when nothing much seemed to be happening, that the partisan opposition would remain silent for long. It is not surprising, therefore, that within a month of the delivery of the President's confidential message to Congress, the Federalists in the Senate sought to force his hand.

The obvious line for critics to take was that the policies of the administration in the face of this crisis were feeble. Early in February, while

---

[34] Yrujo to Cevallos, Dec. 2, 1802 (Donald Jackson, ed., *Letters of the Lewis and Clark Expedition* [1962], p. 4). Pichon also accepted this interpretation (to Talleyrand, Mar. 4, 1803).

Monroe was still awaiting passage, the *New York Evening Post* described the appointment of an envoy extraordinary, under the existing circumstances, as "in every respect the weakest measure that ever disgraced the administration of any country." The editor of this Federalist paper said this in introducing a letter signed PERICLES but written by no less a person that Alexander Hamilton.[35] Impatience was to be expected of this political activist who had described Jefferson's annual message to Congress as a lullaby. Commenting late in December on the embarrassing situation in Louisiana, he had asked: "Yet how is popularity to be preserved with the western partisans, if their interests are tamely sacrificed? Will the artifice be for the chief to hold a bold language, and the subalterns to act a feeble part?"[36] Then he gave his own position with respect to western affairs: "I have always held that the *unity of our Empire*, and the best interests of our nation, require that we shall annex to the United States all the territory east of the Mississippi, New Orleans included. Of course I infer that, on an emergency like the present, energy is wisdom."

A few weeks later, viewing the situation as PERICLES, he regarded it as no less portentous. Claiming that war was undoubtedly justifiable and reducing the question to one of expediency, he recognized two courses only: "First, to negotiate, and endeavor to purchase; and if this fails, to go to war. Secondly, to seize at once on the Floridas and New Orleans, and then negotiate." Being sure that negotiation would fail, he advocated the second plan. France was exhausted at the moment, in his opinion, and British naval aid could be counted on. Naval and military preparations should be made by the United States, to be sure, and negotiations should be pushed with the British, but the plan itself should be adopted and proclaimed before Monroe's departure. "Such measures would astonish and disconcert Bonaparte himself; our envoy would be enabled to speak and treat with effect, and all Europe would be taught to respect us." Also, by pursuing such a course, Jefferson "might yet retrieve his character." Hamilton did not really believe his old antagonist would do that, he said, but he threw out ideas that he himself had long entertained in the hope of strengthening the "current of public feeling in favor of decisive measures."

It is hard to believe that a statesman of his intelligence could have regarded immediate recourse to war as either justifiable or practicable under existing circumstances. The possibility of ultimate recourse to it, in alliance with the British after the European conflict had been re-

[35] *N.Y. Evening Post*, Feb. 8, 1803. The letter is in Lodge, V, 464–467.
[36] Hamilton to Gen. C. C. Pinckney, Dec. 29, 1802 (J.C.H., VI, 551–552). He had heard that the President was "very stout" in conversation.

sumed, had been clearly recognized by Jefferson, but unilateral action such as Hamilton advocated and which at this time would necessarily have been directed against both France and Spain might well have been disastrous. The most natural explanation of his immediate purpose is that as a patriot he was characteristically urging greater military prepa- rations and that as a partisan he was seeking to embarrass Jefferson.

Senatorial critics of the policy of the government advanced similar arguments in support of like proposals. This was in connection with the resolutions introduced by Senator James Ross of Pennsylvania about a week after the letter of Hamilton appeared.[37] From the point of view of Federalist partisans the timing of this verbal attack on the administra- tion was good. Before the former Secretary of the Treasury assumed the mantle of PERICLES, the news got out that the Spanish government had issued an order for the delivery of the province of Louisiana to the French official or officials who should appear to receive it.[38] A transla- tion of this order got into print, and the reference in it to the province of Louisiana "as possessed by the French" when they ceded it to His Catholic Majesty aroused in some minds the fear that the French would claim the entire Mississippi Valley. No special preparations for the de- livery of the province had been reported as yet, but before the debate on the Ross Resolutions was finished the *New York Evening Post*, re- laying word from London that the expedition of the French to Louisi- ana had been expected to sail in January, predicted that they would be in peaceful possession of the province by the time Monroe made his first bow to Bonaparte.[39] That is, his mission would be too little and too late.

Senator Ross's explanation of his move in the Senate was that he was not willing to go home without making an effort to avert the calamity threatening the western country. He had more right to be called a

[37] Ross spoke about them Feb. 14, 1803, and formally introduced them Feb. 16 (*Annals*, 7 Cong., 2 sess., pp. 83-89, 91-97). They were debated Feb. 23-25. Whita- ker gives an admirable account of the entire episode in *Mississippi Question*, pp. 209-217. He takes sharp issue with Lodge's editorial statement that Hamilton parted with his party on the Louisiana question, as at this stage Hamilton certainly did not.

[38] W. E. Hulings, American Vice Consul in New Orleans, after getting from a friend a copy of the order of July 30, 1802, transmitted this to Madison on Dec. 15, 1802, and to Gov. Claiborne on Dec. 24. (To Madison, Jan. 20, 1803 [*A.H.R.*, XXXII, 823]; to Claiborne, Dec. 24, 1802, with translation of order [*Official Letter Books of W. C. C. Claiborne*, I, 256-257].) According to Whitaker, p. 314, note 23, the order was printed in *Constitutional Conservator* of Natchez, Jan. 11, 1803, and appeared in eastern papers before the end of January. It was not "publicly communicated," however, and should not be confused with the order of Oct. 15, 1802, actually calling for the delivery of the province to France.

[39] *N.Y. Evening Post*, Feb. 21, 1803. The arrival in New York of Monroe to take ship was reported at the same time. He did not sail for more than two weeks.

Westerner than any other Federalist in that body since he came from Pittsburgh. "When in possession, you will negotiate with more advantage," he said, echoing Hamilton. The French might be persuaded to sell "if they found us armed — in possession, and resolved to maintain it." [40] The resolutions introduced by him described American rights on the Mississippi and in New Orleans as indisputable, termed the recent infraction of them an aggression hostile to the honor and interest of the country, and asserted that citizens on the western waters were entitled to "complete security" for the enjoyment of their "absolute right." Some of the speakers on the other side objected to this as an overstatement, but no one denied that the American case was strong. If adopted these resolutions would have authorized the President to "take immediate possession of such place or places" on or near the island of New Orleans as he might deem "fit and convenient" for securing the rights previously described. For this purpose he might call out the militia, to the number of 50,000, from five specified southern and western states and the Mississippi Territory. Finally, the sum of $5,000,000 was to be appropriated to carry the resolutions into effect.[41]

Whether the Federalists should be taken at their own valuation as devoted patriots seeking to arouse their countrymen to a due sense of peril, or at that of their opponents as partisans seeking to make political capital out of the Mississippi question, they were desirous that the discussion of the Ross Resolutions, unlike the discussion of this question in the House, be public. It was so ordered after agreement was reached that no confidential information should be revealed by any senator. The debate proper lasted three days and the account of it fills some 150 pages in the *Annals of Congress*.[42] Besides asserting that no efficacious measures had been taken by the administration or proposed by the majority, the Federalist senators, who with the exception of Ross were indubitably Easterners, made strong claims about western discontent and restlessness, adverting to the possibility that the men of the western waters might take matters into their own hands or withdraw from the Union. By contrast, senators from the West, Republicans all, decried these alarms and asserted that their constituents reposed full confidence in the government. Judging from the expressions of these spokesmen, De-Witt Clinton of New York was warranted in saying: "If there be a portion of the United States *peculiarly* attached to republican government and the present Administration, I should select the Western States

---

[40] *Annals*, 7 Cong., 2 sess., p. 88.
[41] Resolutions, *ibid.*, pp. 95–96. The states named were S.C., Ga., Ohio, Ky., and Tenn.
[42] Feb. 23–25, 1803 (*ibid.*, pp. 105–256).

as that portion." [43] Another eastern Republican said that the whole desire of Ross was to stir up the western people to a belief that the government was "insensible to their sufferings, and inattentive to their interests." [44]

When Republicans charged Ross with introducing a war measure
pure and simple, certain Federalists denied that war was imperative,
since the President need not avail himself of the authorization that
would be granted him. This, indeed, was just the point. Being confident
that Jefferson would not seize New Orleans immediately, if at all, his
political enemies sought to put him in the embarrassing position of declining to do so, while they remained free to blame him for whatever
happened. Toward the end of the debate, one of the Virginia senators
characterized the resolutions as unconstitutional on two grounds: (1)
Congress could not transfer to the President the power of declaring
war; (2) the militia could be used only "to suppress insurrections and
repel invasions" — not sent outside the United States for conquest or
revenge.[45] The modern student is most likely to object to this entire
Federalist move as an attempt to interfere with the President's conduct
of foreign affairs.

The day of bipartisanship in that field was far distant, but what was
said by the President's friend John Breckinridge of Kentucky should
have been true: that the only real difference between the Federalists
and the Republicans was with respect to the means of attaining ends
desired by both. In his opinion, the government was pursuing the "only
true and dignified course" and the only one tending to unite all parts of
the country. Recognizing, however, that they must be prepared to redress the situation in case of diplomatic failure, he presented, on the
first day of the full debate, resolutions that he would substitute for
those of Ross. These called for preparations which, in his opinion,
would have a good effect on negotiation. After the defeat of the Federalist proposals by a strict party vote, the Breckinridge resolutions were
adopted unanimously.[46] Without mentioning New Orleans or Louisiana
or the Floridas, these authorized the President, whenever he should
deem it expedient, to require the governors of the several states (eastern included) to organize and make ready for immediate service 80,000
militia. The Federalists called the Breckinridge resolutions "milk-and-
water propositions" and said that but for themselves there would have

[43] Ibid., p. 134.
[44] Wright of Maryland (ibid., p. 160).
[45] S. T. Mason (ibid., p. 216).
[46] Resolutions (ibid., pp. 255–256). See also act of Mar. 2, 1803, regarding militia
(pp. 1566–1567). This required annual reports by states, but proved to have little
value because of inadequate reports.

been no defense measure at all. The British representative regarded the outcome as "no inconsiderable triumph" for them.[47] But the initiative lay with the President, and the moment that he deemed expedient did not arrive.

The public debate on the Mississippi question in the Senate near the end of the congressional session may possibly have had some effect on the negotiations with France, but it had none on the negotiations with Spain about the deposit in New Orleans. The Foreign Secretary of that country had decided to restore the deposit before the debate occurred, and he sent a formal order to that effect before the adjournment of Congress.[48] The individual to whom the country was most indebted for the change in Spanish policy was Yrujo, who was undoubtedly impressed by earlier warlike talk in Congress. At the beginning of the year the Spanish Minister, while praising Jefferson for virtue, moderation, and sanity, had written this to his home government: "I am convinced that if the proclamation of the Intendant is not revoked in three months the clamor of the Federalists, the impulse of public opinion and party policy will force the President and the Republicans to declare war against their wish." [49] In speculating about the reasons for the reopening of the deposit in New Orleans we may suppose that the Spanish had become aware by this time of the likelihood of the resumption of the war in Europe and that they wanted to relieve themselves of needless difficulties and dangers in a place which they were soon to yield to the French anyway. Since consciousness of belligerent sentiment in the United States, as reported by their minister earlier, could hardly have failed to influence them, "Federalist clamor" in Congress before the presentation of the Ross resolutions probably did prove an aid to negotiation. Unwittingly, the President's enemies may have done him a good turn.

He was more than willing for the Spanish and French representatives to become aware of the spirit of belligerency, but he was seeking to prevent that spirit from getting out of hand during the painfully slow course of diplomacy. Shortly after the recess of Congress, when the President was briefly at Monticello, Yrujo renewed his pressure on the Intendant in New Orleans, and both he and Pichon sought to aid the administration in its efforts to tranquilize the country. On receipt of

[47] Thornton to Hawkesbury, Mar. 9, 1803 (FO, 5:38, No. 14).
[48] This was signed Mar. 1, 1803, and became known in Washington Apr. 19.
[49] Yrujo to Cevallos, Jan. 3, 1803 (quoted by Lyon, *Louisiana in French Policy*, p. 176). Other dispatches, soon thereafter, argued to the same effect (see Whitaker, p. 231).

further information from New Orleans, the Spanish Minister wrote Madison a letter which at his own request was released to the press in translation.[50] In this Yrujo stated that his opinion that the action of the Intendant was wholly personal had been verified, and that he was now taking measures which would ensure to the United States the full enjoyment of all its treaty rights. In fact, he was ordering Morales to restore the deposit or designate another place for one.[51] A couple of days later a letter from Pichon to the Governor of Louisiana, protesting in the name of France against the Intendant's action, was also published.[52] In New Orleans nothing came of these letters and they do not appear to have satisfied the more warlike Federalists, but their general effect should have been tranquilizing and reassuring.

The President was back in Washington when decisive news came from Spain. This was communicated to Yrujo, who was to transmit it to New Orleans, and he imparted it to Madison without a moment's delay. On April 20, which happened to be the day before Jefferson sent Dr. Rush a private account of his religious beliefs, a letter from the Spanish Minister to the Secretary of State was published.[53] In this he said that His Catholic Majesty had provided that the deposit should continue at New Orleans until the two governments should agree about another equivalent place. The orders were enclosed and Madison was asked to forward them. In due course they reached the surprised Intendant and the old arrangement was restored.[54]

This was an unquestionable diplomatic victory, but, in private at least, Jefferson used exaggerated terms in speaking of the ills the country had escaped. He said that by peaceful and reasonable procedure the United States had gained in four months what would have required seven years of war and cost 100,000 lives and $100,000,000 of debt, not to speak of vast losses in trade and the demoralization of mind always incident to war. One wonders where he got these estimates and is glad he did not make them public. But he spoke like a realistic statesman and astute diplomat in other things he said: "To have seized N. Orleans as our federal maniacs wished, would only have changed the character & extent of the blockade of our Western commerce. It would have produced a blockade by superior naval force of the navigation of the river

[50] National Intelligencer, Mar. 14, 1803. Madison to TJ, Mar. 10, 14, 1803 (LC, 22467, 22481).
[51] Yrujo wrote Morales, Mar. 11 (Whitaker, p. 311, note 21).
[52] National Intelligencer, Mar. 16, 1803. Madison wrote TJ about this Mar. 17, (LC, 22503).
[53] National Intelligencer, Apr. 20, 1803.
[54] May 17, 1803.

as well as of the entrance into N. Orleans, instead of a paper blockade from N. Orleans alone, while the river remained open." [55]

The "infracted right" had now been restored, and he was assured by the Spanish that the treaty commitments they had so handsomely reaffirmed would be binding on the French. At the moment, he admitted privately that he could not "count with confidence on obtaining New Orleans from France for money," but he did not doubt that he had been wise in seeking to postpone the day of contention and confrontation until the situation should become more favorable.

He penned these reflections and gave this counsel of patience on the last day of April. Writing Monroe privately the next day, Madison said that the orders for the restoration of the deposit had had a good effect on the public mind, and that, despite a strong trend against the party in New England, general political prospects were bright.[56] There was scarcely a cloud except Louisiana, he said. If that were removed the country would be the admiration and envy of the world. He now had important news of impending events which might prove helpful. On or by that day the Secretary of State got word from London that Great Britain and France were about to renew their war. "I hope we shall be wise enough to shun their follies," he said, "and fortunate enough to turn them by honest means to our just interests. You will probably have arrived very critically for the purpose." He and Jefferson did not know that an agreement had already been reached in Paris for the cession to the United States of all the French territory on the continent of North America that was at the disposal of the First Consul.

[55] TJ to Dr. Hugh Williamson, Apr. 30, 1803 (L. & B., X, 386, but quoted here from the original). See also his letter of the same date to John Bacon (Ford, VIII, 229). Presumably he did not learn until the next day of the impending revival of the European war.
[56] Madison to Monroe, May 1, 1803 (MP, 25:66).

[XVI]

The Louisiana Treaty

ON July 3, 1803, two months after the event, word reached Jefferson in Washington that his representatives had signed a treaty whereby the United States would acquire from France the entire province of Louisiana. The news was the most momentous he received while President. He promptly gave it out, with the happy result that the *National Intelligencer* published it on the anniversary of the Declaration of Independence. Writing his son-in-law the next day, he said: "This removes from us the greatest source of danger to our peace." [1] Not until ten days later, when he got the treaty and the two accompanying conventions, did he learn what the cost would be, and not even then did he or anybody else know what the precise boundaries of the acquisition were, but from the first report he concluded that the province extended to the "highlands round the head of the Missouri," and that it was somewhat larger than the whole of the United States.[2]

The chorus of approval that greeted the first announcement was a little less than unanimous: a sour note was immediately sounded in certain quarters in New England, where the news got out unofficially before it reached Washington.[3] From the vantage point of New York, however, the best of the Federalist newspapers discerned that the treaty was favorable to the country and the acquisition important. Also, this paper conceded that the purchase was likely to give *éclat* to the administration. Having made these admissions, it proceeded to add a qualifying statement: "Every man, however, possessed of the least candor and reflection will readily acknowledge that the acquisition has been solely owing to a fortuitous concurrence of unforeseen and unex-

[1] TJ to TMR, July 5, 1803 (LC, 22946).

[2] The formal communication from Livingston and Monroe, dated May 13, 1803 (*A.S.P.F.R.*, II, 558–560), was received July 14. The note in Carter, IX, 4, gives full chronological details with useful references.

[3] The news was brought to Boston by ship from Le Havre by June 28.

pected circumstances, and not to any wise or vigorous measures on the part of the American government." [4]

This was a partisan assertion of an editor who was informed of only external events. William Coleman had not read the official communications which were to be submitted in confidence to the Senate in the fall. He was ignorant of the actual course of the negotiations in Paris and of what the administration in Washington had done behind the scenes to further them. In important respects, however, these negotiations had in fact been beyond the control of the government, and necessarily so.

The President and the Secretary of State lost contact with Monroe the moment he sailed from New York on March 9. Toward the end of May they learned that, on the day before Monroe reached Paris, Talleyrand asked Livingston if the United States wished to buy all of Louisiana. Livingston reported this episode immediately and afterwards intimated, on the strength of it, that there had been no real need for Monroe to come.[5] In midsummer Jefferson and Madison learned that the two Americans — negotiating with Barbé-Marbois, the Minister of Finance — had agreed to terms that went beyond their instructions. Livingston and Monroe did so without consulting their own government, an action that would have delayed matters three or four months. The renewal of the European war already seemed inevitable; it became a reality a couple of weeks after the purchase was agreed to. The two events were reported in the United States almost simultaneously and were obviously connected. In the light of the full information now available it is equally obvious that this epoch-making agreement with France was owing to a concurrence of extraordinarily fortunate circumstances — fortunate, that is, from the American point of view. Some of these circumstances were unforeseen by Jefferson, as they were by Hamilton and other Americans of note.

This is not to say, however, that the administration did not provide for such contingencies as were reasonably to be expected, or that it deserves no credit beyond that of recognizing good luck and seizing upon it.[6] The wisdom of its flexible policy was demonstrated by events, and if its measures had been described as feeble by some partisan critics they were shown to have been vigorous enough. Also, if

[4] N.Y. Evening Post, July 5, 1803.

[5] Livingston to Madison, Apr. 11, 1803 (A.S.P.F.R., II, 552).

[6] Dangerfield introduces his judicious discussion of causation and credit (Livingston, p. 369) by quoting Edward Channing's assertion that Napoleon "threw the province, so to speak, at Livingston, Monroe, Madison, and Jefferson; and they share between them equally — whatever credit there was in catching it and holding it — that is all." (Hist. of the U.S., IV [1917], 319, note 2.)

Jefferson's own words are to be believed, he was ready to use force eventually if his peaceful efforts to meet the imperative needs of his country should fail. The administration was alert and skillful, and, except in minor details, one wonders how its procedure could have been improved upon. Let us see what it sought and what it actually did in Washington.

While the government was physically incapable of playing a direct part in the crucial negotiations in Paris, its aims and anticipations were fully set forth and are a matter of record. They can be most readily perceived in the official instructions to the two ministers, which Madison drew up and Jefferson approved, and in the letters, official and private, of both the President and the Secretary of State to Livingston and Monroe.[7] The papers that reached the ministers before the signing of the treaty show unmistakably that the focus of the administration's interest and effort was still on the unimpeded navigation of the Mississippi River. When Monroe set out the President had not yet learned of the restoration of the deposit at New Orleans. While seeking this, Jefferson rightly judged that it would not be enough. Of course he did not know how much beyond a reaffirmation of treaty rights could be gained from the French at this time by peaceful negotiation. In the instructions to the two ministers, Madison suggested possible alternatives if the French were unwilling to sell the island of New Orleans or a considerable part of it.[8] The United States might get jurisdiction over some other space big enough for a large commercial town. Failing that, it might gain the express privilege of holding real estate for commercial purposes, of providing hospitals, and of having consuls or other officials there. Monroe himself, while hoping to gain all the objects of his mission, regarded sovereignty over a place of deposit as the absolute minimum.[9]

It need not be supposed that the administration would have rested content with this minimum even though compelled to accept it at the moment. Jefferson wrote Livingston: "We must know at once whether we can acquire N. Orleans or not. We are satisfied nothing else will secure us against a war at no distant period." He was repeating with an

[7] The official instructions of Mar. 2, 1803, are in Hunt, VII, 9–30, and *A.S.P.F.R.*, II, 540–544. These were actually drawn up a good deal earlier. TJ approved them Feb. 22 (LC, 22386). His practice was to leave official communications to Madison and to designate his own letters as private. Thus he felt free not to submit these to the Senate at a later time.

[8] The boundaries of the "island" are the Iberville River and the lakes, the Gulf, and the Mississippi.

[9] Monroe to TJ, Mar. 7, 1803 (S.M.H., IV, 4–8).

added note of immediacy what he had said months before. He had already told Monroe that, without hastening war, the United States must begin to prepare for it; and that if Monroe failed on the Continent he might have to cross the Channel. Indeed, the President told the British representative that the emissary would probably do so; and the French representative supposed that consultation with the British was a major object of the mission.[10] That Jefferson was determined to get hold of New Orleans by one means or another in the near future, and would settle for no less, could hardly have been doubted — except by foes who completely mistrusted him.

He was prepared to exercise more patience with respect to the Floridas. He had not yet inquired into their history and into old treaties as he was to do toward the end of the summer, and questions of nomenclature and past boundaries did not now bulk so large as they did then, but he and his associates, especially Gallatin, had familiarized themselves with the geography of the Gulf coast and fully recognized the strategic and commercial importance of West Florida.[11] By any definition this included the part of the present American state of Louisiana that lies above the island of New Orleans and east of the Mississippi (the Baton Rouge district), and also the littoral of the later states of Mississippi and Alabama. Through the strip along the Gulf, containing the port of Mobile, flowed rivers which drained the Mississippi Territory and down which the products of that part of the interior would naturally proceed. From the commercial point of view and that of national security East Florida was considerably less important at the moment. In his official instructions to Livingston and Monroe, Madison estimated the value of the two Floridas in money as one-fourth that of the island of New Orleans; and he regarded East Florida as only half as valuable as West Florida.[12] The intensity of American desires may perhaps be measured in these proportions, but, as Madison wrote Monroe privately, the whole of what the United States wanted was not too much to secure future peace.[13] This view of the vital needs of their

[10] TJ to Livingston, Feb. 3, 1803 (Ford, VIII, 209); to Monroe, Jan. 13, 1803 (Ford, VIII, 191). References to the reports of the foreign representatives are given hereafter.

[11] The terms West Florida and East Florida were employed by the British while in possession of this region for the twenty years (1763–1783) between the peace treaties that ended, respectively, the Seven Years' War and the American Revolution. They divided the two provinces at the Apalachicola River. The American government contended, later in 1803, that Louisiana, as ruled by the French until ceded to Spain in 1763, extended to the Perdido River, and that the nomenclature became confused in 1783, when the Floridas were ceded to Spain. (See below, pp. 303–309.)

[12] A.S.P.F.R., II, 544.

[13] Madison to Monroe, Mar. 1, 1803 (Hunt, VII, 31n.).

country, which was also the view of Alexander Hamilton, was one that neither Jefferson nor Madison ever surrendered.

In the matter of territory, the instructions to the ministers, like the resolutions of Congress, related solely to acquisitions *east* of the Mississippi. Credit for the idea of acquiring land west of the river belongs to Livingston, who, acting independently, suggested the cession of the region above the Arkansas River as a buffer between French possessions and the British.[14] From this seed the idea of disposing of the vast westward stretches of the province of Louisiana may have germinated in the First Consul's mind. In view of the huge unsettled area east of the Mississippi and the necessarily slow process of settlement in that era of transportation, nobody in the administration appears to have perceived any need for mere territory at this time. To Jefferson, however, the desirability of controlling the inland waterways and of preventing the British from moving southward from Canada needed no arguing. Therefore, when informed of the unexpected western acquisition he accepted it with gratitude.

The high officials in Washington did not know just what they were going to get, but they were quite right in their judgment that this was a favorable time to strike for something. In his instructions Madison summed things up as he and Jefferson saw them. He mentioned the instability of the peace of Europe; the attitude of the British — who viewed French colonial ambitions with disfavor and were now friendly to the United States; the condition of French finances; the necessity of their abandoning the West Indies or of sending large armaments to those islands. These circumstances, he said, should predispose the French to an arrangement that would free them of one source of foreign danger and furnish some aid against domestic (financial) embarrassment. Thus the administration recognized the major considerations that are now supposed by scholars to have entered into Bonaparte's decision, though the renewal of the war came sooner than they anticipated.

The timing of the government's actions was affected by the postponement of Monroe's departure, which occurred about a month later than had been expected, because of his illness and the delay in the transmission of his instructions. Livingston learned of the mission before Monroe sailed and duly reported it to the French authorities.[15] The resident Minister Plenipotentiary, who could not have been expected to relish the appointment of the Envoy Extraordinary even though as-

---

[14] Livingston to Madison, Feb. 18, 1803 (*A.S.P.F.R.*, II, 533).

[15] Madison informed Livingston on Jan. 18, 1803, and Livingston acknowledged the letter Mar. 3 (*A.S.P.F.R.*, II, 529, 537).

sured that he himself was to be reinforced and not replaced, claimed that the news of it, along with a report from Pichon of its tranquilizing effect, had given the French an excuse for further procrastination. This, he said, was just after Talleyrand had told him that everything would be arranged.[16] But Pichon's dispatch as a whole was not calculated to encourage French complacency, and it was quickly followed by reports he intended to be alarming. Livingston's authority had not extended to the making of territorial arrangements; he had been instructed merely to inquire into possibilities and prices. Acting on his own, he had strongly argued that Louisiana had slight value to France, thus preparing the way for later negotiations. Being confident that he had gained respect for himself in French officialdom and doubting if Monroe, who had manifested such enthusiasm for democracy when minister to France, would be welcomed by the autocratic First Consul, Livingston thought himself in better position to negotiate than his prospective colleague would be. The mission of Monroe was a blow to his vanity and was regarded by him as needless. From the moment of its announcement, however, it was a reminder to the French that American concern over the situation was too serious to be trifled with — a judgment that Pichon's dispatches soon strengthened — and as such it may be assumed to have contributed to the eventual success of American diplomacy. Jefferson himself was entirely convinced that it was an indispensable factor, as Monroe naturally was.

By the beginning of March, Livingston knew, beyond any doubt, that his government was ready to purchase New Orleans and the Floridas. He was told that Monroe would bring his formal instructions and his commission. Meanwhile, he was to prepare the way for the negotiations the two ministers were to conduct together. The figures given him by Madison were considerably lower than the maximum afterwards mentioned in his official instructions and he was warned not to arouse extravagant French expectations. The President and Secretary of State were not taking Livingston into their full confidence. They did not trust his judgment implicitly; and, as Jefferson told Monroe, their object was likely to assume so many shapes "that no instructions could be squared to fit them." [17] Before clothing with discretionary power an

[16] Livingston to Madison, Mar. 24, 1803, enclosing Talleyrand to Livingston, Mar. 21, 1803, and the latter's reply, which is obviously misdated (ibid., II, 549–551). The dispatch referred to must have been Pichon's of Jan. 21, 1803, which was received Mar. 22 (AECPEU, 55:187). This contained an extended and well balanced account of recent developments, especially in Congress. His more alarming dispatch of Jan. 24 was not received until Mar. 28.
[17] Madison to Livingston, Jan. 18, 1803 (A.S.P.F.R., II, 529); TJ to Monroe, Jan. 13, 1803 (Ford, VIII, 190).

ROBERT R. LIVINGSTON
Portrait by John Vanderlyn, 1804

emissary to whom he could fully reveal his mind, the President was disposed to keep things in his own hands. With the benefit of hindsight we may now judge that it would have been better if Monroe had reached France as soon as the news of his appointment, but that was impossible. The degree of his delay was unexpected, but the nearest thing to a serious miscalculation on the part of the administration was with respect to the speed of events in Europe. Perhaps that also was unavoidable because of the painful slowness of communication in that age of sail.

The diplomatic activity of the administration was by no means limited to its communications with its ministers abroad. What the President and Secretary of State said to Pichon with respect to issues with France, and to Thornton about possible future relations with Great Britain, may have been more influential than any formal American representations to their respective governments. In the informal conversations with these men that the unceremonious society of the village capital facilitated, Jefferson allowed himself more latitude than Madison assumed. If he blew both hot and cold he probably did so designedly. In a fluid and uncertain situation he was not disposed to commit himself to a specific line of action, and he was not unwilling to keep the French and British guessing. His consistency about ends did not extend to means, and some degree of ambivalence was unavoidable in one who was seeking at the same time to calm his own people and to apprise others of grave dangers. And if he should go too far in either cajolery or threat, while talking informally with the representatives of foreign Powers, he always had Madison at hand to restore the balance.

An excellent example of their effective teamwork is afforded by their first discussions of Monroe's mission with Pichon, who was so anxious that good relations between the United States and his own country be maintained. Conversing with him before dinner at the President's House, Jefferson laid great stress on the tranquilizing effect of Monroe's appointment on the West, expressing at the same time the desire of the administration to pursue "pacific means to the last moment," and its hope of French concurrence to preserve harmony. The report of this desire to Bonaparte's government might have tended to relieve the French of their fears of American violence and thus have weakened the hands of American negotiators, as Livingston claimed that one of Pichon's dispatches had already done. But this conversation was reported by the French chargé along with one he had a couple of days later with Madison at the latter's request. If the President used the enticing carrot, Madison, no doubt with his full concurrence, displayed the threatening stick, which as a rule he avoided doing. There could be no enduring peace, said the Secretary, until the United States possessed the lands east of the Mississippi, and he presented an extended argument that France should cede them. That, he claimed, was the only way to protect French possessions west of the river, for Louisiana could not exist without American friendship even in peacetime and would be easy prey on the resumption of the war between France and England. Furthermore, the American government, however friendly, had to allow for powerful public opinion. Pichon gained an impression of Madison's deep concern and judged that the crisis had not lessened but had increased.[18]

In other dispatches, one at least of which reached Paris before Monroe did and another of which got there before the Louisiana treaty was signed, Pichon described the administration as desirous of French friendship, but embittered and humiliated by French silence and unresponsiveness to its moderation. He believed that, under attack by its foes because of its "extreme prudence," it could not hope to escape difficulties and would be compelled to take a course it did not wish to pursue. Speaking of the President, he said:

> It is a necessity that Mr. Jefferson yield his pretensions and scruples against an English alliance. I have remarked at table that he redoubles his kindnesses and attentions to the British chargé. I ought to say also that he treats me with much regard and politeness despite the actual state of things. The language attributed to him as to the danger of our projects is not questionable; it is that of everybody.[19]

The pro-British trend was also perceived by the chargé to whom the President was showing increased attentions. Thornton reported to his government at this time that there had been a great change in the attitude of the ruling party. Its leaders now recognized that cordial cooperation with Great Britain would be imperative if the rights of navigation of the Mississippi could not be procured by peaceful means, and would be desirable in any case. To him Jefferson declared that if necessary the Americans "*would throw away the scabbard.*" Also, after saying that Monroe would probably go to England before returning home, the President had accepted with pleasure Thornton's offer to give the Envoy Extraordinary to France a letter to the British Ambassador in

[18] Pichon reported his conversation of Jan. 12 with TJ, and of Jan. 14 with Madison, to Talleyrand on Jan. 24, 1803 (AECPEU, 55:192–198). Brant describes both interviews in his *Madison*, IV, 116–118. By laying greater emphasis on the harmony of the two men and their supplementary rôles I give the episode a somewhat different shading.

[19] Pichon to Talleyrand, Jan. 28, 1803 (AECPEU, 55:249–251), received Mar. 28. Also, Feb. 18, 1803 (55:300, No. 37).

Paris.[20] Jefferson was quite willing to give the impression that he was preparing for a possible Anglo-American *rapprochement*. The reports of the state of his mind and of American opinion that Pichon sent home appear to have been just the sort he wanted sent; and, arriving when they did, they could hardly have failed to strengthen the arguments that Livingston was advancing.[21]

Since the fate of Louisiana lay with Bonaparte at last, interpreters of these events have been under the necessity of trying to read his mind. This cannot be done with full confidence, but it seems that the First Consul had lost interest in his American colonial venture by or before the time Monroe sailed and that he had decided to renew the war with Great Britain before Monroe landed. The death of General Leclerc in St. Domingo was announced in the *Moniteur* in early January, and his brother-in-law is reported to have said a few days thereafter: "Damn sugar, damn coffee, damn colonies." [22] By the end of the month there were signs that the frustrated First Consul was turning his attention to Egypt, where the position of the British was judged to be weak. Chagrined by the disastrous outcome of the expedition to St. Domingo, where French fortunes could only be retrieved by a large further investment of men and money, he was seeking other fields of action. The Peace of Amiens had been commonly regarded as only a truce, and certain of its provisions had not been carried out. The French were still in Holland, where the expedition for Louisiana was being fitted out, and the British had not yet surrendered Malta. The preparations in Holland, which might have been directed against them, alarmed the British, while the threat against Egypt made them undisposed to withdraw from Malta. Following a royal message to Parliament in early March, calling for additional British measures of precaution — a message that was regarded in England as a precursor of war — Bonaparte, at a reception at the Tuileries, denounced the British in front of their ambassador and loudly asserted that he must have Malta or war.[23] A few days later, Rufus King wrote Madison from London that war appeared inevitable and that Bonaparte had informed the British that the French ships in the Dutch harbors, though intended for America, had now been ordered not to proceed thither.[24] Thus he may have decided by the

[20] Thornton to Hawkesbury, Jan. 31, 1803 (FO, 5:38, No. 8).
[21] Brant says: "Through him, not through Livington, came the impressive, persuasive statements of American policy" (*Madison*, IV, 119).
[22] Quoted by Lyon, *Louisiana in French Diplomacy*, p. 194.
[23] Mar. 12, 1803, reported to TJ by Livingston that day (*A.S.P.F.R.*, II, 547).
[24] King to Madison, Mar. 17, 1803 (*A.S.P.F.R.*, II, 548); Livingston to Madison, Mar. 24, 1803, telling of what had happened a few days earlier (*A.S.P.F.R.*, II, 549).

middle of March to rid himself of Louisiana. That was about the time when Livingston claimed that everything could have been arranged if Monroe's tranquilizing mission had not occasioned a delay.

It was not until April 11, however, that Talleyrand inquired if the United States would like to buy the whole province. In the meantime, more alarming dispatches had come from Pichon and the Ross Resolutions had been reported in Paris.[25] The defeat of these was not yet known and was actually not expected by Livingston. In conjunction with Pichon's dire words about an Anglo-American *rapprochement*, this threat may have played a part in Bonaparte's decision. If he now regarded Louisiana as a military liability he could have retroceded the province to Spain, but his feelings toward that court were ambiguous at the moment and there were financial and political reasons for a sale to the United States. On the French side this was effected in the end at his insistence, against the objections of his brothers Joseph and Lucien and of Talleyrand, all of whom appear to have been involved in an abortive plot with the British Ambassador to put off the war. This seems to have been one reason for Talleyrand's procrastination. Specifically, in return for a large sum of money, they were to persuade Napoleon to withdraw his demand for Malta. Louisiana was involved indirectly, since the sale of that province and the renewal of the war now hung together.[26]

Obviously, Bonaparte wanted to gain from this sale some of the means to carry out his military designs, but to attribute his decision primarily to cupidity or to caprice is to be unjust to his astuteness. There was political realism in his attempt to check the Anglo-American *rapprochement* of which he had received so much forewarning; and, while divesting himself of territories he could not hope to defend against attack in the impending war, he was making sure that the hated British would possess no part of them. By wholly withdrawing from the continent of North America he was removing the major cause of antagonism between his country and the United States, thus turning a potential enemy into a potential friend, or at least a neutral. In the long view the Louisiana Purchase assured the physical greatness of the United States; its more immediate result, as virtually everybody saw, was the removal of the major threat to the security and peace of the

[25] Apr. 8, according to Livingston. See above, pp. 278–280.

[26] This episode is described in detail by C. L. Lokke in "Secret Negotiations to Maintain the Peace of Amiens," *A.H.R.*, XLIX (Oct., 1943), 55–64. It has been taken up by Brant and Dangerfield, but was unknown to Henry Adams who, in his colorful description of the bathroom scene, attributes to patriotic rather than venal motives the objections of Lucien and Joseph to the sale of Louisiana. (*History*, II, 33–39.)

young Republic. That this would also be to the advantage of the French in this era of international strife Jefferson immediately perceived. Shortly after he learned of the treaty he wrote a French philosopher: "Your government has wisely removed what certainly endangered collision between us. I now see nothing which need ever interrupt the friendship between France and this country." [27] Allowance must be made for his proneness to exaggeration in private letters, especially when manifesting good will to fellow intellectuals. The international fraternity of science and philosophy never ceased to be a reality to him, but the uninterrupted friendship between the two nations that he now prophesied was not a matter of kinship of spirit; it was merely the absence of enmity and rival ambitions.

There are signs that the administration became less anxious after learning of the restoration by the Spanish of the deposit in New Orleans and the almost certain renewal of the war in Europe. But, in his later instructions to Livingston and Monroe, Madison sought to provide for various eventualities, specifically authorizing a direct approach to the British and even talk with them of an alliance under certain conditions.[28] Private letters that Jefferson took occasion to write to fellow intellectuals in England just before he learned of the favorable outcome of the negotiations in Paris suggest that he was ready to further a *rapprochement* with the British, if the negotiations did not turn out well, and that in any case he wanted present American friendliness to them to be recognized. No doubt he hoped that his words would reach high places, as in fact they did. Monroe, thinking particularly of Du Pont, questioned the wisdom of Jefferson's private representations, but they illustrate the flexibility of his diplomacy.

He left no doubt that he wanted his country to keep out of the war he now regarded as inevitable. To Sir John Sinclair he said: "Peace is our passion, and though wrongs might drive us from it, we prefer trying every other just principle of right and safety before we would recur to war." To this friend of agriculture, and to another whom he wrote the same day, he also let it be known that he and his countrymen no longer had any sentimental attachment to the French nation. "The events which have taken place in France," he said, "have lessened in the American mind the motives of interest which it felt in that revolution, and its amity toward that country now rests on its love of peace and commerce." At the same time they were concerned about the situation

[27] TJ to P. J. G. Cabanis, July 12, 1803 (L. & B., X, 405).
[28] See especially Madison's official letter of Apr. 18, 1803 (*A.S.P.F.R.*, II, 555–556), and his private letter to Monroe, Apr. 20 (Hunt, VII, 47–48).

of the British and would be "sincerely afflicted were any disaster to deprive mankind of the benefit of such a bulwark against the torrent which has for some time been bearing down all before it." [29]

He soon found out that his own country would not need to rely on British sea power, as he had feared it might, and he assumed a more neutral tone in a letter he wrote another Englishman after he had received news, though no details, of the treaty with France. He went out of his way, however, to express his disappointment with "the issue of the convulsions" across the Channel. "Without befriending human liberty," he said, "a gigantic force has risen up which seems to threaten the world." While expressing sympathy for the British, he thanked God for the Atlantic Ocean and expressed the opinion that American friendship should be of interest to both parties to the conflict. While saying that he and his countrymen would not be "unconcerned spectators," he now had no doubt that they would be onlookers.[30] The Louisiana cession, which he did not yet refer to, would enable them to return to the policy of genuine neutrality that had been worked out and pursued so effectively during his last year as secretary of state under George Washington.

ii

The news of the signing of the treaty that reached Jefferson on July 3, 1803, was official but not direct. It came in a letter from the two ministers to Rufus King, who got this shortly before leaving London, brought it with him on his return home, and transmitted it to Madison from New York.[31] The report of the acquisition of territory west of the Mississippi surprised the American people more than it did Jefferson and Madison. They had learned of this prospect several weeks earlier and had approved the enlargement of the negotiations in a private letter recently dispatched to Paris.[32] Without fear of denial the Na-

---

[29] TJ to Sir John Sinclair, June 30, 1803 (LC, 22918–22920; imperfect in L. & B., X, 396–398); to William Strickland, June 30, 1803 (LC, 22922), expressing similar sentiments. The letter to Sinclair reached Hawkesbury (Perkins, First Rapprochement, p. 217, note 38). Sinclair's reply of Jan. 1, 1804 was cordial (LC 23745).

[30] TJ to the Earl of Buchan, July 10, 1803 (L. & B., X, 399–401; LC, 22983–22985). His Lordship replied in a most agreeable manner on Feb. 4, 1804 (LC, 23864). Strictly speaking there is no inconsistency between TJ's letters to the Britishers and the one of July 12 to Cabanis, though he may be charged with erring on the side of politeness in the latter and sounding more friendly to France than he was.

[31] See note by Carter in Territorial Papers, IX, 4, giving chronological details.

[32] Livingston reported Talleyrand's suggestion to Madison Apr. 11 (A.S.P.F.R., II, 552). He spoke more confidently and enthusiastically in a letter of Apr. 14 to

tional Intelligencer asserted that the Fourth of July was a proud day for the President. As that friendly paper pointed out, this was not so much because he and his countrymen had gained vast and fertile territory, gratifying as that was, but because they had preserved the peace and were now assured that they could continue to do so. "We have secured our rights by pacific means: truth and reason have been more powerful than the sword." The *Aurora*, which got the news later than the *National Intelligencer*, similarly interpreted its significance, laying the emphasis on national security rather than territory.[33]

The news had reached Boston first of all, and, if we may judge from a letter of George Cabot to his friend Rufus King, the Sage of New England Federalism regarded the cession of Louisiana as chiefly advantageous to France. "It is like selling us a ship after she is surrounded by a British fleet," he said. Since France could neither settle nor protect the province, she was "rid of an encumbrance that wounded her pride," while receiving money and regaining the friendship of the American populace. Nothing would satisfy the Essex Junto but an alliance with crazy John Bull, according to the struggling Republican paper of Boston.[34] The grounds of disquietude among New England Federalists were better set forth in a communication to one of their major newspapers about two weeks after the report of the treaty got out. "We are to give money of which we have too little for land of which we already have too much," said the writer. This "unexplored empire, of the size of four or five European kingdoms," would destroy the balance in the Union "A great waste, a wilderness unpeopled with any beings except wolves and wandering Indians" could be cut up into numberless states; and Virginia would be confirmed in her dominion over all the others.[35] Here, before the terms of the treaty were known, was voiced the basic protest of New England. Meanwhile, in the commercial center of New York, Rufus King found that the importance of gaining full control of the Mississippi was immediately recognized, but that there was no discussion as yet of the territorial acquisition west of the river. On all sides, he said, it was agreed that the measure would redound to the authority and popularity of the administration.[36] Nothing that happened subsequently disproved the soundness of that judgment.

TJ (LC, 22586–22590; received June 9). Madison expressed approval to Monroe June 25 (deciphered and quoted by Brant, IV, 132, from Monroe Papers, 8:1342).

[33] *National Intelligencer*, July 8, 1803; *Aurora*, July 7, 8, 1803.

[34] Cabot to King, July 1, 1803 (King, IV, 279); Boston *Independent Chronicle*, July 4, 1803.

[35] Fabricius in Boston *Columbian Centinel*, July 13, 1803.

[36] King to C. Gore, July 10, 1803 (King, IV, 285–286).

In their effort to deny credit to an administration which they would undoubtedly have assailed with bitterness had the negotiations in Paris met with the failure they had predicted, certain Federalists took up Livingston, who had previously been described by partisan critics as a feeble instrument and even as a "rank Jacobin." Some of them now claimed not only that he was chiefly responsible for this deal, but also that he had acted "without authority from his government"— the presumption being that he was more and the government less praiseworthy for that reason. The effort to attribute independent action to him was occasioned by the publication at just this time of the impressive memorial he had addressed to the French government in the previous year on the disadvantages to France of the possession of Louisiana.[37]

The public circulation of this document was regarded by Madison as an indiscretion, and certain anti-British references in it could hardly have been welcome to High Federalists. In fact, their organ in Boston afterwards asserted that both of the ministers were zealous to serve France in her conflict with England. Jefferson remarked that the opposition was "very willing to pluck feathers from Monroe, although not fond of sticking them into Livingston's coat." The position that he himself promptly took, though necessarily vague, was officially correct and historically fair: that both men had "a just portion of merit," that each had rendered special and important service.[38] The *National Intelligencer*, on the day it published Livingston's memorial, derided the "pitiful attempts" of the opposition to derogate from the merit owing the President and his close advisers and to distract attention from a great achievement. At the same time, it gave a sensible answer to the question of the credit rightly due an agent. "Mr. Livingston's merit may have been great," said the paper closest to the administration. "Far be it from us to impair it. But his merit consists, not in standing alone, but in carrying into effect the will of those he represented." [39]

The publication of the document, and the attempt to exploit it for partisan purposes, could not have been expected to improve the standing of Livingston with a President and Secretary of State who had already shown signs of distrust of his judgment and become aware of his proneness to overreach himself. Concerned lest he should try to out-

[37] This essay, a copy of which had been sent Madison by Livingston on Aug. 10, 1802 (*A.S.P.F.R.*, II, 520–524), was published in the *Aurora*, July 7, 1803, in the same issue with the report of the signing of the treaty. It was there described as translated for the *New-England Palladium*. According to Madison, it appeared in all the papers, along with a letter from Paris representing it as the chief cause of the cession (Madison to Monroe, July 30, 1803 [Hunt, VII, 61*n*.]).

[38] *Columbian Centinel*, Aug. 10, 1803; TJ to Horatio Gates, July 11, 1803 (Ford, VIII, 249–250).

[39] *National Intelligencer*, July 11, 1803.

smart the French, Jefferson had privately said: "An American contending by stratagem against those exercised in it from their cradle would undoubtedly be outwitted by them." [40] Madison found in Livingston's own communications justification of Monroe's complaints, soon after he reached Paris, that his colleague was "precipitating the business" in the hope of forestalling him. [41] After he saw the actual terms, Madison expressed the opinion that but for Livingston's precipitancy they could have secured better ones. In any differences between the two ministers, Jefferson and Madison were disposed to uphold Monroe, but the Secretary of State, responding to Livingston's latest expression of uneasiness, assured him that Monroe did not outrank him. It was not in the interest of the government to cast public discredit on either of its representatives, and Madison's considerate treatment of Livingston, while thoroughly characteristic, also reflected his awareness of that minister's embarrassing position. The Secretary of State did not charge him with responsibility for the circulation of his memorial in America but politely suggested the investigation of the source of the "indiscretion" in Paris. Explaining the episode some weeks later, Livingston said that a bad translation of his essay got into the papers through the excessive zeal of his friends, who were mortified by the supposition that Monroe was of a higher grade than he. He blamed friends of Monroe for comparable imprudence and, in presenting his own claims, showed excessive and unbecoming zeal. He did not doubt that Monroe, if placed in the same circumstances, would have been able to do what he did. "But," said Livingston, "he unfortunately came too late to do more than assent to the propositions that were made us, and to aid in reducing them to form." [42] Madison does not appear to have mentioned this matter in later correspondence with Livingston, but the breach which had already opened between the Minister and his government undoubtedly widened, and for this he himself was very considerably responsible.

In important respects Monroe was also unfortunate. If he had arrived in Paris as originally planned no one could have questioned his share in the negotiations, and he might have been more effective if he had not been taken ill soon after he got there. But, because of his closeness to

---

[40] TJ to Madison, Mar. 19, 1803 (MP [Rives Coll.], 2:371). I do not enter into the allegation that Livingston was a "would-be briber" of the French ministry (Brant, *Madison*, IV, 112; Dangerfield, *Livingston*, p. 335).

[41] Monroe to Madison, Apr. 15, 1803 (S.M.H., IV, 9-12); Madison to Monroe, July 30, 1803 (Hunt, VII, 60-61*n.*). Both letters were private and much of the latter was in code.

[42] Livingston to Madison, Nov. 15, 1803 (*A.S.P.F.R.*, II, 573-574), replying to Madison's letter of July 29 (Hunt, VII, 53). Livingston's frenetic efforts to gain credit for the treaty, extending to the changing of dates in his reports, are described by Dangerfield, pp. 377-378.

JAMES MONROE
Portrait by Charles Willson Peale

the administration, he could well afford to be modest. He held that "the transaction ought to rest on its true ground, as a memorable incident in our history tending to prove the wisdom of the measures of the last session." [43] He went to special pains to make his position clear to the senators from his own state, Mason and Nicholas, and to Breckinridge of Kentucky, all of whom would be called on to vote on the treaty and who, as good Republicans, should be in position to proclaim sound party doctrine. While recognizing that the European crisis played an important part, he believed that his country could not have acquired Louisiana without "the wise and firm though moderate measures of the Executive and Congress." The decision of the French to offer the territory was owing to no management of his, he said, since it took place before he got to Paris. Nor was it owing to his colleague, or it would have happened sooner. He believed that it was occasioned by his mission as the manifestation of the purpose and determination of his government. Along with his communication to the three senators he sent a copy of the welcoming letter to him from Livingston in which that seemingly despondent minister spoke of having prepared the way for him. For himself Monroe claimed nothing except, "zeal and industry" after his arrival, and he granted the same merit to his colleague, while obviously trying to spike that colleague's guns.[44] Magnification of the administration whose complete confidence he shared was much easier for him than for Livingston, who naturally feared that he would be overshadowed, but Monroe was wholly warranted in saying that if the measures of the government had failed the blame would have been on it and on him.

As things turned out, most of the credit for this diplomatic triumph went to the administration, as he thought it should. Especially, it went to Jefferson. Until this day, when the Louisiana Purchase is mentioned, Americans think only secondarily of the two ministers and hardly at all of Madison, who had shared the deliberations at every stage and had borne the heavy burden of official correspondence. Speaking of the treaty on the day it became known to him, the British representative in Washington said prophetically: "There seems to be little which can affect the tranquillity of the United States, or shake the firm footing which the President will have obtained, in the confidence of his countrymen." [45] Jefferson was to meet with other difficulties which would

[43] Private letter, Monroe to Madison, June 8 (MP, 2:394).

[44] Monroe to Gen. Mason, Col. W. C. Nicholas, and John Breckinridge, May 25, 1803, enclosed to Madison, with copy of Livingston's letter of Apr. 10 (S.M.H., IV, 31-34). Livingston afterwards claimed that Monroe's friends circulated his letter and objected to this as improper.

[45] Thornton to Hawkesbury, July 4, 1803 (FO, 5:38).

take the edge off his satisfaction, but beyond doubt he was now at the peak of his presidential career.

The official documents that reached Washington on July 14 were not made public, but a summary of them was given out. Jefferson himself described as accurate the one that appeared in the *National Intelligencer* exactly two weeks after that paper had reported the cession.[46] No further information regarding boundaries was or could be released, but the financial terms were now made known: a payment of $11,250,-000 to France in six per cent stock, not redeemable for fifteen years; and the assumption by the United States of the claims of its citizens against France to the amount of $3,750,000. For a period of twelve years French and Spanish ships and merchandise were to pay no higher duties than American in the ports of the ceded territory. Finally, the inhabitants of Louisiana were to be incorporated with the United States as soon as could be done consistently with the Constitution, and were to be secure in their personal rights in the meantime.

The treaty called for the exchange of ratifications within six months of the date of signing (April 30, 1803). Accordingly, the Executive Council decided that Congress should be called to meet October 17; this was three weeks earlier than the scheduled time but was allowing less than two weeks for the action of the Senate and subsequent formalities. They were cutting it pretty fine.[47] In due course the official correspondence was submitted to the Senate, along with the treaty and the conventions. Until that time, however, the letters accompanying the documents were known only within the administration.[48] In their joint letter of May 13, 1803, the two ministers went to pains to give reasons for going beyond their instructions. They need not have been troubled on that score. In a private letter to Monroe, Madison had already approved the extension of the negotiations; and now, on Jefferson's behalf, he assured the two men that they were justified by the "solid reasons" they had given. Neither in official nor in private communications was there objection to the total sum of $15,000,000, though the highest figure previously mentioned to the ministers was 50,000,000 livres, which was less than $10,000,000. Even this economy-minded ad-

[46] *National Intelligencer*, July 18, 1803. The treaty of cession and the two accompanying conventions, dealing with the financial terms and the claims settlement, may be seen in Hunter Miller, *Treaties and Other International Acts of the U.S.A.*, II (1931), 498–528, along with other authoritative information.

[47] The French ratification, already signed, was transmitted June 7 and was in the hands of Pichon by the end of the summer.

[48] Livingston and Monroe to Madison, May 13, 1803 (*A.S.P.F.R.*, II, 558–560). Various private letters to and from Madison and TJ were not submitted to the Senate.

ministration could recognize a bargain. In the uncertainties about boundaries and area, the cost per acre could not well be estimated, but certain of the inhabitants of Louisiana figured that they had cost eleven sous per head, including slaves and cattle.[49] The criticisms that were promptly voiced by Gallatin related to the method of payment. The French could dispose of the stock for cash, as they soon did to the banking houses of Hope in the Netherlands and Baring in London — despite the fact that Great Britain and France were at war. On the other hand, the United States could not begin to curtail this debt for fifteen years. Rufus King, with whom the Secretary of the Treasury conferred in New York toward the end of the summer, "hinted that more advantageous terms might have been obtained," and the two agreed that Livingston's "precipitancy had been prejudicial to the United States."[50] More serious criticism can be made of the claims convention, which was carelessly drawn and led to grave difficulties. Eventually, these caused the administration to lose all patience with Livingston, but they were not anticipated at the moment.[51]

The question of the extent of the territorial acquisition was of more immediate and much greater concern. The treaty itself mentioned no precise boundaries. Quoting the language of the treaty of San Ildefonso, it said that France ceded to the United States what Spain had ceded to her:

> the colony or province of Louisiana, with the same extent that it now has in the hands of Spain, and that it had when France possessed it; and such as it should be after the treaties subsequently entered into between Spain and other states.

Jefferson was not disturbed by the uncertainty of the western boundary, having no doubt that the cession would give full control of the Mississippi and its tributaries. Furthermore, while he had to adjust his mind and policies to a far greater acquisition than he had dreamed of, he showed no inclination whatever to give up any of this land. It will be recalled, however, that he had instructed Livingston and Monroe to put West Florida next after New Orleans on their list of priorities. The day before he received the text of the treaty he got a letter from Liv-

[49] A. R. Ellery to Hamilton, Oct. 25, 1803, quoted by Whitaker, *Mississippi Question*, p. 253, from Hamilton Papers.
[50] Gallatin to TJ, Aug. 18, 1803 (*Writings*, I, 142). Madison reported privately to Monroe, July 30, 1803, that the "pecuniary arrangements" were "much disrelished," especially by Gallatin (Hunt, VII, 61n.).
[51] See Dangerfield, pp. 374-375. TJ's loss of patience was strikingly revealed in a letter of Aug. 18, 1804, to Madison (LC, 24752).

ingston containing the pleasing report that the eastern boundary was the Perdido, according to that minister's construction of the document. That is, he held that most of West Florida was included in the cession. In this letter, which Livingston wrote shortly before he signed the treaty, he stated that the French had been informed of this construction.[52] While seeking to demonstrate his fidelity to his instructions, Livingston was clearly not averse to acquiring credit vis-à-vis Monroe, but by implication at least he associated his colleague with his own interpretation of the treaty's terms.

Jefferson was not yet ready to accept his assurance at face value. In the official letters to him and Monroe, dated more than two weeks after the receipt of the treaty, Madison spoke of the uncertainties about the boundaries and urged further investigation of them. The President wanted to know what understanding with respect to them prevailed in the negotiations, and, particularly, the "pretensions and proofs" for carrying the eastern boundary to the Perdido or including any part of West Florida in the cession. At the time Jefferson and Madison supposed that Monroe would go immediately to Spain after winding up his business in Paris, as he had been authorized to do. He was accordingly instructed to direct inquiries to that question in Madrid.[53] While dubious of the report of Livingston, whose judgment they did not wholly trust and whose desire to gain credit for himself they clearly perceived, the President and Secretary of State recognized the claim as a diplomatic weapon that might be profitably employed in the effort to gain all the rest of the Spanish territory on the continent that they coveted.

Not until the end of the summer did they learn that Monroe supported the "pretensions" to the Perdido boundary and offered "proofs" based on the texts of treaties and the facts of history. Without waiting for him, Livingston had reported in the meantime his own conversations with French officials and explained how he had arrived at his conviction.[54] Marbois had told him, he said, that Mobile was included in the cession by Spain to France. He himself had previously thought otherwise, but when he first saw the text of the secret treaty of San Ildefonso he was immediately convinced — or so at least he claimed — that Spain had retroceded all the country that France had possessed by

[52] Livingston to TJ, May 2, 1803 (LC, 22659–22660), received July 13. He signed later that day, though he had expected to sign the next day. The treaty and conventions were predated Apr. 30.

[53] Madison to Livingston, and to Livingston and Monroe, July 29, 1803 (A.S.P.F.R., II, 566–567); Madison to Monroe, July 29, 1803 (Hunt, VII, 53–60).

[54] Livingston to Madison, May 20, 1803 (A.S.P.F.R., II, 560–561), a letter described by him as private but afterwards transmitted to the Senate with other official communications.

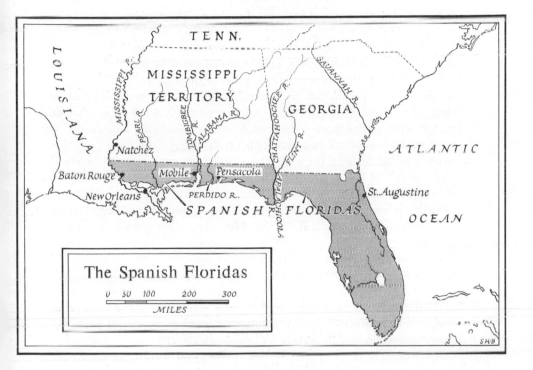

The Spanish Floridas

the name of Louisiana. This extended to the Perdido, as the old maps showed. He would have strengthened his case if he had reported to his government at this time that the exact words of the treaty of 1800 between Spain and France were inserted in the treaty of 1803 between France and the United States at the request of the Americans, who thus sought to lay the groundwork for a claim to West Florida they otherwise would not have had.[55] Monroe was directly involved in this action, however, and Livingston's failure to mention it may perhaps be attributed to his desire to minimize the services of his colleague.[56]

Reporting further conversations with high officials after the signing of the treaty, Livingston said that Marbois would neither assert nor deny that Mobile was part of the cession to the United States, but said merely that it had been a part of French Louisiana. Talleyrand was even more evasive. "I can give you no direction," he said; "you have made a noble bargain for yourselves, and I suppose you will make the most of it." If Livingston had not tried to do just that he would not have been a faithful agent of his country, and his conclusion that the Americans were at liberty to construe for themselves the vague territorial terms of the treaty was natural. His specific recommendation to his government, however, was highly questionable. Expressing confidence that he would gain the concurrence of Monroe but not waiting until he had done so, he recommended "in the strongest terms" that the government insist upon the territory to the Perdido as part of its right and take possession of it. He pledged himself that the right was good and declared that, after the explanations that had been given in Paris, they "need apprehend nothing from a decisive measure."

Monroe was not disposed to join Livingston in this advice to their government until after they had "probed the question to the bottom, and seen that it was founded in principles of justice such as could be demonstrated to the impartial world, even to Spain herself." [57] He soon

[55] See the discussion of this by Brant in *Madison*, IV, 145, citing Livingston and Monroe to Marbois, Apr. 22, 1803, and Monroe to Livingston, April, 1803, from N.Y. Hist. Soc. Brant regards this action on the part of the two ministers as a sufficient answer to the contention that the claim to West Florida was an afterthought (Henry Adams, *History*, II, 44; I. J. Cox, *West Florida Controversy* [1918], pp. 80–81). He holds that the vague language of the treaty of San Ildefonso gave Bonaparte a claim to the Perdido boundary, if that ruler had been disposed to exercise it, and that Bonaparte had some reason to believe that the Spanish King would agree to it after the conclusion of a general peace. According to this ingenious argument, the United States became heir to the French claim. The matter does not appear to have been reported to Madison and TJ in this manner at that time, however.

[56] Monroe refers to the action in his journal (S.M.H., IV, 16).

[57] Undated reply of Monroe to Livingston's letter of May 23, 1803, endorsed as not sent, but reflecting his thinking (S.M.H., IV, 40–43).

concluded from his own investigations, however, that the American right was "beyond all controversy," and he drafted the joint letter they sent to Madison early in June. In this they asserted that "on a thorough examination of the subject" they considered it "incontrovertible" that West Florida was comprised in the cession of Louisiana. The letter contained a brief summary of the arguments and the advice that in all measures relating to the cession the government should act as if West Florida was as much a part of it as New Orleans.[58] The arguments that Monroe summarized in this letter appear in full form in his "Opinion respecting West Florida," a paper he sent to Madison a little later. Jefferson saw this by the end of the summer.[59] Monroe's "Opinion" was an exposition of the territorial article of the treaty, viewed in its relations with other treaties. Directing his attention successively to the three clauses that described the ceded province, he argued that: (1) West Florida had been governed as part of Louisiana while that province was "in the hands of Spain"; (2) Louisiana extended to the Perdido "when France possessed it"; (3) insofar as the treaties "subsequently entered into by Spain" affected the situation, they safeguarded the territorial position and claims of the United States.[60] His main point, actually, was the second. His first allegation could be challenged, as in fact it afterwards was by the Spanish; they asserted that, while West Florida may have been at times under the Governor of Louisiana, it had never been incorporated with that province. But, while boundary lines in North America were not sharply drawn before the Seven Years' War, there was strong historical argument that French Louisiana then extended eastward to the Perdido.

Monroe's exegesis of an obscure text was ingenious; his deductions were logical and his lawyer's brief is impressive. The chief weakness of this strong paper, and of the entire American argument, lay in its emphasis on the treaty as such, with insufficient regard for the interpretation put upon it by the other nations directly involved. The American ministers had not had time to learn that a proclamation had been issued

[58] Livingston and Monroe to Madison, June 7, 1803 (*A.S.P.F.R.*, II, 563-565). Two copies of this letter were sent. One was received Aug. 14 and the other, Aug. 22 (Courtesy of the *Papers* of Madison).

[59] Sent by or before June 19, 1803 (S.M.H., IV, 38-39, 503-509). A copy of this is in LC, 22814-22819.

[60] These were the treaty of 1783, whereby Spain was ceded both of the Floridas by the British, and that of 1795 with the United States, determining the southern boundary. Monroe supplemented Livingston's argument by pointing out that the preliminary articles of the treaty of 1763, whereby France ceded to the British the region from the Iberville to the Perdido, were signed on Nov. 3, 1762, the date of the secret convention whereby she ceded to Spain New Orleans and her possessions west of the Mississippi. Therefore, the cession to the British was not subsequent to this.

by the local Spanish authorities in New Orleans in which West Florida had been excluded from the cession.[61] But one wonders how, from the information available to him, Monroe could have found "many reasons" for the belief that the Spanish government held the same opinion about West Florida that he did. Writing Madison, he said: "I doubt not if it is taken possession of as a part of Louisiana, that the measure will be acquiesced in by that government, or at least that it will not be taken ill by it, or impede an amicable and favorable adjustment relative to the territory of Spain eastward of the Mississippi." [62] The wish must have been father to the thought. To be sure, he and Livingston were aware that the Spanish government was subject to French pressure, such as had been notoriously applied to it in the recent past. Therefore, they could have regarded the attitude of the French government as determinative. They did not have access to documents, available to scholars of later generations, showing that Bonaparte and Talleyrand had no intention whatsoever of supporting an American claim to West Florida against the Spanish. The two Americans read too much into the evasive comments of French officials, but the latter were quite willing for them to deceive themselves and cherish vain hopes of the promised "good offices" of the French government with its Spanish ally.

Monroe soon found out that these would not be immediately available. Bonaparte himself was among those who discouraged him from immediate negotiations with the Spanish regarding Florida, saying that this was not the opportune time, since they had complained of the cession of Louisiana to the United States. Of this complaint and of Bonaparte's own supposed qualms about the cession the administration in Washington was to become painfully aware. Other persons in Paris gave Monroe to understand that they expected the Americans to gain their object ultimately, but that this was not a propitious moment to seek the good offices of the French.[63] In fact he went to England, whence Rufus King had recently departed, and his trip to Spain was delayed for more than a year.

In considering the conduct of Livingston and Monroe in the matter of the boundaries, we should remember that they were not judges in the supreme court of history but lawyers representing their countrymen as clients and advising their own government. If they could register a claim to West Florida and make a case for it, few Americans

[61] May 18, 1803, signed by Salcedo and Casa Calvo (Robertson, II, 169–170). An important collection of documents on the boundary question, mostly from the Spanish but some from the French, is in Robertson, II, 139–214.

[62] Monroe to Madison, June 19, 1803 (S.M.H., IV, 39).

[63] Monroe to Madison, July 20, 1803 (S.M.H., IV, 44–51).

would deny the desirability of their doing so. After their claim had been presented, the President in turn would have been open to condemnation by friends and foes alike if he had rejected it out of hand or failed to make such use of it as should seem legitimate and wise.

Convinced as he had long been that possession of West Florida was necessary for the security and future well-being of his country, Jefferson was predisposed to approve any contention that gave promise of hastening what he regarded as an inevitable consummation. While at Monticello in August and September, availing himself not only of the communications of Livingston and Monroe but also of the facilities of his extensive library, he prepared with his own hands a memoir on the limits and bounds of Louisiana. Besides drawing up a chronological series of facts relative to the region and province, and a list of references, he wrote a historical sketch that can still be consulted with interest and profit. He provided a broad background for Monroe's contentions and what he himself regarded as a full verification of them.[64] His written argument, like that of Monroe, was wholly independent of the expressed opinions of the Spanish and the French. He based it on historical facts as ascertained by him and on the language of treaties. His conclusion was that the purpose of the treaty of San Ildefonso, whose territorial terms had been inserted in the Franco-American treaty of 1803, was to restore the status quo before the Seven Years' War. Accordingly, he arrived at the gratifying judgment that the United States was entitled to demand and Spain was bound to deliver the country as far east as the Perdido. Before Congress met, the validity of the American claim was established to his satisfaction *on paper*, and in his own mind it appears never afterwards to have been shaken; through a succession of experiences that should have been disillusioning it remained a fixed idea. But he let his little treatise remain in his files for the present; and, although he made use of it within the government after a few months, it was not printed for a hundred years.[65]

He had to face another pressing question before presenting to the Senate the treaty of whose approval he was so confident. Whatever the precise boundaries of Louisiana should turn out to be, the United States was acquiring an empire such as had not been anticipated at the Federal Convention of 1787, and had promised to incorporate the inhabitants of

[64] Starting with the summary in Monroe's letter of June 7, he may have satisfied himself before the "Opinion" reached him, but the conclusions were the same in any case.

[65] See pp. 339, 343, below. TJ's memoir, dated Sept. 7, 1803, with a postscript dated Jan. 15, 1804, was printed in 1904 from the original manuscript in Am. Philos. Soc., in *Documents Relating to the Purchase & Exploration of Louisiana*.

the province in the Union. Someone was sure to ask what warrant there was in the Constitution for such actions. Indeed, it might have been supposed that the President himself would be among the first to raise the question, and in fact he was.

⌈XVII⌋

The Constitution and the Expanding Union

SIX months before he learned of the outcome of the negotiations in Paris, Jefferson discussed with his advisers the constitutionality of the "proposed bargain" with France. This was just prior to his nomination of Monroe as envoy in January, 1803. Though he then hoped for no such bargain as was actually arrived at, he anticipated an enlargement of the bounds of the United States and asked an appropriation from Congress for that reason. In fact, he regarded the ultimate acquisition of at least the island of New Orleans as inevitable. But, as he was well aware, the Constitution contains no specific grant of authority to the federal government to make territorial acquisitions of any size; and, in the stress of political conflict, he and his party had become associated in the public mind with strict construction of that document. It seems unlikely that he himself was as closely identified with this doctrine by his contemporaries at this time as he was afterwards by historians who had access to more sources of information. His opinion on the constitutionality of the Bank of the United States had not been published; his authorship of the Kentucky Resolutions was known to very few; and as a rule his private letters were closely guarded. The doctrine of strict construction was so natural for the party of opposition that the Republicans could have been expected to espouse it in some form during the Federalist years irrespective of Jefferson, and his own position cannot be detached from the successive political situations in which he was placed. Neither he nor his partisans operated in a vacuum. Furthermore, he was less rigid in action than he often appeared to be in theory. Nevertheless, his entire career demonstrated his reverence for law, especially fundamental law as embodied in constitutions, and his reluctance to allow much leeway to officials in interpretation. He was in character, therefore, in voicing his constitutional scruples to his closest advisers.[1]

[1] His most important previous expression on strict construction was in the opin-

The Attorney General, who as a New Englander was in good position to anticipate the opposition in his native region to the acquisition of territory to the south and west, suggested that constitutional and political difficulties might be avoided by indirect procedure. Specifically, France might be asked to consent to the extension of the boundaries of the Mississippi Territory and the State of Georgia.[2] Levi Lincoln's observations were submitted by Jefferson to Gallatin, who quickly pointed out that if the acquisition of territory was unconstitutional, it was just as illegal to acquire territory for a state as for the country as a whole. On his own part the Secretary of the Treasury, who was such a stickler for financial regularity, tentatively assumed a constitutional position which was virtually indistinguishable from the liberal construction of his predecessor Hamilton. He summed up his present opinion as follows:

> 1st.   That the United States as a nation have an inherent right to acquire territory.
> 2d.   That whenever that acquisition is by treaty, the same constituted authorities in whom the treaty-making power is vested have a constitutional right to sanction the acquisition.
> 3d.   That whenever the territory has been acquired, Congress have the power either of admitting into the Union as a new state, or of annexing to a State with the consent of that State, or of making regulations for the government of such territory.[3]

This is an admirable description of the constitutional doctrine on which the territorial expansion of the Republic across the continent was to be effected in the next half-century, and at the time Jefferson himself accepted it without qualification except on grounds of expediency. Replying to Gallatin, he said:

> You are right in my opinion, as to Mr. L's proposition: there is no constitutional difficulty as to the acquisition of territory, and whether, when acquired, it may be taken into the Union by the Constitution as it now stands, will become a question of expediency. I think it will be safer not to permit the enlargement of the Union but by amendment of the Constitution.[4]

---

ion on the constitutionality of the Bank which he rendered privately to President Washington. See *Jefferson and the Rights of Man*, ch. XX, esp. pp. 340–349 and note 31. On the Kentucky Resolutions of 1798 and the party attitude toward strict construction, see *Jefferson and the Ordeal of Liberty*, ch. XXV, esp, pp. 402–403.

[2] Levi Lincoln to TJ, Jan. 10, 1803 (LC, 22189–22190). This letter is quoted extensively in E. S. Brown, *Constitutional History of the Louisiana Purchase* (1920), pp. 18–20 (hereafter referred to as Brown).

[3] Gallatin to TJ, Jan. 13, 1803 (*Writings*, I, 111–114; quotation from pp. 113–114).

[4] TJ to Gallatin, January, 1803, in Gallatin's *Writings*, I, 115.

Since he may be assumed to have consulted Madison in this connection, we are warranted in believing that the administration, at this point, recognized as constitutional the *acquisition* of territory by treaty. The question of precisely what should be done with it when acquired was necessarily left in abeyance. For Jefferson to have suggested difficulties and voiced scruples to Congress at this stage would have been to borrow trouble. He was uncertain what could be acquired by peaceful negotiation, and at this time expected no acquisition that would upset the balance and change the character of the Union. Except with respect to the guarantees at New Orleans he perceived no necessity for immediate action. Thus he left the constitutional question sleeping until he learned of the impending acquisition of a province of imperial dimensions. Recognizing as he did the supreme importance of the undisputed control of the inland waterways, he had no hesitancy in accepting the whole of Louisiana, but the sheer size of the cession inevitably magnified and accentuated the constitutional question.

In communications with the chief executive officers and in several private letters in July and August, he said that an amendment to the Constitution seemed necessary. In some of these he appeared to have retreated from his position of six months earlier that there was no constitutional difficulty respecting the *acquisition* of territory. "Our confederation is certainly confined to the limits established by the revolution," he wrote to one of the men of '76. "The general government has no powers but such as the constitution has given it; and it has not given it a power of holding foreign territory, and still less of incorporating it into the Union." [5] After making a similar assertion to Senator John Breckinridge of Kentucky, he described his dilemma in striking language:

The Executive in seizing the fugitive occurrence which so much advances the good of their country, have done an act beyond the Constitution. The Legislature in casting behind them metaphysical subtleties, and risking themselves like faithful servants, must ratify & pay for it, and throw themselves on their country for doing for them unauthorized what we know they would have done for themselves had they been in a situation to do it. It is the case of a guardian, investing the money of his ward in purchasing an important adjacent territory; & saying to him when of age, I did this for your good; I pretend to no right to bind you: you may disavow me, and I must get out of the scrape as I can: I thought it my duty to risk myself for you. But we shall not be disavowed by

[5] TJ to John Dickinson, Aug. 9, 1803 (Ford, VIII, 262).

the nation, and their act of indemnity will confirm & not weaken the Constitution, by more strongly marking out its lines.[6]

By the legislative "act of indemnity" he meant the offering of a constitutional amendment, and in his own effort to "get out of the scrape" he made at least two known attempts to draft one.[7] In neither case did he seek to enlarge the powers of the general government by a specific grant of authority to acquire territory by treaty. The sovereign right of the nation to do this, which was afterwards confirmed unequivocally by the Supreme Court, was doubted by neither Gallatin nor Madison; and, in effect, Jefferson conceded it by bypassing that question. Despite his expressions of devotion to constitutional purism in private letters addressed to persons who might have been expected to harbor scruples, and whom he thus sought to disarm in advance, he may have yielded his own lingering doubts on this point with only slight demur. At all events, he perceived that this particular acquisition would have to be recognized as a *fait accompli* after the ratification which he confidently expected. Therefore, he addressed himself first to the practical problems arising from it.

In his first draft he made a sharp distinction between the southernmost portion of the province, described here as the region below the thirty-first parallel (afterwards the region below the mouth of the Arkansas River), and the vast stretches to the north and west.[8] The former contained virtually all the white settlers. He did not yet know that the United States was bound by the treaty to admit them as soon as possible to the full enjoyment of the "rights, advantages and immunities" of American citizens, but his tentative amendment ended with a declaration that Congress might erect them into a territorial government and vest them with the rights of territorial citizens. At the moment, he was not thinking of the rest of the trans-Mississippi region in terms of settlement. The larger part of his suggested amendment related directly to the Indians, whom he would confirm in their rights of occupancy and self-government as existing. He would assert the right

[6] TJ to J. C. Breckinridge, Aug. 12, 1803 (Ford, VIII, 244n.). The text of this fascinating letter in LC, 23144–23146 differs in only trivial details from the printed version we have quoted.

[7] Two drafts are printed in Ford, VIII, 241–249, in parallel columns, with pertinent correspondence in the notes. The first draft, from an undated paper in LC, 23688 was made by July 9, 1803 — that is, before TJ had learned the precise terms of the treaty. The second seems to have been taken by Ford from TJ's letter of Aug. 30, 1803, to Levi Lincoln (LC, 23232). That version varies in only trivial details from the one in his letter of Aug. 25 to Madison (LC, 23208–23209).

[8] This draft was commented on by Robert Smith (Ford, VIII, 241–242n.) and Gallatin (LC, 22980) on July 9, 1803. For Madison's proposed substitute, see Brant, IV, 142.

of the federal government to maintain military forces and regulate trade throughout the province, to work the mines, open roads, etc., but with respect to the unoccupied lands the only authority he would recognize as yet was that of Congress to grant to the Indians east of the Mississippi the right of occupancy of lands west of the river in exchange for those now possessed by them on the other side. That is, he would seize upon the opportunity to expedite the westward movement of the Indians and free the region east of the Mississippi for white settlement. In his draft he stated explicitly that, except in the southernmost region, Congress should have no further authority to grant lands in the newly acquired province until given such by another amendment. Thus the power that would be granted by his own proposed amendment would be sharply limited. He wanted to prevent emigration except to the southernmost district and to prohibit the establishment of territorial or state governments elsewhere without further constitutional sanction. Quite clearly, he was seeking to postpone the question of the vast expansion of the Union and its consequent transformation.

Secretary Robert Smith, wisely holding that the various provisions about the Indians had better be left to Congress than inserted in the Constitution, drafted a briefer amendment which, in his opinion, better expressed what Jefferson had in mind. Madison drafted an even briefer substitute, but Gallatin, to whom he had also sent his draft, presumed that no immediate action was called for. When the President got the text of the treaty a few days later, he realized not only that the French had exacted certain guarantees about the present settlers in the province but also that they were making rigorous requirements with respect to time. Recognizing that speedy ratification of the treaty was imperative, he called Congress into session three weeks ahead of schedule. That was not all, however: he said in at least one letter that Congress would be "obliged to ask from the People an amendment to the Constitution." [9] In other letters written in the next few weeks he was somewhat more equivocal, saying that an amendment "seemed" necessary, and that he "supposed" Congress should appeal to the country for one, but in these he made some of his most striking statements about exceeding constitutional authority.[10]

Already well aware of the dangers of delay, he became even more so when he received, in August, an alarming letter from Livingston.[11] That agitated minister reported that Bonaparte was less pleased with

[9] TJ to William Dunbar, July 17, 1803 (Ford, VIII, 255n.).
[10] As in his letters to Dickinson and Breckinridge, cited above.
[11] Livingston to TJ, June 2, 1803, received Aug. 17 (LC, 22792–22793, decoded duplicate). TJ wrote Madison, Aug. 18 (LC, 23173), enclosing Livingston's letter.

the treaty and conventions than he had been. In order to speed procedure he had already ratified them, but he now regretted this and would not be sorry if opposition in America should delay ratification until the agreements should become void. The First Consul, said Livingston, "will give express direction to Mr. Pichon not to deliver the [French] ratification in case you make the slightest alteration. It is necessary that you should know this. It is equally necessary that those who oppose the administration should not know it as it will be a trump card in their hands."

This letter, which reached Jefferson at Monticello, aroused in him anxieties that he quickly communicated to Madison at Montpelier. Though the Secretary of State perceived no desire of the French to "retract the bargain" and was strongly supported in this position by Gallatin, both of these officers fully recognized that there must be no American delay.[12] Jefferson himself had immediately concluded that he could not risk giving the French a pretext for retracting, or afford to put a trump card into the hands of his political enemies. He wrote Madison: "I infer that the less we say about constitutional difficulties respecting Louisiana the better, and that what is necessary for surmounting them must be done sub silentio." Without waiting to hear from anybody, he began to write other political friends to the same effect.[13]

This did not mean that he had given up the idea of an amendment, for he soon submitted to members of his official family another draft of one. The opening sentence, taken from a draft of Madison's, implied the constitutional right to acquire territory, while the second sought to carry out the terms of the treaty about the present inhabitants of the province.

> Louisiana as ceded by France to the U.S. is made a part of the U.S. Its white inhabitants shall be citizens, and stand, as to their rights & obligations, on the same footing with other citizens of the U.S. in analogous situations.

As he stated to Levi Lincoln, he had concluded that no attempt should be made to enumerate the powers of Congress over the newly acquired region — that it would be sufficient to give Congress the same powers it had with respect to the other parts of the Union. Indeed, he did not say even that explicitly in this draft, but left it to be assumed, and in what appears to have been a later revision he struck out the

[12] Madison to TJ, Aug. 20, 1803 (LC, 23191); Gallatin to TJ, Aug. 31, 1803 (*Writings*, I, 147–149).

[13] TJ to Breckinridge and to Thomas Paine, Aug. 18, 1803 (Ford, VIII, 244–245n.).

statement about the rights and obligations of the new citizens — presumably because he concluded that these could be taken for granted.[14] Reduced to its ultimate terms, his amendment would have amounted to mere affirmation of a *fait accompli* and tacit acquiescence in congressional authority but for his inclusion of the important limitation he still desired. In his third sentence he said that in the region north of the latitude of the mouth of the Arkansas no new state should be established, and no grants of land made, except to the Indians in exchange for lands occupied by them, until another constitutional amendment should so authorize. The assumption was that the region below the Arkansas might eventually be made into a state; and, again following Madison's suggestion, he provided, in his fourth and last sentence, that Florida, whenever "rightfully obtained," should become a part of the United States. But he was in no hurry to enlarge the Union in the political sense. He was quite willing to leave to the distant future the status of the enormous expanse to the north and west.

The fear that ultimately the Mississippi Valley would be the seat of an independent confederation was voiced chiefly by Federalists rather than by Republicans. Though he took little stock in it, somewhat surprisingly he appeared in some of his private utterances to be indifferent on the subject.[15] In any case the region would assuredly be American, not French or English, he said. Actually, no one did more than he to cement the union of the trans-Appalachian country with the eastern seaboard by his constant regard for western interests, but to him the Union was always a means, not an end in itself. The supremely important consideration was the removal of *foreign* danger, and the consequent freedom of the American experiment in self-government to take its own course. It was to his credit that he did not want the balance in the old Union to be drastically altered without general consent, that he wanted the changes to be gradual, not abrupt. "When we shall be full on this side [of the Mississippi]," he said, "we may lay off a range of states on the western bank from the head to the mouth, and so, range after range, advancing compactly as we multiply."

The best tangible sign of general consent to the gradual expansion of the political Union that he could think of was the adoption of a constitutional amendment, to be followed by one or more afterwards. There appears to be no evidence, however, that any important adviser or sup-

[14] In what may have been a final revision (LC, 23687) TJ drew a line through the second sentence that is quoted above. Apparently Ford either overlooked this or disregarded it because it is undated and bears no mark showing what use, if any, TJ made of it. TJ wrote Madison on Aug. 25, and Lincoln on Aug. 30, 1803.

[15] TJ to John Breckinridge, Aug. 12, 1803 (Ford, VIII, 243–244n.); to Joseph Priestley, Jan. 29, 1804 (Ford, VIII, 295).

porter of his urged either the necessity or the practicality of such constitutional procedure. In an unsolicited opinion his close friend Senator
Wilson Cary Nicholas of Virginia argued strongly against it, saying
that a declaration from Jefferson that the treaty exceeded constitutional
authority would lead to its rejection by the Senate or at least to the
charge of his willful breach of the Constitution.[16]

Jefferson's reply to this letter contains such a striking statement of
his practical difficulties and lingering scruples that historians have
quoted it until this day. After urging the importance of speedy action
on the treaty, he said:

> Whatever Congress shall think it necessary to do, should be done
> with as little debate as possible, & particularly so far as respects
> the constitutional difficulty. I am aware of the force of the obser-
> vations you make on the power given by the Constn to Congress
> to admit new states into the Union, without restraining the subject
> to the territory then constituting the U S. But . . . I cannot help
> believing the intention was to permit Congress to admit into the
> union new states, which should be formed out of territory for
> which & under whose authority alone they were then acting. I do
> not believe it was meant that they might receive England, Ireland,
> Holland, &c. into it, which would be the case on your construc-
> tion.

His extreme illustration weakened his argument, if it did not turn it
into a *reductio ad absurdum*, for there was no likelihood whatever of
expansion into Europe. He voiced his compunctions more appealingly
in the passage immediately following:

> When an instrument admits two constructions, the one safe, the
> other dangerous, the one precise, the other indefinite, I prefer that
> which is safe & precise. I had rather ask an enlargement of power
> from the nation where it is found necessary, than to assume it by a
> construction which would make our powers boundless. Our pe-
> culiar security is in possession of a written Constitution. Let us not
> make it a blank paper by construction. I say the same as to the
> opinion of those who consider the grant of the treaty making
> power as boundless. If it is, then we have no constitution. . . .
> Let us go on then perfecting it, by adding by way of amendment
> to the constitution, those powers which time & trial show are still
> wanting. . . .

This was his counsel of perfection, his prescription of ideal procedure. But, summing things up, he made a significant concession to the

[16] Nicholas to TJ, Sept. 3, 1803, largely printed in Brown, pp. 26–27.

exigencies of the moment, implying that he had already decided to follow another course:

> I confess then I think it important in the present case to set an
> example against broad construction by appealing for new power
> to the people. If however our friends shall think differently, cer-
> tainly I shall acquiesce with satisfaction, confiding that the good
> sense of our country will correct the evil of construction when it
> shall produce ill effects.[17]

To say that he hereby promised to acquiesce in making blank paper
of the Constitution is to overload a metaphor and indulge in extravagance.[18] The decision he faced was between publicly proposing a constitutional amendment and not doing so. If not yet persuaded that the
former was the more dangerous course and the latter the safer, both
with respect to the country's welfare and his own continued leadership,
he was being driven to that conclusion by the pitiless logic of events.[19]
He need not have attributed to the pressure of his friends his willingness to let well enough alone. Among trusted political advisers, however, among those whom he believed to be dedicated to the same ends
as himself, he was characteristically undogmatic about means. One of
the reasons for the extraordinary success of his leadership was that he
forebore to press it unduly, that he was a good party man, that he did
take counsel. To have expressed his constitutional scruples publicly
would have endangered an agreement that he deemed essential to national security, while putting weapons into the hands of his political
enemies; but he wanted his intimate friends to know that these scruples
were still present in his mind, and we may believe that he used highly
colorful language for just that reason. Far from admitting that henceforth all constitutional restraints were off, he was putting himself on
record among his intimates as recognizing dangers of construction
against which they must ever be on guard. As a party leader he was uttering private words of warning while reasserting his faith in the de-
pendability of public opinion in the long run.

A decade earlier, when seeking to convince President Washington
that the bill creating the Bank of the United States was constitutional,
Alexander Hamilton had admitted that there was chance of error and
abuse from the moment that the literal meaning of the basic law was
departed from. "And yet," he added, "an adherence to the letter of its

---

[17] TJ to W. C. Nicholas, Sept. 7, 1803 (LC, 23273–23274). I quote this, but the
differences between it and the printed version in Ford, VIII, 247–248n., are unimportant.
[18] Henry Adams, *History*, II, 90–92.
[19] See the sage comment of Irving Brant (*Madison*, IV, 144).

powers would at once arrest the motions of government." [20] If Jefferson did not recognize this when as secretary of state he believed that his aggressive colleague was pressing broad construction too far, he had to do so when as President he bore the chief responsibility for the government and safety of the Republic. He would have failed if he had not profited by experience. To admit that, while in opposition, he had been too rigid in constitutional theory would have been difficult indeed, but he virtually did that after he had left the presidency. When asked whether circumstances did not sometimes arise that made it a duty of high public officers to assume authority beyond the law, he made this reply:

> A strict observance of the written laws is doubtless *one* of the high duties of a good citizen, but it is not *the highest*. The laws of necessity, of self-preservation, of saving our country when in danger, are of higher obligation. To lose our country by a scrupulous adherence to written law, would be to lose the law itself, with life, liberty, property and all those who are enjoying them with us; thus absurdly sacrificing the end to the means.[21]

He did not cite in this connection the actions of his government in acquiring and incorporating the province of Louisiana, but it is not unlikely that he was thinking of these.

In the summer of 1803 there were unquestionable doubts in his own mind that he thought of resolving by the amending process, but few other people appear to have expressed similar qualms before Congress met. Nobody seems to have said much about constitutional difficulties to the President at any rate. Nathaniel Macon of North Carolina, who has been generally regarded as a firm guardian of pure republicanism, said nothing about them when reporting to Jefferson that news of the acquisition had been received with general satisfaction and that the Republicans had nothing to fear but the "party madness" of their foes. He gave no sign that he feared the assumption of "boundless power" by the government. John Breckinridge, to whom Jefferson had described his dilemma in such moving language, ignored the constitutional issue altogether in his reply. Reporting his efforts to get the western senators and representatives to Washington on time, he said that in Kentucky public anxiety was so great that any neglect of duty would be deemed "treasonable." [22]

One of the few correspondents of the President to tackle the consti-

---

20 Lodge, III, 191; see *Jefferson and the Rights of Man*, p. 347.
21 To John B. Colvin, Sept. 20, 1810 (Ford, IX, 279; see also 281).
22 Macon to TJ, Sept. 3, 1803 (LC, 23257); Breckinridge to TJ, Sept. 10, 1803 (Carter, IX, 47–49).

tutional question was Thomas Paine, who was assuredly a friend of human freedom and a foe to consolidated despotism. His sensible comments deserve quotation at some length:

> It appears to me to be one of those cases with which the Constitution has nothing to do, and which can be judged only by the circumstances of the times when such a case shall occur. The Constitution could not foresee that Spain would cede Louisiana to France or to England, and therefore it could not determine what our conduct should be in consequence of such an event. The cession makes no alteration in the Constitution; it only extends the principles of it over a larger territory, and this certainly is within the morality of the Constitution, and not contrary to, nor beyond, the expression or intention of any of its articles. That the idea of extending the territory of the United States was always contemplated, whenever the opportunity offered itself is, I think, evident from the commencement of the revolution that Canada would, at some time or other, become a part of the United States . . .[23]

Writing his chief from New England, on which he reported periodically, Levi Lincoln said that the Federalists, while "vexed, disappointed, mortified, enraged," had not to his knowledge breathed a syllable on the constitutionality of the cession. He was sure they would take that ground, however, and urged that the administration be prepared. The Attorney General even suggested that Jefferson boldly announce and defend the constitutionality of the purchase in his message to Congress, believing that he would gain a great tactical advantage thereby and preempt the arguments of the opposition. Lincoln admitted, however, that he had no decided views on the subject and conceded that Jefferson's plan to amend the Constitution was the safest after all.[24]

Before summer ended, the President himself had further reason to doubt this. New dangers appeared on the side of the Spanish, who had not yet delivered Louisiana to the French. The week after he penned the warning against making blank paper of the Constitution by construction, he read a letter the Secretary of State had received from the Spanish envoy, the Marqués de Casa Yrujo, containing an unexpected caveat.[25] Jefferson had no difficulty in reading Spanish, but he

[23] Paine to TJ from Stonington, Conn., Sept. 23, 1803 (Foner, *Complete Writings* [1945], II, 1447–1448). There were numerous similar comments about Canada by John Adams and others.

[24] Lincoln to TJ from Worcester, Mass., Sept. 10, 1803 (LC, 23284–23285).

[25] At Monticello he received on Sept. 12, 1803, a copy of this from the State Department in Washington as well as the original with comments from Madison at Montpelier. (Yrujo to Madison, Sept. 4, 1803, copy enclosed in a letter of that day from Jacob Wagner [LC, 23258–23259]; original from Madison with letter of

had a hard time trying to figure out the purpose of this communication. Yrujo, who had protested so vigorously against the closing of the deposit in New Orleans, now reported that the King, his master, was surprised to learn of the sale of Louisiana to the United States, since the French had promised never to alienate the province and therefore had no right to do so. Scholars now know that Yrujo was following specific instructions, and also that he doubted the effectiveness of his representation.[26] He anticipated the line the administration would take in reply, and, while believing that if his letter should be submitted to the Senate, as in fact it was, it would strengthen the hands of the Federalist opposition, he did not flatter himself that they could overcome the large Republican majority and defeat the treaty. But, as they read his threatening letter, Jefferson and Madison could only surmise what was in his mind and that of his government.

Madison promptly took the position that the incident was not serious unless it was the result of a secret Spanish agreement with France or Great Britain. Regarding the collusion of Spain with either as highly improbable, he thought the best explanation to be that she was seeking a price for her consent and putting herself in a more advantageous position to contest American claims about the extent of Louisiana. He never arrived at a better explanation. Jefferson took the threat a shade more seriously. He thought it possible that the Spanish, imagining that by delivering New Orleans they could satisfy the United States, might withhold the peaceable cession of the rest of Louisiana. He and his advisers could discuss the whole matter when they reassembled in Washington about ten days later, he said, but in the meantime a hint might be dropped to Daniel Clark, the consul in New Orleans, and he be instructed to sound out opinion cautiously and report on Spanish forces there. Madison promptly wrote Clark to that effect.[27]

Soon after the chief officers of the government returned to the capital, Yrujo sent Madison another strongly worded letter, reiterating the sentiments of the earlier one and adding the argument that the French had not fully carried out the provisions of the treaty of San Ildefonso.[28] Shortly after that, Madison made calm reply.[29] Speaking for the Presi-

---

Sept. 12 [LC, 23294].) Submitted in translation to the Senate a few weeks later with other documents (*A.S.P.F.R.*, II, 569); modern translation in Robertson, II, 77–79.

[26] Yrujo to Ceballos, Sept. 12, 1803 (Robertson, II, 79).

[27] TJ to Madison, Sept. 14, 1803 (Ford, VIII, 263); Madison to Clark, Sept. 16, 1803 (Carter, IX, 55).

[28] This was in response to another letter from Ceballos. Yrujo to Madison, Sept. 27, 1803; to Ceballos, Sept. 30, 1803 (Robertson, II, 81–85).

[29] Madison to Yrujo, Oct. 4, 1803 (*A.S.P.F.R.*, II, 569–570, with Yrujo's two letters; Carter, IX, 69).

dent, he politely but firmly rejected the Spanish objections to the validity of the cession. Properly refraining from comment on French promises to Spain, which were no concern of his, he quoted an official communication of Ceballos, five months earlier, in which that official
informed the American Minister at the Spanish court that Spain had
retroceded Louisiana to France and that the United States should address to the French its negotiations for such territories as it desired.

In official letters to Livingston in Paris and Pinckney in Madrid,
Madison answered the Spanish objections more fully, providing those
American representatives with ample ammunition in case of need.[30]
What the Spanish were actually complaining of was the conduct of the
French, without whose support their opposition was not to be feared;
and, as Madison pointed out to Pinckney, their charge of perfidy
against the First Consul could not be expected to aid their cause with
him. The attitude of the French continued to be the all-important consideration. Speaking of their representative in America, Madison wrote
Monroe: "Pichon is perfectly well disposed, is offended with the Spanish minister, and if left under the orders he now has will cooperate
zealously, with an honest view to the honor and obligations of his own
country." And among the copies of letters he sent Livingston soon
thereafter was one from Pichon that provided full assurance of the satisfactory French attitude a few days before Congress met.[31] In this the
French chargé pointed out that no stipulation against the alienation of
Louisiana had been inserted in the treaty of San Ildefonso. He claimed
that the promises made in that treaty had been faithfully carried out,
saying that the King of Spain must have thought so when, in October,
1802, he issued an order for the delivery of the province to France.
Pichon had shown this order to Madison, and the Spanish officials in
New Orleans had it in their hands. He expressed the hope, therefore,
that the United States government, undisturbed by the "specious rea-
soning" of the Spanish, would proceed with earnestness to execute the
treaty. He himself had received the necessary orders to exchange ratifications and to effect the repossession of Louisiana by the French and
the transfer of the province to the United States.

While continuing to assert that they expected no resistance by the
Spanish, the high officials of the government believed it necessary to
guard against that contingency. On the day that Madison wrote Yrujo
in the name of the President, the latter met with the Secretaries of

[30] Madison to Livingston, Oct. 6, 1803, P.S., Oct. 14; to Pinckney, Oct. 12 (Hunt,
VII, 67–74).

[31] Private letter, Madison to Monroe, Oct. 10, 1803 (Hunt, VII, 64n.); Pichon
to Madison, Oct. 12, 1803 (A.S.P.F.R., II, 571–572).

State, the Treasury, and War; and they unanimously agreed that force should be used if necessary and should be immediately prepared.[32] The two most important officials to be alerted were Governor Claiborne of the Mississippi Territory, who had already been informed that he was to go to New Orleans to receive the transfer, and General James Wilkinson, the ranking officer in the army, who was in command on the southern frontier. Immediate reliance had to be placed on the regular troops at Fort Adams and other river posts, numbering perhaps 500 men altogether, and the militia in the Mississippi Territory. Early in the year Claiborne had reported that there were about 2000 of the latter and that 600 could take New Orleans from the Spanish. The Secretary of War promptly instructed the General and the Governor to provide boats, provisions, and equipment for all the regulars in the territory and at least 500 militiamen. They were to avoid arousing suspicions as to the real objects of these preparations, however, and the President was not yet calling out the militia.

In this delicate diplomatic situation the President was wise in trying to avoid unnecessary alarm; and, in view of the military weakness of the Spanish forces in New Orleans and the irresolution of the high officials there, these military provisions seemed ample. There was a possibility, however, that reinforcements might come from Havana. It was chiefly for this reason that, after the ratification of the treaty, provision was made to call volunteers from Kentucky and Tennessee.[33] Thus, before Congress assembled, military as well as diplomatic efforts were made to meet the possible Spanish danger. So far as Pichon was concerned, the latter were notably successful; the real danger was that he might get other orders from France and the last thing the administration could countenance was delay. Speed in the ratification of the treaty and the enactment of enabling legislation appeared more imperative than ever.

In his message to the legislature when it met the President said that after the Senate had given constitutional sanction to the treaty and its accompanying conventions, further measures with respect to Louisiana, including those necessary for the immediate occupation of the country, would rest with the two branches of Congress.[34] For him to have urged that a constitutional amendment be adopted would have implied that he had exceeded executive authority during the legislative recess; and, as Gallatin pointed out, if action prior to an amendment

---

[32] Memo. of meeting of Oct. 4, 1803 (Ford, I, 300).

[33] Gallatin to TJ, Oct. 28; TJ to Gallatin, Oct. 29, 1803 (Gallatin, *Writings*, I, 163–167).

[34] Message of Oct. 17, 1803 (Ford, VIII, 269).

were assumed to be unconstitutional, there would be no way for the legislature to avoid unconstitutional procedure while an amendment was being adopted.[35] Many things would have to be done immediately. This was no time to accentuate the difficulties of assuming control of the province by questioning the existing powers of the government. Thus, by force of what appeared to be practical necessity, Jefferson tacitly recognized the authority of the legislature to do what he had previously described in specific or general terms in the successive amendments he had drafted. He did not now mention the limitations on future legislative action that he would have imposed, but left to the good sense of Congress and the people the avoidance of the danger of creating new territories and states too rapidly. Given the circumstances, it is hard to see what wiser course he could have followed.

One of Jefferson's admirers in Tennessee expressed his gratitude to Heaven for permitting him to see, under this wise administration, "the most perfect theory in politics, reduced to genuine practice." Though that was obviously an overstatement, other words of this correspondent showed what the grounds of general gratitude really were. "You have secured to us the free navigation of the Mississippi," he said. "You have procured an immense and fertile country: and all these great blessings are obtained without war and bloodshed." [36] They were not obtained, and could not have been, without changing the character of the Union, but, outside New England, few doubted that the gain would far outweigh the cost.

Besides public support, Jefferson had good reason to count on that of Congress if party lines should hold. In the Eighth Congress, which he was now facing, the Republicans were considerably stronger than they had been in the Seventh. He himself estimated the division to be 25 to 9 in the Senate and 103 to 39 in the House; and as realistic a Federalist as Rufus King, noting that two-thirds of the senators were of the "faithful sect," said that there could be no question of the ratification of the treaty unless some constitutional scruples should arise.[37] Presidential tactics were designed to keep these from arising, or at least to delay their doing so. Congress took matters up in the order he recommended. What he sought was: first, speedy consent to the treaty and conventions by the Senate, which would enable him to exchange ratifications with France within the time limit; second, prompt authorization from

35 In remarks on the President's message, received by TJ on Oct. 4 (*Writings*, I, 158).

36 David Campbell to TJ, Oct. 27, 1803 (LC, 23454–23455).

37 TJ to TMR, Oct. 9, 1803 (LC, 23364); King to C. Gore, Oct. 24, 1803 (King, IV, 316), written after the vote in the Senate but before he had learned of it.

Congress as a whole for taking possession of Louisiana, by force if necessary. Temporary government had to be provided for, and financial requirements had to be met, but the difficult question of a more lasting government could wait. It was the most divisive of all since it bore directly on the future nature of the Union.

The presidential message to Congress was criticized as implying that Jefferson took senatorial consent to the treaty for granted, but the margin of approval was even greater than anticipated. Since there was no Republican defection and Senator Jonathan Dayton of New Jersey deserted his Federalist colleagues, the vote was 24 to 7. This was on October 20, the fourth day after the opening of Congress and the submission to the Upper House of the treaty and conventions with the official correspondence.[38] William Plumer of New Hampshire, whose partisan and sectional zeal must be allowed for but whose account of the proceedings of the Senate in this period is invaluable to historians, lamented the haste of the procedure. "The Senate," he said, "have taken less time to deliberate on this important treaty, than they allowed themselves on the most trivial Indian contract."[39] This disturbed New Englander believed that, but for the requirement of three readings, the treaty would have cleared the Senate the first day. According to him, there was only desultory debate on the second reading. On the third, a Federalist resolution calling for further papers was introduced. These should include those showing that France had actually acquired Louisiana and thus had a clear title to it. Supporters of the administration defeated this resolution, "affirming, with unblushing front," said Plumer, "that the information was unnecessary." Proof that France had taken over the province, in fact, did not yet exist, and the uncertainty of the title was just the point that Yrujo had expected the Federalists to make. His disquieting letters to Madison were among the documents submitted to the Senate, along with Pichon's that answered them. A copy of the treaty of San Ildefonso was not included, as Plumer lamented, but the President did not have that to send. The senators did not have time to digest the mass of material they actually received, but they could not rightly say that the President had not taken them into his full confidence.

He and Madison skillfully avoided a hitch in the exchange of ratifications. The French representative had been instructed to insert a clause saying that the ratification by his country would not be binding in case

---

[38] Documents in *A.S.P.F.R.*, II, 506–572. The actions of the Senate are described, without any record of debate, in its *Journal of Executive Procs.*, I, 449–451.

[39] *William Plumer's Memorandum of Procs. in the U.S. Senate*, ed. by E. S. Brown (1923), p. 13. His record for Oct. 20 begins on p. 3.

the United States did not pay the money within the specified time. In behalf of the President, Madison promptly informed Pichon that proper reciprocity would then require the addition of a clause saying that the treaty would be binding only if the French contract to deliver Louisiana should be fulfilled. Thereupon it was agreed to omit both clauses.[40] Pichon had already sent to New Orleans the documents validating the transfer, though these had not been received as yet. Jefferson may have had more doubts of the entire honesty and sincerity of high officials in France than he could admit in diplomatic intercourse, in which he probably said what he wanted to be repeated, but he had none about Pichon, whose co-operation at this critical stage was invaluable.

After a delay of only a few hours in the exchange of ratifications, Jefferson communicated the treaty and conventions to both houses of Congress for consideration in their legislative capacity.[41] He did not send to the House the official correspondence and other documents which the senators were at liberty to examine. Out of this situation embarrassment might have arisen and very nearly did. In Washington's time, in connection with Jay's Treaty, the Republicans had claimed the right of the House to see the official papers, except such as could not properly be disclosed because of impending negotiations, and Jefferson, then in retirement, had agreed with them.[42] Now, a Federalist congressman offered a resolution calling on the President to lay before the House a copy of the treaty of San Ildefonso and one copy of the deed of cession from Spain to France, if such a document existed, along with other papers bearing on the question of the title to Louisiana. He recognized that the alleged uncertainty of the French title, which led William Plumer to designate the cession as a "naked quit claim," could be made an effective talking point. As finally amended, this resolution was defeated by a vote of 57 to 59. The size of the affirmative vote may have reflected the desire of the Republicans not to be adjudged inconsistent with their past; it certainly indicated no widespread hostility to the purchase, for, unlike Jay's Treaty, that was immensely popular. At all events, Jefferson was spared the embarrassment of saying either that he could not or would not produce the documents.[43]

While seeking to avoid the baffling question of the extent and limita-

[40] Madison to Pichon, Oct. 21, 1803 (Carter, IX, 81); TJ to Livingston, Nov. 4, 1803 (Ford, VIII, 278).
[41] Special message, Oct. 21, 1803 (Ford, VIII, 274).
[42] See *Jefferson and the Ordeal of Liberty*, pp. 256–258.
[43] For the debate of Oct. 24, 1803, see *Annals*, 8 Cong., 1 sess., pp. 385–420; E. S. Brown, *Constitutional History of the Louisiana Purchase* (1920), pp. 49–51. This valuable monograph takes up many matters that cannot be gone into in the present work.

tions of the powers of the House of Representatives with respect to treaties, Jefferson fully recognized that enabling legislation was indispensable and wanted to associate Congress with executive actions that were inescapable. Specific authorization of his taking military possession on Louisiana may not have been strictly necessary — so Gallatin suggested, at any rate — but Jefferson did not want to proceed without legislative sanction. The bill that Senator John Breckinridge introduced on October 22 was based on a draft by Gallatin.[44] This authorized the President to take possession and occupy the territory ceded by France, employing the armed forces for that purpose as he might deem necessary. The bill also provided, in a second section, that until Congress should provide otherwise, all governmental powers exercised by the officers of the present (Spanish) government should be vested in such persons and exercised in such manner as the President should direct. This was interpreted to mean that for the present the existing legal and governmental system should be maintained. Reference was made to the protection of the inhabitants in the free enjoyment of their "liberty, property and religion," but in form at least this temporary government was to be wholly autocratic. The bill passed the Senate on the fourth day by a vote of 26 to 6. Joining the little band of Federalists who said Nay was John Quincy Adams, who had not reached the Senate quite soon enough to vote on the treaty itself. Alone among the Federalist senators from New England he approved of the purchase, but he had qualms about what was happening to the rights of the inhabitants of Louisiana.[45]

Action in the House was likewise quick and decisive, but fear of the grant of governmental powers to the President led to an amendment to the second section of the Senate bill. This provided that the exercise of these powers should cease with the expiration of the present term of Congress if provision for the temporary government of Louisiana had not already been made by that body. In this form the bill passed the House by an overwhelming vote.[46]

Qualms about the delegation of power to the President were not confined to Federalists, but the jibes came chiefly from opponents of the administration. Not without warrant did Senator William Plumer say that if his party had passed such a bill, it would have been denounced as monarchical. Manasseh Cutler alleged that the President

[44] *Annals*, 8 Cong., 1 sess., pp. 17–18; Walters, *Gallatin*, p. 180; Carter, IX, 89, note 7.

[45] Oct. 26, 1803 (*Annals*, 8 Cong., 1 sess., p. 26).

[46] *Ibid.*, p. 546. As signed by TJ on Oct. 31, the act can be readily seen in Carter, IX, 89–91, along with extensive references. The debate is well summarized in Brown, pp. 84–89.

was made "as despotic as the Grand Turk." [47] No one could justly deny, however, that for a time at least the exercise of executive power was the only visible alternative to anarchy. The financial requirements of the treaty also received prompt attention. An administration that had made so much of the reduction of the national debt could expect to be chided for proposing to add so much to it, but there was no threat of increased taxes in connection with this bargain, and the necessary financial legislation had to be enacted in good faith. In the Senate, William Plumer, who had opposed the treaty, joined John Quincy Adams in voting for the bill creating the stock for paying France.[48] Thus one piece of enabling legislation quickly followed another, with recognized inevitability; and thus Jefferson was amply armed with legislative sanction as he and his department heads proceeded to translate the momentous purchase from paper into fact.

In the first congressional debates, which were necessarily restricted because of the obvious need for speedy action, and also in the much more deliberate one, early in the next year, on the government of Louisiana, the main objections of the opposition were constitutional, just as had been expected. The basic Federalist contention was not that the Republic could not acquire territory through the actions of the President and Congress; long before the congressional session was over there was general agreement as to the authority to do that. The argument was that the federal legislature had no constitutional authority to incorporate this in the Union without reference to the existing states. Some Federalists, like William Plumer, held that the consent of each and every one of them was necessary. In pragmatic terms the danger as he saw it was the upsetting of the balance of the Union, to the particular disadvantage of the eastern members. The New Englanders, said Plumer, were undisposed "tamely to shrink into a state of insignificance." They might even be driven to disunion.[49] They objected to the special commercial privileges in Louisiana that were promised to the French and Spanish for a term of years, saying that these gave a preference to the port of New Orleans, whereas the Constitution prescribed that duties must be uniform. The chief ground of objection, however, was the third section of the treaty, promising to incorporate Louisiana and grant its inhabitants the rights and privileges of American citizens.

[47] Plumer, *Memorandum*, p. 27; Cutler, *Life . . . of Manasseh Cutler*, II, 148, quoted by Brown, p. 89.

[48] *Memorandum*, p. 31 (Nov. 3, 1803). A useful note on the financing of the purchase, as carried out in the next two decades, is in Carter, IX, 15, note 20.

[49] *Ibid.*, p. 9. Plumer's private comments on the treaty (Oct. 20, 1803; pp. 3–14) probably reflect the views of all the New England senators except J. Q. Adams at this time, though Plumer does not claim that.

The alternative was to hold the province in subjection as a colony, which was contrary to the historic policy embodied in the Northwest Ordinance. Some Federalists frankly favored that.

John Quincy Adams definitely did not; nor did he make a point of the natural fears of his native New England. He approved the purchase, and, rising above parochialism, he foresaw the day when the American flag would wave over the continent. At the same time, regarding Section Three of the treaty as unconstitutional, he held that the incorporation of Louisiana in the Union should not be effected without the adoption of an amendment to the Constitution on the one hand and a referendum to the people of the province on the other. The most disinterested constitutionalist among the Federalists, he was at this stage perhaps the purest in Congress. A couple of days after the Senate passed the bill enabling the President to take possession of Louisiana, against which Adams had voted, that senator, calling at Madison's office, asked him if the executive had arranged for anybody to bring before Congress a proposal to amend the Constitution. If not, he would think it his duty to do so. In the absence of any comment on this matter from the President at the time, that of his intimate friend and confidant is of particular interest. For one thing, Madison was unaware that the need of an amendment was universally recognized — as, indeed, it definitely was not. For another, he conceded that the Constitution had provided for no such case as this, "that it must be estimated by the magnitude of the object, and that those who had agreed to it must rely upon the candor of their country for justification." Adams agreed to all this, while urging the necessity of removing all doubt on the subject, and he reported Madison as assenting to that. Admitting that he knew of no arrangement that had been made, Madison added that "probably, when the objects of immediate pressure were gone through," the matter would be attended to; and that if he had anything to do with it he would ask that Adams be consulted.[50]

At the time, the members of the administration and the party leaders in Congress were occupied with the "objects of immediate pressure" and the matter was not attended to. About a month later, before Jefferson and his advisers had yet learned of the peaceful delivery of Louisiana to the French by the Spanish, and considerably before it was delivered by the French to the Americans, Adams, again calling on Madison, showed him an amendment he proposed to introduce. In his own words the import of this was as follows: "Congress shall have power to admit into the Union the inhabitants of any territory which has been or may

[50] Oct. 28, 1803 (J. Q. Adams, *Memoirs*, I, 267).

be hereafter ceded to or acquired by the United States." [51] Adams worded his amendment so that it would be applicable to Florida or Canada, if need be; but Madison thought its comprehensiveness would hazard its chances of ratification, saying that a sufficient statement would be: "Louisiana is hereby admitted into this Union." Adams himself was of the opinion that his amendment would be approved by every state. Upon its merits, one might suppose that Jefferson should have approved of it, but immediate practical necessities were still in the forefront of his mind. Furthermore, if we may judge from what they said in Congress, his supporters now saw less need than ever for a constitutional amendment.

When Adams requested the appointment of a committee to report one, no Republican and only two of his Federalist colleagues in the Senate supported him.[52] Several Republican senators strongly denied the need for an amendment, but Breckinridge probably came nearest to expressing the thought of the administration. While recognizing that there was division of opinion on this question, he dismissed the proposal as impracticable. He did not believe that the tedious process of adopting an amendment could be completed before the time within which the purchase money must be paid to France according to the terms of the treaty as already ratified. Therefore, he thought it imprudent even to bring up the question. In view of the anxiety of the President to conclude the transaction with France at the earliest possible moment, there can be little doubt that he took just that position, though the apathy within his own party on the subject was such that he did not have to address himself to it. The constitutional question was by no means dead, for the precise status of the acquired territory was still unsettled, but Adams's particular proposal died of anemia.

Years later, he described the purchase of Louisiana as "an assumption of implied power greater in itself and more comprehensive in its consequences than all the assumptions of implied powers in the years of the Washington and Adams Administrations put together." While in opposition Jefferson and Madison had protested against these, he said, but their later actions showed that they had done so only for political pur-

[51] Nov. 25, 1803, quoted in "Reply to the Appeal of the Massachusetts Federalists" (Henry Adams, *Documents relating to New-England Federalism* [1877], p. 157); full text in J. Q. Adams, *Writings*, III, 20–21.

[52] Pickering of Mass., and Hillhouse of Conn. The motion was on Dec. 9, 1803, following notice on Nov. 25, the day Adams saw Madison. The opinions of various senators are described in Plumer, *Memorandum*, pp. 75–78. There are constitutional implications with respect to the treaty-making power which I do not go into here.

poses.[53] Unlike most critics of past policy, Adams made clear just what he would have done, what he had actually tried to do as a senator. His attitude at the time was one of intellectual honesty and sincere patriotism. It does not follow, however, that the specific proposal he made was wise in the existing situation. Nor was it fair to say, then or thereafter, that the President made a mere convenience of political doctrine, though, like most public men, he indulged in self-justification upon occasion. It is proper to point out that he was generally more realistic when in office than when in opposition, less doctrinaire; and his situation with respect to the treaty and its promises can be best described by saying that he was caught in a chain of inexorable circumstances.

[53] Oct. 20, 1821 (*Memoirs*, V, 364–365).

[XVIII]

The Precarious Periphery

1803—1805

IN the evening of Tuesday, October 31, 1803, the day the President received and signed the enabling act, a post rider set out from Washington, bearing important documents and communications to officials in the Mississippi Territory and New Orleans. Jefferson and his assistants, who had collected and prepared these papers with celerity, transmitted them by the fastest means they knew. Recognizing the need for speedier communication with the Southwest, the Postmaster General, more than a month before, had arranged to run an "express mail" to Natchez and thence to New Orleans. His calculation that one hundred miles could be covered in a day, horses being relieved every thirty miles and riders every hundred, and that Natchez could be reached in fifteen days, proved to be approximately correct.[1] Under the best of circumstances, however, the President would have to wait more than a month for decisive news from the periphery of the Republic.

Because of the delicacy of the diplomatic situation and uncertainties about the attitude of the Spanish, the administration did not take the public into its full confidence, but news of the express and of the possibility of the use of force inevitably got into the papers. Thereupon the *New York Evening Post*, which had differed from other Federalist journals in declaring the cession of Louisiana advantageous to the country, expressed the pious thought or wish that if war should ensue the blood would be "on the heads of those who have resorted to arms to enforce injustice." The editor gloomily added: "In our view nothing can be more critical than the present aspect of our public affairs."[2]

---

[1] Granger to Claiborne, Sept. 27, 1803, and to G. H. Hyndes, Sept. 28 (Carter, IX, 57–58).

[2] *N.Y. Evening Post*, Nov. 5, 1803.

This was a partisan exaggeration, but the administration still faced the task of turning glorious paper promises into physical reality.

The Marqués de Casa Yrujo was aware of the departure of the express. In fact he had been urged by Pichon to avail himself of it to urge the officials of his government in New Orleans to facilitate the transfer of Louisiana to the United States. The French representative was doing just that with respect to *his* government. On the contrary, Yrujo wrote a letter next day to the Spanish Governor in which he delivered a different exhortation.[3] Seizing upon a rumor that an order had been received in New Orleans to suspend the transfer, he urged vigorous resistance to the Americans *if such an order had been received*. Otherwise, he asked that his letter be disregarded. He confidently predicted that the Americans would use force if necessary to carry out their Machiavellian policy of taking what they wanted; indeed, he was sure they would try to possess themselves of West Florida as well as Louisiana and that they would be supported by public opinion in such action. His fears for West Florida were not unnatural, though no orders had been given for military action in that region. His hope was that American attacks would be delayed, since the necessary troops might not be immediately available. Like the American government, he recognized that speed was of the essence, and he sought to guard his warnings against mischance. After dispatching his letter by messenger overland he sent a duplicate by sea. Having also sent warnings to East and West Florida, he believed that he had done all he could to prevent or postpone the transfer. Jefferson and Madison were not in position to read these communications, as modern scholars are, but they knew that Yrujo had dispatched a messenger. Confident of French support, the executive officers were in no mood of desperation, but they would have been relieved if they had known that the Spaniard's letter would not reach New Orleans in time to have any influence on developments, and, what was more to the point, that the officials there had not received, or been sent, the rumored order to suspend the transfer.[4]

The Spanish representative in Washington attributed to his own threats the "extraordinary meeting" of the executive officers on Sunday, October 29, and the prolonged labors in the executive offices on Monday and Tuesday. But much paperwork would have been necessary in any case. Besides copies of the treaty and the enabling act, the papers that were dispatched Tuesday night included commissions to

[3] Nov. 1, 1803 (Robertson, II, 93–99), received Dec. 7. See also Yrujo to Ceballos, Nov. 4 (*ibid.*, II, 99–116).

[4] Ceballos to Yrujo, Jan. 9, 1804 (Robertson, II, 128–129); see also *ibid.*, II, 117. Yrujo's letter to the Governor was received Dec. 7, 1803, a week after the transfer (Whitaker, p. 249).

Claiborne and General Wilkinson to receive the transfer and to the former as temporary governor, along with a proclamation to be issued by him. This was drafted by the President. Besides these formal documents, there were long letters of instruction to the two principals and to Daniel Clark, consul in New Orleans.[5] Jefferson, who did so much laborious paperwork in connection with legislation, relegated most of it to his assistants in this instance, and the instructions given in his name were actually the result of joint deliberations. The high officers functioned effectively as a team. The element of suspense in the unfolding story — suspense of which present-day readers, knowing how things turned out, may not be aware — is revealed in the actions prescribed or suggested in case of Spanish resistance. As the Secretary of State told Claiborne and the Secretary of War told Wilkinson, considerable discretion must be allowed the commissioners, who were in much better position than their superiors to ascertain the actual situation in New Orleans. They were to proceed peacefully if they could, forcefully if they must. If they should learn that the transfer from Spain to France had been made, or were convinced that it would be made peaceably, they were to proceed to New Orleans immediately with the troops already available. If there should be a Spanish refusal, Claiborne and Wilkinson must decide, after consultation with Daniel Clark and Laussat, the French prefect, whether the *coup de main* should be promptly made with the forces in hand or they should await reinforcements that were in prospect. The 500 mounted militia from Tennessee who were being requisitioned were expected to move promptly, and orders had gone to the Governors of Tennessee, Kentucky, and Ohio to prepare and hold in readiness forces of militia totaling 6000. Presumably, the latter would be needed only in case the Spanish were reinforced from Havana. Gallatin, who seemed more concerned than anybody else over that possibility, went out of his way to suggest privately to Claiborne that, having proceeded without delay, they might do something to intercept such a force by putting obstacles in the river.[6] None of the high officials admitted the likelihood of Spanish refusal, but all emphasized the advantages of promptness if there must be a *coup de main*.

Jefferson and his advisers believed that they had provided sufficiently for all *probable* contingencies. Judging from the tardy response to the call for volunteers in the western states, because of the feuds of local

[5] The most important official letters are Madison to Claiborne, Madison to Clark, and Dearborn to Wilkinson, all dated Oct. 31, 1803. With the commissions, they can be conveniently seen in Carter, IX, 91–98, 143–144. The proclamation is in *A.S.P.F.R.*, II, 582.

[6] Private letter of Gallatin to Claiborne, Oct. 31, 1803 (*Writings*, I, 167–168), written in advance of his official letter.

military leaders and the lack of a sense of urgency, we may doubt that the men of the western waters could have quickly offset large Spanish reinforcements from Havana.[7] But, unless the French had changed their minds, the arrival of such a force would have been regarded as an intolerable affront to their government. The administration rightly regarded that prospect as remote, and if it had become a reality the Westerners could probably have been aroused to fury. The immediately available forces were not impressive, but it was supposed that the Spanish were weak from the military point of view and properly believed that they could not challenge French authority.

It was about seven weeks before Jefferson learned that the administration's estimate of the situation had been borne out by events. The news, which came to him as a sort of Christmas gift, that the Spanish had transferred Louisiana to the French, removed the chief remaining uncertainty. The official report that the French flag in New Orleans had been replaced by the American followed about three weeks later.[8]

As the story was relayed to him and his executive heads in installments, he learned that the American documents and instructions arrived virtually on schedule and that the French Prefect was promptly informed and consulted. Expressing entire satisfaction with the arrangements, Laussat promised the most cordial cooperation. Not only so; he said he had been assured of that of the Spanish.[9] But there was a hitch. The Prefect had not yet received the original documents sent him in the middle of October by Pichon, and he was reluctant to proceed on the basis of the copies that had reached him, even though these were authenticated. The Secretary of War had provided an escort through the worst of the wilderness for the bearer of the originals, but this naval officer fell into difficulties when on his own. He could not compete with the express riders dispatched by the Postmaster General. The copies had been authenticated by Madison, after Yrujo declined the request of Pichon that he do so, thus accentuating the resentment of the French representative. The latter's special messenger got to New

[7] See Whitaker, *Mississippi Question,* pp. 241–243, for developments in Tennessee and Kentucky.

[8] The transfer to France on Nov. 30, 1803, was announced in *National Intelligencer,* Dec. 26, 1803, as reported in dispatches received by the last mail. This action was anticipated in Clark to Madison, Nov. 29, received Dec. 19, reported in *National Intelligencer* Dec. 21 (Carter, IX, 123–125). Reports of the transfer to the U.S., Dec. 20, 1803, by Claiborne to Madison (Robertson, II, 225–226) and by Wilkinson to Dearborn (Carter, IX, 138–139) reached Washington Jan. 15. The event was reported to Congress by TJ the next day.

[9] Laussat to Claiborne, Nov. 23, 1803, replying to a communication of Nov. 18, the day after Claiborne got the commissions and instructions and wrote Daniel Clark (Carter, IX, 109–112).

Orleans a couple of days after Laussat bemoaned his tardiness. Yrujo's letter of exhortation and warning had not arrived, and the American Consul was resolved to stop it, if that procedure should seem necessary.[10] Even if it had come earlier, the admonition to suspend the transfer was contingent on the receipt of orders from higher authority, and it would therefore have merely given occasion for procrastination. The silence of the court of Spain was correctly interpreted as implying consent to the transfer, though the administration did not have full proof of this until some months later. Early in the new year the Spanish Foreign Minister repudiated Yrujo's protest against the alienation of Louisiana, while asserting that it was well grounded and approving his conduct. The acquiescence of his government was afterwards formally reported to Pinckney in Madrid, and, later still, by Yrujo himself to Madison.[11]

Though the high Spanish officials in New Orleans gave signs of irresolution almost to the end, they saw no real choice but to follow their existing orders and to set a day (November 30, 1803) for the transfer of the province to the French when Laussat demanded it.[12] The latter forthwith sent to the American commissioners a request that they proceed promptly to the city. He had already conferred in person with General Wilkinson, who passed through New Orleans on a military tour and proceeded thence to the rendezvous at Fort Adams. Claiborne had been unable to enroll volunteers at Natchez to the extent he expected — because of the heavy rains in November, the occupation of the planters with their cotton crops, and the general feeling that no real crisis existed — but under existing circumstances this was a matter of small consequence. The expedition, which was detained at Fort Adams because the boats were not ready, reached New Orleans more than two weeks after the French had taken over the province. Laussat might have had trouble in this interim, but the 450 men whom Wilkinson commanded were sufficient after they got there. According to the American Consul, who often voiced uneasiness, the regular Spanish forces consisted of only 300 men, of whom about half were in hospital or prison. Thus the American troops were adequate to the situation they actually found, and the actions and preparations of the administra-

---

[10] Madison to Clark, Oct. 12, 1803 (Carter, IX, 78–79); Yrujo to Ceballos, Sept. 30, Oct. 16, 1803 (Robertson, II, 84–85, 89–90); Clark to Claiborne, Nov. 23, 1803 (Carter, IX, 119); Clark to Madison, Nov. 28, 1803 (Carter, IX, 112–113), received Dec. 19.

[11] Ceballos to Yrujo, Jan. 6, 9, 1804 (Robertson, II, 127–129; see also 117); extract of letter of Ceballos to Charles Pinckney, Feb. 10, 1804; Yrujo to Madison, May 15, 1804 — both transmitted to Congress Nov. 8, 1804 (A.S.P.F.R., II, 583).

[12] There is a good account of events in Whitaker, pp. 218–253.

tion were vindicated by their complete success. Up to and including the delivery of the province to Claiborne and Wilkinson on December 20, all was peaceful and according to diplomatic propriety.

The President got the news two weeks after New Year's and reported it to Congress next day. "Never have mankind contemplated so vast and important an accession of empire by means so pacific and just," exulted the *National Intelligencer*. About ten days later, this Jeffersonian paper published "copious and interesting details" of the celebration in New Orleans, and at five o'clock that same Friday numerous members of Congress gave a "most superb dinner" in honor of the chief executive and his heads of department.[13] Having been formally escorted to Stelle's Hotel on Capitol Hill and saluted by artillery on his approach, the President, who detested ceremony, entered the door to the strains of "Jefferson's March." As dinners went in that era in the village capital, this was a large one; there were about a hundred in attendance. "An assemblage so numerous, to celebrate an event, at once so glorious and so happy, may not occur again for centuries to come," said the *National Intelligencer*. There had been no such occasion for rejoicing since the adoption of the Constitution, at any rate, and the executives and legislators who were gathered here had abundant grounds for self-congratulation. They could reflect that "without exciting the anguish of one heart, they had extended the blessings of liberty to an hundred thousand beings . . . and by means untainted with the blood of a single victim, they had acquired almost a new world, and had laid the foundation of the happiness of millions yet unborn!"

This language of a staunch journalistic supporter of the administration is subject to some qualification. The Spanish representative in the United States had given the impression of considerable anguish, and the inhabitants of Louisiana, whose number was uncertain, were not enjoying the blessings of liberty as yet. But time was to demonstrate that the jubilation of this hour was abundantly warranted; and, from that day forward, credit for a vast achievement could not be justly denied the administration. The sarcastic references to the "Louisiana Jubilee" by disgruntled Federalists were made with ill grace. Hardly any members of the opposition party were at the dinner. John Quincy Adams showed his independence of spirit by attending, but left early, saying that the food was bad and the toasts too numerous — in which judgment he was probably correct. William Plumer, giving a secondhand report, corroborated him in part by saying that a number of guests

[13] *National Intelligencer*, Jan. 16, 27, 1804, and Jan. 30, reporting the dinner.

drank so many toasts that on departing they left their hats behind them. Congressman Manasseh Cutler, who may be designated as a die-hard Federalist, described the ball of the following Tuesday night as "the second act of the farce." This took place in Georgetown at the assembly rooms and was reported by the *National Intelligencer* as "the most numerous and brilliant" in the history of the locality: 500 were said to have attended.[14] There is no record that the President was one of these, but a transparent portrait of him was displayed. According to friendly Republican report, "the most perfect good order, and the highest flow of hilarity were kept up . . . every difference of opinion or contrariety of intention being melted into one single and unanimous sentiment of social and patriotic joy." Belittling all this jubilation, Manasseh Cutler afterwards asserted that the entire Jubilee turned out to be "a very trifling matter." [15] No one in his right mind could have said that about the acquisition of Louisiana, and national rejoicing was entirely appropriate, but this business was far from finished. Neither the President nor his countrymen yet knew just what the province consisted of, or precisely how it was to be incorporated in the Union.

Jefferson had given much attention to both of these questions since midsummer. Before returning to Washington in late September, he had prepared the historical memoir in which he supported the claim of Livingston and Monroe that, on the east, Louisiana extended to the Perdido. But, although he clung to this claim with the utmost tenacity, he did not communicate the document to Congress, and not until some months later did he have copies of it sent to American ministers abroad.[16] He had barely finished this memoir when he learned that Yrujo was protesting in the name of Spain against the entire cession. Even if the President's contention was meritorious he was wise in refraining from pressing a subsidiary territorial claim at the time. He gave no sign then or later that he proposed to pursue it by force, whatever Yrujo may have said, though admittedly he was prepared to use armed might to get possession of New Orleans. As against the Spanish, he was disposed to delay formal presentation of the claim until a more propitious season.

He could not keep it wholly out of sight, however, and for domestic

[14] Plumer, *Memorandum*, p. 123, saying that Adams, Dayton, and Huger attended; Cutler, *Life*, II, 161; *National Intelligencer*, Feb. 2, 1804, describing the ball of Jan. 30.

[15] Feb. 21, 1804 (Cutler, *Life*, II, 163).

[16] Dated Sept. 7, 1803, with a P.S. dated Jan. 15, 1804. Printed from original ms. in Am. Philos. Soc. in *Documents relating to the Purchase and Exploration of Louisiana* (1904). See above, 309.

reasons probably did not want to, since it made the cession seem all the more advantageous. Letters from Livingston and Monroe, advancing the claim to the Perdido, were among the documents communicated to the Senate with the treaty, and party leaders, such as Senator John Breckinridge and Congressman John Randolph, could hardly have been unaware of the administration's support of this contention. Furthermore, the boundary question must necessarily come up at times in connection with legislation respecting Louisiana.

After dispatching the post riders to Natchez and New Orleans on the last day of October, Jefferson turned his attention to the vital domestic question of providing for the organization and government of the territory of which he expected his country soon to be possessed. Recognizing that the procuring of information about the provinces was a prime necessity, he had sent queries during the summer to a number of persons — Claiborne, Daniel Clark, and others. Besides their replies to him or Madison, information came into the Departments of State and the Treasury from other sources.[17] An abstract of all these materials was made by Jacob Wagner, chief clerk of the State Department, and this was transmitted to Congress by Jefferson a couple of weeks after Claiborne and Wilkinson were sent their instructions.[18] He sent this, he said, in the hope that it might be useful to the legislators in providing for the government of Louisiana. At the same time he promised, and afterwards he sent, a translation of the most important laws of the province. The diligence and foresight of the executive were not applauded by all of Jefferson's countrymen. The description of Louisiana, coming into public as well as congressional view, occasioned partisan ridicule. While not wholly unwarranted, this amounted to distortion.

The first section in this document of description dealt briefly with the question of boundaries. Jefferson probably thought it impossible not to make some reference to these and unwise to define them in a way that would restrict the government in the future. Therefore, while admitting uncertainty about the precise boundaries on the west and

[17] TJ sent similar queries to Claiborne, Clark, and William Dunbar on July 17, 1803. Those sent to Clark (LC, 23029–23031) were forty-three in number and written by different hands; many of them were from Gallatin and often they were repeated in replies, as in Claiborne to TJ, Aug. 24, 1803, and Clark to Madison, Sept. 8 (Carter, IX, 16–25, 28–47). See also Clark to Madison, Sept. 29, 1803, about Indians (*ibid.*, IX, 61–66).

[18] Nov. 14, 1803, "An Account of Louisiana" (*A.S.P. Misc.*, I, 344–356; see also Carter, IX, 47, note 14). It is in *Annals*, 8 Cong., 2 sess., pp. 1498–1525, and appeared in print at the time in newspapers and as *An Account of Louisiana being an Abstract of Documents in the Offices of the Departments of State and the Treasury* (n.d.). An examination of the original document in NA (SD, Orleans Territory Papers, II) leads to the conclusion that Carter was in error in saying that TJ corrected it.

north, which were not yet important, the government publicly reported the claim to the desired eastern boundary, which was of more immediate concern. Without indicating the source of the information, the document said that it was "asserted upon very strong grounds" that, according to the limits of Louisiana "when formerly possessed by France," the province extended at least to the Perdido River. Though this statement was less than an official pronouncement and might have been regarded as tentative, it could also have been interpreted as a commitment. Few may have known that the paragraph of historical summary, immediately following the one containing this statement, reflected Jefferson's memoir on the subject, but anyone could have seen later in the "Account" that the Division of Mobile was listed among those into which Louisiana was divided. There was little descriptive material about it, however, and that was generally uncomplimentary. Though mentioned, the district was not emphasized.

Irrespective of the contestable section on boundaries, "An Account of Louisiana" was a useful, even an invaluable, compendium of information. It dealt with inhabitants, lands and titles, fortifications and militia, officers of government, laws and courts, crime, the church, taxes and duties, the sugar crop, imports and exports. Statistical uncertainties were frankly admitted, but here was the best information that could be readily procured. Special interest attaches to the section dealing with the Indians, about whom Jefferson had gone to particular pains to gain information.

Besides the account of the Indians, there was relatively little about Upper Louisiana, and this reflected the tall tales of hunters and occasional travelers who had visited that wild region.[19] Lewis and Clark had not yet set out. Whoever may have been originally responsible for the extravagances, they were directly attributed to Jefferson in a Federalist editorial that ridiculed him unmercifully. On this topic William Coleman, the brilliant editor of the *New York Evening Post*, outdid himself.[20] Charging the chief magistrate with "a tinsel attempt to flourish and embroider at the expense of good sense, if not of truth and sincerity," he expressed uncertainty whether Jefferson, by describing a "land of promise," was trying to reconcile the people to the huge purchase price, or was merely manifesting "weak credulity." The passages he cited for special ridicule referred to the extraordinary fertility of the region and, most particularly, to an alleged salt mountain. This mountain, which was now gaining fame of a sort, was said to exist a thousand miles up the Missouri and to be forty-five miles wide and 130 miles

[19] *A.S.P. Misc.*, I, 346–347; *Annals.*, 8 Cong., 2 sess., pp. 1503–1504.
[20] *N.Y. Evening Post*, Nov. 28, 1803.

long. The Federalist editor wondered why there was no mention of "an immense lake of molasses and . . . a vale of hasty pudding, stretching as far as the eye could reach."

Since a more friendly editor reported on the same day that the President had received specimens of salt from the "extensive mountain of that substance," one might argue that Republicans were more credulous than Federalists.[21] Also, there is reliable testimony that Jefferson liked to tell large stories of natural wonders. The precise origin of this one remains to be determined, but all that can be said about Jefferson's connection with it is that he let it go to Congress and get into print. Thus was an opportunity provided for a caricature of the man who was dispatching Lewis and Clark in pursuit of accurate geographical knowledge of this largely unknown region, and to whose initiative most members of the legislative body owed virtually all the information about it they now had.

Toward the end of November, a couple of weeks after Jefferson communicated the abstract to Congress and about the time that William Coleman focused attention on the salt mountain, two exceedingly important bills relating to Louisiana were introduced by strong supporters of the administration. One of these, dealing with territorial organization and government, bore directly on the problem of incorporating the ceded province and its inhabitants in the Union.[22] The other, which was translated into law sooner, dealt with duties on imports and tonnage.[23] The Secretary of the Treasury referred to this as the revenue law for Louisiana, but it has gone down in history as the Mobile Act. One of its sections (the fourth) provided for the annexation to the Mississippi Revenue District of all the navigable waters and streams lying within the United States that entered into the Gulf of Mexico east of the Mississippi. Since none of these lay *wholly* within the United States unless some portion of West Florida was regarded as part of the country, this language was equivocal. The eleventh section went further: it authorized the President, whenever he should deem such action expedient, to set up a separate revenue district centering on the Bay and River of Mobile. These particular provisions appear to have attracted

[21] *National Intelligencer*, Nov. 28, 1803. A further example of Republican credulity is provided by a letter of Congressman Jacob Crowninshield to Rev. William Bentley, Nov. 19, 1803, in which the story of the salt mountain is said to have been "well authenticated" (*Historical Magazine*, 2 ser., X, 104).

[22] Introduced in the Senate Nov. 28, 1803; enacted Mar. 26, 1804.

[23] Introduced in the House Nov. 30, 1803; enacted Feb. 24, 1804. Text in *Annals*, 8 Cong., 1 sess., pp. 1253–1258; detailed references in Carter, IX, 189, note 73.

little or no attention in Congress and to have escaped the notice of the Spanish Envoy while the bill was under consideration, though he had abundant opportunity to become aware of them. Afterwards it became evident that his government as well as he regarded them, especially the provisions of Section Eleven, as an affront or at least a grave impropriety. The Foreign Minister of that proud though feeble nation was to say within a year that the Americans had brought forward their "pretensions to this territory," not by recognized diplomatic procedure but by "a solemn legislative act."[24] The conflict that came to light in connection with the so-called Mobile Act was afterwards waged in diplomatic channels, but the historian must wonder why Jefferson caused or permitted the boundary issue to emerge as it did at this time. Questions may properly be asked since this was undoubtedly an administration measure.

Clues to Jefferson's attitude and purposes while the bill was pending can be found in things he wrote to Monroe, who was in his full confidence and to whom he was accustomed to speak freely.[25] That special envoy was now in England, where he was instructed to remain until he had reached some agreement with respect to impressment and other points at issue with Great Britain or had concluded that nothing could be done. He was then to go to Spain to settle the boundaries of Louisiana. The memoir in which Jefferson supported the claim to the Perdido boundary was now taken from the files and sent to Monroe.[26] The President sounded dogmatic and pugnacious when he said: "We scarcely expect any liberal or just settlement with Spain, and are perfectly determined to obtain or to take our just limits." He had left no doubt as to what he believed these just limits were, but when he became specific he appeared more patient. With respect to the part of West Florida lying between the thirty-first parallel and the island of New Orleans — roughly, the Baton Rouge district — he had no fears whatever. Since the inhabitants of that district would soon seek of their own accord to come under American jurisdiction, it could be peaceably acquired by letting things take their natural course. (His immediate hopes were not realized, for a revolt against Spanish authority that year was unsuccessful, but he was warranted in the opinion he had long held that the Spanish government would ultimately have to retire before the tide of American settlement.) For Mobile and East Florida his government would await "favorable conjunctions." He believed that a crisis would arise quickly if American ships were denied the free use of the Mobile

[24] Ceballos to Pinckney and Monroe, Feb. 10, 1805 (*A.S.P.F.R.*, II, 641).
[25] TJ to Monroe, Jan. 8, 1804, postscript Jan. 16 (Ford, VIII, 286–292).
[26] See above, pp. 309, 339, and map of Spanish Floridas, p. 305.

River and Spain should become involved in the European war, but he gave no impression that the situation required any positive action on the part of the government at the moment.

Before Jefferson mailed this letter to Monroe, the new British Minister in Washington wrote home that the American government was disappointed by the refusal of the Spanish to evacuate their troops in the part of the territory east of the Mississippi.[27] But, while there was annoying delay in the removal of troops and departure of high officials from New Orleans, there was no refusal there; and the American commissioners had no orders to request the delivery of the posts in West Florida. Jefferson and Madison knew that the local Spanish authorities, by proclamation some months earlier, had excluded West Florida from the cession, and when they issued their orders they feared that the French Prefect would support the Spanish position, as in fact he did. In the matter of the disputed region, the purpose of the administration was to go over the heads of the local authorities and to negotiate at the highest level when circumstances should seem favorable. Such did not seem the case early in 1804, for the administration had learned from Charles Pinckney that the government in Spain took the same position as the local officials. The situation would become more favorable if Spain should enter the war on the side of France, for the Floridas could then be seized by the British — an eventuality that Napoleon might be expected to regard as less desirable than their cession to the United States.[28] Great as Jefferson's obsession may have been with the idea that his country had a valid legal claim to the Perdido boundary, there were so many good reasons for holding it in abeyance that, as a matter of tactics, even the intimation of the claim in a legislative act would appear to have been unwise. Madison said that Section Eleven was included to avoid inconvenience in the event that Spain should consent to the Perdido boundary before the next meeting of Congress.[29] Thus he pinned responsibility for the most objectionable portion of the act squarely on the administration while lessening its claim to realistic statesmanship and reasonable anticipation. Formal Spanish consent was not to be expected except as the result of Monroe's negotiations, but that diplomat did not reach Madrid until the middle of December, when Congress had been more than a month in session.

[27] Anthony Merry to Hawkesbury, Jan. 16, 1804 (FO, 5:41, pp. 55–59).

[28] Madison presented the American position to Livingston in much this way, Mar. 31, 1804 (Hunt, VII, 123–127); see also letter of Jan. 31, 1804 (Hunt, VII, 114–118).

[29] Brant, IV, 193, reporting a statement to Pichon two or three weeks after the bill became law.

The clearest indication of the purposes of the administration with respect to the Mobile Act is provided by Gallatin's instructions to the Collector of Revenue of the Mississippi District a few days after the bill became law. These reflected Cabinet decisions that were reached after Congress had passed the bill but before Jefferson signed it.[30] After stating that, while the United States claimed the region between the Mississippi and the Perdido, the Spanish government had not yielded possession of that territory, the Secretary of the Treasury uttered these words of counsel:

> This subject being considered as proper matter of negotiation between the two countries, it is not the intention of the President of the United States to occupy the same by force; and you are therefore to exercise no act of Territorial Jurisdiction within the Said limits, though part of your district, nor commit any act which may endanger the peace of the U. States.
>
> But in the meanwhile the inhabitants on both sides should enjoy the advantages of a friendly intercourse; and some regulations are necessary for the protection of the revenue and to prevent the sufferance of possession in Spain from being abused for purposes injurious to the United States.

In laying down specific rules Gallatin made a clear distinction between the Baton Rouge district and the Gulf coast past Mobile (corresponding to the littoral of the present states of Mississippi and Alabama). With respect to revenue laws, the latter was to be considered for the present as a Spanish colony, but commercial intercourse between it and the territory lying on Lakes Ponchartrain and Maurepas must not be interrupted. Boats of less than fifty tons were to be treated as though they were American, and no import duties were to be imposed on native products. Quite obviously no offensive action was anticipated against the region that gave a name to the Mobile Act. The power to set up a separate revenue district in that area was discretionary with the President, and the Council had decided that the port of entry should be Fort Stoddert, which was above the thirty-first parallel and indisputably in the United States.

The main purposes of the regulations with respect to the Baton Rouge district were to control commerce and prevent smuggling. Among these regulations was one prohibiting foreign vessels, including Spanish, from proceeding up the Mississippi beyond New Orleans. But

[30] Gallatin to H. B. Trist, Feb. 27, 1804 (Carter, IX, 192–197); TJ's memo. of meeting of Feb. 18, 1804 (Ford, I, 304–305).

Gallatin modified the rule so as to permit Spanish vessels to ascend to Baton Rouge, and recognized for the present all the Spanish settlements in the disputed region as foreign territory.[31] This modification of the regulations was made on American initiative.

Yrujo had protested violently against the customs act in the meantime, directing his fire against Section Eleven, which contained the word Mobile. Nearly two weeks after Jefferson signed the law the Spaniard stormed into Madison's office, brandishing a local newspaper. He described this act of Congress as an atrocious libel and an insulting usurpation of the rights of his King.[32] While reasserting the American claim to the disputed territory, Madison sought to mollify him with respect to Section Eleven; and, although the American government caused his offensive language to be reported to his court, it did not ask for his recall. Finally, by proclamation some weeks later, Jefferson set up a separate revenue district, naming Fort Stoddert as its port of entry and limiting it to waters lying *within the boundaries of the United States*. He italicized these words as we have, but called it the District of Mobile.[33] He was putting into public form a decision that had been reached by him and his advisers before Yrujo made his protest, but it would have been better if this limitation had been expressly written into the bill in the first place.

One explanation of Jefferson's conduct in this episode which has been advanced by historians is that he wanted to test Spanish resistance to the American territorial claim, and that, finding this greater than he had expected, he altered his stance.[34] Beyond doubt he was capable of blustering against the Spanish; in fact he had done so a decade earlier as secretary of state. But the major threat he held over them was not that of forceful action by the government but by American settlers who, sooner or later, would possess themselves of land to which they believed they had a natural right. The government could best expedite natural processes by removing artificial obstacles through negotiation. That negotiation, as he believed, could be buttressed, and the spirit of the American pioneers — actual or potential — could be quickened, by the claim to most of West Florida as a legal right.

To avoid all definition of boundaries in a revenue act for newly ac-

[31] Gallatin to TJ, Mar. 15, 1804 (*Writings*, I, 179–180); Brant, IV, 196, citing also Gallatin to Trist, Mar. 19, 1804, from NA.

[32] Madison described the episode of Mar. 5, 1804, to Livingston, Mar. 31, and to Pinckney, Apr. 10 (Hunt, VII, 125–126 and note). It is described by Brant, IV, 194–197.

[33] May 30, 1804 (*A.S.P.F.R.*, II, 583).

[34] Cox, *West Florida Controversy*, p. 100; see also on this whole question Henry Adams, *History*, II, 257–263.

quired territories would have been difficult, and Jefferson may be safely assumed to have been unwilling to employ one that would have denied the claim to the Perdido boundary. To have set the line on the east so as to include only the island of New Orleans would have been to surrender a diplomatic weapon he planned to wield. In his stubborn insistence that the rightfulness of the American claim had been irrefutably established by logic, he was perpetuating a rationalization. Yet he viewed the physical future of his country with clear vision and he appears here as a passionate patriot who could overreach himself for his country's benefit. Whether his tactics in this instance served his patriotic purposes well or ill is, of course, another question, but the failure of his pursuit of West Florida can be attributed to something else than lack of diplomatic skill on the part of the administration: it was primarily due to the attitude of the Emperor Napoleon. In the field of international power politics the luck of the American President had begun to turn.

He was a long time in finding this out. During the spring of 1804 Madison did an unconscionable amount of paperwork in preparation for Monroe's mission to Spain, and the continuing hopes of the administration were reflected in the elaborate instructions he drafted for that envoy and the detailed briefing he gave Livingston. Realizing that the position of France was of major importance, he presented a number of excellent reasons why that country should support the American contentions, and at this time, besides sending Livingston Jefferson's memoir supporting the claim to West Florida, he himself presented the official argument in full form.[35] Leaving England in the fall of 1804, Monroe spent several weeks in Paris, where he conferred at length with Talleyrand and others. In the existing atmosphere of venality and intrigue, more powerful arguments than he could advance would probably have been unavailing, and it now appears that there was little point in his proceeding to Madrid.[36] By the winter of 1804–1805 Jefferson knew that the mission of his trusted envoy would inevitably fail, but official news that it had done so was so long delayed that he did not transmit it to Congress until the December after his second inauguration. Thus this diplomatic failure did not enter appreciably into the politics of his first term and mar his domestic success.

[35] Madison to Livingston, Mar. 31, 1804 (Hunt, VII, 123–140, and *A.S.P.F.R.*, II, 575–578).
[36] This mission will be dealt with in the next volume of this work, covering TJ's second term.

[XIX]

The Government and the New Citizens

AMONG those congratulating Jefferson on the acquisition of Louisiana was a future President of the United States who came to be regarded as the embodiment of the West and its democracy. In the summer of 1803 Andrew Jackson wrote: "Every face wears a smile, and every heart leaps with joy." Although Jefferson never went farther west than the Shenandoah Valley nor farther south than his own Virginia, he was speaking of the whole of the Republic when he replied: "The world will here see such an extent of country under a free and moderate government as it has never yet seen." [1] In the long run the prophecy was verified in world opinion, but the Louisianians, whom the nation was bound by treaty to incorporate, were not to enter immediately into the blessings of liberty and self-government as enjoyed by the residents of the states, or even by those of the neighboring Mississippi Territory. They had been living under what Americans regarded as despotic rule, and appeared to have gained only a change of rulers by the act of October 31, 1803, which provided for their temporary government. The President had assumed the role of despot, according to critical Federalists, and his own attorney general held that his power under this law was virtually unlimited. [2]

The territorial act that was signed by him about five months later and became effective the following fall provided for a government that, while admittedly temporary, was unmistakably autocratic. Even in the more populous part of the ceded province, now designated as the Territory of Orleans, authority was vested in appointed officials, and there was no provision for voting. [3] Political enemies of Jefferson, who were

[1] Jackson to TJ, Aug. 7, 1803 (LC, 23114–23115); TJ to Jackson, Sept. 19, 1803 (LC, 23309).

[2] Levi Lincoln to TJ, Apr. 19, 1804 (Carter IX, 227–229).

[3] An Act for the Organization of Orleans Territory and the Louisiana District, Mar. 26, 1804, effective Oct. 1, 1804 (Carter, IX, 202–213, with extensive notes and references).

generally less concerned than he for the rights of the people, did not hesitate to charge him with hypocrisy in connection with this measure, and some of his most loyal supporters were unhappy about it. The judgment of other men entered into this legislative act, but there can be no doubt that it closely followed the line the President himself had marked. At this stage, unquestionably, he was laying major emphasis on the actualities of the situation he faced as a responsible official, rather than on the abstract principles he had proclaimed so eloquently when protesting against tyranny. If there was inconsistency in this he had likewise manifested it on previous occasions when he was seeking to be a realistic interpreter of situations and events. In times past he had shown himself to be a gradualist who could await with patience as well as confidence the attainment of long-range goals. He may have misinterpreted the particular situation, to be sure, and he was by no means incapable of self-deception, but it does not necessarily follow that he forgot or disregarded his principles when he recognized that circumstances alter cases.

For a clue to his attitude at this stage we may turn back, as apparently his mind did, to his observations in France at the outset of the French Revolution. Writing Madison in the autumn of 1788, he predicted that if the people of that country did not promptly obtain as much as they had a right to, they would do so in the long run. "The misfortune," he said, "is that they are not yet ripe for receiving the blessings to which they are entitled." At just the time he was urging the addition of a bill of rights to the new American Constitution, he was doubting if a majority of the French people would accept a habeas corpus law if it were offered them and was hoping that the approaching Estates General would not attempt too much and thus provoke reaction.[4]

The natural assumption that the settlers in lower Louisiana, who had lived under despotic rule, were unprepared for self-government was reinforced by opinions received by him from that part of the country. Claiborne anticipated that the "regeneration" of the autocratic Spanish system would be an arduous task, and feared that the experiment of "sudden and total reformation" might prove hazardous. The future governor of the province laid great stress, not merely on Creole ignorance of American political institutions and the English language, but also on widespread illiteracy.[5] Jefferson himself, saying that his new fellow citizens were acknowledged to be "as yet as incapable of self-

[4] TJ to Madison, Nov. 18, 1788 (Boyd, XIV, 188; *Jefferson and the Rights of Man*, pp. 195–196).
[5] Claiborne to TJ, Sept. 29, 1803 (Carter, IX, 60), received Oct. 23.

government as children," manifested some impatience with those who did not take this into account. Before Congress got around to the question of the government of Louisiana he expressed himself on it in a memorandum to Gallatin, hoping that his hints would be passed on to individual legislators, whom the Secretary of Treasury saw more often than he did.[6] With reference to lower Louisiana, whose political separation from upper Louisiana he anticipated, he favored at the outset the appointment of a governor and three judges, the latter to have legislative powers, subject to the negative of the governor and Congress. Such was the case in the first stage of territorial government under the historic Northwest Ordinance, in which the lines of policy had been laid down.[7] In his memorandum he said:

> The existing laws of the country being now in force, the new legislature will of course introduce the trial by jury in *criminal* cases, first; the habeas corpus, the freedom of the press, freedom of religion &c as soon as can be, and in general draw their laws & organization to the mould of ours by degrees as they find practicable without exciting too much discontent. In proportion as we find the people there riper for receiving these first principles of freedom, Congress may from session to session confirm their enjoyment of them.

If he had been drafting a public paper he might have employed somewhat different phraseology, so as to forestall the charge that "rights" described by him elsewhere as inherent were now referred to as being at the disposal of national authority. But the general procedure suggested by him seemed well adapted to the specific situation. Starting with the laws already existing in the province, he advocated speedy confirmation of basic freedoms and the gradual extension of American political practices and institutions. He might have rounded out his statement by saying that he expected the inhabitants of Louisiana to become full-fledged citizens eventually, but this expectation could hardly have been doubted by Gallatin or anybody else who knew him well. The main question was one of timing. According to the historic Northwest Ordinance, a territory should pass to the second stage of government, with an elective assembly, when its population reached

[6] TJ to DeWitt Clinton, Dec. 2, 1803 (Ford, VIII, 283); to Gallatin, Nov. 9, 1803 (Carter, IX, 100–101; Ford, VIII, 275–276n.).

[7] According to the Northwest Ordinance of 1787, a territory in the first stage was to be subject to laws selected by the governor and judges from the laws of the original states. TJ had concluded that such a provision would turn the laws of Louisiana "topsy-turvy." And he soon decided that "legislative powers" should not be exercised by judges.

5000. The statistics recently submitted by Jefferson to Congress, although unofficial, showed that lower Louisiana already had considerably more inhabitants than that — considerably more, in fact, than the Territory of Mississippi, which had been elevated to the second stage of government during the administration of John Adams. Thus, while he may have been entirely correct in his judgment that the new citizens were unfitted for that degree of self-government, he appeared to be showing uncharacteristic disregard of local expectations. He was rejecting the idea of military rule, however, and could have claimed that under his proposals the Louisianians would have more freedom than they had previously enjoyed.

The legislator on whom fell the task of proposing a constitution for Louisiana was Senator John Breckinridge of Kentucky, who seemed reluctant to draft one. For this ostensible reason, Jefferson sent him some suggestions, saying that he did so with more boldness than wisdom. The boldness lay in expressing himself on a subject to which he claimed he had been able to devote little time. In seeking to keep wholly out of sight, however, he was being exceedingly cautious, for reasons that he expressed in the language of partisan extravagance. In communicating his ideas to Breckinridge, he said: "I must do it in confidence that you will never let any person know that I have put pen to paper on the subject and that if you think the inclosed can be of any aid to you you will take the trouble to copy it & return me the original. I am this particular, because you know with what bloody teeth & fangs the federalists will attack any sentiment or principle known to come from me, & what blackguardisms & personalities they make it the occasion of vomiting forth." Saying that although the caution was unnecessary, it would be "borne in sacred recollection," Breckinridge returned the paper after copying it.[8] Jefferson said he had merely prepared a canvas and given it a few daubs of outline for Breckinridge to fill up, but his draft appeared practically intact in the bill Breckinridge reported. The Senator or his committee made some additions and minor changes, but since these represented no real variance from Jefferson's expressed ideas regarding the executive, legislative, and judicial branches, they may be presumed to have been entirely agreeable to him. To all practical purposes, therefore, the Breckinridge bill was his.

[8] TJ to Breckinridge, Nov. 24, 1803 (Ford, VIII, 279–281); Breckinridge to TJ, Nov. 26, 1803 (LC, 23573); draft in TJ's handwriting (LC, 23695); Breckinridge's bill, reported Dec. 30, 1803, in National Intelligencer, Jan. 4, 1804. Since TJ's draft is neither labeled nor dated, one cannot be absolutely sure that it is the paper referred to here, but its striking similarity to the original bill (which must be distinguished from the one finally passed) leaves little doubt that if Breckinridge did not get it at this time he got it soon thereafter.

His recorded comments on the plan he was submitting so confidentially were largely confined to one feature of it. He now favored granting local legislative authority to what he called an Assembly of Notables. On the basis of past observation, presumably in France, he believed that such a body would be "more familiar and pleasing" to the French settlers than a legislature of judges. Specifically, he proposed that legislative power should be vested in twenty-four of "the most notable, fit and discreet persons of the territory to be selected annually by the Governor from those holding real estate therein who shall have resided one year at least in the said territory." In Breckinridge's bill this body was described as the legislative council and the word "notable" did not appear, but otherwise the proposals were couched in virtually the same language. In the bill as finally passed this body was reduced to thirteen persons, to be appointed by the President — a thing that Jefferson had not recommended. In setting the bounds of legislative authority, he stated that no law should be valid if inconsistent with the Constitution. He made no direct reference to the Bill of Rights and its guarantees of individual liberties, but he specifically denied to the legislature the power to infringe on freedom of religion. This was a question of immediate importance in a predominantly Catholic region that was being incorporated in a predominantly Protestant country.

In his section on the judiciary he specified the right to jury trials in criminal prosecutions of capital offenses, stating that this should be extended to other cases by the legislature "as soon, and under such modifications . . . as the habits and state of the peoples of the territory will admit." He was aware that the inhabitants had had no jury trials whatever under Spanish rule. Though he did not mention the writ of habeas corpus here, he had done so elsewhere, and Breckinridge's addition of it to this section of the bill he introduced was clearly in line with Jefferson's intentions. With respect to guarantees of individual rights, however, the President spoke specifically of only freedom of religion and jury trials in capital cases. This was not much, though it was more than the Louisianians had previously enjoyed.

Despite changes and amendments, the bill for the government of Louisiana, as it passed the Senate by an overwhelming vote in February, was thoroughly compatible with Jefferson's ideas and suggestions.[9]

[9] Bill reported Dec. 30, 1803; passed Feb. 18, 1804, by a vote of 20 to 5, all of the latter being cast by Federalists. The excellent account of the debate in Brown, ch. 7, is based on William Plumer's report of it, which he gives in an appendix, pp. 210–234. This may also be seen in Plumer's *Memorandum* under the appropriate dates. It was not available to Henry Adams. The votes, without the debate, are in *Annals of Congress*. The bill did not include TJ's provision for county courts. The attachment of the upper portion of the ceded region, now called the

Avoiding the question of boundaries, as he had done in his outline, the bill provided for the division of the country "ceded by France" into parts, giving the lower and more settled part the name Orleans, as proposed by the President. Some of the inhabitants afterwards objected to being deprived of the name Louisiana.

Before the debate got under way, John Quincy Adams introduced resolutions asserting that Congress had no right to impose taxes on the people of the province without their consent. These resolutions received only four votes. William Plumer objected to them as mere "abstract propositions," unrelated to any business then before the Senate.[10] Adams continued to contend that no attention was being paid the principle of "consent of the governed," but in the subsequent debate on Breckinridge's bill, objections of this sort were voiced chiefly by Republicans, especially Westerners, while the most extreme expressions on the other side were those of Federalists. Timothy Pickering said that Louisiana was a "purchased province" and should thus be governed, but few senators expressed themselves so harshly.

There were several attempts to provide the Territory of Orleans at this time with a representative government of sorts and more republican institutions. A motion of Senator Worthington of Ohio that it be allowed a non-voting delegate in Congress was defeated 12 to 18. All except one of the Westerners, including Breckinridge, favored this, as did the two senators from Virginia, and presumably it was acceptable to the administration.[11] On the next day, a motion to extend jury trials to all criminal cases, rather than merely to those that were capital, was defeated by almost the same vote.[12] Breckinridge and the two Virginia senators opposed this change, however. A week later, a motion to strike out the provisions for the legislative council, to be appointed by the Governor, and to substitute for it an elected body, was narrowly defeated. The distribution of the vote, following no party pattern, suggests that the senators were of uncertain mind on this question, but the remarks of one of them reflected western qualms. Said Anderson of Tennessee: "This bill has not a single feature of our government in it — it is a system of tyranny, destructive of election rights. We are bound by treaty, and must give that people a free elective government." [13]

District of Louisiana, to the Indiana Territory had not been recommended by him but was in general accord with his ideas.

[10] Plumer, *Memorandum*, pp. 103–104, giving the resolutions. See also J. Q. Adams, *Writings*, III, 25–26; *Memoirs*, I, 286–287.

[11] Jan. 16, 1804 (*Annals*, 8 Cong., 1 sess., pp. 233–234; Brown, pp. 103–105, with a note about the vote).

[12] Jan. 17, 1804 (*Annals*, 8 Cong., 1 sess., p. 235). The vote was 11 to 16.

[13] Plumer, *Memorandum*, p. 111, on debate of Jan. 24, 1804. He does not give

On this very day Jefferson transmitted to Congress a letter just received from Claiborne, expressing the hope that it would "throw light" on the subject of the government of Louisiana.[14] In this the newly arrived Governor spoke of the confidence of the people of Louisiana in "the justice and generous intentions" of the American government, but expressed serious reservations about their political capacity:

> I could wish that the Constitution to be given to this District may be as republican as the people can be safely intrusted with. But the principles of a popular Government are utterly beyond their comprehension. The Representative System, is an enigma that at present bewilders them. Long inured to passive obedience they have, to an almost total want of political information, superaded an inveterate habit of heedlessness as to measures of Government, and of course are by no means prepared to make any good use of such weight as they may prematurely acquire in the national Scale. . . . Not one in fifty of the old inhabitants appear to me to understand the English Language. Trials by Jury at first will only embarrass the administration of Justice; tho I presume a short experience would be sufficient to convince any reasoning society of the inestimable advantages of that happy System. . . .

This communication from the responsible civil official of the territory could have been expected to strengthen the position of those supporting Breckinridge's original provisions for its government.

The most extended and heated debate in the Senate was over a question not covered by the Kentuckian's proposals. By an overwhelming vote the Senate approved the inclusion of an amendment closing the territory to the slave trade, both foreign and domestic. It went beyond Jefferson's earlier suggestion to Gallatin, though it was in line with that: "slaves not to be imported except from such of the U.S. as prohibit importation." [15] The sweeping prohibition of the importation of

---

the vote. The figures in *Annals*, 8 Cong., 1 sess., p. 239, do not agree with the list of Yeas and Nays, but presumably the motion to strike out was defeated by a tie vote of 14 to 14.

[14] Jan. 24, 1804. Presumably Claiborne's letter of Jan. 2 to Madison (*Official Letter Books of W. C. C. Claiborne*, I, 322–329). His letter of Jan. 10, 1804, was to the same effect (*ibid.*, I, 329–333).

[15] TJ to Gallatin, Nov. 9, 1803 (Carter, IX, 100). Besides forbidding importation from a foreign country, the amendment prohibited the importation of slaves brought into the U.S. from abroad since May 1, 1798 — that is, into South Carolina, which reopened the foreign slave trade after that date. It also prohibited other domestic importation except by citizens of the U.S. who were removing to the territory for actual settlement and were bona fide owners of the slaves imported. Jefferson, who had come to believe that the diffusion of the slaves already in the country would tend to weaken rather than strengthen the

slaves was the provision in the act that excited most vocal protest from the Creole planters.

The desire to extend self-government to the inhabitants of the territory was more manifest in the House of Representatives than in the Senate. Objection to the Senate bill centered on the provisions for a legislative council, all of whose members were to be appointed. By an overwhelming vote, following the original motion of Nathaniel Macon of North Carolina, one of the staunchest of Republicans and most loyal supporters of the administration, the entire legislative section was stricken out.[16] That section had few defenders and many critics. One of the most severe of these was George W. Campbell of Tennessee, who said that the bill established "a complete despotism," that it evinced not "a single trait of liberty," that it did not confer "one single right" to which the inhabitants were entitled under the treaty, that it extended to them none of the benefits of the Constitution and failed to declare when they would receive any.[17] This western congressman was unwilling to separate liberty from the right of self-government, and, without saying so, he emulated Jefferson himself in taking the position that freedom was far less likely to be abused than despotism. The President's partisans showed little disposition to chide him for inconsistency, but a number of them now sounded more republican than he.

The practical difficulties of carrying these characteristically American principles into effect were reflected in the relatively close vote by which the House adopted a fresh section to replace the one that body had overwhelmingly rejected.[18] The substitute section provided for a legislative council such as the Senate had approved, but limited its life to one year. After that, the thirteen members previously appointed were to be elected from districts that the original council should set up. Thus the House sharply limited the duration of the form of government that had been described as despotic and specifically provided for a more representative local government in the near future. In the bill as finally passed by both houses, after a conference between their respective managers, the first provision was retained, but the second was not. Going into effect October 1, 1804, the law was to continue a year

---

institution he detested, did not suggest the last prohibition, but there is no record that he opposed it.

[16] On Feb. 29, 1804, the vote was 80 to 15, and on Mar. 15, it was 74 to 23 (*Annals*, 8 Cong., 1 sess., pp. 1078, 1193). For an account of the debate, see Brown, ch. 8.

[17] *Annals*, 8 Cong., 1 sess., pp. 1063–1064.

[18] The vote on Mar. 15, 1804, in favor of the substitute was 58 to 42. For the voting and substitute section, see *Annals*, 8 Cong., 1 sess., 1192–1194. TJ's son-in-law T. M. Randolph was among those voting Nay.

thereafter and thence to the end of the ensuing session of Congress. That is, there would soon have to be another act. The right to vote was denied the inhabitants in the meantime, and no promise regarding it was made. Congress adopted a temporizing measure, and the civil authorities were to conduct a holding operation.[19]

Jefferson believed that this was all the government could do at the moment. He does not appear to have said much about the act, but Madison, writing Livingston while the bill was before the Senate, gave a summarizing statement that may be safely assumed to have reflected the position of the administration:

> It is pretty certain that the provisions generally contemplated will leave the people of that District for a while without the organiza-ion of power dictated by the Republican theory; but it is evident that a sudden transition to a condition so much in contrast with that in which their ideas and habits have been formed, would be as unacceptable and as little beneficial to them as it would be difficult for the Government of the United States. It may fairly be expected that every blessing of liberty will be extended to them as fast as they shall be prepared and disposed to receive it. . . .[20]

In the light of the information available to him the President favored a measure that seemed realistic. Perhaps he may be fairly charged with trying to avoid the allegation of a departure from republican orthodoxy by allowing the onus to fall on Breckinridge and other congressional leaders. Unquestionably there was political astuteness in the effort to keep his public image unmarred, but the sincerity of his concern for the new citizens need not be doubted for that reason. Since he took the long view, he was willing to be patient while seeking to attain an empire for freedom.

It was some months before he was fully informed of the impatience that certain prominent persons in lower Louisiana manifested with respect to the government act. Meanwhile, early in June, he received from New Orleans a letter voicing fears, which, as the author of the Virginia Bill for Establishing Religious Freedom, he took particular pleasure in quieting. This was from Sister Thérèse de St. Xavier Farjon

---

[19] *Annals,* 8 Cong., 1 sess., pp. 1229–1230. For the act, as approved Mar. 26, 1804, see pp. 1293–1300. We have not considered other important features of this, such as the extension to the territory of more than a score of previous acts of Congress. Nor have we gone into the confusing question of land grants. A close relation seems to exist between a draft of TJ's (LC, 23694), the amendment introduced in House on Mar. 14, 1804, by Rhea of Tennessee (*Annals,* 8 Cong., 1 sess., pp. 1186, 1187, 1196), and Section 14 of the act.

[20] Madison to R. R. Livingston, Jan. 31, 1804 (Hunt, VII, 115–116).

and a dozen other nuns of St. Ursula and related to the property in their possession. While they believed that this was secured to them by the treaty of cession and the American sense of justice, they sought formal confirmation of what they regarded as a "sacred deposit." Addressing them as "holy sisters," the President assured them that the principles of the Constitution and government of the United States were a guarantee that their property would be preserved to them "sacred and inviolate" and that their institution would be permitted to govern itself wholly without interference from the civil authority. "Whatever diversity of shade may appear in the religious opinions of our fellow citizens," he said, "the charitable objects of your institution cannot be indifferent to any." And he added the promise that it would have all the protection his office could give it.[21]

The appeal of the Sisters called for assurance, not action. This he could give firsthand, but in seeking to administer the remote province in his executive capacity the President had to act through appointed officials on the ground, especially the Governor. Not until late summer did he get round to sending a commission as Governor of the Territory of Orleans to Claiborne, whose status had been that of a temporary appointee. Jefferson never regarded him as the best possible choice for this difficult position, and had named him in the first place because he seemed the best man who was readily available. Now he frankly told Claiborne that he had originally intended to give the post to "a person whose great services and established fame would have rendered him peculiarly acceptable to the nation at large." He was referring to Lafayette. Congress had recently voted to the Marquis a large grant of land, and the administration surveyed the possibility of locating this in lower Louisiana, where also he might be useful as governor. Jefferson dismissed the idea of appointing him as impracticable, however, since he could not wait for his old friend to get there from France.[22] Neither could geographical difficulties be overcome quickly enough by James Monroe, to whom Jefferson would have gladly given the appointment but who himself regarded it as incompatible with his unfinished task abroad. Andrew Jackson was recommended by the Tennessee delegation in Congress, but the President was also warned against him as a violently passionate man and does not appear to have considered him

[21] Ursuline Nuns to the President, Apr. 23, 1804; received June 8 (Carter, IX, 231–232); TJ's reply, July 13 or 14, 1804 (LC, 24602).
[22] See his letter of Nov. 4, 1803, in *Letters of Lafayette and Jefferson*, ed. by Gilbert Chinard (1929), p. 225. Other letters in that collection bear on the question of the lands. TJ's letter of Aug. 30, 1804, to Claiborne, with numerous references bearing on the consideration of Lafayette and others for this post, is in Carter, IX, 281–284.

seriously.[23] Lafayette would have had one distinct advantage — the ability to speak French — but we may doubt that the governorship of this territory would have enhanced his fame, or Monroe's for that matter. Andrew Jackson would doubtless have ruled with a firmer hand than any of them, but one of the merits of Claiborne, in Jefferson's eyes, was that he abjured the use of force and was conciliatory in spirit. "There were characters superior to him whom I wished to appoint, but they refused the office," said the President several years later, adding that he did not yet know a better man who would accept it.[24] He could also have said that he never doubted Claiborne's loyalty to the administration.

Though he sometimes rebuked the Governor, Jefferson trusted him. He asked and generally followed Claiborne's advice about appointments and naturally tended to view local developments through the eyes of the man who officially reported them to him. One of the grievances of which he was first informed was over the prohibition of the slave trade, with which objections to the division of the province were soon coupled. Whether the inhabitants of French stock, if left to their own devices, would have formally protested against the failure to extend self-government to them at this time is an unanswerable question; but Claiborne believed that the leaders of the opposition to the measures of the government were self-seeking Americans who were now championing the "rights" of Louisiana. He referred especially to Edward Livingston, a recent arrival from New York, and Daniel Clark, the American Consul whom Jefferson had frequently consulted in the recent past, and who, in Claiborne's opinion, thought his services had been insufficiently rewarded. Livingston, formerly district attorney of New York, was under a court judgment for a shortage of his accounts in that office. He had come to New Orleans to restore his fortunes and was far from friendly to the administration. He played a major part in a meeting in New Orleans on May 31, at which it was determined to remonstrate against provisions of the recent act and to petition for its repeal; and he drafted the memorial that was adopted at a later meeting, circulated for signatures, and afterwards presented to Congress. This able man was destined to remain a thorn in poor Claiborne's side and a vexation to Jefferson.[25] The Governor feared that the flame he and a

23 *A.H.R.*, III, 286–287.
24 TJ to John Dickinson, Jan. 13, 1807 (Ford, IX, 9).
25 His troubles in New York, on which I pass no judgment here, and his early years in New Orleans are described in W. B. Hatcher, *Edward Livingston* (1940), pp. 93–99, ch. 7. The meeting of May 31, 1804, was reported to Claiborne, June 1, 1804, and he commented on Livingston and Clark in a letter to Madison, June 3 (Carter, IX, 241–243). Among letters in which Claiborne reported on later

few other Americans had kindled would not soon subside. Believing that they were demanding statehood, he expressed his own opposition to that, but was now of the opinion that the representative system should be introduced by making the legislative council elective.

The thought and labor devoted by Jefferson to nominations for that body, in the effort to make it broadly representative, were largely wasted, for of the thirteen who were originally invited eight declined to serve. Among these were Daniel Clark and Evan Jones, who were active in the protest movement, and important members of the French group. Claiborne was duly inducted as governor on October 2, 1804; and, by filling in blank commissions the President had sent him, he managed to attain a quorum by December.[26] The party of the opposition had not succeeded in paralyzing his government, and he claimed that the situation was better than it might appear to be, but his operations had been greatly impeded.

When Jefferson sent his annual message to Congress in November, 1804, he was not as fully informed of local difficulties as he was a little later. Nonetheless, he reported that the commencement of the territory had been retarded. Recognizing that the form of government was temporary and open to such improvements as "further information of the circumstances of our brethren there might suggest," he said that of course Congress would give consideration to this matter.[27] The three agents arrived with the "Remonstrance" about three weeks later. They visited the President, and, according to Senator William Plumer, reported that he "studiously avoided" conversation relating to their mission.[28] No disapprobation of the agents was manifest, however, in what Jefferson wrote Claiborne: "They will find a disposition in the great majority here to do whatever circumstances will admit for our new fellow citizens, to do as much for them as we do for our own brothers and children settling in new territories, and only to refuse them what the principles of our constitution and government refuse equally to all." [29] He had reappraised the circumstances and correctly sensed the mood of Congress. He was continuing to avoid the appearance of dictating to that body and in this matter apparently did not

developments were those of June 29 to Madison, and July 1 to TJ (Carter, IX, 245–248); July 1 to Madison (*Official Letters*, II, 233–234); July 13 to Madison (Carter, IX, 261). He summed things up to TJ, Oct. 27, 1804 (Carter, IX, 314–316), letter received Dec. 4.

[26] Claiborne to TJ, Dec. 2, 1804, with attached list (Carter, IX, 344–346). TJ did not get this until Feb. 20, 1805, but he had learned of some of the declinations a number of weeks earlier.

[27] Nov. 8, 1804 (Ford, VIII, 329).

[28] Plumer, *Memorandum*, p. 223, under date of Dec. 15, 1804.

[29] Dec. 2, 1804 (Carter, IX, 343).

need to, but there is no reason to doubt that the congressional action was in full accord with his wishes.

No one could have justly denied that the "Remonstrance of the People of Louisiana," which was duly presented to the two houses, was an able and stirring presentation of republican principles.[30] Some of its references and phrases could hardly have failed to discomfit the author of the Declaration of Independence. Among the disconcerting questions it asked was this: "Do political axioms on the Atlantic become problems when translated to the shores of the Mississippi?" The answer of Jefferson as a responsible executive, rather than a purveyor of abstractions, had been that in fact they did. Edward Livingston had no difficulty in demonstrating that the government now established in the Territory of Orleans was autocratic in form, and he recognized no generosity of spirit in those who were administering it. The "Remonstrance" itself was marked by the spirit of impatience — greater impatience, in Claiborne's opinion, than characterized the people of the territory as a whole. It asked for the repeal of the entire act of the last session of Congress, and the immediate grant, as a matter of right, of a degree of self-government that could have been exercised only under statehood. It specifically objected to the prohibition of the slave trade, which, along with the conduct of the public business in an unfamiliar language, appears to have been the chief grievance of the French element. It asked for the same degree of self-determination in this respect as was allowed by the Constitution to the States — that is, the right to legalize the foreign slave trade until the year 1808 if they wanted to. Jefferson was one of the many who regarded this constitutional provision as unfortunate, and few members of Congress showed a disposition to perpetuate in the name of consistency what they regarded as an evil.[31]

The comments of John Randolph of Roanoke on this memoir when he reported on it to the House of Representatives, while colored by his distinctive personality and phraseology, clearly reflected the attitude of the administration.[32] He believed that the grievances complained of were inseparable from the "sudden transition of government" to which the inhabitants of Louisiana had been subjected by late political events.

[30] *Annals,* 8 Cong., 2 sess., pp. 1597–1608. Brown discusses this, quoting some of the more striking passages (pp. 157–159).

[31] As has already been noted, the Territory of Orleans was under greater restrictions than the Territory of Mississippi regarding the importation of slaves from other states. Apparently, TJ would not have objected at this time to putting these two territories on the same basis in this respect, though Congress did not do so. His insuperable objection was to the increase in the slave population in the country as a whole.

[32] Jan. 25, 1805, in *Annals,* 8 Cong., 2 sess., pp. 1015–1017.

He could not agree that these grievances should be ascribed to a denial by the United States of rights to which the inhabitants were entitled by the treaty. He regarded this interpretation as "tortured" and would countenance no charge of breach of faith. At the same time, his committee earnestly recommended that "every indulgence, not incompatible with the interests of the Union" be extended to the people of the territory, and that, without recourse to force, every effort be made to bind them to the sovereign government by ties of affection. Certain restrictions must be placed on them, such as the prohibition of the foreign slave trade and a denial of the power to infringe on the basic rights of individuals; but, without specifying just how this was to be done, he and his committee recommended the extension to them by law of the right of self-government.

The act of March 2, 1805, which originated in the Senate and occasioned little debate in either branch of Congress at a time when interest centered on the trial of Justice Chase, granted self-government to the extent of providing for a representative assembly.[33] This act extended to the inhabitants of Orleans Territory "all the rights, privileges, and advantages" that were secured by the Northwest Ordinance of 1787 and then enjoyed by the people of the neighboring Territory of Mississippi. Slavery as then existing in the new territory was recognized, and the slave trade was not mentioned, but the prohibition of it in the act of the previous year, which was more stringent than the corresponding provision in Mississippi, remained in force despite the strong objection of leading inhabitants to it. Finally, the admission of the territory as a state was promised whenever it should be ascertained by actual census or enumeration that the number of free inhabitants amounted to 60,000.[34] In effect, this meant the postponement of statehood until after the census of 1810, by which time no state would have the right to legalize the foreign slave trade.

Impressions regarding the acceptability of this act to the inhabitants varied with the reporters, but so far as official expressions went the next stage of territorial government in the remote Southwest was commenced under propitious circumstances. Following the organization of the territorial House of Representatives in the fall of Jefferson's second term, it adopted a brief address to him. This was prepared by a member who had been consistently friendly to the Governor and the administration, but it was signed by one of the agents who had borne the

---

[33] For the act, see Carter, IX, 405–407, with bibliographical note; *Annals*, 8 Cong., 2 sess., 1674–1676. Details regarding the assembly are in Sections 2 and 3.

[34] The right of Congress to alter the boundaries prior to such admission, though not in such a way as to delay it, was reserved.

"Remonstrance" to Washington a year before and was now Speaker of the House.[35] Too much stress should not be laid on the complimentary expressions in what may be regarded as a ceremonial paper, but in the "first moments of their legislative existence" these elected representatives assured the President of their "esteem and confidence." They also said this: "If any circumstance could enrich the fame of a statesman already conspicuous by a firm and able support of the civil and religious rights of men, it would be your conduct in the acquisition of Louisiana."

He acknowledged this address gratefully in a gracious letter.[36] The "sound discretion" displayed by the new citizens in their choice of representatives, to which he referred, may have reassured one who had seriously doubted their political capacity, but in any case he now sounded the note of faith, not fear. He confidently asserted that the day that added to the United States "a country so highly favored by nature, and, to the great American family, a people so worthy of the blessings of freedom, and zealous to maintain them," would ever be among the most fortunate in the annals of the Republic. And he hoped that it would ever be commemorated as "the birthday of a political well-being too rare among men."

However, his troubles with lower Louisiana were far from over. Midway in his second term he said that great discontents existed there.[37] So far as the French inhabitants were concerned, he attributed these to their continued resentment at their inability to import slaves, the administration of justice in American forms and in the English language, and the requirement that they show title to their lands. Of these, he regarded the second as the most important. Among the American inhabitants, he perceived the old division between Federalists and Republicans. Partisan considerations were undoubtedly present in his mind and entered into this business, but the main troubles arose, as John Randolph had said, from the speedy transition of government. This was not to be the last time in history that things desirable in themselves happened too fast.

In the discharge of his official duties from day to day as the responsible head of government, Jefferson was well aware of immediate difficulties, but he never abandoned the faith that was to be justified by time. Shortly after he left office he wrote his successor: "I am persuaded no constitution was ever before so well calculated as ours for

[35] Address of Nov. 14, 1805, drafted by Dr. John Watkins and signed by Jean Noel Destrehan (Carter, IX, 521).

[36] TJ to the Speaker and House of Representatives of the Territory of Orleans, Dec. 28, 1805 (Carter, IX, 551–552).

[37] TJ to John Dickinson, Jan. 13, 1807 (Ford, IX, 8–9).

extensive empire and self government." [38] Within this framework, as he believed, the American political experiment would proceed by its own momentum if subjected to no foreign interference. Thus "empire," as he used the term, was in no conflict with liberty; on the contrary, the security of the domain of freedom was furthered by its expansion.

[38] TJ to Madison, Apr. 27, 1809 (W. C. Rives Papers, LC). In this letter he used the expression "empire for liberty" and expressed the desire for further physical expansion with a view to greater national independence.

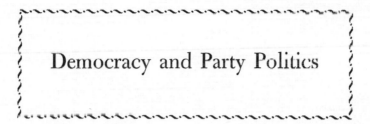

Democracy and Party Politics

[XX]

Without Benefit of Protocol:
The Merry Affair

BY the winter of 1803–1804, when the President was struggling with
the problems of remote territories, there were some signs that a
new era had begun in the physical history of the straggling village
which was the incongruous seat of empire. Anyone could see that
young Lombardy poplars had been set out on Pennsylvania Avenue
between the President's House and the Capitol. The drawing that
Jefferson sent early in the previous spring to Thomas Munroe, the superintendent of public buildings, called for four rows of trees with a
gravel carriage road in the middle, and walks or canals on the sides as
might be afterwards determined. Whether or not these young trees
were boxed or whitewashed for protection against horses and cattle, as
was suggested, is not clear, but they served to mark the capital's only
real thoroughfare as a street rather than a road, and they were expected
to grow quickly.[1]

Benjamin H. Latrobe, whose appointment as surveyor of public
buildings — about the time Munroe was setting out the poplars — most
sharply marked the commencement of a new architectural chapter, had
begun to raise the walls of the South Wing of the Capitol while still
uncertain about the interior plans, which he sought to modify from
those originally drawn by Dr. William Thornton. Also, he had shored
up the walls of the "Dutch Oven" in which the representatives sat, and
made extensive repairs on the North Wing, where the roof leaked and
the senators, by contrast with their fellows in the House, suffered from
the cold.

These actions were made possible by a congressional appropriation
of $50,000, to be applied to the public buildings under the President's

[1] Thomas Munroe to TJ, Mar. 14, 1803; TJ to Munroe, Mar. 21, 1803, with
drawing (Padover, pp. 297–299, 300–301).

direction. Since Jefferson was determined that most of this should be applied to the Capitol and the accommodation of the legislators, expenditures on the President's House were kept as low as possible. Work was still in progress on the roof, but that was not totally renewed before another winter. Prior to that time the unfriendly local newspaper, protesting against the expense, had suggested that this work was provided Latrobe as a reward for past political services.[2] Partisanship stretched credulity very far in those days. Though Latrobe had stopped the leaks, put up the staircase between the public dining room and the library, done the necessary plastering, and sunk a well to provide good water, he himself held that the big house still lacked accommodations generally regarded as indispensable in a private dwelling.[3] Though more habitable than heretofore, it was still barnlike and forbidding.

During this winter it was not graced by the presence of either of Jefferson's daughters, nor brightened by the laughter of any of his grandchildren. Martha was in Albemarle, where she had another baby in the autumn without mishap; and Maria was with her, anxiously awaiting her deliverance in the new year. The two young husbands, Thomas Mann Randolph and John Wayles Eppes, were in Washington as members of Congress, living at the President's House. There was plenty of room for them to sleep upstairs, where, to Maria's dismay, her father had been quite alone after she and Martha left him the previous winter. At that time Meriwether Lewis was still camping in the unfinished East Room. Just where the Captain's successor, Lewis Harvie, lived is uncertain. Probably he had one of the rooms upstairs and there pursued legal studies during most of his afternoons and evenings, as Jefferson had assured him he might. A young Virginian of twenty-five, who had been studying law in Georgetown, he remained in the secretarial post only about a year. Since it was expected for a time that he would carry to France the balance of the stock for the purchase of Louisiana, the newly arrived British Minister described him in one of his dispatches home. Harvie could hardly have been as impressive a courier as Meriwether Lewis, being of only average height and inclined to corpulency, and he was not needed as a scribe. Jefferson was still writing his letters, and before this winter was out was beginning to use a "precious" polygraph. It need not be assumed that Harvie was arrogant in manner because a hypercritical British diplomat said he

[2] *Washington Federalist,* Nov. 7, 1804.

[3] Reports on the public buildings, Feb. 20, Dec. 1, 1804 (Padover, pp. 335–340, 347–350). TJ had invited Latrobe to be surveyor of public buildings Mar. 6, 1803 (*ibid.,* pp. 296–297). I do not enter here into the disagreement between him and Thornton respecting plans for the Capitol.

BENJAMIN HENRY LATROBE
Portrait by Charles Willson Peale

was, and no doubt he helped with the guests as Lewis had. Along with the two sons-in-law, he was regularly at the President's bountiful table.[4]

What Jefferson called his winter campaign began with the congressional session. The widower, who was now in his early sixties, wrote his daughter Martha: "I dread it on account of the fatigues of the table in such a round of company, which I consider as the most serious trials I undergo."[5] He made this statement some months after his social encounter with Anthony Merry, the highlight of the winter campaign of 1803–1804, and no doubt his weariness during his presidency was cumulative, but from the beginning he imposed a heavy burden on himself not only by his continuous hospitality but also by his constant accessibility.

Normally, his dinner was served at half past three or soon thereafter. Reporting a dinner at which the company numbered seventeen, Senator John Quincy Adams said that he and his wife left at six, but there is record that the guests sometimes stayed till eight.[6] The President is known to have received visitors after dinner, including diplomats, but the two hours before bedtime were generally free. For some years he had made it a rule not to go out at night, he usually retired at ten, and he habitually arose at dawn. We may presume that nobody disturbed him in the early morning hours, but otherwise, until he went riding about one o'clock, he was accessible to all comers. They had to take him in his working — or possibly his riding — clothes. The surviving comments on his sartorial indifference relate chiefly to his morning dress or undress, rather than to his attire at dinner. He did not give much heed to fashion in either case, but two comments by William Plumer within a period of less than a month suggest that there was ground for a distinction. Describing a dinner at which a group of Federalist senators and congressmen were guests and the Republicans were

---

[4] Anthony Merry described him in a letter to Hawkesbury, Jan. 30, 1804 (FO, 5:41, p. 80), referring to his proposed trip to France which was subsequently abandoned. TJ invited Harvie to become his secretary, Feb. 28, 1803, after William Brent of Washington had declined an offer made through Lewis. Harvie accepted Mar. 12, 1803, but did not assume his duties until some weeks thereafter (LC, 22420–22421, 22478, 22627). On his proposing to leave TJ's service to practice law, TJ, on Mar. 26, 1804, asked William A. Burwell to succeed him (Bixby, pp. 105–106), as the latter did some weeks later.

[5] TJ to Martha, Oct. 7, 1804 (*Papers, MHS*, p. 115).

[6] Manasseh Cutler and a group of Federalist legislators remained that long on Dec. 13, 1802 (Cutler, *Life*, II, 113). Adams reported a dinner of Nov. 7, 1803 (*Memoirs*, I, 272), saying that three Republican congressmen came in before he left.

represented by the President, his two sons-in-law and his secretary, Plumer said of the host: "He was well dressed — A new suit of black — silk hose — shoes   clean linnen, & his hair highly powdered." [7] He seems to have prepared himself well for that particular encounter. With this not unflattering account may be coupled the same senator's report of a visit he made the President a few weeks earlier to pay his respects. He then found Jefferson better dressed than he had ever seen him in the *morning*. "Though his coat was old and thread bare," said Plumer, "his scarlet vest, his corduroy small cloths, and his white cotton hose, were new and clean — but his linnen was much soiled, and his slippers old. His hair was cropt and powdered." [8] The reference to soiled linen is hard to reconcile with the statement of his ardent feminine admirer Margaret Bayard Smith that he was fastidiously neat in his personal habits, but devoted followers described his clothes as plain and old-fashioned, and the frequent mention of his slippers permits of no doubt that he wore them often, if not invariably, in the morning. Just what sort of slippers they were was not made clear, except that they had heels, but there is ample reason to believe that the third President of the United States was no more concerned about the looks of his working garments in Washington than at Monticello, and that in both places this elderly man sought warmth and comfort.

The most uncomplimentary descriptions of him emanated from political enemies, of whom William Plumer was one of the less virulent, or from persons with an antidemocratic bias. Perhaps no description of him in his presidential years has been more widely quoted — or more gleefully by those who would make him seem vulgar or bizarre — than that of the young diplomat Augustus J. Foster, who measured all men by the standards of the aristocratic society of England. After mentioning Jefferson's red freckled face and neglected gray hair, Foster described him thus: "He wore a blue coat, a thick grey-coloured hairy waiscoat, with a red under-waiscoat lapped over it, green velveteen breeches with pearl buttons, yarn stockings and slippers down at the heel, his appearance being very much like that of a tall large-boned farmer." [9] Jefferson himself would hardly have objected to the com-

[7] Dec. 3, 1804 (Plumer, *Memorandum*, p. 212). With this may be contrasted the comment of Frances Few on TJ's shabbiness at a dinner in 1808–1809, when she was a guest at what appears to have been virtually a family meal (*Jour. Sou. Hist.*, August, 1963, pp. 350–351). There may be similar comments by others, at the height of TJ's presidency, but I have not chanced to see them.

[8] Nov. 10, 1804 (Plumer, *Memorandum*, p. 193).

[9] Based upon Foster's impressions of 1804, though he did not compose his "Notes on the United States" until three decades later. The quotations may be seen in *Jeffersonian America*, ed. by R. B. Davis (1954), p. 10. Foster came to America as secretary of the British legation about a year after Anthony Merry, and shared

SENATOR WILLIAM PLUMER OF NEW HAMPSHIRE
Portrait by C.B.J.F. de Saint-Mémin

parison and it may be recognized as an apt one, but he was more sympa-
thetically described by a traveler a few years later. After remarking
that his manners were modest and affable, this writer said: "An enemy
to luxury and parade, he lives at Monticello in the simple and negligent
style of a man wholly devoted to rural and philosophical pursuits.
When the sitting of Congress required his presence at Washington, he
carried with him the same *negligent simplicity*." [10]

Such negligence might have been attributed to the indifference to
externalities of an elderly man of learning who had insufficient feminine supervision. It appeared to another astute observer, however, that
Jefferson was by no means untrue to the traditions of the region
whence he came and of the social group to which he belonged. Joseph
Story, who met him when he was sixty-four, was much taken with his
unaffected manner and pleasant speech, but was somewhat surprised at
the negligence of his dress. After making the customary reference to
slippers and old-fashioned clothes that were rather out of order, the
future Justice of the Supreme Court said this in a private letter: "You
know Virginians have some pride in appearing in simple habiliments,
and are willing to rest their claim to attention upon their force of mind
and suavity of manners. The President is a little awkward in his first
address, but you are immediately at ease in his presence. His manners
are inviting and not uncourtly; and his voice flexible and distinct. . . .
His smile is very engaging and impresses you with cheerful frankness.
His familiarity, however, is tempered with great calmness of manner
and with becoming propriety. *Open to all, he seems willing to stand the
test of inquiry, and to be weighed in the balance only by his merit and
attainments*." [11]

Political enemies and hostile critics were disposed to attribute Jefferson's apparent unconcern for dress and appearance to deliberate political purpose. Partisanship was evident in the conflicting reports of physical details in the various descriptions. Whereas the aristocratic young
British diplomat Foster, who consorted with New England Federalists,
referred to the "very red freckled face" of the President, his supporters
spoke of his complexion as fresh or ruddy and described him as "rather
freckled." References to his "shifty glance" date back to his secretaryship of state and accord with the image of a deceitful intriguer that
the Hamiltonians sought with no little success to establish. On the

that minister's sentiments about TJ. Among Americans, his favorite associates were
Federalists from New England.
[10] John Lambert, *Travels through Canada, and the United States of North
America in the Years 1806, 1807 & 1808* (1813), II, 355. Italics added.
[11] Joseph Story to S. P. P. Fay, May 30, 1807, in W. W. Story, *Life and Letters
of Joseph Story* (1851), I, 151. Italics added.

other hand, admirers of him as President spoke of his "clear and pene-
trating eye," his "free and intelligent eye," and of a hazel eye that was
"very animated." Foster thought his expression rather cynical, and to
the wife of John Quincy Adams his countenance "indicated strongly
the hypocrisy of his nature," but to the wife of the editor of the *National Intelligencer* it seemed to beam with benignity. The young
Britisher spoke of his "grey neglected hair," while a more sympathetic
observer said it was "worn in negligent disorder, though not ungrace-
fully." Observers of this multi-dimensional and at times paradoxical
man tended to see in him just what they wanted to. We shall not try to
reduce him to an average, but we can note that his ardent supporters
did not claim that he was handsome or even distinguished looking, and
that his political enemies did not deny his characteristic friendliness to
his visitors and guests.

There was general agreement regarding the bountiful excellence of
his dinners. Though himself a gourmet, he probably needed to give
only general instructions to his French chef. In his own diet he laid
great stress on vegetables; and at his table fruits abounded, along with
sweetmeats. His wines were constantly remarked upon; William
Plumer said that he served eight varieties. Ever since his stay in France,
when he made a special study of the subject, he had been ordering
foreign wines, and these constituted a major item of expense. He continued to give personal attention to his cellar while President. Once,
sending an order for 400 bottles of champagne, he remarked to the
importer: "The expanding wants of my position oblige me to be more
extensively troublesome than I could wish." [12] In the federal city of his
day thirst for champagne appears to have been great and growing.
While his wines were justly renowned, no toasts or healths were drunk
at his table. "You drink as you please, and converse at your ease," said
one congressman. "In this way every guest feels inclined to drink to the
digestive or the social point, and no further." [13] It would seem that a
policy of self-determination was conducive to the maintenance of equilibrium. That there was style as well as bounty at these dinners was
recognized by observers who were otherwise critical. According to
Louisa Catherine Adams, everything about the "ruling demagogue"
was aristocratic except his ungainly and ugly person. Describing a
dinner she attended in November of 1803, she said: "The entertainment was handsome. French servants in livery, a French butler, a
French cuisine, and a buffet full of choice wine: had he had a tolerable

---

[12] TJ to Theodorus Bailey, June 21, 1804 (LC, 24492). In his papers there is
much interesting correspondence about wines with Bailey and others.
[13] Dr. S. L. Mitchill to his wife, Jan. 10, 1802 (*Harper's Mag.*, LVIII, 743-744).

fire on one of the bitterest days I ever experienced, we might almost have fancied ourselves in Europe." [14] When longing for a warm dining room, the good lady could hardly have been thinking of England; she might even have said that in this one respect the President was unwittingly emulating the British.

Her husband, John Quincy Adams, who obviously enjoyed the President's conversation, faithfully recorded interesting bits of it in his diary. At one of these dinners Jefferson, after urging the importance of acquiring French and Spanish, described the latter as an amazingly easy language: he claimed that with the help of a copy of *Don Quixote* and a grammar he had learned it on his voyage to Europe, when he was only nineteen days at sea. "But Mr. Jefferson tells large stories," said the humorless Adams, apparently without suspicion that his host might have been pulling his leg. "You never can be an hour in this man's company without something of the marvelous, like these stories." [15] The President's humor was likely to assume the form of exaggeration, and at times this generally reasonable man seems to have found a certain pleasure in being shocking. In social matters, however, he usually sought to please. This was in the tradition of the Virginia gentry and in his own nature.

His dinner guests had little chance to hear partisan political talk, for this he sedulously avoided. William Plumer thought it unfortunate that he had only Federalist legislators one day and only Republicans another, but the purpose of this practice was to avoid controversy upon social occasions. He undoubtedly hoped and sought to increase good will, but he did not expect to convert hardened sinners. One explanation of his continuance of the practice of issuing invitations as "Th: Jefferson," rather than as President of the United States, was that as an individual he would be under no obligation to invite his bitterest critics in Congress. He does not appear to have invited all the members of that body, but sooner or later he got around to most of them. His enemies were not above attributing to cowardice his avoidance of controversial talk at social gatherings, but that appears to have been his general practice throughout mature life. Foster said that because of his "principles of general philanthropy," he was "ever ready to excuse all offences not political, though with regard to these he was violent and vindictive." [16] That he was amiable in most respects was generally recognized, and it seems clear that as a host he tried to keep above party and to recognize

[14] From her autobiographical sketch in Adams Papers, MHS, microfilm reel 269, p. 159.

[15] Nov. 23, 1804 (J. Q. Adams, *Memoirs*, I, 316–317).

[16] August or September, 1807, in an account of a visit to Monticello (*Jeffersonian America*, p. 153).

no distinctions whatever except the one decreed by Nature between men and women.

Though there were unfavorable comments on his morning undress almost from the beginning of his administration, very little appears to have been said about the egalitarianism and unceremoniousness of his dinners until after the middle of his first term, when a note of alarm was sounded in diplomatic circles. William Plumer, at a stag dinner, noted his custom of following his guests into the dining room, as a private gentleman would do at home, but gave no sign that he himself objected to it. One may doubt that Jefferson paid any attention whatever to precedence in seating his small official family of department heads either at their meetings or at his own table, and nobody gave much heed as yet to seniority in Congress. There may have been a degree of democratic affectation in Jefferson's designation of his dinners in Washington as those of a private gentleman, and they must have been more formal than those he customarily gave at Monticello. But ceremoniousness would have seemed much more artificial in the village capital than in Philadelphia; and, while his avoidance of it was probably not without political motivation, Americans at that place and time apparently did not object to the disregard of what we now call protocol. That word was unknown to them as related to etiquette, and that issue was not raised until a British representative of ministerial rank appeared upon the scene, along with his insistent wife.

At the outset of Jefferson's "winter campaign" of 1803–1804, the principals of the diplomatic corps numbered four: the Marqués de Casa Yrujo, envoy extraordinary of Spain, who had so strongly manifested his vexation at the cession of Louisiana; Louis A. Pichon, chargé of France, who was so helpful to the United States government in connection with the transfer of the province; Peder Pederson, chargé of Denmark, the only newcomer since the inauguration; and Edward Thornton, secretary of the British legation, who had visited Jefferson at Monticello and was described by the President as plain and sensible. While Thornton did not believe that British interests had suffered in his hands during the three years since Robert Liston's departure, he recognized that times had changed and important events impended. Therefore, in March, 1803, he recommended the appointment of a minister of appropriate rank who could surround himself with more fitting splendor.[17] Admittedly it would be difficult, he told Lord Hawkesbury, to persuade a man of rank and distinction to come to America, where

17 Thornton to Hawkesbury, Mar. 11, 1803 (FO, 5:38).

he would find few men of education to associate with, and still fewer who were gentlemen in sentiment and manners. The President and the Secretary of State were not mentioned as exceptions in this rather obsequious letter from a minor official to his chief. Thornton did say that he himself had uniformly received from them "every possible mark of deference and attention," despite the fact that he lacked the "outward circumstances of advantage." He had been embarrassed, however, by his inability to show any hospitality and believed that the adequate support of British interests now required "a more elevated character."

Anthony Merry, who reached America in the autumn following this recommendation, bore the title of minister but otherwise fell short of Thornton's specifications. In fact he was the man the Foreign Office had had in mind for this post from the time Liston relinquished it, and this seems to have been essentially a routine appointment. There was some talk of a worse one — that of Francis James Jackson, who came to America in Madison's administration and then fully substantiated Rufus King's earlier description of him as "positive, vain and intolerant." The year before Merry arrived, he was regarded by the same observer as "a plain, unassuming and sensible man," who was the reverse of Jackson in nearly every point of character.[18] The son of a London merchant who dealt in Spanish wines, he had not inappropriately done most of his diplomatic service in Spain. He did not qualify as a man of rank and splendor among his own countrymen. Ignored by them in later years, he has emerged from the footnotes of history only because of his mission of three years to the court of Thomas Jefferson. It began with a comic episode that was also ironic. This humorless official did not live up to his name — or to the punning nickname or motto, "Toujours Gai."[19] Rufus King in his advance notice made no mention of Mrs. Merry, who was far from unpretentious. It seems that Merry acquired her shortly before he sailed for America. Said to have been a rich widow, she brought with her so many servants and so much baggage that, according to her own report, members of Congress were staggered. But, as she wrote from Washington to the poet Thomas Moore, who made the voyage with them (he parted with them at Norfolk, proceeding thence to Bermuda), trifles became giants in the mouths of

[18] Merry was mentioned as the likely successor to Liston on Sept. 30, 1800 (*I.B.M.*, p. 186 and note 25). King characterized Jackson and Merry in a letter of Apr. 10, 1802, to Madison (King, IV, 100).

[19] Brant, *Madison*, p. 162, says he bore this nickname in the Foreign Office. In the useful brief account of him by Bernard Mayo in *I.B.M.*, p. 197, note 13, it is said to have been his family motto. There is no sketch of him in the *Dictionary of National Biography*.

Americans.[20] The Merrys, who had had a stormy crossing, endured further grave discomforts en route to the federal city. They were six days by boat from Norfolk to Alexandria and proceeded thence by "coachie" over intolerable roads to Georgetown, where they lodged until they could find a "hovel" of their own. Mrs. Merry said she laughed all the way in the unfamiliar coachie; her husband's "*quiet* astonishment and *inward groaning*" excited her "mirth and risibility." Probably she viewed him with elevated amusement, as she did the raw scene on the banks of the Potomac. There, as she correctly said, a traveler found poor reward for the "innumerable difficulties and impositions" that befell him. Her husband did not report his official grievances to his home office until after this lady had received what he regarded as an affront at the President's table, though he then complained also of the form, or rather the formlessness, of his own reception a few days earlier.

The Envoy Extraordinary and Minister Plenipotentiary of His Britannic Majesty presented his credentials toward the end of November, 1803. Presumably the President was apprised beforehand, as Merry supposed, though specific appointments appear to have been exceptional. At any rate, the Secretary of State escorted the Minister, who was in full uniform and made a short speech, after which Madison retired. Indignantly reporting his reception to Lord Hawkesbury a week later, Merry said the President was in his "usual morning-attire," and according to another report he was wearing slippers.[21] This was only Jefferson's second reception of a diplomatic representative since his assumption of office, and Merry learned that he was equally informal in receiving Pederson the Dane a couple of years before. That officer, however, was only a "minister of the third order." According to Merry's understanding, Presidents Washington and Adams had received foreign ministers more respectfully. His suspicions afterwards increased, but at this time he did not believe that the present government meant to show particular disrespect to the British King. What he did believe was that they had seized on his arrival to alter customary procedure and debase foreign ministers generally in order to raise their

[20] Extracts from letter of Mrs. Merry to Moore, quoted by Beckles Willson in *Friendly Relations: A Narrative of Britain's Ministers and Ambassadors to America* (1934), pp. 39–40. A readable account of the Merry mission, based largely on Foreign Office correspondence, is in this work, ch. III. H. M. Jones, in *The Harp That Once — A Chronicle of the Life of Thomas Moore* (1937), p. 67, speaks of the lady as Merry's "bride, a rich widow who was bringing a large retinue of servants and a well-developed sense of punctilio to the conquest of barbarous Washington."

[21] Merry to Hawkesbury, Dec. 6, 1803, separate (FO, 5:41); R. King to C. Gore, Jan. 4, 1804 (King, IV, 340).

own consequence. The position of the government, on the other hand, was that this particular President altered his customary procedure for nobody, not even a foreign minister. He dressed the same for all. Merry in his full uniform commands sympathy, and one could wish that Madison had intimated that he should don more informal garments, though the Secretary might have given offense by so doing. Among other alleged departures from the "rules of distinction" as observed toward his predecessor, Merry mentioned the requirement that foreign ministers make the first visit to all the heads of department and not merely to the Secretary of State. Apparently he raised this question at his first conference with Madison, claiming his right to receive the first visit from the others, and was then informed that he was in error. He acceded to the requirement for practical reasons, he said, but in fact was asked to do no more than was expected of foreign representatives in his own country.

What most shocked the self-conscious new Minister from Britain was the "absolute omission of all distinction" in his and Mrs. Merry's favor at a dinner at the President's House.[22] Jefferson claimed that he merely followed his usual practice, which nobody had previously objected to. Pichon supported this claim, saying that even Yrujo, whom he regarded as the vainest of men, had acceded to it. When one of the Secretaries' ladies was serving as the President's hostess, he offered her his arm and seated her at his right. Dolley Madison was the favored lady in this instance, and, whether by accident or design, the wife of the Spanish Minister was on his left, while Yrujo sat beside Mrs. Madison, and Mrs. Merry below him. Poor Merry, hastening to seat himself next to Yrujo's wife, had to give way to a more agile congressman. To his plight he claimed that the President was wholly indifferent. Merry had already learned that Jefferson never observed formality at his table but regarded his conduct in this instance as studied.

Not unnaturally assuming that the dinner was given for him, Merry could not understand the inclusion of Pichon among the guests when France and Great Britain were at war. He concluded that this could not have been regarded as a dinner for the entire diplomatic corps since the Danish representative was not present. It afterwards appeared that the Dane was omitted because he had been a very recent dinner guest; and Jefferson would probably have denied that there ever was a guest of

[22] Described in Merry's letter of Dec. 6, 1803, to Hawkesbury (FO, 5:41). Henry Adams quotes from this and other dispatches from Merry, Pichon, and Yrujo in his brilliant account of the entire episode (*History*, II, ch. XVI). Heightening contrasts for dramatic effect and emphasizing paradox, he achieved a work of art that is unlikely to be matched, but his assessment of motives is open to question and a fairer story can be told.

honor at his table. Merry was the diplomatic newcomer, nonetheless, and others besides him have wondered just why the Frenchman was invited. According to that official's own account, Jefferson, in order to make sure of his attendance, urged him to expedite his return from Baltimore, whither he had to go on business, and he complied out of respect for the President and also out of curiosity.[23] Some embarrassment on his part as well as on Merry's might have been anticipated.

Seeking to explain Pichon's inclusion to Monroe in England, Madison afterwards said it was supposed that at the President's table "a liberal oblivion of all hostile relations ought to take place." [24] In view of Jefferson's general policy of avoiding the mingling of Federalists and Republicans at dinner, however, his action in this case may appear to have been both inconsistent and maladroit. Since there was some deliberation in it, this cannot be viewed merely as an instance of thoughtlessness on the part of an elderly man who had no vigilant wife to forewarn him, though unquestionably he needed one. It may perhaps be regarded as an act of bravado, or as a deliberate attempt to cut a pompous diplomat down to size. But it was not characteristic of him consciously to humiliate a guest, and at this particular time, when he was still awaiting news from New Orleans, his policy was not anti-British. A possible explanation of his invitation to Pichon is that the absence of the Frenchman, who had been so helpful in connection with Louisiana, would have been noted and have given a false impression — and this all the more if Yrujo were there. The President might have omitted him, as well as Pichon, but in that case his action might have been interpreted as punitive against the Spaniard for his obstructiveness with respect to the transfer of Louisiana, which the government was seeking to minimize. Yrujo's own report that the President showed marked preference for him and his wife over the Merrys may be attributed, however, to the vanity of that gentleman.[25] Jefferson seems to have wanted to give the impression of genuine neutrality as well as that of complete equality at his table. By erring on the side of inclusiveness this generous host, who went to such pains to provide the best of food and drink and who generally radiated good will in social intercourse, gave the impression of social naïveté and lack of consideration. But if this episode as a

[23] Pichon to Talleyrand, Feb. 5, 1804 (AECPEU, 56:342–351); quoted at considerable length by Adams (History, II, 368–369), with the assertion that he did this "in order to have the pleasure of seeing Jefferson humiliate his own guest in his own house," and that Pichon was "gratified by the result." I do not feel warranted in describing Jefferson's purpose or in reading Pichon's mind so precisely.

[24] Madison to Monroe, Jan. 19, 1804 (MP, Rives, 2:458–463).

[25] Adams, History, II, 370, quoting a passage from a letter of Yrujo to Cevallos, Feb. 7, 1804, accepts his statement at face value.

whole provides an example of his love of exaggeration and paradox, he himself did not regard it as amusing and Anthony Merry was certainly not the man to laugh it off.

The physical situation of that gentleman in the "savage" federal city was thoroughly miserable. With great difficulty he acquired two small houses, which he described as mere shells with bare walls and no fixtures, not even a pump or well, and he had difficulty in getting provisions, especially vegetables, at any price. He also found the city very short on common etiquette, but he attributed to deliberate design, rather than to ignorance and awkwardness, the embarrassment he suffered at Mr. Madison's a few days after his ordeal at the President's.[26] He experienced the same lack of distinction, preference being given the wives of the Secretaries — "a set of beings as little without the manners as without the appearance of gentlewomen" — while the diplomats and their ladies were left to their own devices. "In short," he said, "the latter are now placed here in a situation so degrading to the countries they represent, and so personally disagreeable to themselves, as to have become almost intolerable." According to soberer account, the Secretary of State had offered his arm to the wife of the Secretary of the Treasury. The resulting confusion was described by Pichon as *"une sorte de dérangement dans le salon."* [27] The British Minister reported that he himself took care of Mrs. Merry. According to other report, as received by Jefferson, he conducted her to the head of the table where Mrs. Gallatin was standing, and that lady then withdrew in her favor, receiving no thanks.[28] Madison did not follow his customary procedure at this dinner, but he afterwards explained that he had to follow that in the President's House once the issue had been raised. They could not accept the dictates of a foreign minister in so domestic a matter. Merry, on the other hand, was determined henceforth to avoid such occasions until he should have received authority from Lord Hawkesbury to acquiesce in such deprivation of "distinction." [29]

The best information about what happened next in the social vendetta comes from the report of Pichon.[30] Laying the chief blame for fanning the flames on Yrujo, whose pretentiousness and superiority of

[26] Merry to George Hammond, Dec. 7, 1803, private (FO, 5:41).

[27] Pichon to Talleyrand, Feb. 5, 1804.

[28] TJ to William Short, Jan. 23, 1804 (*A.H.R.*, July, 1928, p. 833).

[29] Merry to Hawkesbury, Dec. 31, 1803, separate (FO, 5:41). At the same time he reported that by action of the Vice President he had been deprived of the seat previously allotted to the British Minister in the Senate. He still could attend, however, and this particular action appears to have been connected with some indiscretion on the part of Yrujo.

[30] Pichon to Talleyrand, Feb. 5, 1804. This part of his letter is sufficiently quoted by Adams, *History*, II, 373–374.

manner he had long found objectionable, he said that the Spaniard "concerted reprisals" with the Merrys. Actually the British Minister had a low opinion of Yrujo in the first place, and the vanity of the Spanish Envoy had been wounded by developments on the diplomatic front before the social issue arose. The "reprisals" included the refusal by Merry of an invitation to tea from the Secretary of War and his failure to appear at a tea given by the Secretary of the Treasury, after he had accepted the invitation. They included also the conspicuous failure of both the diplomatic ladies to come to the President's House on New Year's Day, when everybody else was there, though Yrujo made it entirely clear at the time that his wife's health was perfect. Finally, the two aggrieved diplomats declined to dine with the President when invited without their wives.

Jefferson understood that the Merrys would dine only with private citizens, after having received advance assurance that they would have the precedence they deserved.[31] During her first weeks in the desolation of Washington, however, Mrs. Merry attended a ball given by Secretary and Mrs. Robert Smith. Her dress attracted great attention. According to Mrs. Samuel Harrison Smith, "it was brilliant and fantastic, white satin with a long train, dark blue crape of the same length over it and white crape drapery down to her knees and open at one side, so thickly covered with silver spangles that it appeared to be a brilliant silver tissue." [32] She also made considerable display of diamonds. "She is a large, tall well-made woman," said Mrs. Smith, "rather masculine, very free and affable in her manners, but easy without being graceful. She is said to be a woman of fine understanding and she is so entirely the talker and actor in all companies, that her good husband passes quite unnoticed; he is plain in his appearance and called rather inferior in understanding."

There was no doubt whatever in the mind of Jefferson that this large lady, rather than her plain husband, was the major reason for the disturbance of social harmony. If he did not think well of Merry he said he did, describing him to Monroe (in words which no doubt he expected that minister to repeat in England) as being "personally as desirable a character as could have been sent us," while his wife was an opposite character in every point. The President described the lady as a virago, saying that in a few weeks she had "established a degree of dislike among all classes which one would have thought impossible in so short a time." After a few weeks, Pichon reported that all the

31 TJ to Short, Jan. 23, 1804.
32 *First Forty Years*, p. 46.

women were "to the last degree exasperated against Mrs. Merry." [33]

This did not mean that they all treated her as a social pariah, however. Dr. and Mrs. Thornton had the British couple for dinner, along with their own close friends and neighbors the Madisons and the two sons-in-law of Jefferson among others. No information about the seating arrangements is available, but we know that Mrs. Thornton also invited the Pichons, with whom she was very friendly. It may have been for prudential reasons that they did not come.[34] Mrs. Thornton appears to have been on good terms with Mrs. Merry, but for unstinted praise of that lady we must turn to Federalist sources, such as a report by Congressman Manasseh Cutler of Massachusetts on a formal visit he made her husband in company with Senator John Quincy Adams of the same state and General James Wadsworth of Connecticut. (Cutler, a frequent dinner guest of the President, referred to him as "his Democratic majesty.") After saying that the Minister and his lady had received repeated affronts and been treated very improperly, he thus described them:

> Mr. Merry is a well-formed, genteel man, extremely easy and social. But I was especially pleased with the lady, who is a remarkably fine woman. It happened that I was seated by her. She entered instantly into the most agreeable conversation, which continued during the visit, while the other gentlemen were conversing with each other. She was just as easy and social as if we had been long acquainted, and continued so as long as we tarried, which was about a couple of hours.[35]

Besides the "affronts" at the tables of the President and the Secretary of State, this "remarkably fine woman" fancied that she had received another *in absentia* at the hands of the former. Early in the new year, further social complications were created by the arrival in the village capital of Jerome Bonaparte and his young bride from Baltimore (neé Patterson). The marriage put Jefferson in a rather ticklish situation, because the Emperor might have expected him to prevent it. Accordingly, he had instructed Livingston to explain that he did not have the power to do this. Also, he had gone out of his way to point out the wealth and social standing of the Patterson family — circumstances which, he said, "fix rank in a country where there are no hereditary

[33] TJ to Monroe, Jan. 8, 1804 (Ford, VIII, 290–291); Pichon to Talleyrand, Feb. 5, 1804.

[34] Dinner of Feb. 8, 1804, and invitations of Feb. 3, reported in Mrs. Thornton's Diary (LC).

[35] Cutler to his daughter, Mrs. Poole, Feb. 28, 1804 (Cutler, II, 164).

titles." [36] He was certainly not describing his own social philosophy, but he was seeking to mollify Napoleon at a time when, so far as his knowledge went, the situation in Louisiana was still uncertain, by assuring him that his brother had married well. The dinner at which the President had the newlyweds as guests was a sort of family party — including, besides Pichon, Senator Samuel Smith of Maryland and his wife (aunt of the bride), and the Senator's brother, Robert, Secretary of the Navy, and his wife. The President, who bowed to convention in this instance, offered his hand to the bride — giving her precedence over a Secretary's lady, as the Merrys said.

i i

The sanest comment on the miniature social tempest was that of Pichon, who discreetly kept out of it. Writing Talleyrand, he said that, while he believed that Jefferson could have avoided the uproars of Merry and Yrujo by the exercise of tact, their indiscreet actions were lacking in proper respect for him, and they had deprived him of all the means of making reparation, even though he had the best intention of doing so.[37] If the Frenchman charged Jefferson with tactlessness in the first place, he blamed the Englishman and the Spaniard for vain intransigence in the second. In the case of the insecure and uxorious Merry this might have been attributed to stupidity, in that of proud and impetuous Yrujo to frustration. The net result was "much reciprocal acrimony," and in the meantime the Federalists gleefully took up the matter and made a "burlesque of the facts." A couple of months after the famous dinner Pichon reported that the government had done nothing to correct the misstatements by the opposition press.

Some efforts had been made to buttress the social edifice, however. One of the first actions was to seek precise information about ceremonial and social usage in England. Madison asked some questions of Rufus King, recently back from his mission there, expressing mortification at the necessity of troubling him about so trivial a matter. King promptly sent a lengthy reply, and Jefferson put this into outline form.[38] Among other things this showed that in Merry's own country

---

[36] TJ to Livingston, Nov. 4, 1803 (Ford, VIII, 277).

[37] This is a less than literal translation of a long sentence in Pichon's letter of Feb. 5, 1804, to Talleyrand (AECPEU, 56:345–351), dealing with Merry episode. Henry Adams does considerable violence to this, especially by his translation of the first clause and his omission of the rest of it. For the exact passage and comments, see Appendix III, below. In this letter Pichon also described the dinner to the Bonapartes.

[38] Madison to King, Dec. 18, 1803 (King, IV, 332–333); King to Madison, Dec. 22, 1803 (LC, 23718–23720); TJ's outline (LC, 23651).

the highest official an American envoy was likely to dine with was the minister for foreign affairs, who gave two dinners a year to the members of the diplomatic corps *without* their wives. In society the titled took precedence over the untitled in all cases; and the ladies proceeded into the dining room in advance of the gentlemen, the highest in rank taking the lead. In King's opinion, the English really placed slight value on etiquette, and he had found that diplomats had little part in society. Judged by these standards and the invitations the Merrys received during their first weeks in America, they fared very well.

Presumably it was after the receipt of this information that rules or canons of etiquette for the guidance of the executive officers were drawn up. Perhaps there would have been no attempt to formalize the ceremonial policy of an unceremonious administration had not Yrujo insisted that the official position of the government on this momentous question of precedence be made known. Madison said that the subject was distasteful to the President, and he was apologetic whenever he mentioned it in his letters to others. "I blush to have to put so much trash on paper," he wrote Monroe. The question was taken up by the Council, though no record remains of the decisions reached except for certain undated fragments in Jefferson's own files.[39] These are in agreement about the main points at issue, however, and they set down in black and white the principle that he called pell mell.

The basic principle was that perfect equality should obtain in all social intercourse. No distinctions of grade among diplomats were to be recognized; and members of the executive were to practice at home and recommend to others "adherence to the ancient usage of the country, of gentlemen in mass giving precedence to the ladies in mass, in passing from one apartment where they were assembled into another." In formal language this pronouncement sounds rather absurd, but, judging from a comment of Madison's, it was in accord with prevailing custom. "In this country," he told Merry, "people were left to seat themselves at table with as little rule as around a fire."[40] There was to be somewhat less mass movement in the President's House, since Jefferson expected to continue to give his hand to a lady. However, he would merely pick the nearest, thus disregarding the claims of the Secretaries' ladies as well as those of the wives of diplomats. He explained his position to his old secretary, William Short, who had been a dinner guest along with the Merrys:

[39] The fullest discovered by me is in LC, 23714. Ford (VIII, 276-277) seems to follow the rough draft in LC, 41634-41636, making the changes and corrections that he supposed TJ had indicated. Because of the statement that this contained what was agreed on, I quote from it.

[40] Reported in his letter of Jan. 19, 1804, to Monroe (MP, Rives, 2:458-463).

I thought it more honorable if an act of mine could be construed into a departure from the true principle of equality, to correct it at once, and get into the right road rather than by perseverance in what was incorrect, to tangle myself in inconsistencies. I presume the courts of these agents will have too much good sense to attempt to force on us their allotment of society into ranks or orders, as we have never pretended to force on them our equality. Our ministers with them submit to the laws of their society; theirs with us must submit to ours. They plead the practices of my predecessors. These practices were not uniform: besides I have deemed it my duty to change some of their practices, and especially those which savoured of anti-republicanism.[41]

Not only did Jefferson appear here as an egalitarian but also as a would-be isolationist. "I have ever considered diplomacy as the pest of the peace of the world," he said, "as the workshop in which nearly all the wars of Europe are manufactured." He had got rid of half the foreign representatives of the United States and wished he could have dispensed with all; only in commerce did he want to mix in the affairs of Europe. No doubt he was blowing off steam in this private letter, as he had done at other times in writing Short. His words need not all be taken at face value. But, if Pichon's report is to be believed, he was deeply wounded by the refusal of Merry and Yrujo to dine with him without their wives, regarding their concerted response as insulting.[42] They could no longer accept his invitations, they said, until after they had received from their courts responses to their representations. The President said it was unheard of that a foreign minister had to have the permission of his court before seating himself at the table of the chief of state. Madison had conferred with both of the offended gentlemen, who remained adamant. Yrujo contended that they had a right to demand the continuance of the usages under previous Presidents until changes had been officially announced. Madison pointed out that Yrujo had conformed for three years without protest, and Jefferson made it perfectly clear that he would never let the idea get out that importance was determined by anybody's place at his table.

Writing his daughter Martha on the same day he wrote Short, he said that no foreign ministers would be invited to the dinner in honor of the acquisition of Louisiana, so that no questions of etiquette would be

---

[41] TJ to William Short, Jan. 23, 1804 (*A.H.R.*, July, 1928, p. 833). This letter is of special value as showing TJ's interpretation of the entire episode.

[42] Pichon to Talleyrand, Feb. 13, 1804 (AECPEU, 56:369–371), reporting conversations with TJ and Madison at and after dinner at the President's with Jerome Bonaparte. Apparently no women were present. Pichon said this was the first time they had opened their mouths on the subject.

raised.[43] "The brunt of the battle now falls on the Secretary's ladies, who are dragged in the dirt of every federal paper," he said. He was glad that Martha and Maria had not been with him that winter, for they would have been "butchered the more bloodily" because of their closeness to him. Among the newspaper accounts that give him special umbrage was one in which he was alleged to have ordered that the Secretaries and their wives, referred to here as "a pretty set," should be preferred to all others, with the result that at his dinner their "ladyships" were led and seated according to their rank while Mr. and Mrs. Merry were left to view the procession. As for the President himself, referred to here as "our polite philosopher," his conduct was attributed to a combination of "pride, whim, weakness and malignant revenge."[44] The assertion that the heads of department and their wives ranked diplomatic characters was repeated in a communication to the *Washington Federalist*, obviously based on hearsay. Though generally humorless, this ended with a bright suggestion: namely, that thenceforth at official functions the ladies should be led into the dining room "according to *seniority, the oldest first.*" Maiden ladies above seven and twenty, however, should go in as they pleased, without any question.[45]

To this paper Jefferson drafted a reply, which was printed with only minor alterations in the *Aurora*, just as though William Duane had written it. It represented one of Jefferson's few departures from his pre-presidential policy of writing nothing anonymously for the papers — in which respect he had differed so sharply from his antagonist Hamilton and his friend Madison. Also, it was in effect an official statement of the position of the government. Recognizing its importance, Pichon put the printed version into French and sent a copy to Talleyrand.[46] Jefferson asserted many times that he had no direct connection with the *National Intelligencer*, which appears to have ignored this episode completely, or with the *Aurora*, and there can be no real doubt of the editorial independence of the two most influential Republican papers. His action in this case was exceptional and under existing circumstances probably had to be surreptitious. At any rate, he avoided the magnification of a petty quarrel by publicly ignoring it and letting Duane speak for him. This procedure was politically advantageous, since the editor

[43] TJ to Martha, Jan. 23, 1804 (*Family Letters*, 254–255).

[44] *Gazette of the U.S.*, Jan. 17, 1804; extract of a letter from a gentleman in Washington, Jan. 2, 1804. TJ referred specifically to this in his letter to Short.

[45] *Washington Federalist*, Feb. 1, 1804, courtesy American Antiquarian Society. While designated as a communication, this piece was signed by no pseudonym and was given the position of an editorial.

[46] The undated paper in TJ's handwriting is in LC, 19124½. It appeared in the *Aurora*, Feb. 13. Pichon's French copy is in AECPEU, 56:372–373. See Appendix III, below.

could assail Federalist critics in a way the President could not afford to do.

The communication had an undeniable partisan flavor. It referred to "unfounded stuff" in the papers of a party that sought to "excite misunderstandings with other nations" — even with England if they could not do so with Spain and France. It rightly denied that the actions of the American government were owing to unfriendliness to the British government. There was, however, both patriotic and partisan appeal in the assertion that there had been no "court of the United States" since March 4, 1801. The author said: "That day buried levees, birthdays, royal parades, and the arrogation of precedence in society by certain self-stiled friends of order, but truly stiled friends of privileged orders." This verbal slap at relatively innocuous Federalist ceremonialism, allegedly in imitation of foreign courts, was a Republican cliché. But the specific "rules of social intercourse" that were laid down here, insofar as they related to the visits of officials at least, were entirely sensible. They followed British practice in stipulating that heads of department received the first visits from foreign ministers, but went beyond that in saying that these were returned. No claim of priority was made for the Secretaries over the members of the legislature, and it was recognized that visits between the latter and the diplomats depended on individual inclination. In case these should take place, however, the latter, as newcomers, might claim the right to the first visit, according to English and American custom.

The emphasis on unceremoniousness and social equality was largely confined to the final paragraph:

> In social circles all are equal, whether in, or out, of office, foreign or domestic; & the same equality exists among ladies as among gentlemen. No precedence therefore, of any one over another, exists either in right or practice, at dinners, assemblies, or any other occasions. "Pell-mell" and "next the door" form the basis of etiquette in the societies of this country.

The expressions "pell mell" and "next the door" suggest more chaos and unseemly competition than may be supposed to have characterized American social gatherings of the better sort. And Jefferson himself did not like disorderly scrambling, averse to artificial distinctions of all kinds though he was and believed his countrymen to be. Perhaps, in using these words, he was indulging his fondness for hyperbole. At any rate, they gave color to the charge that Merry made to his lordly superior in England and no doubt repeated in Federalist circles in America, that, for reasons of domestic politics, the government had sought to

place him "on a level with the lowest American citizen." [47] In commenting on the supposed ideals of a democratic society, he unwittingly anticipated Gilbert and Sullivan:

> The Noble Lord who rules the State —
> The Noble Lord who cleans the plate —
> The Noble Lord who scrubs the grate —
> They all shall equal be! [48]

This episode clamors for comic treatment and defies rational analysis.
Since there was as little likelihood that Merry would meet one of the
lowest American citizens at dinner in Washington as that the great
body of the American people would cringe before ranks and titles, it
would appear that one absurdity provoked another. But, whatever lack
of discrimination and fondness for hyperbole Jefferson may have
shown in presenting the American "principle" of social relations, he
was very generous in assessing the motives of the diplomatic gentlemen
who had opposed it — easier on them, in fact, than they deserved. Thus
he said for his countrymen:

> Not that they question the right of every nation to establish or
> alter its own rules of intercourse, nor consequently our right to
> obliterate any germs of a distinction of ranks, forbidden by our
> constitution: but that it is part of their duty to be watchful for
> the relative standing of their nation, and to acquiesce only so soon
> as they see that nothing derogatory of that is contemplated.

Merry had soon come to believe that derogation of his King and
country *was* intended, an idea that Thornton came to share, and he
clung to this belief stubbornly despite Madison's representations. But
he had taken the business out of his own hands by referring it to higher
authority in England. His somber dispatches, describing his injured
dignity and his lady's wounded pride along with their unquestionable
personal discomforts, led to some talk in official circles in London
shortly after they were received. Christopher Gore, who remained
there for a time after Rufus King's departure and who viewed the administration through disdainful Federalist eyes, feared that this "silly
business" might have an ill effect on Anglo-American relations, but
Lord Hawkesbury, his host at dinner, agreed with him at the time that
these should not be affected by "personal considerations and trivial circumstances" and the Foreign Secretary did not afterwards change his
mind.[49] James Monroe reported a month later that no one of the officials

---

[47] Merry to Hawkesbury, Dec. 31, 1803.
[48] *The Gondoliers*, Act I.
[49] C. Gore to R. King, Feb. 8, 1804 (King, IV, 341–342).

had spoken to him on the subject of Merry's situation, though he was inclined to believe that they regarded the circumstance as vexatious. Other people with whom he had talked unofficially agreed that, if an issue of precedence should be raised, the home government and department heads were always superior. While determined to raise no such an issue on his own account, Monroe made it clear that, in the matter of precedence, his position was far from satisfactory. "In respect to the ministers of other powers we appear to hold the lowest grade," he wrote Jefferson. At a diplomatic dinner at Lord Hawkesbury's precedence was given, seemingly by design, to all the others. Also, hardly any of his visits to high British officials, or of his wife to their wives, had been returned. He had found, in fact, that the opinion he had held of the respect due his office and his government was not shared by the British government. What disturbed him more than the indifference of the British was their colossal ignorance of America. One Lord was surprised to learn that Americans had carriages like those in England.[50] No doubt Merry's reports of "savage" Washington, bandied about, fell on ready ears.

Jefferson and Madison were well aware, however, of the friendliness of the Addington ministry; and events proved, during its few remaining weeks, that it was not disposed to let a trivial matter of etiquette affect the relations between the two countries. In May, following the resignation of Addington and the formation of the second ministry of Pitt, Lord Harrowby succeeded Lord Hawkesbury as foreign secretary. In his first instructions to Merry, late in the summer, he made no reference whatever to that envoy's social troubles.[51] Relations between the two countries had deteriorated somewhat since the Louisiana Purchase, though to no such degree as Merry and Thornton supposed and not at all for social reasons. Now feeling more self-reliant, the American government had revived discussion of impressment. Not until the summer and autumn after Jefferson's second inauguration as President, however, was there a marked change in the American attitude. Jefferson talked of a British alliance after the failure of Monroe's mission to Spain and the entrance of that country into the war on the side of France.[52]

Anthony Merry did not contribute perceptibly to this continuing amicability. Though his major instruction had been to cultivate good understanding with the individuals composing the American govern-

[50] Comments from letters of Monroe to Madison, Mar. 3, 1804, and to TJ, Mar. 15 (S.M.H., IV, 148–152, 153–163).
[51] Aug. 3, 1804 (I.B.M., pp. 204–206).
[52] Bradford Perkins, in The First Rapprochement (1955), ch. 15, gives an admirable account of Anglo-American relations in this period.

ment, he quarreled with the President and Secretary of State, while consorting with their bitterest political enemies. As we shall see hereafter, he connived with New England separatists and Aaron Burr. Meanwhile, in the late summer of 1804, when Madison and Jefferson were in the Virginia hills, he showed persistent intractability in the matter of official prestige. He then questioned the authority of the Clerk of the Department of State to correspond with him, an accredited minister, in the absence of the Secretary. He afterwards wrote Jacob Wagner a private letter, explaining that his object was to call attention to the fact that no mention of Wagner had been made to him. This omission he regarded as part of the system of "withholding from Foreign Ministers the attentions due to them." In this system, he had *"not yet been instructed by his Court to acquiesce."* [53] On this point, in fact, he appears never to have received any instructions of any sort.

The local social scene had been brightened for him and his wife by a brief visit paid them by Thomas Moore in the spring of 1804, after the poet's gay season in Bermuda. It is said that this small man received little attention when introduced to the President — according to one account he was taken for a boy — and that the poem about the City of Washington published by him a couple of years later constituted his revenge.[54] There is humor in a number of references, such as the one to

> This fam'd metropolis, where Fancy sees,
> Squares in morasses, obelisks in trees.

But those to Jefferson's "black Aspasia," to "false liberty," "Gallic garbage of philosophy," and courting the rabble's smile, reveal it as a thinly veiled anti-Jefferson diatribe.

Both the poet and the minister proceeded northward, the latter alleviating his situation by spending the summer in Philadelphia, which was relatively civilized though hot. Merry was back in September, but his poor wife was taken ill, and unable to return to Washington until the first of the year. By that time Augustus John Foster had succeeded the faithful but less glamorous Thornton as secretary of the legation. He gave loyal support to Merry and accepted the explanation that an ambassador, as compared with a minister, would have received distinguished attention, and that the Americans really wanted the British to send them a peer.[55]

Again taken ill, Mrs. Merry was confined at home several weeks

[53] Wagner to Madison, Sept. 1 and Sept. 15, 1804 (MP, 28:2, 10). Italics added.
[54] "Epistle VII. To Thomas Hume, Esq. M.D.," in Moore's *Epistles, Odes, and Other Poems* (London, 1806), pp. 209–215. See account of his visit in H. M. Jones, *The Harp That Once*, pp. 77–81, and in Foster's *Jeffersonian America*, pp. 10–11.
[55] *Jeffersonian America*, p. 54.

more, but she saw company there. Manasseh Cutler again found her agreeable and thought highly of her accomplishments, especially in the field of botany. "The dreary, uncultivated state of this part of the country is extremely disagreeable to her," he said. "She expresses her astonishment at the want of taste in gardens, walks, etc., and that the ladies in this country have no relish for the most beautiful productions of nature." Very likely her point was well taken, but this condescending visitor should at least have allowed for the botanical knowledge and taste of the President of the United States, to whom she had returned her best thanks for "the very valuable and scarce seeds" he had sent her soon after she was his guest at dinner.[56]

Admiring Manasseh Cutler also described an elegant dinner with the Envoy of His Britannic Majesty and his spouse. The company numbered twenty-eight; the table, lighted by six double-branched silver candlesticks, was superb. The plate was in the center; and in the last service the knives, forks, and spoons were of gold. Coffee was in the drawing room. "A very pleasing entertainment," said this guest, and no doubt it was to him, especially if the thirteen members of Congress present were all Federalists, as no doubt they were.[57] He made no mention of any member of the executive branch, though it was with this, rather than with the legislature, that a diplomatic representative was supposed to deal. And it may be added, to the further discredit of the judgment of the Merrys, that they had exiled themselves from the best table in Washington.

[56] Cutler to Mrs. Torrey, Feb. 21, 1805 (*Life*, II, 190). Mrs. Merry to TJ, Dec. 26, 1803 (MHS).
[57] Feb. 12, 1805 (Cutler, *Life*, II, 183).

[XXI]

Partisans and Irreconcilables

1803 – 1804

CONSORTING with Federalists was a well-established custom among British representatives to the United States, but Edward Thornton viewed the party of opposition more objectively than Anthony Merry — or at least he did so before that ceremonious minister arrived. In the fall of 1803, Thornton rightly anticipated that Federalists would oppose the attempt to amend the constitutional provision for the election of the President and Vice President that was sure to be made in the ensuing session of Congress. Since there was slight prospect of defeating Jefferson in any other way, they clung to the hope of doing so by intrigue, said the British observer disapprovingly. So long as the electors should cast their ballots for two men, without designating one of them for the first and the other for the second office, Jefferson's enemies could support his running-mate, thus seeking to escape a greater evil by embracing a lesser.[1] They had actually supported Burr, in defiance of public opinion, when the unexpected tie between him and Jefferson was referred to the House in 1801. That sort of situation might never recur but the original electoral system unquestionably lent itself to intrigue. John Adams had good reason to know that such was the case *within* a party. In fact the original system was thoroughly incompatible with parties, and from 1796 onward discontent with it could be found in both of them. The events of 1800–1801 served to crystallize this dissatisfaction, however, and the lead in the movement to change the system naturally came from supporters of Jefferson, who had lacked so little of being victimized by it.[2]

In the first session of Congress after the election in which the system

[1] Thornton to Hawkesbury, Sept. 30, 1803 (FO, 5:38).
[2] The events of 1800–1801 are described in *Jefferson and the Ordeal of Liberty*, pp. 493–505.

had such unexpected results, a constitutional amendment designed to correct it was passed by considerably more than the required two-thirds majority in the House and lacked only one vote in the Senate, where the tally was 15 to 8.[3] The question came up in the next two sessions but was deferred. Time was growing short when it was raised in the fall of 1803, since there would be a presidential election in the following year. The Federalists made a partisan issue out of the amendment, and, being short on argument as well as votes, had recourse to tactics of obstruction. Defeated, 22 to 10, on the crucial vote in the Senate, they claimed that this was insufficient since it did not represent two-thirds of the total membership. The vote in the House was precisely two-thirds of those voting, including the Speaker. A few "democratic members," chiefly New Englanders, voted with the minority. The House resolution, requesting the President to transmit copies of the amendment to the executives of the several states for submission to the legislatures, was concurred in by the Senate on December 12, 1803.[4] Since this question had been before Congress about seven weeks, there was ample time for deliberation; and, as things turned out, the Twelfth Amendment was declared ratified on September 25, 1804 — that is, before the election. Such a fortunate outcome could not have been confidently predicted at the moment, however. Hailing the action by Congress as a "deathblow to faction," the *National Intelligencer* thus summarized the language of its foes: *"we will divide you by stratagem if we cannot overcome you by force."* [5] At the present time we may regret that the legislators did not go further in remedying the complicated and artificial electoral system, but the requirement that there be an unmistakable distinction between the President and Vice President, while denigrating the latter, could be expected to facilitate majority rule and make intrigue against the major candidates more difficult.

Early in the new year, on receiving notification of the favorable action of one of the state legislatures, that of Pennsylvania, Jefferson ex-

[3] The history of the passage of the Twelfth Amendment is well summarized by H. V. Ames in "Proposed Amendments to the Constitution," *Annual Report A.H.A. 1896*, II (1897), 77–80, with notes pp. 324–325. On the events in 7 Cong., 1 sess., see note #345, with references.

[4] *Annals*, 8 Cong., 1 sess., p. 214. The dates of the crucial votes were, respectively, Dec. 2 and 9. Plumer comments on the House vote in his *Memorandum*, Dec. 9, 1803 (pp. 78–79). When the amendment was before the state legislatures, the Federalists continued to contend that it had not been adopted by the requisite majority. Thus the legislature of Delaware, one of the few states that rejected it, declared the proceedings of Congress on the subject "inconsistent with the interest, peace, and happiness of the several states, and also *unconstitutional*" (*National Intelligencer*, Jan. 20, 1804, italics added).

[5] *National Intelligencer*, Dec. 12, 1803.

pressed the opinion that the Federalists would continue to oppose the amendment for party reasons. Writing Governor Thomas McKean, he said: "They know that if it prevails, neither a President or Vice President can ever be made but by the fair vote of the majority of the nation, of which they are not." [6] He also said that he himself had more reason than others to approve of the specific designation of the President in the vote, for thus the verdict on him would be unequivocal. Then, in a roundabout way, he announced that he expected to stand for re-election. Apparently this is his first recorded statement to that effect. "The abominable slanders of my political enemies have obliged me to call for that verdict from my country in the only way it can be obtained," he said, "and if obtained, it will be my sufficient voucher to the rest of the world and to posterity, and leave me free to seek, at a definite time, the repose I sincerely wished to have retired to now." Actually, the slanders of his enemies had not noticeably increased of late; and the peaceful acquisition of Louisiana, which had just been officially reported to him, made a favorable verdict as clearly predictable as things ever can be in politics. He could well afford to assume a silent and passive role with respect to his own candidacy. He did this, also, with respect to the choice of his running-mate. Writing to McKean, who had been looked upon as a possibility but who now explicitly stated that he was unwilling to be considered, the President said that he did not permit himself even to make inquiries as to the persons who were to be placed "on the rolls of competition for the public favor." It need not be believed, however, that he was left in ignorance of what was going on, and it can be supposed that he saw no occasion to exercise a veto.

Had there been any likelihood of the renomination of Aaron Burr, his attitude would doubtless have been much less nonchalant, but the standing of the Vice President within his own party had continued to decline. By now his old political base in New York had largely eroded. George Clinton was governor of the state, and his nephew DeWitt Clinton had become its dominant Republican figure. In effect, Jefferson had sided with the Clintonians by the fall of 1801, when he ceased to heed Burr's recommendations regarding appointments, but he had carefully avoided the appearance of doing so. Trying to keep out of local factional quarrels in New York and everywhere else, he sought to maintain the unity of the party. Among his intimate advisers, Gallatin was dubious of the stories about Burr's intrigue against Jefferson in the last election and regarded the attacks on him by James Cheetham in

[6] TJ to McKean, Jan. 17, 1804 (Ford, VIII, 292–293), replying to McKean's letter of Jan. 8 (LC, 23773).

1802 as injurious to the Republican cause. On the other hand, Jefferson's fellow Virginian, Senator Wilson Cary Nicholas, believing that the party would never again support Burr, thought it desirable to break with him well in advance of the next election. With this advice to De-Witt Clinton he coupled a word of warning: "There are the most urgent reasons why everything should be avoided that will induce a belief that personal regard to Mr. Jefferson has in any manner excited this attempt to unveil this modern Machiavel." [7] The Clintons and Livingstons were out to get Burr on their own account, however, and Cheetham continued his attacks in further pamphlets in 1803. Jefferson had all of these, along with the reply of William P. Van Ness to them in the ARISTIDES pamphlet. Besides being a defense of Burr, the latter was a bitter attack on his local foes and some of its language seemed designed to drive a wedge between the Clintonians and Jefferson. Meanwhile, there was talk of Burr's running for governor in the spring of 1804.

DeWitt Clinton did not mention Burr's name in a letter he wrote Jefferson in late November, but in his reference to a certain gentleman who was ambitious to be governor he quite clearly had the Vice President in mind. The surest way to forestall this gentleman would be to gain the consent of George Clinton to run again, but, as Jefferson was now informed in confidence, the Governor had indicated to a few intimates his intention to decline. Hoping that he could be prevailed upon to change his mind, his nephew suggested that a letter from Jefferson might be a "singular service." The President declined to render this service, thus maintaining his policy of not intermeddling in local political contests. [8] He clearly implied his approval of the present administration in New York, however, and circumstances soon permitted an exchange of felicitations with the Governor. George Clinton, after reading in the "scurrilous" pamphlet of ARISTIDES the charge that in 1800, at Burr's house, he had made remarks "highly derogatory" of Jefferson's political character, hastened to write the President that this was "abuse and dishonorable misrepresentation" which was contradicted by the uniform tenor of his conduct. He said that he did not then suspect that he was "under the roof of a corrupt intriguer, surrounded by his worthless minions." [9] In his very prompt reply, Jefferson referred to

[7] W. C. Nicholas to DeWitt Clinton, Aug. 13, 1802; quoted by Cunningham, *Jeffersonians in Power*, p. 207. This author gives an excellent account of Burr's declining fortunes in New York (pp. 203–213).

[8] DeWitt Clinton to TJ, Nov. 26, 1803 (LC, 23574); TJ to DeWitt Clinton, Dec. 2, 1803 (Ford, VIII, 282).

[9] George Clinton to TJ, Dec. 22, 1803 (LC, 23652), received Dec. 30. This episode is described by E. W. Spaulding in *His Excellency George Clinton* (1938), ch. 21.

the pamphlet as "libelous," saying that he found it so false that he quickly tossed it aside. As for Clinton's alleged remark, no contradiction was needed. He had long been aware of "a design to sow tares between particular republican characters" — that is, he was fully aware of the purposes of the Burrites. Their own business, he said, was to march ahead to the object that had occupied them since the Declaration of Independence. One might have supposed that he and this one time opponent of the Constitution had always agreed on everything. Such, in fact, was not the case, and Jefferson was not the architect of the historic Virginia–New York axis. He now said: "In confidence that you will not be weary in well doing, I tender my wishes that your future days may be as happy as your past ones have been useful." [10] Though he had committed himself to nothing, his language was effusive, as it tended to be when he was waxing complimentary. He might have reflected that George Clinton was no such spoilsman as his nephew; in the matter of appointments, which was the main issue between Republican factions, he thought more like Jefferson. And he was unquestionably a friend of the administration — a thing which certainly could not have been truthfully said of Aaron Burr.

Before he again heard from Clinton, the President made some critical memoranda about the Vice President. In one he merely recorded a report, received from a supporter, of alleged conversations at the time of the electoral tie in which Burr manifested his expectation of becoming President. The other was Jefferson's own account of a visit from Burr. [11] In this Burr made the surprising statement that he acceded to the vice presidential nomination with a view to promoting Jefferson's fame and advancement, and from the desire to be with one "whose company and conversation had always been fascinating to him." The object of his flattery was not at all taken in. Burr, charging that the "calumnies" against him had been excited by his political enemies, the Clintons and Livingstons, professed unchanged attachment to Jefferson. He admitted that it would be to the Republican interest for him to retire, but he did not want to do so without some sign of favor and confidence from Jefferson. In his response, the President asserted that his policy had always been one of non-interference, except that in the last election he had sought to gain unanimous support in Virginia for his running-mate. It was still his policy: he would not even let people talk to him about the election. But he promised Burr nothing whatever, except to give his request consideration; and in this private memorandum he

[10] TJ to George Clinton, Dec. 31, 1803 (L. & B., X, 439–441); see *Jefferson and the Rights of Man*, pp. 457–458.
[11] Memoranda of Jan. 2, 26, 1804 (Ford, I, 301–304).

stated that he had long distrusted the man and had warned Madison against him. He claimed that there had been no intimacy and little association between himself and Burr, and said that the latter's claim on him for gratitude rested solely on his extraordinary activities and success in New York in the election of 1800. Quite obviously, Jefferson saw no reason to be grateful now.

A few days after he received this visit and recorded these reflections, he had from George Clinton a letter in which the Governor expressed himself as "highly gratified by the generous and very friendly sentiments" in Jefferson's letter to him, and claimed that he really had expected no reply. The most significant thing he said, however, was that because of age and ill health he would not stand for re-election in New York.[12] This was a confirmation rather than a revelation, to be sure, but if the Governor knew what DeWitt Clinton had already told the President he did not mention it. He gave the impression of taking Jefferson into his confidence; and while he talked as though he expected to return to the ranks, his announcement could have been regarded as a suggestion of his willingness to occupy the honorable but unexacting post of Vice President. By the time of the election he would be sixty-five years old.

About a month later, at a caucus of the Republican members of Congress, after Jefferson had been unanimously nominated for the first office, this available veteran was nominated as his running-mate by a majority that approximated two-thirds. This was on the first ballot, which was taken in secrecy without speeches on the proposal of particular persons.[13] The next highest vote was received by John Breckinridge but he was far behind the leader, while nobody voted for Aaron Burr. This nomination represented a consensus, presumably arrived at after numerous conversations at dinner tables and in lodgings. Into these Jefferson did not need to enter.[14] There was some objection to Clinton in the West, where Breckinridge was favored, but the Senator himself soon quieted that, and there was no serious protest against the assumption by the congressional caucus of the right to speak for the party. The chief significance of these events lies in the emergence of

[12] George Clinton to TJ, Jan. 20, 1804 (LC, 23817).

[13] Feb. 25, 1804. The Report in *National Intelligencer*, Feb. 29, said that 110 were in attendance but did not give the precise vote. The *Aurora*, Mar. 6 (cited by Cunningham, p. 104), said that of 108 votes cast, Clinton got 67, John Breckinridge 20, Levi Lincoln 9, John Langdon of N.H. 7, Gideon Granger 4, and Samuel Maclay of Pa. 1. Cunningham gives an excellent account of the caucus, pp. 103–108.

[14] The hostile *New York Evening Post* anticipated it, Feb. 17, 1804.

that body from the veil of secrecy and its acceptance as an instrument or institution.

In view of the possibility that the Twelfth Amendment might not be ratified before the election, another action was significant. A committee was named with the ostensible purpose of promoting the success of the ticket, but with the particular purpose of effecting the election of Clinton without endangering that of Jefferson. There was to be no repetition of the accidental tie of 1800, and the second man was to be kept in his place.[15] The *National Intelligencer*, after saying that any attempt to eulogize Jefferson would be a work of supererogation, proceeded to describe him lengthily as the "man of the people" in public as in private life. In a much briefer account Clinton was thus described: "Firm, cool, collected, plain in his manners, and assiduous in the discharge of duty, he is beloved by his friends, and esteemed by his enemies." [16] Presumably no one recalled the charge that four years earlier he had referred to Jefferson as an "accommodating trimmer," and nobody seems to have inquired into his skill in the only task he was really expected to perform, that of a presiding officer, though time was to show it to be slight. This vice presidential nomination was based on political expediency, pure and simple — like most of those in later years.

The caucus impressively demonstrated Republican unity on the congressional level. Jefferson was well aware that there were rifts on the local level, but until this time these had borne little on his personal popularity. Rival factions generally vied with each other in professing the utmost loyalty to him. In the previous summer, speaking of Pennsylvania where factionalism was specially rife, he had said: "I verily believe our friends have not differed with us [the administration] on a single *measure* of importance. It is only as to the distribution of office that some difference of opinion has appeared." [17] He had just received a lengthy address from the Ward Committees of Philadelphia in which the memorialists, while insisting that their confidence in him had never wavered, objected to the continued presence in public office of avowed enemies of the government.[18] William Duane of the *Aurora* was a leader in the faction responsible for this. Jefferson decided not to answer the address, but he drafted a long letter to Duane, whose partisan zeal seemed excessive but whom he respected and whose support he

[15] Cunningham, pp. 104–105.

[16] *National Intelligencer*, Mar. 2, 1804.

[17] TJ to William Duane, July 24, 1803 (Ford, VIII, 259), in a letter he wrote but did not send.

[18] Received July 17, 1803 (LC, 23042 23043a). It had been in preparation for some weeks.

highly valued. Besides explaining why he could not in propriety answer such a memorial, he sought to explain and justify his policy of removals and appointments, the moderation of which had been objected to. On Gallatin's advice, however, he did not send this. Had Duane been aware of the circumstances, no doubt he would have been confirmed in his opinion that the President was too much under the influence of the Secretary of the Treasury.[19]

This particular uproar died down, as Gallatin believed it would, but in the late winter and spring of 1804 there were factions within factions among the Republicans of Pennsylvania — they had got into a "jumble of subdivision," as Jefferson said. Assuring a member of one such subdivision that he himself had received no charge against him as an intended schismatic, Jefferson recommended mutual indulgence among the brethren, "and that we be content to obtain the best measures we can get, if we cannot get all we would wish." [20] The Republicans all looked to him, whatever they might say about one another.

Though the congressional caucus had decisively disposed of Burr as a Republican on the national level, he was still a divisive factor in the politics of New York. Before the meeting in Washington at which Clinton was nominated for Vice President, a legislative caucus of the party in Albany, which was attended also by a number of other Republicans from various parts of the state, unanimously resolved to support Morgan Lewis for governor.[21] At that stage in the development of party machinery, this was as near an official nomination as one could get, and Lewis may be said to have had the Organization behind him. In the meantime, however, a rival faction had nominated Burr. Though Jefferson's preference for the candidate of the dominant Clinton-Livingston faction cannot be doubted, he followed his consistent policy in declining to express himself with respect to this local election. Some of Burr's supporters took advantage of this policy of ostensible neutrality by claiming that the President thought Burr as good a Republican as

[19] TJ to Duane, dated July 24, 1803, not sent, and to Gallatin, July 25, 1803 (Ford, VIII, 255–260); Gallatin to TJ, Aug. 11, 1803 (*Writings*, I, 134–135). The factional quarrels in Pennsylvania at this time are described in Cunningham, pp. 213–217, and Higginbotham, pp. 39–65. TJ had removed a threat to party unity in 1802 by appointing to the collectorship of the port of Philadelphia Peter Muhlenberg, a rival of McKean for the governorship. Other appointees of his, notably A. J. Dallas, U.S. Attorney, were from the rival faction. Interesting comments on Republican divisions, especially in Philadelphia, are in various letters to TJ from his old landlord Thomas Leiper, such as Sept. 9, 1802 (LC, 21754–21755).

[20] TJ to Joseph Scott, Mar. 9, 1804, and to Thomas Leiper, June 11 (Ford, VIII, 304–305).

[21] Feb. 20, 1804. For an excellent account of developments in New York, see Cunningham, pp. 148–152, 209–213.

Lewis.[22] On the other hand, supporters of the "regular" candidate denied that he regarded Burr's "little band" as genuinely Republican and asserted that Burr himself was hostile to the administration. Gideon Granger had reported that the President retained the confidence of everyone.[23] In this statement, however, the Postmaster General could hardly have intended to include Burr.

Shortly before the vote in New York was reported in Washington, the unsympathetic British minister said that the only thing that could cause the President trouble would be the election of Burr as governor.[24] Anthony Merry was well aware of what this would mean to the bitterest of Jefferson's political foes, some of whom had been talking of disunion. Jefferson seems to have known less of their machinations than Merry did; and he certainly did not know as much about them as we do now, since he did not have access to their private correspondence. No doubt he quickly learned that many of the Federalists in New York talked of supporting Burr; and before the election there he was apprised of a scheme to form a coalition between Federalists and dissident Republicans in seven eastern states. After one of his chief sentinels, Gideon Granger, told him about this in conversation, he said that the idea was new to him. Presumably this was shortly before April 1. He left Washington for his dying daughter's bedside on that date and remained away for six weeks. On reflection he was in no doubt that the idea was "to form the basis of a separation of the Union," but he was in neither the mood nor the position to do anything about it. Apart from what he said in one letter written at Monticello, there seems to be no record of his having made any reference to this particular threat at the time.[25]

He was well aware that he was faced by a hard core of irreconcilables and often referred to them as desperate. He had told Governor McKean that their attacks on him had compelled him to seek vindication at the polls. His words to his former secretary, William Short, put issues on a higher plane and were actually more in character: "They can never now excite a pain in my mind by anything personal," he said, "but I wish to consolidate the nation, and to see these people dis-

[22] Cunningham, p. 210, reprints a handbill containing an assertion to that effect.
[23] Granger to DeWitt Clinton, Mar. 27, 1804 (quoted by Cunningham, p. 211, from DeWitt Clinton Papers, Columbia University).
[24] Merry to Hawkesbury, Apr. 29, 1804 (FO, 5:41, No. 31, pp. 163–165).
[25] TJ to Granger Apr. 16, 1804 (Ford VIII, 298–300). He referred in this letter to his latest conversation with Granger. A letter of Apr. 8 from the latter gave information about the elections in New Hampshire but made no reference to New York or schemes of disunion. The election in New York was on Apr. 25. TJ was back in Washington on May 13.

armed either of the wish or the power to injure their country." [26] He
believed they had spurned his attempts at reconciliation and wholly
failed to credit him with resistance to extreme partisan zeal among his
own supporters, especially in the matter of removals and appointments.
Paradoxical though it may seem, this extraordinarily effective party
leader, who was so markedly successful in inspiriting his followers, was
in fact a moderating influence on them during their ascendancy. Also,
this enemy of governmental consolidation had narrowed the gap between the executive and the legislative majority (thus occasioning
charges of encroachment), and this alleged advocate of state rights, by
pressing the national as well as the popular interest, had served to unify
the country. That is, most of it. Judging from the growth of his party
in New England, his efforts to bring that region within the fold were
far from futile, but the focus of unyielding opposition to him was still,
and now more than ever, in the northeastern part of the country. The
Louisiana Purchase had augmented the desperation of irreconcilables,
accentuating fears in the East and increasing resentment of the political
dominance of Virginia.

More than a decade earlier, acidulous Senator William Maclay of the
Pennsylvania backcountry had predicted that with the removal of the
government to the banks of the Potomac it would probably fall under
fresh influences, and that the New Englanders might then become "re-
fractory" and endeavor to "unhinge" it. His judgment of the character
of the Easterners led him to believe that they would "cabal against and
endeavor to subvert" any government they could not manage.[27] Basic in
this political conflict, as in most others, was the struggle for power, and
there was danger of resentful obstruction on the part of the displaced leaders. Senator John Quincy Adams, who had broader vision
than most of his Federalist colleagues and regarded himself as a man of
principle rather than partisanship, deplored the intensity of the latter.
In his diary he recorded these reflections: "The country is so totally
given up to the spirit of party, that not to follow blindfold the one or
the other is an inexpiable offence. The worst of these parties has the
popular torrent in its favor, and uses its triumph with all the unprincipled fury of a faction; while the other gnashes its teeth, and is waiting
with all the impatience of revenge for the time when its turn may come
to oppress and punish by the people's favor." [28] While objecting to the
Republicans more than to the Federalists, he would pronounce a plague

---

[26] TJ to William Short, Jan. 23, 1804 (*A.H.R.*, XXXIII, 834).
[27] July 22, 1790. *Journal of William Maclay* (1927), pp. 331–332; see *Jefferson
and the Rights of Man*, p. 303.
[28] Dec. 31, 1803 (J. Q. Adams, *Memoirs*, I, 282–283).

on both their houses. His fears of the former were increased by the impeachment proceedings against federal judges, and he drew closer to Timothy Pickering on this issue, but Adams had no sympathy whatever with the spirit of disunion, which was so strongly manifested at this time by his senatorial colleague. From the private correspondence of the time Pickering emerges as the best symbol of embittered sectionalism and the chief proponent of "a new confederacy, exempt from the corrupt and corrupting influence and oppression of the aristocratic Democrats of the South." [29]

Since this disunionist movement was secret as well as abortive, it is chiefly significant as a revelation of the mood of a few irreconcilable Federalist leaders — of the violence of their hostility to the administration, and, at the same time, of the basic weakness of their position vis-à-vis the President. Though fears of the subordination of New England in the enlarged Republic were by no means unnatural, and reasonable men might have been concerned for the independence of the judiciary and the maintenance of balance in the government, the dangers anticipated at the hands of the present "rulers" of the country, as described in the private correspondence of these Federalist leaders, now seem quite fantastic. Jefferson himself referred to "certain Jacobinical, atheistical, anarchical, imaginary caricatures" which had been created to frighten the credulous.[30] Though his arch foes referred to the danger of both anarchy and despotism, which were in fact antithetical, and assumed the mantle of virtue and constitutionalism according to immemorial political practice, what they really feared was democracy. George Cabot regarded this as "the government of the worst"; and John Adams, yet unmellowed in his retirement, likened it to a rake, full of fair promises, who seduced a trustful maid.[31]

Pickering thus described and commented on Jefferson: "The coward wretch at the head, while, like a Parisian revolutionary monster, prating about humanity, could feel an infernal pleasure in the utter destruction of his opponents. We have too long witnessed his general turpitude

---

[29] Pickering to Richard Peters, Dec. 24, 1803 (Henry Adams, *Documents Relating to New England Federalism* [1887], p. 338). Contemporary correspondence bearing on the "secession plot" of 1804 is given in this work, pp. 338–366, along with the later account by J. Q. Adams (pp. 144–170, passim). See also the letters of King, IV, ch. 23. Henry Adams's account of this episode in his *History*, II, ch. 8, is a classic requiring virtually no retouching. An excellent recent account is that of L. W. Turner in *William Plumer of New Hampshire* (1962), ch. 8; see also his Appendix A.

[30] TJ to Timothy Bloodworth, Jan. 29, 1804 (L. & B., X, 443).

[31] Cabot to Pickering, Feb. 14, 1804, in Henry Adams, *Documents*, p. 346–349; John Adams to William Cunningham, Mar. 15, 1804, in his *Correspondence* with the latter (1823), pp. 18–19.

— his cruel removals of faithful officers, and the substitution of corruption and baseness for integrity and worth." [32] Detestation of those who disagreed with him was in Pickering's character, but his bitterness was accentuated by the President's extraordinary political success, and the New Englander's natural gloom was intensified by the acquisition of Louisiana. This seemed to assure the continued dominance of the slave-holding South and the West — to the habits, views, and interests of which the East could not reconcile itself. In this desperate situation the logical procedure, as he saw it, was to move toward separation. The first steps must be taken in New England, where both virtue and indignation reached their highest point, but New York was indispensable to the eastern confederacy, and New Jersey might be expected to join it. There appears to have been no hope of Pennsylvania, and little Delaware seems to have been quite overlooked, despite its rejection of the Twelfth Amendment — which New Jersey promptly approved, as did Vermont and Rhode Island along with Republican New York. At no time did Pickering as a would-be separatist receive any encouragement from the major Federalists in New York, Alexander Hamilton and Rufus King. Worst of all, he quickly learned that the disunionists could not rely on the Federalist leaders of Massachusetts, the state which he had hoped would take the lead.

The comments on Pickering's proposals by sagacious George Cabot, who undoubtedly spoke for others besides himself, ought to have thoroughly squelched the secession movement and did serve to deflect it. While readily agreeing with respect to existing evils and dire future prospects, he doubted if separation in itself would cure the ills of democracy; and he regarded disunion as thoroughly impracticable in the absence of a sufficiently appealing grievance. Such a grievance might be a war against Great Britain, provoked by the country's rulers, as indeed, in the next decade, the War of 1812 was adjudged by certain New Englanders to be. Meanwhile, Cabot believed that a "wholly popular" government would inevitably go from bad to worse until intolerable evils would "generate their own remedies." That is, the course of wisdom was to wait. [33]

Negotiations in connection with this stillborn plot seem to have been generally if not always bilateral; there appears to be no record of the meeting of a group. Its main strength lay in the Connecticut River Valley, whence nearly all of its known participants except Pickering

[32] Pickering to King, Mar. 4, 1804 (King, IV, 364).
[33] Cabot's letter of Feb. 14, 1804, to Pickering is extensively quoted and admirably discussed by Henry Adams in his *History*, II, 164–167. He regards Cabot's reply as too gentle.

came.[34] Roger Griswold and Uriah Tracy of Connecticut were involved in it, though the latter did not give John Quincy Adams that impression. Senators Samuel Hurt and William Plumer of New Hampshire were in it, though the latter was not a prime mover and John Quincy Adams did not learn of his involvement until two decades later, when Plumer described his participation as his greatest political mistake.[05] Adams was unalterably opposed to it at all times, and disunionism was not in the spirit of Hamilton or Rufus King.

Rebuffed by the wisest and ablest leaders of their own party, the persistent irreconcilables turned their eyes to Burr, thus compounding the political mistake they had made in 1801. Claiming that he spoke for the congressional Federalists in general, Pickering expressed the belief that only Burr could break the "Democratic phalanx" in New York. Writing Rufus King, he said:

Were New York detached (as under his [Burr's] administration it would be) from the Virginia influence, the whole Union should be benefited. Jefferson would then be forced to observe some caution and forbearance in his measures. And if a *separation* should be deemed proper, the five New England States, New York and New Jersey would naturally be united. Among those seven States there is a sufficient congeniality of character to authorize the expectation of practicable harmony and a permanent union; New York the centre. Without a separation, can those States ever rid themselves of negro Presidents and negro Congresses, and regain their just weight in the political balance? . . .[36]

Before he got this letter King had already received one from Hamilton, urging him to run for governor, so as to keep Federalist votes *away from* Burr. King declined to do this, but he gave slight comfort to Pickering. He believed that with certain exceptions (of whom Hamilton was the most eminent) the Federalists of New York would vote for Burr, but that they would not be enough to elect him.[37] Hamilton was so alarmed that he actively opposed Burr, using language which occasioned, in the summer, the most famous of American duels and the loss to the Federalist party of its greatest mind.[38] Burr would probably have lost the election anyway. It was held on April 25, while Jefferson

---

[34] Turner, *Plumer,* p. 142.

[35] Plumer to J. Q. Adams, Dec. 20, 1828 (H. Adams, *Documents*, pp. 144–146).

[36] Pickering to King, Mar. 4, 1804 (King, IV, 365). His reference to "negro Presidents" and "negro Congresses" relates to the constitutional provision for representation on the basis of free persons plus three-fifths of the slaves.

[37] Hamilton to King, and King to Hamilton, Feb. 24, 1804 (King, IV, 351–354); King to Pickering, Mar. 9, 1804 (King, IV, 367–368).

[38] See below, ch. XXIII.

was still at Monticello, and the full report on it was slow to come in. When he got back to Washington in the middle of May, he was assured that Morgan Lewis had administered a decisive defeat to Burr. George Clinton sent him a letter to that effect and he could soon read a long editorial about it in the *National Intelligencer*. That paper described it as "glorious to the cause of republicanism" and conclusive evidence of the "almost universal prevalence of principle among the republicans of the United States." [39] At any rate, there could be little doubt that in New York they were overwhelmingly loyal to the administration. Also, the failure of the attempt to strike at Jefferson through promoting the fortunes of Burr demonstrated anew the political unwisdom of his bitterest enemies, who showed themselves here to be abysmally poor judges of public opinion as well as of human character.

What would have happened to their reputations if their private letters had been exposed to public view can readily be imagined. Anthony Merry, who relished disunionist talk, reported to his government after the defeat of Burr that word had got into the papers of secret meetings of certain Federalist members of Congress during the last session, looking toward the separation of the eastern states, but the extent of this publicity remains to be determined. He reported that, following this discovery, the Federalists were completely silent; and to him it seemed that the influence of the democratic party had extended itself into every quarter. In effect he agreed with George Cabot that its influence would continue to increase until it should have produced "so much injustice and disorder throughout the country as to occasion a revolt." [40] The British Minister looked toward an eventual separation, and, as his later actions showed, was disposed to encourage it. Later events were also to show that certain irreconcilables in New England had merely shelved the idea, and were keeping it for future reference. At the moment, however, the inescapable political fact was that the President and his party were undermining the Federalists in their own sanctuaries.

Nowhere was this more strikingly manifest than in the state of New Hampshire, both of whose senators were involved in the secession

[39] George Clinton to TJ, May 7, 1804 (LC, 24303), received May 14; *National Intelligencer*, May 16, 1804. The report of May 11 in that paper left no doubt of Burr's defeat.

[40] Merry to Hawkesbury, June 2, 1804 (FO, 5:42). In a letter of May 7 (FO, 5:41, p. 166) he referred to a "public suggestion" of the separation of the eastern states, with an exhortation from "an individual of New England." I have not learned just what or whom he was talking about. It may be noted that the Boston *Independent Chronicle*, July 23, 1804, in connection with the announcement of the death of Hamilton, mentioned and deplored talk of the secession of Massachusetts, but spoke in vague and general terms.

movement. The March elections there were so favorable to the Republicans that the Assembly not only ratified the Twelfth Amendment; it also adopted resolutions approving of the conduct of the administration in Washington and deploring the abuse and vilification of the President and principal officers in the press. The Governor proceeded, however, to veto both actions, whether or not he had the constitutional right to do so.[41] Thus William Plumer's state was not listed among those that voted affirmatively, but actually only three rejected the amendment: Delaware, Massachusetts, and Connecticut. And, although it could not be proclaimed until late September, the virtual certainty of the amendment's adoption before the election was recognized by as unfriendly an observer as Anthony Merry in the month of May. When the President got back to Washington after six weeks at Monticello he faced political prospects that had never been brighter. But he had left behind him in the graveyard on the hillside the younger of his two daughters, cut down long before her time. To his old college friend John Page he wrote: "Others may lose of their abundance, but I, of my want, have lost even the half of all I had. My evening prospects now hang on the slender thread of a single life." [42]

[41] *National Intelligencer*, July 4, 1804; resolutions in issue of July 2. The actions were taken in late June.
[42] TJ to Page, June 25, 1804 (L. & B., XI, 31).

[XXII]

Tragic Interlude

THE most noteworthy fact about the President's family in the winter of 1803–1804 was that the men were all at the seat of government in Washington while the women and children were rusticating in
Albemarle County. Though he could not have his daughters and grandchildren with him, Jefferson gained great pleasure from the presence of
his two sons-in-law in the President's House. Their independent political careers occasioned him some embarrassment, however. Through the
years, sensitive and quick-tempered Thomas Mann Randolph, who was
now thirty-five, presented his solicitous father-in-law with more problems than did John Wayles Eppes, who was about five years younger.
Mr. Randolph, as both Jefferson and Martha always referred to him,
had entered the race for Congress from the President's own district in
the spring of 1803 without consulting that astute gentleman and to the
great annoyance of the incumbent, Samuel J. Cabell, who had spent
two nights on his blanket to make Jefferson President (during the balloting in the House to break the electoral tie with Burr), and who now
believed that the ungrateful beneficiary had set up his son-in-law
against him.[1] After hearing this report, Jefferson, in a letter to Cabell,
denied that he had instigated Randolph to challenge his old friend, and
said that, when he heard of it, he tried to prepare his son-in-law for a
failure. Otherwise, he had stuck to his policy of non-interference in
local elections.

This one was all the more embarrassing because of its indecisive-
ness. Randolph had a tiny majority, but there were "bad votes" on both
sides, and the count was contested.[2] His situation would have been

[1] JWE reported this to TJ, Apr. 14, 1803 (Edgehill-Randolph Papers, UVA).
[2] TJ to Cabell, Apr. 25, 1803 (LC, 22638); TMR to TJ, Apr. 29, 1803 (Edgehill-
Randolph Papers, UVA); TJ to TMR, May 5, 1803 (LC, 22670); TMR to TJ,
May 22, 1803 (LC, 22736).

more tolerable, he said, if he had been defeated. He was seated, along with Eppes, on the first day of the congressional session in the fall; but a memorial by Cabell, with depositions and other documents relating to the contested election, was presented the next day and referred to the Committee on Elections. The committee did not report for nearly five months, attributing its delay to the request of Cabell that he be allowed to produce further documents and to his failure to appear, when requested, to present his case. After examining the documents submitted to them, the committee saw no sufficient ground for invalidating Randolph's claim.[3] Cabell did not push his case, and at this distance we cannot determine whether or not it had merit. Almost immediately upon becoming assured of his seat, the President's elder son-in-law made his first and longest congressional speech.[4] He played a negative role until nearly the end of the congressional session, presumably because of the uncertainty of his position. Though often brash, he was an insecure person, whom his father-in-law frequently took occasion to reassure.

Eppes was less given to self-questioning and suffered from no doubt about his status in Congress. He had been elected to the seat from Southside Virginia that was voluntarily vacated by the redoubtable William Branch Giles for reasons of health; and he tangled, perhaps unwittingly, with the even more redoubtable John Randolph early in his first session. He then offered a resolution calling for instructions to the Ways and Means Committee which the high-spirited chairman of that committee regarded as unnecessary if not presumptuous. In opposing this resolution, John Randolph asserted his freedom to exercise his own judgment "without any consideration of the quarter from which a motion comes."[5] The opposition press quickly seized upon this expression as a slap at the President, but John Randolph hastened to assure Jefferson that such was not the case, saying that he would not directly or indirectly attack "a character for which I have uniformly felt and expressed the highest esteem and veneration." In his reply to this the President said that no explanation was necessary from one who had given so many proofs of friendship. Adopting the most favorable interpretation of the expression, he claimed to understand perfectly that the reference was not to his own fireside but to the Republican quarter of

---

[3] *Annals*, 8 Cong., 1 sess., pp. 373 (Oct. 18, 1803), 1128 (Mar. 9, 1804).
[4] TMR spoke, Mar. 10, 1804, on the question of Georgia claims (*Annals*, 8 Cong., 1 sess., pp. 1138–1153); described in W. H. Gaines, Jr., *Thomas Mann Randolph* (1966), pp. 54–56.
[5] Nov. 25, 1803 (*Annals*, 8 Cong., 1 sess., p. 626).

the House.[6] He went on to say that no one should presume that what came from his sons-in-law came from him:

> No men on earth are more independent in their sentiments than they are, nor any one less disposed than I am to influence the opinions of others. We rarely speak of politics, or of the proceedings of the House, but merely historically, and I carefully avoid expressing an opinion on them, in their presence, that we may all be at our ease.

He may have had his relations with the Majority Leader particularly in mind when he suggested that "mutual delicacy" had prevented as full an exchange of opinions between him and members of Congress as was desirable. At all events, he sought to be reassuring. "I see too many proofs of the imperfection of human reason, to entertain wonder or intolerance at any difference of opinion on any subject," he said, "and acquiesce in that difference as easily as on a difference of feature or form." With reference to the irreconcilable Federalists this was an overstatement, but it unquestionably represented his characteristic attitude toward those who were in basic political agreement with him, and certainly toward the adult members of his own family. To his sons-in-law he manifested generosity which at times must have seemed overwhelming, but in intimate personal relations he was a disciple of *laissez faire*.

As good Republicans and sensible men, Messrs. Randolph and Eppes voted for the Twelfth Amendment early in December, and soon after that they went to Albemarle to see their respective families. Congress did not recess for Christmas, but while waiting for news from Louisiana it did little more than meet and adjourn. The President did not stir from Washington; he had to be there when word came from New Orleans, and he paid little heed to Christmas anyway. Had he been at Monticello on that day he could have seen his latest grandchild, a little girl, then less than two months old, whom his prolific elder daughter had named Mary. Though inclined to indulge in marital jokes, especially with men, Jefferson generally had recourse to circumlocutions when speaking to his daughters of pregnancies and accouchements. Having informed Eppes in June that Patsy was "fattening for an autumn exhibition," he remarked to her in November that she was approaching an "interesting term." He suggested precautions, but, judging from the past, probably expected her to have no more trouble bearing her seventh child than she had had with the others. Apparently there was no

[6] John Randolph to TJ, Nov. 30, 1803 (LC, 23587); TJ to John Randolph, Dec. 1, 1803 (Ford, VIII, 281–282).

thought that her young husband should leave Congress and make the three-days' journey to be with her, and the report of events that duly came was good. Rejoicing that Martha and her "new bantling" were both well, her father hoped that her example would be an encouragement to Maria.[7]

The Christmas visit from her husband could not have failed to raise the spirits of that anxious young matron, but Eppes was back in Washington before the President held court on New Year's, and if Thomas Mann Randolph did not return with him he came soon thereafter.[8] Martha and Maria were at Edgehill, counting the days until the latter's deliverance and hoping for the earliest possible adjournment of Congress. The letter the President wrote his younger daughter the day after Christmas, while solicitous, may not have encouraged her as much as he supposed. Of her "expected indisposition" he said: "You are prepared to meet it with courage I hope. Some female friend of your Mama's (I forget whom) used to say it was no more than a knock of the elbow." [9] This comment was of a kind with his jocular but rather insensitive earlier remark about a woman's "trade." In the light of the gynecology, obstetrics, and pediatrics of our own time, it is easier for us than it was for him to recognize how onerous and precarious that trade was in the early nineteenth century. Martha, who bore children with such ease, soon reported to him about her sister. "Maria's spirits are bad," she said, "partly occasioned by her situation which precludes every thing like comfort or chearfulness, and partly from the prospect of Congress not rising till April which Mr. Randolph writes us is the general opinion. I hope we shall do as well as if Mr. Eppes was here but certainly her mind would be more at ease could he be with her." [10] They were also worried about little Francis, whose general health was good but who had "dreadful fits" which Martha feared were epileptic. Her father expressed the hope that these would be outgrown, as he did that Congress would rise in March instead of April.

Maria wrote her husband early in February that if she could believe this it would revive her more than anything.[11] She often found it hard to bear up against sickness, confinement, and separation from him, she said. Her health had grown steadily worse. Her stomach had become so weak that she could hardly retain anything, yet she dared take no medicine in her present condition. She told him not to be uneasy, however.

---

[7] TJ to JWE, June 19, 1803 (UVA); to Martha, Nov. 7, 1803, and to Maria, Nov. 27 (*Family Letters*, pp. 248–249).
[8] JWE voted in Congress Dec. 29, 1803, and TMR on Jan. 2, 1804.
[9] TJ to Maria, Dec. 26, 1803 (*Family Letters*, p. 250).
[10] Martha to TJ, Jan. 14, 1804 (*Family Letters*, p. 252).
[11] Maria to JWE, Feb. 6, 1804 (UVA).

She would soon be able to give him "the intelligence most interesting and most desired." When they should meet she would present him with "so sweet an addition" to their felicity that it would compensate for almost any suffering. Also, Francis had improved so much in talking that the little boy would be able to carry on a conversation with him when he returned. At all times this fading young woman spoke with deep affection of her own father, but her thought was centered on her absent husband, whom she addressed here as "best beloved of my soul" and from whom she hoped she would never again be parted.

Jefferson continued to be relatively optimistic about the end of Congress and suggested that Mr. Eppes might join her even sooner. He was hoping, however, that she would let them all see that she had within herself "the resources of a courage not requiring the presence of any body." [12] He and his granddaughter Anne Cary had been corresponding on the subject of raising bantams. He reported that he had received two pairs of beautiful fowls from Algiers. When they met in March all of them would discuss this fascinating subject, he predicted, and soon thereafter they would begin leveling Pantops for Maria and build a henhouse there. Because of her low health and spirits Maria left his letters long unanswered, but she managed to write him one before her hour came. In it she reminded him of his promise to let Saint-Mémin do his picture at the first chance. Expecting the artist to be in Washington that month, she asked that he grant her and her sister this favor. "If you did but know what a source of pleasure it would be to us while so much separated from you to have so excellent a likeness of you, you would not I think refuse us. It is what we have always most wanted all our lives and the certainty with which he takes his likenesses makes this one request I think not unreasonable." Saint-Mémin did make a portrait of Jefferson, after tracing his profile with the aid of the physiognotrace, but this was some months too late to do Maria any good.[13]

Within two weeks of his receipt of this letter, the last she is known to have written him, Jefferson was writing Maria to congratulate her on the "happy accession" to her family. The reports he had received led him to believe that the crisis was over and all was well. Within a week, however, he learned that such was far from the case. Only the impossibility of leaving Congress to proceed on its business without him prevented his instant departure, he then said. But, Congress or no Congress, her husband would be on his way, and her father hoped that

[12] TJ to Maria, Jan. 29, 1804 (*Family Letters*, p. 256).
[13] Maria to TJ, Feb. 10, 1804 (*ibid.*, p. 256); the portrait was drawn Nov. 27, 1804. See below, pp. 437–439.

his arrival would "render her spirits triumphant over her physical debility."[14]

Young Mr. Eppes had a terrible journey. Because of high winds he could not cross the Potomac by ferry and had to proceed by the bridge upstream and thence by unfamiliar roads on which he lost his way. Impeded by ice thereafter, for long stretches he had to walk his horse. On his arrival at Edgehill he promptly wrote his father-in-law, as he did by every post thereafter, though this could be no oftener than twice a week and some of his letters took more than the customary three days to get to Washington.[15] The first one was encouraging. Since Maria was free from fever, sitting up, and at the moment had no complaint but weakness, her husband now had no fear but that she would soon be restored to health. The baby, a little girl named for her mother, was thriving. During her illness Maria had wholly lost her milk, but Martha was nursing the infant with her own.

Much relieved in spirit by this firsthand report, Jefferson suggested recourse to light food and cordial wines to overcome his daughter's debility.[16] "The sherry at Monticello is old and genuine," he said, "and the Pedro Ximenes much older still and stomachic. Her palate and stomach will be the best arbiters between them." By the time he got home, which he now believed might be on April 1, he hoped Maria would be well enough to go to Monticello. He wrote her husband: "The house, its contents, and appendages and servants, are as freely subjected to you as to myself and I hope you will make it your home till we can get you fixed at Pantops." He did not think that Maria should be ventured "below" — that is, in Southside Virginia. Her husband shared this sentiment and promptly agreed to Jefferson's proposal, for that spring and summer at least. He could report no improvement in his wife's condition, however; she was threatened with an abscess in her breast and virtually unable to take nourishment of any sort. Hoping that the change of air would do her good, they took her to Monticello before the Master himself returned. She made the journey from Edgehill to her birthplace in a litter borne by human hands. The burden was light but the way was four miles long, and the bearers had to cross a ford and ascend a little mountain.

Congress did not adjourn until March 27, and the President of the

[14] TJ to Maria, Feb. 26, Mar. 3, 1804, and to Martha, Mar. 8, 1804, after the receipt of a more encouraging report (*ibid.*, pp. 258–259). The child was born Feb. 15. Eppes was expected to arrive Mar. 6. He was not in Congress when TMR gained assurance of his seat and made his long speech.
[15] JWE to TJ, Mar. 9, 12, 19, 23, 26, 1804, in Edgehill-Randolph Papers, UVA.
[16] TJ to JWE, Mar. 15, 1804 (Randall, III, 98–99).

United States could not leave town until April 1, the day on which he had hoped to arrive at Monticello. The last word he had received had been moderately reassuring: at least his daughter was no worse. While champing the bit in Washington, this incessantly industrious man, besides performing his normal official tasks, did something to set his house in order. He offered the post of private secretary to William A. Burwell, since Lewis Harvie was leaving him to practice law. And this generous host, taking a look at his cellar, engaged in a characteristic calculation — no doubt relieving his troubled mind in the process. The 651 persons who had dined at his table since December 1 had consumed 207 bottles of champagne — that is, one bottle had sufficed for $3\frac{1}{7}$ persons. He concluded, therefore, that he needed 500 a year to be safe, and actually ordered forty dozen.[17] It may be asusmed that he allowed for the time he was normally out of Washington — which was to be beyond the average this year — and for less dining and drinking during the blessed intervals between congressional sessions. It was about the time Congress rose that Gideon Granger gave him an inkling of the designs of certain eastern Federalists, whom he rightly suspected of being disunionists. He gave some thought to them after he got home, and, while he could dismiss from his mind the past social season, including the antics of Merry and Yrujo, he always had to attend to routine official business at Monticello. But affairs of state were not what was at issue there.

A few days after his arrival he described the situation to Madison: "I found my daughter Eppes at Monticello, whither she had been brought on a litter by hand, so weak as barely to be able to stand, her stomach so disordered as to reject almost every thing she took into it, a constant small fever, & an imposthume [abscess] rising in her breast." He himself had regulated her food, he said. Her first imposthume had broken, but they feared a second, which might "countervail the effect of her present regimen." Though not without hope of restoring her by wine and digestible food, he gave no impression of confidence, nor did he display any emotion in what amounted to a clinical report. "Her spirits and confidence are favorably affected by my being with her," he said, "and aid the effects of regimen." [18]

He did more to give himself away in what he wrote his most intimate political associate on his own unmentioned birthday, though here, also, he was starkly factual:

[17] Account Book, Mar. 20, 1804; to James Taylor, Mar. 25, 1804 (MHS). After he got back to Washington he ordered more.
[18] TJ to Madison, Apr. 9, 1804 (MP-Rives, 2:486).

Our spring is remarkably uncheary, A North West wind has been blowing three days. Our peachtrees blossomed the 1st day of this month; the poplar began to leaf, so as to be sensible at a distance about the 7th. Asparagus shewed itself about 5 days ago; perhaps we may have a dish to-day or tomorrow. But my beds are in a state of total neglect, & therefore not a fair measure of the season My daughter exhibits little change. No new Imposthume has come on, but she rather weakens. Her fever is small & constant. Affectionate salutations.[19]

Ten days later he added to a routine letter to Madison about public business a personal paragraph in which he said: "On the 17th instant our hopes and fears here took their ultimate form. I had originally intended to have left this towards the end of the present week. But a desire to see my family in a state of more composure before we separate will keep me somewhat longer." Giving the probabilities of his schedule, he asked his secretary of state to inform the other heads of department, so that they might govern themselves accordingly with respect to his mail.[20] This may also have been his roundabout way of informing them of just what had happened. It was a week later that a notice appeared in the *National Intelligencer;* in this Mrs. Maria Eppes was designated as the wife of John W. Eppes, Esquire, and daughter of Thomas Jefferson, Esquire.[21] In his ever-present Account Book, where he recorded momentous personal events along with all varieties of expenditure, the latter gentleman had made a laconic entry, presumably in the evening of April 17: "This morning between 8 & 9 o'clock my dear daughter Maria Eppes died." Born on August 1, 1778, at 1:30 A.M., as he had also recorded, she had not yet reached twenty six. He could not have failed to remember that her mother, after having borne him six children of whom only two grew up, had died when she was nearing thirty-four. Nor could this natural philosopher have failed to reflect on the gross wastefulness of Nature.

He once told Maria that she had been a source of pure and unmixed happiness, but if ever he drew a pen picture of her, which is most unlikely, he took care that no profane eye should ever see it. And, so far as the existing record shows, he revealed his grief in words to very few. As he himself said, it was inexpressible. The most intimate account of her last days — and one of the few of her as a person — is from the hand of one of Martha's daughters, who was eight years old when her

[10] TJ to Madison, Apr. 13, 1804 (MP-Rives, 2:488).
[20] TJ to Madison, Apr. 23, 1804 (Ford, VIII, 300).
[21] *National Intelligencer*, Apr. 30, 1804.

aunt died and drew on family tradition as well as childish recollection in writing to her grandfather's biographer half a century later.[22] The memory of Maria's beauty and her indifference to it, of her modesty and her fear that she could never equal her sister in her father's eyes, persisted in the family. But in her expressions of devotion to her prodigious father, effusive though these sometimes were, she rarely went as far as Martha; and Jefferson himself had long ago perceived that her affections were not and could not be expected to be concentrated on him to the same degree. Deprived of her own mother, she had spent her early childhood at Eppington, not at Monticello, and she had not wanted to leave that pleasant home for a strange place and unknown people when her father summoned her to join him and her elder sister in Paris.[23] Her Aunt Eppes was a mother to her long before becoming her mother-in-law, and her Cousin Jack was a playmate long before he became a husband to whom she was passionately devoted.

While Jefferson was well aware, during the early years of separation from her, that he was in danger of losing his daughter, he refused to recognize any clash of loyalties in her maturity. He genuinely liked her husband and treated him, as he did Martha's, like a son. Though he tried to get the young couple established near him at Pantops and insisted on their periodic visits to Monticello, he was genuinely concerned for their health and well-being and can hardly be adjudged possessive on these grounds alone. But, though excessively generous and extraordinarily tender, he had an all-pervading personality. In her teens he had expected too much of the less intellectual and more beautiful of his two daughters, and, even after she had grown up, Maria probably was uncomfortable at times, more so than her sister ever was, in the shadow of this giant. Less outgoing than Martha and saddened by ill health, Maria was more conscious of her inadequacies and probably more aware of the clash of loyalties than anybody else. She may have reproached herself that in being an Eppes she was less a Jefferson than she would have liked to be, and less than Martha always was. This is somewhat speculative, but in death her father's claim to her was unquestioned. Of the funeral services we only know that an old schoolmate of his, the Rev. Matthew Maury, officiated.[24] She was buried in the hillside graveyard where for more than a score of years her mother had lain sleeping and

[22] Ellen Wayles Coolidge (née Randolph) to H. S. Randall, Jan. 15, 1856 (Randall, III, 101–103; also, *Domestic Life*, pp. 299–302).

[23] See *Jefferson and the Rights of Man*, p. 134.

[24] In his Account Book, Apr. 25, 1804, TJ wrote: "Inclosed to Mr. Maury 16 D. for attendance at funeral." Matthew Maury, son of James Maury, TJ's old teacher, had succeeded his father as rector of Walker's Church and as a school-master.

where John Wayles Eppes never was to join her. Indisputably in death, if not wholly in life, she was her father's daughter.[25]

Jefferson's own ties with the Eppes family were far from being severed. They could not be as long as he remembered his own wife, and the immediate effect of Maria's untimely death was actually to strengthen them. Before the President went back to Washington, Francis and Elizabeth Eppes, who had cared for Polly after her mother's death, arrived from Eppington. They soon took charge of the motherless infant, who had been named Maria. Little Francis and Anne Cary Randolph also accompanied them when they returned home; and they later sent the carriage back for Martha, who visited them for several weeks. The supposition was that all the children would be at Monticello when Jefferson was there in August; and events until then disproved his forebodings about summers spent away from the mountains, since they thrived under grandpaternal care. Fortunately he did not yet know how brief little Maria's span of years would be.

Writing her father in early June, Jefferson said: "While I live, both of the children will be to me the dearest of all pledges; and I should consider it as increasing our misfortune, should we have less of your society." He had given up none of his plans for Pantops, he said; it could become little Francis's place of residence some day.[26] They afterwards engaged in considerable talk about Pantops and Poplar Forest, but this need not concern us yet. It is worth noting here, however, that when the young widower announced his intention of keeping his son with him as a constant companion, Jefferson expressed the hope that they would have him at the President's House next winter. This they did, to the great satisfaction of his maternal grandfather, who called him a "charming boy." Throughout Jefferson's years young Francis was to remain a living link with a cherished portion of his past.

According to family tradition, Martha, toward the end of the day her sister died, found her father, after hours of solitude, with a Bible in his hands. Such may have been the case, for he was thoroughly familiar with the Scriptures and found in them great comfort, though this was not the sort of thing he often talked about. The letter of consolation his dearest college friend wrote him reflected more conventional piety than he himself displayed. In his response to John Page, however, he came closer to lamentation than he seems to have come in any other

[25] John W. Eppes, who remarried several years later with TJ's full understanding, died Sept. 13, 1823, several years before TJ, and was buried in the Eppes family cemetery near Curdsville, Va.
[26] TJ to JWE, June 4, 1804 (Randall, III, 99).

contemporary letter. It was to this very old friend that he said he had lost half of all he had — that his evening prospects now hung on the thread of a single life.[27] Also bemoaning the loss of friends — by political alienation as well as death — he wondered if a very long life was really desirable. "But," he added, "whatever is to be our destiny, wisdom, as well as duty, dictates that we should acquiesce in the will of Him whose it is to give and take away, and be contented in the enjoyment of those who are still permitted to be with us."

His chief stay and comfort, now and ever thereafter, was his daughter Martha, whose disposition, as her own daughter was to say, "seemed to have the sunshine of heaven in it." [28] Writing her after reaching Washington about the middle of May, her father went into greater detail than usual in describing an exhausting journey through the rain and mud. Never again, he said, would he so forget his age as to subject himself to such fatigue. He was apologetic for writing such a gloomy self-centered letter, but Martha responded with one of her most effusive declarations of devotion:

> No apology can be necessary for writing lengthily to me about your self. I hope you are not yet to learn that no subject on earth *is* or *ever can be* so dear and interesting to me. I speak so entirely without an exception that I do not hesitate to declare if my other duties could possibly interfere with my devotion to you I should not feel a scruple in sacrificing them, to a sentiment which has litterally "grown with my growth and strengthened with my strength," and which no subsequent attachment has in the smallest degree weakened. It is truly the happiness of my life to think that I can dedicate the remainder of it to promote yours. It is a subject however upon which I ought never to write for no pen on earth can do justice to the feelings of my heart.[29]

This extraordinarily robust young woman had recently suffered from stomach cramps, which made breathing difficult. She was convinced that her husband was wholly wrong in attributing these to hysterics and blamed them on eating at the same meal radishes and milk, both of which were unfriendly to her stomach. She was now her healthy self again, however, and there was no reason for her to show her husband her letter of filial devotion.

[27] TJ to John Page, June 25, 1804 (LC, 24511; L. & B., XI, 30–32), replying to Page's letter of May 25 (LC, 24360).
[28] Ellen W. Coolidge to H. S. Randall, Jan. 15, 1856.
[29] TJ to Martha, May 14, 1804; Martha to TJ, May 31, 1804 (*Family Letters*, pp. 259–261).

Jefferson spent ten weeks in Washington (until July 23) before re-turning to Monticello for his customary long visit. No member of his family was with him in the President's House, but his loneliness was relieved by the presence there of his new secretary, William A. Bur-well, a young Virginian aged twenty-four. Anyone who goes through this President's voluminous papers, and observes the innumerable and often trivial details to which he gave personal attention, must wonder what use he actually made of a secretary. He informed Burwell in ad-vance that he wrote his own letters, copying them on a press.[30] This had long been his practice, but he was already experimenting with the polygraph, whereby two or more pens could be operated simultane-ously and, in theory at least, produce identical copies. The American rights to the invention were held by the artist and museum director Charles Willson Peale, with whom Jefferson was on the friendliest of terms for artistic, scientific, and political reasons. Peale sold a two-penned polygraph to Benjamin H. Latrobe, from whom Jefferson pro-ceeded to borrow it. After trying this out he ordered one for himself, making certain comments and particular specifications. Sending this to him, Peale asked him to report every possible objection, since his own purpose was to perfect the machine. Jefferson promptly agreed to communicate such criticisms as might occur to him, saying that it was much easier to object than to solve. This was a couple of days before he left Washington on the springtime visit home that was darkened by the fatal illness of Maria. A week after her death he wrote Peale: "Your Polygraph gave me so much satisfaction that I thought it worth while to bestow some time in contriving one entirely suited to my own con-venience: it was therefore the subject of my meditations on the road, and on my arrival here I made the drawings which I now send you." He then described at length the changes he proposed.[31] That he was able to think of anything but his daughter at this time may seem sur-prising; his ruminations on a bit of mechanism may suggest the triumph of utility over sentiment. But life had to go on, and a fascinating inven-tion provided him with salutary distraction in a period when grave so-licitude was followed by deep grief.

[30] TJ's description of his secretary's duties in his letter of invitation to Burwell, Mar. 26, 1804 (Bixby, pp. 105–106), is the fullest I have seen.
[31] TJ to C. W. Peale, Apr. 23, 1804 (LC, 24210–24211). Interesting earlier letters on this topic are: TJ to B. H. Latrobe, Feb. 26, 1804, and to Peale, Feb. 27 (LC, 23968a, 23976); TJ to Peale, Mar. 1, 1804 (LC, 23988); Peale to TJ, Mar. 5, 1804, and TJ to Peale, Mar. 9 (LC, 24008); Peale to TJ, Mar. 13, 1804 (LC, 24020). For an excellent brief account of the polygraph, see C. C. Sellers, *Peale*, II, 159–161.

JEFFERSON'S POLYGRAPH

The delicacy of its mechanism was a major reason for the failure of the polygraph to gain wide adoption, but this was no deterrent to Jefferson, who enjoyed few things more than tinkering. For months he and his friend Peale corresponded on this subject with the utmost enthusiasm. By the summer after Maria's death, he was fully committed to the polygraph. Before returning to Monticello for his late summer visit, he ordered from Peale another machine for use there, sending him more suggestions and more drawings. When this arrived, after a voyage from Philadelphia to Richmond and thence to Albemarle, an important spring was found broken, but Jefferson ordered another after patching things up. At the same time he declared that after five months' trial he regarded the polygraph as "a most precious invention." So superior to the copying press had he found it that he had wholly discarded the latter.[32] Afterwards, when giving a polygraph away, he referred to it as a "portable secretary." He wanted no other for purposes of writing.

Like his predecessors, Burwell served as a sort of aide-de-camp. His main duties consisted of running errands and helping entertain guests. There was relatively little company during the congressional recess, but, a few weeks after he got back to the capital, Jefferson had visitors who delighted him. Conducted by the irrepressible Peale, the Baron Alexander von Humboldt came to town expressly to see the President.[33] Freshly arrived in Philadelphia from Mexico, Humboldt wrote that gentleman a long letter, voicing his high admiration for Jefferson's actions and writings and the liberalism of his ideas, and describing in considerable detail his expedition of more than four years in South and Central America. Jefferson, who would have been fascinated in any case by the account of such travels and was particularly desirous of learning more about Spanish America, gave him a warm welcome, first by pen and then in person. Accompanied by Peale and two other members of the American Philosophical Society (to which the Baron was soon elected), he visited Washington in June and had dinner with the President. Peale described this as "very elegant" and was much pleased that they drank no toasts and avoided all politics. They discussed natural history, the manners of different nations, and the improvements in life's conveniences — including the polygraph, no doubt.[34] Humboldt himself wrote: "I have had the good fortune to see the first Magistrate

[32] TJ to Peale, Aug. 19, 1804 (LC, 24760). He ordered the second machine June 14 (LC, 24449).

[33] Humboldt's correspondence with TJ (May 24, 1804–Feb. 27, 1825) was published by Helmut de Terra in *Proc. Am. Philos. Soc.*, Vol. 103, pp. 787–795 (Dec., 1959). His letters, written in French, appear there in translation.

[34] Account of visit in Sellers, *Peale*, II, 182–184, including diary entry of June 4, 1804; TJ wrote Dr. Caspar Wister about it June 7 (LC, 24408).

of this great republic living with the simplicity of a philosopher who received me with that profound kindness that makes for a lasting friendship." [35] His correspondence with this "first Magistrate," while not extensive, was indeed lasting: it spread over more than a score of years. To Jefferson himself the meeting was indeed a delightful experience, atoning for the contretemps with Merry and Yrujo and helping keep his mind off his recent domestic tragedy. Shortly before he had the Baron for dinner, however, he received from Abigail Adams a letter of condolence which was not wholly solacing — although, with more care on the part of both of them, it might have been.

About a month after Maria's death, Mrs. Adams wrote him: "Had you been no other than the private inhabitant of Monticello, I should e'er this time have addrest you, with that sympathy which a recent event has awakened in my Bosom. But reasons of various kinds withheld my pen, until the powerful feelings of my heart have burst through the restraint, and called upon me to shed the tear of sorrow over the departed remains of your beloved and deserving daughter, an event which I most sincerely mourn." [36] The account she had read in a newspaper had freshly reminded her of the attachment she had formed for Polly Jefferson, when the little girl was in her care after a long voyage across the Atlantic to join a virtually forgotten father and sister in Paris. That was some seventeen years before, when the Adamses were on Grosvenor Square.[37] For a period of three weeks the sensitive child found another mother in the wife of the Minister to the Court of Saint James's, and that lady, recalling the scene with the utmost tenderness, avowed that the attachment she had then formed for the little girl had endured through all the ensuing years. But, unfortunately, she admitted that she was writing Jefferson only because of this, along with consciousness of parental sorrow arising from her own experience; and, while counseling him to seek comfort in God, she sent him no personal good wishes. Instead, she signed herself as one who had *once* taken pleasure in subscribing herself his friend. Thus she imparted a grudging tone to what might have been, with a few omissions and changes of phrase, a beautiful and wholly compassionate letter.

Before replying to it, the recipient sent it to Maria's husband, asking

[35] Letter of June 27, 1804.

[36] Abigail Adams to TJ, May 20, 1804, received June 2 (punctuation slightly modified). The correspondence between the two, May 20–Oct. 25, 1804, is in *A.-J. Letters*, I, 268–282.

[37] See *Jefferson and the Rights of Man*, pp. 135–137.

him to show it to Martha and then return it.[38] Recognizing Mrs. Adams's expressions of sentiment about Maria as wholly sincere, he incorrectly interpreted her letter as proof that her own friendship for him was in fact unbroken. "It has been a strong one," he wrote his son-in-law, "and has gone through trying circumstances on both sides, yet I retain it strongly both for herself and Mr. Adams." Years later he told Dr. Benjamin Rush that he had recognized the unpromising complexion of her letter, but at this time he gave no sign that he did so. Instead, he said it offered him a welcome opportunity to say that he had never ceased to esteem John Adams. Admitting, however, that one act of his predecessor had given him personal displeasure, the "midnight appointments," he told Eppes that candor would require him to mention that. Presumably he expected the wife of his predecessor to be impressed with his assurance that this had been the *only* one that displeased him. He might have anticipated that she would seize upon it, and he would undoubtedly have been wiser to have written less.[39]

In his reply, he attested graciously to Maria's abiding regard for Mrs. Adams and made appreciative references to his long association with and friendship for her husband — such, in fact, as he often made to his own partisans, who were generally less magnanimous than he. Minimizing his political rivalry with Adams, he took the position that honest differences of opinion constituted no real obstacles to friendship. His predecessor's last appointments, however, he regarded as personally unkind. "It seemed but common justice," he said, "to leave a successor free to act by instruments of his own choice." But, while admitting that he had brooded over this action of Adams's and sometimes talked about it, he said that by now he had cordially forgiven it. Obviously he had not let himself forget it. He claimed that he maintained for Adams "an uniform and high measure of respect and good will" and for Mrs. Adams "a sincere attachment." Having voiced his main personal grievance, there is good reason to believe that he did. He gained relief by unbosoming himself, he said, but he did so at heavy cost, for Mrs. Adams availed herself of this opportunity to express her sentiments on certain actions of *his* which she adjudged unkind, and their correspondence stretched out over a period of five months without getting anywhere.[40]

---

[38] TJ to JWE, June 4, 1804 (Randall, III, 99–100).

[39] As he would also have been in 1791, when his desire to maintain Adams's personal friendship led him to say too much. (See *Jefferson and the Rights of Man*, pp. 364–370.)

[40] TJ replied to her letter June 13, 1804; she replied July 1; he replied July 22; she replied Aug. 18; he replied Sept. 11; and she had the last word on Oct. 25.

He could not possibly explain to her satisfaction the pardoning of James Thomson Callender, whom she regarded as the base libeler and vile slanderer of her husband, though his explanations are of no inconsiderable value to the historian. He made a satisfying reply to her allegation that he had deliberately deprived her son of a minor office, but she voiced her continuing fear that, in his zeal to rectify what he supposed to be the errors of the previous administration, he was being led into measures still more fatal to the Constitution, and even more derogatory to his honor and character. With respect to politics, into the discussion of which they should never have entered, she was irreconcilable and unyielding, and she could not bring herself to extend to him her personal good wishes.

After reading at her request the entire correspondence, of which he had been wholly unaware, John Adams declined to comment on it. Jefferson kept it to himself for seven years. Sending it to Benjamin Rush at the time their common friend was seeking to reconcile him and Adams, he said it was "highly disgraceful" to both parties, "as indicating minds not sufficiently elevated to prevent a public competition from affecting our personal friendship." Dr. Rush, who was then much more concerned with the state of John Adams's mind than with that of his wife, acquitted Jefferson of all impropriety in refusing to renew correspondence with the latter, and claimed to be "delighted with the kindness, benevolence, and even friendship" discovered in his letters. Less than a year later, when Jefferson was indicating his willingness to resume correspondence with John Adams, he told Rush that he could not give Mrs. Adams friendship in return for the sentiments she had expressed, and that she would naturally be excluded from the "fusion of mutual affections." He added: "It will only be necessary that I never name her." [41] A few weeks later, however, her husband, when writing Jefferson, said that she joined him in good wishes. Some months after that she added a postscript to one of her husband's letters to him, and he made this the occasion of a cordial letter to her.[42] This was more than nine years after she bemoaned the death of his "beloved and deserving daughter." Though neither the third President nor the wife of the second said so, their memories of Maria remained green while the animosities of politics were slowly fading.

[41] TJ to Rush, Jan. 16, 1811 (L. & B., XIII, 8); Rush to TJ, Feb. 1, 1811 (Butterfield, II, 1078); TJ to Rush, Dec. 5, 1811 (Ford, IX, 299–301n.).
[42] TJ to Abigail Adams, Aug. 22, 1813 (A.-J. Letters, II, 366–367), after seeing her postscript of July 15.

[XXIII]

An "Interview" and an Election

1804

IN mid-July, less than a week before he left Washington for his long
annual visit to Monticello, Jefferson added a postscript to a letter to
his daughter: "I presume Mr. Randolph's newspapers will inform him of
the death of Colo. Hamilton, which took place on the 12th." The next
day, bringing a friend in Europe up to date on happenings since his last
letter, he listed "remarkable deaths lately." Among these, following
Samuel Adams and Edmund Pendleton, both of whom had died in the
previous autumn, was the name of Hamilton. Then he referred with
"inexpressible grief" to the loss of his own daughter.[1] This was one of
his very rare references to that; and, before he set out for home, he
appears to have made no other written mention of the most startling
death of the year. From his recorded words no one would have suspected that it resulted from a duel (destined to be the most famous in
American history) between two men who in different ways had been
conspicuous rivals of his. We do not know what he may have said to his
secretary, to whom he paid a quarter's salary before leaving, or to James
Madison, from whom he had no secrets, or to the members of his own
family after he got home. Upon the face of the record, however, no
contrast could be greater than that between this extraordinarily dramatic and deeply tragic episode and the virtual silence with which he
greeted it.

The newspapers, to which he referred his son-in-law, were full of it.
This was especially true of the *New York Evening Post*, whose editor,
William Coleman, devoted himself for weeks to the collection and pub-
lication of materials bearing on the "melancoly event" and the character

[1] TJ to Martha, July 17, 1804 (*Family Letters*, p. 262); TJ to Philip Mazzei,
July 18, 1804 (L. & B., XI, 41).

and achievements of "the greatest and most virtuous of men." [2] It may be presumed that the President, who was a subscriber to the *Evening Post,* saw the elaborate account of Hamilton's funeral in that paper, along with Gouverneur Morris's oration.[3] Mr. Jefferson, an inveterate civilian, must have noted that Hamilton was repeatedly referred to as "General" and that the "funeral obsequies" had a distinct military character. The dead General's hat and sword lay on top of his coffin, which was preceded and flanked by militiamen and followed by his gray horse with reversed boots and spurs. In the procession, however, were high civil officials as well as officers of the army and navy, representatives of professions, agents of foreign powers, professors and students from Columbia College, members of various societies including Tammany, and vast numbers of citizens. As a public manifestation of grief and respect this was without American parallel since the demonstrations following the death of Washington. Commenting on these events to Jefferson a dozen years later, John Adams, while recognizing that the death of Hamilton, "under all its circumstances, produced a general grief," remarked that Samuel Adams, John Hancock, and other noted patriots had been buried in "comparative obscurity." [4] Though he did not say so in this connection, Jefferson favored that sort of burial for everybody, and he was undoubtedly relieved that his presence was not expected at the last rites of a former antagonist who had met death at the hands of a discredited colleague. Fortunately, on the issue between them he did not have to commit himself in any way.

The circumstances of the confrontation in Weehawken which was euphemistically designated by principals and seconds as an "interview" were made known with unusual fulness and remarkable speed. The *Evening Post* quickly published in its columns the documents in the case, including the notes exchanged; and William Coleman soon gathered these into a volume, along with comments, orations, sermons, and eulogies that these events inspired.[5] Jefferson does not appear to have possessed this volume, but he could not have failed to be aware of its main contents. That partisans of Hamilton accused Burr of murder was

[2] On Aug. 20, 1804, in *N.Y. Evening Post,* Coleman said he would now resume his customary duties after having neglected them for a month. He soon recurred to the topic, however.

[3] *N.Y. Evening Post,* July 17, 1804.

[4] Adams to TJ, Sept. 3, 1816 (*A.-J. Letters,* II, 488).

[5] The best place to see the relevant sources is *Interview in Weehawken: The Burr-Hamilton Duel as Told in the Original Documents,* ed. by H. C. Syrett and J. G. Cooke with an Introduction & Conclusion by W. M. Wallace (1960). The book William Coleman edited and published in 1804, *A Collection of the Facts and Documents, relative to the Death of Major-General Hamilton . . . ,* was reprinted in 1904.

a matter of common knowledge, as was the verdict to that effect of a coroner's jury in New York, which actually had no jurisdiction. Also, it was well known that a grand jury in New Jersey, where the deed occurred, had indicted Burr.

Jefferson was not one to palliate recourse to a duel. To his own son-in-law, a couple of years later, he described it as "the most barbarous of appeals," pointing out that the real victims of this sort of knight-errantry were helpless women and children.[6] The plight of Hamilton's family afforded ample proof of this contention, and no one could doubt that Jefferson shared the general sympathy for the impoverished widow and children. Like everybody else he knew that the eldest of Elizabeth Hamilton's sons had also fallen in a duel a few years earlier. Since Jefferson did not recognize the authority of the code duello, he would not have been likely to contend that Burr was amply justified in demanding retribution for repeated reflections on his private as well as his public character, though Hamilton himself virtually admitted this in one of the published documents. It probably would not have occurred to Jefferson to say, as John Randolph did after reading the correspondence leading to the duel, that Burr actually showed up better in the preliminaries.[7] Jefferson's relative judgment of the two men could not be based on such grounds as these, and in the long view he clearly preferred the victim to the victor.

Shortly after the funeral, Gallatin wrote him from New York that "much artificial feeling, or semblance of feeling" had been added to the natural and sincere regret for Hamilton. For this he blamed "the combined Federal and anti-Burrite party spirits."[8] Looking backward on this period, John Adams concentrated attention on the former and perceived an ulterior motive. Writing Jefferson, he said that Hamilton's party (by which he meant Hamilton's segment of the Federalists) "seized the moment of public feeling to come forward with funeral orations and printed panegyricks reinforced with mock funerals and solemn grimaces. . . . And why? Merely to disgrace the old Whigs, and keep the funds and banks in countenance." In his response to this assertion, Jefferson contented himself with a general reference to the abuses of grief, avoiding mention of this particular episode.[9] He was then in position to reflect that the partisans of Hamilton gained little or no political advantage from their exploitation of genuine public sorrow

---

[6] TJ to TMR, June 23, 1806 (Edgehill-Randolph Papers, UVA).

[7] Randolph to J. H. Nicholson, Aug. 27, 1804 (Bruce, Randolph, I, 297–299). Wallace, in Interview in Weehawken, p. 171, agrees with him.

[8] Gallatin to TJ, July 18, 1804 (Writings, I, 201).

[9] Adams to TJ, Sept. 3, 1816 (somewhat modernized), and TJ to Adams, Oct. 14, 1816 (A.-J. Letters, II, 488, 490).

for him and of public indignation against the man who killed him. Though Vice President of the United States, Burr could not be identified with the administration, and he had already been repudiated by the dominant Republican faction in his state, some of whose prominent members joined in the hue and cry against him. Hamilton's death could be rightly regarded as the ultimate rebuke to those Federalists who had pinned their hopes on the man he had dubbed Catiline.

There was profound irony in the lamentations of Hamilton's party over their lost leader, for he had ceased to be the recognized leader of the party, if indeed he had ever been of the whole of it. In the parochialism and negativism into which it had fallen this nationalistic activist was already repudiated, except by a faithful few. The historian must recognize, also, that the most significant public services of the first Secretary of the Treasury now lay a decade behind him. A couple of years before his death he had lamented that "this American world" was not meant for him, and there is little reason to believe that he would ever again have been a potent public figure if he had lived on.[10] As is often the case, the eulogies of him claimed far too much. The tragic circumstances of his death inevitably caused his excesses to be minimized or forgotten and his unquestionably impressive stature as a patriotic statesman to be magnified. In these abnormal circumstances he could not easily be viewed on balance. Gouverneur Morris reflected on the difficulties before and after delivering the moderate funeral oration, which, in his opinion, fell below expectations.[11] And there appears to be no contemporary evidence that Hamilton's old-time antagonist, now the President, even attempted to sum him up.

Among Jefferson's known comments at other times on the man who was now the subject of so many eulogies, those contained in a letter to President Washington a dozen years earlier were the bitterest he ever made. Then Secretary of State, he was being violently attacked in the newspapers by his brilliant and intemperate colleague, the Secretary of the Treasury. In the effort to drive him from an office that he had actually been trying for some time to relinquish, Hamilton was hurling offensive epithets from behind an easily penetrated veil of pseudonymity and, to an even greater degree than Jefferson realized, was seeking to nullify his colleague's foreign policy offstage. To Washington, who was well aware of Jefferson's intention to leave the government and was reluctant to yield to it, the latter wrote: "I will not suffer my retirement to be clouded by the slanders of a man whose history, from the moment at which history can stoop to notice him, is a tissue of

[10] Hamilton to Gouverneur Morris, Feb. 27, 1802 (Lodge, VIII, 591).
[11] July 11–14, 1804 (Morris, *Diary and Letters*, II, 455–458).

machinations against the liberty of the country which has not only received and given him bread, but heaped its honors on his head." [12] Rarely if ever again did he advert to Hamilton's rise from obscurity or speak in disparaging terms of him as a person.[13] He might have been expected to dislike his imperious colleague intensely as a human being, and he probably did although he did not say so, for they were thoroughly incompatible in temperament. He was willing to go far in the effort to maintain amicable relations with his fellows — in fact his enemies described him as hypocritical for just that reason — but nobody could get along with Hamilton without agreeing with him. As John Quincy Adams said a score of years later, "he had within him to a great degree that which subdues the minds of other men, perhaps the first of all qualities for the commander of an army." [14] This eminent though not disinterested interpreter, who recognized that Hamilton had talents of the highest order, added comments which cannot be matched in Jefferson's writings. He said that Hamilton "was of that class of characters which cannot bear a rival — haughty, overbearing, jealous, bitter and violent in his personal enmities, and little scrupulous of the means which he used against those who stood in the way of his ambition." The enduring personal resentment of Hamilton by John Adams and son cannot be doubted. It must be recognized that Hamilton, who contributed to John Adams's defeat in the election of 1800 by writing an outrageous letter about him, did less harm to Jefferson. His most vicious attacks on Jefferson occurred when they were colleagues, and these actually served to build up the Secretary of State, making him the public symbol of anti-Hamiltonianism. He could hardly have been fully aware of this service at the moment, or deeply grateful for it, but, even in the period of their most intense rivalry, he rarely descended to personalities, and there seems to be no record that he did so at all in later years. He objected to Hamilton's "system," which, in his opinion, flowed from "principles adverse to liberty," and to his actions in particular public matters. As for Hamilton's ability, he had profound respect for that. When he himself was for a time withdrawn from the battle, he described his former colleague as a Colossus, saying that without numbers he was a host in himself. Aaron Burr elicited no such praise from him at any time.

The circumstances of Jefferson's election to the presidency might

[12] TJ to Washington, Sept. 9, 1792 (Ford, VI, 109). For the entire episode, see *Jefferson and the Rights of Man*, ch. XXVII.

[13] Even in the episode of the Giles Resolutions, which quickly followed, TJ's concern was with the *official* conduct of the Secretary of the Treasury. See *Jefferson and the Ordeal of Liberty*, ch. II.

[14] J. Q. Adams, *Parties in the U.S.* (1941), p. 26.

have been expected to temper his hostility to Hamilton, who let his preference for him over Burr be clearly known when there was an accidental electoral tie between the two Republicans, and the Federalists in the House of Representatives were unwisely supporting Burr.[15] But if Jefferson had been permitted to read the private letters of the former Secretary of the Treasury, which are now available to any interested person, he could not have found them gratifying to himself as a human being. After saying that he was "not very mindful of the truth," and describing him as "a contemptible hypocrite," Hamilton finally admitted that there was "no fair reason to suppose him capable of being corrupted," but this concession could hardly have taken the edge off the previous characterizations.[16] There is no way of knowing how aware Jefferson was of the names he was being called by his old rival at this time, but in view of past experience they could hardly have surprised him, and the realization that he was preferred to Burr as the lesser evil must have been considerably less than exhilarating.[17]

Had he been as fully informed as we are of the "secessionist plot" of 1804 and the machinations of certain Federalist leaders with Burr, which Hamilton opposed so strongly and with such fatal consequences, his sympathies could not have failed to be with the latter. While he never ceased to regard Hamilton's admiration for the existing British government as uncritical and to find this incomprehensible, he afterwards referred approvingly to "the known principle of General Hamilton, never, under any views, to break the Union." [18] This was after his own return to private life, when he was beginning to make occasional mention of the fallen Colossus about whom he was so silent during his presidency. Such comments as he is known to have made on him in the early years of his own retirement are notably devoid of personal recrimination. In one of the first of them, speaking of their service in Washington's administration, he said: "We had indeed no personal dissensions. Each of us, perhaps, thought well of the other as a man, but as politicians it was impossible for two men to be of more opposite principles." [19] He did well to insert "perhaps" and might have done better to underline the word, but if political differences rather than personal did not predominate in his memory he thought they should and sought

[15] For the electoral tie in 1800–1801, see *Jefferson and the Ordeal of Liberty*, pp. 493–505.

[16] These particular quotations are from Hamilton's letter to J. A. Bayard, Jan. 16, 1801 (Lodge, VIII, 581–582).

[17] His son-in-law said that his own suspicions of Hamilton were deepened rather than allayed by the letter's expressed preference (TMR to James Monroe, Feb. 14, 1801, cited in *Jefferson and the Ordeal of Liberty*, p. 503).

[18] TJ to John Melish, Jan. 13, 1813 (Ford, IX, 375).

[19] TJ to Joel Barlow, Jan. 24, 1810 (Ford, IX, 269).

to give the impression that they did. Shortly after this, writing Dr. Benjamin Rush, he drew a contrast between John Adams, "honest as a politician as well as a man," and Hamilton, who was honest as a man but, as a politician, believed in "the necessity of either force or corruption to govern men." [20] He cast no reflection on the latter's personal integrity, recognizing that he had gained nothing for himself by "corruption." If any demonstration of that was needed, the state of Hamilton's finances at his death provided it. Under his "system," in Jefferson's opinion, favors were deemed indispensable to gain support for government, whereas he himself advocated complete and consistent *laissez faire* and relied on popular support, which his antagonist belittled. This foe of special privilege never ceased to use the term "corruption" in connection with the benefits accruing to particular individuals and groups as a result of Hamilton's policies, but the major contrast he perceived, and which the historian must perceive with him, lay in their respective attitudes toward the citizenry as a whole. It was because Hamilton did not share his profound faith in self-government and had a contemptuous attitude toward the generality of mankind that Jefferson regarded him as antirepublican. In a paper he drafted at the age of seventy-five, which constitutes a sort of apologia for his conduct as Secretary of State and is distinctly partisan in tone, he designated Hamilton as a monarchist and again stressed his reliance on "corruption," after the example of the British government. Here he referred to his ancient foe as a "singular character." [21] On the credit side he said that Hamilton, besides being possessed of acute understanding, was personally disinterested, honest, honorable, and amiable in society. As the paper he was then writing showed unmistakably, the political differences between the two men were far from forgotten; at this time, in fact, he was freshly recording them. But he was still trying to distinguish between what was public and what was private, and, while condemning the "system" of Hamilton, he was seeking to view him fairly, even generously, as a man. The patriarch may be blamed for failure to recognize the benefits that had flowed from his old rival's achievements, but he may be honored for having made no mention of the violent personal attacks he had suffered at that rival's hands.

While Burr's "interview" with Hamilton in Weehawken need not be supposed to have lessened Jefferson's distrust of him, there is no evi-

[20] TJ to Rush, Jan. 16, 1811 (L. & B., III, 3-4).
[21] In the foreword to the so-called Anas, dated Feb. 4, 1818 (Ford, I, 166). The partisan tone is partially attributable to TJ's extreme annoyance at the treatment of these events in John Marshall's *Life of Washington*.

dence whatever that the President joined with the local Republican enemies of the victorious duelist in their outburst against him. He had not taken the lead in the movement within the party against Burr in the first place, though he had tacitly supported the Clintonians in New York and would have been politically unwise if he had not done so.[22] And he was now participating in no campaign of persecution.[23] Actually, the clamor against Burr in New York and New Jersey, which occasioned him to keep out of those states, did not follow him to Washington in the fall. There he resumed his seat as Vice President as though nothing had happened. In fact, he returned to the Senate sooner than usual. One Federalist member of that body claimed that the Republicans were manifesting their joy at Hamilton's death by "caressing his murderer." William Plumer, who afterward suffered from a guilty conscience because of his connection with the secession plot, said that Jefferson, along with Gallatin and Madison, showed the "murderer" marked attention, having invited him to the President's House more often than previously. These assertions would be hard to prove, and nothing more may have been involved than a maintenance of proprieties. Most of the Republicans in the Senate signed a petition to the Governor of New Jersey asking that a nolle prosequi be entered on Burr's indictment. Noting that other individuals of the same *sect* had co-operated, he himself correctly predicted that nothing hostile would be attempted by that state and appeared to be nonchalant about his situation.[24]

It was still colored by politics to some extent. Even William Plumer believed that the Republicans would not trust Burr unnecessarily, but as the presiding officer in the Senate he still had some importance in the impeachment trial of Justice Chase, which was coming up. The President must have perceived this, as the congressional leaders did, and he would not have been in character if he had not sought to maintain party unity. No doubt he contemplated with satisfaction the prospect of Burr's retirement to private life at the end of the congressional session, and it would have been like him to preserve the amenities in the meantime. Of his personal feelings, so far as the records show, he gave

---

[22] The assertion of J. C. Miller, in *Alexander Hamilton* (1959), p. 569, that Burr might properly have challenged TJ instead of Hamilton, and the implication that TJ had been the "prime mover" against Burr behind the scenes, seem to me quite unwarranted by the known facts with respect to the conduct of both Hamilton and TJ.

[23] He resisted pressure to remove from office Burr's supporter, Swartwout (to DeWitt Clinton, Oct. 6, 1804 [Ford, VIII, 322–323]).

[24] Plumer, *Memorandum*, pp. 203–204; Burr to Joseph Alston, Dec. 15, 1804 (*Memoirs*, II, 353).

no sign, but his own political position had never seemed more secure than in the autumn of 1804, for it was then that he was triumphantly re-elected. At this stage he could not have been expected to anticipate that Burr, as a man without office as well as without party, would embark on a career of desperation that would threaten the security of the country.

Less than a month after the fatal confrontation on the banks of the Hudson, the President, then at Monticello, sent the Secretary of State the ratification of the Twelfth Amendment by South Carolina. Presuming that Madison would receive that of Tennessee within a week, he supposed that the adoption of the amendment should then be announced.[25] Though the formal declaration was not made until late September, he knew by early August that the last discernible obstacle to his re-election had been removed. The electoral vote was not fully reported until the very end of the year, several weeks after the beginning of the congressional session, but as the returns filtered in the only surprise was in the extent of the victory. Few presidential nominees have approached it in the whole of American history. Losing only the states of Connecticut and Delaware and two electors in Maryland, Jefferson and Clinton got 162 votes to 14 for their opponents.[26] The highly respectable Federalist candidates, Charles Cotesworth Pinckney of South Carolina and Rufus King of New York, were so deeply buried by this landslide that their countrymen have had difficulty in remembering them in connection with it. And, after the sensational Burr-Hamilton duel, which appears to have affected the result in no way, the presidential election of 1804 was notably lacking in excitement.

Contrasting the public state of mind with that of four years earlier, the *National Intelligencer,* without seeking to subtract a cubit from Jefferson's stature, observed that he had been re-elected "without awakening either the rapturous exultation of his friends or the angry passions of his enemies." [27] Friends of the administration had smothered its foes almost everywhere. Even in the stronghold of his bitterest enemies, New England, the President had gained the support of all the states but one. "In Connecticut," said Gideon Granger, "the Republicans are more severely treated than anywhere else, and on their part

---

[25] TJ to Madison, Aug. 3, 1804 (MP, 27:108).

[26] Precise information about the method of electing electors and about the votes in this instance is given in C. O. Paullin, *Atlas of the Historical Geography of the U.S.* (1932), table on p. 89, and summary on p. 93. In six states, including Connecticut and Delaware which Jefferson lost, electors were still chosen by the legislature. Maryland was one of the five states in which they were chosen by districts.

[27] *National Intelligencer,* Dec. 21, 1804.

strike bolder strokes." Later events were to confirm the accuracy of this observation. In Massachusetts, however, John Quincy Adams, while deploring the President's "itch of popularity," recognized that the contagion was widespread in the state and believed that the revolution there was completed.[28] The Republicans were well organized in New England, but so were the Federalists.[29] Therefore, it would appear that they owed their success in this region as elsewhere to the peace and prosperity of the country, the popularity of the President, and the inability of the Federalists to find an appealing issue. For these reasons, also, they had been unable to divide the Republicans, though large credit must be given Jefferson himself for the maintenance of party unity on the national front. His major contribution, to be sure, was in his own person as a symbol, and in the successful and popular policies he had espoused, but wherever he saw a good chance he sought to reduce intraparty rivalry and dissension, as his letters to leaders of opposing Republican factions clearly show. And, in interpreting his prodigious victory, he took greatest satisfaction in the degree of national unity that had been attained. Indeed, some of his comments lead one to wonder what place he was really willing to allow the opposing party.

His own election four years earlier stands forth in history as a vindication of the right of political opposition, and his inauguration marked the peaceful transfer of rule from a political group that had lost popular support to one that had gained it. At first glance his accession may seem to have signified the recognition of the historic American two-party system. Yet he deplored the divisive spirit and sought to unify the country. One way to do that would have been to obliterate the opposing party. Writing a friend in Europe after the election, he said that the two parties, formerly so violent in their antagonism, were "almost melted into one"; and he sounded as though he hoped the process would be completed.[30] While admitting that Delaware would remain uncertain till her Anglomany had yielded to Americanism, he said with unwarranted optimism, "Connecticut will be with us in a short time." If these hopes should be fulfilled, the United States would be little short of a one-party country.

In the course of his long life, and especially in his old age, Jefferson had a good deal to say about parties, though, as was usual with him, his

[28] Granger to TJ, Sept. 2, 1804 (LC, 24831); comment of J. Q. Adams, Nov., 1804 (*Writings*, III, 81).

[29] For an account of Republican organization on both the national and local levels, see Cunningham, chs. 5–6. He points out that organization was best on both sides where the conflict was greatest.

[30] TJ to Volney, Feb. 8, 1805 (Chinard, *Volney et L'Amérique*, p. 175).

comments were chiefly *ad hoc* and not thrown into the form of a balanced disquisition. During his first term as President he had shown himself to be one of the most effective party leaders in American history, but he had not wholly thrown off the distrust of parties he had inherited from the past and had not ceased to dislike squabbling. He did not like it among his own supporters and, for all his lifelong emphasis on freedom of opinion, he found divisive partisanship an unpleasant thing. When in the minority he had said: "Perhaps this party division is necessary to induce each to watch and relate to the people the proceedings of the other." [31] It should not be supposed, however, that by the time of his presidency he had arrived at the conception that was to be so well summed up in the British phrase "His Majesty's Opposition." Actually, that expression did not enter the political vernacular until the last year of his life and the two-party system did not approximate modern form in the United States until after his death.[32]

Whether or not he was familiar with the classic definition of Edmund Burke, which antedated the American Revolution, Jefferson also defined parties in terms of principles.[33] He could not concede that they were rival organizations, merely struggling for power, and least of all would he admit that the contest between them was chiefly for the spoils of office. The major differences between the two existing American parties as he saw them were set forth in a letter he wrote shortly before his re-election:

> The one desires to preserve an entire independence of the executive and legislative branches on each other, and the dependence of both on the same source — the free election of the people. The other party wishes to lessen the dependence of the Executive and of one branch of the Legislature on the people, some by making them hold for life, some hereditary, and some even for giving the Executive an influence by patronage or corruption over the remaining popular branch, so as to reduce the elective franchise to its minimum.[34]

[31] TJ to John Taylor, June 1, 1798 (Ford, VII, 264).

[32] See the admirable article by Caroline Robbins, " 'Discordant Parties': A Study of the Acceptance of Party by Englishmen," *Pol. Sci. Quarterly*, Dec., 1958. The expression was that of John Cam Hobhouse in the House of Commons in April, 1826. The American two-party system crystallized in the 1830's.

[33] Burke defined party as "a body of men united for promoting by their joint endeavours the national interest upon some particular principles in which they are all agreed." TJ owned a copy of Burke's *Thoughts on the Cause of the Present Discontents* (1770), in which this definition appears, but I have found no direct reference he made to it.

[34] TJ to John F. Mercer, Oct. 9, 1804 (L. & B., XI, 54).

It cannot be maintained that in his own administration the executive and legislative branches were entirely independent, or that they should have been. No previous President had influenced Congress to the degree that he did or had even sought to do so, and one may doubt if any successor ever surpassed him in this regard. He himself would have claimed with very considerable justification that his methods were personal and indirect, that he relied on neither force nor corruption, that he employed patronage without sacrifice of the public interest; but there was inconsistency between his theory and practice in his relations with the legislature. To have admitted this would have been difficult and embarrassing. It would probably have been bad politics. But he would have served posterity better if he had said that the President had a constitutional share in the legislative process and had frankly admitted the necessity of presidential leadership.

In their recognition of the popular will and dependence on it, he and his party had unquestionably kept the faith. Therein lay the basic difference between them and their opponents, as it did between him and Hamilton. Therein also lay the abiding significance of Jefferson's victory. What he called "Anglomany" and contrasted with "Americanism" was not yet dead; issues growing out of foreign affairs were to arise again. But, increasingly, the Federalists had to accommodate themselves to public opinion and give lip service, at least, to political democracy. As has been said, they came to sound like Jeffersonians.[35] In many ways the Federalist leaders of the Old School, who were frankly opposed to or highly skeptical of democracy, were more attractive than those of the New, whose hostility or skepticism was covert rather than overt, and Jefferson himself in later years was suspicious of newly espoused "republicanism." He had battled chiefly with the older group and if they were as monarchical as his language would lead us to suppose, if they were really counter-revolutionary, there could be no reconciliation with them. He himself had abandoned all hope of it, and, as he wrote his old secretary, William Short, had ceased to care what they thought, said, or did. Speaking of the Federalists as a group, he said: "To me will have fallen the drudgery of putting them out of condition to do mischief." [36] His view of the uses of political opposition was not wholly clear and varied with circumstances, but by his outstanding success in the conduct of a temperate popular government he had won over the moderates and checked the counter-revolutionary

---

[35] D. H. Fisher, *The Revolution of American Conservatism: The Federalist Party in the Era of Jeffersonian Democracy* (1965), p. 153. General discussion in ch. VIII.

[36] TJ to William Short, Nov. 10, 1804 (LC, Vol. 144, without folio no.).

movement. This achievement gave him a unique place among the contemporary heads of state in the Atlantic world.

Toward the end of the year, John Taylor of Caroline well characterized Jefferson's lifelong purposes and main aim as President. The rural philosopher referred to the effort "to subdue tyranny by intellect" and the sublime object of "exhibiting republicanism to the world, in an experiment, fair, full and final." Disturbed by reports, which, in his own opinion, were reprobated by "firm consistent republicans," that the President would retire at the end of the term to which he had just been elected, Taylor asked if the success of this experiment should be thus hazarded. And he urged Jefferson, whatever his inclination might be, to postpone his final decision. In his reply Jefferson, while reporting that he had given up the idea of a public declaration, said that he had freely let it be known in private conversation that he fully intended to follow the example of George Washington and strengthen the wholesome two-term precedent. Only one circumstance could engage his acquiescence in another election, he said: "such a division about a successor as might bring in a monarchist." This circumstance, however, he believed to be impossible.[37] Meanwhile, his main task as party leader was to maintain essential unity within his own following.

Two portraits of him were made shortly after his triumphant re election. One was the work of Saint-Mémin and the other of Rembrandt Peale. Shortly before her death in the previous spring his daughter Maria had asked him to let Saint-Mémin do his picture at the first opportunity.[38] Thus he was making belated response to what was virtually a dying request when he went, in late November, to the house on F Street where this émigré artist had set up his physiognotrace. After tracing a profile of his subject by means of this instrument, Saint-Mémin made a drawing, and then two engraved copperplates. Jefferson got one of these, along with a considerable number of prints and the drawing. The artist used the other to make prints which he afterwards offered for sale at the inauguration. Maria had been confident that Saint-Mémin would get a good likeness. So far as the profile is concerned, we may assume that he did, but, judging from other portraits of Jefferson, the face is too full and the oversized eye too protruding. There is a certain comic quality in this informal portrait, but there is no mistaking the firmness of the mouth and the strength of the slightly jutting chin. Jefferson's family appear to have approved of it, and, since so many

[37] Taylor to TJ, Dec. 26, 1804 (LC, 25334); TJ to Taylor, Jan. 6, 1805 (Ford, VIII, 338–340).
[38] See above, p. 412.

JEFFERSON IN PROFILE
Portrait by C.B.J.F. de Saint-Mémin, 1804

prints were made, he was relatively well known to his contemporaries in this cheerful likeness.[39]

The portrait painted by Rembrandt Peale in the President's House in January was done in a much grander manner, though there is a quality of homeliness about it. Jefferson was wearing a coat with a fur collar, characteristically guarding himself against the cold. The son of his admiring friend and inveterate correspondent Charles Willson Peale had painted a notable portrait of him in 1800, before his future presidential status was assured.[40] The young artist was now more sophisticated, since his visit abroad, and his second life portrait of Jefferson has been regarded by many as his best work. The face is somewhat thinner, the nose a little sharper than in the first portrait, and it does not give quite the same sense of strength, though, as in Saint-Mémin's portrait, the lips and chin suggest determination. To a notable degree it reflects intelligence and benignity, and there is at least the suspicion of a twinkle in the eyes. Whether or not the artist flattered the subject, this is a handsome portrait. For long years it looked down from the walls of the Peale Museum in Philadelphia, being specially illuminated on the eve of Jefferson's second inauguration, but Rembrandt appears to have had very few commissions to do replicas of it and it was not engraved in that century. In the twentieth century it has been a great favorite, and probably we are in better position than the contemporaries of the President, though certainly not of the Peale family, to perceive how intelligent and benevolent he was.[41]

The period between his overwhelming electoral victory and his second inauguration turned out to be the most frustrating part of his presidency thus far, but, judging from his portraits and his temperament as already manifested, he entered upon it with serenity.

[39] A. L. Bush gives an excellent brief account of it in *Life Portraits of Thomas Jefferson* (1962), pp. 65–67, with references. The fullest account is H. C. Rice, Jr., "Saint-Mémin's Portrait of Jefferson" in *Princeton University Library Chronicle*, XX, No. 4 (summer, 1959). TJ's Account Book shows that on Nov. 27, 1804, he paid the artist $29.50.

[40] Used as the frontispiece in *Jefferson and the Ordeal of Liberty*.

[41] This portrait appears as the frontispiece in this volume. The sittings for it were on Jan. 23, 24, 31, 1805. See the account by Bush, pp. 69–70, with references, and Sellers, *Charles Willson Peale*, II, 189–190.

[XXIV]

John Randolph and the Yazoo Question

IN no other congressional session of his first term did Jefferson play so passive a role as in the one immediately following his triumphant re-election. During the winter of 1804–1805, while he seemed aloof, public interest was centered on domestic issues and attention focused on Capitol Hill. There John Randolph stormed against the proposed settlement of the Yazoo claims, and the impeachment trial of Justice Samuel Chase created intense excitement.

Meanwhile in Pennsylvania, the chief seat of discord within the dominant party, there was a turbulent sideshow in which the President did not let himself get involved. Late in the summer, he had said: "Pennsylvania seems to have in its bowels a good deal of volcanic matter, and some explosion may be expected." [1] The vote for him in the presidential election was unaffected by the violent feuding there, but by winter the "Keystone in the Democratic Arch" appeared to be splitting down the middle.[2] The leaders on one side, which perhaps we may call the right, were Governor Thomas McKean, Alexander J. Dallas, and Dr. George Logan, with Congressman Michael Leib and Editor William Duane on the left. The reverberations of this waxing feud had already reached the President in connection with appointments. The partisan clamor for the more rapid removal of Federalist officeholders came from the Duane-Leib faction, termed by Jefferson the "high-fliers," and the editor of the *Aurora* had a further grievance against the administration in the matter of printing, of which he believed he did not get enough. He remained loyal to Jefferson, who was exceedingly patient with him and against whom he had little complaint except that the President was too much under the influence of Gallatin.

---

[1] TJ to Robert Smith, Aug. 28, 1804 (Ford, VIII, 318).

[2] I have borrowed the expression from the excellent monograph of S. W. Higginbotham, *The Keystone in the Democratic Arch: Pennsylvania Politics 1800–1816* (1952). See, especially, ch. III.

In the political sniping of this time Federalists continued to direct their fire against Jefferson and his moral character. In the fall he was castigated for his "wanton disrespect" for the Sabbath in his travels to and from Monticello, and early in the new year the Walker affair was gloatingly exhumed in hostile newspapers and debated in the legislature of Massachusetts.[3] Within the party, however, barbs were rarely loosed against him; when hurled at the government they were generally directed against his lieutenants. Essentially, the conflict in Pennsylvania was over local issues and was incident to the struggle for power between groups of Republican leaders, but the animus of one of these groups against the Secretary of the Treasury was an occasion for concern to the administration. Furthermore, the struggle over the judiciary of the state, which reached a climax in the winter of 1804–1805, reverberated in Washington.

Neither of the two major domestic controversies in the capital resulted from specific recommendations of the President to this session of Congress. Both revolved around items of unfinished congressional business. In foreign affairs, which Jefferson was always disposed to keep in the hands of the executive, there were also important matters of unfinished business, along with some fresh problems. He did not ignore these in his annual message to the legislators, but he appeared to view the world scene with relative complacency.[4] Not yet had the armed conflict between France and Great Britain "extended its flames to other nations, nor been marked by the calamities which sometimes stain the footsteps of war." (This he said in one of his more rhetorical sentences. In general his language was so temperate that he was credited in a hostile newspaper with having learned, since his inaugural address, "not again to cut his fingers by handling metaphors he could not manage.")[5] Infringements on American rights and laws in coastal waters and in the country's own harbors constituted virtually the only development in foreign relations that occasioned a call for congressional action. After consultation with his advisers, Jefferson shortly communicated to Joseph H. Nicholson, chairman of the appropriate select committee of the House, a draft of a proposed act "for the more effectual preservation of the peace in the harbours and waters of the U.S. and on board vessels."[6] The purpose of this was to provide for the enforcement of

[3] See above, pp. 219–221. The reference to the Sabbath is to an item entitled "Jefferson's Religion," reprinted from *Boston Repertory* in *N. Y. Evening Post*, Oct. 15, 1804.

[4] Message of Nov. 8, 1804 (Ford, VIII, 323–332).

[5] *Washington Federalist*, Nov. 17, 1804.

[6] Draft in TJ's writing (LC, 25069–25070). He mentions this in his letter of Nov. 19, 1804, to John Randolph (Ford, VIII, 333–336; with marginal comments by Gal-

prescribed regulations on foreign armed vessels and to empower the President to remove them or forbid their entrance. The law along the lines of Jefferson's proposal that was enacted by this Congress did not prevent the abuse of American hospitality but that was more flagrant in his second term than during the rest of his first.[7]

Connected with this question was that of gunboats, which had proved useful in the shallow waters off the Barbary Coast and were expected to be effective in the defense of harbors. They had the further merit of being cheap. Jefferson commended them in his message, and, on request, set forth his ideas more fully in a private letter to Congressman Nicholson. The country already had ten, built or building. For the present he favored only modest expansion of the program and sought to avoid public discussion which would expose defense policy too much. The gunboats, on which he was to rely increasingly, were to be derided before he left office, but his proposals perturbed few as yet. Congress promptly passed a bill calling for the construction of not more than twenty-five of these small vessels and appropriating $60,000.[8]

Grave danger seemed remote, but by now Jefferson was well aware that he was approaching an impasse in his efforts to acquire West Florida. The passage in his message bearing on relations with Spain did not suggest the difficulties of the situation. He would have been unwise, however, if he had described them with full candor in public or even in confidence to Congress before the results of Monroe's mission were reported. The West Florida question did not become a burning and divisive domestic issue until his second term. Therefore, we shall follow his lead and put it out of sight for the present. So, also, with the Tripolitan War, which seemed to drag on interminably.

On the domestic side, he recognized that the temporary government of the Territory of Louisiana was susceptible of improvement; and, as we have already seen, considerable improvement in it was made by this Congress.[9] Negotiations with the Indians were proceeding well, he thought, and no one could deny that the state of the country's finances was admirable. Jefferson made a highly favorable ad interim report, foreshadowing no fresh executive action of consequence and leaving

---

latin in footnote). The matter was referred to in several letters to Robert Smith, Gallatin, and Lincoln during the previous summer and he undoubtedly discussed it with Madison. The "insults" ranged from defiance of peace officers to smuggling and impressment.

[7] Approved, Mar. 3, 1805 (*Annals*, 8 Cong., 2 sess., pp. 1694–1698). A notorious later insult was that by the *Leander* in 1806.

[8] TJ to J. H. Nicholson, Jan. 29, 1805 (L. & B., XI, 59–62). Act approved Mar. 2, 1805 (*Annals*, 8 Cong., 2 sess., p. 1684).

[9] See ch. XIX, above.

domestic matters largely to the wisdom of Congress. Events were to cast very considerable doubt, however, on the wisdom of this particular Congress, and especially on that of John Randolph, leader of the Republicans in the House.

It should be remembered that the majority leader of the House was neither named by the President nor formally elected by his fellows. The position was not created; it evolved as, in the course of events, a leader emerged and gained recognition. The confidence of the administration was an important factor in this process and no floor leader could have maintained himself without it. Yet the closeness of the tie with the executive varied with individuals, and to describe anybody as the President's congressional "lieutenant" who sought to carry out his "commands" would be to indulge in exaggeration.[10]

Of all the majority leaders of the House during Jefferson's presidency the one closest to him while in that position was the first one, William Branch Giles, although that pugnacious representative from Southside Virginia manifested a degree of partisanship considerably beyond that shown by Jefferson himself. The extraordinary success of the first session of the Seventh Congress (1801–1802) was owing to a number of favorable factors, but one of these unquestionably was the close collaboration of Giles with the President. Because of the state of his health, however, this doughty debater and skillful parliamentarian was unable to serve during the second session of that Congress and did not stand for re-election. Succeeded in the House by Jefferson's son-in-law, John W. Eppes, he did not resume his legislative career until the fall of 1804, when he took his seat in the Senate.

The emergence of John Randolph as majority leader in 1802–1803, when Giles was incapacitated, need not be attributed directly or primarily to the favor of the administration. A few weeks after the session began, Jefferson, regretting the dilatoriness and ineffectiveness of Congress and its lack of "men of business," expressed the wish that Congressman-elect Caesar A. Rodney of Delaware were there. It will be recalled that he had induced Rodney to run against James A. Bayard — partly because of his desire to get rid of Bayard, no doubt, but also because he wanted to strengthen party leadership in the House.[11] This

[10] These words appear in the useful pioneer study of R. V. Harlow, *History of Legislative Methods in the Period before 1825* (1907), p. 177. The best study I have seen of the matters dealt with here is the dissertation of A. B. Lacy, "Jefferson and Congress"; especially, ch. IV.

[11] TJ to Rodney, Dec. 31, 1802 (Ford, VIII, 187); see p. 142, above, for their earlier correspondence. Rodney, elected in the fall of 1802, began his service the following fall.

particular reinforcement could not arrive until another year and for a variety of reasons did not then come up to expectations. Meanwhile, according to Federalist report some weeks after the session of 1802–1803 started, the Republicans in the House lacked "an acknowledged, bold and determined leader." William Plumer said that Randolph, "a pale, meagre, ghostly man," had more talents than any of the others, but that they were unwilling to acknowledge the leadership of one who looked so boyish.[12] Then only twenty-eight years old, he was often referred to by his foes as "Johnny." He has gone down in history as "John Randolph of Roanoke," but it was not until after Jefferson's administration that he thus designated himself to avoid confusion with a detested kinsman. His present home was the paternal seat in Southside Virginia, "Bizarre" — a word which suggests his almost incredible appearance and personality. It may be doubted if any public man of his era was ever described more often or so vividly. A congressman from New England, himself a clergyman, spoke of him thus to another minister:

> As to Mr. John Randolph you can scarcely form an idea of a human figure whose appearance is more contemptible. He is rather taller than middle size, extremely slender, he never had a razor on his face and has no more appearance of beard than a boy of 10 years old, and his voice is the same. . . . By his appearance one would suppose him to be either by nature, or manual operation fixed for an Italian singer, indeed there are strong suspicions of a physical disability. . . .[13]

That there was a "physical disability" — impotence in fact — was revealed by post-mortem examination, and Randolph's excesses of arrogant belligerency may perhaps be explained, in terms of modern psychology, as over-compensation for his lack of virility. By any reckoning he was a weird figure and an odd character — willful, capricious, neurotic. That he received high public preferment may perhaps be regarded as a sign that his age was more tolerant than ours of personal divergence from the norm, but he got it at the outset because he was born to high estate; as a Randolph he was related to virtually everybody of note in Virginia, including Thomas Jefferson. Furthermore, this bizarre young aristocrat gave clear evidence of unusual ability, especially in the realm of speech. Whether his voice was regarded as piping or flutelike may have depended on the political sensibilities of

---

[12] Plumer to Nicholas Emory and to Jeremiah Mason, Jan., 1803 (William Plumer, Jr., *Life of William Plumer* [1856], pp. 248–249).

[13] S. Taggart to Rev. John Taylor, Jan. 13, 1804 (Taggart "Letters," p. 125).

CONGRESSMAN JOHN RANDOLPH
Portrait by Chester Harding

his auditors, but he was probably the greatest of congressional orators between Fisher Ames and Daniel Webster.[14]

Besides Randolph, the chief contenders for the post of leadership formerly held by Giles were Samuel Smith of Maryland, who was unpopular, and his well-liked colleague from the same state, Joseph H. Nicholson, who, as a member of the last Congress under John Adams, had conspicuously manifested his devotion to Jefferson. Too ill to stand, he was borne on a litter to the Capitol day after day that he might cast his vote, and but for this heroic action the vote of Maryland would have gone to Burr. He showed great deference to the wishes of the President he had helped elect, and perhaps Jefferson was thinking of him when he told Rodney that an "ill-judged modesty" prevented those who were equal to the task of congressional leadership from assuming it. At all events, Nicholson was a friend of Randolph's and his ally against Samuel Smith. The fiery Virginian had great capacity for intimate friendship. Of prime importance in the career of Randolph was his deep friendship with Speaker Nathaniel Macon, who, at the first opportunity, appointed him chairman of the newly created and increasingly important Committee on Ways and Means. This gave him a position of prominence and influence of which he quickly availed himself, and, after he once got into the spotlight, his theatrical talents kept him there. Macon, Randolph, and Nicholson constituted a congressional triumvirate comparable to the executive triumvirate of Jefferson, Madison, and Gallatin. The tie between the two trios was chiefly provided by Gallatin, who had been a close friend of Randolph's since they served together in Congress, and whose wife Randolph particularly liked. Also, she was Nicholson's first cousin. Madison had no particular contacts with Randolph, social or otherwise, and ultimately became that congressman's *bête noir* in the administration. Jefferson's relations with him were friendly without being intimate. He recognized Randolph's usefulness in a House where the Republican representatives were mediocre. The Majority Leader handled the business relating to New Orleans and the Louisiana treaty with notable skill.

Randolph reached his peak in the session of 1803–1804, but even then some Republicans said they hated their arrogant congressional leader. So at least William Plumer reported on the eve of the feast at Stelle's Hotel in celebration of the acquisition of Louisiana, adding discerning comments of his own:

[14] W. C. Bruce, *John Randolph of Roanoke* (2 vols., 1922), is the standard biography.

His manners are far from concilating — Many of the party dislike him — & on trifling measures they quarrel with him, but on all measures that are really important to the party they unite with him. He is *necessary* to them — they know it — he knows it — & they dare not discard him. These frequent quarrels may eventually sour their minds against him, & prevent a reunion — A *few* of them consider themselves as *personally* injured by him, they will probably never *cordially* unite with him — but at present, with the majority of them its like the bickerings of lovers who contend but afterwards unite with greater zeal.[15]

The brief clash between the Chairman of the Committee on Ways and Means and Congressman John W. Eppes, son-in-law of Jefferson, occurred early in this session, when affairs were in such an uncertain state that Randolph probably appeared to the President as indispensable. Federalist exploitation of that episode occasioned the Majority Leader to assure Jefferson of his continued esteem and veneration. In the magnanimous reply in which he referred to Randolph's many past proofs of friendship, Jefferson intimated that Randolph had consulted him less than he would have liked and there can be no doubt that he recognized the delicacy of their relations.[16] At this time, however, his main reservation about the Majority Leader arose from no personal pique: he would have preferred someone who would do more to promote the unity of the government and of the party. Some weeks later, when expressing regret at the decision of Rodney not to seek re-election, he wrote that congressman: "I had looked to you as one of those calculated to give cohesion to our rope of sand." [17] By then John Randolph, who was descended from Pocahontas and is said to have looked it, was on the warpath — not against the administration as such, but against the settlement of the disputed Yazoo claims that had been recommended by the three high executive officers constituting the federal commission. Making his opposition to this unmistakable early in 1804, he caused a postponement of the question. When it came up again in the next session, the last of Jefferson's first term, he attacked the proposed settlement with unrivaled fury, demonstrating his extraordinary skill in obstructing as well as in promoting measures backed by the administration. He greatly oversimplified what was in fact a very complicated question, reducing it to an issue between right and wrong. On the other hand, the federal commissioners, while well aware

[15] Jan. 26, 1804 (Plumer, *Memorandum*, p. 123).
[16] See above, pp. 409–410, and his letter of Dec. 1, 1803 (Ford, VIII, 281–282).
[17] TJ to C. A. Rodney, Feb. 24, 1804 (Ford, VIII, 296).

of legal uncertainties and moral implications, spoke for the national interest in the language of common sense.

The conflict over the Yazoo claims, which was not to be resolved while Jefferson was President or John Randolph in Congress, must be set against the background of what has been aptly described as "the greatest land speculation in American history." [18] In 1795 the legislature of the relatively undeveloped state of Georgia, which had not yet ceded to the Union the region between its present western boundary and the Mississippi River, sold to four companies of speculators for $500,000 some 35,000,000 acres of land, comprising the larger part of the present states of Mississippi and Alabama. Of all those voting for the Yazoo Act of 1795, by which this deed was done, every legislator but one was personally interested because of bribe or investment. The notorious act was repealed a year later under circumstances of great public indignation. John Randolph, who visited a friend in Georgia that year, became thoroughly informed of both past corruption and present resentment. One ground for repeal to which he afterwards referred in Congress was that the state had no right to make the sale in the first place, since the Indians had not yet yielded title to the lands in question and only the federal government had constitutional authority to treat with them. In connection with an earlier sale that never became effective, Jefferson, while in George Washington's official family, had taken the same position.[19] Furthermore, the state appeared to have surrendered to the companies, for a time at least, political sovereignty over this vast area. The most popular argument for repeal, however, then and thereafter, was that the circumstances of notorious corruption were sufficient to invalidate the contract.[20] So intent were the Georgians on removing from their record every trace of this outrageous transaction that they tore from the legislative journal the pages bearing on it, and by means of a microscope called down fire from Heaven to ignite them.

These circumstances played a vital part in occasioning the state to yield to the federal government its western lands, including those granted to the companies.[21] One provision of the Convention of 1802,

[18] T. P. Abernethy, *The South in the New Nation*, p. 168; authoritative account in that work, ch. VI. Besides the pioneer study of C. H. Haskins, "The Yazoo Land Companies," in *A.H.A. Papers*, V (1891), the following general accounts are among the most noteworthy: A. J. Beveridge, *Marshall*, III, ch. X; W. C. Bruce, *John Randolph of Roanoke* (1922), I, 180–200; Brant, *Madison*, IV, ch. XVII.

[19] Opinion of May 3, 1790 (Boyd, XVI, 406–408).

[20] This argument was overruled by John Marshall in the famous case of Fletcher *vs.* Peck (1810), when he declared the repeal unconstitutional, bypassing the question of the constitutionality of the Act of 1795 itself. See Abernethy, p. 167.

[21] See p. 246, above.

which Jefferson's appointees (Madison, Gallatin, and Levi Lincoln) negotiated with the commissioners of the state, was that 5,000,000 acres might be set aside to settle such claims as might arise. That the original Yazoo speculators did not afterwards appear as claimants was owing to their foresight and celerity in selling out their claims at a profit. And, although more than half of their own payments to the state were refunded, they appear to have made virtually no refunds to those who had purchased from them. Many of these purchasers, including some big ones, appear to have been innocent, though they may be assumed to have been infected with the virus of speculation. By the time the claims became a national issue most of these were held by Easterners. The New England Mississippi Company, which figured prominently in the later controversy, was formed to protect the interests of the largest body of them. Thus the controversy took on a sectional aspect.

The federal commissioners who had negotiated the Convention of 1802 were authorized to examine claims and report to Congress. This they did early in 1803.[22] Far from overlooking the corruption that accompanied the Yazoo Act of 1795, they abundantly documented it. They did *not* recognize the validity of the title of claimants under that act.[23] Nonetheless, the commissioners believed that the interests of the country, the tranquility of future inhabitants of the territory (where, in fact, no titles would be secure until this matter was settled), and "various equitable considerations" that might be urged in behalf of *most* of the claimants, made a reasonable compromise expedient. The compromise they specifically recommended was that, after provision had been made for certain settlers, the 5,000,000 acres referred to in the Convention of 1802 with Georgia be used to satisfy the Yazoo claimants. That is, the claims of the latter were pared down to a fraction of the original grant but not rejected. The commissioners had to deal with what a Federalist congressman described as "a very perplexed and iniquitous business," and they had recognized that to make honest men of the corrupt Georgia legislature and the greedy land speculators would have been even beyond "Jeffersonian omnipotence."[24] Actually, the proposal was Jeffersonian only in the sense that it was made to Congress by three high-ranking members of the government in whose in-

[22] Feb. 16, 1803. For this report and accompanying documents see *A.S.P. Public Lands*, I, 132–164.

[23] It may be noted that Hamilton, when his legal counsel was sought in 1796, upheld it, and that Robert Goodloe Harper gave the same assurance in promotion literature, quoting Hamilton (R. G. Harper, *Case of the Georgia Sales on the Mississippi, Considered* . . . [1799], p. 109; quoted by Beveridge, *Marshall*, III, 569n.). See also Abernethy, p. 152.

[24] Samuel Taggart to Rev. John Taylor, Jan. 13, 1804, speaking particularly of the task facing Congress ("Letters," p. 126).

tegrity and patriotism the President reposed complete confidence. We may assume that he approved their recommendation and may suppose that a large majority of the members of Congress would have regarded it as moderate and sensible had not John Randolph challenged it as iniquitous. That he did so, and with such vehemence, was ironical in view of the fact that the man chiefly responsible for it was Albert Gallatin, his most intimate and trusted friend in the administration.

It would be impossible to give a wholly rational interpretation of the conduct of as neurotic a person as the Majority Leader, but it may be observed that in opposing this plan of settlement he appeared as a purist who would make no compromise whatever with corruption or countenance the orgies of speculation in any way. His sincerity need not be questioned even though his excesses were deplorable. Whether or not his passionate speeches against the proposal may be regarded as parliamentary classics, as has been claimed, he himself would have relished a comparison between his philippics and those of Demosthenes — or between his denunciations and those of Catiline by Cicero.[25]

On January 29, 1805, the Chairman of the House Committee on Claims, Samuel W. Dana of Connecticut, presented a resolution authorizing the commissioners to settle the disputed Yazoo claims within the limits prescribed by the Convention of 1802 with Georgia. The debate centered on a proposed amendment declaring that no part of the 5,000,-000 acres should be employed as compensation to claimants under the Act of 1795. This amendment was defeated by a vote of 63 to 58, and the resolution was consequently agreed to. But, far from being discouraged, Randolph congratulated his friends on this showing. "We are strong in the cause of truth," he said, "and gentlemen will find that truth will ultimately prevail." He then proclaimed the policy he was determined to follow thereafter: "In whatever shape the subject may be again brought before the House, it will be my duty, and that of my friends, to manifest the same firm spirit of resistance, and to suffer no opportunity to pass of defeating a measure so fraught with mischief." The success of his tactics of obstruction was shown by the failure of the House to act on the bill that was subsequently introduced in accordance with the resolution.[26] The vote showed that he had carried nearly all of the southern Republicans with him, including Jefferson's

[25] Bruce uses the expression "parliamentary classics" and quotes extensively from these speeches (*Randolph*, I, 186–197) without reference, however, to the orators of classical antiquity.
[26] *Annals*, 8 Cong., 2 sess., proceedings, Jan. 29–Feb. 2, 1805, pp. 1022–1174. Anyone who samples the speeches will find them extremely interesting.

two sons-in-law. The resolution was supported by Federalists and
northern Republicans. Whether or not Randolph detested the latter, as
his critics claimed, his words and actions tended to draw a divisive sectional line within his own party.

The compromise this unrelenting man abhorred was not merely with
corruption, but with what he called "the spirit of Federalism." With
this he associated "the plunder of the public property" in behalf of
favored individuals and groups — a "set of speculators" in this instance.[27] "A monster generated by fraud, nursed in corruption" —
this was the image he conjured up, well aware that a major charge of
the partisan critics of Hamilton in his heyday, Jefferson among them,
was that the Secretary of the Treasury condoned speculation in public
securities. Furthermore, he held that if the monstrous Yazoo fraud
should be sanctioned, there would be no point in talking of the "crimes
and follies" of the administration of Adams. In other words, no one
who favored this compromise settlement could regard himself as a true
Republican. Such dogmatism was inevitably resented by congressional
colleagues whose records of devotion to the party were as unsullied as
his but who would not go along with him in denying all flexibility or
compromise in the conduct of government. This undisciplined young
orator was employing tactics of verbal terrorism in the name of rectitude as he himself defined it. William Plumer, who viewed the stormy
scene as a Federalist from New England, privately recorded his own
view of Randolph's language:

> His speeches were too personal — his allusions to brothel-houses &
> pig stys too course & vulgar — his arraigning the motives of mem-
> bers charging them with peculation, bribery, & corruption, were
> insufferable — He lashed demo's & feds indiscriminately — He
> treated no man that was opposed to him with either respect or
> decency. The Speaker ought to have called him to order — for his
> conduct was insufferable; but the Speaker dared not offend him.[28]

While administering to his congressional opponents in both parties
tongue lashings that occasioned talk of duels, the Majority Leader made
no direct attack on the executive branch. He vouched for the freedom
of the great departments of the government from corruption, and described the commissioners as men of ability, sagacity, fidelity, and impartiality than whom no better could be found. However, he charged
them with incredible inconsistency in having recommended compro-

---

[27] *Ibid.*, pp. 1032–1033.
[28] Feb. 2, 1805 (Plumer, *Memorandum*, p. 269).

mise with the corruption they had so clearly recognized and so abundantly described. He would not admit that there was anything else at
issue.

Least of all did he directly attack the President, who in Republican
eyes was still inviolate. He referred to Jefferson as "the great and good
man who now fills, and who (whatever may be the wishes of our opponents) I hope and trust will long fill the Executive chair, not less to
his own honor than to the happiness of his fellow-citizens." The orator
left no doubt, however, of his certainty that consistency would require
this great and good man to follow without deviation the straight and
narrow path of public virtue that Randolph himself had pointed out. If
the President should put his hand to the monstrous act that had been
proposed he would sign "a libel on his whole political life." That he
would never thus "tarnish the unsullied lustre of his fame" Randolph
predicted confidently, thereby seeking to make it impossible for Jefferson to support the pending settlement.[29]

No President could have acquiesced in the delimitation of his course
of action by a congressional leader without abdicating his own position
of leadership, and subsequent events showed that this was something
Jefferson would not do. But Randolph, while employing his characteristic language of exaggeration, had pointed to the dilemma which was
implicit in this problem. Jefferson, who detested speculation and had
himself sedulously avoided it in an era when public men of integrity
often engaged in it with respect to lands, might have been expected to
be sensitive to the charge that the government was countenancing and
abetting it. Furthermore, the attacks on his policy of moderation in the
matter of removals from office had made him fully aware that he was
regarded by some of his own partisans as not partisan enough. Now
added to these complaints was the charge by a political fundamentalist
that the government was yielding to the *spirit* of the Federalists. Both
as the head of a party that he was seeking to hold together and as the
chief of state who was striving to unify the country, Jefferson could
not have failed to deplore the division between Northerners and Southerners that Randolph's outburst had accentuated. The desirability of
equitable treatment of the claimants was increased rather than diminished by the residence of so many of them in New England, the most
disaffected region and the one that Jefferson had striven hardest to win
over. And, although he would almost certainly have agreed that the
state of Georgia had no right to make a sale to the speculating companies in the first place, no one was more desirous than he of expediting

[29] *Annals*, 8 Cong., 2 sess., pp. 1025, 1107.

the settlement of the Territory of Mississippi, which a compromise of this perplexed business and an assurance of valid titles would have furthered. To him no doubt, as to his most trusted advisers, the compromise seemed the lesser of two evils, but his difficulties were magnified when in the hall of Congress it was described as monstrous. Judging from the negative character of the surviving record, he pursued a hands-off policy throughout this controversy. Whether this was wise or unwise no man can say, but presidential intervention even though indirect might have done more harm than good, and this was too confused an issue to warrant his putting his party leadership and presidential prestige to the test by picking up a challenge which was not directed to him anyway.

The nearest thing to a direct attack on the executive branch that was made by John Randolph was on the Postmaster General, Gideon Granger, who was not in the executive council but had at his disposal no inconsiderable amount of federal patronage in the form of contracts to deliver mail. John Randolph denounced him as a claimant on his own part and as the agent of the largest body of claimants (in the New England Mississippi Company), who had had the effrontery to seek to influence Congress in their behalf. In the fall of 1804, Granger and another Republican from New England had presented a memorial in behalf of their clients. This was in fact a moderate document indicating a willingness to compromise their claims within the limits set by the Convention of 1802.[30] The extent of his lobbying beyond this has not been determined, but John Randolph directly charged him with trying to bring to bear upon congressmen the "tremendous patronage" at his command. Referring to an alleged intermediary, Randolph asserted that the Postmaster General maintained a jackal to do his dirty work for him at night.[31] Smarting under these charges, made in such language, Granger addressed a letter to the Speaker of the House in which he asserted that they were "absolutely and altogether untrue" and requested an investigation of his conduct. So inflamed was the House by this letter that for a time a congressman from New England thought that body "bore more resemblance to a French revolutionary convention than the legislature of a free, enlightened, and independent nation."[32] Granger was roundly condemned by some for indecency in

[30] Memorial of Perez Morton and Gideon Granger, submitted Nov. 30, 1804, and referred to a committee (*Annals*, 8 Cong., 2 sess., p. 725).

[31] In his speech of Jan. 31, 1805 (*ibid.*, p. 1106). He had already attacked Granger on Jan. 29 (*ibid.*, pp. 1031–1032).

[32] Granger's letter of Feb. 1, 1805, to the Speaker, and debate on resolution that this be referred to a committee (*ibid.*, pp. 1110–1118); comment of Samuel Taggart, Feb. 3, 1805, in "Letters," p. 152.

asserting that a congressman (Randolph) had spoken untruthfully, and warmly commended by others for his restraint under great provocation.

The chief excitement was created by Matthew Lyon, formerly of Vermont and now of Kentucky, a supporter of the Yazoo compromise who had mail contracts and regarded himself as one of those accused by Randolph of having been bribed. When this rugged democrat bluntly said that both he and the Postmaster General had been "egregiously belied" by the member from Virginia, he was called to order by the Speaker. When he again arose and was recognized by the Speaker, Randolph's coterie sought to have him again ruled out of order, but his right to speak was upheld by a decisive vote under conditions of intense excitement. He yielded the floor, however, until after a resolution to refer Granger's letter to a select committee was passed without recorded dissent. Then he vigorously defended himself and Granger, giving a detailed account of his mail contracts and repaying Randolph in his own currency of abusive language.[33] Lyon called himself a plebeian, and the refinement of the man who had responded to the insulting language of Congressman Roger Griswold in earlier days by spitting on him, and who had defended himself against assault with firetongs, was questionable. But his courage was certainly open to no doubt and the staunch Republicanism of this victim of the Sedition Act was indisputable. Thus the confrontation between him and the haughty Majority Leader, whom he taunted as a possessor of unearned lands and slaves who was ignorant of the basic facts of life, strikingly illustrated the extreme and conflicting elements comprised in Jefferson's party. There was much common sense in Lyon's speech, but it was rendered sensational by its scurrilous references to Randolph. He did not think that the character of the Postmaster General could be injured by "the braying of a jackal or the fulminations of a madman," and he thanked God that he himself had been given the face of a man, "not that of an ape or a monkey." Though Randolph was said to be trying to goad Congressman Dana of Connecticut into a duel, he would not have condescended to challenge a vulgarian like Lyon. On the other hand, he never accepted the challenge of that robust Republican that he produce proof of his charges and allegations about mail contracts.

By referring Granger's letter to a committee the House buried it. Thus the charges against him were not investigated and remained unproved. He himself sought to disprove them by writing another letter to the Speaker in which he set forth in detail his relations with the Yazoo claims, and soon thereafter he presented his case in virtually

33 *Annals*, 8 Cong., 2 sess., pp. 1121–1126.

the same words in a broadside.[34] He said that he accepted the agency before there had been any congressional objection to the report of the commissioners, and also that he had consulted the Attorney General, who said unofficially that he could perceive no objection. The Postmaster General, flatly denying that he had tried to make use of any kind of improper influence in behalf of the company he represented, again urged an investigation.[35]

Congress was now too much occupied with other matters to give further attention to this sideshow. As for Jefferson, he could hardly have failed to regret Granger's connection with the New England Mississippi Company, and he might have been expected to question its propriety. But obviously he saw no reason to take any sort of public action on the basis of unproved charges against an official whom he regarded as competent and loyal. And there were a number of practical reasons for ignoring the matter altogether. Among these was the fact that Granger was one of the most active and influential of New England Republicans — a group that John Randolph had aggrieved. A further consideration was that Granger's adviser, Levi Lincoln of Massachusetts, had informed the President that, for personal reasons, he would leave the government at the end of the year. The President was looking for a new attorney general and there was little likelihood that he would find one in New England. He did not want to be without a representative from that region in his government and he had found Granger highly useful as a political sentinel. His personal confidence in him appears to have remained unshaken through the years. Besides retaining him throughout his own presidency, he commended him afterwards to President Madison for the vacancy on the Supreme Court created by the death of Justice William Cushing of Massachusetts, which called for the selection of someone from New England. Jefferson rated him as second only to Levi Lincoln among possible appointees from that region. "His abilities are great," said the ex-President, "I have entire confidence in his integrity, though I am sensible that J.R. has been able to lessen the confidence of many in him." [36] Madison did not fully share Jefferson's high opinion of the man who was still Postmaster General,

[34] Granger to the Speaker, Feb. 7, 1805 (*ibid.*, pp. 1110*n.*–1113*n.*). A copy of the broadside, dated Feb. 25, 1805, is in LC, 25662. I have found no record of any other explanation made by him to TJ, but no doubt one was made orally.

[35] In the next Congress a select committee, which had been appointed at the instance of a strong opponent of the Yazoo compromise to inquire into his conduct, reported that time was insufficient for an inquiry and recommended a postponement which turned out to be permanent; Apr. 17, 1806 (Plumer, *Memorandum,* p. 485; *Annals,* 9 Cong., 1 sess., pp. 244–245).

[36] TJ to Madison, Oct. 15, 1810 (Ford, IX, 283). Lincoln, TJ's first choice, was offered but declined the appointment, and Madison finally appointed Joseph Story.

but the fact that Granger was tinctured with "Yazooism" would have given him pause in any case, for John Randolph gave currency and long life to the term as one of reproach and had attached it to Madison himself. That was one of many ill effects of the Majority Leader's intemperate and inveterate hostility to the wise compromise the three federal officers had recommended.

Four years after Marshall's decision in Fletcher vs. Peck (1810) and five years after Jefferson left office, this long controversy was finally settled along the lines of the commissioners' original proposal. The ex-President's full approval of the Chief Justice's disposition of the case cannot be rightly claimed, since he referred to this as another one of the "twistifications" whereby Marshall reconciled law to his personal biases.[37] What he himself would have done at this stage he did not say, but the most practical procedure at the outset would have been to waive the question of the validity of the original Yazoo grants and to make a settlement on grounds of expediency and equity just as the commissioners had recommended. One of the ill results of the defeat of the compromise was to force the issue of legal validity. Thus Marshall was confronted with a constitutional dilemma, just as Jefferson had been with one that was political and in Randolph's eyes moral. The Chief Justice met it by declaring the Repeal Act of 1796 unconstitutional as a violation of the provision forbidding any state to violate the sanctity of contracts. Thereby he gave a handle to critics of the Court, who could say that it was indifferent to corruption and denied recourse to remedial measures. Also, he bypassed the question of the constitutionality of the notorious Yazoo Act of 1796, which was an infringement on national sovereignty by the state of Georgia.[38] Jefferson probably regarded this act as unconstitutional, but for Marshall to have declared it so in 1810 would have been to deprive the claimants of any legal grounds and probably to make even a compromise impossible. This famous decision was no unmixed blessing. It was without legislative effect until after John Randolph left Congress. Since nothing was gained and much lost by the long delay in effecting a reasonable settlement of this important and deeply divisive question, he may be safely said to have rendered disservice to his country.

The duration of his relentless obstructionism could hardly have been anticipated when he blocked the Yazoo compromise early in the year 1805, but before entering upon the decisive phase of the impeachment

[37] TJ to Madison, May 25, 1810 (Ford, IX, 276). Beveridge, in *Marshall*, III, 592–593, makes the unsupported assertion that TJ and Madison "ardently desired" this disposition of the case.

[38] See Abernethy's pointed comments on this aspect of Marshall's decision (*South in the New Nation*, pp. 166–167).

trial of Justice Chase he had strained his relations with the administration and furthered dissension in his own party. While wasting his strength, he had unmistakably demonstrated his proneness to excess. In the meantime the President — for a variety of reasons, including the unmanageability of the Majority Leader of the House — remained aloof from the legislative battle.

$\begin{bmatrix} X X V \end{bmatrix}$

Judges on Trial

THE trial of Justice Samuel Chase of the United States Supreme Court before the Senate on articles of impeachment adopted by the House of Representatives, which ended only three days before Jefferson's second inauguration as President, was the most dramatic political episode of his first term. Since the Louisiana Purchase involved a series of events, extending over many months and marked by no clearly recognizable climax, its dramatic effect was dissipated. The Burr-Hamilton duel had important political implications but was nonetheless a private confrontation, whereas the Chase trial was a public spectacle. The trial proper followed hard on the Yazoo debates and lasted about a month, but in a sense this case dominated the entire congressional session and it was in definite prospect months before that. It was the last of a series of trials of impeached judges, and if we would understand it we must view events in the order of their happening. Before we get to it, therefore, we should consider developments in Pennsylvania and the sad case of Judge John Pickering of New Hampshire. Also we should inquire into Jefferson's attitudes and actions in this connection.

i

Early in the first congressional session of his presidency, speaking of his political foes, he said privately: "On their part, they have retired into the judiciary as a stronghold. There the remains of federalism are to be preserved and fed from the treasury, and from that battery all the works of republicanism are to be beaten down and erased." [1] If the crucial terms are capitalized and allowance is made for exaggerated partisan forebodings, the essential truthfulness of the assertion can hardly be denied, for the national judiciary, one hundred per cent Federalist, amounted to an arm of that party. Within the next few weeks the

[1] TJ to John Dickinson, Dec. 19, 1801 (L. & B., X, 302).

united Republicans, by repealing the Judiciary Act of 1801, leveled the outworks that had been erected during the final days of the Adams administration, thus restoring the *status quo ante bellum*.[2] Of the remaining judges the President might have said, as he did of officeholders as a group, that few died and none resigned. This was an undoubted grievance to his own hungry partisans, of whose claims he was well aware but whom he and Gallatin usually sought to moderate.

Before there was any overt move against Federalist judges on the national level, action was taken in Pennsylvania on a state level. Reform of the inadequate state judiciary was a burning and became a divisive issue there, since Governor McKean wanted to increase the number of judges while the Duane-Leib faction sought to democratize the judicial function by extending the powers of the justices of the peace. The latter group evinced a spirit of hostility to judges generally such as was not to be found in the Governor or in Alexander J. Dallas, whom Jefferson had appointed federal district attorney and who was in close touch with Gallatin. The two factions united, however, in the effort to remove Alexander Addison, presiding judge of the fifth or western judicial district, who was described as the "transmontane Goliath" of Federalism in the state and had demonstrated his intransigence by continuing his partisan offenses after the Republicans had won an unquestionable popular mandate. Though he himself delivered political harangues from the bench, he denied to a Republican colleague the right to address a grand jury. In Pennsylvania, judges might be removed by joint address of the two houses of the legislature, and the now-dominant Republicans might have disposed of Addison in that way, but his case was held by the lower house to warrant impeachment. In January, 1803, he was convicted and removed from office. Dallas conducted the prosecution, and the Federalists, while supporting the accused Judge with partisan unanimity, made little of the case afterwards. This inaction may have been because of their political impotence in the state, but it may also have reflected a recognition of the weakness of Addison's position. Even if it be granted that in moving against him the Republicans were motivated chiefly by considerations of party, his conduct seems indefensible — except on grounds of Federalist partisanship.[3]

Early in February, 1803, about a week after Judge Addison's removal

[2] See ch. VII, above.

[3] Political developments in this state and the antijudiciary fight there are well described in S. W. Higginbotham, *The Keystone in the Democratic Arch*, chs. 4, 5; comments on the Addison case, pp. 53–55. Beveridge (*Marshall*, III, 164), reflecting the Federalist point of view, regards the evidence against Addison as trivial and his address in defense of himself as historically important. Its importance, however, lies chiefly in its revelation of a state of mind.

from the bench of Pennsylvania, Jefferson sent to the House of Representatives of the United States a communication which led to the first impeachment proceedings against a member of the federal judiciary. Since the complaints he had received against District Judge John Pickering of New Hampshire were not "within Executive cognizance," he said, he was transmitting the documents containing them to the body to which the Constitution had "confided a power of instituting proceedings of redress," if its members should believe that the case called for them.[4] About three weeks after the transmission of this message, Chief Justice Marshall announced his decision in the case of Marbury *vs.* Madison.[5] And in May, after the adjournment of Congress, the President called the attention of an influential congressman to a recent performance of Justice Samuel Chase which should not be permitted to go unnoticed. In the perspective of history it is difficult to regard this sequence of events as wholly fortuitous. Thrust seems to have been followed by counterthrust in a duel of eminent antagonists. But the conflict over the judiciary was between rival political parties, and the ultimate failure of the impeachment movement is attributable to the divisions within the majority in Congress, where for a variety of reasons decisive action was delayed. In the winter and spring of 1803 the climate of Republican opinion seemed favorable, and Jefferson may have thought this a good time to anticipate or counter the moves of a Chief Justice whom he regarded as crafty, but he could have justly claimed that he was trying to meet situations as they arose. The complaints against Judge Pickering were so serious that some action seemed to be called for, and he transmitted the documents to Congress only a few days after he got them.

These documents had been collected on the instructions of Gallatin, who had received an earlier complaint of the extraordinary conduct of the Judge in the case of the ship *Eliza*, which had been seized by the Republican Surveyor of Customs at Portsmouth, along with goods claimed by him to have been illegally unladen. Whereupon the Federalist owner of the vessel sought legal redress from Pickering, who promptly released the vessel. Thereafter, at a trial brought on by the Republican Collector of Customs, at which the case of the government was presented by the Republican District Attorney and the Federalist merchant was represented by a strongly Federalist lawyer, the Judge,

[4] Message of Feb. 4, 1803 (*Annals,* 7 Cong., 2 sess., p. 460). The fullest and ablest account of the entire case is that of Lynn W. Turner, "The Impeachment of John Pickering," in *A.H.R.,* LIV, 485–507 (April, 1949). The congressional history is well told by Lacy in his dissertation "Jefferson and Congress," pp. 239–247; he includes a useful chronological table of the proceedings.

[5] See pp. 148–151, above.

in a state of distressing intoxication, ruled for the Federalist owner and, in denying an appeal, employed offensive language. The fact of the business is that Pickering, who had had a distinguished career of service to his state, was now insane and not responsible for his actions. It is also a fact that this case was enmeshed in partisan politics from start to finish. Federalist friends blamed the Judge's plight on the repeal of the Judiciary Act of 1801, under a wise provision of which the circuit judges might appoint one of their number to perform the duties of an incapacitated district judge — as in fact had been done in his case during the brief lifetime of that law. In his present condition he had neither the mind nor the will to resign, and he could not afford to do so because he was in greatly reduced circumstances as the result of recent heavy losses by fire. How aware Gallatin may have been of the total situation when he ordered the collection of the documents, we have no way of knowing. Senator William Plumer of New Hampshire went to see him in Washington in the fall of 1802, shortly after these shameful doings in Portsmouth, and was then informed that complaints against the Judge had been received. Gallatin's hints that Pickering resign to avoid severe action were not heeded, however, for Plumer and other Federalists feared the appointment in his stead of John S. Sherburne, the district attorney, a political foe whom they especially detested.

The documents that were duly submitted to the President by the vigilant Secretary of the Treasury reflected the point of view of the local governmental officials who were involved in the case and thus may be said to have been one-sided.[6] There were mitigating circumstances which might have been expected to touch the heart of any compassionate man, and Jefferson may not have been as informed of these at the outset as he should have been, but not even the Judge's friends, well aware of his personal problems and past repute, could deny his demonstrated unfitness for the high office he held on a life appointment. Since Pickering did not resign the office and his fellow Federalists advised against his doing so, the President was confronted with a problem for which the Constitution and existing law had made no provision beyond the grant of authority to the House to impeach and the Senate to try civil officers for treason, bribery, or other high crimes and misdemeanors. If the offense of this mentally irresponsible judge could not be interpreted as falling within one of these categories there was no legal way to remove him. Confronting this dilemma, at a time when partisanship was extremely rancorous and the scope of the impeachment process untested, Republicans and Federalists respectively seized the horn pointing to their immediate political advantage.

[6] Turner, p. 491.

By passing the problem on to Congress, Jefferson clearly sought to initiate the impeachment process, and afterwards, when the case was pending, he seems to have had no doubt that Pickering's intoxication on the bench and denial of an appeal would lead to his conviction, regardless of his insanity. He told William Plumer, however, that the removal of judges by impeachment was "a *bungling way*," and he had previously expressed the opinion that the Constitution should be so amended that "the President, on application of Congress should have authority to remove any Judge from office." [7] More than a score of years later, when William Plumer's political complexion had changed, he asserted that if such a provision had been present in the Constitution, every senator would have voted for the removal of Pickering; and, while doubting this, a careful and judicious modern student of the episode has expressed the opinion that the President and his party missed a golden opportunity to correct a serious defect in the existing Constitution.[8]

The idea of the removal of judges by the executive on joint address of the legislature was by no means novel at the time, since there was provision for such procedure in a number of states, including New Hampshire as well as Pennsylvania. Judge Edmund Pendleton, deeply revered in Virginia, had recommended it for the federal government during the first year of Jefferson's presidency. But the amending process was slow, and we may doubt if his impatient followers would have been willing to resort to it until after they had tested the possibilities of impeachment. Judging from the obstructionism of the Federalists in Congress, and in particular from their delaying tactics with respect to the Twelfth Amendment, there is little reason to doubt that they would have opposed this one. Their main purpose was to keep the judges just as they were, and they would have described any talk about their removal as an attack on the independence of the judiciary. If this provision had included the requirement of a two-thirds vote in each branch of Congress, it does not seem likely that it would have been resorted to often; and, unlike the trial on impeachments, it would also have required the agreement of the President. Unquestionably, it would have been a useful procedure in the case of poor Judge Pickering and also in that of Justice Chase. The Federalists might have been expected to oppose it for just that reason.

From the surviving written record it is impossible to determine whether or not Jefferson, after referring this difficult and unpleasant

[7] Records of Jan. 5, 7, 1804, in Plumer, *Memorandum* (pp. 100–102). He said that TJ made the latter statement in the previous congressional session (1802–1803).
[8] Turner, p. 492, quoting Plumer's "Autobiography."

business to the House ("passing the buck," as we might say), did anything more about it. He cannot be fairly held responsible for all the words and actions of the Republican leaders in Congress, but the Federalists regarded this impeachment as a measure of the administration, and party discipline was clearly manifest in connection with it. Within a month the House voted to impeach Judge Pickering and notified the Senate to that effect, though formal charges were not approved until the next congressional session and the trial did not take place until March, 1804, a year after the receipt of the President's message. This "grand inquest of the nation," as the managers for the House described it, had many of the characteristics of a partisan brawl. The Federalists alleged that the procedure of the men who served as prosecutors for the House — John Randolph, Nicholson, Rodney, and others — and that of the Senate majority was ruthless and inhumane. Though ordered to appear on short order, the erring Judge did not and presumably could not do so. Only with reluctance was testimony with respect to his insanity admitted, and this was disregarded by more than two-thirds of his senatorial judges when they convicted him by a strict party vote.

The most striking feature of the procedure was the phraseology of the voting formula. Saying merely that Pickering was "guilty as charged" in a particular article, not that he was "guilty of high crimes and misdemeanors" upon that charge, this formulation relieved the consciences of some who doubted if the Judge's offenses fell within the language of the Constitution. That he was guilty of the stipulated offenses was indisputable, but this case seemed to show, as Senator Plumer observed, that the impeachment process was to be considered, in effect, as "*a mode of removal*, and not as a charge and conviction of high crimes and misdemeanors." Such indeed was the interpretation the Republican congressional leaders sought to give the process at this stage. Shortly after the event one of the highest of the High Federalists said: "The *demon* of party governed the decision." [9] Timothy Pickering (not to be confused with the Judge) might well have said that the *demon* had dominated the case from its very beginning, but, suffering from the astigmatism so common among politicians, and indeed among human beings generally, he recognized no Federalist responsibility for the party spirit that engulfed this case. Members of the Judge's own party strongly opposed his resignation for purely political reasons; and,

[9] Plumer to Isaac Lyman, Mar. 17, 1804, quoted by Lacy, p. 247, from Plumer Papers; Timothy Pickering to Theodore Lyman, Mar. 14, 1804 (Adams, *Documents Relating to New England Federalism*, p. 359).

while championing the independence of the judiciary, they were in fact defending a Federalist judiciary. Their self-righteousness did not become them.

A great many people must share the discredit for this confused and tragic episode; but, while the Federalists should bear the onus of trying to keep a man of demonstrated incompetence in office, the Republicans bore that of disregard for an unfortunate human being. And the President himself, after the conviction, gave a handle to his critics by the appointments he quickly made. To the vacant judgeship he named Sherburne, the district attorney, and to the attorney generalship he named the clerk of the court. There may have been practical as well as political reasons for promoting two men already on the scene whose qualifications had been previously gone into, especially since the picking among Republican lawyers in New Hampshire was scanty. But both of these men had been witnesses for the prosecution, and Sherburne had been accused in the locality of plotting against Pickering with a view to succeeding him. When as judge he himself proceeded to appoint another witness as clerk it appeared that the major local actors in this case had received their political reward. Thus the partisan complexion of the affair was deepened.[10]

ii

As things turned out, the Pickering case set no constitutional precedent, but this ostensible success encouraged the Republican leaders of the House to proceed formally against Justice Chase, into whose conduct they had been inquiring. The impeachment trial of this redoubtable man could hardly have failed to become a *cause célèbre* because of his stature and temperament and the feelings he aroused. He towered in the Supreme Court, both physically and intellectually, before the advent of Marshall, and throughout his long and distinguished career he had been a tempestuous character. His political course had been marked by inconsistency as well as turbulence. Espousing the cause of the Patriots in the preliminaries of the American Revolution, he was not averse to rioting; and as a signer of the Declaration of Independence he belonged to the goodly company that the author of that document held in such high honor. In the course of the Revolution, however, when involved in a dubious financial operation, Chase excited the indignation

[10] Turner (pp. 505–506) reports that Steele, who was appointed to succeed Sherburne but who had hoped to succeed Pickering, declined the appointment on alleged grounds of propriety and ultimately left the party; and that Sherburne himself lost his mind a score of years later as though by divine interposition, being then relieved of his duties by other judges and drawing his salary till death.

of Alexander Hamilton, who went so far as to say that he was "universally despised." [11] He opposed the Constitution but afterwards turned Federalist; and as a judge in Maryland he barely escaped removal from office on joint address of the Assembly, where there was a majority against him but not the requisite two-thirds.

On the national scene he had been a particular object of Republican dislike from the time that he presided, as a justice on circuit, over the trials of Thomas Cooper and James Thomson Callender under the Sedition Act — especially the latter, which took place in Richmond. Jefferson's son-in-law, Congressman John W. Eppes, engaged in only slight exaggeration when he said that there was only one sentiment in Virginia as to the Judge's conduct in the Callender case: namely, that it was *"indecent and tyrannical."* [12] The President himself was undoubtedly of that sentiment, and very many believed that Chase had not merely browbeaten the lawyers, as he had also in the earlier case of Fries, but had insulted the Commonwealth. This white-haired man of large bulk and powerful mind reminded Joseph Story of Dr. Samuel Johnson, but to many this harsh and implacable judge seemed an American Jeffries. He was considerably less than that, but in his official capacity he was so intemperate and indiscreet that District Judge Richard Peters said he never sat with him without pain, and the victims of his wrath found him intolerably overbearing.[13] Thus he became the conspicuous symbol of the judicial arrogance that Republicans found so infuriating and that extremists among them were disposed to attribute to federal judges as a group and even to state judges.

The specific occasion for the initiation of proceedings against this highhanded Justice of the Supreme Court was provided by him in a charge to a grand jury in Baltimore in May, 1803. In this he used language of grave impropriety and manifested political intransigence along with characteristic self-assurance and self-righteousness.[14] The observations by means of which he sought to inculcate "correct principles of government" included a direct attack on political democracy, and specific references to the late alteration of the federal judiciary by

[11] Quoted, with references, in article by E. S. Corwin in *D.A.B.*, which is the best brief account of Chase I am familiar with.

[12] Quoted by Plumer in his *Memorandum*, pp. 103–104. I have described the proceedings briefly in *Jefferson and the Ordeal of Liberty*, pp. 471–472.

[13] Peters' comment, in 1804, is quoted by Warren, I, 281. There was some talk among Republicans in the House about including Peters in the impeachment proceedings, but this idea was wisely abandoned.

[14] The charge of May 2, 1803, supposedly in the form that Chase read it, is Exhibit No. 8 in the account of the trial (*Annals*, 8 Cong., 2 sess., pp. 673–676). The claim that he departed from this written paper and made other critical comments on the government was denied at the trial and cannot be proved.

the abolition of the offices of sixteen circuit court judges (that is, the repeal of the Judiciary Act of 1801), the adoption of universal suffrage by the State of Maryland, and alterations in the existing state judicial system that had been proposed. In the passage that was destined to be most quoted he said that the independence of the judiciary of the nation was "already shaken to its foundation" and could be restored only by the virtue of the people; and that the independence of the state judges would be "entirely destroyed" if the legislature should pass the bill abolishing the two supreme courts.[15] Then he attacked an action which had already been taken in Maryland:

> The change of the State constitution, by allowing universal suffrage, will, in my opinion, certainly and rapidly destroy all protection of property, and all security to personal liberty; and our republican constitution will sink into a mobocracy, the worst of all possible government.

Besides making a plea for an electorate of property holders and directly attacking political democracy, he alluded unmistakably to Jefferson. The Justice asserted that "visionary and theoretical writers" and the doctrines of modern reformers "that all men in a state of society are entitled to enjoy equal liberty and equal rights" had brought upon the country "this mighty mischief." Jefferson undoubtedly regarded this utterance as a repudiation of the Declaration of Independence which he and Chase had signed. Himself an intellectual and champion of education, he was never so much the democrat as to condone rule by massive ignorance, but the Justice had denied the faith in the citizenry generally by which the President's steps had long been lighted. Furthermore, in the political harangue he presumptuously delivered from the bench, Chase, a high official of one co-ordinate branch of the United States government, had specifically condemned an act of Congress, signed by the President and already upheld by the Supreme Court. Also, he had condemned a past action of his own state and sought to influence the future conduct of its government. It would appear that this single judge, regarding himself as inviolate in his sanctuary, was defiant of all authority but his own and that, while warning against mobocracy, he was exemplifying judicial irresponsibility and inciting lawlessness. Whether or not the *National Intelligencer* was warranted in seeing in this charge "humiliating evidence of the unfortunate effects of disappointed ambition," that paper had good ground for pronouncing it the

[15] We do not enter into the merits of that particular issue, on which Chase may have taken a wise position.

most extraordinary that the "violence of federalism" had yet produced.[16]

Congress was not in session at the time and the President never referred this speech to the House, as he did the complaints he had received against Judge Pickering. He took no official cognizance of this matter. From his reference to it in a private communication, however, the movement for the impeachment of Justice Chase may be dated. This was at the end of a long letter to Representative Joseph H. Nicholson, a member of the Republican triumvirate in the House and a citizen of Maryland. After discussing the perennial problem of appointments and removals in response to a communication from Nicholson and reporting briefly on recent foreign developments, Jefferson said:

You must have heard of the extraordinary charge of Chace [sic] to the Grand Jury at Baltimore. Ought this seditious and official attack on the principles of our Constitution, and on the proceedings of a State, to go unpunished? And to whom so pointedly as yourself will the public look for the necessary measures? I ask these questions for your consideration. For myself, it is better that I should not interfere.[17]

Lacking other comments from Jefferson on the performance of the Justice, we have only this brief private reference to go on. We may take exception to his designation of Chase's action as "seditious." It was not thus described afterwards in the formal articles of impeachment. But few can now deny the gross impropriety of the Judge's conduct or be at all surprised that the President thought him deserving of removal from office. Though Jefferson had told William Plumer that impeachment was a bungling method of removing judges, no other method was sanctioned by the Constitution. The House had already voted to impeach Pickering, but had presented no articles as yet. Quite clearly Jefferson wanted the untested impeachment process to be pursued, while he himself kept out of it. Impeachment was wholly within the province of Congress; the President did not have to approve its actions as in the matter of legislation. Had he participated publicly in this case he might well have been charged with impropriety by Republicans and almost certainly would have been so charged by his political enemies. How far beyond the impeachment, conviction, and consequent re-

[16] *National Intelligencer*, May 20, 1803. A condensed version of the charge followed. Apparently the full text was not secured until later. This paper, on Aug. 5, 1803, said that Chase had sent a copy "with great reluctance."

[17] TJ to J. H. Nicholson, May 13, 1803 (LC, 22701; L. & B., X, 390, in slightly different form).

moval of Chase he would have liked for things to go, no man can say, since there is no record of his having told anybody. All we surely know is that he privately suggested that action be taken against a particular justice for a designated offense, and unless evidence to the contrary should appear, we must assume that thenceforth he left this matter wholly in the hands of the Republican leaders in Congress.

Nicholson was not to be the prime mover in the business, however. When he took counsel with his friend Nathaniel Macon in the summer of 1803, the Speaker strongly urged him not to be, since he would be regarded as a likely successor to Chase. Furthermore, while Macon believed Chase more culpable than poor Judge Pickering, he expressed doubts of the applicability of the impeachment process to the Justice's expressions of political opinions in a charge to a grand jury.[18] One of the pointed questions he asked was couched in Jefferson's own language: "Is error of opinion to be dreaded where enquiry is free?" The questions the Speaker had raised may have occasioned the search for other offenses; but it was John Randolph rather than Nicholson who introduced, at the next congressional session, a resolution calling for the appointment of a committee to inquire into Chase's official conduct. The Federalist request that evidence of wrongdoing be presented before the taking of the vote on this was denied, and the resolution was adopted by more than a two-thirds majority, including the President's two sons-in-law. An occasional Republican voted the other way, but this was viewed on both sides as an out-and-out party measure. John Randolph was chairman and Nicholson a member of the committee named in pursuance of the resolution. This report, recommending impeachment, was approved by an overwhelming vote immediately after the conviction of Pickering.[19] This timing was regarded by the opposition as unseemly, but the session of 1803–1804 had been laborious and the leaders wanted to bring it to an end, as they did about two weeks later. Much important legislation had been enacted, especially with respect to Louisiana, and the President personally concerned himself with that part of it. In this connection the Majority Leader of the House had reached the highest point of his collaboration with the administration and his usefulness to it.

There is no evidence that Jefferson tried either to guide or to restrain John Randolph in his procedure with respect to the impeachment of

[18] Letters of Macon, July 26, Aug. 6, 1803, quoted by Lacy, pp. 248–249, from Nicholson Papers.
[19] Resolution and debate, Jan. 5–7, 1804 (*Annals*, 8 Cong., 1 sess., pp. 805–876); report and action of Mar. 12 (*ibid.*, pp. 1171–1181).

Chase, in which he continued to be the prime mover. As chairman of
the committee to draw up articles, he presented a report on the day
before adjournment.[20] Formal action on this was deferred, but copies of
the articles were provided for each representative and senator and they
got into the papers. The President was now in position to observe, if he
had not been earlier, that Chase's charge to the grand jury at Baltimore,
the only offense he had called to the attention of Nicholson a year
before, entered into only the last of seven articles.[21] The others dealt
chiefly with the Justice's conduct in the trials of Fries and Callender,
especially the latter, and thus were involved in legal technicalities and
questions of judgment. Time was to show that Randolph, untrained in
the law, could not cope with these, and that they served to distract
attention from Chase's direct attack on the legislative and executive
branches of the federal government and the constitutional proceedings
of a state.

From the outset the Federalist papers attributed the move against the
jurist to presidential lust for power, vindictive partisanship, and Republican hunger for office. Referring sarcastically to the "Man of the
People," the *New York Evening Post* made this early comment: "The
simple truth is, Mr. Jefferson has been determined from the first to
have a judiciary, as well as a legislature, that would second the views of
the executive." And, following the adoption of the resolution presented
by "Mr. Jefferson's leading democrat" in the House, which led to the
appointment of what the *Evening Post* called the "Inquisitorial Committee at Washington," that paper said: "No, let us not be deceived,
justice is not the object, party rage is still unsatisfied, our Courts are
filled by federal [that is, Federalist] Judges; here is the mighty crime,
here the high misdemeanor. . . . The bench in short is to be cleared of
its present incumbents, no matter by what means, and filled with men
subservient to the views of the powers that be, no matter altho' at the
expense of all that renders a court of justice respectable."[22] Throughout this affair the Federalists continued to contend that the Pickering
and Chase impeachments were the opening phase of a concerted party
move against the entire bench, up to and including the Chief Justice,
and, through the years, they have been echoed by numerous historians.
The utterances of some of Jefferson's supporters lent color to a claim
which would probably have been made in any case, but it was war-

[20] Mar. 26, 1804 (*ibid.*, pp. 1237–1240).

[21] In the articles approved in the fall it was No. 8. Another article was based on
Chase's treatment of a grand jury at Newcastle.

[22] *N.Y. Evening Post*, Jan. 20, 1804; other quotations from issues of Jan. 11, 13 and
Mar. 3, 1804.

ranted by nothing he himself or his ministers said, and was not in accord with John Randolph's personal attitude toward John Marshall.[23]

Shortly after Congress rose, Chase himself entered the fray by issuing what the leading and wholly partisan Federalist organ described as an "interesting, forcible, and eloquent appeal . . . to the justice of his country, against an unheard of, cruel, and detestable party persecution." This was a memorial to the House of Representatives, undelivered because of the adjournment of that body, which Chase requested the editors of the newspapers of the country to publish along with the reported articles of impeachment. In complying with this request, the *National Intelligencer* said that under the circumstances a declination would have been denounced as "partial or pusillanimous." [24] Samuel Harrison Smith's relatively moderate paper, saying that until now it had avoided comment on the grounds of impeachment, and that it had hoped the Republican papers "would not provoke a conflict of prejudice and passion," described the late action of Chase as unprecedented, undignified, and provocative. Characterizing as extraordinary his strictures on the conduct of the House of Representatives and certain of its individual members "in the discharge of delegated powers," it sought to answer his arguments point by point.

In the memorial he prepared before the articles of impeachment had been reported Chase requested that these be drawn up before adjournment, so that he might have ample time to form his defense and vindicate his innocence. His position was by no means unnatural, but actually the testimony on which the charges were to be based was already available to him in print and he showed that he was familiar with it. He denounced the method by which the resolution calling for his impeachment had been adopted and trembled at the thought of future excesses that might follow such a precedent. In the letter he wrote after the articles had been reported he said they contained "the most aggravated and inflamed construction" that "passion and party spirit" could put on the ex-parte evidence. Therefore, he made his undelivered memorial public as an appeal to his country, the world, and posterity "against the injustice and illegality of the proceedings in this case, and as a solemn protest against the principles on which they are founded."

[23] W. C. Bruce points out that, in the Chase trial, Randolph repeatedly expressed "profound admiration" for Marshall, and adds that he entertained this throughout life.

[24] The memorial, dated Mar. 24, 1804, and a letter of Mar. 29, 1804, from Chase, were printed in both *N.Y. Evening Post* and *National Intelligencer* on Apr. 4, 1804. The latter paper, which had already published the articles, commented at some length on the memorial. I have used its text.

Since there could be no further action until Congress reassembled in the fall, Chase had seven months to ponder over the articles of impeachment that had been reported, as he wished, and become public. In this interim there were important political developments of which we may remind ourselves. The "secession plot" in New England, already foiled by Burr's defeat in New York, went wholly under cover; and, before the end of the long summer, the ratification of the Twelfth Amendment virtually assured the re-election of the President, who retained the support of all Republican factions. Largely bypassing the troublesome question of the Floridas, he was able to send a highly optimistic message to Congress when that body met in November, and soon everybody knew that his victory in the election was overwhelming. His prestige was at its height, but he did not put it on the line in the impeachment fight, as President Franklin D. Roosevelt was to do more than a century later when seeking to reform an obstructive Supreme Court. He did not mention impeachment or the judiciary in his message and, so far as we know, had referred to the proceedings against Chase in private until this time only in his letter of a year and a half before to Congressman Nicholson. He was charged by William Plumer with showing unmerited hospitality to Vice President Burr, who would preside over the trial of Chase in the Senate, but the focus of attention was on Congress, and particularly on John Randolph, whose self-confidence tended to be excessive and appears to have become overweening. Well aware of Randolph's vanity and sensitiveness, the President went out of his way to explain why he had sent to Nicholson, rather than to him, the draft of a proposed measure for the protection of harbors.[25] That the Majority Leader sought Jefferson's counsel with respect to the Chase affair is as unlikely as that the President voluntarily offered it. John Randolph had assumed the dominant role in these proceedings and was now relying on his extraordinary powers of speech and parliamentary skill, along with the backing of the large Republican majority in Congress.

He reported articles of impeachment on November 30. These differed little from those reported by him at the end of the last session. Two articles bearing on the Fries trial were combined, and one relating to Chase's conduct in the Callender trial, with which the Virginians were so obsessed, had been added, but these proved to be weakest of the lot, which now numbered eight altogether. The charge to the grand jury at Baltimore was last, presumably because it was last in point of time. While the testimony on which these articles were based was in

[25] Nov. 19, 1804 (Ford, VIII, 333-336); see pp. 441-442, above.

print and fully available to the members of the House, only a small part of it was actually brought into what now appears to have been an inadequate discussion, and we may doubt if the legal technicalities were well understood. The articles were adopted by an overwhelming party vote on December 4, and on the next day seven managers were elected — the list being headed by John Randolph, Rodney, and Nicholson. It was then ordered that the Senate be informed and the articles exhibited.[26]

William Branch Giles of Virginia, whose health was sufficiently restored to permit his return to Congress as a member of the Senate, assumed the leadership in this business in that body. It will be recalled that he had been dubious of Jefferson's moderation at the beginning of the administration and had himself then advocated an "absolute repeal" of the federal judicial system.[27] Subsequently, in the House of Representatives, he led the fight to repeal the Judiciary Act of 1801. Though his sentiments about the judiciary were more radical than any Jefferson ever expressed, the two men were fully agreed on this particular action and worked together with notable harmony during the first congressional session of this presidency. To what extent Giles consulted the President in the session of 1804–1805 we do not know, but during the preliminaries of the Chase trial that senator was reported as consulting with John Randolph every day. John Quincy Adams lamented that the issue of Chase's prosecution would be settled *out of doors*. What he and other Federalist senators feared and expected at the outset was that the will of the House of Representatives would prevail. This will was embodied in John Randolph, whom he particularly detested. The utterances of Giles at this stage, as reported by the unsympathetic pens of Adams and William Plumer, reflected a political view of the impeachment process which those diarists abhorred for reasons that were ostensibly constitutional and could hardly have failed to be partisan as well. In Giles's opinion, mere error in a judge — or mere inability to perform his duties, as in the case of Judge Pickering — was warrant for his impeachment, conviction, and removal from office.[28] The pugnacious Senator from Virginia is said to have been more specific and even more alarming in private conversation. Thus John Quincy Adams reported him as saying that "if the Judges of the Supreme Court should dare, *as they had done*, to declare an act of Congress unconstitutional, or to

[26] Nov. 30–Dec. 5, 1804 (*Annals*, 8 Cong., 2 sess., pp. 726–763). Lacy, in his account of these events (pp. 250–252), emphasizes the inadequacy of the debate.

[27] Anderson, *Giles*, pp. 76–80; see above, pp. 116, 127–128.

[28] Plumer's entry of Dec. 20, 1804 (*Memorandum*, pp. 229–230), reporting observations of Giles in a discussion of rules for the trial which is not reported in the *Annals*.

send a mandamus to the Secretary of State, *as they had done*, it was the undoubted right of the House of Representatives to impeach them, and of the Senate to remove them, for giving such opinions, however honest or sincere they may have been in entertaining them." [29] These unguarded expressions, thus reported, gave countenance to the assertions of numerous subsequent historians that the weapon of impeachment would have been employed against Marshall if it had proved effective against Chase. Also, the reported statement of Giles that they wanted offices, in order to give them to men who would fill them better, gave color to the contention of certain later writers that the major motive of the entire impeachment movement was hunger for spoils and emoluments, as was claimed by the Federalist press at the time.[30]

Even if it be assumed that Giles at this stage voiced not only his personal opinions but also those of the appointed managers for the House, especially John Randolph with whom he was so much in conference, it does not follow that his accent was that of Jefferson, who remained inaudible, or of Madison, on whom the President was disposed to rely most in constitutional matters, or of Gallatin, who had so stubbornly resisted the spoilsmen in the party and was already at odds with the antijudiciary faction in his own state of Pennsylvania. Furthermore, though the Republican senators may have been and very probably were agreed with respect to the gross impropriety of Chase's actions, Giles was not able to carry enough of his Republican colleagues with him to make this a political inquest instead of a trial. It was determined that each senator take an oath at the very beginning that he would do impartial justice according to the Constitution and laws of the United States, and the rules of procedure were modeled on those of courts, not those of legislative bodies. If the extreme political view of the impeachment process was not rejected at the very start, it was certainly not accepted. Justice Chase, to whom a copy of the articles of impeachment was delivered along with a summons, duly appeared on the second day of the new year. The refusal of his request that he be allowed until the next session of Congress — that is, about ten months — to prepare an answer may perhaps be viewed as a victory for Giles, but he was allowed a month (until February 4, 1805). In view of the fact that he had long been familiar with all the important charges, this seems to have been ample, even though the Federalists claimed otherwise.

Developments during this interim of a month, before the beginning

[29] J. Q. Adams, *Memoirs*, I, 322–323.
[30] Beveridge, *Marshall*, III, 157, begins his chapter on impeachment by quoting this statement.

of the trial proper, turned out to be favorable to the accused Justice. The increasingly bitter struggle between Republican factions in Pennsylvania had other important aspects, but at the moment the dominant issue lay between the critics and defenders of the state judiciary. In the spring of 1804 the lower house of the legislature had voted to impeach three Federalist judges of the state supreme court because of their punishment of Thomas Passmore for contempt. The circumstances were confused and their actions may have seemed highhanded and tyrannical, but the episode had strong overtones of partisanship.[31] The sole Republican judge on the court, Hugh Henry Brackenridge, was not involved in the case, but, since he supported the position of his colleagues, he publicly asked that he be included in the impeachment. Thereupon, the angry legislators in joint address asked the Governor to remove him, a thing which McKean declined to do. The trial of the other three judges by the Senate took place in January, 1805. Alexander J. Dallas served as counsel for the judges, and such was the support of the latter by the legal fraternity that for a time it looked as though there would be no counsel for the prosecution. Eventually, the services of Congressman Caesar A. Rodney of Delaware, one of the House managers in the Chase trial, were procured. On January 25, the Senate acquitted the judges. There was a majority for conviction but not two-thirds. The situation continued to be confused, but the antijudiciary group appeared to many moderate Republicans to have overreached themselves and party unity was shattered in Pennsylvania. That it was not being maintained in Washington was evident in this same month, when John Randolph's bitter attack on the proposed Yazoo compromise heightened his unpopularity with his fellow Republicans, especially those from the North, and foreshadowed his ultimate breach with the administration.

iii

The stage for the trial was well set in the Senate chamber, with crimson-covered benches for members of that body on each side of the Vice President's seat, chairs for the representatives, boxes for counsel and stenographers, diplomats and high American officials, an elegant special gallery for ladies (which, however, the gentlemen invaded), and the regular gallery for the general public, who were freely admitted. The arrangements had been left to the Vice President, the anomalies of whose situation did not pass unnoticed. One Federalist paper, after remarking that it had always been sure that Burr would be *"in at the*

[31] On this case and the impeachment, see Higginbotham, pp. 55–58, 66–67.

JUSTICE SAMUEL CHASE
Portrait by J. W. Jarvis

death," quoted another as saying that formerly "it was the practice in Courts of Justice to arraign the *murderer* before the *Judge*, but now we behold the *Judge* arraigned before the *murderer*." [32] The suave and elegant presiding officer, whose good graces the Republicans were charged with cultivating, irritated certain Federalists by his early rulings but in the end received their plaudits for his impartiality. The central figure, however, was the big, white-haired, red-faced Justice. At the Maryland bar they called him "Bacon face," but his admirers now described him as "covered with the frost of seventy winters" and made frequent reference to his physical infirmity. After the testimony was all in he was permitted to withdraw because of the state of his health — he suffered from the gout — but while there he was a dignified and impressive figure.

On the appointed day, February 4, 1805, with the assistance of two of his counselors, he read his Answer to the Articles of Impeachment, consuming two and a half hours in the process. Of special interest to us here is his reply to Article Eight, referring to the charge to the grand jury in Baltimore, the only offense specifically mentioned by Jefferson. While denying that the sentiments expressed by him were seditious or intemperate and inflammatory, he asserted that there was no law forbidding him to express his opinions to a grand jury, even though these should be incorrect and unfounded, and that there could be no offense without the breach of a law. It had long been the custom in America for judges to express their political opinions to grand juries, he said, and, by not forbidding the practice, the legislative authority had given it implied sanction. Admitting nothing improper or unusual in his own action, he held that if this article of impeachment should be sustained, "the liberty of speech on national concerns, and the tenure of the judicial office" must hereafter depend on the "arbitrary will" of Congress, declared after the acts were done. Thus, while pointing to a real danger, he continued to claim what amounted to judicial irresponsibility, recognizing no restriction on his own conduct but that of specific laws which were themselves subject to judicial interpretation. [33]

The representatives listened, with whatever attentiveness they could muster and maintain, to the reading of the massive document in which Chase powerfully defended himself against the articles of impeachment one by one. A copy of it was made available to John Randolph and his fellow managers next day, but he can hardly be supposed to have digested it when, on that very day, he reported to the House a "replica-

---

[32] *N.Y. Evening Post*, Feb. 6, 1805.
[33] The Answer is in *Annals*, 8 Cong., 2 sess., pp. 101–150; discussion of Art. VIII, pp. 143–149.

tion" to it. This was described by William Plumer as "very concise, but conceived in very bitter, indecent, and abusive language."[34] A motion was made to omit a portion of it, as follows:

> That the said Samuel Chase has endeavored to cover the high crimes and misdemeanors laid to his charge, by evasive insinuations, and misrepresentation of facts; that the said answer does give a gloss and coloring, utterly false and untrue, to the various criminal matters, contained in the said articles.[35]

After this motion had been decisively defeated the "replication" was adopted by a majority of more than two-thirds, and it was presented to the Senate by John Randolph on the following day. Even if he had been compelled to omit the passage we have quoted, he would still have asserted that "the said Samuel Chase did, in fact, commit the numerous acts of oppression, persecution, and injustice of which he stood accused." This would have been quite enough. Partisan invective did not befit the solemnity of this occasion and was an inadequate weapon against legal argument anyway. John Randolph, exhausted and ill, had made a bad beginning. The events of the trial were to show that, for all his parliamentary skill and rare gifts of speech, he and his fellow managers were no match for the counselors Chase had wisely assembled: Robert Goodloe Harper, Joseph Hopkinson, Luther Martin (the Federalist bulldog who had an obsessive hatred of Jefferson), Philip Barton Key, and Charles Lee, former attorney general. Furthermore, while Chase and his advisers had used the month of January to good effect in studying the legal aspects of the case and planning the defense, Randolph had wasted his powers in the Yazoo fight. He was not really prepared for this legal battle, but, throughout it, he was the major performer on the side of the prosecution. Though miscast, he played the stellar role. Among the witnesses, the most distinguished was the Chief Justice, John Marshall, who was called for the defense but was too conciliatory toward the prosecutors for William Plumer's liking. Apparently he was playing it safe, and the contrast in temper between him and Chase that Randolph drew was warranted.[36] He was not disposed to provoke unnecessary conflict with Congress. As for the President, he did not appear at the trial even as a spectator. In a narrative centering

---

[34] Plumer, *Memorandum*, p. 277.

[35] Feb. 6, 1805 (*Annals*, 8 Cong., 2 sess., p. 1182). We have followed the wording of the motion, which varies slightly from the "replication." The motion was defeated 41 to 70, and the "replication" was then adopted by a vote of 77 to 34.

[36] Plumer's comment of Feb. 16, 1805, is in *Memorandum*, p. 291. John Randolph contrasted Marshall and Chase in his opening speech (*Annals*, 8 Cong., 2 sess., pp. 160–161) and made other complimentary references to the Chief Justice.

on him, therefore, it is more important to consider the outcome and significance of this case than the proceedings.[37]

The crucial question throughout these, and the question of most enduring interest, was that of the nature and limitation of impeachment within the constitutional framework. Opinions ranged from the one most strikingly voiced by Senator Giles at the outset, that impeachment was a mere political inquest into which the question of criminality did not enter, to the Federalist contention that no offense was impeachable if not indictable. Against the latter John Randolph and others argued that to limit impeachment to offenses which the courts might be expected to deal with on their own account would be to render meaningless and unnecessary the elaborate procedure prescribed by the Constitution.[38] As between the threat of the employment of impeachment by a dominant party as an instrument for the removal of politically objectionable officials, and the danger of rendering it essentially innocuous, the senators might have preferred the latter anyway, especially since many of them were genuinely concerned to maintain the independence of the judiciary. But the emphasis in the articles and in the trial on Chase's conduct in particular cases tended to becloud an issue that transcended party.

The question of how to rid the country of an unfit judge who was neither corrupt nor criminal remained unanswered, while the senators invoked the precise language of the Constitution. This they did officially when they determined on the final day of the trial the question which should be addressed to each of them when he cast his vote. In the Pickering trial this was whether or not the accused Judge was guilty as charged, and the answer was either Aye or No. It was now decided that each senator should be asked whether or not Chase was guilty of *high*

[37] The detailed and colorful accounts of the proceedings in Beveridge, *Marshall,* III, ch. 4, and Henry Adams, *History,* II, ch. 10, reflect in the one case the traditional Federalist interpretation of the events and in the other the view of them that was transmitted in the Adams family, which was not wholly lacking in discrimination but was hypercritical of John Randolph. The account by W. C. Bruce, in *Randolph,* II, 200–221, including long extracts from Randolph's speeches and sensible comments on them, provides a desirable corrective. The chief contemporary accounts on which later writers have drawn are those of J. Q. Adams in his *Memoirs* and letters and of William Plumer in his *Memorandum* and letters. These represent both men in a highly partisan phase of their careers. The Republicans lacked comparable diarists and the reports in their leading papers, *National Intelligencer* and *Aurora,* were largely factual. The comments in the Richmond *Examiner* reflected the obsession of Virginians with the Callender case. The Federalist *N.Y. Evening Post* was wholly partisan.

[38] See the passage from his closing speech quoted by Bruce, I, 209–210. In this he pointed out that if a President should undiscriminatingly veto every act of Congress presented to him he would commit no indictable offense though he would clearly deserve impeachment.

crimes and misdemeanors, as charged in a particular article. This wording was proposed by Federalist Senator Bayard, and John Quincy Adams informed his father that the precedent of the Pickering case was abandoned "almost without a struggle," though "not without very strong signs of reluctance." He privately recorded that Giles, while continuing to insist that the House could impeach and the Senate convict for other causes, announced his willingness to take the question as proposed by Bayard because Chase had actually been charged with high crimes and misdemeanors. He protested, however, against this being established as a precedent. Other Republican senators must have concluded that there was no escape from the words of the Constitution and of the articles of impeachment on this particular occasion, for the majority of one by which Bayard's resolution was adopted would have been quite impossible without their support; 17 voted for it, and there were only 9 Federalists in the Senate.[39] The latter supported Chase completely on every test, but at no time was there comparable unity among the twenty-five Republicans. Virtual unanimity on their part would have been required to convict the Justice, since twenty-three votes were necessary. It now appears that under the existing circumstances of confusion and fear the procuring of that number would have been beyond the power of what Congressman Taggart called Jeffersonian omnipotence, and there seems to be no evidence that the President himself sought to bring any influence to bear on his wavering partisans.

He was not among the anxious spectators who crowded the Senate chamber on March 1, 1805, and witnessed the final scene of the trial, beginning at noon. Public interest, which had been great throughout the proceedings, was now at its highest pitch; and, recognizing the importance and gravity of the occasion, the senators were all there. Uriah Tracy of Connecticut had arisen from his sickbed and appeared with a smelling bottle. As their names were called in alphabetical order all thirty-four of the members of the upper house voted Guilty or Not Guilty on each and every article of impeachment. After two hours the Vice President declared that, since there was no constitutional majority on any article, Samuel Chase was acquitted. The absent President undoubtedly received the news promptly, and presumably he availed himself of the table published by the *National Intelligencer* a few days later in making a tabulation of his own and an analysis of the vote.[40]

[39] Adams speaks of this matter under the dates Feb. 28, Mar. 1, 1805 (*Memoirs,* I, 360 362), and in his letter of Mar. 14 to his father (*Writings,* III, 114–116). Plumer refers to it and gives the vote of Mar. 1, 1805, as 17 to 16 in *Memorandum,* p. 308.

[40] A table appeared in *National Intelligencer,* Mar. 4, 1805, following an account of the proceedings, TJ's table is in LC, 27104. The votes were also tabulated by

He did not view the memorable scene, but he had indisputable facts and figures to ponder over. Though two-thirds of the senators had adjudged Chase guilty on no one of the articles, a majority had done so on three. Thus the result could not be properly regarded as a full vindication of the accused Justice, who appears to have been considered by most senators as guilty of more than the casual indiscretions common to all mankind that were admitted by his counsel, and of more than mere errors of official judgment. Furthermore, Jefferson would have been warranted in perceiving a vindication of his own judgment in the fact that the largest vote against Chase, 19 to 15, was on Article VIII, the only one bearing on the offense to which he had originally called attention, the charge to the grand jury in Baltimore. Although relatively little stress was laid on it in the trial, it was the strongest article in the lot. There was also a majority against Chase on two articles (III and IV) growing out of his conduct in the trial of Callender, but the two articles relating to his alleged disregard of Virginia procedure in that trial — the two that had been inserted by Randolph in the fall — commanded virtually no support. Not a single senator pronounced Chase guilty on Article V and only four did so on Article VI. This rebuff suggests that in emphasizing the grievances of his own state the Majority Leader overreached himself. The two senators from Virginia did not follow him in this instance. Indeed, Giles voted Guilty on only four of the eight articles, and his colleague, Andrew Moore, did so on only five. Jefferson's political analysis showed that six Republican senators joined the entire body of Federalists to acquit the respondent on all counts. Three of them, including a conservative South Carolinian, had entered the Senate since the Pickering trial. One of the six hailed from Ohio, two were from New England, and two from New York.[41] The Republican "defectors" were chiefly Northerners. These men may have been more concerned for the independence of the judiciary than the body of Southerners and Westerners, but they may also be supposed to have been alienated by John Randolph in the fight over the Yazoo compromise. At any rate, he failed to gain the support of a large segment of the Republican majority in the Senate, though his control of it seemed undiminished in the House.

There, later in the day of Chase's acquittal, after delivering a phillipic

---

J. Q. Adams (*Memoirs*, I, 362–363) and William Plumer (*Memorandum*, pp. 309–310). They are reported, article by article, under the date Mar. 1, 1805, in *Annals*, 8 Cong., 2 sess., pp. 664–669.

[41] The six were Stephen R. Bradley and Israel Smith of Vt., John Smith and Samuel Mitchill of N.Y., John Smith of Ohio, and John Gaillard of S.C. The political significance of the voting pattern is discussed, among other things, by Lacy, pp. 261–264.

against Chase and the Senate, he introduced a resolution proposing a constitutional amendment which would require the President to remove a federal judge on joint address of both houses of Congress requesting him to do so. While action on this was deferred until the next session, more than two-thirds of the members indicated their desire to consider it. This proposal was no more radical than the extraordinary private suggestion made by John Marshall some weeks earlier, that Congress be granted authority to overrule judicial decisions, which he regarded as preferable to the power to remove judges — a suggestion which one of his biographers attributes to his extreme fear of the outcome of the Chase impeachment.[42] The proposal of Randolph called for only a majority, not two-thirds, and left no discretion to the President. Actually, it was only a gesture of bravado made in a moment of frustration. His fellow prosecutor, Nicholson, made another empty one that manifested resentment against the Senate. He offered a resolution calling for an amendment which would have permitted any state legislature to recall that state's senators at any time. This also was postponed, after a debate in which Randolph and Nicholson are reported by William Plumer to have been "very warm and passionate." He also said the administration "disapproved of this violent measure," as no doubt Jefferson and his advisers did, along with the senators.[43] Describing to his father the situation when the Eighth Congress terminated its existence on the evening of Sunday, March 3, John Quincy Adams said that the two houses were "in positions of direct opposition against each other, with the House of Representatives aiming . . . at the same moment a cut at the supreme judiciary and a thrust at the Senate."[44] Also, there was an unseemly squabble over the expenses of the witnesses in the recent trial. The representatives wanted to reimburse only the witnesses for the prosecution, while the senators, Republicans and Federalists alike, wanted to meet the expenses of all. The deadlock was not broken before the session ended. Giles was one of those most exercised by the unfairness of the position taken by the House and admitted that the edge of his partisanship had been blunted in the course of recent events. The bad manners of the frustrated leaders of the House might have been expected to have that effect on any Republican senator, however loyal to the party.

The Secretary of State is reported to have been amused by their petulance. John Randolph afterwards attributed the failure of the proceedings against Chase to Madison's disapproval of them. Madison him-

[42] Beveridge, III, 177–178.
[43] Plumer, *Memorandum*, p. 311; *Annals*, 8 Cong., 2 sess., pp. 1213–1214.
[44] Letter of Mar. 14, 1805 (*Writings*, III, 122).

self said after the event that the heads of department did not inter-meddle with a matter belonging exclusively to the legislature and that it would now be improper for them to express themselves on it.[45] Randolph's old friend Gallatin, whose judgment had been repudiated by him in the Yazoo fight and who was so dubious of the antijudiciary movement in Pennsylvania, must have taken precisely this position. And so, apparently, did the President himself, however disappointed he may have been in the outcome and however disillusioned with John Randolph he may have become. Such comments as he made afterwards on impeachment — which appear to have been few — were general rather than specific. A couple of years after the acquittal of Chase he said in a letter to Giles that impeachment was a farce which would not be tried again. He gave what was probably the best summary of his mature position in a letter to Editor Thomas Ritchie when he was nearing seventy-eight. At the time his fears of judicial encroachment and irresponsibility had been freshly aroused.

> Having found, from experience, that impeachment is an im-practicable thing, a mere scare-crow, they [the federal judges] consider themselves secure for life; they sculk from responsibility to public opinion, the only remaining hold on them . . . A ju-diciary independent of a king or executive alone, is a good thing; but independence of the will of the nation is a solecism, at least in a republican government. . . .[46]

He had not yet become aware of any means, other than the pressure of public opinion, whereby untouchable judges could be made respon-sive to the will of a democratic society. The test case in his own admin-istration showed that this could not be done by the evocation of legisla-tive omnipotence — or, more particularly, the omnipotence of the majority of the popularly elected House. Unquestionably that case was bungled, and undoubtedly the prosecutors overreached themselves. Advocates of a viable government may have regarded the constitu-tional definition of impeachment as too restrictive. But many besides Federalist partisans, believing that the antijudiciary movement had got out of hand, were relieved by the conspicuous demonstration that im-

---

[45] Brant, *Madison*, IV, 250; N. K. Risjord, *The Old Republicans* (1965), p. 42.
[46] TJ to Thomas Ritchie, Dec. 25, 1820 (quotation from Ford, X, 170–171). I have omitted the part of the passage relating to Marshall and his method of an-nouncing decisions. Quoting from this letter, Henry Adams (*History*, II, 243) omits the crucial reference to public opinion and does not get to the last sentence, which best sums up TJ's position. See also TJ's letters of Apr. 20, 1807, to Giles, and of Sept. 6, 1819, to Spencer Roane (Ford, IX, 45–46; X, 140–143).

peachment could not be readily employed as an instrument of political persecution. Nonetheless, the charges and votes against Chase constituted a rebuke and this lesson was not lost. The overt partisanship of the federal bench declined thereafter and eventually became unthinkable.

After the event, one of the major journalistic critics of the administration made this assertion: "It is perfectly understood that the impeachment of Judge Chase was Mr. Jefferson's measure, and that of his confidential advisers, and that Randolph was only his creature to carry it through." [47] No one familiar with John Randolph's personality can think of him as anybody's creature at any time, and his congressional contemporaries regarded him as the embodiment of this prosecution. One senator, noted for his own loyalty to the Republican party, is reported to have said that "Mr. Randolph had boasted with great exultation that this was *his* impeachment — that every article was drawn by *his* hand, and that *he* was to have the whole merit of it." [48] Thus the man who would have taken the full credit for success was blamed for a cause that failed. This was not wholly fair, to be sure, but the Majority Leader of the House was a fitting scapegoat. The available records show that, on the Republican side, he dominated the case from the moment that he took it over from Nicholson; and it will be recalled that Jefferson's letter to that congressman was private.

Shortly before leaving for home, William Plumer commented in his diary on the political talent of the President. "It seems to be a great and primary object with him never to pursue a measure if it becomes unpopular," said the Senator, giving as an example his abandonment of the removal of Chase.[49] Once the movement against the Justice was started, he could hardly have stopped it, even if he had wanted to; but, either for reasons of propriety or political sagacity, and probably for both, he had remained aloof after his original suggestion, and doubts of the wisdom of the proceedings must have gathered in his mind before the end. He did not say so; indeed, he does not appear to have said anything, and this was to his political advantage. His political enemies had nothing they could really pin on him, and, although his party was far from united, he himself still retained the loyalty of all factions. It was unfortunate for his presidential image, however, that an event which could be hailed by his foes as a glorious victory for their side should have brought his administration to an anticlimactic close.

[47] *N.Y. Evening Post*, Mar. 9, 1805.
[48] Senator William Cocke, in conversation with J. Q. Adams after the acquittal, recorded in the latter's *Memoirs*, I, 364.
[49] Mar. 3, 1805 (Plumer, *Memorandum*, p. 316).

On the eve of his second inauguration he could have gained little gratification from contemplating the course of public affairs since his re-election. While he himself had seemed so remote and inactive that the period might almost be described as an interregnum, things got out of hand. He appears to have been in a fatalistic mood at this juncture, and he was never one to indulge in vain regrets. It was characteristic of him to take the long view, and if at this moment he had looked back on his administration as a whole he could have done so with very considerable and thoroughly justifiable satisfaction. Though the latest congressional session had been marked by excessive turbulence and discord, he could reflect that the country was much more united in spirit than it had been when he took office, and that the unique American experiment in self-government had been pursued for four more years with success which, though not invariable, was undeniable. In a free society the die-hard Federalists had remained irreconcilable and some of his own followers had become obstreperous, but he had attached to his government the large majority of his countrymen — not by bestowing positive favors on any group, but by convincing the citizens generally that the government was truly theirs and was being conducted with due regard for their historic rights and liberties. No small part of the credit for the success of the Republican party in elections must go to local leaders and workers, whom Jefferson consistently left to their own devices, but virtually all of these recognized him as the party's major asset. His appeal as a symbol of freedom and democracy appears to have increased rather than diminished while he was President, and he had attained and maintained enormous personal popularity despite unexampled personal attacks. This popularity may be attributed in considerable part to the general awareness of his unfailing interest and abiding faith in individual human beings.

He could not foresee how much less skillful and effective than he most of his successors would be in their relations with Congress, but he could reflect that the legislators had responded favorably to virtually all his important recommendations, that his legislative failures had been minor, or in matters he did not press. Except for the actions against the Barbary pirates, he had kept the peace; and by the acquisition of Louisiana the administration had removed a major cause of western discontent while doubling the area of the Republic. The country was prosperous; its finances were in admirable shape despite the abolition of excise taxes, and the affairs of the government were competently and honestly administered.

Some of the most notable of these successes could hardly have been achieved if the international situation had not been favorable. The administration had been fortunate in external circumstances. Most of Jefferson's presidential voyage had been blessed with good weather. No doubt this lover of the land would have preferred not to go to sea at all, but according to such tests as historians apply his first voyage had been fruitful and memorable. There were already signs that his good luck was not lasting, but fortunately he did not know what storms would beset him.

⌈APPENDIX I⌋

The Charge of a "Deal" in 1801

I F there were any rumors at the beginning of Jefferson's presidency that he had gained office by means of a "deal" or "bargain" with James A. Bayard, these seem to have died down quickly. He himself referred to the allegation in a memorandum of April 15, 1806, which began with a reference to Aaron Burr, then in private life and at a very low point in his political fortunes.[1] Early in his vice presidency Burr had been charged with intriguing with the Federalists in connection with the election of 1801, and the allegation about Jefferson may be regarded as a countercharge. For use in legal actions against Burr's detractors — actions which, in fact, were not pursued — depositions were procured in 1806 from two key congressional figures, James A. Bayard of Delaware and General Samuel Smith of Maryland. The allegation against Jefferson was that Bayard had sought and Smith, speaking for Jefferson, had given certain assurances about the latter's future conduct on the strength of which Bayard and the Federalist congressmen most closely associated with him in the fight over the presidency in the House of Representatives permitted the deadlock to be broken.[2]

In his private memorandum of 1806 the President said:

I do not recollect that I ever had any particular conversn with Genl. Saml. Smith on this subject. Very possibly I had however, as the general subject & all its parts were the constant themes of conversation in the private *tête à têtes* with our friends. But certain I am that neither he, nor any other republican ever uttered the most distant hint to me about submitting to any conditions or giving any assurances to anybody; and still more certainly was neither he nor any other person ever authorized by me to say what I would or would not do.[3]

[1] Ford, I, 311–314.
[2] Bayard's deposition of April 3, 1806, and Smith's of April 15, 1806, are in M. L. Davis, *Memoirs of Aaron Burr*, II, 129–137. The entire matter is summarized and discussed by Morton Borden in *The Federalism of James A. Bayard*, pp. 80–93. It is dealt with in part in ch. I, pp. 13–14, above.
[3] Memo. of Apr. 15, 1806 (Ford, I, 314).

Earlier in this same memorandum he stated that he could see no purpose in Bayard's deposition except to calumniate him and described the
Senator's pretensions as "absolutely false." [4] Also, shortly before his
election, he had privately recorded the report, which he had from
Edward Livingston and W. C. Nicholas, that Bayard was trying to win
Samuel Smith over to Burr's side by offering him a high appointment
and was also tempting Livingston. [5]

Jefferson's private comments on Bayard, as made in his memorandum
of 1801, became public when they appeared in the first edition of his
writings, after his death. This publication occasioned a spirited defense
of Bayard in the Senate of the United States by John M. Clayton of
Delaware, one of his successors in that body, and statements of exonera-
tion by Samuel Smith and Edward Livingston, both of whom were
members at that time. [6] A little later, Bayard's sons discovered in TJ's
published writings his memorandum of April 15, 1806, and, after an
arduous search, the depositions which their father and Samuel Smith had
made at the instance of representatives of Aaron Burr. They afterwards
reported that they published these, along with extracts from the senatorial discussion, in a newspaper in Philadelphia (December, 1830) and
in a pamphlet. Thus, four or five years after TJ's death, the charge that
he had made a "deal" for the presidency came into public view as an
intended refutation of private memoranda of his reflecting on Bayard
that were now in print.

A quarter of a century later, Bayard's son and namesake, then a member of the Senate, reopened the matter. This was after he saw a copy of
the Washington edition of TJ's writings (1853–1855), published by
order of Congress, containing the two memoranda he and his brother
had objected to. They sought refutation of these in more public and
enduring form. Accordingly, the remarks in the Senate in 1830, the
depositions of Bayard and Smith in 1806, and other documents appeared
in 1855 in the *Appendix to the Congressional Globe*, and afterwards in
a pamphlet. [7] Bayard's sons did not include, however, a letter of April 3,
1830, to them from Samuel Smith in which he gave his interpretation of
the episode most in question and advised them to stop the whole business. [8] If their father's deposition of 1806 reflected on TJ as party to a
bargain, it also reflected on the man with whom he was said to have
made one, a man to whose high character former political foes were
now gladly attesting.

[4] *Ibid.*, I, 312.
[5] Memo. of Feb. 12, 1801 (Ford, I, 291). The post he mentioned specifically,
that of secretary of the navy, would not have been alluring, for Smith declined it
when offered it by Jefferson.
[6] Jan. 28, 1830. *Register of Debates in Congress*, VI (1830), 93–95 (21 Cong.,
1 sess.).
[7] 33 Cong., 2 sess. (New Series, Vol. XXXI [1855], 135–141).
[8] Davis, *Memoirs of Burr*, II, 106–110.

In his deposition Bayard candidly stated that, in 1801, he and certain other members of the House of Representatives who were in position to determine the outcome of the presidential election tried to get the best "terms of capitulation" they could. First he approached Jefferson's friend Representative John Nicholas, seeking assurance on the points that were consistently pressed at this juncture by the Federalists, from John Adams down: namely, maintenance of the public credit, support of the navy, and the retention of Federalists in public office. With respect to the last, Bayard went to pains to explain that he was referring to subordinate officers, who, in his opinion, should not be removed "on the ground of their political character, nor without complaint against their conduct." [9] Nicholas gave his own opinion that Bayard's points accorded with the views and intentions of Jefferson. On the basis of his intimate knowledge, Nicholas was warranted in saying this, except perhaps with respect to the navy.

Bayard was not content with general assurances anyway; he wanted "an engagement," and Nicholas was unwilling to seek one from Jefferson. Therefore, by his own account, Bayard turned to General Samuel Smith, and in his conversation with this congressman he left no doubt that the real crux of the matter was the question of removals of Federalists from office. He went into particulars, mentioning two men who held the lucrative post of collector, at the ports of Philadelphia and Wilmington respectively: George Latimer and Allan McLane. As Bayard reported the events, Smith readily agreed to consult Jefferson and brought back the desired assurances, whereupon he and the other gentleman named by him withdrew their opposition — that is, they withheld their votes from Burr — and Jefferson was elected President. Writing his friend McLane on the day of the election, Bayard reported that he had direct information that Jefferson would not engage in a proscription of Federalist officeholders and expressed the belief that his friend was safe.[10]

The deposition of Samuel Smith in 1806 describes conversations he had in 1801 with several Federalists and shows that he gave them the same general assurances that Nicholas had given Bayard. He based these more specifically, however, on recent conversations with Jefferson, which were easy for him to have since he also lodged at Conrad's. With respect to the particular officers for whose continuance Bayard was so concerned, he reported that Jefferson did not think that such men should be dismissed on political grounds alone, except where they had made improper use of their offices to force their subordinates to vote against their own judgment. He also said that, on the basis of reports he had on McLane's character, Jefferson regarded him as a meritorious official. We have already referred to the President's comments when he

[9] Davis, II, 131.
[10] Bayard to McLane, Feb. 17, 1801 (*A.H.A. Report for 1913*, II, 128–129).

saw Smith's deposition, five years after the events it described. At that time he blamed Bayard, a bitter political enemy who, he believed, was trying to injure him. He did not reproach Smith for presumption.

A quarter of a century later, Smith, writing to Bayard's sons, took most of the blame upon himself.[11] He then said that he conversed with Jefferson about the matter that Bayard had broached to him, but that the Republican leader did not have "the remotest idea" of his object. Later still, Albert Gallatin, describing this election and attributing Bayard's final and decisive part in it to his "pure patriotism," had this to say about Smith: "One of our friends who was very erroneously and improperly afraid of a defection on the part of some of our members, undertook to act as an intermediary, and confounding his own opinions and wishes with those of Mr. Jefferson, reported the result in such a manner as gave subsequently occasion for very unfounded surmises." [12] Gallatin's charitable judgment of both Bayard and Jefferson commends itself to those who try to see great public servants on balance, but his comments on Samuel Smith must be viewed in the light of the factional opposition of the latter to himself. His comments make sense, nonetheless.

It need not be supposed that Jefferson was so ingenuous as not to realize that his views on current questions would be passed on. Indeed, he expected them to be. But, since Smith was living in the same house, the General did not need to seek a special interview; he could easily have engaged in casual conversation with his fellow lodger with a view to drawing him out. Writing to Bayard's sons, he said:

> Mr. Jefferson was a gentleman of *extreme frankness* with his friends; he conversed freely and frankly with them on all subjects, and gave his opinions without reserve. Some of them thought that he did so too freely. Satisfied with his opinion on the third point [dealing with removals from office], I communicated to your father the next day — that, from the conversation that I had had with Mr. Jefferson, I was satisfied in *my own mind* that his conduct on that point would be so and so. But I certainly never did tell your father that I had any authority from Mr. Jefferson to communicate any thing to him or to any other person.

While it seems safe to say that Smith was presumptuous and overreached himself, his report to Bayard was in general accord with views Jefferson expressed elsewhere and policies he afterwards pursued. He did not intend a sweeping proscription of Federalist officeholders. At his first meeting with his executive council the general rule was adopted that no collectors were to be removed until called on for account; then it could be determined who were defaulters. This question is inseparable

11 Smith to R. H. and J. A. Bayard, Apr. 3, 1830 (Davis, II, 108).
12 Gallatin to H. A. Muhlenberg, May 8, 1848 (Adams, *Life*, p. 250).

from the total policy of the administration about removals, which is discussed elsewhere, but if Jefferson saw no present reason for displacing
the Collector of the Port of Wilmington he may have said just that,
without committing himself for the future.[13] There was nothing here
which could be properly called a deal. Furthermore, the later bitterness
between Bayard and Jefferson can be amply explained without reference to the fate of particular holders of appointive office. Bayard became the leader of the congressional opposition to the administration,
and Jefferson induced Caesar A. Rodney to run against him in Delaware
in 1802, encompassing his defeat.

George Latimer, one of the two men about whose security Bayard
was particularly concerned, remained as collector of the port of Philadelphia until July, 1802, when he resigned this highly desirable post
under pressure from the administration. The administration was itself
under powerful pressure from certain partisan Republicans in that city,
but the new appointee, Peter Muhlenberg, was regarded as conservative.[14] The case of Allan McLane, who was not removed, is one of the
most confused on record. In a monograph on Jefferson's appointments
a chapter could be devoted to it.

Early in the administration, complaints against McLane, a Revolutionary hero with a war record which he himself made much of and Jefferson respected, were made by Delaware Republicans, who saw him as a
violently partisan Federalist and resented his holding the best appointive
office in the state. In the election of 1800, he was reported to have proclaimed that the Jacobinical Democrats, if victorious, would drown
everybody in Kent and neighboring Sussex.[15] Those counties remained
Federalist in 1800, and the chief clamor for his removal came from hard-
pressed Republicans in Kent, where he had formerly lived. The charges
against him bore on maladministration and electioneering activity. John
Dickinson, from whom Jefferson sought a dispassionate judgment,
doubted if any man in the United States had been more zealous as an
electioneer.[16] The administration took cognizance of only the charges
of official misconduct, however, and McLane was cleared of these after
a formal inquiry. The comptroller, John Steele, thought him an effective collector, and this disposition of the case was in line with the policies of Gallatin, who was especially averse to removals for political
reasons. For the moment, therefore, Jefferson let well enough alone.

But McLane, who appears to have been a highly opinionated and self-

[13] See ch. V, above.
[14] Gallatin to TJ, July 17, 1802, reporting Latimer's resignation (LC, 21488).
On his own list TJ did not designate this as a removal (LC, 20545).
[15] John Munroe, *Federalist Delaware, 1775–1815* (1954), p. 208.
[16] TJ to Dickinson, June 21, 1801 (LC, 19504 19505); Dickinson to TJ, June 27
and July 18, 1801 (LC, 19557, 19608–19609); TJ to Dickinson, July 23, 1801 (LC,
19683–19684). N. E. Cunningham discusses this case in *Jeffersonian Republicans in
Power*, pp. 44–49.

righteous man, was so obnoxious to certain local Republicans that they continued to clamor against him. The matter came to a head in the spring of 1802, when Jefferson received petitions for his removal and he addressed himself to Gallatin and the Comptroller with an air of injured innocence.[17] The petitioners described the Federalists as irreconcilable and the Collector as obnoxious, but they did so in such general terms that Jefferson was unsure whether McLane had done anything since his acquittal that warranted his removal. Accordingly, he himself consulted Caesar A. Rodney, a prominent Delaware supporter whom he regarded as reasonable. While regretting the extreme partisanship of the local Republicans, Rodney believed that the current against McLane was too strong to be resisted without hazard. The Collector's political conduct, in his opinion, was much the same as before Jefferson's inauguration, though less open. Jefferson's own judgment, which undoubtedly was influenced by that of Gallatin, was that McLane's removal at this time would be adjudged vindictive, because overt electioneering *since* his trial and acquittal had not been shown. After a conference with Rodney and Governor Hall in Washington, he believed they were satisfied that McLane could be left alone if that official did not take an active part in elections.[18]

This *cause célèbre* strengthens the impression that Jefferson resisted the pressure of his own partisans to remove Federalists from office on purely political grounds. In local terms his inaction appears to have been politically unwise. After the election of 1802, Rodney, who barely defeated Bayard in the congressional contest, said that the failure to act against McLane deeply discouraged the Republicans in Kent County and was the main cause of party reverses there.[19] Rodney still believed that the retirement of the Collector was necessary for the "cause" in Delaware and he cherished the hope of a resignation. It turned out that McLane, while still fearing removal, had no intention of resigning.[20] Therefore, the campaign continued through another year and more, being marked by a petition from merchants of Philadelphia in his behalf as well as further attacks on him.[21] He was still in office when Jef-

[17] An address from a meeting in Dover, Del., Mar. 24, 1802, is in LC, 20581–20582. Gov. David Hall, a Republican, writing TJ on May 31 (LC, 21279), sent another with his own approval. McLane wrote to John Steele, Apr. 10, 19, 1802 (*Papers of Steele*, I [1924], pp. 266–268) and on June 12, 1802, to Gallatin and to Steele (LC, 21329–21331).

[18] TJ to Rodney, June 14, 1802 (Ford, VIII, 154–155); Rodney to TJ, June 19–21, 1802 (LC, 21361–21364); TJ to Gallatin, July 13, 1802 (LC, 21464), after Gallatin had conferred with Rodney and Hall in Baltimore.

[19] Rodney to TJ, received Nov. 4, 1802 (LC, 22965–22968). TJ himself blamed the reverses in Kent on the attacks there on his own morals and religion.

[20] Gallatin to TJ, Dec. 20, 1802 (LC, 22089).

[21] Petition of Feb. 2, 1803, signed by TJ's friend Thomas Leiper, among others (LC, 22293).

ferson retired, and Republican fortunes did not soon brighten in Delaware.

Jefferson justified his inaction in this case on grounds of broad policy. Whatever his motives may have been, it seems safe to say that the influence of Gallatin on him was a far more potent factor than any sense of obligation to James A. Bayard.

$\lceil$ APPENDIX II $\rceil$

The Miscegenation Legend

THE miscegenation story, as elaborated after Jefferson's death, assigned to him the paternity of the children borne by Sally Hemings during his presidency, two of them in his second term.[1] He was even accused of casting out, toward the end of his life, an allegedly beautiful mulatto daughter and forcing her into a life of shame. The latter charge can be disproved by testimony and information now available. The former assumed that, despite the publicity Callender and the Federalist newspapers gave his alleged liaison, he continued it during his sixties while holding the highest office in the land, thus defying public opinion and wholly disregarding the feelings of his beloved daughters and grandchildren. To charge him with that degree of imprudence and insensitivity requires extraordinary credulity.

Merrill D. Peterson, in his brief but admirable account of the development of the miscegenation legend,[2] attributes its rise and progress to three factors: (1) Federalist hatred, with which the efforts of British critics like Mrs. Trollope to discredit democracy should be associated; (2) the institution of slavery and, especially, the efforts of Abolitionists to discredit it by showing that Jefferson, though himself a conspicuous champion of freedom, was contaminated and victimized by the slave system; (3) certain factors in his own life, including the discreditable Walker affair and his special concern, through many years, for the members of the Hemings family among his slaves.

Since we have given considerable attention to the Federalists in the text, we may now turn to the Abolitionists. Mr. Peterson's fresh treat-

---

[1] Her surviving children were: Beverley (b. 1798), Harriet (1801), Madison (1805), and Eston (1808). A daughter, also named Harriet, born in 1795, died before 1798.

[2] *The Jefferson Image in the American Mind* (1960), pp. 181–187. The treatment of this matter by Winthrop D. Jordan in his excellent book *White over Black* (1968), pp. 461–469, is well documented but in his psychological speculations, suggestive though these are, it seems to me that he has ventured far beyond the demonstrable.

ment of them in this connection is of special pertinence and interest, since those who have revived the miscegenation story in our own time have made allegations and used illustrations strikingly similar to and often identical with those of antislavery writers more than a century ago. In the earlier instance the moral discredit cast on Jefferson, whom in other respects the Abolitionists extolled, was incidental to the struggle against slavery rather than an object in itself. In the later instance, it is incidental to the fight against segregation and in behalf of the rights of Negroes. To enter into a discussion of these causes would be inappropriate, but at least it may be said that the abuse of his moral reputation in their behalf is ironical indeed in view of his lifelong abhorrence of the institution of slavery, his notable solicitude for the bondsmen and bondswomen whom fate assigned him, and his supreme emphasis on the dignity of every human being. Quite obviously, the truth must be sought in the life he actually lived, not in what political enemies or social reformers have said about that life for their own purposes, good or bad. Insofar as there is any ground whatever for credulity with respect to this long-lived legend, it must lie in the third of Peterson's categories.

From various sources of information about Jefferson's slaves and their life at Monticello we can learn a good deal about the Hemings family.[3] Unfortunately, however, the perplexing question of the paternity of the numerous children of Betty Hemings cannot be answered with finality. This prolific woman, who is said to have been the daughter of an English sea captain and a full-blooded African Negress, had at least ten children when Jefferson acquired her and her brood in 1774, on the settlement of the estate of his father-in-law, John Wayles, and she bore two thereafter.[4] In the persons of her children and grandchildren, some of whom were "bright" and others darker in their coloring, she provided most of the household servants and artisans on the mountain. Any special favors the Master may have shown the artisans — including Betty's son John Hemings and her grandsons Joe Fosset and Burwell — may be attributed to their recognized merit; and when Jefferson pro-

[3] Among the most important of these are *Thomas Jefferson's Farm Book* (1953), ed. by E. M. Betts, containing detailed information about his slaves; Isaac Jefferson, *Memoirs of a Monticello Slave* (1951); H. W. Pierson, *Jefferson at Monticello* (1862), the reminiscences of Edmund Bacon, his chief overseer. In the edition of Pierson's work by J. A. Bear, Jr. (1967), the *Memoirs* of Isaac Jefferson are included. Among examples of the exploitation or uncritical employment of the miscegenation theme in recent years may be cited an article, "Thomas Jefferson's Negro Grandchildren," in *Ebony*, Nov., 1954; Pearl M. Graham, "Thomas Jefferson and Sally Hemings," *Journal of Negro History*, April, 1961; J. C. Furnas, *Goodby to Uncle Tom* (1956), pp. 140–141; R. L. Bruckberger, *Image of America* (1959), pp. 76–77. The two latter were selections of the Book-of-the-Month Club.

[4] A genealogical chart of the family, drawn from TJ's *Farm Book* by the late John C. Wyllie, Jr., is in Bear's edn. of *Jefferson at Monticello*, opp. p. 24. Valuable information about the family was compiled by the late Douglass Adair, from whom I received helpful suggestions.

vided in his will for their emancipation, he had reason to believe they could maintain themselves as freedmen by their skills.[5]

More talk was occasioned by Jefferson's continuing solicitude for other descendants of Betty Hemings whose color was light enough to be remarked upon. The particular reference is to the six youngest of the children she brought to Monticello, of whom Sally was the last. Two of her sons in this group, Bob and James, were freed by their master in the 1790's, apparently without exciting any special comment. This action of Jefferson's met another test: he was confident at the time that as freedmen they could take care of themselves.[6] Betty's daughter Thenia was sold to James Monroe, who could be expected to be kind to her. Two others, Critta and Sally, remained at Monticello as household servants and were apparently treated with indulgence, but this was the rule rather than the exception there.

Thomas Jefferson Randolph said that Sally was treated no better and no worse than the other servants, but his grandfather freed her daughter Harriet in 1822, when that reputedly handsome girl became twenty-one. This action occasioned a good deal of talk at the time, according to Edmund Bacon, the overseer. Indeed, it was the basis of the later charge that Jefferson ejected his own daughter, forcing her into a life of prostitution. But Bacon stated explicitly that she was *not* Jefferson's daughter and that he himself knew who her father was, having seen this man emerge from Sally's room many times in the early morning.[7] Harriet was given $50 and put on the stage for Philadelphia, where she may be presumed to have joined her brother James. The action seems to have been designed to protect her virtue, not to imperil it. In his will, Jefferson provided for the emancipation of Sally's sons Madison and Eston when they should reach the age of twenty-one. Until then they were to continue as apprentices to their uncle John Hemings; after that, presumably, they could support themselves as carpenters. This action, again, was in line with the policy Jefferson followed with respect to other men slaves he freed.

A rational explanation can be given for his actions in all these cases, but his concern, in life and death, for the descendants of Betty Hemings could hardly have failed to excite some local comment and thus to have laid some foundation, albeit unsubstantial, for the legend that arose and

[5] John Hemings, born at Monticello and the best carpenter among the slaves, may have been the son of a white woodworker. Joe Fosset, the son of Betty's eldest known daughter, was an ironworker. Burwell, son of another of the elder daughters, Bett Brown, was not only a painter and glazier but a sort of factotum, and perhaps the most esteemed of the men slaves.

[6] See *Jefferson and the Ordeal of Liberty*, pp. 208–209.

[7] *Jefferson at Monticello* (1967 edn.), p. 102. Actually Bacon was not at Monticello until considerably after the conception of Harriet, but he seems to have known whose mistress Sally was after he arrived; and he was there well before the birth of her son Eston in 1808.

grew. Perhaps no valid distinction can be drawn between his consideration for John Hemings, Joe Fosset, and Burwell on the one hand, and
for James and Bob Hemings and Sally's children on the other; but it is
possible and may be probable that he regarded himself as especially responsible for the welfare of the latter group. If we can accept the oral
tradition, handed down by certain of the slaves themselves, that Betty
Hemings was the concubine of John Wayles after the latter's third
wife died, and that he was the father of the six youngest children she
brought to Monticello, Jefferson's actions take on fresh significance
and poignancy. If this tradition is correct, he shouldered and bore
quietly for half a century a grievous burden of responsibility for the
illegitimate half brothers and sisters of his own adored wife. There is
material here for the tragedian, but the historian must recognize that
oral tradition is not established fact. Jefferson himself would have been
the last person to mention such a relationship, and I should be extremely
reluctant to do so here had not others previously mentioned it in print.
Since it is already in the public domain, I should be remiss if I ignored
it, even though, in my opinion, Jefferson's conduct toward these slaves
of his can be explained, though less poignantly, on other grounds. It
was quite in his character as a private man.[8]

The question of the paternity of Sally's children remains. So far as I
know, nothing is said about this in any of Jefferson's records. Paternity
is exceedingly difficult to prove, and in this case at this distance it may
be quite impossible. But Thomas Jefferson Randolph made a categorical
statement long years ago, which has only recently come to light. Swear-
ing to secrecy the biographer Henry S. Randall, he said that, while there
was no shadow of suspicion at Monticello that his grandfather had commerce with female slaves at any time, the connection of two of his very
near relatives with two women of the Hemings family was notorious
on the mountain and scarcely disguised by them. Specifically, he said
that Sally was the mistress of Peter Carr, favorite nephew of Jefferson
and treated by him as a son, while Betsey Hemings was the mistress of
Samuel Carr, Peter's brother.[9] One of Jefferson's granddaughters,
though speaking to the same effect so far as his character and reputation were concerned, shifted the other characters. Writing to her
husband while on a visit to her brother, Ellen Randolph Coolidge
reported a "general impression" that all four of Sally's children were
the children of Sam Carr, whom she described as "the most notorious

[8] The tradition is mentioned in Isaac Jefferson's *Memoirs*, p. 10. It is given in
detail in the autobiography of Madison Hemings, originally published in *Pike
County Republican* (Ohio), Mar. 13, 1873, and made much of by certain recent
writers.

[9] H. S. Randall to James Parton, June 1, 1868, first printed in M. E. Flower,
James Parton (1951), pp. 236–239. It should be noted that Randall was repeating
from memory what T. J. Randolph had told him more than a decade earlier.

good-natured Turk that ever was master of a black seraglio kept at other men's expence." [10] We are left in doubt as to the family designation of the chief villain in the piece, which may be just as well, but in any case Jefferson's grandson advanced a further reason for his silence on this subject. At the same time he provided an explanation of the persistence of the miscegenation legend. Some of the children of these young Hemings women — especially Sally's — strikingly resembled Jefferson. The one who was said to look most like him must have been Madison Hemings, born in 1805, and perhaps it was he who startled the dinner guests when he waited on table. It was he who claimed, long years later, that he was the son of the President.[11] Thomas Jefferson Randolph said that his mother would have liked to send the whole brood away but that they all knew his grandfather would never consider the suggestion. Such an action would itself have looked like a confession that something was wrong on the mountain. Silence appeared the wisest course, and Jefferson was wholly in character in maintaining it in family matters.

If all the records now available and referred to here had been open to the Abolitionists, they would have found fresh materials for their favorite allegation that the best of Southern blood was mixed with that of slaves. Miscegenation was a legend in his case, but its existence in the plantation households he knew best was an undeniable fact. He was a victim of the slave system he abhorred, though not in the way his political enemies asserted at the time, or that certain moral and social reformers claimed afterwards.

[10] Ellen Randolph to Joseph Coolidge, Oct. 24, 1858 (courtesy of Harold Jefferson Coolidge and Alderman Library). This granddaughter of TJ engaged in considerable correspondence with his biographer. To her husband she was reporting what her brother had recently told her. Therefore, her memory was fresher than that of Randall and may have been more accurate.

[11] In the autobiography cited in note 8 he says that his mother so informed him. While the autobiography checks with known facts in certain respects it is clearly erroneous in others, and one can argue that Sally's claim, if made, may be attributed to vanity. At all events, it must be weighed against the testimony of Jefferson's grandchildren, his categorical denial of the alleged liaison, and his own character.

⌈APPENDIX III⌋

Notes on the Merry Affair

(Chapter XX, note 37).

HENRY ADAMS'S use of Pichon's letter of Feb. 5, 1804, to Talleyrand.

The quotation I have paraphrased on p. 384 reads as follows: "Je sens qu'avec de l'addresse de la pars de M. Jefferson, il avait pu éviter tous ces éclats; mais d'un autre côté l'indiscretion avec laquelle on s'est conduit, n'a nullement été conforme au respect qu'on lui doit, et avec la meilleur intention de raccommoder ce qui s'est fait on lui en ôté tous les moyens." (Pichon to Talleyrand, Feb. 5, 1804; AECPEU, 56:345–351.) Henry Adams did considerable violence to this balanced judgment (*History*, II, 374). He quoted only the first clause of this long sentence, placing a period rather than a semicolon after it, as though it represented Pichon's full judgment. Thus the impression was created that TJ alone was blameable, whereas in fact Pichon was highly critical of Merry and especially Yrujo. Furthermore, Adams tacked this single clause on to a long quotation from a much earlier part of Pichon's letter: the omission he indicated actually amounted to four pages largely devoted to Yrujo. He translated "éclats" as scandals, but the word is better translated as "uproars," as its use elsewhere in the letter shows. Brant (*Madison*, IV, 166–167), who thus translates it, paraphrased or translated the part of the letter Adams ignored. Adams also speaks of Pichon as "delighted," while I gain the impression that he regretted the episode.

(Chapter XX, note 46).

"Etiquette of the Court of the U.S.": TJ's draft of reply to account in *Washington Federalist*, Feb. 1, 1804 (LC, 19124½); published with minor changes in *Aurora*, Feb. 13, 1804.

"The Washington Federalist of the 1st inst. has published what he calls the 'Etiquette of the court of the U.S.' In his facts as usual, truth is set at nought, & in his principles little correct to be found. The Editor having seen a great deal of unfounded stuff on this subject, in that &

other papers of a party whose first wish it is to excite misunderstandings with other nations (even with England, if they cannot with Spain or France) has taken pains to inform himself of the rules of social inter-course at Washington, and he assures his readers that they may rely on the correctness of the following statement of them.

"In the first place there is no 'court of the U.S.' since the 4th of Mar. 1801. That day buried levees, birthdays, royal parades, and the arroga-tion of precedence in society by certain self-stiled friends of order, but truly stiled friends of privileged orders.

"The President receives but does not return visits, except to the Vice-President.

"The Vice-President pays the 1st visit to the President, but receives it from all others, and returns it.

"Foreign ministers pay the 1st visit here, as in all other countries, to all the Secretaries, heads of department.

"The Secretaries return visits of the members of the legislature & for-eign ministers, but not of others; not from any principle of inequality, but from the pressure of their official duties, which do not admit such a disposal of their time.

"No distinction is admitted between Senators & Representatives. That pretension of certain would-be Nobles was buried in the grave of fed-eralism on the same 4th of March. The members of both houses & the domestic ministers interchange visits according to convenience, without claims of priority.

"Members of both houses & foreign Ministers also interchange visits, according to convenience & inclination; no intercourse between them being considered as necessary or due. Were it necessary, the former, as newcomers, might claim the 1st visit from the latter as residents, ac-cording to the American & English principle.

"In social circles all are equal, whether in, or out, of office, foreign or domestic; & the same equality exists among ladies as among gentlemen. No precedence therefore, of any one over another, exists either in right or practice, at dinners, assemblies, or any other occasions. 'Pell-mell' and 'next the door' form the basis of etiquette in the societies of this country. It is this last principle, maintained by the administration, which has produced some dissatisfaction with some of the diplomatic gentlemen. Not that they question the right of every nation to establish or alter its own rules of intercourse, nor consequently our right to obliterate any germs of a distinction of ranks, forbidden by our con-stitution: but that it is a part of their duty to be watchful for the rela-tive standing of their nation, and to acquiesce only so soon as they see that nothing derogatory of that is contemplated."

Acknowledgments

MY first expression of appreciation is to the Directors of the Thomas Jefferson Memorial Foundation, to whom I had the pleasure of dedicating the previous volume in this series. They have continued to contribute to the support of a project which has been considerably more prolonged than was anticipated, and among them I have found wise and helpful counselors. During most of the period in which this book was written, I had from the American Council of Learned Societies a grant which was applied to secretarial and office expenses. I am grateful to that admirable organization for this help, as I am to its president, Frederick H. Burkhardt, for the personal interest he has manifested in this series through the years. A grant from the National Endowment for the Humanities, which has been in effect during the past year, has served chiefly to expedite the work on Jefferson's second term, but I would not fail to express my appreciation of it here.

Virtually all of my research on Jefferson's presidency has been done in the Alderman Library of the University of Virginia and in the Library of Congress. Although a scholar is still a handicraftsman in our machine age and a pedestrian in a world of speed, his work as an investigator is greatly facilitated by modern photographic devices and inter-library loans. Therefore, he does not need to leave home as often as he used to. I have availed myself increasingly of the microfilm with which the Alderman Library is abundantly supplied and have had many things sent me on loan from Washington. Nonetheless, most of the unprinted papers of Jefferson and his contemporaries that I have used in preparing this book were first seen by me in the Division of Manuscripts of the Library of Congress, long one of my favorite haunts. I am most grateful for the continued cooperation and kindness of the officials and attendants there. The same can be said for the Rare Book Room, though I have repaired to that treasure house less often.

In recent years I have had little occasion to work in the rich collections of the Massachusetts Historical Society, since its Jefferson papers are on microfilm, but its director, Stephen T. Riley, has always been ready to answer queries. Equally responsive have been Julian P. Boyd, editor of the *Papers of Thomas Jefferson;* William T. Hutchinson and William M. E. Rachal, editors of the *Papers of James Madison;* and others engaged in publishing the writings of Jefferson's contemporaries. The director of the National Historical Publications Commission, Oliver W. Holmes, has sent me valuable information from the National Archives.

During most of the time the seat of my research activities has been the Alderman Library, which has invaluable collections of manuscripts and books bearing on the life of the Father of the University of Virginia, along with an abundance of microfilm. This book has been wholly written in my study there, except for what has been done in summers on Cape Cod. I may be properly described as a resident of the Alderman Library, and I shall always be grateful for the ample quarters that have been so generously provided me, and the services that have been so graciously rendered me for so long a time. If I should try to give names I should almost certainly leave somebody out. Thanks are due the former librarian and my long-time friend the late John C. Wyllie, Jr., and his successor, my friend Ray W. Frantz, Jr., and everybody else who has been on the staff in recent years. Since it is at the library that I most often see the curator of Monticello, James A. Bear, Jr., I will say here, as I did in the previous volume, that he has given me free access to source materials he has collected and has helped me in many other ways.

Throughout my labors on this book I have been most fortunate in my secretaries. All have worked on part time but all have shown a full measure of interest and devotion. I salute these helpful young companions of my long, slow journey and list them in the chronological order of their service: Judith True, Suzanne Berry, Mary F. Crouch, and Katherine M. Sargeant.

During the academic year of 1968–1969, Steven Hochman has been my part-time research assistant. Though he has worked chiefly on Jefferson's second term and will receive more thanks in my next volume, he is gratefully mentioned here.

I have made use of materials from contemporary newspapers that were collected several years ago by my friend and former student Jerry W. Knudson in connection with his study of Jefferson's relations with the press. I thank him now and shall do so again.

In the notes on particular episodes I have acknowledged my indebtedness to many scholars and their writings. I hope there are no grave omissions. Among those who have permitted me to read works of theirs in advance of publication are: Harry Ammon, Richard E. Ellis, Richard Hofstadter, and Donald G. Morgan. The latter scholar also did me the kindness of reading two of my chapters. I do not attempt to list all those who have aided me by their counsel, but have thanked some of them in the notes.

In connection with this volume my publishers, Little, Brown and Company, have shown the patience and cooperation that I have come to expect of them. I especially appreciate the continued kindness and solicitude of Larned G. Bradford.

Finally, I want to express again to my long-suffering wife my regret that I have been so slow, and my hope that this volume will seem worth the long wait.

List of Symbols and Short Titles[1]
Most Frequently Used in Footnotes

Account Book	Jefferson's informal account books, in various repositories. Cited by date only.
Adams, *History*	*History of the United States* (during the administrations of Jefferson and Madison), by Henry Adams. Of the nine volumes, the first two chiefly concern us here.
AECPEU	Affaires Étrangères, Correspondance Politique, États-Unis (transcripts in Library of Congress from French Archives).
A.H.R.	*American Historical Review.*
A.-J. Letters	*Adams-Jefferson Letters,* ed. by L. J. Cappon.
Annals	*Annals of Congress.*
A.S.P.F.R.	*American State Papers, Foreign Relations,* ed. by Lowrie and Clarke. References are to Vol. II (1832).
Beveridge	*Life of John Marshall,* by A. J. Beveridge, references chiefly to Vol. III.
Bixby	*Thomas Jefferson Correspondence Printed from the Originals in the Collections of William K. Bixby.*
Boyd	*Papers of Thomas Jefferson,* ed. by Julian P. Boyd (Princeton, 1950–).
Brant	*James Madison,* by Irving Brant. Referred to by volume number, chiefly to Vol. IV, *Secretary of State, 1800–1809.*
Bruce	*John Randolph of Roanoke,* by W. C. Bruce.

[1] Repositories are designated by roman capitals run together, the names of editors and authors are in roman type, and the abbreviated titles of printed works are in italics. Further details about these works, and about others frequently used but more easily identified from the references in the notes, are in the Select Critical Bibliography which follows. To avoid excess of italics in the lists, long titles are printed there in roman except in cases where a magazine or other work is italicized to distinguish it from an article in it.

Butterfield	*Letters of Benjamin Rush*, ed. by L. H. Butter-field.
Carter	*Territorial Papers of the United States*, ed. by C. E. Carter. The volumes dealing with particular territories are designated by number.
Cunningham	*Jeffersonian Republicans in Power*, by Noble E. Cunningham.
D.A.B.	*Dictionary of American Biography*.
Domestic Life	*Domestic Life of Thomas Jefferson*, by Sarah N. Randolph (1871).
Family Letters	*The Family Letters of Thomas Jefferson*, ed. by E. M. Betts and J. A. Bear, Jr.
Farm Book	*Thomas Jefferson's Farm Book*, ed. by E. M. Betts.
FO	Despatches of the British Ministers to the United States to the Foreign Office (transcripts in Library of Congress).
Ford	*Writings of Thomas Jefferson*, ed. by P. L. Ford (10 vols.).
Garden Book	*Thomas Jefferson's Garden Book*, annotated by E. M. Betts.
Hunt	*Writings of James Madison*, ed. by Gaillard Hunt.
I.B.M.	"Instructions to the British Ministers to the U.S., 1791–1812," ed. by Bernard Mayo, *Ann. Report A.H.A. 1936*, Vol. III.
J.C.H.	*Works of Alexander Hamilton*, ed. by J. C. Hamilton
J.-D. Correspondence	*Correspondence between Thomas Jefferson and Pierre Samuel du Pont de Nemours*, ed. by Dumas Malone.
JWE	John Wayles Eppes, son-in-law of Jefferson.
King	*Life and Correspondence of Rufus King*, ed. by C. R. King. References to Vols. III, IV.
L. & B.	*Writings of Thomas Jefferson*, ed. by Lipscomb and Bergh.
LC	Library of Congress. Unless otherwise indicated the references are to the Jefferson Papers there.
Lodge	*Works of Alexander Hamilton*, ed. by H. C. Lodge (10 vols.).
MHS	Massachusetts Historical Society. Unless otherwise indicated the references are to the Jefferson Papers in the Coolidge Collection.
MP	Papers of James Madison, Library of Congress.

NA	National Archives, Washington.
Padover	*Thomas Jefferson and the National Capital*, ed. by S. K. Padover.
Papers, MHS	*Jefferson Papers, Collections Massachusetts Historical Society*, 7 ser., I.
Plumer, *Memorandum*	*William Plumer's Memorandum of Proceedings in the United States Senate, 1803–1807*, ed. by E. S. Brown.
Randall	*Life of Thomas Jefferson*, by H. S. Randall.
Robertson	*Louisiana under the Rule of Spain, France and the United States*, ed. by J. A. Robertson.
S.M.H.	*Writings of James Monroe*, ed. by S. M. Hamilton.
Sowerby	*Catalogue of the Library of Thomas Jefferson*, compiled by E. M. Sowerby (5 vols.).
TJ	Thomas Jefferson.
TMR	Thomas Mann Randolph, Jr., son-in-law of Jefferson.
UVA	Alderman Library, University of Virginia. Unless otherwise indicated the references are to the Jefferson manuscripts.
Va. Mag.	*Virginia Magazine of History and Biography*.
W. & M.	*William and Mary Quarterly Historical Magazine*.
Warren	*Supreme Court in United States History*, references chiefly to Vol. I.

Select Critical Bibliography

A. *Manuscripts*

THE years of Jefferson's first term as President are covered by Volumes 110–147 in the major collection of his papers, that in the Library of Congress (referred to as LC). These papers can be most conveniently used in the Division of Manuscripts at that great repository, where a card index is accessible, but they are also available on microfilm in a number of libraries, including the Alderman Library at the University of Virginia. They consist not only of letters and other documents received by him but also of copies of those he himself wrote. The press copies are not always legible, but those he made during the latter part of his first term, when he was using the polygraph, are notably so. His own writing is nearly always clear, though the same cannot be said for that of Albert Gallatin, who wrote him at least a brief note almost every day when they were in Washington together and who flooded him with lengthier communications when he was at Monticello. The inside story of the administration has gaps in it, since conversations were rarely recorded, but there is a rich record of it in the President's own files. I have used these materials extensively, but it would be impossible to do full justice to them in a book like this.

There are materials bearing on his public life in the Coolidge Collection of his papers at the Massachusetts Historical Society (MHS), though that collection is weighted on the private side. This is even more the case with the chief collection at the University of Virginia (UVA); and the supplementary collections there, such as the Edgehill-Randolph Papers, are predominantly personal and familial. I have referred specifically to these and other relatively small collections whenever I have had occasion to draw on them.

Jefferson's Account Book for a particular period constitutes a sort of diary — an external sort. The one he kept through the year 1803 is in the New York Public Library, and the one covering the rest of his life is in the Massachusetts Historical Society. Photostat copies of these books can be seen in the Library of Congress and the Alderman Library, as they probably can elsewhere. This personal record leaves many financial questions unanswered but it shows where he was at any particular time. Also invaluable is his Index to Letters (LC), showing not merely those he wrote but those he got on any day.

In the Madison Papers in the Library of Congress (MP), Volumes 22–28 of the main collection and Volumes 2 and 3 of the Rives Collection cover Jefferson's first term. When they were both at the seat of government, the correspondence between the President and the Secretary of State declined to a much greater degree than that between Jefferson and Gallatin and his other secretaries. The total amount of their correspondence, however, is very large; and, although Jefferson carefully preserved copies of his own letters, Madison's Papers are a valuable supplement to his. They contain private correspondence with American ministers abroad which did not become part of the public record. These papers are available on microfilm, and an *Index* to them has been published by the Library of Congress (1965). Equally useful is the *Index to the James Monroe Papers* (1963), and this is even more welcome since his handwriting is less legible. Among other manuscripts in the Library of Congress that are of lesser but special value for this period are the Papers of Joseph H. Nicholson, Volume 2 (1801–1805); the Diary of Mrs. William Thornton, Volume 1; and the Private Memoir of William A. Burwell, Jefferson's secretary. As in previous volumes, I have made extensive use of the printed papers of Jefferson's contemporaries.

In connection with foreign affairs, which bulked so large in his presidency, the transcripts from foreign archives in the Library of Congress are of great value. For this period I have made special use of:

> Despatches of the British Ministers to the United States to the Foreign Office, 1801–1805 (referred to as FO with the appropriate volume numbers). These include the despatches of Edward Thornton and Anthony Merry.
>
> Affaires Étrangères, Correspondance Politique, États-Unis. Vols. 54–57 (referred to as AECPEU). These contain the despatches of Pichon and Turreau.

Among relevant materials of importance in the National Archives are:

> Miscellaneous Permanent Commissions (containing copies or forms of commissions and names of appointees). Jefferson's first appointees to what came to be known as the Cabinet are in Volume B. Those of the rest of his administration fall in Volume C (Mar. 26, 1801–Nov. 17, 1812).
>
> Applications and Recommendations for Office, 1797–1901. A guide to those that concern us here was issued by the National Archives in a pamphlet accompanying Microcopy No. 418: *Letters of Application and Recommendation during the Administration of Thomas Jefferson, 1801–1809* (1963).

These largely unexplored sources offer rich materials for the mono-graph on appointments to office by Jefferson which remains to be writ-ten.

B. *Jefferson's Published Papers*

The following work, which contains letters to Jefferson as well as those from him, along with other important materials and extensive notes, continues to supersede all other printed collections as it pro-gresses:

> The Papers of Thomas Jefferson. Julian P. Boyd, ed. (Princeton, Princeton University Press, 1950–   ; cited as Boyd).

Of the fifty-odd projected volumes seventeen have been published at this writing. Unfortunately for the purposes of the present work, these lack some ten years of reaching the presidency, but I have made good use of some of the volumes in securing background material for certain episodes. Because of the form of citation I have employed (giving names and dates as well as indicating sources), my references to both manuscript and printed collections can be readily translated into refer-ences to this great edition as it catches up with me. Meanwhile, I con-tinue to refer to less adequate editions, citing printed sources whenever I can for the convenience of the curious reader. I have continued to refer chiefly to the two following printed collections:

> The Writings of Thomas Jefferson. Paul Leicester Ford, ed. 10 vols. (New York, 1899). This is cited as Ford but should not be con-fused with the same editor's work in 12 volumes containing the same materials. Since it is more dependable than any of the other printed collections prior to that of Boyd, I cite it in preference to them, calling attention to such inaccuracies as I have perceived if these seem worth mentioning. Ford prints some letters to Jefferson in his notes. Unlike most editors he is unfriendly to his subject.
> The Writings of Thomas Jefferson. A. A. Lipscomb. and A. E. Bergh, eds. 20 vols. (Washington, 1903). Less accurate than Ford in text and more extensive. This work is often referred to as Me-morial Edition, but is cited here as L. & B.

The following smaller collections are very useful within their re-spective limits:

> The Jefferson Papers. Collections of the Massachusetts Historical So-ciety, 7 ser., I (Boston, 1900). Referred to as *Papers, MHS*.
> Thomas Jefferson Correspondence. Printed from the Originals in the Collections of William Bixby. With notes by W. C. Ford (Boston, 1916). Referred to as Bixby.
> Glimpses of the Past. Correspondence of Thomas Jefferson, 1788–

1826. Missouri Historical Society, Vol. III, April-June, 1936 (St. Louis, 1936). Contains about a dozen letters from the period 1801–1805.

Thomas Jefferson and the National Capital, 1783–1818. Saul K. Padover, ed. (Washington, Government Printing Office, 1946). A convenient collection of notes, correspondence, and reports from various repositories and publications. (Referred to as Padover.)

Family Letters of Thomas Jefferson. E. M. Betts and J. A. Bear, Jr., eds. (Columbia, Mo., University of Missouri Press, 1966). Correspondence between Jefferson and his daughters and grandchildren, collected from various repositories and generously made available to me long in advance of publication. (Referred to as *Family Letters.*)

The Adams–Jefferson Letters: The Complete Correspondence between Thomas Jefferson and John and Abigail Adams. Lester J. Cappon, ed. Vol. I, 1777–1804 (Chapel Hill, published for the Institute of Early American History and Culture at Williamsburg, Va., by the University of North Carolina Press, 1959). Referred to as *A.-J. Letters.*

The Letters of Lafayette and Jefferson. Introduction and notes by Gilbert Chinard (Baltimore, The Johns Hopkins Press, 1929).

Correspondence between Thomas Jefferson and Pierre Samuel du Pont de Nemours, 1798–1817. Dumas Malone, ed., translations by Linwood Lehman (Boston and New York, Houghton Mifflin Co., 1930).

Correspondence of Jefferson and du Pont de Nemours, with an introduction on Jefferson and the Physiocrats, ed. by Gilbert Chinard (Baltimore, The Johns Hopkins Press, 1931). Du Pont's letters are in their original French.

Volney et L'Amérique, d'après des documents inédits et sa correspondance avec Jefferson, par Gilbert Chinard (Baltimore, The Johns Hopkins Press, 1923).

Thomas Jefferson and James Thomson Callender. By W. C. Ford. (Originally in *New England Historical and Genealogical Register*, Vols. L, LI; published separately, 1897).

The two following works, edited by Edwin M. Betts, are invaluable:

Thomas Jefferson's Garden Book, 1766–1824, with relevant extracts from his other writings (Philadelphia, American Philosophical Society, 1944). The extracts are more important than the entries in these years.

Thomas Jefferson's Farm Book, with commentary and relevant extracts from other writings (published for the American Philosophical Society by Princeton University Press, 1953). Jefferson's agricultural activities in this period were limited, but his correspondence about agricultural matters is of great interest.

The personal letters in Henry S. Randall's *Life of Thomas Jefferson* (3 vols., New York, 1858), a work of enduring merit in itself, impart to it something of the character of a source book. Sarah N. Randolph's *Domestic Life of Thomas Jefferson* (New York, 1871) has a good deal of the same material.

Besides containing detailed information about his major collection of books, E. Millicent Sowerby's *Catalogue of the Library of Thomas Jefferson* (5 vols., Washington, The Library of Congress, 1952–1959) gives pertinent comments that he made on them.

In the previous bibliographies I commented on the contemporary memoranda known as the "Anas." I have continued to use these as notes of the moment. More frequent and more lengthy during Jefferson's presidency than any other period but his secretaryship of state, they are the best source for the proceedings of the executive council (later Cabinet).

The works listed below contain original materials of the first importance which cannot be described as writings but may be classified under Jefferson's papers:

Thomas Jefferson, Architect. Original Designs in the Collection of Thomas Jefferson Coolidge, Jr. With an essay and notes by Fiske Kimball. (Boston, printed for private distribution, 1916.) A classic work.
The same, with a new introduction by Frederick D. Nichols (New York, DaCapo Press, 1968).
Thomas Jefferson's Architectural Drawings. Compiled and with commentary and a check list by Frederick D. Nichols. (Boston, Massachusetts Historical Society; Charlottesville, Thomas Jefferson Memorial Foundation and University of Virginia Press, Revised and enlarged second edition, 1961.) Supplements Kimball's work.

C. *Official and Semi-Official Collections*

American State Papers. Documents, Legislative and Executive. Selected and edited, under the authority of Congress, by Walter Lowrie and Matthew St. Clair Clarke. 38 vols. (1832–1861).
Foreign Relations, Vol. II (referred to as *A.S.P.F.R.*), is more frequently cited in the text than any other volume in this official series.
Varying use has been made of volumes covering this period that are entitled Finance, Military Affairs, Naval Affairs, Indian Affairs, Public Lands, and Miscellaneous (referred to as *A.S.P. Finance*, etc.).

State Papers and Correspondence bearing upon the Purchase of the Territory of Louisiana (Washington, Government Printing Office, 1903). This official publication contains materials not in *A.S.P.F.R.*

Dispatches from the United States Consulate in New Orleans, 1801–1803 in *American Historical Review*, XXXII, 801–824 (July 1927); XXXIII, 331–359 (January, 1928).

Documents relating to the Purchase and Exploration of Louisiana (Boston and New York, 1904). Contains Jefferson's "Examination into the Boundaries of Louisiana," from the manuscript in the library of the American Philosophical Society.

Annals of Congress, 7 and 8 Congress, 1801–1805. 4 vols. (1851–1852). Invaluable, despite the imperfect reporting of the debates.

Journal of the Executive Proceedings of the Senate of the United States. Vol. I, 1789–1805 (1828).

Instructions to the British Ministers to the United States, 1791–1813. Bernard Mayo, ed. (referred to as *I.B.M.*). Annual Report of the American Historical Association for the Year 1936, Vol. III (1941). Very illuminating.

Treaties and Other International Acts of the United States of America. Hunter Miller, ed. Vol. II, 1776–1818 (1931).

Territorial Papers of the United States. Clarence E. Carter, ed. Of this invaluable series (referred to as Carter), the following are specially useful for this period:

Vol. III   Territory Northwest of the River Ohio (1934).
Vol. IV   Territory South of the River Ohio (1936).
Vol. V   Territory of Mississippi (1937).
Vol. IX   Territory of Orleans (1940).

A Compilation of the Messages and Papers of the Presidents, 1789–1897. By James D. Richardson. Published by authority of Congress. Vol. I (Washington, 1896).

Louisiana under the Rule of Spain, France, and the United States, 1785–1807. Edited and translated by James A. Robertson. Vol. II (Cleveland, 1911). Contains many important Spanish documents. (Referred to as Robertson.)

Transactions of the American Philosophical Society Held at Philadelphia for Promoting Useful Knowledge. Especially Vol. VI (1809).

D. *Contemporary Writings*

1. CORRESPONDENCE AND OTHER PAPERS

ADAMS, HENRY. Documents relating to New England Federalism, 1800–1815 (Boston, 1877).

ADAMS, JOHN. Works. C. F. Adams, ed. 10 vols. (Boston, 1856).

———. Correspondence between the Hon. John Adams and the Late

William Cunningham (1823). Contains comments on events dealt with in this volume.

ADAMS, JOHN QUINCY. Writings. Worthington C. Ford, ed. Vol. III (1914).

———. Memoirs. Charles Francis Adams, ed. Vol. I (1874). Full of interesting comments, including a number on Jefferson.

AMES, FISHER. Works, with a Selection from His Speeches and Correspondence. Seth Ames, ed. 2 vols. (Boston, 1854).

BAYARD, JAMES A. Papers, 1796-1815. Elizabeth Donnan, ed. Annual Report of the American Historical Association for the Year 1913, Vol. II (1915).

BENTLEY, WILLIAM. Diary of William Bentley, D.D., Pastor of the East Church, Salem, Massachusetts. Vols. II, III (1907-1911). A Jeffersonian in the country of the Essex Junto.

BURR, AARON. Memoirs of Aaron Burr with Miscellaneous Selections from his Correspondence. By Matthew L. Davis. 2 vols. (New York, 1836-1837).

CABOT, GEORGE. Life and Letters. By Henry Cabot Lodge (Boston, 1878). Contains many letters.

CLAIBORNE, W. C. C. Official Letter Books. Dunbar Rowland, ed. Vols. I-III (Jackson, Miss., 1917).

CUTLER, MANASSEH. Life, Journals, and Correspondence. By W. P. and J. P. Cutler. 2 vols. (Cincinnati, 1888).

DUANE, WILLIAM. Letters, in *Proceedings of the Massachusetts Historical Society*, 2 series, XX (1907), 257-394. A number of these are to Jefferson.

GALLATIN, ALBERT. Writings. Henry Adams, ed. Vol. I (Philadelphia, 1879). This invaluable collection can be supplemented by the *Life* by Adams, which contains a number of letters.

HAMILTON, ALEXANDER. Works. John C. Hamilton, ed. 7 vols. (New York, 1850-1851). I have used this (referring to it as J.C.H.) almost interchangeably with the Lodge edn. Neither is adequate.

———. Works. Henry Cabot Lodge, ed. 9 vols. (New York, 1885-1886). Difficult to use because of the topical arrangement and marred by extreme partisanship.

HUMBOLDT, ALEXANDER VON. Correspondence with Jefferson, Madison, and Gallatin. Helmut De Terra, ed. In *Proceedings of the American Philosophical Society*, December, 1959.

KING, RUFUS. Life and Correspondence. Charles R. King, ed. Vols. III, IV (New York, 1896-1897) cover this period, and, because of the letters to King from so many leaders of his party, they continue to be an invaluable source for High Federalist opinion.

LELAND, JOHN. Writings of the Late Elder John Leland . . . with additional sketches, etc. by Miss L. F. Greene (New York, 1845).

MADISON, JAMES. Writings. Gaillard Hunt, ed. 9 vols. (New York, 1900-

1910). This edn. requires much supplementation but is indispensable.
————. Letters and Other Writings. Published by order of Congress. 4 vols. (1894). Contains some letters not in Hunt.

MITCHILL, SAMUEL LATHAM. Dr. Mitchill's Letters from Washington, 1801–1813, in *Harper's New Monthly Magazine*, Vol. LVIII (1879), pp. 740–755.

MONROE, JAMES. Writings. S. M. Hamilton, ed. (Referred to as S.M.H.) 7 vols. (New York, 1898–1903).

MORRIS, GOUVERNEUR. Diary and Letters. Anne Cary Morris, ed. Vol. II (New York, 1888).

PAINE, THOMAS. Complete Writings. Philip S. Foner, ed. 2 vols. (New York, Citadel Press, 1945).
————. Writings. Moncure D. Conway, ed. Vols. III, IV (New York, 1895–1896).

PLUMER, WILLIAM. Memorandum of Proceedings in the United States Senate, 1803–1807. Everett S. Brown, ed. (New York, Macmillan, 1923). Invaluable for opinions and gossip as well as for proceedings (referred to as Plumer, *Memorandum*).

PRIESTLEY, JOSEPH. Life and Correspondence. By John T. Rutt (1831).

RUSH, BENJAMIN. Letters. L. H. Butterfield, ed. Vol. II (published for the American Philosophical Society by Princeton University Press, 1951). Referred to as Butterfield.

SMITH, MARGARET BAYARD. The First Forty Years of Washington Society. Gaillard Hunt, ed. (New York, Scribner's, 1906). Because of its contemporary letters, an important source for Jefferson's presidency.

STEELE, JOHN. Papers. H. M. Wagstaff, ed. Vol. I (Raleigh, North Carolina Historical Commission, 1924).

SYRETT, H. C. and COOKE, J. G. Interview in Weehawken: The Burr-Hamilton Duel as Told in the Original Documents. Introduction and conclusion by W. M. Wallace (Middletown, Wesleyan University Press, 1960).

TAGGART, SAMUEL. Letters of Samuel Taggart, Representative in Congress, 1803–1814. Introduction by George H. Haynes. In *Proceedings of the American Antiquarian Society*, XXXIII (1923), Part I, covering 1803–1807, pp. 113–226.

TAYLOR, JOHN. Letters, May 11, 1793–April 19, 1823. In *John P. Branch Historical Papers of Randolph-Macon College*, II (June, 1908), 252–353.

2.   TRAVELS AND RECOLLECTIONS

BERNARD, JOHN. Retrospections of America, 1797–1811 (New York, 1887). Contains recollections of Jefferson, 1801–1803, by this English actor.

DAVIS, JOHN. Travels of Four Years and a Half in the United States of America; during 1798, 1799, 1800, 1801, 1802 (London and New York, 1803). More important for the later years than the earlier ones.

FOSTER, SIR AUGUSTUS JOHN. Jeffersonian America. Notes . . . Collected in the Years 1805-6-7 and 11-12. Edited with an introduction by Richard Beale Davis (San Marino, Huntington Library, 1954). First drafted 1833-1835.

JANSON, CHARLES WILLIAM. The Stranger in America, 1793-1806. Reprinted from London edn. of 1807 with introduction and notes by Carl S. Driver (New York, Press of the Pioneers, 1935). Anti-Jeffersonian, mostly dealing with the period after 1800.

JEFFERSON, ISAAC. Memoirs of a Monticello Slave, as Dictated to Charles Campbell in the 1840's. Edited by Rayford W. Logan (Charlottesville, University of Virginia Press, 1951; "popular" edn., with somewhat modernized spelling and additional materials, 1955).

PIERSON, HAMILTON W. Jefferson at Monticello (New York, 1862). Reminiscences of Edward Bacon, "chief overseer and business manager" of Jefferson's estate for twenty years.

E. *Newspapers, Magazines, and Contemporary Pamphlets*

In this volume I have made considerable use of newspapers — sometimes because of the documents and information they contain, sometimes in order to determine the dates at which information became public, and most often, probably, to illustrate the varying response to policies and events. Allowance must be made for partisanship, which was extreme in this era though probably less so than the extravagant journalistic language of the time would imply. The editorial was more frequently employed than heretofore and some editors managed to be relatively judicious and moderate. On the Republican side this was true of Samuel Harrison Smith of the *National Intelligencer* in Washington, which was a sort of official reporter though not really a governmental organ, and Thomas Ritchie of the Richmond *Enquirer*, a paper which did not get started, however, until 1804. William Duane of the Philadelphia *Aurora* was an ardent Republican and consistently loyal to Jefferson, though he disapproved of Gallatin and would have preferred a more partisan administration. Among other Republican papers, mention should be made of the Boston *Independent Chronicle*, edited by Abijah Adams, which fought gallantly against the Federalist Establishment in New England.

The most distinguished Federalist paper was the *New York Evening Post*, established in the autumn of 1801 and ably edited by William Coleman. The most scurrilous was the Richmond *Recorder*, edited by the notorious James Thomson Callender, but happily for Jefferson it lasted only half through his first term. The *Washington Federalist*, supported by Federalist congressmen and Georgetown merchants, was the local antiadministration paper. A Republican representative said: "The *Washington Federalist* is a vile and infamous thing, and purposely misrepresents the transactions in Congress." * The other Federalist papers most often referred to in this volume are the Boston *Columbian Centinel*, edited by Benjamin Russell, and the Philadelphia *Gazette of the United States*, edited by Enos Bronson. The influence of the latter paper, which had been so great when Jefferson was secretary of state in Washington's administration, declined after the government moved to Washington.

Most if not all of these papers are available on microfilm. Detailed information about them and their attitudes (except for the *Washington Federalist*) is given in Jerry W. Knudson's dissertation "The Jefferson Years: Response by the Press, 1801–1809" (UVA, 1962). This is still unpublished but two of his chapters have appeared in print: "The Rage around Tom Paine" (*New York Historical Society Quarterly*, January, 1969, pp. 34–63); and "Newspaper Reaction to the Louisiana Purchase" (*Missouri Historical Review*, January, 1969, pp. 182–213). I have greatly benefited from his study and the extracts which he so generously provided me with. A detailed study of the Federalist press has been made by David Hackett Fischer in *The Revolution of American Conservatism: The Federalist Party in the Era of Jeffersonian Democracy* (New York, Harper and Row, 1965). See especially chapter VII and Appendix III. He believes that the Federalist papers were more moderate than the much less numerous Republican in the election campaign of 1800. Such may have been the case, but it would have been natural for the situation to be reversed during Jefferson's administration and my own impression is that it was. This period in journalistic history was dark by any reckoning and there can be no possible doubt that the incumbent President was much maligned.

Later magazines containing correspondence or other materials drawn on in the text are referred to sufficiently in the notes. Special mention should be made, however, of one contemporary magazine, the *Port Folio*, established in Philadelphia in 1801, and edited as a weekly throughout Jefferson's administration by Joseph Dennie. As the citations from it in this volume show, it was extremely Federalist.

In view of the fact that in this era political pamphlets generally appeared in newspapers and that I myself have generally seen them there, I will make no attempt here to list pamphlets extensively. The following, however, are of special interest:

AUSTIN, BENJAMIN. Constitutional Republicanism, in opposition to Fallacious Federalism (Boston, 1803). The author, described by

---

* Jacob Crowninshield to William Bentley, No. 12, 1803, in *Historical Magazine*, August, 1871, p. 162.

Jefferson as "one of the valuable advocates of human nature," may be designated as a doctrinaire republican.

HAY, GEORGE. An Essay on the Liberty of the Press, Shewing, that the Requisition of Security for Good Behaviour Is Perfectly Compatible with the Constitution and Laws of Virginia (Richmond, 1803). The author was afterwards the chief prosecutor of Aaron Burr.

TAYLOR, JOHN. A Defense of the Measures of the Administration of Thomas Jefferson. By CURTIUS (Providence, R.I., 1805). Originally in *National Intelligencer* (1804) and thoroughly approving up to that time.

WORTMAN, TUNIS. Treatise concerning Political Enquiry, and the Freedom of the Press (New York, 1800).

YOUNG, ALLEN. The Defence of Young and Minns, Printers to the State, before the Committee of the [Massachusetts] House of Representatives, with Appendix, Containing the Debates (Boston, 1805). This bears on the scandalous charges against Jefferson originally launched by Callender.

CHEETHAM, JAMES. A View of the Political Conduct of Aaron Burr (New York, 1802). This and Cheetham's other pamphlets were bitterly hostile to Burr.

ARISTIDES (William Peter Van Ness). An Examination of the Various Charges Exhibited against Aaron Burr (New York, 1803).

CHEETHAM, JAMES. A Reply to Aristides (New York, 1804). Jefferson had all these pamphlets.

F. *Secondary Works and Articles**

ADAMS, HENRY. History of the United States of America [during the administrations of Jefferson and Madison]. 9 vols. (New York, 1889–1890). Referred to as Adams, *History*.

――――. The Life of Albert Gallatin (Philadelphia, 1879).

ADAMS, JOHN QUINCY. Parties in the United States (New York, Greenberg, 1941).

ADAMS, MARY P. "Jefferson's Reaction to the Treaty of San Ildefonso," in *Journal of Southern History*, XXI (May, 1955), 173–188.

――――. Jefferson's Military Policy with Special Reference to the Frontier, 1805–1809 (doctoral dissertation, University of Virginia, 1958).

ALLEN, GARDNER W. Our Navy and the Barbary Corsairs (Boston, 1905).

AMBLER, CHARLES HENRY. Thomas Ritchie: A Study in Virginia Politics (Richmond, 1913).

* This very select list contains the titles of indispensable works and others to which I am specially indebted.

AMES, HERMAN V. "The Proposed Amendments to the Constitution of the United States during the First Century of Its History, in *Annual Report of the American Historical Association*, 1896, Vol. II (1897).

AMMON, HARRY. James Monroe: The Quest for National Identity (seen in manuscript).

————. The Republican Party in Virginia, 1789 to 1824 (doctoral dissertation, University of Virginia, 1948).

ANDERSON, DICE R. William Branch Giles: A Study in the Politics of Virginia and the Nation from 1790 to 1830 (Menasha, Wis., George Banta Publishing Co., 1914).

BALINKY, ALEXANDER. Albert Gallatin. Fiscal Theories and Policies (New Brunswick, Rutgers University Press, 1958).

BEARD, CHARLES A. Economic Origins of Jeffersonian Democracy (New York, Macmillan, 1915).

BEVERIDGE, ALBERT J. The Life of John Marshall. Vol. III (Boston and New York, Houghton Mifflin Co., 1919). Reflects Marshall's unfriendly view of Jefferson and his party.

BOORSTIN, DANIEL J. The Lost World of Thomas Jefferson (New York, Holt, 1948).

BORDEN, MORTON. The Federalism of James A. Bayard (New York, Columbia University Press, 1955).

BOWERS, CLAUDE G. Jefferson in Power (Boston and New York, Houghton Mifflin Co., 1936).

BRANT, IRVING. James Madison: Secretary of State, 1801–1809 (Indianapolis and New York, Bobbs-Merrill, 1953).

BROWN, GLENN. History of the United States Capitol. (56 Congress, 1 session, Senate Document No. 60, Washington, 1800).

BRUCE, WILLIAM CABELL. John Randolph of Roanoke. 2nd edn., 2 vols. in one (New York, Putnam's, 1922).

BRYAN, WILHEMUS BOGART. A History of the National Capital. Vol. I, 1790–1814 (New York, Macmillan, 1914).

BURT, A. L. The United States, Great Britain, and British North America (New Haven, Yale University Press, 1940).

BUSH, ALFRED L. The Life Portraits of Thomas Jefferson. Catalogue of an exhibition at the University of Virginia Museum of Fine Arts, April 12–26, 1962 (Charlottesville, Thomas Jefferson Memorial Foundation, 1962). Supplementing Kimball's study, this is the latest authoritative word on the subject.

BUTTERFIELD, LYMAN H. "Elder John Leland, Jeffersonian Itinerant," in *Proceedings of the American Antiquarian Society*, LXII, Part II (October, 1952), pp. 155–242.

CALDWELL, LYNTON K. The Administrative Theories of Hamilton and Jefferson (University of Chicago Press, 1944).

CHINARD, GILBERT. "Jefferson and the American Philosophical Society," in *Proceedings of the American Philosophical Society*, LXXXVII, No. 3 (1943), pp. 263–276.

COMETTI, ELIZABETH. "John Rutledge, Jr., Federalist," in *Journal of Southern History*, XIII (May, 1947), 186–219.

Cox, ISAAC J. The West Florida Controversy, 1798–1813 (Baltimore, The Johns Hopkins Press, 1918).

———. "The Louisiana-Texas Frontier," in *Southwestern Historical Quarterly*, July, 1913; October, 1913. Specially valuable for Spanish attitudes and actions. Deals with years 1803–1805.

CUNNINGHAM, NOBLE E., JR., The Jeffersonian Republicans in Power: Party Operations, 1801–1809 (University of North Carolina Press, for Institute of Early American History and Culture at Williamsburg, 1963).

DANGERFIELD, GEORGE. Chancellor Robert R. Livingston of New York (New York, Harcourt, Brace, 1960).

DARLING, ARTHUR B. Our Rising Empire (New Haven, Yale University Press, 1940).

DAUER, MANNING J. The Adams Federalists (Baltimore, The Johns Hopkins Press, 1953).

DUMBAULD, EDWARD. Thomas Jefferson: American Tourist (Norman, University of Oklahoma Press, 1946). Useful for this, as for earlier periods.

ELLIS, HAROLD MILTON. Joseph Dennie and His Circle: A Study in American Literature from 1792 to 1812. Bulletin of the University of Texas, July 15, 1915. Studies in English No. 3.

ELLIS, RICHARD E. The Jeffersonian Crisis: Courts and Politics in the Young Republic (doctoral dissertation, University of California, Berkeley, 1969).

ERNEY, RICHARD ALTON. The Public Life of Henry Dearborn (doctoral dissertation, Columbia University, 1957).

FISCHER, DAVID H. The Revolution of American Conservatism: The Federalist Party in the Era of Jeffersonian Democracy (New York, Harper and Row, 1965).

FOOTE, HENRY WILDER. Thomas Jefferson: Champion of Religious Freedom, Advocate of Christian Morals (Boston, Beacon Press, 1947).

GAINES, WILLIAM H., JR. Thomas Mann Randolph, Jefferson's Son-in-Law (Baton Rouge, Louisiana State University Press, 1966).

GREEN, CONSTANCE McLAUGHLIN. Washington: Village and Capital, 1800–1878 (Princeton University Press, 1962).

HALSEY, ROBERT H., M.D. How the President, Thomas Jefferson, and Doctor Benjamin Waterhouse established vaccination as a public health procedure (privately printed, New York, 1936).

HAMLIN, TALBOT. Benjamin Henry Latrobe (New York, Oxford University Press, 1955).

HIGGINBOTHAM, SANFORD W. The Keystone of the Democratic Arch: Pennsylvania Politics, 1800–1816 (Harrisburg, Pennsylvania Historical and Museum Commission, 1952).

HOFSTADTER, RICHARD. Jeffersonian Democracy and Political Parties: Notes on the Intellectual History of the Virginia Dynasty (seen in manuscript, January, 1969).

HUNT, GAILLARD. "Office-Seeking during Jefferson's Administration," in American Historical Review, III (January, 1898), 270–291.

JORDAN, WINTHROP D. White over Black: American Attitudes toward the Negro, 1550–1812 (Chapel Hill, University of North Carolina Press, 1968).

KIMBALL, FISKE. Thomas Jefferson, Architect (Boston, 1916).

———. "The Life Portraits of Jefferson and Their Replicas," in Proceedings of the American Philosophical Society, LXXXVIII, No. 6 (December, 1944), pp. 497–534.

KIMBALL, MARIE G. "The Original Furnishings of the White House," in Antiques, June, 1929; July, 1929.

KOCH, ADRIENNE. Jefferson and Madison: The Great Collaboration (New York, Knopf, 1950).

LEVY, LEONARD W. Jefferson and Civil Liberties: The Darker Side (Cambridge, Harvard University Press, 1963).

———. Legacy of Suppression: Freedom of Speech and Press in Early American History (Cambridge, Belknap Press, 1960).

LOKKE, CARL L. "Jefferson and the Leclerc Expedition," in American Historical Review, XXXIII (January, 1928), 322–328.

LYON, E. WILSON. Louisiana in French Diplomacy, 1759–1804 (Norman, University of Oklahoma Press, 1934). Contains excellent bibliography.

MALONE, DUMAS. The Public Life of Thomas Cooper, 1783–1839 (New Haven, Yale University Press, 1926. Reprint, Columbia, University of South Carolina Press, 1961).

———. Jefferson the Virginian (Boston, Little, Brown, 1948).

———. Jefferson and the Rights of Man (Boston, Little, Brown, 1951).

———. Jefferson and the Ordeal of Liberty (Boston, Little, Brown, 1962).

MARTIN, EDWIN T. Thomas Jefferson: Scientist (New York, Henry Schuman, 1952).

MAYS, DAVID J. Edmund Pendleton, 1721–1803. Vol. II (Cambridge, Harvard University Press, 1952).

MILLER, JOHN C. Alexander Hamilton: Portrait in Paradox (New York, Harper and Bros., 1959).

MORGAN, DONALD G. Congress and the Constitution: A Study of Responsibility (Cambridge, Harvard University Press, 1966).

MORISON, S. E. The Life and Letters of Harrison Gray Otis. Vol. I (Boston, Houghton Mifflin Co., 1913).

Mott, Frank L. Jefferson and the Press (Baton Rouge, Louisiana State University Press, 1943).

Munroe, John A. Federalist Delaware, 1775–1815 (New Brunswick, Rutgers University Press, 1954).

Palmer, Robert R. The Age of the Democratic Revolution (Princeton University Press, 1959).

Pelzer, Louis. "Economic Factors in the Acquisition of Louisiana," in Proceedings of the Mississippi Valley Historical Association, VI (1912–1913).

Perkins, Bradford. The First Rapprochement: England and the United States, 1795–1805 (Philadelphia, University of Pennsylvania Press, 1955).

Peterson, Merrill D. The Jefferson Image in the American Mind (New York, Oxford University Press, 1960).

Phillips, Edward Hake. "Timothy Pickering's Portrait of Thomas Jefferson," in Essex Institute Historical Collections, XCIV (October, 1958), 309–327.

Prucha, Francis Paul. American Indian Policy in the Formative Years: The Indian Trade and Intercourse Acts, 1790–1834 (Cambridge, Harvard University Press, 1962).

Quincy, Edmund. Life of Josiah Quincy (Boston, 1868).

Risjord, Norman K. The Old Republicans: Southern Conservatism in the Age of Jefferson (New York, Columbia University Press, 1965).

Robbins, Roy M. Our Landed Heritage: The Public Domain (Princeton, Princeton University Press, 1942).

Saricks, Ambrose. Pierre Samuel du Pont de Nemours (Lawrence, University of Kansas Press, 1965).

Schachner, Nathan. Aaron Burr: A Biography (New York, F. A. Stokes Co., 1937).

———. Alexander Hamilton (New York, Appleton-Century, 1946).

Sellers, Charles C. Charles Willson Peale, Later Life 1790–1827. (Philadelphia, Memoirs of the American Philosophical Society, Vol. XXIII (1947).

Setser, Vernon G. The Commercial Reciprocity Policy of the United States, 1774–1829 (Philadelphia, University of Pennsylvania Press, 1937).

Shackelford, George G., ed. Collected Papers to Commemorate Fifty Years of the Monticello Association of the Descendants of Thomas Jefferson (published by the association, 1965). Valuable for genealogies and materials about the family.

Shulim, Joseph H. The Old Dominion and Napoleon Bonaparte (New York, Columbia University Press, 1952).

Simms, Henry H. Life of John Taylor (Richmond, William Byrd Press, 1932).

SPAULDING, E. WILDER. His Excellency George Clinton (New York, 1938).

SPROUT, H. H. AND MARGARET. The Rise of American Naval Power, 1776–1918 (Princeton, Princeton University Press, 1939).

TOLLES, FREDERICK B. George Logan of Philadelphia (New York, Oxford University Press, 1953).

TURNER, LYNN W. "The Impeachment of John Pickering," in *American Historical Review*, LIV (April, 1949), 485–507.

———. William Plumer of New Hampshire (Chapel Hill, University of North Carolina Press, 1962).

WALTERS, RAYMOND, JR. Alexander James Dallas: Lawyer-Politician-Financier, 1759–1817 (Philadelphia, University of Pennsylvania Press, 1943).

———. Albert Gallatin: Jeffersonian Financier and Diplomat (New York, Appleton-Century, 1934).

WARREN, CHARLES. The Supreme Court in United States History. Vol. I (Boston, Little, Brown, 1922).

WHITAKER, ARTHUR P. The Mississippi Question, 1795–1803 (New York, Appleton-Century, 1934).

WHITE, LEONARD D. The Jeffersonians: A Study in Administrative History (New York, Macmillan, 1951).

WOOD, GORDON S. The Creation of the American Republic, 1776–1787 (Chapel Hill, University of North Carolina Press, 1969).

WOODFIN, MAUDE HOWLETT. "Contemporary Opinion in Virginia of Thomas Jefferson," in *Essays in Honor of William E. Dodd*, Avery Craven, ed. (University of Chicago Press, 1935).

WOODRESS, JAMES. A Yankee's Odyssey: The Life of Joel Barlow (Philadelphia and New York, J. B. Lippincott Co., 1958).

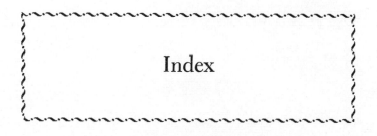

Index

Adams, Abigail (wife of John), opinion of President's House, 37–38, 46; correspondence with TJ, 155, 422–24

Adams, Henry, on TJ and strict construction, 319 and note; on Merry affair, 379n., 384n., 499

Adams, John, xiii, 35, 63, 98, 393; leaves Washington, 3, 4, comments on Republican victory, 5; converses with TJ, 8, 12; letter to TJ (1801), 32; last appointments, 33, 73, 113, 423; horses and carriages, 41; procedure as President avoided by TJ, 51; on Thomas Paine, 192, 200; on TJ's religion, 205; on democratic government, 403; on Hamilton, 426, 427

Adams, John Quincy, 370, 434, 481; on popularity of administration and rejection of Federalist policies, 139; position as senator on Louisiana treaty, 329, 330–32; attends dinner celebrating acquisition, 338; on taxation of people of Louisiana, 353; on TJ's large stories, 375; deplores spirit of party, 402–3; on Hamilton, 429; reports Giles on impeachment, 472–73, 479

Adams, Louisa Catherine (wife of John Quincy), describes TJ, 374

Addison, Judge Alexander, 459

Amendatory Act (Apr. 29, 1802), 131–34 (see Judiciary, federal)

Amendment, Twelfth, 393–94, 407, 433

American Philosophical Society, relations of TJ with, 177–78, 182

Ames, Fisher, 122, 225

Anderson, Joseph, senator from Tennessee, 353

Army, reduction of, 104, 148, 248, (see Dearborn, Henry)

Aurora (Philadelphia), 30, 129, 131; on Louisiana treaty, 297; prints "Etiquette of the Court of the U.S.," 387–89, 499–500 (see Duane, William)

Baldwin, Abraham, senator from Georgia, 90

Baptists, support TJ, 109, 191, 206

Barbé-Marbois, François, Marquis de, French minister of finance, negotiates Louisiana treaty, 285; on boundaries of Louisiana, 304, 305

Barlow, Joel, 181

Bayard, James A., 36, 88; alleged deal with TJ, 11, 13–14, 487–93; opposes repealing act, 127, 128, 129; scores Amendatory Act, 131, 132; defeated for Congress, 142; in Senate in Chase trial, 479

Beckley, John, advises about appointments, 71; clerk of House of Representatives, 90

Bentley, Rev. William, 228

Beveridge, Albert J., on Federalist judiciary, 115; on Marshall's motives in case of Marbury vs. Madison, 145–46

Bishop, Abraham, 77, 78

Bishop, Samuel, 77, 78

Bonaparte, Jerome, 383–84

Bonaparte, Napoleon, 347, 383; seeks to revive colonial empire, 251; sells Louisiana to U.S., 283; reasons for action, 293–94; discourages Monroe from Spanish negotiations, 308; reported as dissatisfied with Louisiana treaty, 315–16

Brackenridge, Hugh Henry, writes TJ about electoral crisis (1801), 10; about appointments, 71; as judge in Pennsylvania supports impeached colleagues, 474

Breckinridge, John, senator from Kentucky, 241, 270, 398; and repeal of Federalist judiciary act, 117, 119, 120; resolutions of (1803), 280; letter of TJ to, about constitutionality of Louisiana Purchase, 313–14, 320; introduces act (1804) for government of Louisiana, 351, 353

Brown, David, 35, 207

Brown, John, senator from Kentucky, 241

Burr, Aaron, 391; Vice President, 4, 90; accidental tie with TJ, 5; loses influence on appointments, 88–89, 141; actions in fight over judiciary (1802), 123–24; charged with disloyalty to party, 141; defended by Callender, 211; TJ's memoranda on (1804), 397–98; in gubernatorial campaign in N.Y., 400–01, 405–06, 430; duel with Hamilton, 425, 426, 427; treatment in Washington, 432–33; presides over Chase trial, 474, 476

Burwell, William A., TJ's private secretary, 414, 419, 421; refers to Walker affair, 217, 218

Cabell, Samuel J., congressman from Virginia, 408, 409

Cabinet, Presidential (see Council, Executive)

Cabot, George, on French cession of Louisiana, 297; on democracy, 403; on separatist movement (1804), 404

Callender, James Thomson, 232, 424; grievances, 207–10; attacks on administration, 211; death, 211–12; on TJ's character, 212–13, 216–18, 494

Campbell, George W., 355

Capitol, U.S., North (Senate) Wing, 3, 46; South (House) Wing, 46, 367

Carlton, William, printer of Salem *Register*, 227–28

Carroll, John, Roman Catholic bishop, letter to, 191

Caucus, Republican congressional, 398–99

Chase, Samuel, justice of Supreme Court, 35, 134, 207; career, 464–465; charge to grand jury in Baltimore, 465–67; impeachment, 468–469, 471–72, 473; memorial to House, 470; trial and acquittal, 474–80

Cheetham, James, attacks Burr, 123, 395–96; altercation with Callender, 211

Claiborne, William C. C., governor of Mississippi Territory, 243, 245–246, 266; on militia, 273; in transfer of Louisiana to U.S., 324, 335; acting governor of Louisiana, 335; on Louisiana territorial act, 349, 354; governor of Orleans Territory, 357–58, 360

Clark, Daniel, consul in New Orleans, 322, 335, 337; in protest movement there, 358, 359

Clinton, DeWitt, on loyalty of Westerners to administration, 279; and gubernatorial campaign (1804) in N.Y., 395–96

Clinton, George, 232, 406; governor of N.Y., 88, 395; correspondence with TJ (1804), 396–97; nominated for Vice President, 398–99; elected, 433

Cocke, William, senator from Tennessee, 243

Coleman, William, collects materials on Hamilton and his death, 425, 426 (see *New York Evening Post*)

Columbian Centinel (Boston), 4, 31, 298; condemns TJ's offer to Paine, 195

Congress, TJ's attitude to and relations with, xvi–xvii, 90–92, 110–

113, 436, 440; pattern of procedure, 119–20; party strength in, 141, 325; role in constitutional matters, 152–156; (*see* House of Representatives, Senate, specific acts)

Cooper, Thomas, 465; letter to, 137

Council, Executive, harmony in, 51; meetings, 52, 61 62, 373 74 (*see* individual members)

Cranch, William, 113, 115

Croswell, Harry, editor of *The Wasp*, tried for libel, 232–33

Cutler, Manasseh, congressman from Massachusetts, 108; thinks TJ embarrassed by Paine, 197; on "Louisiana Jubilee," 338; describes dinner with Merrys, 392

Dale, Commodore Richard, 98

Dallas, Alexander J., district attorney, Pennsylvania, 80; opposes repeal of judiciary act, 124; in conservative faction, 440; prosecutes Judge Addison, 459; defends impeached judges, 474

Davis, Matthew L., 89

Dawson, John, congressman from Virginia, 37, 95, 194

Dayton, Jonathan, senator from N.J., 326

Dearborn, Henry, secretary of war, 34, 35, 36; described and characterized, 57–58; activities for frontier defense, 272–73; letter to, about Indian policy, 274

Debt, national, reduction, 100, 101, 104–06; for purchase of Louisiana, 302–03

Democratic-Republican party (*see* Republican party)

Dennie, Joseph, editor of *Port Folio*, prosecution, 228, 330–31

Deposit, closure of (1802), 240, 260; responsibility for action, 264–65; protests against, 266; legislative action, 268 69, 280; restoration, 281–83

Dexter, Samuel, 35

Dickinson, John, 491

District of Columbia, extent and population, 47 (*see* Washington, D.C.)

Duane, William, 35, 251; and removals from office, 80; and Thomas Paine, 196, 198–99; replies to Callender, 211; characterized, 215; factional leader, 399, 440, 459 (*see Aurora*)

DuPont de Nemours, Pierre Samuel, correspondence with TJ, 91, 255–257, 271; on TJ's election to Institut National de France, 178

Edwards, Pierpont, consulted by TJ, 75, 76

Elections, presidential (1801), 6–7; state and congressional (1802), 139–41; gubernatorial, N.Y. (1804), 406; presidential (1804), 433–34

Ellicott, Andrew, 180, 245

Eppes, Francis, grandson of TJ, 412, 417; birth, 160; health, 162, 174, 411

Eppes, John Wayles, TJ's son-in-law (referred to as JWE), buys horses for TJ, 41; affectionate relations with him, 174; electioneering, 175; at President's House, 368, 417; in Congress (1803–05), 409–410, 450–51; writes TJ during wife's illness, 413; on Chase's conduct in Callender case, 465

Eppes, Maria Jefferson, younger daughter of TJ, children, 160, 368, 413, 417; reluctant to visit Washington, 163; descriptions, 167, 171; visits TJ in Washington, 170–74; illness and death, 411–15; relations with her father, 415–17; with Abigail Adams, 422

Executive Council (*see* Council, Executive)

Federalists, xiv, xv, 268, 279; unwilling to accept outcome of election (1800), 4–5, 15; critical of Gallatin at first, 54–55; intransigent in Connecticut, 75–77; on TJ's removal policy, 82–84; popular rejection of their policies, 139; attack TJ's moral character, 211, 219–21, 441; relatively indifferent to West, 241; partisan in foreign affairs, 280; deny administration credit for Louisiana treaty, 284–85, 298; question constitutional authority to incorporate Louisiana, 329; oppose 12th amendment, 393–95; support Burr in N.Y., 405; Old and New School, 436; in case of Judge Pickering, 461, 462, 464; in Chase impeachment and trial, 469, 470, 480

Fletcher vs. Peck, case of, 456

Florida, East, 271, 287

Florida, West, 271, 287, 334; claimed as included in Louisiana Purchase, 303–09; districts, 343, 345; negotiations regarding, 346–47, 442

Foster, Augustus John, secretary of British legation, 391; describes TJ, 371, 373, 374, 375

France, peace with Great Britain, 95, 239; convention with U.S. ratified (1801), 95; TJ's attitude to, 96, 253–58, 295; retrocession of Louisiana to, 240, 248; Louisiana treaty with, 302–03 (see Bonaparte, Napoleon; Pichon, L. A.)

Fries Rebellion, 104

Fulton, Robert, 181

Gallatin, Albert, secretary of the treasury, 29, 34, 244, 395, 400; in electoral crisis (1801), 6, 7, 8, 10, 11; on conduct of John Adams, 33; description and characterization, 54–57, 66; differences with Robert Smith, 59, 99, 263; attitude and services in appointments, 80–82, 88–89; financial policy, 100–04; relations with Congress, 111; on repayment of Callender's fine, 209n.; attacked by Callender, 211; on financial provisions of Louisiana treaty, 303; on constitutional questions involved in purchase, 312, 315, 324–25; on Mobile Act, 342,

345–46; on mourning for Hamilton, 427; ties with congressional triumvirate, 446; and Yazoo claims, 449–50; and Pickering impeachment, 460, 461; and Chase trial, 482; on alleged deal of TJ with Bayard, 490

Gallatin, Hannah Nicholson (wife of Albert), 56, 381, 446

Gazette of the United States (Philadelphia), 30

Gelston, David, 80, 89

Georgia, cession of western lands to U.S., 246, 448–49; cession of Indian lands in state, 247 (see Yazoo claims)

Gerry, Elbridge, 74

Giles, William Branch, desires purge of Federalist office holders, 72; desires repeal of judiciary system, 116; overstates case in debate, 127–128; retires from House because of health, 143; attacked by Callender, 211; majority leader in House, 443; opinions and actions in Senate in Chase trial, 472–73, 480, 481

Goodrich, Elizur, and collectorship of port of New Haven, 75–79

Gore, Christopher, 389

Granger, Gideon, postmaster general, appointed, 79–80; political sentinel, 75, 76, 401, 433; on TJ's reply to Danbury Baptists, 109; attacked by Callender, 211; provides "express mail" to New Orleans, 333; in Yazoo controversy, 453–55

Great Britain, peace with France, 95, 240; convention with U.S. (1802), 97; TJ's attitude to, 96, 293, 295–296; talk of alliance with, 253, 255, 256, 257, 291 (see Thornton, Edward; Merry, Anthony)

Greenville, treaty of, with Indians, 241

Griswold, Roger, congressman from Connecticut, 263, 405; resolution of, 268–69

Habersham, Joseph, 36, 79

Hamilton, Alexander, xiv, 94, 465;

financial policy, 12; comments on TJ's inaugural address, 21; ideas compared with TJ's, 25; criticizes TJ's first annual message, 98, 99, 104; attitude toward national debt, 105; relations with Congress when Secretary of Treasury, 111; gloomy reflections (1807), 137, 138; Reynolds affair, 217, 218; counsel for Harry Croswell, 233; on TJ's second annual message, 262; advocates forceful annexation of New Orleans and Floridas, 277–78; on strict and liberal construction of Constitution, 319–20; opposed to disunionists, 404, 405; condemns Burr, 405; duel and funeral, 425–428; comments and judgments on, 428–31

Harper, Robert Goodloe, 449*n*., 477

Harrison, Gov. William Henry, letter to, about Indian policy, 274–75

Harrowby, Lord, British foreign secretary, 390

Harvie, Lewis, TJ's private secretary, 368, 414

Hawkesbury, Lord, British foreign secretary, 389, 390

Hemings, Sally, 212–13, 214, 494, 496, 497–98

Hoban, James, 38, 46

Hopkinson, Joseph, 477

House of Representatives, quarters, 46 47, 90; party alignment in, 90, 325; majority leaders, 443; triumvirate, 446; in opposition to Senate (1805), 481 (*see* Congress)

Humboldt, Baron Alexander von, 421–22

Impeachments, of judges in Pennsylvania, 459, 474; of federal judges (*see* Pickering, John; Chase, Samuel)

Independent Chronicle (Boston), 297

Indians, land cessions of, 247, 275; TJ's policies respecting, 273–75, 315; in Louisiana, 341

Institut National de France, elects TJ a member, 178–79

Jackson, Andrew, 348, 357

Jackson, James, senator from Georgia, fears army of judges, 126

Jefferson, Thomas, subject of this book and referred to as TJ:

Personal Life

At Conrad and McMunn's, 29; removes to President's House, 37; domestics, 40; finances, 40, 42–43; horses and carriages, 41; neighborly relations in Washington, 48; hospitality, 94, 374–76; normal regimen, 370; social vendetta with Merry and Yrujo, 378–89

Finds real happiness only in family life, 159; visits home, 64–65, 160–61, 165–67; relations with sons-in-law, 161, 164–65, 174–76, 368, 408–10; family correspondence, 161–63; efforts to get daughters to visit him in Washington, 163–65; is visited by them (1802–03), 170–74; comments on "woman's trade," 411; loses younger daughter, 415–418; corresponds with Abigail Adams, 422 24

Relations with American Philosophical Society, 177–78; with Institut National de France, 178–79; philosophical and scientific correspondence, 180–84; services to vaccination, 185; correspondence about health, 185–89; attends divine services, 199; correspondence about religion, 200 01, 203 04; attacks on personal character, 206, 211–23, 494–98; uses polygraph, 419–21; entertains Baron von Humboldt, 421

Public Career

Inauguration, 3–4; previous electoral crisis, 5–11; alleged deal with Federalists, 11–14, 487–93; delivers inaugural address, 17; pardons victims of Sedition Act, 35, 207; seeks to improve physical facilities of capital, 46–48; qualifications as executive, 51, 66; relations with chief assistants, 51, 57, 60–61; struggles with problem of appointments and removals, 69–89

Sends message to Congress, 92, 95; financial policy, 100–06; receives "mammoth cheese" and "mammoth veal," 106–08; leadership over Congress, 110–13, 436; gains repeal of Federalist judiciary act, 116, 119, 120–21, 130; approves amendatory act, 132–33; restraint as party leader, 112, 141; intervenes in cases of Mason and Rodney, 142

Actions leading to case of Marbury vs. Madison, 73, 144–45; rebuked in Marshall's opinion, 149–150, 151; supported by Baptists, 109, 191; opposed by dominant clergy in New England, 190–91; actions with respect to Thomas Paine, 192, 194–95, 197–99; connection with libel cases, 227–33; and freedom of press, 233–35

Relations with West before Louisiana Purchase, 240–47; learns of retrocession of Louisiana, 248; considers diplomatic effects, 253–258; position regarding St. Domingo, 251–53; seeks asylum for insurrectionist slaves, 252–53; proposes drydock, 263; nominates Monroe as minister extraordinary, 269; secures appropriation, 270–71; actions for frontier defense, 272–273; Indian policies, 273–75; secures authorization of exploring expedition, 275–76; patience condemned by Hamilton, 277–78; authority threatened by Ross resolutions, 279–80; gains restoration of deposit, 281–82

Policies, procedure, and activities leading to acquisition of Louisiana, 285–88, 291–92, 295–96; prepares memoir on bounds of province, 309; considers constitutionality of acquisition, 311–19; learns of possible difficulties with French and Spanish, 315–16, 322; implements treaty, 324–29, 335; learns of transfer of province to France, 336; to U.S., 338; procures and submits account of province to Congress, 340–42; purposes regarding Floridas, 343–47; actions and opinions regarding government of Louisiana, 348–52, 356–60; 362

Decides to stand for re-election, 395; unanimously nominated by caucus, 398; supported by all factions in party, 399, 401, 406; attitude to irreconcilable Federalists, 401–02; re-elected, 433–34; significance of victory, 436–37; passive role in congressional session (1804–05), 440, 457; hands-off policy in Yazoo controversy, 452–53; submits documents regarding Judge Pickering, 460; favors removal of judges on joint address, 462; makes partisan appointments in New Hampshire, 464; calls attention to conduct of Samuel Chase, but otherwise does not enter into impeachment and trial of the Justice, 467–68, 471; analyzes vote, 479–80; concludes impeachment is a farce, 482; administration in retrospect, 484–85

Papers
(*see* Bibliography)

First inaugural address, 17–28; reply to New Haven merchants, 78–79; first annual message, 92, 95, 248; reply to Danbury Baptist Association, 108–09; *Manual of Parliamentary Practice*, 119–20; *Notes on Virginia*, 191, 214; Bill for Establishing Religious Freedom, 191, 226; Syllabus of an Estimate of the Merit of the Doctrines of Jesus, 201–04; *Life and Morals of Jesus of Nazareth*, 204; second annual message, 262–64; memoir on limits and bounds of Louisiana, 309, 339,

343, 347; third annual message, 326; draft of bill for government of Louisiana, 351; "Etiquette of the Court of the U.S.," 387–89, 499–500; fourth annual message, 441, 442–43; draft of act to preserve peace in harbors, 441–42

Philosophy and Opinions
(see Papers)

General statement of political principles, xiii–xix; confidence in American experiment in self-government, 21, 27–28, 235, 437; belief in sovereignty of people, 24, 99–100, 435–36; in limited government, xx, 22, 25–26, 27, 136–37; separation of powers and balanced government, 154, 435 (see Congress; judiciary, federal); majority rule with minority rights, 18–19; spheres of federal and state governments, 23, 102; egalitarianism, 93, 388–89; elitism, xv, 79, 87–88; representative character of presidency, 94; on political parties, 434–35; emphasis on harmony, 60–61, 91; on peace, xx, 95, 262, 295; freedom of opinion, 20; freedom of press, xix, 227, 229–30, 233; religious position, 108–09, 190–92, 200–05; on science and invention, 179, 181, 184; state of medicine, 184

Comments and Descriptions

In songs and celebrations, 30–31; by John Quincy Adams, 375; Louisa Catherine Adams, 374; Augustus J. Foster, 371, 373, 374, 375; Alexander Hamilton, 430; John Lambert, 373; John Marshall, 22; Samuel Lathrop Mitchill, 94; Timothy Pickering, 177, 403; William Plumer, 370–71; Margaret Bayard Smith, 18, 371; Joseph Story, 373; Edward Thornton, 167; portraits, 437–38

Jones, Evan, 359
Jones, Gabriel, 212

Jones, Meriwether, 209
Jones, William, 36
Judiciary Act (Federalist of 1801), provisions, 113–14; legislative battle over, 121–30; repeal affirmed by Supreme Court, 134
Judiciary, federal, 71; Republican hostility to, 114–15, 458–59; TJ's attitude to, 116, 133, 151–52, 462; as affected by Amendatory Act, 131; impeachments (see Pickering, John; Chase, Samuel)

Kentucky, strongly Republican, 141; memorial of legislature, 269
Key, Philip Barton, 477
King, Rufus, minister to Great Britain, 37, 253, 291, 296; removal sought by Republicans, 72, negotiates convention with British (1802), 97; on retrocession of Louisiana, 248, 249; on expedition to St. Domingo, 251; on terms of Louisiana treaty, 303; on Anthony Merry, 377; on etiquette in England, 384–85; against disunionist plot, 404, 405; vice-presidential candidate (1804), 433
Kinloch, Francis, 219

Lafayette, Marquis de, 357
Lambert, John, describes TJ, 373
Langdon, John, 36
Latimer, George, 13, 489, 491
Latrobe, Benjamin H., surveyor of public buildings, 369; and President's House, 37, 45, 368; and Capitol, 47, 367; plan of drydock, 263
Laussat, Pierre Clement, French prefect, New Orleans, 336, 337
Leclerc, General Charles V. E., arrives St. Domingo, 251; early success, 259; death, 272, 293
Lee, Charles, in case of Marbury vs. Madison, 145, 149; counsel for Chase, 477
Lee, Henry (Light-Horse Harry), actions in Walker affair, 222, 223

Leib, Michael, congressman and factional leader in Pennsylvania, 440, 459

Leiper, Thomas, 209

Leland, John, on TJ's removal policy, 84; and "mammoth cheese," 107–08

Lewis, Meriwether, private secretary of TJ, 29, 40, 210; duties and quarters, 43–44, 368; exploring expedition authorized, 275–76

Lewis, Morgan, 400, 406

Lincoln, Levi, attorney general, 34, 208, 348; acting secretary of state, 34, 36, 145; comments of Gallatin on, 57–58; consulted about New England affairs, 75, 79, 109; receives TJ's syllabus on doctrines of Jesus, 204; letter to, about Walker affair, 222; opinions on constitutionality of acquisitions from France, 312, 321; and Yazoo claims, 449, 456; resigns, 455

Livingston, Edward, 358, 488

Livingston, Robert R., minister to France, 34, 37, 42, 347; arrives in France, 96; instructions and qualifications, 250; letters of TJ to (1802), 254–57; memoir on Louisiana, 258, 298–99; reports prospects, 258–59; denies value of Monroe's mission, 285, 289, 299; is taken up by Federalists, 298; standing with administration, 298–299, 303; claims inclusion of West Florida in Louisiana Purchase, 303–04; reports dissatisfaction of Bonaparte, 315–16

Louisiana, xix; retrocession to France, 240, 248–50; anticipated effects on American foreign policy, 253–58; importance to France asserted, 259; cession to U.S., 283; comments on, 284, 297, 325; assignment of credit for treaty, 298–300; cost, 302–03; boundaries, 303–09; enabling act, 328; transfer to U.S., 338; celebrations of, 338–39; account of province, 340–42; governmental acts, 342, 348, 351–56, 361; "Remonstrance of the People," 360

Lyon, Matthew, congressman from Kentucky, attacks John Randolph, 454

McKean, Thomas, governor of Pennsylvania, 97, 440; in electoral crisis (1801), 7, 10–11; policy in appointments, 71; and prosecutions for libel, 228–31; letter of TJ to (1804), 395, 401; in controversy over state judiciary, 459, 474

McLane, Allen, and alleged deal of TJ with Bayard, 13–14; struggle for removal, 82, 489, 491–92

Maclay, Senator William, 402

Macon, Nathaniel, Speaker of House of Representatives, 90, 93, 320, 355; on opinion in Marbury vs. Madison, 149; in congressional triumvirate, 446; on impeachment of Chase, 468

Madison, Dolley (wife of James), 173, 379

Madison, James, secretary of state, xiv, 9, 145; delayed in assumption of duties, 34; stays at President's House (1801), 40, 42; characterization at outset of administration, 52, 57, 66; guest at Monticello (1802), 166; dealings with Callender, 210; in Walker affair, 218, 223; teamwork with TJ in diplomacy, 254, 290–92; on importance of Mississippi River, 266; on renewal of European war, 283; in Louisiana negotiations, 286, 288, 301; on constitutionality of purchase, 314, 316, 330; answers Spanish objections to cession, 322–23; on Mobile Act, 344, 346; on claim to West Florida, 347; in Merry affair, 379–381, 385, 389; letters from TJ about illness and death of daughter, 414–15; relations with John Randolph, 446; and Yazoo claims, 449, 456; and Chase impeachment, 481–82

Marbois (*see* Barbé-Marbois)

Marbury *vs.* Madison, case of, preliminary motion, 117–18; questions at issue, 143–48; opinion of Chief Justice, 149–50; contemporary reception of this, 151; contemporary significance, 156

Marbury, William, 73, 118, 144, 145, 146 (*see* Marbury *vs.* Madison)

Marshall, Humphrey, 241

Marshall, James M., 115

Marshall, John, chief justice, 4, 23, 113; comments on TJ and inaugural address, 22, 111; acting secretary of state, 29, 34, 144; grants preliminary motion in case of Marbury *vs.* Madison, 117–18; in later years praises amendatory act, 131; favors acceptance of repealing act, 133–34; purposes in case of Marbury *vs.* Madison, 145–48; opinion, 149–51; decision in Fletcher *vs.* Peck, 456; witness in Chase trial, 477; suggests grant to Congress of authority to overrule judicial decisions, 481

Martin, Luther, counsel for Chase, 477

Mason, Stevens Thomson, in struggle to repeal judiciary act, 117, 126; persuaded by TJ to remain in Senate, but dies soon thereafter, 142

Massachusetts, House of Representatives debate on article attacking TJ's character, 220–22

Meredith, Samuel, 56

Merry, Anthony, British minister to U.S., 344; appointment, 377; complains of indignities, 378–79, 381; feud with administration, 382–392; on political situation, 401, 406, 407

Merry, Mrs. Anthony, 377, 391–92; described, 382, 383

Mississippi River, free navigation of, xix, 239, 255, 266, 286

Mississippi Territory, factionalism, 244–46; militia, 273

Mitchill, Samuel Lathrop, describes TJ (1802), 94; on violence of congressional speeches, 136; on Thomas Paine, 197

Mobile Act, 342–47

Monroe, James, governor of Virginia, in electoral crisis (1801), 7, 9, 11; advises TJ about appointments, 71–72; against postponement of Supreme Court session, 132; disinclined to enter Senate, resumes law practice, 142; relations with Callender, 207, 209, 210; privy to Walker affair, 218; correspondence with TJ about slave revolts, 252–53; appointed minister extraordinary, 269–70; delay in departure for France, 272, 288; value of his mission, 289, 299–301; "Opinion respecting West Florida," 306–308; minister to Great Britain, 343; mission to Spain, 344, 347; and governorship of Orleans Territory, 357–58; on Merry affair and protocol in England, 389–90

Monticello, descriptions of (1802), 166–68

Moore, Thomas, 377, 391

Morales, Juan de Dios, Intendant at New Orleans, actions in closure of deposit, 264, 265–66

Morocco, 262, 263

Morris, Gouverneur, 12, 42, 120; presents farewell address to TJ in Senate, 15; in fight over repeal of Judiciary Act, 121, 122, 126; comments on administration (1802), 138; on opposition of Senate Republicans to petition of Marbury, 146; on TJ's policy (1803), 272; funeral oration on Hamilton, 426, 428

Munroe, Thomas, superintendent of public buildings, 367

Murray, William Vans, 37

National Intelligencer, 17, 200, 284, 387, 406, 415; comments on repealing act, 129; on congressional session (1801–1802), 135; moderation, 225; on Louisiana treaty, 296–97; on Livingston's merit, 298; rejoices at acquisition of Louisiana, 338; on 12th amendment, 394; on Republican nominees (1804), 399; on TJ's re-election, 433; on Chase's charge to grand jury, 466–67 (*see* Smith, Samuel Harrison)

Navy, reduction of, 102–03, 248–49; proposed drydock, 263; gunboats, 442

New England, efforts of TJ to win over, 58, 452, 455; fears aroused by Louisiana Purchase, 297; disunionist plot, 402–06

New England Palladium (Boston), attacks TJ's character, 220

New Hampshire, and 12th amendment, 407

New Haven merchants, protest of 77–78; reply to, 78–79

New Orleans, dangers in French possession of, 254, 255, 256; TJ determined to acquire, xix, 287 (*see* Deposit; Louisiana)

Newspapers, TJ's attitude toward, 224–25, 226–27, 233–35; status and character, 225–26; prosecutions of editors, 227–33; (*see* individual papers; Bibliography)

New York Evening Post, 251; comments on TJ's removal policy, 83–84; on elections (1802), 139; exploits TJ's gifts to Callender, 211; belittles appointment of Monroe, 277, 278; denies government credit for Louisiana treaty, 284–85; on gloomy prospects in Louisiana, 333; attacks account of province, 341–42; on Chase impeachment, 469 (*see* Coleman, William)

Nicholas, John, congressman from Virginia, 13, 489

Nicholas, Wilson Cary, senator from Virginia, 6, 74, 97, 119; correspondence with TJ about constitutionality of Louisiana Purchase, 318–19; advocates break with Burr, 396

Nicholson, James, 88

Nicholson, Joseph H., congressman from Maryland, 441, 442, 463; defends postponement of Supreme Court session, 132; in congressional triumvirate, 446; in Chase impeachment and trial, 467–68, 472; resentment against Senate, 481

Ohio, 241; formation of state government, 243–44

Orleans, Territory of, 348, 353, 361 (*see* Louisiana)

Pace, Henry, 211

Page, John, appointed to office, 86–87; letter to TJ, 218; letter from TJ on death of Maria, 407, 418

Paine, Thomas, American opposition to, 192–94; letter of TJ to, offering passage to U.S., 194–95, 199–200; arrival and reception, 196; treatment by TJ, 197–99; comments of John Adams on, 260; discusses constitutionality of Louisiana Purchase, 311

Peale, Charles Willson, 107; admiration and regard for TJ, 178; miscellaneous correspondence with him, 180; mastodon, 182–84; dines with TJ, 411; polygraph, 419–21

Peale, Rembrandt, portrait of TJ, 439

Pederson, Peder, chargé of Denmark, 376, 379

Pendleton, Judge Edmund, author of "The Danger Not Over," 118–19; on removal of judges, 462

Pennsylvania, factional conflicts in, 399, 440–41; anti-judiciary controversy, 459, 474

Perdido River, claimed as eastern boundary of Louisiana, 304, 306, 307, 341, 343

Peters, Judge Richard, 465

Peterson, Merrill D., on miscegenation legend, 494–95

Philadelphia, inaugural celebration in, 29–30; address of Ward Committees, 399

Pichon, L. A., French chargé, 259, 281, 376; reports TJ's friendliness, 96; on St. Domingo, 252; on political situation (1802), 264; reports conversations with TJ and Madison (1803), 290–92; cooperates in transfer of Louisiana, 323, 327, 334; in Merry affair, 379–80, 381–382, 387, 499

Pickering, Judge John, impeachment and trial, 148, 460–64

Pickering, Timothy, comments on TJ, 177, 403; prosecutes printer for libel, 227–28; on Louisiana, 353; in separatist plot (1804), 404–05; on case of Judge John Pickering, 463

Pinckney, Charles, minister to Spain, 88, 250, 323

Pinckney, Charles Cotesworth, presidential candidate, 433

Pinckney, Thomas, 219, 239

Plumer, William, senator from New Hampshire, 353, 481; comments on Thomas Paine at President's House, 197; on hasty action on Louisiana treaty, 326; on constitutional question, 329; on Louisiana dinner, 338; describes TJ, 370–71; on TJ's dinners, 374, 375, 376; and separatist plot, 405; describes John Randolph, 444, 446–47, 451; and Pickering impeachment, 461, 462; reports Giles on impeachment, 472; comments on Randolph's replication, 477; on TJ's abandonment of removal of Chase, 483

Polygraph, 368, 419–21

Port Folio, quoted, 167, 228, 230–31 (see Dennie, Joseph)

Presbyterian General Assembly, 206

President's House, description of, 37–38; furnishings, 41–42; use of rooms, 43–46; physical improvements, 368

Press (see Newspapers)

Priestley, Dr. Joseph, 9; letters to, 27; corresponds with TJ about religion, 200–01, 203–04

Randall, Henry S., 497

Randolph, Anne Cary, eldest granddaughter of TJ, 162, 412

Randolph, David M., removed from office, 74; connection with Callender case, 208; with Walker affair, 219

Randolph, Ellen Wayles, granddaughter of TJ, 162; visits Washington, 170; description, 172; on Sally story, 497

Randolph, John, congressman from Virginia, xii; on repeal of judiciary act, 126–27; majority leader in House, 143, 443, 446–47; on Walker affair, 223; resolution for papers on removal of deposit, 264, 269; on grievances of people of Louisiana, 360–61; relations with TJ, 409–10, 447; on Burr and Hamilton, 427; described, 444; on Yazoo claims, 447, 450–52; attacks Granger, 453–54; is attacked by Matthew Lyon, 454; divisive influence on party, 451, 455, 457; in Chase impeachment and trial, 468–469; 471–72, 476–78, 483; proposes amendment for removal of judges, 481

Randolph, Martha Jefferson, elder daughter of TJ, children, 160, 368, 410, correspondence with TJ, 161–163; descriptions, 167, 171; visits TJ in Washington (1802), 170–74; letter to, 386–87; devotion to her father, 418

Randolph, Thomas Jefferson, grandson of TJ, 162; visits Washington (1802), 170, 172; on Sally story, 496, 497

Randolph, Thomas Mann, Jr., son-in-law of TJ (referred to as TMR), is offered land by TJ, 43; relations with TJ, 161, 175; projects and abandons land purchase in Georgia, 164, 165, 175–76; congressional career, 176, 408–09, 410, 411, 450–51; at President's House, 368

Randolph, Virginia, granddaughter of TJ, birth, 160

Repealing Act (*see* Judiciary Act)

Republican party, attitudes of leaders in electoral crisis (1801), 6–8; doctrines, xvi, xviii, 435–36; schisms and factions, 124, 141, 399–401, 440; congressional caucus (1804), 398–99; best organized where conflict was greatest, 434 and note 29; sectional lines, 451–52

"Revolution of 1800," 26; TJ's interpretation of, xiii, xv

Richmond *Enquirer*, 225–26 (*see* Ritchie, Thomas)

Richmond *Examiner*, 209, 211

Richmond *Recorder*, vehicle of Callender's attacks on administration and TJ, 211, 223

Ritchie, Thomas, publisher of Richmond *Enquirer*, 225–26, 482

Rodney, Caesar A., 463, 492; runs for Congress at TJ's request, 142, 443; on Thomas Paine, 198; in Chase trial, 472; prosecutes judges in Pennsylvania, 474

Roosevelt, Franklin D., 98

Ross, James, senator from Pennsylvania, opposes repealing act (1802), 124; resolutions of (1803) authorizing forceful action against Spanish, 148, 278–81

Rush, Dr. Benjamin, 72, 431; on TJ's inaugural address, 24, 32; corresponds with TJ about latter's health, 185–88; about religion, 200–01, 203–04; on TJ's correspondence with Abigail Adams, 424

Rutledge, John, Jr., 128

St. Clair, General Arthur, 243–44

St. Domingo, French expedition to, 251–53, 259; failure of, 272, 293

Saint-Mémin, C. B. J. Fevret de, portrait of TJ, 412, 437–39

St. Xavier Farjon, Sister Thérèse de, 356–57

San Ildefonso, treaty of, 322, 327

San Lorenzo, treaty of, 239, 240

Sargent, Winthrop, 244, 245

Sedgwick, Theodore, 3, 82

Senate, farewell address to TJ, 15; party alignment in, 91, 123, 325; majority leaders, 117, 472; debate on Marbury petition, 146; impeachment trials in, 463–64, 474–480; in opposition to House, 481 (*see* Congress, specific acts and treaties)

Short, William, 385, 401, 436

Sinclair, Sir John, letter of TJ to, 295

Slave trade, prohibited in Louisiana, 358, 360

Smith, Margaret Bayard (wife of Samuel Harrison), on TJ's inaugural address, 17–18, 24; at President's House, 42; describes TJ's daughters and granddaughter, 171–172; on his dress, 371

Smith, Robert, secretary of the navy, 315, 382, 384; differences with Gallatin, 59, 99, 263; letter to, about Walker affair, 222

Smith, Samuel, 384; and alleged deal of TJ with Bayard, 13–14, 487–90; temporary secretary of navy, 36, 59; congressman, 446

Smith, Samuel Harrison, publisher of *National Intelligencer*, 17, 115; reports judiciary debate, 120; reserved about Paine, 196; attacked by Callender, 211; declines communication regarding him, 215

Spain, treaty of San Lorenzo with, 239–40, 266; retrocedes Louisiana to France, 240; objects to cession to U.S., 322–23; acquiesces, 337; protests against Mobile Act, 343; mission of Monroe to, 344, 347 (*see* Yrujo, Marqués de Casa)

Steele, John, 56, 491

Stoddert, Benjamin, 12, 36

Story, Joseph, describes TJ, 373

Stuart *vs.* Laird, case of, 134

Stuart, Gilbert, 44, 54, 55

Supreme Court, as affected by judiciary act (1801), 113; session abolished (1802), 131–32; affirms repealing act, 134 (*see* specific decisions; Marshall, John)

Swartwout, John, 88

Talleyrand, Charles M., French foreign minister, 250–51, 260, 294; on boundaries of Louisiana, 306, 308

Taxes, repeal of internal, 100, 102

Taylor, John (of Caroline), 100; on judicial reform, 119, 120; on TJ's continuance in office, 437

Tennessee, strongly Republican, 141; militia, 335

Thornton, Edward, British chargé, comments on TJ's ministers, 57–58; on his unceremoniousness, 93; reports his attitude to France and Great Britain, 96; political success of financial program, 100; comments on judiciary debate, 136; on political divisions of country, 140; on Monticello, 167; on reduction of army, 248; on anti-French sentiment, 253–54, 260; on TJ and Navy, 263; reports pro-British trend, 292; recommends appointment of minister, 376–77; comments on Federalist opposition, 393

Thornton, Dr. William, 382; visits TJ at Monticello, 166; architect of Capitol, 367

Thornton, Mrs. William, 382; account of Monticello, 166–68

Tiffin, Edward, 243; first governor of state of Ohio, 244

Toussaint Louverture, General, 251, 252, 253, 259

Tracy, Uriah, senator from Connecticut, 120, 405, 479; seeks papers on Walker affair, 219

Tripoli, war with, 97–99, 262–63

Trollope, Frances, 213, 494

Troup, Robert, comments on administration (1801), 24, 25; on Gallatin, 54

Van Ness, William P., 396

Wagner, Jacob, chief clerk, department of state, 340, 391

Walker, John, and episode relating to his wife, 217–23

Walker, Mrs. John, episode relating to, 216–23

Warren, Charles, comments on decision in case of Stuart vs. Laird, 134

Washington, D.C., 47; TJ's unique relations with, 48; physical changes, 367 (see District of Columbia)

Washington Federalist, 387

Washington, George, xiv; portrait, 44; procedure as President followed by TJ, 51, 61–62; precedent of address to Congress abandoned, 92; attacked by Paine, 193, 195; letter from TJ about Hamilton, 428–29

Waterhouse, Dr. Benjamin, 185

Wayles, John, 495, 497

Wayne, Anthony, 241

West (trans-Appalachian region), TJ's interest in, 240–41; his support by, 241, 279; unrest over Mississippi question, 269

White House (see President's House)

Whitney, Eli, 181

Wilkinson, General James, 36; and transfer of Louisiana to U.S., 324, 336–38

Wilson, Woodrow, addresses Congress, 91; legislative record compared with TJ's, 110

Worthington, Thomas, 243, 244, 353

Yazoo claims, background of controversy over, 246, 448–50; congressional debate (1805), 450–55; Marshall's decision on, 456

Young and Minns, printers of State of Massachusetts, attack TJ's character, 220–21

Yrujo, Marqués (earlier Chevalier) de Casa, Spanish minister, 97, 376; protests against closure of deposit, New Orleans, 265, 266, 281; opposes transfer of Louisiana to U.S., 322–23, 334, 339; protests against Mobile Act, 343–46; in Merry affair, 379–80, 381–82, 384, 385